Capital Allowances

2021-22

Ray Chidell
Jake Iles

Company number 07658388
VAT number 114 9371 20

Law date

The text is based on the tax law as at 20 April 2021.

First (2012-13) edition August 2012
This tenth (2021-22) edition May 2021

WORLD LAND TRUST™

www.carbonbalancedpaper.com
UPM FINE

The carbon emissions of the paper used to produce this book have been offset via the World Land Trust's Carbon Balanced Paper scheme.

This product is made of material from well-managed, FSC®-certified forests and other controlled sources.

Capital Allowances

2021-22

Ray Chidell
Jake Iles

Published by:

Claritax Books Ltd
6 Grosvenor Park Road
Chester, CH1 1QQ

www.claritaxbooks.com

ISBN: 978-1-912386-37-6

Main titles from Claritax Books

General tax annuals

- Capital Gains Tax
- Income Tax
- Inheritance Tax *
- Stamp Duty Land Tax

  * First published October 2020, this will be part of the general tax annuals series from its second (2022-23) edition.

Specialist tax annuals

- Advising British Expats
- A-Z of Plant & Machinery
- Capital Allowances
- Financial Planning with Trusts
- Pension Tax Guide
- Property Investment

Other specialist titles

- Construction Industry Scheme
- Discovery Assessments
- Disguised Remuneration
- Employee Share Schemes
- Employment Status
- Enterprise Investment Scheme
- Furnished Holiday Lettings
- Living and Working Abroad
- Main Residence Relief
- Personal Representatives
- Research and Development
- Residence: The Definition in Practice
- Schedule 36 notices
- Tax Appeals
- Tax Losses
- Taxation of Partnerships
- Taxpayer Safeguards and the Rule of Law

See claritaxbooks.com for details of all our titles.

About the authors

Ray Chidell, MA (Cantab), CTA (Fellow)

Ray has worked as a tax specialist for more than 30 years and is recognised as one of the UK's leading authorities on capital allowances. Ray originally qualified as a tax inspector but switched to the accounting profession in 1989, working for Baker Tilly and later Mazars, the latter role including six years as a tax partner.

Ray is now a technical director of Six Forward Capital Allowances, supporting the provision of a full capital allowances service to accountants and their clients.

Ray has written about capital allowances matters for more than two decades. After working as a senior technical author for other publishers for eight years, he launched Claritax Books in 2011, a role he continues to enjoy alongside his technical capital allowances work.

Ray can be contacted by phone on 01244 342179, or by email to raychidell@claritax.co.uk.

Jake Iles MBA, MCMI

Jake has worked as a capital allowances specialist for the last 15 years, having originally qualified as a mechanical and electrical engineer. In 1997 he moved into senior programme management on an unrivalled multinational collaborative project. His responsibilities on that project included, among other things, the life cycle cost, funding, improvements and environmental issues facing the construction and management of buildings and facilities in four European countries.

Jake has been the managing director of Six Forward Capital Allowances for 11 years and, along with his multi-skilled team, is responsible for the provision of a full capital allowances service, that includes in-house survey and valuation, to more than 250 UK accountants and their clients, analysing expenditure of over £1 billion per year.

Jake has written capital allowances articles for the accounting institutions and is a regular presenter and speaker, sometimes with Ray, to tax specialists, accountants and solicitors.

Jake can be contacted on 0800 0787 964 or by email to jiles@sixforward.com.

Preface to 2021-22 edition

For this 2021-22 edition, we have once more taken full account of statutory and case law developments, and of updated HMRC guidance material. Examples have all been reviewed and updated as appropriate.

Key changes for this edition

Key changes for this 2021-22 edition have included:

- HMRC guidance re capital allowances and general anti-abuse rule (GAAR) (**1.1.2**);
- case of *Steadfast Manufacturing* re distinction between capital and revenue expenditure (resurfacing of yard) (**1.5.2**);
- overview of capital allowances for freeports (**1.14**);
- HMRC guidance relating to furnished holiday accommodation that fails to meet the criteria in some years (**3.4**);
- FTT decision in *Inmarsat* (successor to trade not entitled to allowances for expenditure on leased satellites) upheld by Upper Tribunal (**4.1.2**);
- HMRC lose in Court of Appeal in *SSE Generation* case, mainly re interpretation of CAA 2001, s. 22 (**4.2.3**);
- Court of Appeal observation, again in *SSE Generation*, on the time taken to reach agreement on capital allowances matters (**4.3.2**);
- *Cheshire Cavity* Upper Tribunal commentary on distinction between plant and premises (**4.3.4**);
- new commentary re creation of ambience (**4.3.4**);
- new HMRC guidance re meaning of "use in a dwelling-house" (not necessarily accepted by the authors) (**4.14.2**);
- text and all examples updated for extension of £1 million annual investment allowances (**5.2.8**);
- cars: updated thresholds for first-year allowances (**5.4.6**) and for writing-down allowances (**9.3.2**);
- detailed coverage of first-year allowances for plant and machinery used in freeports (**5.12**);
- detailed coverage of the new regime for super-deductions and other temporary first-year allowances (**5.13**);

- brief reference to the *Cape Industrial Services Ltd* case re long funding lease regime (**7.3.5**);
- super-deduction for software costs (**8.3**);
- lower threshold for car hire restriction (**9.9**);
- more recent HMRC guidance on "sampling" to identify fixtures for largest businesses (**11.6**);
- major new section added on practicalities of advising the buyer of a commercial property re fixtures claims (**12.13**);
- additional HMRC example re time limit for short-life asset election (**15.4.2**);
- technical change re long-life assets and associated companies (**16.3.3**);
- brief reference to *Szymusik* case re seafarers and ships (**20.1**);
- clarification re entitlement to claim structures and buildings allowances where there are different interests in the same property (**24.6.1**);
- new HMRC example re change in rate of SBAs (**24.7.1**);
- practical issue concerning NHS grants made to doctors and others (**31.2.6**);
- HMRC toolkit notes updated (e.g. re cars) (**Appendix 3**).

As before, changes in this edition once more reflect real issues addressed in our roles at Six Forward Capital Allowances, where we have continued to work together on a wide range of cases. Jake's business and valuation skills complement my own detailed knowledge of the *Capital Allowances Act*, and once more I am delighted to have Jake as supporter and co-author.

The accompanying *A-Z of Plant & Machinery*, written by the same authors, is also available from Claritax Books. This book takes a detailed look at more than 300 types of common expenditure, showing whether (or in what circumstances) the expenditure is likely to qualify for plant and machinery allowances.

Ray Chidell
April 2021

Abbreviations

AIA	Annual investment allowance
AQE	Available qualifying expenditure
Art.	Article
ATA	Assured tenancy allowance
ATT	Association of Taxation Technicians
BIM	Business Income Manual
BLM	Business Leasing Manual
BPRA	Business premises renovation allowance
BTC	British Tax Cases
CA	Capital Allowances (manual)
CAA 2001	Capital Allowances Act 2001
CG	Capital Gains (manual)
CGT	Capital gains tax
Ch.	Chapter
CIOT	Chartered Institute of Taxation
CIR	Commissioners of Inland Revenue
CIRD	Corporate Intangibles Research & Development (manual)
CoACS	Co-ownership authorised contractual schemes
CPSE	Commercial property standard enquiries
CT	Corporation tax
CTA	Corporation Tax Act
CTM	Company Taxation Manual
EBITDA	Earnings before interest, tax, depreciation and amortisation
ECA	Enhanced capital allowances
EEA	European Economic Area
EIM	Employment Income Manual
ESC	Extra statutory concession
EU	European Union
EWHC	England and Wales High Court
FA	Finance Act
FCA	Flat conversion allowance
FHL	Furnished holiday letting
FPE	Foreign permanent establishment
FRS	Financial reporting standard
FY	Financial year
FYA	First-year allowance
GAAP	Generally accepted accounting principles
GAAR	General anti-abuse rule
GREIT	Guidance on Real Estate Investment Trusts (manual)
HMIT	HM Inspector of Taxes
HMRC	HM Revenue and Customs
HP	Hire purchase
HVAC	Heating, ventilation and air conditioning

IBA	Industrial buildings allowance
ICTA 1988	Income and Corporation Taxes Act 1988
IFRS	International financial reporting standards
INTM	International Manual
ITA 2007	Income Tax Act 2007
ITEPA 2003	Income Tax (Earnings and Pensions) Act 2003
ITTOIA 2005	Income Tax (Trading and Other Income) Act 2005
JPUT	Jersey property unit trust
LFL	Long funding lease
LLP	Limited liability partnership
MEA	Mineral extraction allowance
NACE	Nomenclature statistique des activités économiques
NIC	National Insurance contributions
Oao	On the application of
OT	Oil Taxation (manual)
P&M	Plant and machinery
PMA	Plant and machinery allowance
Pt.	Part
RDA	Research and development allowance
RPI	Retail prices index
RQE	Residue of qualifying expenditure
REIT	Real estate investment trust
S.	Section
SBA	Structures and buildings allowance
Sch.	Schedule
SDLT	Stamp duty land tax
SDLTM	Stamp Duty Land Tax Manual
SI	Statutory Instrument
SLA	Short-life asset
SME	Small or medium sized enterprise
TC	Tax Chamber
TCC	Tax and Chancery Chamber
TCGA 1992	Taxation of Chargeable Gains Act 1992
TDR	Total disposal receipts
TDV	Total of any disposal values
TIIN	Tax information and impact notes
TIOPA 2010	Taxation (International and Other Provisions) Act 2010
TMA 1970	Taxes Management Act 1970
UKFTT	United Kingdom First-tier Tribunal
UKHL	United Kingdom House of Lords
UKUT	United Kingdom Upper Tribunal
UQE	Unrelieved qualifying expenditure
UT	Upper Tribunal
VAT	Value Added Tax
WDA	Writing-down allowance
WLR	Weekly Law Report

Table of contents

GENERAL PRINCIPLES

1.   Introduction and general principles

1.1   Introduction

1.1.1   Scope of this book

Capital allowances are relevant for almost every business in the UK, as well as for property investors and for some employees. The legislation is familiar to all accountants, yet it contains numerous complexities that can cause headaches even for those working with the allowances on a daily basis. Changes to the capital allowances rules are made on a frequent basis, some minor or very specific but others having a major impact.

Two key questions dominate when considering a possible claim for allowances: how much expenditure can qualify for relief, and how (and when) that relief is given in practice.

This book aims to provide clear and comprehensive guidance on those topics met by the vast majority of practitioners. Full guidance is given, for example, on annual investment allowances, on integral features and on the transitional rules that operate when rates of allowances or thresholds are changed. There is also extensive coverage (with worked examples) of the issues that arise in respect of fixtures in property, where the value of capital allowances can be particularly high (and where the issues are often least well understood).

To keep the content at a reasonable level, however, certain topics have been covered at more of an overview level (e.g. long funding leases and the wide array of anti-avoidance measures that generally trouble only those who are going out deliberately to the edges of the statutory provisions). Some very specialist topics (including ships and measures affecting only the mining and oil industries, between them with more than 40 sections of legislation) have been afforded just a token coverage. The coverage of allowances that have now been withdrawn is kept very brief (see **Chapter 30**).

1.1.2   Legitimacy of claiming allowances

Capital allowances have been around for many decades and are an entirely legitimate, recognised part of the UK tax system. There is no sense at all in which the claiming of these allowances is either morally or legally dubious.

There has been a lot of talk in recent years about tax avoidance. HM Revenue and Customs (HMRC) have drawn a distinction between:

- using tax reliefs in the way they were intended; and
- exploiting them in ways that were never envisaged.

A properly formulated capital allowances claim falls clearly into the former category and should never be provocative to the tax authorities, though there may on occasions be proper discussion about the quantum of a claim for tax relief.

In 2015, HMRC issued a document *Tackling tax evasion and avoidance.* In that document, HMRC drew a distinction between tax avoidance that bends the rules and tax planning that "involves using tax reliefs for the purpose for which they were intended, for example, claiming tax relief on capital investment".

David Gauke, speaking for the government in February 2016, was discussing the corporation tax rate and specifically affirmed the legitimacy of claiming capital allowances:

> "Just to be clear, the statutory rate is 20% and that applies to everybody. There are businesses that will have a lower effective rate, entirely lawfully and in accordance with the spirit of the law, because, for example, they make use of capital allowances or they might have losses that they are making use of. Someone having an effective rate below the statutory rate does not mean that they are conducting avoidance activity."

Similarly, Hansard of 11 April 2016 records the following words by Nigel Mills in the context of scrutinising the tax records of large companies:

> "We should know which companies have made aggressive calculations, or used strange reliefs or funny payments that we do not understand, and which are paying the right amount and happen to have losses brought forward or capital allowances that they have not used."

HMRC's official guidance on the general anti-abuse rule (GAAR) specifically states as follows (at para. B4.4):

> "Using statutory incentives and reliefs to support business activity and investment in a straightforward way (for example business

property relief, Enterprise Investment Scheme (EIS), capital allowances, Patent Box) are also not caught by the GAAR."

The paragraph does, however, go on to warn that "experience has shown that incentives and reliefs can be abused".

The GAAR guidance later comments on potentially abusive tax arrangements that "[result] in deductions or losses of an amount for tax purposes significantly greater than the amount for economic purposes". However, it then adds the following (at para. C5.11.3):

"As above, it is explicitly provided that such features will not be indicators of abuse if it would be reasonable to assume that they were anticipated (or indeed intended) when the relevant tax provisions were enacted.

For example the capital allowance legislation may deliberately allow a taxpayer to claim a deduction for tax purposes in relation to capital expenditure on plant or equipment that is, in a particular period, substantially greater than the depreciation on those assets which is recognised for accounting purposes for that period. This result would clearly have been intended when the legislation was enacted."

So in an era of greater scrutiny of taxes by the general public and by the media, capital allowances remain a legitimate tool for reducing tax liabilities. Indeed, the greater risk for advisers is to ignore the potential tax-saving opportunities that capital allowances afford (especially, perhaps, in relation to commercial property). The foreword to the CIOT/ATT document *Professional Conduct in Relation to Taxation*, which became effective from March 2017, comments on the "vital" need for a tax profession that offers "proper and effective representation". That document lists activities forming part of the "vital role" carried out by tax agents and advisers, a list that includes advising clients on the mitigation of their tax liabilities "by making reasonable and appropriate use of the legislative framework and the choices available".

In summary, capital allowances are legitimate and fully approved, and it is a proper (and indeed essential) part of the tax adviser's role to ensure that his or her clients are able to benefit from such allowances. This book aims to help tax advisers to achieve that goal.

Guidance: https://tinyurl.com/y65aq4qr (GAAR guidance)

1.1.3 Reducing tax rates and new restrictions on other tax reliefs

The rate of corporation tax reduced to 19% from April 2017. Any reductions to income tax or corporation tax rates lessen somewhat the value of capital allowances. Even at 19%, however, a business buying a property for £2 million, and claiming allowances for fixtures of £700,000, will potentially save £133,000. The comparative potential saving for an individual paying tax at 45% would be £315,000.

Despite falling headline rates of corporation tax in recent years, there are nevertheless reasons why capital allowances may be of more relevance, rather than less, for larger corporate entities today than in the past. Such reasons include the restrictions for interest relief and for losses brought forward.

The interest relief changes, introduced from April 2017, mean that deductible interest is in certain cases restricted to 30% of UK EBITDA (earnings before interest, tax, depreciation and amortisation). See also section **1.12.3** below.

There is a *de minimis* threshold, however, such that the restrictions will only apply to companies or groups with net interest expenses in excess of £2 million.

For loss relief (see, generally, **1.11.3**), changes also came into effect from April 2017. First, a relaxation allows corporate losses incurred after April 2017 to be set against any future profits, rather than just the profits of the same trade, and brought forward trading losses are now available for offset against profits of another group company.

At the same time, however, the amount of taxable profits that can be covered by losses brought forward is restricted. Such losses are unrestricted for set-off against the first £5 million of current taxable profits, but it is only possible to offset brought forward losses against half of any profits in excess of that figure.

Example

A company has trading losses brought forward of £60 million, but makes profits of £12 million in the year to 31 March 2021. The losses it can offset against the £12 million will be restricted to £8.5 million (i.e. the first £5 million and half of the remaining £7 million). As this leaves £3.5 million of potentially taxable profits in the year, capital allowances (which may hitherto have been deemed an irrelevance) may play an important part in mitigating the tax liability.

The details are quite complex, and certainly beyond the scope of this book, so the above is very much a simplification of the rules. Broadly speaking, however, the restriction applies to losses incurred before April 2017 and to certain other specified losses such as those arising from uncommercial activities.

Both of these restrictions – for interest relief and for losses – mean that certain companies that have not needed to worry about capital allowances in the past will now need to make greater use of them to reduce corporation tax bills. This may be the case for large companies with substantial historic trading losses, for example, or for those with very large interest payments.

With corporation tax rates now set to rise substantially in the coming years, for larger companies, the importance of claiming capital allowances will only increase.

1.1.4   Northern Ireland

The *Corporation Tax (Northern Ireland) Act* 2015 was passed in March 2015 and has wide-ranging potential implications for capital allowances claims, though subject to commencement provisions. The Act applies (in the words of the *Explanatory Notes*) to "the trading profits of a company if that company is a micro, small or medium-sized enterprise (SME), and the company's employee time and costs fall largely in Northern Ireland". See **1.13** and **Appendix 1** for further details.

1.2   How capital allowances work

1.2.1   The function of allowances

As the name suggests, capital allowances give tax relief for certain capital expenditure. The allowances have been described as the tax equivalent of the depreciation charge shown in the business accounts.

Although it would be simpler if the depreciation charge in a set of accounts were to be allowable for tax purposes, the capital allowances regime has many advantages from the government's point of view. In general terms, it simply gives greater control to the tax authorities. At a more detailed level, it allows tax relief to be given or denied by statutory principle, rather than by virtue of accounting standards. The rate of tax relief can be varied according to the economic cycle, permitting the flow of tax relief to be slowed down or accelerated at particular times. The system may also be used to encourage behaviour that is deemed to be laudable, for example by penalising cars with higher levels of polluting emissions.

1.2.2   Giving effect to allowances

Capital allowances (and, where appropriate, balancing charges) are given effect in calculating income (for income tax purposes) or profits (for corporation tax) of a chargeable period. As such, the allowances are deducted (or the balancing charges are added) as part of the calculation of the taxable income or profits.

This general principle is, however, expanded or modified in relation to particular types of allowance.

See **1.6** for the meaning of "chargeable period".

Law: CAA 2001, s. 2
Guidance: CA 11110

1.2.3   Interaction with income tax basis periods

As noted above, capital allowances are given in calculating taxable profits. It follows that allowances due must be deducted before any apportionment between basis periods.

Example

Morris starts trading on 1 September 2020 and draws his first accounts up to 30 April 2021, with annual accounts to 30 April thereafter.

Before deducting capital allowances, he calculates that his tax-adjusted profits for the eight months to 30 April 2021 are £18,000. However, he bought a machine just after he started his trade, paying £3,000, and he wishes to claim annual investment allowances on that amount. He therefore reduces the £18,000 to £15,000, and this is done before calculating the taxable profits for the various basis periods.

So for 2020-21, the taxable business profit will be calculated as £13,450 (i.e. 217/242 x £15,000, based on counting days from 1 September 2020 to 5 April and then to 30 April 2021).

For 2021-22, the basis period will be the first 12 months, i.e. the period from 1 September 2020 to 31 August 2021. The taxable business profit for that year will therefore include the whole of the £15,000, as well as one third of the profits (after deducting any further capital allowances due) for the year to 30 April 2022.

In this sense, therefore, the value of capital allowances may be given more than once. This does not mean, however, that expenditure incurred can ever be treated as qualifying expenditure in more than one basis period. This is illustrated at **1.6.2** below.

Law: CAA 2001, s. 2; ITTOIA 2005, s. 198*ff.*
Guidance: CA 11110

1.2.4   Losses

As a general principle, capital allowances reduce taxable profits, turn a profit into a loss, or increase an existing loss. Relief for the loss thus created or augmented will be given in the usual way, depending on whether it is a company or not, and depending on the nature of the activity (trading, property investment, etc.). See **1.11** below.

1.3   Legislation and guidance

1.3.1   Legislation

The main body of tax legislation relating to capital allowances is the *Capital Allowances Act* 2001 (abbreviated in this book to CAA 2001). CAA 2001 now contains the following Parts:

Part 1:	Introduction
Part 2:	Plant and machinery allowances
Part 2A:	Structures and buildings allowances
Part 5:	Mineral extraction allowances
Part 6:	Research and development allowances
Part 7:	Know-how allowances
Part 8:	Patent allowances
Part 9:	Dredging allowances
Part 10:	Assured tenancy allowances
Part 11:	Contributions
Part 12:	Supplementary provisions

This book follows broadly the same structure.

Former Parts 3 and 4 (dealing respectively with industrial and agricultural buildings) were repealed in 2011. The rules relating to flat conversions (former Part 4A) were repealed by FA 2012. Business premises renovation allowances (former Part 3A) ceased to be available from April 2017.

CAA 2001 also has three schedules, containing abbreviations, defined expressions, consequential amendments that arose from the enactment of CAA 2001, and a series of "transitionals and savings" that are still of occasional interest. Schedule A1 (re first-year tax credits) was inserted in 2008, but was subsequently repealed in relation to expenditure incurred from 1 April or 6 April 2020.

In practice, the allowances relating to plant and machinery are the most complex and are also, by some margin, the allowances of relevance to most businesses. That is all the more true since the abolition of the allowances for industrial and agricultural buildings. Plant and machinery allowances therefore dominate both the legislation and this book. The newer regime for structures and buildings allowances is important for those investing in commercial property, though even here much of the relief is given under the plant and machinery regime (i.e. for fixtures).

Allowances for capital expenditure on know-how and patents are, nowadays, mostly given under the separate tax regime relating to intangible assets.

Law: CAA 2001

1.3.2   *Guidance*

Extensive HMRC guidance may be found in the *Capital Allowances Manual*, which is sold commercially by some publishers but which is also available online at www.hmrc.gov.uk/manuals/camanual. References in this book to that manual are noted as CA followed by a number, so (for example) CA 20000 for the start of the guidance relating to plant and machinery allowances.

HMRC have a "helpsheet" – HS252 Capital allowances and balancing charges (2018) – which can easily be found online. It offers a somewhat simplistic overview of capital allowances but may be of use for someone coming to the subject for the first time.

HMRC also publish a "toolkit". This is useful as far as it goes, but is again fairly basic in its scope. The toolkit may be found by searching the internet or at https://tinyurl.com/y48uwrbk.

In a less structured manner, HMRC have also, over the years, issued an odd array of notes on a wide range of capital allowances issues, covering everything from football grounds to the pig industry.

Official HMRC guidance is invariably of value in gaining an understanding of how the sometimes complex legislation will be applied in practice. Nevertheless, such guidance sometimes represents just one side of the story and the authors have not been afraid to highlight, in this book, areas where businesses and their advisers may wish to challenge the HMRC line. Furthermore, the guidance falls far short in some areas, most notably in relation to property fixtures.

Online guidance from other sources may also be found, some of which is very useful but other parts of which are misleading or even simply wrong. Care should be taken accordingly.

1.3.3   Case law precedents

Numerous references are made in this book to First-tier Tribunal decisions, and to other legal decisions at all levels. It is worth being aware of the force that such decisions carry, and the following guidance – though given by HMRC in the context of inheritance tax – is of much wider application:

> "The Special Commissioners and First-tier Tribunal can publish their decisions. Their decisions do not create legally binding precedents but they may be referred to in correspondence from taxpayers or their advisers. The conclusions reached may be more relevant if no appeal is made to a higher Court or tribunal against their decision.
>
> You may get correspondence that refers to such decisions in other cases where it is suggested that a similar point arises. Where that decision is or may be the subject of an appeal, you will need to explain to the taxpayer or their agent that you are not able to enter into any discussion of the case because of this."

The fact that these decisions are not binding cuts both ways, of course, and the HMRC guidance goes on to say (addressing HMRC employees):

> "Although you may refer to Special Commissioners' and First-tier Tribunal decisions in HMRC's favour, you should do this with care and you should not refer to any unpublished decision. Instead, you should put forward your own view on the point in contention, and state the authorities on which you rely. You should also say, if appropriate, that this view was upheld by the Special Commissioners or First-tier Tribunal in the particular case. In appropriate   cases,   particularly   where   a   taxpayer   is

11

unrepresented, you should state that the decision is not legally binding in other cases."

The decisions of the higher courts are, by contrast, binding both on lower tribunals and on HMRC and taxpayers.

Guidance: IHTM 02085

1.4   Claims

1.4.1   General rule

No allowances may be given unless a claim for allowances is made.

The general rule is that any claim must be included in a tax return. The return must be required to be made under TMA 1970 (for income tax) or under FA 1998, Sch. 18 (for corporation tax). The general rule for capital allowances claims thus overrides the usual claims legislation.

Claims for structures and buildings allowances (SBAs – see, generally, **Chapter 24**), must be separately identified as such in the tax return.

In *Ayeni v HMRC*, which concerned a number of different tax issues including the now defunct flat conversion allowances, the tribunal considered whether a letter from the taxpayer could be treated as an amendment to his tax return. The tribunal concluded that it could not "since it was not in the form of a tax return and did not contain a signed statement confirming its accuracy".

A person may exceptionally be entitled to an allowance without any assessment being made (e.g. a person paying tax under PAYE who has a one-off capital expense). In such a case, allowances may be given on the basis of a written agreement.

Making a reduced claim

A claim may be for less than the statutory entitlement, in which case the amount claimed must be specified. There are various circumstances in which it may be appropriate to claim less than the maximum amount:

- An individual may have unused personal allowances, which will simply be wasted if full allowances are claimed in the year. By reducing the claim, the balance of the capital allowances pool carried forward (in the case of plant and machinery allowances) will be greater, allowing for higher claims in future years where the taxable income perhaps exceeds the personal allowance. (This will not be a relevant consideration for corporation tax purposes.)

- An individual may be aware that he or she will face higher tax rates in a future year. This will be a more complex calculation, but in principle a person may prefer to have higher writing-down allowances (WDAs) in the future (perhaps saving tax at 40% or 45%) rather than lower allowances (at 20%) in the current year. The benefit of any such tax savings may, however, be more than offset by the cash flow cost of postponing the claim.

- As capital allowances can augment tax losses, or even convert profits to losses, it may be appropriate to consider how any losses would be used (for either income tax or corporation tax purposes, as appropriate). It is possible that the deferral of relief will create different options for offsetting losses, bearing in mind that the relief for current year losses is different from the relief for losses brought forward. (See, generally, *Tax Losses*, available from Claritax Books.)

- If the business is to be sold in the near future, the disclaiming of allowances may allow for a larger terminal loss claim, with the broader options that such a claim offers for tax relief.

- If the business knows that an asset is to be sold in the near future, and that the asset is likely to gain a good price on sale, the disclaiming of allowances may prevent a future balancing charge. A decision to defer on these grounds will be exceptional.

In all cases, it should be remembered that annual investment allowances (AIAs) and first-year allowances (FYAs) can only be claimed for the year in which the expenditure is incurred. So if, for example, a business could claim AIAs of £40,000 for an asset in year one, but decides to defer the claim to the following year, no AIAs will be available and the maximum WDAs for the asset in year two will be either £7,200 (at 18%) or just £2,400 (at 6%). The balance of relief may still be given over future years, but at a much slower rate.

In the case of fixtures in property, it is possible that a deferred claim will lead to a permanent loss of relief (rather than merely a cash flow disadvantage). This is considered at **11.2** below ("Retention of benefit of allowances").

HMRC's *Company Tax Return Guide* includes numerous references to the claiming of capital allowances.

Law: CAA 2001, s. 3, 565
Case: *Ayeni v HMRC* [2016] UKFTT 592 (TC)
Guidance: CA 11120; CTM 98000*ff.*

1.4.2 Time limits for claims

As the claim has to be included in a tax return, the time limit for making a claim is the same as that for submitting or amending a return.

For income tax purposes, this means that the claim must be made in a return by 31 January following the end of the tax year, and may be amended for a further 12 months. *But, I thought that CA claims can be made at any time*

Example 1

A sole trader draws accounts up to 31 December each year. The accounts to 31 December 2021 are assessed for 2021-22. The capital allowances claim must be submitted as part of the return for that year, for which the deadline is 31 January 2023. The claim may be amended at any time up to 31 January 2024.

Where a business is carried on in partnership, the partners are not permitted to submit individual capital allowances claims but must make a single partnership return. This would apply, for example, to cars used by partners.

For corporation tax purposes, the deadline for making a claim (as part of the CT return) is normally 12 months from the end of the accounting period. Once more, there is a further 12 months during which the return may be amended. See CTM 98020 for illustrations of unusual CT time limits.

In each case, the time limit is extended if the return is subject to HMRC enquiry. In this case, it remains possible to amend a claim until 30 days after the enquiry is concluded. This may be by virtue of the issue by HMRC of a notice of completion, by amendment by HMRC of the return or by determination of any appeal.

This last point raised an interesting technicality in the *Dundas Heritable* case, heard in 2018. The company submitted its return late, including a substantial claim to capital allowances. As the return was late, HMRC opened an enquiry to deny the otherwise valid capital allowances claim. By opening the enquiry, however, HMRC validated the claim because the enquiry extended the window for making that claim. This was a logical result of the way the legislation is worded, and is a rather Alice in Wonderland outcome, but the principle has been confirmed by the Upper Tribunal.

Subject to the above, HMRC policy is that the time limit for claiming allowances will not be extended "unless circumstances beyond the company's control prevented it being able to make the claim within the normal time limits". HMRC also make the following point:

> "A company may make a capital allowance claim 'out of order' – that is, for an accounting period when a return for a later accounting period has already been made. This capital allowance claim may reduce the capital allowances due for that later accounting period. For example, a claim for plant and machinery allowances will reduce the qualifying expenditure in a plant and machinery pool and so the capital allowances due for later periods. Where this happens the company has 30 days to make the necessary amendments to its return for that later period."

Law: FA 1998, Sch. 18, para. 82; CAA 2001, s. 3
Case: *Dundas Heritable Ltd v HMRC* [2018] UKFTT 244 (TC), [2019] UKUT 208 (TCC)
Guidance: CA 11130-11150

Missed claims for earlier years

A particular issue arises where a claim has been missed in an earlier year. Typically, this is in relation to a late claim for fixtures in a commercial property.

The same principles as above apply in these cases. It is not possible to go back and re-open computations from many years ago. However, the costs may be brought into account as qualifying expenditure in a later year.

Example 2

The proprietor of a care home had the property built in 2009. Claims were made for some items, including a lift, but it is now apparent that a much larger claim could have been made at the time for fixtures in the property.

It is too late to re-open the 2009 accounts, but a claim for the additional fixtures may be made for a later year that is still open. A condition of this is that the fixtures are still owned at some point in the year for which the claim has been made.

The claim will be for WDAs only. No AIAs are due, as explained and illustrated at **5.2.1** below. There is a similar restriction on claiming FYAs in these circumstances (see **5.4.1**).

If the property was bought from a third party who was able to claim allowances, changes introduced by FA 2012 will prevent the current owner from claiming if certain conditions were not met. See below.

As mentioned, a claim can only be made in a later year if the asset was still owned at some point in that year. Indeed, in their "toolkit", HMRC highlight the issue of ownership in these circumstances as a particular risk area:

> "Where expenditure incurred in earlier accounting periods is introduced into the pool it is important to establish that the relevant asset(s) are still owned by the business at the time of their introduction."

Where a property has been bought from a third party, it is also now necessary to consider the FA 2012 requirements for pooling of expenditure (see, generally, **12.4**). In most cases, a property vendor who could have identified qualifying expenditure on fixtures in the property, but who has not done so, will be required to do so as a condition of the sale. As the sale and purchase process is already complex enough, this is one of several reasons why property owners are well advised to make full claims for fixtures as soon as the expenditure is incurred.

Guidance: https://tinyurl.com/y48uwrbk (HMRC toolkit)

1.4.3   Exceptions

The requirement to make a claim in an income tax return does not apply to special leasing of plant or machinery (see **3.8**) or to patent allowances (see **Chapter 28**) in respect of non-trading expenditure. In each case, these claims are instead subject to the provisions of TMA 1970, s. 42 (procedure for making claims and claims not included in returns).

The requirement to make a claim in a corporation tax return does not apply to claims under CAA 2001, s. 260(3)(b) (claim to carry back allowances in respect of special leasing of plant or machinery). Such claims are instead subject to FA 1998, Sch. 18, para. 54-60.

For claims made by partnerships, these general rules are subject to TMA 1970, s. 42(6) and (7) (special provisions relating to partnerships).

Special rules apply for REITs (see **1.12.4** below) and for CoACS (see **1.12.5** below).

Law: CAA 2001, s. 3; CTA 2010, s. 599(8)
Guidance: CA 11120

1.5   Capital expenditure

1.5.1   Relevance

The *Capital Allowances Act* 2001 begins with a statement that it is concerned with allowances in respect of capital expenditure. If expenditure is not capital in nature (or is not deemed to be such by virtue of some special provision) then no capital allowances will be due. Tax relief may or may not be available by virtue of other provisions.

As a general principle, capital expenditure is not otherwise deductible when computing trading profits for corporation tax purposes (CTA 2009, s. 53(1)) or for income tax purposes (ITTOIA 2005, s. 33). In each case, the statutory prohibition is reinforced by accounting principles.

Law: CAA 2001, s. 1

1.5.2   Meaning

The concept of capital expenditure is initially defined, for capital allowances purposes, in negative terms. As such, it does *not* include any of the following:

- any amount that may be deducted in calculating the profits or gains of a trade, profession, vocation or property business;
- any amount that may be allowed as a deduction under certain specified provisions (e.g. as mileage allowance relief) from the taxable earnings from an employment or office; or
- certain amounts paid under deduction of income tax (annual payments, patent royalties, and certain royalties etc. where the usual place of abode of the owner is abroad).

Capital expenditure is defined to include any contribution to capital expenditure. Special rules apply to contributions (see **Chapter 31**).

Capital expenditure includes VAT unless the VAT is allowable as input tax. In more detail, HMRC guidance in relation to VAT reads as follows:

> "The purchase price of an asset on which you can claim capital allowances sometimes includes VAT. If you are registered for VAT

and can offset that VAT against your output tax when you make your VAT returns, you should only claim capital allowances on the net cost of the asset.

If you are registered for the VAT Flat Rate Scheme and enter details of your income and expenses net of VAT (that is, with the VAT taken off), you should only claim capital allowances on the net cost of the asset.

If you are not registered for VAT or can only claim an element of the VAT you have incurred, for example, because you are partly exempt, include the irrecoverable VAT paid in the capital costs on which you claim capital allowances."

Beyond these statutory provisions, the concept of capital expenditure relies on judicial interpretations, and goes beyond the scope of this book. One of the most famous definitions is that of Lord Cave in the *Helsby Cables* case, when he stated that:

"when an expenditure is made, not only once and for all, but with a view to bringing into existence an asset or an advantage for the enduring benefit of a trade, I think that there is very good reason (in the absence of special circumstances leading to an opposite conclusion) for treating such an expenditure as properly attributable not to revenue but to capital".

It is also worth mentioning the much more recent *Steadfast Manufacturing* case, in which expenditure incurred on resurfacing a yard used for unloading lorries was held to be revenue expenditure. HMRC had argued that the works were such as to create an enduring advantage, but the First-tier judge ruled otherwise:

"The appellant's evidence is clear that the grassy areas, which HMRC considered meant that the useable area had increased, were the result of the deterioration of the original surface, rather than a previously unsurfaced area which was now being surfaced and brought into use. ...

Accordingly, I consider that there was no improvement in the yard compared to its original condition, and that the works only returned the yard to its previous standard. There was no increase in the useable area compared to the original. There also was no evidence of any increase in the load bearing capacity of the yard. ...

The reduced need for repairs does not of itself make the expenditure capital – in this case, it would be an inevitable result of repairing the yard properly, rather than in patches. In order to be capital, the reduced need for repairs would have to result from the bringing into existence of something new that had an enduring benefit to the business. In my view, the works restored the yard to its original state and did not bring something new into existence."

DRE

The distinction between revenue and capital expenditure is covered in greater depth in the *A-Z of Plant & Machinery*, also available from Claritax Books.

Cases: *Atherton v British Insulated and Helsby Cables Ltd* (1925) 10 TC 155; *Steadfast Manufacturing & Storage Ltd v HMRC* [2020] UKFTT 286 (TC)

Guidance: HMRC helpsheet 252: *Capital Allowances and Balancing Charges*

Lease premiums

no CA

In some circumstances, a person paying a lease premium will be able to claim tax relief for part of the premium paid. Relief is given by spreading the chargeable amount over the period of the lease and treating it as additional rent due.

If relief is given in this way, s. 4 applies to deny capital allowances for the amount concerned. This is explained as follows in the *Property Income Manual* at PIM 2310:

> "Where relief is given under CTA09/S227 or ITTOIA05/S287 onwards, capital expenditure for capital allowances purposes must exclude sums taken into account in computing rental business profits."

The guidance goes on to add that "similarly, amounts chargeable to tax as property income cannot also be taxed under the capital allowances provisions".

Trading stock

Allowances may be given where revenue expenditure is appropriated permanently to fixed assets. HMRC guidance in this respect reads as follows:

> "If expenditure on the provision or construction of an asset was revenue expenditure and the asset is later permanently appropriated to fixed assets WDAs may be given. The expenditure that qualifies for WDAs is the original expenditure incurred and

e.g selling cars but later becomes a company car

not the market value of the asset at the time of the appropriation. You should not accept that an asset has been permanently appropriated to fixed assets unless you are satisfied that any profit on sale would be capital rather than revenue."

HMRC have also given the following view in relation to the specific issue of TV rental:

"You may have to deal with a business that both hires out television sets and sells them. If so, the television sets which are hired out will be plant if the hiring is a separate and distinct business activity and the stock of sets for hiring out is separate from the stock of sets for sale."

In *Waterloo Car Hire*, the tribunal concluded that the cars being discussed were "fixed assets subject to capital allowance legislation and not items that could properly be included in 'cost of sales' ".

Law: CAA 2001, s. 4, 10

Cases: *Atherton v British Insulated and Helsby Cables Ltd* (1925) 10 TC 155; *Waterloo Car Hire (a partnership) v HMRC* [2016] UKFTT 752 (TC)

Guidance: CA 11530, 21200

1.5.3 Timing of expenditure – general rule

The legislation provides a definition of when capital expenditure is treated as incurred.

The general rule is that it is treated as incurred as soon as there is an unconditional obligation to pay it. This is the case even if some or all of the expenditure does not have to be paid until a later date, though this general rule is subject to the exceptions and anti-avoidance rules listed below.

HMRC have given the following advice in relation to this general principle:

"A person buying goods is legally required to pay for them on delivery unless there is a special agreement as to terms of payment. If the buyer is legally required to pay on delivery the obligation to pay becomes unconditional when the goods are delivered.

If goods are sold subject to reservation of title ... the obligation to pay becomes unconditional when the goods are delivered. The supplier has then fulfilled his or her part of the contract. This means that the buyer incurs capital expenditure as soon as the goods are delivered.

The date on which the obligation to pay for an asset becomes unconditional and the date on which the purchaser is legally required to pay for that asset may not be the same. For example, the sales agreement may require payment to be made within four weeks of delivery. If so the obligation to pay becomes unconditional on delivery but the purchaser is not legally required to pay until four weeks after delivery."

Example 1

A company draws accounts up to 30 April. It orders some new office furniture, which is delivered on 28 April. Payment is required within 21 days and a BACS payment is in fact made on 11 May. The expenditure is treated as incurred before the year end.

A different consideration arises if the order is placed before the year end but is not delivered until after that date.

Example 2

Another company draws accounts up to 30 April 2021. It orders some new office furniture on 14 April which is being customised to fit the area in which it will be used. As such, the contract states that the order cannot be cancelled once it has been placed. The furniture is delivered in July 2021.

The correct interpretation here would appear to be that the obligation to pay remains conditional until the furniture is delivered in July, and that allowances are therefore only due for the year to April 2022. A query in *Taxation* magazine of 24 September 2009 confirmed that this is how the legislation is interpreted and applied by HMRC.

HMRC provide further guidance on the meanings of various terms at CA 11700, as summarised below:

Expenditure under a contract

Expenditure will only be treated as incurred "under a contract" or "in pursuance of a contract" if the contract is legally binding and "the expenditure is expenditure to which the taxpayer was contractually committed by that contract".

If the taxpayer incurs expenditure by exercising a contractual option, the HMRC view is that the expenditure is not incurred under the original contract but rather is incurred "under the new contract which the taxpayer enters into when the option is exercised".

When a contract is performed

The question may arise of when a contract is performed, and the two parties may perform their contractual obligations at different times, as illustrated in the following HMRC example:

Example 3 – HMRC example

Barry enters into a contract to buy a guitar for £15,000. Under the contract he pays a deposit of £5,000, he pays £7,000 when he takes delivery of the guitar and he pays the balance of £3,000 two weeks after delivery.

The supplier performs his obligations under the contract when he delivers the guitar to Barry. Barry does not perform his obligations under the contract until he has paid the full amount due. This means that Barry does not perform his obligations under the contract until he has paid the final amount of £3,000 and so performance of the contract is when Barry pays £3,000 to the supplier two weeks after delivery.

Conditional

In deciding when a contract becomes unconditional, HMRC guidance is that the word "condition" may refer either to an event ("upon which the contract as a whole is conditional") or to a contractual term (a "promissory condition").

In the absence of other agreements, the obligation to make payment arises when delivery is made. This is also the case if there is a "concurrent promissory condition" whereby the parties agree that the performance of their respective promises will be simultaneous.

However, HMRC illustrate other possibilities as follows:

- "George contracts with Andy for Andy to repair his car. Under the contract, George promises to pay Andy once Andy has finished the repairs. George's legal obligation to pay Andy does not become unconditional until Andy has completed the work." HMRC call this a "condition precedent promissory condition".

- "Cass contracts with Oliver for Oliver to build a machine. Cass is required to make payment two months from the date the contract was entered into. Cass's payment is conditional only on the passage of time and is independent of any obligation imposed on Oliver." HMRC call this an "independent promissory condition".

Romalpa contract

Under these arrangements, goods are sold subject to reservation of title. The supplier fulfils his obligation on delivery. The buyer can choose when to make payment, but title to the goods does not pass until he does so.

Hire purchase agreements

Under HP agreements, also referred to as lease purchase agreements, the agreement specifies either that the hirer will eventually become the owner or that the hirer has an option to purchase the asset.

Law: CAA 2001, s. 5
Guidance: CA 11700, 11800

1.5.4   Timing of expenditure – payment due after four months

Sometimes there is a delay in the date by which payment has to be made. The general rule does not apply to the extent that any amount falls due for payment four months or more after the unconditional obligation to pay has come into being. Instead, any such amount is treated as incurred on the date by which it has to be paid.

HMRC illustrate this with the following example:

HMRC example

Bob buys a car for £15,000. Under the terms of the contract he has to pay £12,000 one month after delivery of the car and the balance of £3,000 five months after that. He takes delivery of the car on 24 May and his obligation to pay becomes unconditional then. He is legally required to pay:

- £12,000 on 24 June, and
- £3,000 on 24 November

The first payment is due four months or less after his obligation to pay becomes unconditional but the second one is not. He incurs expenditure of £12,000 on 24 May and £3,000 on 24 November.

Law: CAA 2001, s. 5(5)
Guidance: CA 11800

1.5.5 Timing of expenditure – payment conditional upon certificate (milestone contracts)

A different rule applies where the capital expenditure is on the provision of an asset and where the following further conditions are met:

- an unconditional obligation to pay an amount of the expenditure comes into being as a result of the giving of a certificate or any other event;
- the giving of the certificate, or other event, occurs within the period of one month after the end of a chargeable period; and
- at or before the end of that chargeable period, the asset has become the property of, or is otherwise under the agreement attributed to, the person subject to the unconditional obligation to pay.

In these circumstances, the expenditure is treated as incurred on the last day of the chargeable period in question.

The scope of this provision is fairly limited.

Example

A hotel draws accounts up to 31 December. It is paying for a luxury spa development, at a cost of £3.5 million. The spa contains extensive levels of plant and machinery.

The architect supervising the work issues certificates at various stages. The special rule above will only apply if one such certificate is issued during January for works that have already become the property of the hotel before the end of the calendar year.

This rule is subject to the anti-avoidance provision described below.

Law: CAA 2001, s. 5(4)
Guidance: CA 11800

1.5.6   Anti-avoidance rule

Without special provisions, it would be possible to exploit the above rules to obtain allowances earlier than those drafting the legislation had intended.

To counter this, expenditure is treated as incurred on the date by which it has to be paid, and not the earlier date on which the unconditional obligation to pay arises, if:

- "there is an unconditional obligation to pay an amount of capital expenditure on a date earlier than accords with normal commercial usage"; and
- "the sole or main benefit which might have been expected to be obtained thereby is that the amount would be treated, under the general rule, as incurred in an earlier chargeable period".

Law: CAA 2001, s. 5(6)
Guidance: CA 11800

1.5.7   Overriding rules

All of the above provisions are subject to two overriding rules.

First, they do not apply if any other provision of CAA 2001 treats expenditure as incurred on a later date. Different rules apply, for example, to pre-trading expenditure (see **4.17.2** in relation to plant and machinery) and to hire purchase agreements (see **Chapter 6**).

Second, they do not apply to expenditure treated as incurred as a result of a person incurring an additional VAT liability (see **Chapter 23**).

Law: CAA 2001, s. 5(7)
Guidance: CA 11800

1.5.8   Measuring the qualifying expenditure

In most cases, it will be obvious how much expenditure has been incurred: if a person buys an asset at arm's length, the amount paid (net of recoverable VAT – see **1.5.2** above) will be the amount on which allowances are due.

Where a new property is built, the claim should always be based on a proper analysis of the construction costs if possible. Exceptionally, if the documentation is insufficient to allow such an analysis, the claim may be based on a valuation approach (which should obviously be carried out by a suitably qualified/experienced valuer).

Where property is acquired from a third party, for whom the expenditure constituted capital expenditure, the qualifying expenditure on any plant or machinery will normally be determined by means of a fixtures election (under s. 198). In some circumstances, however, a valuation approach will be required (even since the changes introduced from April 2012 and from April 2014). The principles are discussed in depth at **Chapters 10 to 14**.

Law: CAA 2001, s. 4, 198

1.6 Chargeable periods

1.6.1 Corporation tax

For corporation tax purposes, a chargeable period is simply an accounting period. In this respect, it should be remembered that an accounting period is not always the same as the period for which accounts are in fact drawn up. For example, accounts may be drawn up for longer than 12 months, but an accounting period may never exceed that length of time.

More specifically, the legislation specifies that a corporation tax accounting period will come to an end on the first occurrence of any of the following:

"(a) the ending of 12 months from the beginning of the accounting period,

(b) an accounting date of the company,

(c) if there is a period for which the company does not make up accounts, the end of that period,

(d) the company starting or ceasing to trade,

(e) if the company carries on only one trade, coming, or ceasing to be, within the charge to corporation tax in respect of that trade,

(f) if the company carries on more than one trade, coming, or ceasing to be, within the charge to corporation tax in respect of all the trades it carries on,

(g) the company becoming, or ceasing to be, UK resident,

(h) the company ceasing to be within the charge to corporation tax,

(i)   the company entering administration, and

(j)   the company ceasing to be in administration."

Law: CAA 2001, s. 6(1)(b); CTA 2009, s. 10

1.6.2   Income tax

For income tax, the starting point is that a chargeable period is the same as a period of account, but more complications arise.

The term "period of account" has its own definition for these purposes.

Non-traders

For any person who *cannot* claim allowances in calculating the profits of a trade, profession or vocation, the period of account is the tax year ending on 5 April.

Traders

The rules are more complex in the case of a person who can claim allowances in calculating the profits of a trade, profession or vocation.

The starting point is that a period of account is simply the period for which accounts are drawn up. However, this is subject to certain exceptions. These exceptions are to address the complications of overlapping periods of account or of gaps between such periods.

The first exception deals with overlapping periods of account and with cases where one period of account is contained within another. This is a different concept from that of overlapping basis periods.

For capital allowances purposes, the period common to both is treated as part of the first period of account only, as illustrated by HMRC at CA 11510:

Example 1 – HMRC example

Accounts may be drawn up for the year ended 30 June 2008 and then the 12 months to 31 December 2008. The period 1 January 2008 to 30 June 2008 is in both periods. It falls within the period of account 1 July 2007 to 30 June 2008. It does **not** fall within the period of account 1 January 2008 to 31 December 2008.

That HMRC example actually illustrates a rather rare occurrence, where accounts are drawn up for overlapping periods. A much more common scenario is where accounts are drawn up consecutively but where basis periods overlap, especially at the commencement of a business.

Example 2

George starts trading on 1 February 2021 and draws accounts up to the end of each calendar year, so his first accounts cover a period of 11 months.

George's basis period for 2020-21 is 1 February 2021 to 5 April 2021 and his basis period for 2021-22 is 1 February 2021 to 31 January 2022.

If George incurs capital expenditure of £10,000, on which capital allowances are due, in the period from 1 February to 5 April 2021, this is treated as falling within the first period only. So whether annual allowances or WDAs are claimed, the £10,000 is treated as incurred in the first period only.

As it happens, George will still enjoy an element of double relief for the £10,000: although that figure is deducted only once in calculating profits for the 11 months to 31 December 2021, those profits will affect his tax liability for more than one tax year. This is illustrated at **1.2.3** above.

The second exception is where there is a gap between two periods of account, in which case the gap is treated as part of the first period only.

The third exception is where a period of account would otherwise be longer than 18 months. Such a period must be divided into shorter periods of account, none of which may exceed 12 months. The first such period starts with the start of the actual period of account and each subsequent one begins on the anniversary of that date.

Example 3

A sole trader starts business on 1 September 2019 and draws up his first set of accounts to 30 April 2021, a period of 20 months.

For these purposes, he is treated as having one period of account that runs from 1 September 2019 to 31 August 2020, and a second period of account that runs from 1 September 2020 to 30 April 2021.

Law: CAA 2001, s. 6, 58(2); ITTOIA 2005, s. 198*ff.*
Guidance: CA 11510

1.7 Exclusion of double relief

1.7.1 General principle

As a general principle, an allowance may not be made under two different Parts of CAA 2001 (e.g. as both plant and machinery and as expenditure on research and development). This applies to particular expenditure but also to the provision of any asset to which that expenditure relates.

If the same capital expenditure potentially qualifies under two different headings, the taxpayer may choose to claim allowances under one part of the statutory code rather than another. However, the decision once made is considered by HMRC to be irrevocable, a point that came into sharp focus when allowances for industrial and agricultural buildings were withdrawn, leaving many businesses with substantial amounts of unrelieved expenditure. For these purposes, the reference to capital expenditure includes expenditure treated as capital for the purposes of s. 270BJ(1) – expenditure on repairs, renovation and conversion for the purposes of the code re structures and buildings allowances.

Law: CAA 2001, s. 7, 8

1.7.2   Know-how and patents

This general rule does not, however, apply in relation to Part 7 (know-how allowances) or Part 8 (patent allowances). This rather odd and seemingly unwarranted exclusion was explained, in the *Explanatory Notes* accompanying the 2001 legislation, by stating that "the nature of patents and know-how is such that it seems unlikely that the subject matter of patent and know-how allowances could in practice lead to claims for double relief". For companies, such expenditure is in any case now claimed under the rules relating to intangible assets.

Law: CAA 2001, s. 7, 8
Guidance: CA 16000

1.7.3   Plant and machinery

Further restrictions apply specifically to plant and machinery, in respect of pooling (s. 8: see **5.3**) and of fixtures claims (s. 9: see **12.7.5**).

1.8   The cap on income tax reliefs

1.8.1   Background

A cap is imposed on the amount of income tax reliefs that may be set against an individual's income. The argument is that "wealthy individuals should not be able to reduce their income tax bills to zero, year after year by using these income tax reliefs to excess".

1.8.2 Capital allowances

The question therefore arises of the effect of these proposals on capital allowances. More specifically, will an individual be restricted in the amount of capital allowances he or she can claim?

The point was specifically addressed in a technical consultation issued in July 2012. The broad principle is that allowances are given effect in calculating the amount of taxable income, rather than in reducing the tax due on that income. As such, allowances are not generally affected by the cap.

However, allowances may also create (or augment) an income tax loss, and this may in turn be offset against general income. To this extent, the loss relief will be capped under the proposals.

Law: ITA 2007, s. 24A

Guidance: www.hmrc.gov.uk/tiin/2012/tiin2426.pdf

1.9 Cash basis for small businesses

1.9.1 Background

A "cash basis for small businesses" is an option for some individuals carrying on a trade or profession. The cash basis, which only applies if the individual elects for it to do so, replaces the requirement to calculate profits in accordance with generally accepted accounting practice.

Special capital allowances rules apply where the profits of a trade, profession, vocation or property business (a "relevant activity") are computed on the cash basis.

Law: CAA 2001, s. 1A; ITTOIA 2005, s. 25A

1.9.2 Treatment of capital expenditure

With the exception of expenditure on a car, capital expenditure that would have qualified for capital allowances is allowed as a revenue deduction for those using the cash basis.

A person calculating taxable income on the cash basis is therefore not entitled to claim capital allowances on new expenditure, other than for the cost of a car.

For vans and motorcycles, no capital allowances are due under the cash basis. Owners have the option to claim tax relief using the simplified mileage rates (45p for the first 10,000 miles, and then 25p), or to claim a deduction for the full capital cost of the vehicle, and then to claim actual running costs.

Law: CAA 2001, s. 1A; ITTOIA 2005, s. 33A

1.9.3   Joining the cash basis

A person joining the cash basis may have a pool of unused qualifying expenditure on plant and machinery.

The cash basis has a mechanism to grant relief for a "relevant portion" of the expenditure, i.e. "the amount of the expenditure for which a deduction would be allowed in calculating the profits of the trade on the cash basis for a period if the expenditure was paid during that period". This relief is by way of a deduction in calculating the taxable profits, and not by way of capital allowances.

This relevant portion is to be determined on a just and reasonable basis. The calculation would reduce the deduction where there is private use of an asset (by the sole trader or partner).

Example

Tony runs a computer consultancy business. He has a balance of £3,000 on his main plant and machinery pool immediately before he elects to calculate his profits on the cash basis. The pool only includes computer equipment that is used wholly and exclusively for the purposes of his trade. In his first year on the cash basis he can claim a revenue deduction for the full amount of £3,000.

If, instead, Tony accepts that 20% of the use of the equipment is private, he will be able to claim a deduction for £2,400.

A plant and machinery pool (either the main pool or the special rate pool) may include both the cost of a car and the cost of other assets. As capital allowances continue to be given for cars under the cash basis, it will be necessary to identify the part of the pool that relates to the car. This, once more, is to be computed on such basis as is just and reasonable in all the circumstances. Capital allowances will continue for the car but a revenue deduction will be given for the remaining expenditure (subject, as above, to any adjustments required, for example in relation to private use).

In practice, these rules will often *not* apply, as AIAs will have covered all expenditure apart from the cost of a car.

Restrictions apply to expenditure that has been pooled but not yet fully paid for, the details of which are beyond the scope of this book.

Law: CAA 2001, s. 1A, 59; ITTOIA 2005, s. 240A-240E, 334B-334E

Guidance: https://tinyurl.com/wrfudbkc (HMRC guidance: entering cash basis)

1.9.4   Leaving the cash basis

A person may choose to leave the cash basis for a particular year, or may be forced to do so because the business has grown above the threshold. The following rules apply if the individual in question has incurred expenditure that would have been qualifying expenditure were it not for the cash basis applying.

First, the "relieved proportion" of the expenditure must be calculated. This is the amount for which a deduction was allowed under the cash basis, or would have been allowed if the expenditure had been incurred wholly and exclusively for the purposes of the trade etc.

The remaining expenditure is said to be "unrelieved". This will arise only rarely as the normal process will be to grant full tax relief for capital expenditure as if it were a revenue cost. It might, however, apply to an asset that has been bought under an HP arrangement.

The person is then treated as incurring the unrelieved proportion of the expenditure in the first chargeable period for which the cash basis no longer applies. This deeming provision means that annual investment allowances (AIAs) or first-year allowances may be available, subject to the usual conditions.

Example

A piece of equipment has been purchased over three years at £100 per month of capital expenditure. After one year of payments the business leaves the cash basis.

The £1,200 already paid (and so already deducted) would be the relieved proportion; the remaining £2,400 would be the unrelieved proportion. This unrelieved proportion of £2,400 is deemed to have been incurred in the first chargeable period after leaving the cash basis. In principle, the whole amount could be relieved by way of AIAs.

For the purposes of calculating other allowances and charges, the whole of the expenditure is allocated to the appropriate pool or pools, but the available qualifying expenditure is reduced by the relieved portion.

Law: CAA 2001, s. 66A

1.10   Capital gains tax

1.10.1   Introduction

It is sometimes suggested that any benefit gained by claiming capital allowances will be lost because of a corresponding increase in liability to capital gains tax (or to corporation tax on the gain, as the case may be).

In practice, this is rarely the case. The starting point is certainly that a capital allowances claim does *not* increase the amount of any capital gain on disposal of the asset.

Law: TCGA 1992, s. 41

1.10.2   General principles

There is a natural instinctive view that if capital allowances are given for the cost of an asset, the same cost cannot be taken into account when calculating a capital gain. On the face of it, that would amount to giving tax relief twice for the same expenditure.

The issue arises most commonly in relation to fixtures in property. The thinking is that if part of the cost of the property is allocated to fixtures, on which allowances are claimed, the base cost for the remainder of the property must be reduced. It would seem to follow that there will be a higher capital gain if the property comes to be sold at a profit.

In reality, however, the capital allowances claim does *not* mean that an adjustment has to be made to the capital gain when the property is sold.

The statutory starting point is section 39 of the *Taxation of Chargeable Gains Act* 1992. Section 39(1) includes the following wording:

> "There shall be excluded from the sums allowable under section 38 as a deduction in the computation of the gain any expenditure allowable as a deduction in computing the profits or losses of a trade, profession or vocation for the purposes of income tax or allowable as a deduction in computing any other income or profits or gains or losses for the purposes of the Income Tax Acts and any expenditure which, although not so allowable as a deduction in

> computing any losses, would be so allowable but for an insufficiency of income or profits or gains."

Capital allowances are (nowadays) given in calculating trading or other profits (see, for example, CAA 2001, s. 247). So if TCGA 1992, s. 39 were the end of the matter, the capital gain would indeed have to be adjusted by reference to capital allowances claimed.

Fortunately, however, section 41 of that Act comes to the rescue, providing that:

> "Section 39 shall not require the exclusion from the sums allowable as a deduction in the computation of the gain of any expenditure as being expenditure in respect of which a capital allowance or renewals allowance is made."

In most cases, that *is* the end of the matter.

This general principle, which applies for nearly all categories of capital allowances (not just plant and machinery allowances, but see also below), is amended in two circumstances:

- where property is sold at a loss (considered at **1.10.4** below); and
- where the asset is a wasting asset (see **1.10.6** below).

The interaction of CGT with structures and buildings allowances (SBAs) works differently, however, as explained in detail at **24.10**. This distinction between SBAs (on the one hand) and the allowances available for fixtures under the plant and machinery code (on the other) is one of several reasons why the latter will be the more attractive allowances to claim as far as possible.

Law: TCGA 1992, s. 39, 41; CAA 2001, s. 2, 247
Guidance: CG 15400*ff.*

1.10.3   Selling property at a profit

The general principle – that claiming capital allowances does not increase a capital gain when property is sold at a profit – can be illustrated with the following examples.

Example 1

Tradingco One Ltd buys the freehold of a small office for £500,000 and sells it some years later for £600,000. The company makes no claims for capital allowances in the property. Ignoring legal and other incidental costs, the company has a capital gain of £100,000.

Example 2

Tradingco Two Ltd buys an identical property next door for the same price at the same time, and again sells it for £600,000. This company, though, claims capital allowances for fixtures in the property. It identifies fixtures with a value of £160,000 and, when it sells, it signs an election under CAA 2001, s. 198 with a figure of £90,000 for the fixtures. It therefore obtains tax relief, by way of capital allowances, on a net amount of £70,000. This has no bearing on the calculation of the capital gain, which is still £100,000.

The principle is also confirmed by HMRC, as follows (subject only to the exceptions referred to at **1.10.2** above):

> "The computation [of the capital gain] is unaffected by the fact that capital allowances have been given. In particular
>
> - the capital gains allowable expenditure is not restricted simply because capital allowances or renewals allowances have been given, TCGA92/S41 (1),
> - nor is the capital gains disposal consideration reduced because there is, as a result of the disposal,
>   - a capital allowances balancing charge, or
>   - an adjustment under CAA01/S55 (plant and machinery) ... ."

Law: TCGA 1992, s. 41
Guidance: CG 15401

1.10.4   Selling property at a loss

Overview

There is an important modification of the general rule where property is sold at a loss. In this case, the loss is restricted, broadly by reference to capital allowances that have been given and retained on the property. In HMRC's words, the purpose of the restriction "is to prevent relief being given twice for the same expenditure, once under the capital allowances code and once under the capital gains code".

The effect of the restriction may be to reduce the loss or to eliminate it altogether. It cannot convert a capital loss into a capital gain (but see below regarding indexation).

Section 41(1) of TCGA 1992 states the general principle that:

> "The amount of any losses accruing on the disposal of an asset shall be restricted by reference to capital allowances and renewals allowances."

This is then expanded in the following subsection:

> "In the computation of the amount of a loss accruing to the person making the disposal, there shall be excluded from the sums allowable as a deduction any expenditure to the extent to which any capital allowance or renewals allowance has been or may be made in respect of it."

So the adjustment is made in computing the amount of any capital loss, and this is achieved by excluding qualifying expenditure to the extent to which that expenditure has attracted capital allowances (or a renewals allowance). The allowances to take into account are net of any balancing adjustments made in relation to the disposal in question.

Example 1

Doris buys a property for £200,000 and sells it two years later for £195,000. She claims allowances of £25,000 initially and she signs a section 198 election at the time of sale, allocating £10,000 to fixtures in the property. As such, she has had net allowances of £15,000.

Her capital loss is initially calculated as £5,000. However, this is reduced to zero because of the capital allowances claim. The capital loss does not convert to a chargeable gain.

If, instead, the sale price of the property had been £172,000, she would initially have calculated a capital loss of £28,000. As a result of the capital allowances claimed, this loss would have reduced to £13,000.

See **1.10.8** below for discussion of the tax planning angles.

In practice, it may be impossible to calculate the allowances given in respect of a particular asset, because expenditure on plant and machinery is pooled in most cases. Where pooling has applied, the allowances are calculated as the difference between the amount of expenditure treated as incurred for capital allowances purposes on the asset in question and the disposal value that has to be brought into account in respect of that asset.

For these purposes only, capital allowances are defined to include any deduction made under s. 311A of ITTOIA 2005 or s. 250A of CTA 2009 (replacement domestic items relief)

Pooling requirement

There is no reason why a concern about capital losses should prevent a person from meeting the pooling requirement.

Example 2

A tax adviser is discussing the potential purchase of a property with his client. It is clear that the vendors have not claimed allowances. The vendors' accountants, however, are concerned that valuable CGT relief will be lost if the vendor is required to pool the assets.

This is not a real concern, as the vendors can pool the value of the assets and then transfer the whole value to the purchasers by means of a s. 198 election. The capital gains tax position is affected only if the vendor retains the value of some of the allowances.

Indexation

The treatment of any indexation allowance goes beyond the scope of this book (but is covered with examples in the *Capital Gains* manual, at CG 17434). Broadly, however, any indexation allowance is calculated on the amount as reduced by s. 41. Note also that an unindexed loss can become an unindexed gain. See also CG 16900 for an example illustrating the link between indexation, the capital allowances restriction and rebasing to 31 March 1982.

Asset acquired at written down value

In certain circumstances, a person may acquire an asset at its capital allowances written-down value. This may be under s. 268 (successions by beneficiaries) or under s. 569 (election to treat sale as being for alternative amount – where there is a change of control, or certain transfers between connected persons).

In these cases, any adjustment of the capital loss must take account of allowances made to the transferor (or to previous transferors) as well as of those made to the transferee.

The same adjustment will be needed where either of the following has applied:

- section 264(3) – partnership using property of a partner; or
- section 558 (succession to trades, etc.).

Law: TCGA 1992, s. 41
Guidance: CG 15410*ff.*; CG 17434

1.10.5   Part disposals

There may be a part disposal of an asset that has qualified for capital allowances. In these cases, any apportionment required by TCGA 1992, s. 42 (part disposals) must be made *before* any restriction for losses under s. 41.

Any loss accruing on a subsequent disposal (or further part disposal) will then be restricted by capital allowances or renewals allowances to the extent that they have not already been used to restrict an earlier loss.

See CG 15421 for an illustration of this principle, and see CG 17442 for a discussion of the issues of rebasing in the case of part disposals.

Law: TCGA 1992, s. 42
Guidance: CG 15420, 15421

1.10.6   Wasting assets

An important technicality needs to be addressed in respect of wasting assets, as these are subject to special CGT rules.

The starting principle is that no chargeable gain can arise on the disposal of an asset that is "tangible movable property" (i.e. a chattel) and that is also a wasting asset.

The general definition of a wasting asset is that it has a predictable useful life not exceeding 50 years. However:

- freehold land is never a wasting asset; but
- plant and machinery is always a wasting asset.

As "land" is defined for the purposes of the capital gains tax legislation to include "buildings", this raises the question of whether fixtures in a freehold property are never wasting assets (because they are part of the property which is part of the land) or are always wasting assets (because they are plant and machinery).

HMRC guidance is clear that land includes all buildings situated on it and all fixtures attached to it, and also that "where a chattel has become a fixture, it should not be treated as a separate asset unless it is physically detached from the land and sold independently". So an individual asset may initially be a chattel, but once it becomes a fixture it is part of the property and is not treated as a wasting asset.

This issue does not arise in connection with a leased property with a term of less than 50 years as this will be a wasting asset.

The chattel exemption does not apply if the asset in question has qualified for capital allowances throughout the period of ownership, and an apportionment is made (per s. 45(3)) where the asset has had mixed use. HMRC guidance is that "in making the apportionment of the expenditure you should have regard to the extent to which the asset qualified for capital allowances over the whole period of ownership". The guidance goes on to say that "the apportionment of the consideration should follow any apportionment of the consideration which has been made for capital allowances purposes".

The detailed CGT rules are beyond the scope of this book but, broadly, the normal calculation is modified for assets that *are* wasting assets. The gain is in principle exempt if the disposal value is £6,000 or less, and is restricted where the value is higher.

Law: TCGA 1992, s. 45, 288(1)

Guidance: CG 15400, 15452, 70205, 70207

1.10.7   *Companies – relevant circumstances*

One party may step into the shoes of a previous owner for the purposes of calculating capital allowances in particular circumstances. For example, a two companies under common control may transfer assets at written down value.

Any restriction of losses will in such a case take account of capital allowances given to the previous owner, or to any number of previous owners in an unbroken series of such transfers.

Law: CAA 2001, s. 41(3)

Guidance: CG 45922

1.10.8   *Tax planning issues*

The interaction of the capital allowances rules with those applying for CGT purposes raises some important tax planning considerations. This is especially true in the context of property fixtures, where the vendor may have significant control – by means of the fixtures election – over the proceeds figure to be brought into account.

The "obvious" (but not necessarily appropriate) thinking may be to adjust the fixtures election value to ensure that there is no restriction of capital losses.

Example

A Ltd is selling for £1m a property it bought some years earlier for £1.1m, so it will have a capital loss of £100k. It has not claimed any capital allowances but has identified fixtures with a value of £240k, which are now to be added to the main capital allowances pool. The company is now considering the figure to go into the fixtures election.

One possibility is that it agrees to put the maximum £240k into the election, so that it passes the full value of the allowances to the new owner. In that scenario, there will be no restriction on the capital loss, so there is a potential value in the £100k of losses, but there is no capital allowance tax relief for any of the property fixtures.

In many cases, this will not be the best way of approaching the matter. Even for a company, the best scenario is that any capital loss will be offset against other gains in the same period, and any remaining losses will be carried forward to be set against chargeable gains in a future accounting period. It may be possible to end up with a better outcome.

Example (cont.)

Suppose that A Ltd, from the example above, is making trading profits of around £100k per year. Suppose, too, that it does not have any capital gains in the current accounting period, and that it does not anticipate having any in the near future. In that case, the only benefit of preserving the capital loss is a possible future reduction of liability on a capital gain that may never materialise.

Suppose that the purchaser of the property is willing to accept a fixtures election value of £40k. This would then mean that A Ltd could gain immediate tax relief on £200k by way of capital allowances, as long as it is ready to sacrifice the capital loss. On the face of it, that is a much better overall result.

There are all sorts of permutations here. Another possibility is that the company in question has substantial trading losses and cannot immediately use either capital allowances or a capital loss. In that case, the better option should probably be to maximise the sale value.

Example (cont.)

As A Ltd cannot use either capital allowances or capital losses, it may be appropriate to seek to negotiate the sale price upwards, in return for additional capital allowances tax relief for the buyer. Further allowances of £200k are potentially worth £38k to a corporate buyer, assuming a 19% corporation tax rate. A Ltd might therefore wish to approach the buyer and offer a fixtures election figure of £240k in return for an additional £20,000 of sales consideration. In this way, A Ltd would also preserve its capital loss for possible future offset.

Timing of tax relief

In addition to the points illustrated in the above examples, a number of further factors may merit consideration.

One of these will be the timing of any tax relief. The examples above have considered the possible delay in claiming relief for capital or indeed trading losses, but the timing of any capital allowances should also be built into the equation. This will in turn involve an analysis of the extent to which annual investment allowances are available.

Another key issue will be the rate of tax payable, by the two parties to the transaction or simply by the vendor. A company pays 19% corporation tax on both income and gains, but the position is more complex where income tax and capital gains tax are involved. If, in the last part of the example above, the purchaser was a partnership paying tax at 45%, the argument for passing maximum tax relief to that purchaser is correspondingly stronger.

For a vendor paying income tax, the comparison between the liability to CGT and the benefit of capital allowances may need more detailed consideration, taking into account the rates at which the two taxes would be payable in all the given circumstances. It may be better to retain the highest possible value in capital allowances, gaining tax relief at a higher income tax rate and accepting a capital gains tax charge at a lower rate.

The key message here is that there are tax issues that merit proper consideration based on all the relevant circumstances, so a "one size fits all" approach is unlikely to give the optimal outcome in all cases.

1.11   Losses

1.11.1   Introduction

Capital allowances are given as a deduction in computing profits. For a profitable taxpayer, they will therefore reduce the tax liability on those profits. It is possible, however, that capital allowances will be sufficient to convert what would otherwise be a profit to a loss, or that they will augment an existing loss. The question of how relief may be given for such a loss is therefore important.

Tax relief may be available for losses incurred, including those created or augmented by capital allowances, but the statutory rules vary according to the nature of the activity giving rise to the loss. The income tax rules also differ in some respects from those applying for corporation tax purposes.

1.11.2   Income tax – trading losses

Trading losses (including losses arising from carrying on a profession or vocation) may be carried forward for offset against future profits from the same trade (ITA 2007, s. 83).

Trading losses (including losses arising from carrying on a profession or vocation) may also be offset against the person's net income from all sources for the year in which the loss is made or for the previous tax year (or both) (ITA 2007, s. 64). If a trader cannot offset the whole of the loss against general he may treat the unused part as an allowable loss for CGT purposes (ITA 2007, s. 71 and TCGA 1992, s. 261B and 261C).

A more generous form of loss relief applies for a person who makes a loss in a trade, profession or vocation in the first four tax years in which he or she carries on the activity in question. In such cases, the loss may be set against the individual's net income for the three years before the year in which the loss arose (ITA 2007, s. 72).

Similarly, losses incurred by a person making a loss in a trade, profession or vocation in (broadly) the final tax year of the business may be offset against that person's net income for that final year and for the previous three tax years (ITA 2007, s. 89).

Numerous restrictions and anti-avoidance provisions apply in respect of these loss reliefs, and full reference must therefore be made to the appropriate legislation. For example, restrictions apply to individual partners seeking to obtain sideways loss relief for AIAs or FYAs, where there is a tax avoidance motive. More generally, the £50,000/25% cap for sideways loss relief may need to be considered. See also *Tax Losses* from Claritax Books.

Law: TCGA 1992, s. 261B, 261C; ITA 2007, s. 24A, 64, 71, 72, 76, 78, 83, 89

1.11.3   Corporation tax – trading losses

The corporation tax legislation specifically states that the same rules apply "in calculating losses of a trade as apply in calculating profits" (CTA 2010, s. 47).

Trading losses may be carried forward for offset against future profits from the same trade (CTA 2010, s. 45). There has been some relaxation of the rules governing the use of such loss relief – see **1.1.3** above.

Trading losses may also be offset against the company's total profits of the accounting period in which the loss is made or total profits of previous accounting periods to the extent they fall within the 12 months immediately before the start of the loss-making period (CTA 2010, s. 37). If a company makes a loss in the accounting period in which the trade ceases, the 12-month carry back period is extended to three years (CTA 2010, s. 39).

Group relief provisions allow a trading loss to be offset in certain circumstances against the profits of another group company (CTA 2010, s. 99 and 100). Once more, there has been some relaxation of the rules governing the use of loss relief in these circumstances – see **1.1.3** above.

Numerous restrictions and anti-avoidance provisions apply in respect of these loss reliefs, and full reference must therefore be made to the appropriate legislation.

Law: CTA 2010, s. 37, 39, 45, 47, 99, 100

1.11.4   Furnished holiday letting losses

Losses arising from the carrying on of a qualifying furnished holiday lettings (FHLs) business are subject to various restrictions. In particular, it is not possible to offset losses from such an activity against an individual's total net income, or against corporate profits arising from other activities.

In the case of income tax, the restriction is imposed by ITA 2007, s. 127(3A). This states that the loss relief provisions apply in a way that broadly means that the only relief for FHLs losses is to be carried forward against profits from the same qualifying activity.

A similar effect is achieved for corporation tax purposes by CTA 2010, s. 65(4A) (and, for EEA FHL businesses, by s. 67A(5)).

1.11.5 *Property business losses*

By default, property losses (as opposed to FHL losses – see above) are carried forward to be set against future profits from the same property business. However, property losses attributable to capital allowances may be set against total income of the year of the loss or of the following year ("sideways relief"). Such losses may not be carried back.

This extension of the standard relief for property losses applies where the loss "has a capital allowances connection". (It also applies if the business has a "relevant agricultural connection" but that aspect is beyond the scope of this book.) However, structures and buildings allowances are ignored for these purposes.

A loss is said to have a capital allowances connection if there are net allowances after adjusting for any balancing charges.

A claim for this relief must specify whether the deduction is to be made for the loss-making year or for the following year, but if the loss for the specified year is not fully deducted then the excess may be set against general income of the other year. The taxpayer therefore has some scope to plan for the more effective use of the loss in question. However, it is not possible to restrict the claim for one year so as to preserve personal allowances that would otherwise be wasted.

Reference is made to Step 2 of the calculation at ITA 2007, s. 23, and details of how the relief works are given at s. 121.

A claim for relief under these provisions must be made by the first anniversary of the self-assessment filing date for the tax year specified in the claim. So if a 2020-21 loss is to be set against general income of 2021-22, the deadline for the claim will be 31 January 2024.

On the face of it, this may seem attractive for buy-to-let investors who wish to offset any allowances against income from other sources, such as from an employment. However, the restrictions for allowances in dwelling-houses (CAA 2001, s. 35 – see **4.14**) will often preclude such a claim in practice.

Law: ITA 2007, s. 120-124

1.12   Special situations

1.12.1   Property allowance

A new £1,000 income tax allowance is available for "micro-entrepreneurs" with very small levels of property income.

If the total property income does not exceed the limit, the income is tax-free and does not have to be reported to HMRC.

If gross receipts from the property income are in excess of the £1,000 allowance, the individual may deduct the £1,000 figure rather than keeping records of actual expenditure, paying tax only on the excess over £1,000.

In this case, no deduction will be given for "relevant expenses", including capital allowances. (Allowances for those carrying on an ordinary UK property business are given effect in calculating the profits of the business, treating an allowance as an expense of that business. The new rules specify that relevant expenses include all amounts that would otherwise be brought into account in calculating the profits of the business.)

A parallel relief exists for trading income – see immediately below. If an individual has both trading and property income, the total amount of the allowance cannot exceed £1,000.

Law: CAA 2001, s. 248; ITTOIA 2005, s. 783B-783BQ

1.12.2   Trading allowance

As for property income (see immediately above), a £1,000 income tax allowance is available for "micro-entrepreneurs" with very small levels of trading income.

If the total trading income does not exceed the limit, the income is tax-free and does not have to be reported to HMRC.

If gross receipts from the trading income are in excess of the £1,000 allowance, the individual may deduct the £1,000 figure rather than keeping records of actual expenditure, paying tax only on the excess over £1,000.

In this case, no deduction will be given for "relevant expenses", including capital allowances. (Allowances for those carrying on a trade are given effect in calculating the profits of the trade, treating an allowance as an expense of that trade. The new rules specify that relevant expenses include all amounts that would otherwise be brought into account in calculating the profits of the business.)

If an individual has both trading and property income, the total amount of the allowance cannot exceed £1,000.

An election may be made for full or partial relief under these provisions.

Law: CAA 2001, s. 247; ITTOIA 2005, s. 783A-783AR

1.12.3 Corporate interest restriction

A restriction applies to the amount of interest and other financing amounts that a company may deduct in computing its profits for corporation tax purposes.

For the purposes of calculating the restriction, it is necessary to establish the company's "tax-EBITDA", broadly speaking the earnings of a company or group before interest, tax, depreciation and amortisation.

The rules specify that capital allowances (and balancing charges) are to be excluded in arriving at the tax-EBITDA figure for any given period of account.

For companies suffering this restriction, capital allowances may be of greater relevance now than before, as discussed at **1.1.3** above.

Law: TIOPA 2010, s. 407

1.12.4 REITs

The general rules regarding capital allowances claims do not apply for the purposes of real estate investment trusts (REITs).

REITs are beyond the scope of this book but, broadly speaking, a REIT is a UK-resident corporate vehicle through which a person may invest in property. A REIT is obliged to pay out, in the form of dividends, 90% of the profits it derives from its property rental business. Those profits are calculated as they would be for tax purposes. Broadly speaking, the tax liability is transferred to the shareholders, who therefore pay tax as if they had invested directly in the properties making up the portfolio.

Full guidance is given in the *Guidance on Real Estate Investment Trusts* manual, but the following extract from that manual gives an overview of the capital allowances issues:

> "The income of the property rental business is based on the computation of profits for the purposes of taxing a property

business. One element in arriving at the profit is capital allowances, and normally, a company has to make a claim for the amount of capital allowances it wants to deduct in the period (section 3(1) CAA 2001).

The section 3(1) CAA requirement to claim and the choice of how much to claim are set aside in calculating the income of the property rental business (section 599(8) CTA 2010). Instead, the maximum allowances available under CAA must be taken into account in the calculation of the profits of the property rental business.

This means that a capital allowances 'shadow' regime operates within the property rental business. The result of this is that capital allowances are taken into account in calculating the profits of the property rental business and thus have the effect of reducing the property income distribution to, and so also the tax liability of, shareholders. Shareholders receive a distribution from the profits of the property rental business after capital allowances: there are no provisions that allow shareholders to access directly capital allowances on property rental business assets.

Otherwise, apart from some modifications when the company joins or leaves the regime, and when assets move from between the property rental and residual businesses (see GREIT04015), all the normal capital allowance rules apply to the property rental business. For more information see the Capital Allowances Manual. Apart from on joining and leaving the regime, and on transfers between the property rental and residual businesses, this includes the ability to make section 198 and section 199 CAA 2001 elections to apportion the sale price between fixtures and property when a property is disposed of or acquired by the company. See GREIT03015 for how to obtain a tax reference for capital allowance purposes."

The paradoxical result of this statutory approach is that capital allowances are of great value to REITs, even though they cannot claim the tax relief as such. By taking account of notional relief, through a system of shadow capital allowances, the REIT is able to reinvest funds within the business that would otherwise have to be paid out to investors.

The use of capital allowances can also have a beneficial effect on the balance between ordinary dividends and mandatory "property income distributions".

Law: CAA 2001, s. 3; CTA 2010, s. 599(8)
Guidance: GREIT 01005, 04010

1.12.5   CoACS

Co-ownership authorised contractual schemes (CoACS) exist "to satisfy industry demand for a UK based tax transparent fund vehicle". These schemes are transparent for the purposes of taxing income, in that the income accruing to the CoACS is automatically treated as the income of the investors in the CoACS, in proportion to their investment.

The reason for introducing special rules for CoACS was explained as follows in an (undated) technical note issued by HMRC as follows:

> "Because CoACS are transparent for the purposes of capital allowances, the investor – not the scheme – may be entitled to claim capital allowances subject to the normal rules. However, the operator of the CoACS holds the information which investors require to calculate their entitlement to capital allowances.
>
> To avoid the need for exchanges of information between the operator and investors, the government introduced a simplified scheme of calculating capital allowances whereby the operator of a CoACS may calculate the allowances and allocate them to investors."

The legislation effecting the changes is in Part 2, Chapter 20 of CAA 2001, beginning at s. 262AA. The rules are voluntary because:

> "some CoACS have only or mainly investors who are exempt investors, and who therefore are not entitled to claim capital allowances. To impose the new scheme on those CoACS would be an unnecessary administrative burden."

If the operator chooses not to elect in to the simplified scheme then individual investors will be able to claim on the normal basis if they meet the usual conditions.

If the operator does elect to calculate allowances at CoACS level, the calculation must be made as if all investors were taxable; the calculation is made according to a number of specified assumptions. If there is more than one qualifying activity, allowances must be separately calculated (and allocated – see below) for each activity.

The allowances as so calculated must then be allocated to each investor on a just and reasonable basis, taking into account the relative size of the investor's holding of units in the scheme. The operator is not entitled to take into account the investor's liability to tax, so it may be that some allowances are allocated to an investor who cannot use them.

Various administrative burdens are imposed on the operator of the CoACS, but these are not meant to be unduly onerous.

Law: CAA 2001, s. 262AA-262AF

Guidance: https://assets.publishing.service.gov.uk/government/uploads/system/uploads/attachment_data/file/670522/ACS_autumn_17_technical_note.pdf

Buying from a CoACS

Special rules apply to a person buying property from a CoACS, if the operator has elected into the simplified scheme. In these circumstances, the purchaser must (within two years from the date of purchase) obtain from the operator a written statement of the assumed tax written-down disposal value of the fixtures in the property. The purchaser's qualifying expenditure is then limited to this value. If no such statement is obtained within the two-year limit, the purchaser's qualifying expenditure on the fixtures in question is treated as nil.

This is a variant of the "disposal value statement requirement" that applies for fixtures more generally.

Law: CAA 2001, s. 262AE

Guidance: https://tinyurl.com/s6vcrce8 (HMRC guidance re CoACS)

1.12.6   Jersey property unit trusts

The following brief notes will hopefully provide a useful starting point for anyone considering capital allowances matters in the context of these trusts. The authors do not claim specialist expertise in relation to Jersey trusts, however, and therefore stress the need to take advice from those with day-to-day experience of working with such trusts.

Jersey property unit trusts (JPUTs) may be used to acquire and hold commercial UK property. It is understood that JPUTs will typically be "Baker" trusts, such that the trust income accrues automatically to the unit holders, rather than being held within the trust for future distribution.

The trustees of a Baker trust will not claim capital allowances. Instead, the individual unit holders in the trust can in principle claim the allowances, their claim being *pro rata* to the units held by each individual investor. (The trustees may, however, coordinate the claim and advise the individual unit holders of the claims they are entitled to make.)

Those acquiring units, and all unit holders when a commercial property is acquired (or improved/extended), will need to protect their interests to ensure that they will be entitled to claim allowances in relation to fixtures in the property. In either case, consideration should be given to the usual requirements for property fixtures, considered in depth later in this book, beginning at **Chapter 10**. In particular, it will be necessary to consider the pooling and fixed value requirements (see **12.4** and **12.5** below respectively).

By the same token, if unit holders sell their units, that will constitute a disposal of their share of the plant or machinery. Similarly, if a property is sold by the trust, there will be a disposal by all of the unit holders. Once more, the usual considerations will need to be given due attention.

1.12.7   *Fixed rate deductions for cars etc.*

For many years, employees have claimed mileage relief – rather than capital allowances – for business mileage (see **9.1.3**). The claiming of capital allowances by employees for their cars is specifically prohibited, so mileage allowances offer the only form of tax relief.

As an option, so without obligation, the use of mileage allowances was extended to the self-employed from April 2013. From April 2017, it was further extended (again, only as an option) to unincorporated property businesses. Transitional rules applied to allow landlords to claim mileage relief even if capital allowances had been claimed in the tax years 2013-14 to 2016-17. However, no balance could be carried forward in respect of the car once mileage relief was claimed.

Law: CAA 2001, s. 59; ITTOIA 2005, s 94E

1.13   **Northern Ireland**

1.13.1   *Background*

The *Corporation Tax (Northern Ireland) Act* 2015 received Royal Assent on 26 March 2015. However, the Act contains a commencement clause and the UK government have said that the legislation will not be implemented until the finances of the Northern Ireland Executive are "on a sustainable footing". The start date is also "subject to HMRC having sufficient time to develop the necessary IT systems". HMRC and the Department of Finance and Personnel in Northern Ireland have signed a "memorandum of understanding" which sets out the proposed arrangements.

Guidance: www.gov.uk/government/publications/memorandum-of-understanding-on-northern-ireland-corporation-tax

1.13.2   Capital allowances

Schedule 2 of the *Corporation Tax (Northern Ireland) Act* 2015 contains an extensive number of amendments to the capital allowances legislation. The proposed changes are set out in *Explanatory Notes*, which are reproduced at **Appendix 1**.

1.14   Freeports

1.14.1   Background

A "bidding prospectus" for freeports was published in November 2020, following a consultation earlier in the year. Fuller details of a number of enhanced capital allowances were then announced in the Budget of March 2021 and in the associated documentation. The measures provide capital allowances advantages for certain expenditure on plant and machinery, and on structures and buildings, incurred in freeport tax sites.

A "freeport" is defined as "an area which is identified as a freeport in a document published by, or with the consent of, the Treasury for [these] purposes".

An may only be designated by regulations as a "special area" for capital allowances purposes – a "freeport tax site" – if, when the regulations are made, the area is situated in a freeport or where the Treasury "consider that the area is being used, or is likely to be used, for purposes connected with activities carried on, or likely to be carried on, in a freeport".

For English freeports only, there are also SDLT benefits not covered in this book (but see *Stamp Duty Land Tax* from Claritax Books).

Any designation must specify the date on which the designation takes place.

According to the official documentation, the establishment of "at least 10" freeports is "intended to support the policy of levelling up the towns, cities and regions" of the UK. The idea is to make use of freedoms offered by Brexit to encourage investment in designated parts of the country.

Law: FB 2021, cl. 109, Sch. 21

1.14.2   Specific measures for freeport sites

For certain expenditure incurred by companies (only) on plant and machinery, 100% first-year allowances are available, subject to various conditions being met. These rules are considered in detail at **5.12** below.

For certain expenditure qualifying for structures and buildings allowances (SBAs), accelerated allowances (giving relief over 10 years rather than 33.33 years). These enhanced SBAs are available for income tax as well as corporation tax. For details, see **24.14**.

PLANT AND MACHINERY
ALLOWANCES

2. Introduction

2.1 Scope

Plant and machinery allowances are of value for virtually every business in the UK. From the window cleaner's ladder to the fixtures in the premises of every retailer, factory or office, plant and machinery allowances reduce the tax liability that would otherwise arise.

The legislation that governs the giving of allowances for expenditure on plant and machinery is extensive and in places complex. It is also subject to frequent change, whether in relation to the types of expenditure that may qualify for allowances or the rate at which such tax relief may be given.

Law: CAA 2001, Pt. 2
Guidance: CA 20000*ff.*

2.2 Statutory overview

2.2.1 Legislation

The main legislation relating to plant and machinery allowances may be found in Pt. 2 of CAA 2001. That legislation is divided into numerous chapters, as below:

Chapter 1:	Introduction
Chapter 2:	Qualifying activities
Chapter 3:	Qualifying expenditure
Chapter 3A:	AIA qualifying expenditure
Chapter 4:	First-year qualifying expenditure
Chapter 5:	Allowances and charges
Chapter 6:	Hire purchase etc. and plant or machinery provided by lessee
Chapter 6A:	Interpretation of provisions about long funding leases
Chapter 7:	Computer software
Chapter 8:	Cars, etc.
Chapter 9:	Short-life assets
Chapter 10:	Long-life assets
Chapter 10A:	Special rate expenditure
Chapter 11:	Overseas leasing

Chapter 12:   Ships
Chapter 13:   Provisions affecting mining and oil industries
Chapter 14:   Fixtures
Chapter 15:   Asset provided or used only partly for qualifying activity
Chapter 16:   Partial depreciation subsidies
Chapter 16ZA: Asset provided or used only partly for NI rate activity
Chapter 16A: Avoidance involving allowance buying
Chapter 16B: Cap on first-year allowances
Chapter 17:   Other anti-avoidance
Chapter 18:   Additional VAT liabilities and rebates
Chapter 19:   Giving effect to allowances and charges
Chapter 20:   Supplementary provisions

To keep the size (and cost) of this book at a more moderate level, the main focus of this book is on those areas that are relevant for the vast majority of businesses and practitioners, including (for example) the various provisions relating to allowances and charges. By contrast, there are only passing references to the rules for ships and for provisions affecting the mining and oil industries.

Law: CAA 2001, Pt. 2

2.2.2 General conditions

The essential principle is that plant and machinery allowances are available if a person carries on a qualifying activity and incurs qualifying expenditure.

If a person carries on more than one qualifying activity (e.g. a sole trader who also has an investment property), allowances are to be calculated separately for each activity.

For the meaning of "qualifying activity" see **Chapter 3**.

For the meaning of "qualifying expenditure" see **Chapter 4**.

Law: CAA 2001, s. 11

2.2.3 Manner of giving relief

Tax relief may be given by means of a variety of allowances, including first-year allowances, annual investment allowances, writing-down allowances and balancing allowances. Relief once given may be recaptured by way of a balancing charge. All of these are considered in **Chapter 5**.

The way in which effect is given to such allowances is considered at **5.10**.

2.3   HMRC toolkit

HMRC have produced a "toolkit" to help those claiming plant and machinery allowances. According to HMRC:

> "This toolkit is aimed at helping and supporting tax agents and advisers by providing guidance on the errors we find commonly occur in relation to capital allowances for plant and machinery. It may also be helpful to anyone who is completing a Company Tax Return or Income Tax Self Assessment tax return."

Key elements of this toolkit are included at **Appendix 3**.

Guidance: https://tinyurl.com/mu63ua7h (HMRC toolkit 2020-21)

3. Qualifying activities

3.1 Introduction and overview

The following are qualifying activities for the purposes of claiming plant and machinery allowances:

- a trade, profession or vocation;
- an ordinary UK property business;
- a UK furnished holiday lettings business;
- an ordinary overseas property business;
- an EEA furnished holiday lettings business;
- a concern listed in ITTOIA 2005, s. 12(4) or CTA 2009, s. 39(4) (mines, transport undertakings etc.);
- managing the investments of a company with investment business;
- special leasing of plant or machinery; and
- an employment or office.

However, these are all qualifying activities "to the extent only that the profits or gains from the activity are, or (if there were any) would be, chargeable to tax".

Allowances are to be calculated separately for each qualifying activity (s. 11(3)).

At the time of writing in April 2021, the authors are not aware of any move to change the rules in relation to EEA properties, following the UK's departure from the EU.

Restriction re dwelling-houses

For ordinary UK or ordinary overseas property businesses, and for special leasing of plant or machinery, the general principle is subject to the restriction in s. 35 re plant or machinery for use in a dwelling-house (see **4.14**).

The restriction does not apply in relation to other activities (e.g. for trades).

Further restrictions

Other restrictions apply in relation to offices or employments (s. 36: see **4.13.5**). No allowances are due for privately owned vehicles used for the purposes of an office or employment (s. 80: see **9.1.3**).

Foreign permanent establishments

A special rule has applied since 19 July 2011 in relation to any business carried on through one or more permanent establishments outside the UK by a company in relation to which an election under CTA 2009, s. 18A has effect (exemption for profits or losses of foreign permanent establishments). Such a business is a separate activity and is to be regarded as "an activity all the profits and gains from which are not, or (if there were any) would not be, chargeable to tax".

Law: CAA 2001, s. 15

3.2   Trade

The meaning of "trade" has been the subject of much discussion and case law over many decades. The implications of whether or not a particular activity constitutes a trade go far beyond capital allowances matters, and a full analysis is therefore beyond the scope of this book.

Nevertheless, the distinction – between a trade on the one hand and a different activity on the other – does have important capital allowances consequences, and it is therefore worth making a few general observations here.

The courts have identified various "badges" of trade – indicators that would lead to the conclusion that a particular activity is likely to constitute a trade for tax purposes.

A key such indicator is the profit-seeking motive, and a distinction is drawn here between the purchase of an asset with an intention of re-selling at a profit, perhaps after modifying the asset in some way, and a purchase made for the purposes of generating an income.

So a person who buys a property with a view to selling it at a profit may be carrying on a trade, whereas a person who buys it with a view to generating a rental income may instead be carrying on a property business.

Where necessary, the underlying evidence may be explored to determine the true intention when the property was acquired. If (for example) it was marketed almost as soon as it was bought, and/or if the funding of the purchase was such that it was clear from the outset that the property would need to be sold quickly, that would point to a trading transaction. On the other hand, if it can be shown that there was a genuine attempt to generate a long-term rental income, but that that did not succeed and this forced the owner to sell the property, then this may indicate that it was not a trading transaction, even if the property was in the event sold quite quickly, without ever having a tenant in place.

Serviced accommodation

In recent years (from say 2018 onwards), the authors have noticed a steep increase in the number of people seeking to badge their property activity as one of providing "serviced accommodation". Typically, this is to try to sidestep the capital allowances restrictions applying to residential property, or to gain a broader range of options for relieving losses, whilst avoiding the sometimes onerous conditions that apply if a property is to be classified as a furnished holiday let (FHL) property. (If a property is used for a trade or for an FHL business, the restrictions for residential property do not apply – see **4.14**).

If capital allowances are to be claimed, the activity must be a qualifying activity, as listed at **3.1** above. So the label "serviced accommodation" is not a statutory one, and the capital allowances legislation requires us to determine whether it is in fact a trade, an ordinary property business, an FHL business or (possibly) some other qualifying activity. If it does not meet the FHL criteria, and if the property is residential in nature, allowances will only be due on the fixtures in the property if the activity amounts to a trade.

The potentially dangerous idea that seems to be taking root is that the provision of a few additional services will easily convert an activity from being an ordinary property business to being a trade (such that the FHL criteria can simply be ignored). This was explored most notably in the *Nott* case at the FTT in 2016. The case referred back to a court decision, *Salisbury House Estate*, from 1930, where Lord Macmillan had stated:

> "A landowner may conduct a trade on his premises, but he cannot be represented as carrying on a trade of owning land because he makes an income by letting it. The relatively insignificant services for which the company makes charges to its tenants are not in my opinion sufficient to convert the company from a landowner into a trader ..."

Reference was also made in the *Nott* case to HMRC's *Property Income Manual* at PIM 4300, with the following words quoted:

"The whole letting activity will only constitute a trade where the owner remains in occupation of the property and provides services over and above those usually provided by a landlord. The provision of bed and breakfast, for example, is clearly trading. Essentially the distinction lies between the hotelier (who is carrying on a trade) and the provider of furnished accommodation (who is not). An important difference is that in a hotel etc the occupier of the room does not acquire any legal interest in the property."

The requirement to be in occupation was given significant weight in the *Nott* case. So in comparing the taxpayer's situation with that of a provider of hotel or bed and breakfast accommodation, the tribunal commented:

"The first issue for consideration is the extent to which the relevant case law supports the "occupation plus services" test referred to in the two extracts and, if so, the extent to which those features are present in Mr Nott's case."

The tribunal held that Mr Nott was not in "actual" occupation of the units that were being discussed (a reference to the 1982 *Conelee Properties* case), even though he did live in one of eight units on the estate.

In terms of services, cooked breakfasts were offered (usually for an additional charge) but no other meals. The units were cleaned at the end of the guests' stay, or daily for an additional charge. Various additional facilities were available to guests, including a pool, a pool house, a communal garden area, a games area, a working farm and a concierge service. Nevertheless, the tribunal held that it would have been misleading to describe the units to guests as a hotel or bed and breakfast.

The tribunal sided with HMRC, mainly on the grounds that the taxpayer was not truly in occupation of the property in question – a requirement that the tribunal held must constitute physical occupation rather than merely the holding of legal title – but also because the tribunal was not convinced that the package provided to guests was of a nature to convert it from a property rental business to one of providing services akin to those of a hotel or bed and breakfast.

Another leading case, in which the special commissioner gave detailed consideration to the distinction between a trade and a property business, is that of *Maclean*.

In conclusion, a taxpayer who does occupy the property in the sense required, and who also provides a broad range of services, may possibly be able to cross the line and to be treated as having a trade of providing serviced accommodation, rather than as generating income from property rental.

However, such an approach is likely to attract detailed HMRC scrutiny and quite possibly a further tribunal hearing, unless the facts can be very clearly distinguished in the taxpayer's favour from the case law referred to above. The HMRC view, at BIM 22001, is that "it is only treated as a trade when the landlord remains in occupation of the property and provides services substantially beyond those normally provided by a landlord" – broadly quoted in the *Mervyn Jones* FTT decision, which HMRC won.

At present, therefore, the classification of a property activity as a trade may be seen as a relatively high risk strategy. To prevent the risk of penalties, and of a future "discovery" assessment, anyone going down this route will be well advised to make a full and open disclosure of the facts to HMRC.

Cases: *Salisbury House Estate Ltd v HMRC* (1930) 15 TC 266; *Webb v Conelee Properties Ltd* [1982] BTC 368; *Maclean and Anor v HMRC* (2007) SpC 594; *Mervyn Jones and Anor v HMRC* [2009] UKFTT 312 (TC); *Nott v HMRC* [2016] UKFTT 106 (TC)
Guidance: BIM 22001; PIM 4300

3.3 Ordinary UK property business

This term is defined to mean any UK property business except a UK furnished holiday lettings business.

According to ITTOIA 2005, s. 264:

> "A person's UK property business consists of:
>
> (a)   every business which the person carries on for generating income from land in the United Kingdom, and
>
> (b)   every transaction which the person enters into for that purpose otherwise than in the course of such a business."

Law: CAA 2001, s. 16; Sch. 1, Pt. 2; ITA 2007, s. 989; CTA 2009, s. 1119

3.4   UK furnished holiday lettings business

This term is defined to mean any UK property business consisting (or to the extent that it consists) of the commercial letting of FHL accommodation.

If a person (or partnership, or body of persons) makes more than one such commercial letting of FHL accommodation, all such lettings are treated as a single qualifying activity for the purposes of claiming capital allowances.

For income tax purposes, the concept of "commercial letting of furnished holiday accommodation" is defined by reference to ITTOIA 2005, s. 323. The letting must be on a commercial basis, with a view to the realisation of profits. The person paying to use the accommodation must also be entitled to use the furniture. Various rules apply as to the number of days in the year on which the property must be let.

For corporation tax, the definition is by reference to CTA 2009, s. 265, which imposes almost identical conditions.

Accommodation that is let may qualify as holiday accommodation only in part. If so, just and reasonable apportionments must be made to determine the correct calculation of capital allowances.

A property may meet the qualifying criteria in one year but fail to do so in another. HMRC take a pragmatic (and reasonably relaxed) view about this, as explained in the *Property Income Manual* (at PIM 4115) under the heading of "Non-qualifying years":

> "Strictly, if a property qualifies in one year but does not do so in the next, the disposal value of plant and machinery should be brought into account. If income from a property temporarily ceases to qualify solely because not all the tests are satisfied for that year, capital allowances may be continued. But if a property is let on a long-term basis, or sold, or otherwise seems unlikely to qualify in the foreseeable future, disposal value should be brought into account."

Losses incurred on FHL activities may only be carried forward against profits from the same trade. Sideways loss relief is no longer available for such activities. Terminal loss relief is similarly denied. See also **1.11.4** above.

For a detailed discussion of the rules, see *Furnished Holiday Lettings* by John Endacott, available from Claritax Books.

Law: CAA 2001, s. 17; ITA 2007, s. 127(3A)
Guidance: PIM 4115

3.5 Ordinary overseas property business

This term covers any overseas property business except insofar as it is an EEA furnished holiday lettings business (see **3.6**).

According to ITTOIA 2005, s. 265:

"A person's overseas property business consists of:

(a) every business which the person carries on for generating income from land outside the United Kingdom, and

(b) every transaction which the person enters into for that purpose otherwise than in the course of such a business."

Law: CAA 2001, s. 17A; Sch. 1, Pt. 2; ITA 2007, s. 989; CTA 2009, s. 1119

3.6 EEA furnished holiday lettings business

This term covers any overseas property business consisting (or to the extent that it consists) of the commercial letting of furnished holiday accommodation in one or more EEA states.

If a person (or partnership, or body of persons) makes more than one such commercial letting of furnished holiday accommodation, all such lettings are treated as a single qualifying activity for the purposes of claiming capital allowances.

The same definitions as given at **3.4** above apply regarding the meaning of "commercial letting of furnished holiday accommodation".

It is possible that accommodation that is let will qualify as holiday accommodation only in part. In such a case, just and reasonable apportionments must be made to determine the correct calculation of capital allowances.

At the time of writing in April 2021, the authors are not aware of any move to change the rules in relation to EEA properties, following the UK's departure from the EU.

Law: CAA 2001, s. 17B

3.7   Managing the investments of a company with investment business

This activity is defined to mean the pursuance of purposes on which expenditure would qualify as management expenses within CTA 2009, s. 1219 (expenses of management of a company's investment business).

A "company with investment business" is a company, other than a credit union, whose business consists wholly or partly of making investments.

Law: CAA 2001, s. 18, CTA 2009, s. 1218

3.8   Special leasing of plant or machinery

The term "special leasing" refers to the hiring out of plant or machinery otherwise than in the course of a trade or of any other qualifying activity. References to a lessor or lessee in the context of special leasing are interpreted accordingly.

HMRC give the following example of an activity that might constitute special leasing:

> "Jason is a professional musician. He owns a yacht for the private use of himself, family and friends, which he sometimes charters out. The profits from chartering out the yacht are taxed as miscellaneous income [ITTOIA 2005, s. 574*ff*.]. The chartering out of the yacht is a special leasing. [Plant and machinery allowances] on the yacht are calculated separately from ones relating to his profession as a musician.
>
> Jason buys a powerboat, which he also leases out occasionally. PMA are calculated separately on the yacht and the powerboat."

A qualifying activity consisting of special leasing begins when the plant or machinery is first hired out in such circumstances. Such a qualifying activity is permanently discontinued if the lessor permanently ceases to hire out the plant or machinery otherwise than in the course of any other qualifying activity.

A person may have more than one item of plant or machinery that is the subject of special leasing. In that case, he is treated as having a separate qualifying activity in relation to each item.

Modified rules apply for a company carrying on life assurance business.

Law: CAA 2001, s. 19
Guidance: CA 20040

3.9 Employments and offices

The term "employment" – in the context of qualifying activities – does not include employment as a diver or diving supervisor, where such work is treated as the carrying on of a trade under ITTOIA 2005, s. 15.

Special rules apply if the earnings for any duties of an office or employment fall within ITEPA 2003, s. 22 (chargeable overseas earnings for year when remittance basis applies and employee ordinarily UK resident) or s. 26 (foreign earnings for year when remittance basis applies and employee not ordinarily UK resident).

In such a case, the plant and machinery rules apply "as if the performance of the duties did not belong to that employment or office". What this means is that if an employee pays tax only on earnings that are UK based, plant and machinery allowances will be available only to the extent that the assets in question are used in the performance of the UK duties. No allowances are available for general earnings that are charged on a remittance basis.

Restrictions

Restrictions apply in relation to offices or employments (s. 36: see **4.13.5**). No allowances are due for privately owned vehicles used for the purposes of an office or employment (s. 80: see **9.1.3**).

Law: CAA 2001, s. 20

4. Qualifying expenditure

4.1 Introduction

4.1.1 Significance

One of the fundamental conditions for giving plant and machinery allowances is that a person must incur qualifying expenditure.

Law: CAA 2001, s. 11

4.1.2 General rule

The "general rule" is that expenditure constitutes qualifying expenditure if:

"(a) it is capital expenditure on the provision of plant or machinery wholly or partly for the purposes of the qualifying activity carried on by the person incurring the expenditure, and

(b) the person incurring the expenditure owns the plant or machinery as a result of incurring it."

See **1.5** for a discussion of "capital expenditure".

If a person incurs abortive expenditure, no allowances will normally be due as the ownership condition is not met. (The position is different in the case of a hire purchase arrangement, however, as explained at **6.1.2**.)

The concept of expenditure being "on the provision of" plant and machinery comes up repeatedly in the legislation, but is not specifically defined. In *Inmarsat*, the FTT ruled that the launch costs of satellites did not constitute expenditure on their provision. This ruling was subsequently upheld by the Upper Tribunal.

This general rule is, however, modified by various other provisions. In particular, Chapter 3 of the plant and machinery legislation is entitled "Qualifying expenditure".

See also **4.13** and **4.14** for discussion of various exclusions from qualifying expenditure. These include cars owned and used by employees, and (in some circumstances) plant and machinery in dwelling-houses.

In *Barclays Mercantile*, certain payments were held to be qualifying expenditure despite a complex set of ultimately circular payments.

Law: CAA 2001, s. 11

Cases: *Barclays Mercantile Business Finance Ltd v HMIT* [2004] UKHL 51; *Inmarsat Global Ltd v HMRC* [2019] UKFTT 558 (TC)

4.2 Buildings, structures and land

4.2.1 Introduction

The area of plant and machinery in buildings is an important one. Often poorly understood in practice, the topic needs to be tackled head on as substantial amounts of tax are invariably at stake. Changes introduced from April 2012 further added to the need to grasp the relevant concepts.

The plant and machinery legislation contains two Chapters that are particularly important for understanding the relationship between buildings on the one hand and plant and machinery on the other.

Chapter 3 (of Part 2 of CAA 2001) deals specifically with "Buildings, structures and land" and is considered in this section **4.2**.

There is then a need for a second tier of legislation, dealing with the problems that arise in relation to ownership. This may be, for example, because a tenant installs plant and machinery in a building that belongs to the landlord: complications need to be addressed as to who, if anyone, is then entitled to claim allowances. These rules are found in Chapter 14 of the legislation ("Fixtures") and are dealt with at **Chapters 10 to 14** below.

In a sense, the headings used in the legislation are unhelpful, for Chapter 3 is in reality also concerned primarily with fixtures.

4.2.2 Buildings

The relevant legislation (s. 21) begins with the bald statement that "expenditure on the provision of plant or machinery does not include expenditure on the provision of a building". For clarity, it goes on to state that "the provision of a building includes its construction or acquisition".

Without further statutory provisions, no allowances could be given for assets that form part of a building. Quite specifically, there could be no allowances for fixtures, as that term is for capital allowances purposes defined to mean "plant or machinery that is so installed or otherwise fixed in or to a building or other description of land as to become, in law, part of that building or other land".

Matters are in fact made worse, as the term "building" is then defined to include any asset that:

    a. is incorporated in the building,

    b. although not incorporated in the building (whether because the asset is moveable or for any other reason), is in the building and is of a kind normally incorporated in a building, or

    c. is in, or connected with, the building and is in list A.

For a discussion of the term "incorporated in the building" (and of "normally incorporated in the building") reference may usefully be made, albeit in a different tax context, to the *Taylor Wimpey* case heard in the Upper Tribunal in 2017. The case makes the point that " 'incorporates' is not the same as 'installed as fixtures' ".

In *Urenco*, the tribunal gave its view that section 21 (unlike the common law test for whether an item qualifies as plant) "requires consideration of the nature and characteristics of a structure including whether or not the functions it is intended to perform are typical functions of a building". It went on to say that "a structure which has four walls and a roof might naturally be described as a building, whatever specialist function it might have in a trade." In relation to a kiln facility and a condenser facility, for example, the tribunal accepted that their predominant function was to support machinery and other equipment or to provide containment rather than shelter, but "those characteristics do not mean that the structures are not buildings". This gives a greater impact to the restrictive effect of s. 21 than had been seen in previous case law. Repeatedly, the tribunal returned to its conclusion that a particular asset was "naturally described as a building", and ultimately concluded that all the disputed expenditure was on buildings.

List A – assets treated as buildings

List A reads as follows:

    1. Walls, floors, ceilings, doors, gates, shutters, windows and stairs.

    2. Mains services, and systems, for water, electricity and gas.

3. Waste disposal systems.

4 Sewerage and drainage systems.

5. Shafts or other structures in which lifts, hoists, escalators and moving walkways are installed.

6. Fire safety systems.

Exceptions

If that were the end of the matter, there could be no plant and machinery allowances for any such items. In fact, however, these provisions are all subject to the all-important rules to be found at s. 23 (see **4.2.5** below).

As regards building alterations incidental to the installation of plant and machinery (s. 25), see **4.4**.

The restrictions in s. 21 do not apply to expenditure incurred before 30 November 1993 (or in some cases 6 April 1996), a point that could still be relevant today in relation to historic claims (Sch. 3, para. 13).

Law: CAA 2001, s. 21
Cases: *Taylor Wimpey plc v HMRC* [2017] UKUT 34 (TCC); *Urenco Chemplants Ltd & Anor v HMRC* [2019] UKFTT 522

4.2.3   Structures

The restrictions relating to buildings, as described immediately above, have a parallel in further restrictions covering "structures, assets and works".

The legislation states that expenditure on the provision of plant or machinery does not include expenditure on the provision of a structure or other asset in list B, or on any works involving the alteration of land. The provision of a structure is defined to include its construction or acquisition.

For these purposes, a structure must be a fixed structure other than a building. "Land" is defined to exclude buildings or structures, but is otherwise defined to mean "land covered with water, and any estate, interest, easement, servitude or right in or over land".

List B – excluded structures and other assets

List B reads as follows:

1. A tunnel, bridge, viaduct, aqueduct, embankment or cutting.

2. A way, hard standing (such as a pavement), road, railway, tramway, a park for vehicles or containers, or an airstrip or runway.

3. An inland navigation, including a canal or basin or a navigable river.

4. A dam, reservoir or barrage, including any sluices, gates, generators and other equipment associated with the dam, reservoir or barrage.

5. A dock, harbour, wharf, pier, marina or jetty or any other structure in or at which vessels may be kept, or merchandise or passengers may be shipped or unshipped.

6. A dike, sea wall, weir or drainage ditch.

7. Any structure not within items 1 to 6 other than–
   a. structure (but not a building) within Chapter 2 of Part 3 (meaning of "industrial building"),
   b. structure in use for the purposes of an undertaking for the extraction, production, processing or distribution of gas, and
   c. a structure in use for the purposes of a trade which consists in the provision of telecommunication, television or radio services.

The *SSE Generation* case explores in detail the meanings of some of these concepts. Reference should generally be made to the Upper Tribunal (UT) decision as some of the reasoning (though not the ultimate outcome) of the First-tier Tribunal was criticised in the higher court. The UT decision was upheld on all points (other than one relating to a technicality about requiring permission to appeal) when the case reached the Court of Appeal.

Alteration of land

Section 22(1) disqualifies expenditure on:

(a) the provision of a structure or other asset in list B (see above); or

(b) any works involving the alteration of land.

The precise meaning of this restriction was considered in depth in the *SSE Generation* case, at FTT level and subsequently at the UT and in the Court of Appeal. Those decisions are analysed in greater detail in the accompanying volume to this book, the *A-Z of Plant & Machinery*.

In brief, however, the tribunals both sided with the taxpayer in saying that the "works" restriction is narrower than HMRC were suggesting. As the UT put it:

> "List B does not in our view exclude expenditure on the alteration of land to the extent that it was required in the provision of a structure or other asset."

And again:

> "If expenditure on the asset is not disqualified because of the operation of any of the exceptions listed in Item 7 then that is the end of the enquiry and the expenditure is allowed. There is no separate consideration as to whether the construction of the structure or asset involved the alteration of land."

This has now received approval in the Court of Appeal, following HMRC's unsuccessful appeal.

Industrial buildings

The statutory meaning of "industrial building" (in item 7(1)) is defined by reference to Chapter 2 of Part 3 of CAA 2001. Part 3 was concerned with industrial buildings allowances (IBAs), and was "omitted" by FA 2008 for chargeable periods beginning from 1 or 6 April 2011. Nevertheless, we still need to refer to the omitted legislation for the purposes of item 7(a) above (as confirmed in *SSE Generation*).

The term "industrial building" was defined at s. 271 to include:

- a qualifying hotel or qualifying sports pavilion;
- in relation to qualifying enterprise zone expenditure, a commercial building or structure; and
- a building or structure in use for the purposes of a "qualifying trade" (see below).

For IBA purposes (as still now applied for these s. 22 purposes), a qualifying trade was either a trade of a kind described in Table A at s. 274, or an "undertaking" (see below) of a kind described in Table B of that section, if the undertaking was carried on by way of a trade.

Qualifying trades listed in Table A included trades, as there defined, of manufacturing, processing, storage, agricultural contracting, working foreign plantations, fishing, and mineral extraction.

Undertakings listed in Table B were those, again as described, of electricity, water, hydraulic power, sewerage, transport, highway undertakings, tunnels, bridges, inland navigation, and docks.

In *SSE Generation*, for example, it was agreed by all parties that the activities carried on by the company constituted a qualifying trade, on the basis that it was "an undertaking for the generation, transformation, conversion, transmission or distribution of electrical energy".

Cases: *SSE Generation Ltd v HMRC* [2018] UKFTT 416 (TC); *HMRC v SSE Generation Ltd* [2019] UKUT 332 (TCC), [2021] BTC 6

Undertaking

The meaning of "undertaking" in this context was considered in the *Cheshire Cavity Storage* case. The tribunal said that the term might on the one hand refer to an entity (e.g. a company or partnership) but might on the other refer to "the doing of an action or task". The tribunal sided with HMRC in deciding that the latter meaning was the intended one in this context. The tribunal also took a narrow view (arguably too narrow a view) of the meaning of "undertaking for the ... processing or distribution of gas".

Case: *Cheshire Cavity Storage 1 Ltd and EDF Energy (Gas Storage Hole House) Ltd v HMRC* [2019] UKFTT 498 (TC)

Tunnels

Tunnels are referred to in both s. 22 (list B, item 1) and s. 23 (list C, item 25). The Upper Tribunal and subsequently also the Court of Appeal in *SSE Generation* held that the word has different meanings in the two sections, in each case needing to be interpreted according to the immediate statutory context. Once more, this is considered in greater depth in the accompanying volume to this book, the *A-Z of Plant & Machinery*.

Cases: *HMRC v SSE Generation Ltd* [2019] UKUT 332 (TCC), [2021] BTC 6

Exceptions

There could be no plant and machinery allowances for any items caught by sections 21 or 22 if that were the end of the matter. In fact, however, these provisions are again subject to the s. 23 rules (see **4.2.5** below).

See also case study 2 at **Appendix 2** in relation to the question of marinas and associated expenditure.

The restrictions in s. 21 do not apply to expenditure incurred before 30 November 1993 (or in some cases 6 April 1996), a point that could still be relevant today in relation to historic claims (Sch. 3, para. 13).

Law: *Interpretation Act* 1978, Sch. 1 (re "land"); CAA 2001, s. 22

4.2.4   *Precise effect of sections 21 and 22*

The effect of sections 21 and 22 is to deny allowances for certain expenditure on buildings and structures (albeit subject to the s. 23 relieving provisions).

Counsel for the taxpayer in the *SSE Generation* case successfully argued that these restrictions were narrower than they had previously been deemed to be. The argument was that these sections merely prevented allowances from being given for certain items, but did not determine that the items in question were in fact not plant and machinery.

So, for example, item 3 at list A of s. 21 denies allowances for the cost of waste disposal systems, but the statutory wording was that *expenditure* on such systems is not treated as *expenditure* on plant or machinery. That did not mean, however, that the legislation was saying that the systems do not in fact constitute plant or machinery. In some cases, this made a real difference, especially in relation to relief given for the costs of "the alteration of land for the purposes only of installing plant or machinery".

The argument was a clever one, and prevailed in that case (and indeed was confirmed as correct by the Upper Tribunal). The success was short-lived, however, as the matter was reversed by legislation at FA 2019, s. 35, amending sections 21 and 22. The intention of the amended legislation, as per the relevant *Explanatory Notes*, was "to put it beyond doubt that land excavation costs for the purpose of creating an asset that functions as plant in common law are not allowable if the asset is excluded under section 21 or 22 CAA 2001".

The amended legislation applies to claims made from 29 October 2018, whenever the expenditure was incurred.

The question of whether the statutory rules of sections 21 to 23 should be considered before or after the case law principles (i.e. of what is meant by plant) was also aired in *SSE Generation*, but in the end it has little practical significance, as both tests must be met. As the tribunal judge put it in *Cheshire Cavity Storage*, "the order in which I considered them did not seem to matter and this dispute was therefore rather anodyne".

Cases: *SSE Generation Ltd v HMRC* [2018] UKFTT 416 (TC); *Cheshire Cavity Storage 1 Ltd and EDF Energy (Gas Storage Hole House) Ltd v HMRC* [2019] UKFTT 498 (TC)

4.2.5   Exceptions to the restrictions

The initially severe restrictions for allowances for buildings and structures have been outlined at **4.2.2** and **4.2.3** respectively. Those restrictions are subject to some very important exceptions, given at s. 23.

To avoid confusion, it is advisable to look at s. 23 as constituting two halves that work independently from one another. First, s. 23 lists certain particular provisions to which the restrictions for buildings and structures (given by s. 21 and s. 22 respectively, as described immediately above) do not apply. These provisions relate to thermal insulation, personal security, integral features, and software.

For each of these categories, the legislation has particular rules saying that the expenditure in question specifically qualifies for plant and machinery allowances. For example, allowances for integral features or for thermal insulation are given "as if ... the expenditure were capital expenditure on the provision of plant or machinery". Section 23 thus ensures that sections 21 and 22 cannot override those deeming provisions that allow certain types of expenditure to qualify as plant or machinery. The relevant provisions are all considered in their context later in this book.

List C

The remaining part of s. 23 works differently, though. This provides a long list of assets ("list C"), being "expenditure unaffected by sections 21 and 22". The key point to note is that inclusion in list C does not guarantee that expenditure on the item in question will qualify as plant or machinery; the effect of this part of s. 23 is merely to remove the automatic bar on claiming allowances on the items in question. The background to what is now list C was a perception that the Courts were starting to err too much in favour of the taxpayer in various appeals regarding plant and machinery. Consider, for example, these words in the Revenue response to the Institute of Taxation back in 1994:

"As you know, court cases have, over the years, increasingly reclassified expenditure on buildings and structures as being expenditure on plant. This erosion in the plant/structure boundary has affected Exchequer receipts and has in itself created continuing uncertainty.

The intention behind the legislation is therefore to strengthen the current boundary, and to ensure that no further erosion takes place. It would of course be difficult for the new rules to replicate past treatment in every case. Nevertheless, the broad aim is to provide exclusions for assets currently regarded as plant as a result of Court decisions, so as to leave the present position unchanged."

The point was made in stronger terms by Stephen Dorrell, speaking for the government when the clauses were debated in Parliament. He was clear that the purpose of the new legislation was "to prevent further changes in the law" and again "to prevent further development of case law". He stated specifically that "we are not seeking to revisit the law established by the Courts" and again that "it is not our intention to change the capital treatment of any class of asset". Once more, he stated that "nothing in the clause is intended to change existing practice of how cases are treated". Occasionally, in areas of doubt, the Courts will try to fathom the intentions of Parliament. In such cases, it may be useful to refer to these assurances that the government was not seeking to change "existing practice".

"Thus far but no further" was the approach. This was a strange concept, for it meant that if an asset happened to have been the subject of a successful appeal the tax treatment of that particular asset was frozen into the legislation. The statutory rules were being made subservient to the case law, rather than the other way round. This accounts for the bizarre range of assets captured in list C that have little internal logic (though even that unusual approach does not account for other oddities such as the doubling up of refrigeration equipment at items 5 and 9).

To reiterate the key point, inclusion in list C does not guarantee that an item qualifies as plant or machinery. If an asset is initially caught by s. 21 or s. 22 (in broad terms, being respectively a building or a structure) the effect of inclusion in list C is simply to remove the statutory restriction that would automatically prevent a claim. The actual tax treatment of the asset can then be considered on its own merits, using the case law precedents established before or since the statutory rules were introduced in 1994.

Two words of caution are also needed about the wording at s. 23(4) that introduces list C. The relieving provisions of items 1 to 16 of list C do not apply if the principal purpose of the asset is to insulate or enclose the interior of a building or to provide an interior wall, floor or ceiling that is intended to remain permanently in place. See **4.11.3** for HMRC guidance on this wording in the context of integral features.

The second caveat is based on a point that was raised in the 2019 *Urenco* case, a First-tier decision that went entirely in HMRC's favour, and is concerned with installation costs. HMRC made an argument that may be summarised as follows (and that was accepted by the tribunal):

- Section 21 denies allowances for expenditure on the provision of a building.
- List C at s. 23 undoes the statutory restriction in relation to certain items.
- Section 23(3), which introduces list C, states that the relieving provisions apply to "expenditure **on** any item described in list C" and not to "expenditure **on the provision of** any item described in list C".
- Items 23 to 33 at list C refer to "the provision" of the assets in question (e.g. to the provision of dry docks) but that wording is absent from items 1 to 22.
- If we take item 1 (machinery) as an example, the effect of this – according to HMRC – is that installation costs of machinery (as opposed to the cost of the machinery itself) are not rescued by list C.

This is one possible interpretation of this wording, but is certainly not universally accepted as the correct interpretation. The conclusion of the FTT in this case (which is not binding, of course – see **1.3.3**) was nevertheless that "if a piece of machinery or equipment is incorporated in a building or connected with a building then the cost of installation remains part of the expenditure on the provision of the building" (and is therefore not allowable).

Case: *Urenco Chemplants Ltd & Anor v HMRC* [2019] UKFTT 522

List C – expenditure unaffected by sections 21 and 22

List C reads as follows:

1. Machinery (including devices for providing motive power) not within any other item in this list.

2. Gas and sewerage systems provided mainly–
   a. to meet the particular requirements of the qualifying activity, or
   b. to serve particular plant or machinery used for the purposes of the qualifying activity.

3. [Omitted by FA 2008, s. 73(1)(b)(ii).]

4. Manufacturing or processing equipment; storage equipment (including cold rooms); display equipment; and counters, checkouts and similar equipment.

5. Cookers, washing machines, dishwashers, refrigerators and similar equipment; washbasins, sinks, baths, showers, sanitary ware and similar equipment; and furniture and furnishings.

6. Hoists.

7. Sound insulation provided mainly to meet the particular requirements of the qualifying activity.

8. Computer, telecommunication and surveillance systems (including their wiring or other links).

9. Refrigeration or cooling equipment.

10. Fire alarm systems; sprinkler and other equipment for extinguishing or containing fires.

11. Burglar alarm systems.

12. Strong rooms in bank or building society premises; safes.

13. Partition walls, where moveable and intended to be moved in the course of the qualifying activity.

14. Decorative assets provided for the enjoyment of the public in hotel, restaurant or similar trades.

15. Advertising hoardings; signs, displays and similar assets.

16. Swimming pools (including diving boards, slides and structures on which such boards or slides are mounted).

17. Any glasshouse constructed so that the required environment (namely, air, heat, light, irrigation and temperature) for the growing of plants is provided automatically by means of devices forming an integral part of its structure.

18. Cold stores.

19. Caravans provided mainly for holiday lettings.

20. Buildings provided for testing aircraft engines run within the buildings.

21. Moveable buildings intended to be moved in the course of the qualifying activity.

22. The alteration of land for the purpose only of installing plant or machinery.

23. The provision of dry docks.

24. The provision of any jetty or similar structure provided mainly to carry plant or machinery.

25. The provision of pipelines or underground ducts or tunnels with a primary purpose of carrying utility conduits.

26. The provision of towers to support floodlights.

27. The provision of–
    a. any reservoir incorporated into a water treatment works, or
    b. any service reservoir of treated water for supply within any housing estate or other particular locality.

28. The provision of–
    a. silos provided for temporary storage, or
    b. storage tanks.

29. The provision of slurry pits or silage clamps.

30. The provision of fish tanks or fish ponds.

31. The provision of rails, sleepers and ballast for a railway or tramway.

32. The provision of structures and other assets for providing the setting for any ride at an amusement park or exhibition.

33. The provision of fixed zoo cages.

In item 19 of the above list, the term "caravan" is defined to include, in relation to a holiday caravan site, anything that is treated as a caravan for the purposes of–

a.   the *Caravan Sites and Control of Development Act* 1960; or

b.   the *Caravans Act (Northern Ireland)* 1963.

To illustrate all this with a practical example, take the question of a hut put up by a builder to provide canteen and toilet facilities for workers at particular sites. The reasoning to follow will be:

- Assuming that the hut is to be kept in use for at least two years, it should be clear that the cost is capital expenditure.

- The cost of the hut is potentially caught by either s. 21 (as a building) or by s. 22 (as a structure).

- There is nothing relevant at s. 23(2), but item 21 at list C refers to "moveable buildings intended to be moved in the course of the qualifying activity".

- That does not of itself mean that the hut can qualify for allowances, but it can at least be considered using case law principles.

- Case law coverage of moveable buildings is not always helpful, but HMRC guidance does in this case come to the rescue, as allowances are specifically permitted for such buildings.

If, instead, the huts in question were used for some other trade – perhaps for selling items at trade fairs around the country – the HMRC guidance is less favourable. It would then be necessary to apply general principles to determine the correct outcome. In this case, it may be appropriate to question the HMRC view, so as to see if it can stand up to scrutiny.

See the complementary title *A-Z of Plant & Machinery* – also available from Claritax Books – for a similar approach to more than 300 categories of expenditure.

Meaning of "equipment"

Item 4 in the above list refers to "equipment" and the meaning of this word – especially in the context of storage – was considered in some detail in the *Cheshire Cavity Storage* case. The term "equipment" is a common one, and therefore of some importance. For this reason, the following lengthy quotation has been included (unedited) from this First-tier Tribunal decision:

"193. The first relevant item of List C was no. 4 which applied to:

4. Manufacturing or processing equipment; storage equipment (including cold rooms); display equipment; and counters, checkouts and similar equipment.

While I have set out no 4 in full, in reality the appellant's case was that the gas cavities were 'storage equipment'.

194. While HMRC accepted (rightly) that the gas cavities were for storage, they did not accept that they were 'equipment'. HMRC relied on the definition in the Shorter English dictionary that

Articles used or required for a particular purpose; apparatus

HMRC's position was that underground cavities could not be described as articles or apparatus, however much they might have a purpose.

195. The appellant's position was that the cavities were equipment because they were, or served as, pressure vessels for storage of gas. Moreover, if a cold room is 'equipment' it naturally followed that another storage structure, such as a gas cavity, was also equipment. They were both permanent, fixed man-made spaces for storage under particular conditions.

196. I'm going to consider what Parliament meant by the use of 'equipment' in this context by considering the normal meaning of 'equipment' and then whether a different and wider meaning was intended because it was said to include cold rooms.

197. With the exception of the reference to cold room, everything else in item 4 is some sort of 'equipment' in the normal meaning of the word even though some of them might be well be fixtures when used (eg manufacturing equipment and counters). Were it not for the reference to cold rooms, I would consider that Parliament intended 'equipment' to be used with its normal meaning.

198. It follows, therefore, that although Mr Aron's evidence was that industry would not consider a cavity to be equipment, I do not consider that matters as the question is its normal and not technical meaning. I am not clear whether Mr Aron's view that equipment had to have moving parts was a personal view or a view which reflected that of industry, but I do not accept that it is relevant. The normal meaning of equipment would not require moving parts, only that it is an article with a purpose.

199. However, I agree with HMRC that the word 'equipment' would not in normal usage encompass an underground cavity, even one that was man-made for a particular purpose. The word 'equipment', as well as the words 'article' and 'apparatus' used to define it, imply a thing that is not a part of the land (although it might include something that has been fixed to the land in order to use it). Equipment may not be portable but it is not a part of the landscape. The cavity, however, is formed in rock. It is part of the land and not fixed to it.

200. But should 'storage equipment' be understood to have a wider than normal meaning as it is stated to include cold rooms, which, if fixed, are a part of land? I would not consider a cold room to be an article. I would assume it was a purpose built structure or part of a structure with design features which enable (normally only when powered) a cold temperature to be maintained. So should other structures with a storage function be considered storage equipment?

201. It seems to me that drafter understood that 'storage equipment' would not include cold rooms, and so specifically included it as Parliament wished cold rooms to have the benefit of capital allowances (perhaps to reflect the *Union Storage* case). I do not think there was an intention to widen the meaning of 'equipment' generally as the drafter said 'including' cold rooms and not 'such as' cold rooms. I have already said I do not think Parliament meant the exemptions to be widened by analogies with function.

202. My conclusion is that item 4 is fairly narrowly drawn and would not ordinarily extend to structures with a purpose although it would appear to extend to fixed apparatus. While it was clearly intended to extend to cold rooms, it was

not intended to extend to store rooms, or it would have said more than simply 'including cold rooms'. So Item 4 does not cover the cavities as they are not equipment. They are part of the sub-surface rock."

Case: *Cheshire Cavity Storage 1 Ltd and EDF Energy (Gas Storage Hole House) Ltd v HMRC* [2019] UKFTT 498 (TC)

Poor HMRC reasoning

In the *Telfer* case, HMRC sought to argue that an implicit restriction must apply if an item within list C removes that restriction. More specifically, HMRC were arguing that as item 19 removes a restriction on claiming for certain caravans, it must follow that caravans generally are within the restrictions for buildings and structures in the first place. This, in the view of the authors, was an inexcusable stance from HMRC: if they wished to bring sections 21 or 22 into play, the onus was entirely on HMRC to demonstrate that the caravans in question were either buildings or fixed structures. In reality, of course, they were clearly neither.

In rejecting the HMRC stance on this point the tribunal commented as follows:

> "This is an argument from redundancy – that is, an argument that it would be redundant for a class of caravans to be excluded from the application of sections 21 and 22 by section 23 CAA, if section 21 or section 22 did not apply to caravans. Lord Hoffmann famously said that he seldom thought that an argument from redundancy carried great weight (*Walker v Centaur Clothes Group Ltd* [2000] 1 WLR 799 at 805D), and we respectfully agree. Further, it seems to us that section 21 or section 22 CAA could only apply to fixed caravans and plainly Mr Telfer's caravans were not fixed."

Case: *Telfer v HMRC* [2016] UKFTT 614 (TC)
Guidance: CA 22110

4.2.6   Interests in land

Expenditure on land does not constitute expenditure on plant or machinery.

For these purposes, the term "land" is defined to exclude buildings, structures or any asset that is "so installed or otherwise fixed to any description of land as to become, in law, part of the land".

83

Subject to these points, "land" is defined to include "land covered with water, and any estate, interest, easement, servitude or right in or over land".

Again subject to the exclusion of buildings etc. (as above), an "interest in land" has the meaning applied to it for the purposes of the fixtures legislation (s. 175: see **10.1.4**).

Law: *Interpretation Act* 1978, Sch. 1 (re "land"); CAA 2001, s. 24

4.3   The meaning of "plant" and "machinery"

4.3.1   Introduction

Before allowances can be given for "plant or machinery" it is obviously necessary to know what that term encompasses, yet this is often far from clear. Certainly, not all capital expenditure qualifies for plant and machinery allowances. This point is well established but was confirmed in the *Bowman* case, where certain consultancy payments were held to be capital in nature but did not qualify for allowances.

Statutory rules introduced in the 1990s went some way towards creating a firmer definition, but those rules, now starting at s. 21 of CAA 2001 (see **4.2** above), are limited in their scope and still leave many questions unanswered. In essence, the distinction is drawn between the premises or setting within which a qualifying activity is conducted, and the apparatus used in the course of that activity. In practice, the setting and the apparatus can overlap and there are many grey areas. Dozens of cases have been taken to court where it has not been possible for a business to reach agreement with the tax authorities about where the line should be drawn.

One complication is that the correct capital allowances treatment of a particular asset is coloured by its context. A ship, for example, will normally qualify quite clearly as an item or plant or machinery, yet the best known capital allowances case concerning a ship determined that it did not so qualify in the particular circumstances of the case (as it was functioning only as the premises for the business in question). Readers may usefully refer to the accompanying volume from Claritax Books Ltd – the *A-Z of Plant & Machinery* – which provides item-by-item guidance in relation to more than 300 different types of asset, explaining the circumstances in which they are likely or not likely to qualify as plant or machinery.

There has been some judicial disagreement over whether the term "plant" is still used in its natural sense, or whether it has developed its own meaning in the tax context. On the whole, the prevailing view is that the term has now gained a specialist meaning. Oliver LJ, in *Cole Bros* opined that:

> "it is now beyond doubt that [the term 'plant'] is used in the relevant section in an artificial and largely judge-made sense".

Cases: *Cole Brothers Ltd v Phillips* [1982] BTC 208; *Grant Bowman t/a The Janitor Cleaning Company v HMRC* [2012] UKFTT 607 (TC)

4.3.2   Illogical distinctions

Case law shows that it is notoriously difficult to pin down the meaning of "plant". As Stephenson LJ commented in his judgment in *Cole Bros*:

> "The more definitions multiply, the less enviable grows the task of H.M. Inspectors of Taxes. If they 'traverse the whole gamut of reported cases' crossing the border into Scotland and the seas to Australia in their search for guidance, they find plant in the most unlikely objects, from a horse to a swimming pool, from a dry dock to a mural decoration. Faced with such applications of the word, all supported by cogent reasoning, they may be pardoned for finding anything, or almost anything, to be or not to be plant and may be justified in making any number, or almost any number, of inconsistent concessions and illogical distinctions. It all depends on the circumstances, especially the work of the particular taxpayer, and (I feel bound to add) on how it strikes the particular judges of the question, whether in tax administration or on the judicial bench."

It is unfortunate that such a fundamental concept, affecting all businesses and often involving substantial amounts of expenditure, should have been left so open to the whims of individual interpretation. The comments quoted above pre-date the legislation now beginning at s. 21 (and indeed the concept of "integral features") but in reality that legislation has been of limited help in defining the slippery notion of "plant".

The Court of Appeal in *SSE Generation* made the wry observation that the complex hydroelectric scheme that was the subject of that case was opened less than three years after construction work began, but "the arguments about the tax treatment of various components that make up the project ... still remain to be resolved over ten years after the project was completed". The arguments were primarily about which expenditure was on plant or machinery.

In the end, the Courts have on occasion been ready to admit that the term is not clearly defined, and to fall back on more fundamental principles, as stated by Lord Wilberforce in the *Scottish & Newcastle* case:

> "I do not think that the courts should shrink, as a backstop, from asking whether it can really be supposed that Parliament desired to encourage a particular expenditure out of, in effect, taxpayers' money and perhaps ultimately, in extreme cases, to say that this is too much to stomach."

At least the 2008 legislation, whereby certain assets are categorised as "integral features", brought a greater degree of certainty to some common types of expenditure, including electrical work and cold water systems. These developments are very welcome, though they are limited and, even here, the precise scope of the legislation is at times unclear.

Case: *Cole Brothers Ltd v Phillips* [1982] BTC 208; *HMRC v SSE Generation Ltd* [2021] BTC 6

4.3.3   All goods and chattels

Given that the capital allowances legislation contains no positive definition of "plant or machinery" it has fallen to the courts to develop an interpretation over the years.

The meaning of "machinery" has caused relatively few problems in practice. Defining "plant" has been a far greater challenge, but at least the starting point is agreed by all parties. Lindley LJ attempted a definition in a case, *Yarmouth v France*, heard back in 1887 on a matter that had nothing to do with taxation:

> "There is no definition of plant in the Act: but, in its ordinary sense, it includes whatever apparatus is used by a businessman for carrying on his business – not his stock-in-trade which he buys or makes for sale; but all goods and chattels, fixed or moveable, live or dead, which he keeps for permanent employment in his business."

This quotation has been approved over and over again, in all courts, in discussions of the meaning of plant for capital allowances purposes. It can be seen as the cornerstone definition and – subject only to statutory provisions that restrict or expand its scope – it is thus of pre-eminent importance in determining what does or does not qualify as plant.

The key concepts to be drawn out of the quotation are the use of the term "apparatus" and the breadth of the definition, encompassing "all goods and chattels, fixed or moveable, live or dead". In other words, Lindley gave to the word "plant" the widest possible meaning. The term "apparatus" has sometimes been given a narrow interpretation, but "whatever apparatus" clearly indicates that it actually embraces a wide category of assets. That wide interpretation is made explicit in the last part of the quotation, encompassing "all goods and chattels".

The definition also draws a contrast between plant on the one hand and trading stock on the other, but that distinction has in practice not caused any difficulty. Nor is the question of "permanent employment" of any great significance, as anything that fails on that ground alone is likely to be allowed as an ordinary revenue deduction rather than by way of plant or machinery allowances.

The broad meaning of plant was brought out further in the *Scottish & Newcastle* case, where – in the House of Lords – Lord Lowry stated:

> "I think that much difficulty is caused by seeking to place limitative interpretations on the simple word 'plant': I do not think that the classic definition propounded in *Yarmouth v France* suggests that it is a word which is other than of comprehensive meaning."

Cases: *Yarmouth v France* [1887] 4 TRL 1; *CIR v Scottish & Newcastle Breweries Ltd* [1982] BTC 187

4.3.4   Plant or premises

The references in the quotation above to apparatus, goods and chattels can also be used to differentiate between plant and premises, a more important theme that was to emerge more fully and specifically in later case law. This was developed, nearly a century later, in the *Cole Bros* case where the judge explicitly drew out the etymological link between the taxation use of the term "plant" and its more familiar botanical use:

> "I think it worthwhile spending a moment's time in reflecting briefly on what the botanical analogy is. In the field of botany 'plant' is used in three quite separate contexts. It can mean a vegetable organism synthesizing its nourishment from inorganic materials by the use of chlorophyll. In this sense an oak tree is a plant, whilst the Matterhorn is not. It can mean a vegetable organism with a soft stem. In this sense a bluebell is a plant, but an oak tree is not. Neither of these senses affords the analogy. But

the word can mean a vegetable organism deliberately placed in an artificially prepared setting.

A gardener can say 'I am going to dig my flower beds in readiness for my plants' or, 'I am going to buy some plants at my garden centre'. It is this sense which gives it its analogical meanings, e.g. in medicine ('an organ transplant'), in crime ('it was planted on me'), or in industry, which is the sense we are now discussing, as the means by which a trade is carried on in an appropriately prepared setting. In each case, the contrast is between the thing implanted, i.e. the plant, and the prepared setting into which it is placed."

Apparatus

In practice, particular focus has been given to the word "apparatus" and the courts have to some extent driven a wedge between apparatus on the one hand, and the setting or premises on the other. Even ignoring the statutory enactments from 1994, mentioned at **4.2** above, there is a legitimate divide here.

The point was brought out in a second world war compensation claim case, that of *J. Lyons & Co*, where it was held that "the electric lamps and fittings were not part of the apparatus used for carrying on the business, but were part of the setting in which the business was carried on, and, therefore, were not 'plant' ". In reaching that conclusion, the judge noted that the items in question presented "no special feature either in construction, purpose or position".

In the case of *St John's School*, too, a school laboratory and a gymnasium were held not to be plant as "the building was only the structure within which the function of educating the boys was carried on"; neither the laboratory nor the gymnasium had any function to perform other than to shelter the pupils. Similarly, allowances were refused for the ship in the *Yard Arm Club* case as it functioned only as the premises and not as apparatus used for carrying on the trade.

But the divide between setting and apparatus is not black and white. In *Jarrold v Good*, the judge specifically commented that "the setting in which a business is carried on, and the apparatus used for carrying on a business, are not always necessarily mutually exclusive".

In *Wimpy*, Hoffman J provided a useful summary of the earlier case of *Scottish & Newcastle Breweries*, explaining it as follows:

> "The items in dispute in that case were wall decor, plaques, tapestries, murals (which were in fact detachable), pictures and metal sculptures used to decorate hotels. All of these were held to be chattels or trade fixtures and not integral parts of the premises. The Revenue refused them capital allowances as plant on the ground that they formed part of the 'setting', which in one sense, and probably the most obvious sense, they certainly did. But the House of Lords held that they nevertheless passed the business use test because they were used to please and attract customers, and therefore were for the promotion of the trade."

One of the best cases to explore the boundary between apparatus and setting is that of *Andrew*, which considered whether a gazebo in a pub garden was an item of plant. The taxpayer was successful in the claim but various particular facts influenced the outcome and it does not follow that a gazebo would qualify in all circumstances. The arguments and the reasoning of the tribunal were clear, however, so the case does provide a useful precedent.

The argument essentially turned on whether the gazebo merely formed part of the *premises in which* the pub trade was conducted, or whether it could properly be described as *apparatus with which* the trade was conducted.

HMRC argued that the gazebo was part of the premises, and relied on the reasoning of *Fitch's Garage* and of *St John's School*. For the taxpayer, it was argued that the gazebo provided seating to which the covering was incidental. It was "a movable piece of wood garden furniture purchased as a decorative asset for the enjoyment of customers who may sit there to enjoy the views of the South Downs".

The tribunal considered whether the gazebo was caught by s. 22 by virtue of being a "structure". However, s. 22(3) defines a structure as a "fixed structure of any kind". The tribunal found as a fact that it was not a fixed structure as "it could be moved and looking at it gave the impression that it could be moved". As it provided only limited shelter or security, it was not properly described as a building either. The reasoning of the tribunal was then as follows:

> "25. We have no doubt that if the gazebo was simply a polygonal bench surrounding a table then it would be plant: it would be a permanent asset provided for the comfort of customers during

their stay in the pub and such provision would be a function of the conduct of the pub trade. It would not matter whether the bench were used or intended to be used by customers to sit, eat, read, talk, wait, or smoke: its provision would be part of the way the publican discharged the function of his trade, and it would not have been premises in which they were conducted.

26. If on the other hand the gazebo was simply a fixed roof on pillars to which customers could resort to smoke outside the pub building it would seem more likely that it could properly be described as part of the premises within which the customer is given licence to put himself where the giving of such licence was part of the trade. In such a case the gazebo, like the roof of the pub, is housing to which customers are given access rather than some further benefit or comfort whose provision is part of the publican's trading function."

After considering the issue in this way, the tribunal reached its conclusion as follows:

"On this basis we conclude that the gazebo is plant: it does not look like part of the garden, rather it looks as if it rests upon it; it is attached simply by its own weight and not in any permanent way; without it the gardens of the pub would still be complete; it is movable and possibly may be moved; it provides some shelter but remains open on all sides to wind and some rain. Overall the gazebo looks to us more like an embellishment of the garden, and, rather than something which simply performs the function of housing the business, it provides facilities for its customers to sit and eat and drink."

The tribunal went on to make the following important distinction:

"This is not saying that, because the gazebo performs another function as well as housing, it is plant – that approach was eschewed by the Court of Appeal in *Wimpy*, rather it is saying that regarded as a whole it is more appropriate to call it apparatus than to call it premises."

The case was distinguished from *Fitch's Garage* on the basis that the gazebo did not simply house the delivery of food but provided services that were a function of the business.

As the gazebo was considered to be neither a building nor a (fixed) structure, it was not necessary to consider whether or not it was a decorative asset. Nevertheless, the tribunal noted its view that it would be wrong to describe the gazebo as such. The tribunal left open the question of whether – if the gazebo had been more correctly described as a building – it would have been right to exempt it under the category of "moveable buildings intended to be moved in the course of the qualifying activity".

The more recent case of *Rogate Services* provided little difficulty for the tribunal. The case concerned buildings described by the company as "car valeting bays" but that consisted of floor, walls and a roof. As the tribunal commented:

> "The Building keeps out the elements and some dust and similar matters and is like an office or workshop in the sense of being a place where people work. It is not a tool of the trade. It is a place of work which does not amount to plant."

HMRC were successful in *Telfer* (despite losing two of their three lines of argument) because the caravans in that case "played no part in the carrying on of [the] duties, but were merely the place within which they were carried on".

The "plant or premises" distinction was considered once more in the *Cheshire Cavity* case, in which HMRC were successful at the FTT and again at the Upper Tribunal. The latter tribunal referred back to the *Anduff* decision, and commented as follows:

> "That suggested that to answer the question of whether the item functioned as premises or plant might involve deciding 'whether it is *more appropriate* to describe the item as apparatus for carrying on the business or as the premises in or upon which the business is conducted'. The conclusion of that decision results in a binary outcome. The language of 'more appropriate' reflects that, in reaching an eventual decision on the issue, there might be elements of the item's purpose which point towards both the premises and plant function. Ultimately, however, it must be decided which description the item falls into. In directing itself to examine which function predominated the FTT was describing just that sort of task."

Ambience/atmosphere

Case law has drawn out an extended meaning of "plant" for those involved in the hospitality or similar trades, a point that is now preserved to some extent by item 14 of list C at s. 23 (see, generally,

4.2.5). In the *Scottish & Newcastle* case, the principle of providing a certain "ambience" was explored as follows by Lord Wilberforce:

> "It seems to me ... that the taxpayer company's trade includes, and is intended to be furthered by, the provision of what may be called 'atmosphere' or 'ambience', which (rightly or wrongly) they think may attract customers. Such intangibles may in a very real and concrete sense be part of what the trader sets out, and spends money, to achieve. A good example might be a private clinic or hospital, where quiet and seclusion are provided, and charged for accordingly. One can well apply the 'setting' test to these situations. The amenities and decoration in such a case as the present are not ... the setting in which the trader carries on his business, but the setting which he offers to his customers for them to resort to and enjoy."

It should be noted, however, that despite the reference in the above quotation to "a private clinic or hospital" the statutory relaxation at s. 23 (list C, item 14) refers to a narrower range of businesses that may be able to claim for the costs of creating "ambience" – namely "hotel, restaurant or similar trades".

Specialist structures

In *May*, by contrast, a grain silo was held to be plant because it was performing a plant-like role: the facility was not only used but was also built and designed both to dry the grain and then to keep it dry. Reference was made to the *Barclay Curle* case, concerning a dry dock, in which Lord Reid had commented that "I do not say that every structure which fulfils the function of plant must be regarded as plant, but I think that one would have to find some good reason for excluding such a structure."

The tribunal went the other way in *Urenco*, in which the First-tier tribunal sided with HMRC in a complex case concerning a nuclear facility. The construction methods included protection in the event of an earthquake such as might be expected once in 10,000 years, and the tribunal accepted that the methods went "well beyond conventional health and safety requirements and building regulations". Other parts, providing radiation shielding, were "far from conventional". Indeed, the tribunal noted that "the various structures and their components are all specifically and uniquely designed to ensure that radiation dosages to employees, visitors, members of the public and the environment are minimised".

So there was no doubt that these were very specialist constructions, but that was not enough for them to qualify as plant. The tribunal held that – with the exception of certain separately identified assets – the structures were the setting in which the trade was carried on, rather than apparatus with which it was carried on. The tribunal took the view that "the safety functions of shielding, containment and seismic qualification are properly viewed as part of the setting in which that trade is carried out". In other words, the structures merely provided a safe setting for the processes, but those processes could still be carried out without them.

In reaching this conclusion, the tribunal felt entitled to ignore the regulatory environment within which the plant had to operate. And it rejected the arguments of the taxpayer that "all the features of the structures, namely their containment, shielding and seismic qualification are an essential and necessary part of the trade processes. They performed a trade function and not simply a premises function. Even if they were the setting in which the processes were carried out, they also enabled those processes to be carried out safely and performed a plant-like function." Another tribunal might perhaps have accepted this taxpayer argument – certainly the point seems arguable on the facts.

As such, however, the structures in question were held not to be plant. (As the tribunal had stated that "if a structure is both the setting and the means by which the business is carried on then it will be plant", it follows that the tribunal must have considered that the structures were *merely* the setting and did not have any apparatus function at all. This case therefore serves as a reminder of a point that had been brought out many years earlier: the fact that premises are well suited to the trade carried on within them does not mean that those premises are functioning as plant – see the analysis of the *Wimpy* case at **4.3.5** below.)

Furthermore, all the structures were buildings and the separately identified assets were "in or connected with" the buildings. As such, allowances were denied by virtue of s. 21 (see **4.2.2** above). The expenditure was not saved from that statutory restriction by s. 23 (see **4.2.5**) as it was not expenditure on "machinery, manufacturing or processing equipment or the alteration of land for the purpose only of installing plant or machinery".

Despite its conclusion in favour of HMRC, the *Urenco* tribunal did acknowledge that the function of plant may be either active or passive. ("For example, moveable partitioning might be said to perform its function passively but it may still be plant.")

Alteration of land

The *Urenco* case also pondered the meaning of "alteration of land" in s. 23 (list C, item 22), which provides a potential exemption from the s. 21 restrictions for the costs of "alteration of land for the purpose only of installing plant or machinery". The question was raised of whether "land" in this context includes buildings and other structures or whether, as HMRC argued, "constructing a building on land cannot sensibly be regarded as being on the alteration of land". The arguments are rehearsed at paragraphs 145 to 153 of the judgment but no decision was given, as the tribunal already came down on HMRC's side based on other aspects of the case. It may be noted, however, that the general definition of land (to include buildings) is specifically disapplied for the purposes of s. 22 (per s. 22(3)(b)) but not for the purposes of s. 23.

Cases: *Yarmouth v France* [1887] 4 TRL 1; *J. Lyons & Co Ltd v Attorney General* [1944] Ch 281; *Jarrold v John Good & Sons Ltd* (1963) 40 TC 681; *CIR v Barclay, Curle and Co Ltd* (1969) 45 TC 221; *St. John's School (Mountford and Another) v Ward* (1974) 49 TC 524; *Benson v The Yard Arm Club Ltd* (1979) 53 TC 67; *CIR v Scottish & Newcastle Breweries Ltd* [1982] BTC 187; *Cole Brothers Ltd v Phillips* [1982] BTC 208; *Wimpy International Ltd. v Warland* [1987] BTC 591; *Andrew v HMRC* [2010] UKFTT 546 (TC); *Rogate Services Ltd v HMRC* [2014] UKFTT 312 (TC); *Telfer v HMRC* [2016] UKFTT 614 (TC); *May v HMRC* [2019] UKFTT 32 (TC); *Urenco Chemplants Ltd & Anor v HMRC* [2019] UKFTT 522; *Cheshire Cavity Storage 1 Ltd & Ors v HMRC* [2021] BTC 513

Storage trades

The taxpayer was unsuccessful in *Cheshire Cavity Storage*, a dual appeal from two connected companies. The companies operate gas storage facilities on adjoining sites in Cheshire, together holding up to one fifth of the UK's daily delivery capacity. The tribunal determined that the appellants were not in the business of either processing gas or distributing gas (even though they carried out, incidentally, both of these activities), but only of storing gas. The tribunal also determined that the cavities could not be described as pumps (even though they might in some circumstances be said to act as a substitute for a pump or compressor).

The companies spent tens of millions of pounds on a process of "de-brining" and "leaching" the cavities – the technicalities of which need not concern us unduly – to make them suitable for gas storage. HMRC accepted that related costs (boreholes, pipework, pumping and dehydration equipment, and control mechanisms) qualified for plant and machinery allowances. The dispute was therefore over the costs of preparing the cavities themselves.

The claim was rejected by the First-tier Tribunal, and the reasoning of this borderline case is relevant for other circumstances, especially those involving storage trades:

- The gas cavities were central to the appellants' business, but that would not in itself make them plant: premises and plant can both be essential.

- The cavities were not merely fixed to the land, but were clearly a part of it, like an underground reservoir.

- That did not rule out the possibility that they were plant: the matter depended on whether the cavities functioned as premises or as plant.

- The function of the cavities was to store gas in such a way that it did not dissipate and that it remained in a suitable condition.

- Despite the tribunal's finding that the cavities did perform a plant-like function (equivalent to pumps/compressors, but using natural forces), this was held to be an "incident of the construction" and not the reason they were constructed in that manner.

- A plant-like function "does not necessarily make premises plant, in circumstances where the premises also functions as premises". It is a "matter of degree":
  - The water tower in *Lowestoft Water* was used to store water, but its *purpose* was to increase pressure (so the Lords in *Barclay Curle* said that it should have been treated as plant).
  - The silo in *Schofield* was used to store grain, but had the *purpose* of discharging the grain at speed, for the business was one of distribution not storage ("it was the speed of input and output into the silos which were important and not their capacity to protect and contain").
  - Here, by contrast, the purpose of the cavities was to store gas, for however short a period, so as to profit from price fluctuations. Storage is a premises-like function and not a plant-like function.

- So the "significant and predominant" function of the cavities was the premises-like function of shelter and containment.

- An analogy with a cold room did not help, as the main function of the cold room was to reduce the temperature of what was stored, whereas altering the temperature of the gas was not a function of the cavity.

- The fact that the cavities could be used to store gas at high pressure merely meant that they were very good at performing their premises-like storage function.

The case also considered the meaning of the word "install" – see **4.4** below/above.

HMRC were also successful in *Urenco*, and the following observation of the tribunal is relevant here:

> "A structure does not take on the character of plant simply because it is used for storage by a trader carrying on a storage business, even where that storage business is highly specialised."

Cases: *Margrett v The Lowestoft Water and Gas Company* (1935) TC 481; *Schofield v R & H Hall Ltd* (1975) 49 TC 538; *Cheshire Cavity Storage 1 Ltd and EDF Energy (Gas Storage Hole House) Ltd v HMRC* [2019] UKFTT 498 (TC); *Urenco Chemplants Ltd & Anor v HMRC* [2019] UKFTT 522

4.3.5 Function

Another test to have emerged from the courts is that of function, but this test has rarely proved helpful in practice. Going back more than half a century, knives and lasts were held to be plant in the *Maden & Ireland* case as they "performed an indispensable function in the process of manufacture".

In reality, though, every asset has a function of some sort and the test generally leads back to the question of whether it functions as apparatus or as setting. Particular weight was given to the concept of function in the case of *Fitch's Garage* ("the right test is the functional test") but the House of Lords in *Cole Brothers* (Lord Hailsham) suggested that *Fitch's Garage* had been incorrectly decided. In *St John's School*, Templeman J did not attach much importance to the notion of function:

"It is necessary to find, not the name of the building or its function, but whether the building is in truth a building within which the business is carried on or ... whether it is apparatus used by the businessman for carrying on the business."

HMRC specifically agree that the functional test leads back to the distinction between apparatus and setting:

"Note that the functional test is not whether an asset has a function. All business assets have a function. The functional test is whether the asset functions as apparatus used in carrying on the activities of the business. For example, an asset that functions as the business premises is not plant. It is not apparatus used in carrying on the activities of the business."

It is, though, worth making the point that a building that is designed in a particularly suitable way does not thereby become an item of plant. This was noted by Fox in the *Wimpy* case, as follows:

"It is proper to consider the function of the item in dispute. But the question is what does it function as? If it functions as part of the premises it is not plant. The fact that the building in which a business is carried on is by its construction particularly well-suited to the business, or indeed was specially built for that business, does not make it plant. Its suitability is simply the reason why the business is carried on there. But it remains the place in which the business is carried on and is not something with which the business is carried on."

In *Urenco*, the tribunal commented that:

"It is not sufficient to say that "but for" the structures the process could not be carried out. It is necessary to identify a specific function of the structures."

Cases: *Yarmouth v France* [1887] 4 TRL 1; *Hinton v Maden & Ireland Ltd* (1959) 38 TC 391; *St. John's School (Mountford and Another) v Ward* (1974) 49 TC 524; *Dixon v Fitch's Garage Ltd* (1975) 50 TC 509; *Cole Brothers Ltd v Phillips* [1982] BTC 208; *Wimpy International Ltd v Warland* [1989] BTC 58; *Urenco Chemplants Ltd & Anor v HMRC* [2019] UKFTT 522

Guidance: CA 21100

4.3.6   Machinery

Until recently, the meaning of "machinery" has seemed to be relatively clear cut. HMRC have taken a relatively relaxed view, applying a commonsense approach and at times accepting quite a generous interpretation of the term (e.g. for door handles with moving parts, and antique watches).

The writer became aware in 2017 and 2018 of a much tougher line from HMRC, however. The case concerned the automated ticket barriers commonly seen at railway and underground stations, where HMRC sought to analyse the expenditure on the units into qualifying elements (e.g. the card reader) and non-qualifying elements (e.g. the opening flaps that allow the passenger to pass), even though the units in question were both designed and installed as single items of machinery.

The authors disagree strongly with the HMRC line, as explored in more depth in the accompanying volume from Claritax Books Ltd – the *A-Z of Plant & Machinery*.

4.3.7   Piecemeal approach

The question may also arise of the level at which the nature and function of an asset should be considered (as in fact illustrated in the section immediately above concerning machinery). So it may suit one party or the other to argue that the asset in question is a "single entity" to be considered as such, the whole asset qualifying or not as plant or machinery. Or one of the parties may argue that a "piecemeal" approach is more correct, whereby the overall asset is divided into its constituent parts, each being considered separately to decide whether or not it is plant or machinery.

There is no right or wrong answer here, and each case will be considered on its merits. In *Cole Bros*, for example, the House of Lords accepted the piecemeal approach adopted by the special commissioners. And in *Anchor International*, the synthetic carpets were considered separately from the stone base on which it was laid.

In *Urenco* (at the First-tier), the tribunal sought to identify assets that "can readily be seen to form a separate structure and to function as such". Each structure had its own separate visual identity.

As such, the tribunal concluded that "to a large extent each structure comprises a whole". Within each structure, the components were "closely physically connected" and largely supported each other and worked together in providing their respective functions. This is a matter of degree, however, as HMRC had already accepted that certain individual items within each structure (e.g. kilns and a condenser) retained their identity, could properly be separately identified, and qualified as plant.

Cases: *Cole Brothers Ltd v Phillips* [1982] BTC 208; *Anchor International Ltd v IR Commrs* [2005] BTC 97; *Urenco Chemplants Ltd & Anor v HMRC* [2019] UKFTT 522

4.4   Building alterations connected with the installation of plant or machinery

4.4.1   General principle

A person is treated as incurring expenditure on plant or machinery if:

- a.   he is carrying on a qualifying activity;
- b.   he incurs capital expenditure on alterations to an existing building; and
- c.   those alterations are incidental to the installation of plant or machinery for the purposes of the qualifying activity.

The alterations are then treated as if they were part of the plant or machinery. It follows that if the plant is an integral feature, the incidental costs will also need to be allocated to the special rate pool rather than to the main pool.

Law: CAA 2001, s. 25

4.4.2   Existing building

There is no statutory definition of "existing building". It is clear that the legislation does not apply to works incurred in the course of a new construction. However, it may be possible to argue that a business could make a claim if it buys a new building but then has some alterations made before moving in.

There may also be uncertainty if a tenant takes the lease of a new property and incurs costs in fitting it out. Most fitting-out costs will qualify on normal principles, but there may be other costs (such as a new lift shaft) where the claim would rely on the s. 25 rules.

It is not clear whether or not HMRC would accept a claim in these circumstances. One factor may be the question of whether the certificated of practical completion has been issued for the property. It may also be helpful to see if the rating completion notice has been issued.

4.4.3   Scope of rules

According to HMRC:

> "The legislation is intended to cover the direct costs of installation, that is those works which are brought about by the installation of the plant and which are associated with it in such a way that their cost can properly be considered to be part of the cost of providing the plant. The use of the word 'incidental' makes it clear that the primary purpose of the work must be the installation of plant or machinery."

The HMRC guidance goes on to refer to Lord Reid's guidance in the *Barclay, Curle* case, very slightly misquoting his words. The original version of the words quoted by HMRC is that:

> "the exigencies of the trade require that, when new machinery or plant is installed in existing buildings, more shall be done than mere installation in order that the new machinery or plant may serve its proper purpose".

The Upper Tribunal in the *Wetherspoon* case commented that the relevant legislation is:

> "a deeming provision which requires expenditure on certain alterations to existing buildings to be treated as expenditure on the provision of plant or machinery even if, apart from the section, it would not have been so treated".

With that starting point, the tribunal then went on to give the following commentary:

> "The touchstone for that deeming provision is that the expenditure on alterations be 'incidental to the installation of the machinery or plant'. Viewed purposively, the focus of the section is on the point that if plant is installed in an existing building rather than in a purpose-built new building, it is entirely possible that something will not fit, and that this will lead to alterations having to be made to the existing building. In the case of a purpose-built new building, there will generally be no equivalent need for such expenditure. Thus [s. 25] levels the playing field between new and existing buildings by affording taxpayers relief for expenditure on existing buildings which would not be needed

in relation to the installation of the same plant in new buildings, or in the open."

In rejecting part of the claim made by the company, the tribunal noted that:

"There appears to be no ground for assuming some Parliamentary purpose that an additional subsidy should be given for renovations, and the re-use of existing buildings, to account for the asymmetry that the Appellant's contentions would generally involve."

HMRC guidance states that there must be a direct link between the incurring of the expenditure and the installation of the relevant plant:

"The main purpose of the alterations must be the installation of plant or machinery. Work done for some other purpose such as the better operation of the asset does not qualify."

Elsewhere, HMRC mention a lift shaft as an example of expenditure that would qualify under this heading, the cost being incidental to the expenditure on the lift itself, which is an item of plant or machinery.

Reference may usefully be made to the *Wetherspoon* decision and to the commentary on that decision in the complementary title from Claritax Books, the *A-Z of Plant & Machinery*.

Cases: *CIR v Barclay Curle* (1969) 45 TC 221; *J D Wetherspoon plc v HMRC* [2012] UKUT 42 (TCC)

4.4.4   Meaning of "install" and of "provision"

The meaning of "install" was considered in the joint *Cheshire Cavity* and *EDF Energy* appeal, where the FTT judge argued as follows (in relation to existing cavities prepared for holding large quantities of gas):

" 'Install' carries the implication that something pre-existing is put in position. Creating a space where previously there was none does not install the space. It creates it but it does not install it."

Quoting from a non-tax case where a distinction was drawn between installing and creating an asset, the tribunal ruled that something could be installed only after it was created. At the time it gave this view, the *Cheshire Cavity* ruling differed from that of the *SSE Generation* appeal, also at the FTT. However, *SSE Generation* proceeded to the Upper Tribunal, which confirmed the *Cheshire Cavity* decision on this point (despite upholding the company's appeal on other grounds). The Upper

Tribunal in *SSE Generation* (at para. 128) made the following observations in this respect:

> "In our view there is a clear distinction drawn in the statute between the 'provision' of a structure or asset, which as we have seen, includes its construction and may embrace as part of the construction process the 'installation' of plant, and those items of plant which by their nature are constructed separately and then need to be 'installed.' It seems to us that item 22 in List C is confined to items which need to be installed separately from the process of manufacture or construction. ... the saving [in item 22] applies in circumstances where 'installation' occurs in circumstances where it is necessary to make alterations of the land only to enable 'installation' of the plant to take place, not in circumstances where the alteration is made in order to build or construct the asset in question."

More simply, at para. 117, the Upper Tribunal referred to the House of Lords decision in *Barclay Curle* and concluded as follows:

> "We can see nothing in what their Lordships said which gives authority for the proposition that creating an asset through the excavation of land alone is to be regarded as 'installation'. "

The Upper Tribunal also gave more explicit guidance on the meaning of "provision" of a structure as the term is used in s. 22. Subsection 22(2) already makes it clear that the provision of a structure or other asset includes (for the purposes of that section) its construction or acquisition. The Upper Tribunal clarified that the term "will include all of the costs of construction, which in this case will include the necessary preparatory work in excavating the land before the structure was built, its building in situ and its subsequent covering over".

Cases: *Cheshire Cavity Storage 1 Ltd and EDF Energy (Gas Storage Hole House) Ltd v HMRC* [2019] UKFTT 498 (TC); *HMRC v SSE Generation Ltd* [2019] UKUT 332 (TCC)

4.5   Demolition costs

Tax relief, by way of plant and machinery allowances, is available for costs incurred on demolishing plant or machinery that has been used for the purposes of a qualifying activity. The treatment depends on whether or not the item in question is replaced.

If the person replaces the item(s) in question with other plant or machinery then the net cost of the demolition is treated as expenditure incurred on the provision of the new plant or machinery.

If the item is not replaced, the net demolition cost is allocated to the appropriate pool for the chargeable period in which the demolition takes place. For these purposes, the appropriate pool is the one to which expenditure on the demolished plant or machinery has been (or would be) allocated.

The net demolition cost is the amount by which the cost of demolition exceeds any amount received for the remains of the plant or machinery.

Different rules may by election apply for general decommissioning expenditure before the cessation of a ring-fence trade (s. 164(4)).

Law: CAA 2001, s. 26

4.6   Deemed capital expenditure

Plant and machinery allowances are available for certain expenditure that would not otherwise qualify for relief. In such cases, the rules are applied as if "the expenditure were capital expenditure on the provision of plant or machinery for the purposes of the qualifying activity in question". The person incurring the expenditure is deemed to own plant or machinery as a result.

The categories of expenditure that can potentially qualify by virtue of these special measures are the following:

- thermal insulation (see **4.7**);
- certain costs connected with safety at sports grounds (for now, but see **4.8**); and
- certain personal security costs (see **4.9**)

These special rules override all the restrictions that would otherwise apply by virtue of s. 21 or s. 22.

Law: CAA 2001, s. 23(2), 27

4.7   Thermal insulation

4.7.1   General principles

See **4.6** immediately above for a general comment about this type of expenditure.

Expenditure on thermal insulation is in certain circumstances deemed to constitute capital expenditure on the provision of plant or machinery. The detailed rules depend on the nature of the qualifying activity: see **Chapter 3** for detailed definitions of the various activities.

HMRC take the view that the rules apply only to insulation added to an existing building. It is assumed that this is based on an interpretation of the wording "adding insulation ... to a building occupied by him" which would deny relief unless the building is occupied before the insulation is added.

Any costs qualifying by virtue of these rules are treated as "special rate" expenditure, attracting a slower rate of tax relief (see **Chapter 17**). If there is a disposal event, the disposal value is treated as nil.

Law: CAA 2001, s. 28, 63(5), 104A(1)(a)
Guidance: CA 22220

Loss of heat

The rules apply only for insulation against loss of heat; they would not apply if the insulation were primarily against noise, or if it was to keep a building cool. HMRC guidance reads as follows:

> "Give the expression 'insulation against loss of heat' its ordinary meaning. Treat capital expenditure on things like roof lining, double-glazing, draught exclusion and cavity wall filling as expenditure on thermal insulation. Sometimes expenditure may be incurred for more than one reason. For example, double-glazing may be installed to insulate against both noise and loss of heat. The expenditure will qualify under Section 28 provided that it is clear that insulation against loss of heat is one of the main reasons why it was incurred."

Guidance: CA 22220

4.7.2   *Ordinary property business*

Relief is available if a person carrying on an ordinary UK property business or an ordinary overseas property business incurs expenditure in adding insulation against loss of heat to a building let by him in the course of the business.

This is subject to the restrictions of s. 35 (plant or machinery in a dwelling-house: see **4.14**).

No relief is available under this heading if a deduction for the cost is already available under CTA 2009, s. 251 or ITTOIA 2005, s. 312 (energy-saving expenditure, sometimes known as "Landlord's Energy Saving Allowance" or "LESA"). To avoid a circular statutory reference, s. 251(1)(e) and s. 312(1)(e) are for these purposes ignored.

Law: CAA 2001, s. 28(2)-(2C)

4.7.3   Any other qualifying activity

The rules are simpler for other activities. In these cases, relief is simply available if the person carrying on the other qualifying activity incurs expenditure on adding insulation against loss of heat to a building occupied by him for the purposes of that activity.

Law: CAA 2001, s. 28(1)

4.8   Safety at sports grounds

Special reliefs for expenditure on safety at sports grounds were repealed from April 2013.

Law: CAA 2001, s. 30-32
Guidance: CA 22240; https://tinyurl.com/y5dqynze

4.9   Personal security

The legislation has a particular section dealing with assets provided for personal security. These may qualify for plant and machinery allowances but the provisions apply only in cases where there is an exceptional security risk. Numerous conditions must be met and it is clear that the legislation will rarely apply.

The following conditions are listed:

- the expenditure must be incurred by an individual, or partnership of individuals, in connection with the provision for, or for use by, the individual, or any of the individuals, of a security asset;
- the individual or partnership must be carrying on a relevant qualifying activity;

- the asset must be provided or used to meet a threat which is a special threat to the individual's personal physical security, and which arises wholly or mainly because of the relevant qualifying activity;
- the person incurring the expenditure must have the sole object of meeting that threat in incurring that expenditure;
- he or she must intend the asset to be used solely to improve personal physical security (though any incidental use is ignored, as is any protection also provided for members of the individual's family or household).

If expenditure has a dual purpose, the legislation does allow an apportionment so that relief may be given for "the proportion of the expenditure attributable to the intended use to improve personal physical security". According to HMRC, "the appropriate proportion is that attributable to the intended use to improve physical security".

The legislation cannot apply to a car, ship or aircraft. Nor does it apply to "a dwelling or grounds appurtenant to a dwelling" (for which purposes HMRC apply the CGT private residence principles). The rules can, however, cover "equipment, a structure (such as a wall) and an asset which becomes fixed to land". HMRC have indicated that "assets like alarm systems, bullet resistant windows, reinforced doors and windows, and perimeter walls and fences are the sort of assets that may qualify as security assets".

The capital allowances legislation is similar to that applying for employees. In the latter context, HMRC have updated their guidance but formerly stated that a deduction was due for individuals whose work exposed them "to a very real threat to their physical safety from terrorists, extremists and others who may resort to violence". In *Hanson*, a claim for security expenditure was allowed but the commissioners stated that the facts of the appeal and the appellant himself were unique (which could, however, be said of every appellant and probably of every appeal).

The point was tested once more in the *Brockhouse* case, which considered whether the cost of fencing round business premises was for the security of the partners (and to one in particular) because of a special threat. Facts were in short supply for the appeal but the tribunal found no evidence of a special security threat to the individual in question, especially as there had been an 11 year gap from the date of a particular incident to the time at which the fence in question was erected.

Furthermore, the evidence clearly suggested that at least part of the reason for erecting the fence was to protect the land and stock, which meant that the "sole object" condition was not met.

Law: CAA 2001, s. 33

Cases: *Lord Hanson v Mansworth (HMIT)* (2004) Sp C 410; *Brockhouse (t/a A5 Aquatics) v HMRC* [2011] UKFTT 380 (TC)

Guidance: CA 22270; EIM 21811

4.10   Notional expenditure

4.10.1   Assets brought into use for trade, etc.

A person may already own an asset before it is brought into use for the purposes of the qualifying activity. By way of example, a consultant setting up his own business, working from home, may bring into business use his computer, car, office furniture, etc.

In such a case, the person is treated as incurring notional expenditure on the date on which the asset is brought into use for the purposes of the qualifying activity.

The value to be used is normally the market value at the time the asset is first used for the purposes of the business. However, the amount of the actual expenditure previously incurred is used if this is less than the market value. This is also subject to anti-avoidance rules (s. 218: see **22.3.2**) in certain cases (e.g. certain transactions between connected parties). It is also subject to transitional rules (Sch. 3, para. 11) if the plant or machinery was brought into use before 21 March 2000.

Appropriate adjustments are made if the asset is used only partly for the purposes of the qualifying activity (see, generally, **5.8**).

Different rules can apply to pre-trading expenditure on mineral exploration and access (s. 161: see **21.2**).

Annual investment allowances are not available in these circumstances (s. 38B, general exclusion 5 – see **5.2.3**).

Example

Anita bought a house in Swindon for £200,000 back in 2007. She inherits another property from a deceased aunt in 2019 and decides to renovate the inherited property and then live in it. She then starts to let her Swindon house out as an FHL property.

Anita can claim for the cost of fixtures in the property, but the claim must be based on the actual expenditure she incurred in 2007 (s. 13(5)), assuming that this is lower than the valuation in 2019.

The effect of s. 13 is to treat Anita as incurring capital expenditure on the date on which the property starts to be used for the qualifying activity, so some time in 2019. The integral features rules apply to expenditure incurred from 1 April 2008 so it is necessary to separate the main rate and special rate expenditure.

It might be thought that the transitional rules in FA 2008, Sch. 26 would prevent a claim for the pre-commencement integral features, but this does not appear to be the case.

On the face of it, this is rather an odd outcome. If Anita's neighbour in Swindon, Bert, bought the next door property in 2007 and immediately used it for an FHLs business, he would be unable to claim for those integral features that did not then qualify. But as Anita lived in her property first, the problem seems to go away.

Law: CAA 2001, s. 13

4.10.2   Assets previously used for long funding leasing

Special rules may apply if a person has been using plant or machinery for the purpose of leasing it under a long funding lease ("LFL") (see **Chapter 7**). In principle, such a person will have been unable to claim tax relief as, very broadly, the LFL provisions transfer the entitlement to claim from lessor to lessee.

If that person ceases to use it for that purpose, but continues to use it for the purposes of *another* qualifying activity, he may be treated as incurring notional capital expenditure for the purposes of that other activity. The amount of the notional expenditure is defined as "an amount equal to the termination amount, determined in accordance with section 70YG".

This rule applies only if, at the cessation of the LFL, he owned the asset as a result of incurring capital expenditure for the purposes of the qualifying activity. The asset is treated as if it were a different one from that leased out under the LFL provisions.

Law: CAA 2001, s. 13A

4.10.3   *Assets rotated between property businesses*

Special rules may apply where plant or machinery is used in rotation for a variety of property-related activities.

For these purposes, the legislation introduces the concept of "relevant qualifying activity" which covers any of the following:

- an ordinary UK property business;
- a UK furnished holiday lettings business;
- an ordinary overseas property business; and
- an EEA furnished holiday lettings business.

The special rules apply where a person ceases to use plant or machinery for one such activity but continues to use it for another, the expenditure having originally been incurred for the purposes of that other activity. The way the rules work was explained in the *Explanatory Notes* to the 2011 *Finance Bill* as follows:

> "Where a person carrying on a property business of any of the four types listed ... uses plant or machinery in rotation between different types of property business, whilst still retaining ownership, that person is treated as if the plant or machinery was first acquired at the date it started to be re-used for the first property business after ceasing to be used in the second property business."

In these circumstances, the person is treated as incurring notional expenditure on new plant or machinery for the purposes of the ongoing activity. The figure to use for the notional expenditure is the lower of market value at the date of cessation and the amount of the actual expenditure.

There is a potential pitfall here in that the cessation of use for the earlier activity (e.g. an FHL business) will mean that a disposal value must be brought into account at market value. In the context of a disposal of fixtures in the property, it will not be possible to control the disposal value by means of a fixtures election under s. 198 as the disposal will not fall within items 1 or 9 of the table at s. 196 (and the condition at s. 198(1) is therefore not met). A market value disposal will therefore be required and the recipient business may well be denied allowances on the grounds that the property is a dwelling-house (s. 35 – see, generally, **4.14**). This is discussed and illustrated at **12.7.1** below.

The practical effect of the market value disposal will depend on the overall circumstances, and especially on whether there are any other FHL properties. In principle, there will be a pool of expenditure, covering all the FHL properties that are owned by the person concerned (s. 53), and the disposal proceeds will therefore reduce the balance in that pool of expenditure, rather than necessarily triggering an immediate balancing charge.

Law: CAA 2001, s. 13B

4.10.4   Plant or machinery received as a gift

A person may be given an item of plant or machinery which he then brings into use for the purposes of a qualifying activity.

In such a case, the market value of the asset, calculated on the day it is brought into use for the qualifying activity, is treated as qualifying expenditure.

Appropriate adjustments are made if the asset is used only partly for the purposes of the qualifying activity (see, generally, **5.8**).

Different rules can apply to pre-trading expenditure on mineral exploration and access (s. 161: see **21.2**).

The HMRC view is that the anti-avoidance legislation beginning at s. 214 applies in these circumstances:

> "The anti-avoidance legislation applies to assets received as a gift. The recipient of the gift is treated as buying it from the giver and the giver is treated as selling it to the recipient at a price equal to market value when it is brought into use for a qualifying activity …. This means that if the asset has appreciated since it was bought and the giver was connected with the recipient, the recipient's qualifying expenditure is restricted to the giver's cost."

The point does not seem to the author to be entirely free from doubt, for various reasons.

First, most gifts are between connected persons, so it is odd that the legislation at s. 14 does not at least say "this is subject to the anti-avoidance rules".

More specifically, s. 14 states that the capital expenditure "is to be treated as being the market value". It is not wholly clear that this is overridden by the wording of s. 218.

Finally, it is arguable that a gift is not within the anti-avoidance rules at all. Section 213(3) makes it clear that a person (B), who is treated as incurring expenditure under s. 14 because of a gift from another person (S), is treated as purchasing it from S. It does not, though, specify that S is treated as selling it to B, which is a requirement if the avoidance rules are to be in point.

The HMRC stance seems clear, but whether that stance would win in front of a tax tribunal remains to be seen.

Law: CAA 2001, s. 14, 213(3), 214, 218
Guidance: CA 28200

4.11   Integral features

4.11.1   Introduction

The introduction (in 2008) of the rules for integral features represented an important development in the plant and machinery legislation. The key effects were to broaden the range of assets qualifying for plant and machinery allowances but to slow down the rate at which allowances are typically given for certain types of expenditure.

According to HMRC, the intention was "to re-draw the boundary between buildings, including their main features, and other equipment".

Guidance: CA 22310

4.11.2   Effect of rules – overview

The rules apply where a person carrying on a qualifying activity incurs expenditure on the provision, or sometimes the replacement, of an "integral feature" (as defined) of a building or structure used for the purposes of his qualifying activity.

The rules treat certain expenditure "as if" it were capital expenditure on the provision of plant or machinery for the purposes of a qualifying activity. The person incurring the expenditure is treated as owning the plant or machinery as a result. The rules only apply to expenditure incurred from 1 or 6 April 2008.

What this means in practice is a little more complex than it may at first seem. The effect for the taxpayer may be beneficial, because an asset that would otherwise not qualify for relief (e.g. general office lighting) may now do so. The effect may be to reduce the rate at which tax relief is given (e.g. an air conditioning system that would otherwise have qualified for standard plant and machinery allowances but that would now qualify for allowances at a slower rate). Finally, the effect may be to convert revenue expenditure (that would have been fully deductible in the year) to capital expenditure (where the tax relief is typically spread over many years).

The slower rate of tax relief applies not only to integral features but also to certain other specified types of asset. The rules are considered under "Special rate expenditure" at **Chapter 17** below.

A short-life asset election is not permitted for integral features. By contrast, expenditure on integral features (including replacement expenditure) may be subject to a claim for annual investment allowances (AIAs). Indeed, if a business incurs expenditure in the same year on both integral features and general plant and machinery, it will normally wish to claim AIAs against the integral features first.

Law: CAA 2001, s. 33A, 84 (table: item 4)
Guidance: CA 22360, 23084

4.11.3 Definition

The statutory definition of integral features encompasses five categories of expenditure, as follows:

(a)   an electrical system (including a lighting system),

(b)   a cold water system,

(c)   a space or water heating system, a powered system of ventilation, air cooling or air purification, and any floor or ceiling comprised in such a system,

(d)   a lift, an escalator or a moving walkway,

(e)   external solar shading.

However, the definition excludes "any asset whose principal purpose is to insulate or enclose the interior of a building or to provide an interior wall, floor or ceiling which (in each case) is intended to remain permanently in place". HMRC have given guidance on this, as follows:

"If, for example, a business installs a new, permanent false ceiling in its premises, in order to conceal new wiring and service pipes, expenditure on that ceiling would not qualify for PMAs.

On the other hand, if a business installs in its premises a plenum floor or plenum ceiling, the principal purpose of which is to function as an integral part of the heating or air conditioning system (for example, the plenum floor or plenum ceiling may form the fourth side of a duct or channel through which stale air is extracted and treated air is discharged), that expenditure would qualify for PMAs as part of an 'integral feature' of the building or structure."

Law: CAA 2001, s. 33A(5), (6)
Guidance: CA 22320

Electrical systems

There is no statutory definition of "electrical systems" but the HMRC view is that:

"The term takes its ordinary meaning: a system for taking electrical power (including lighting) from the point of entry to the building or structure, or generation within the building or structure, and distributing it through the building or structure, as required. The system may range from the very simplest to the most complex.

The term does not include other building systems intended for other purposes, which may include wiring and other electrical components. For example, communication, telecommunication and surveillance systems, fire alarm systems or burglar alarm systems."

The last items mentioned (alarms, etc.) will normally qualify as plant or machinery in their own right, attracting allowances at the standard rate rather than at the lower "special" rate.

Ducting should be allocated as appropriate to integral features or to general plant, apportioning as necessary on a just and reasonable basis.

Guidance: CA 22320

Cold water systems

Again, there is no statutory definition of this term. According to HMRC, it would cover "a system for taking water from the point of entry to the building or structure and distributing it through the building or structure, as required". Once more, such a system "may range from the very simplest to the most complex".

Guidance: CA 22320

Active façades

When the concept of "integral features" was introduced back in 2008, there was discussion about whether a category of "active façades" (e.g. two layers of glazing separated by an air cavity that is actively ventilated) would be included. The reason for not doing so is explained by HMRC as follows:

> "It is already accepted that the external skin of the active façade system is not eligible (as it is basically a window and so excluded by section 33A (6) CAA01), but that the inner skin is eligible, because it is, in effect, creating a duct within which the cooling/heating air circulates. In short, the relevant parts of these systems already qualify as 'integral features', by virtue of being considered part of the air cooling or heating systems of the building, so there is no need to specify this expenditure separately in the list."

Guidance: CA 22320

4.11.4   Interaction with other rules

The rules have the effect that the person in question is treated as incurring capital expenditure on the provision of plant or machinery.

The various exclusions in relation to buildings and structures do not need to be considered as the integral features rules override those exclusions (by virtue of s. 23(2): see **4.2.5**). The whole of lists A, B and C can therefore, in principle, be ignored once it is known that an asset can be categorised as an integral feature.

There is one (apparently unintended) complication, however, which may be illustrated by reference to a lift. It seems possible to argue that the lift can in fact qualify under general principles, thus attracting a faster rate of write-off, on the grounds that a lift is undoubtedly a machine.

The statute does not appear to give precedence to one interpretation or the other but as the mention of lifts at s. 33A is so specific, it may be that a court would take the view that the "integral features" rules take priority. On the other hand, the integral features rules apply only "as if" certain expenditure were on plant and machinery; the view could be taken that an asset that *in fact* qualifies as plant and machinery on normal grounds cannot then be classified as an integral feature.

The point was raised by one of the authors with HMRC, who replied as follows:

> "I don't think we would argue with you that a lift is machinery. However we take the view that the legislation is clear that lifts are integral features and expenditure on integral features has to be allocated to the special rate pool.
>
> So in our view the person making the claim does not have a choice, it may be qualifying expenditure on machinery but more specifically it is qualifying expenditure on a lift which is an integral feature and that qualifying expenditure has to be allocated to the special rate pool."

Ultimately, the point may have to be tested in the courts to gain clarity on the matter.

Law: CAA 2001, s. 23(2), 33A

4.11.5   Revenue deduction

If expenditure on integral features is qualifying expenditure, no revenue deduction may be given for the cost in computing the income of the qualifying activity. This rule is necessary because the integral features sometimes have the effect of converting revenue expenditure to notional capital expenditure. The rule does not apply in calculating the profits of a trade on the cash basis.

However, it is not always the case that expenditure on an integral feature will be qualifying expenditure for capital allowances purposes. This is because there are various exclusions (see, generally, **4.13** below) that state that certain expenditure is not qualifying expenditure. This applies, for example, in relation to employments or offices, or to plant or machinery used (in some circumstances) in a dwelling-house.

If the expenditure on integral features is not qualifying expenditure for capital allowances purposes, the integral features rules are simply ignored in deciding whether or not a revenue deduction is due.

Law: CAA 2001, s. 33A(3), (4); ITTOIA 2005, s. 55A(2)

4.11.6   Replacements

Expenditure on replacing all or most of an integral feature is automatically treated as new capital expenditure on the feature (even if it would be treated as revenue expenditure on ordinary accounting principles). No revenue deduction is therefore available for expenditure of that sort. The policy aim of the rule is explained by HMRC as follows:

> "The broad policy purpose underlying these rules is to ensure that both new and replacement expenditure on an 'integral feature' is afforded the same tax treatment.

> 'Replacement' expenditure is defined and brought within these new capital allowances rules to prevent some businesses from seeking to claim that they have really incurred a revenue expense on a repair to a larger asset such as the building itself, in other words, that they have not incurred capital expenditure.

> The test of 'replacement', by reference to expenditure on replacing more than 50% of the integral feature within 12 months, is intended to discourage any attempts to avoid the application of the replacement rules by businesses, say, splitting replacement expenditure over two or more chargeable periods."

In simple terms, the rule applies where expenditure on an integral feature amounts to more than half of the cost of replacing the item in question at the time the expenditure is incurred.

Example 1

A company has an air conditioning system that was installed some years previously. A new system would cost £16,000 which would be capital expenditure on integral features. The company is considering repairing the old system instead, and receives a quotation for £9,000. As this is more than half the current replacement cost, it will be treated as capital expenditure on a new integral feature if the work is undertaken in this way.

A more complicated situation arises, however, where expenditure on the asset (which might otherwise be revenue expenditure) is spread over a period of up to a year.

If the total of the initial expenditure and any further expenditure in the following year amounts to more than half of the cost of replacing the asset then both the initial and the later expenditure are treated as if they were capital expenditure on the integral feature. Note that the initial expenditure does not refer here to the original cost of the asset but to the first tranche of costs subsequently incurred on it.

Example 2

To get round the problem of having to capitalise the cost for tax purposes, the company considers doing the repair work in two successive accounting periods, with a six month interval. This possible approach is caught by the special rules and the cost will still have to be treated as capital expenditure for these tax purposes.

As the later expenditure may have a bearing on the tax computations for the earlier period, the rules allow for the making of all such assessments, and adjustments of assessments, as may be required to put them into effect.

The rule applies only if the further expenditure is incurred within 12 months of the initial expenditure. HMRC suggest that a "light touch" approach will be used in deciding whether or not the 50% figure applies – there is, for example, no onus on the business to obtain different quotations, one of which might have brought the replacement costs within the 50% band.

HMRC guidance material includes various examples illustrating the application of the 50% principle. HMRC have also written, however, that "the policy intention is to adopt a 'light touch' approach, so that any additional administrative burdens are kept to a minimum".

Law: CAA 2001, s. 33A(1), 33B
Guidance: CA 22340, 22350

4.11.7   Connected parties

The need for special rules

One of the effects of introducing the rules for integral features was that certain assets started to qualify for plant and machinery allowances for the first time. The main examples were general electrical/lighting costs and cold water systems.

A business that already owned such assets before April 2008 was not entitled to make a claim by virtue of the new rules. However, a person buying such an asset from a third party could then make a claim.

Without special rules, this would have created an obvious tax-saving opportunity. So, for example, A Ltd might have incurred non-qualifying costs in 2007. By transferring the property containing the fixtures to a connected company (B Ltd), it would have enabled B Ltd to claim allowances for the integral features.

To prevent this, anti-avoidance provisions restrict claims in certain circumstances.

Details of the restrictions

The anti-avoidance provisions have effect if there is a sale between connected persons (per s. 575: see **32.9.5**) of an integral feature that would not have qualified for tax relief before the introduction of the 2008 rules (labelled in the legislation as a "pre-commencement integral feature"). In these circumstances, the new owner will not be able to claim allowances on the integral features.

Law: FA 2008, Sch. 26, para. 15

4.11.8   Transfers within groups

In contrast to the restrictions outlined at **4.11.7** above, there is a provision to ensure that groups of companies are not penalised by making a transfer of an integral feature. If the asset qualified as plant and machinery before April 2008 and is now transferred to another company, the new company would (without this special provision) only be able to claim allowances at the lower rate. An example would be the transfer of an air conditioning system as part of the overall transfer of a property.

The two companies may jointly elect, within two years of the transfer, to move the asset in question across at a value that produces no balancing adjustment for the seller. The buyer may then claim standard allowances, normally in the main pool, rather than having to classify it as special rate expenditure.

The companies must be members of the same group in accordance with TCGA 1992, s. 170(3) to (6).

In the event of a future sale, the disposal proceeds will be capped at the original cost figure rather than at the written down value at the time of the inter-group transfer.

Law: FA 2008, Sch. 26, para. 16, 17
Guidance: CA 22370

4.12   Shares in plant and machinery

A person may own part of an asset, or a share in an asset. Unless the context otherwise requires, such a part or share is treated as an asset in its own right for the purposes of claiming plant and machinery allowances.

A share in plant or machinery is treated as used for the purposes of a qualifying activity so long as (but only so long as) the asset in question is used for the purposes of that activity.

Law: CAA 2001, s. 270, 571

4.13   Exclusions from qualifying expenditure

4.13.1   Introduction

Various exclusions apply to prevent particular types of expenditure from qualifying for plant and machinery allowances.

The exclusions that are of the greatest importance relate to dwelling-houses (considered in depth at **4.14** below) and to claims by directors and employees (at **4.15** below).

Other exclusions are covered in the paragraphs that follow.

4.13.2   MPs and others

Allowances are restricted for Westminster MPs and for members of the Scottish Parliament, the National Assembly for Wales or the Northern Ireland Assembly.

Expenditure incurred by such individuals will not be qualifying expenditure for plant and machinery purposes if:

- it is incurred "in or in connection with the provision or use of residential or overnight accommodation"; and
- the purpose of the expenditure is to enable the member to perform his or her duties at or near the place where the body sits, or the constituency or region that the member represents.

Law: CAA 2001, s. 34

4.13.3   Long funding leasing

Expenditure is not qualifying expenditure if it is incurred on the provision of plant or machinery for leasing under a long funding lease.

In such circumstances, allowances will normally be available instead to the lessee, but subject to the complex rules applying to long funding leases generally (see **Chapter 7**).

Law: CAA 2001, s. 34A
Guidance: BLM 39025

4.13.4   Sums payable in respect of depreciation

A person may receive a subsidy to cover the deprecation of plant or machinery used for the purposes of a qualifying activity. The subsidy may be intended to cover either the whole or part of any depreciation suffered.

If any such receipts are taken into account in calculating the taxable income or profits then they are ignored for capital allowances purposes. In other cases, allowances will be restricted: see **5.9**.

Law: CAA 2001, s. 37, 210*ff.*

4.13.5   Production animals

Farmers may elect to treat certain creatures on the "herd basis" under ITTOIA 2005, s. 111*ff.* or under CTA 2009, s. 109*ff.* If an election is made, the expenditure on such animals (or on shares in such animals) is not qualifying expenditure for plant and machinery purposes.

Animals not treated in this way may, however, qualify as plant and machinery if they do not form part of the trading stock.

Law: CAA 2001, s. 38

4.13.6   Qualifying care providers

Individuals who are paid to provide "qualifying care" may be exempt from any income tax liability or may benefit from an "alternative method" of calculating liability.

Entitlement to capital allowances (in practice, almost certainly to plant and machinery allowances) is suspended for any period for which the person enjoys either the tax exemption or the reduced liability. The individual is treated as making a disposal at the start of such a period, but there is no balancing adjustment as the disposal proceeds are deemed to equal the unrelieved qualifying expenditure.

A person who ceases to benefit from the exemption, or to use the alternative method, can start to claim allowances once more if he or she is carrying on a qualifying activity. Assets that are still owned and that are used for the purposes of the activity may be brought in at market value.

Law: ITTOIA 2005, s. 824*ff.*

4.14   Plant or machinery used in a dwelling-house

4.14.1   Details of restriction

This is an important exclusion from qualifying expenditure, but it is of limited application.

Expenditure is not qualifying expenditure if it is incurred on plant or machinery for use in a dwelling-house to be used in one of the following qualifying activities:

- an ordinary UK property business;
- an ordinary overseas property business; or
- special leasing of plant or machinery.

As such, the restriction does not apply to all qualifying activities, including in particular to trades or to a furnished holiday lettings business. See **Chapter 3** for definitions of the various qualifying activities.

This rule means that it is important to consider the implications of moving a property between companies.

Example

Trader Ltd owns a number of residential properties and provides a service of housing and supervising young adults with troubled backgrounds, receiving payments from local authorities. It is accepted that this constitutes a trade, so it is not necessary to consider the dwelling-house restrictions.

As the scope of the activities grows, the decision is taken to create a simple structure of parent company (owning the properties) and trading subsidiaries (providing the service). The parent company therefore leases the properties to the trading subsidiary.

The company owning the properties is now an ordinary UK property business. As such, it is now necessary to consider whether or not the properties are dwelling-houses, a matter that must be considered on the facts of the case. If they are, the parent company will not be able to claim allowances, as s. 35 will operate to prevent the claim.

This needs advance planning. It may be possible to sign a fixtures election under s. 198 (see, generally, **12.7**), at the point of transfer from the original company to the new parent company, so as to retain the full benefit of the allowances within the trading subsidiary.

If plant or machinery is used for mixed purposes, a just and reasonable apportionment must be made to determine how much of the expenditure is disqualified under this rule.

In some cases where no capital allowances are available, relief may instead be given for the cost of replacing certain domestic items. See below.

Law: CAA 2001, s. 35
Guidance: CA 23060

4.14.2   Meaning of dwelling-house

HMRC have given the following view on how this term is defined:

> "There is no definition of 'dwelling house' for the purpose of CAA 2001, s. 35 so it takes its ordinary meaning. A dwelling house is a building, or a part of a building. Its distinctive characteristic is its ability to afford to those who use it the facilities required for day-to-day private domestic existence. In most cases there should be little difficulty in deciding whether or not particular premises comprise a dwelling house, but in difficult cases the question is essentially one of fact.

> A person's second or holiday home or accommodation used for holiday letting is a dwelling house. The common parts of a building which contains two or more dwelling houses will not comprise a dwelling house, although the individual dwelling houses within the building will do so. A hospital, a prison, nursing home or hotel (run as a trade and offering services) are not dwelling houses.

> ...

> The common parts (for example, the stairs and lifts) of a building which contains two or more dwelling houses will not, however, comprise a dwelling-house."

It should be emphasised that this is the HMRC view but is not necessarily entirely correct. It is understood, for example, that HMRC formerly took the view that holiday accommodation used for letting was *not* a dwelling-house, and the point is at least debatable. (In relation to furnished holiday lettings, this is not an issue in practice as the s. 35 restriction does not apply to such properties, but the change of view could make a big difference to other let properties that do not meet the criteria to qualify as furnished holiday lettings.)

Elsewhere, HMRC give the following specific guidance in relation to central heating systems:

> "A lift or central heating system serving the common parts of a building which contains two or more dwelling houses will not comprise part of either dwelling house. A central heating system serving an individual residential flat does not however qualify for PMA.
>
> Expenditure on a central heating system serving the whole of the building containing two or more dwelling houses should be apportioned between the common parts should be apportioned between the common parts, which part qualifies for PMA, and the residential flats or individual dwelling houses which do not."

HMRC have also issued more specific guidance, in connection with student accommodation, as considered immediately below.

Communal areas and houses in multiple occupation

Particular issues may arise in relation to houses in multiple occupation (HMOs). The fact that a property is in multiple occupancy does not in itself, of course, mean that shared parts of the property qualify; the test is to determine what constitutes the dwelling-house, and in many cases the whole property will constitute a single dwelling. HMRC guidance at CA 23060 (which, incidentally, was quietly re-worded in 2019) is as follows:

> "Some advisers have encouraged taxpayers to claim PMAs for plant and machinery used in shared areas (sitting rooms, kitchens etc.) of houses in multiple occupation. They contend that the shared areas are not part of the 'dwelling house' and that allowances are therefore available. We disagree."

And the focus of the HMRC guidance at CA 11520 is on the other areas of such properties:

> "We are aware that some taxpayers have submitted claims for plant and machinery allowances in respect of shared parts of houses in multiple occupation (such as hallways, stairs, landings, attics and basements within the houses). They contend that these

> shared areas are not part of the 'dwelling-house' and that allowances are therefore available. We disagree with this position."

It is helpful to think of an analogy with an ordinary private dwelling, such as a family home. In this case, it is clear that all areas of the property form part of the dwelling-house; the same principle applies to HMO properties. However, HMRC recognise that it is also possible for a single property to contain more than one HMO, in which case there may be areas of the property that do not form part of any of the HMOs, and in relation to which a fixtures claim may be possible.

In the opinion of the authors, this HMRC interpretation is clearly correct. It was also reinforced by the 2019 FTT case of *Tevfik*. The case contained a catalogue of disasters for the ill-advised taxpayer. The case report quoted an HMRC letter which does helpfully bring out the distinction between different types of property:

> "HMRC responded that in their view, where a house has a number of separate bedrooms with or without en-suite facilities occupied by a number of unconnected individuals who share other facilities such as kitchen, bathroom and lounge, then the whole of the house is a dwelling-house. He further commented that (conversely) for a dwelling-house that has been converted into a number of individual flats, each flat with its own entrance, cooking, washing and sleeping facilities, then each separate flat is a dwelling-house and that all areas within each flat comprise the dwelling-house. The officer added that common areas between the flats such as hallways and stairways are not part of the dwelling-houses."

Law: CAA 2001, s. 35

Case: *Tevfik v HMRC* [2019] UKFTT 600 (TC)

Use "in" a dwelling-house

HMRC have stated that:

> "The plant or machinery doesn't necessarily have to be located in a dwelling house in order to be 'for use in' it. For example, if a landlord installs ground-mounted solar panels in the garden of a house he lets and the electricity generated will be used in that house, the solar panels will not qualify for PMAs."

Some property businesses may not wish to accept this interpretation. The statutory test is whether expenditure is incurred in providing plant or machinery for use in a dwelling-house. The author would argue, in the example given by HMRC, that although the electricity may be used in the house, the plant or machinery is clearly not.

Guidance: CA 20020, 23060

Whether usage of property is a relevant consideration

In deciding whether a given property is a dwelling-house, one area of uncertainty is the question of whether it is appropriate to look at the nature of the activities carried on in a property, or merely at its construction.

At **4.14.1** above, an example was given of a company providing care services to young adults. It may be the case that the young people are housed in ordinary flats, which on the face of it are clearly dwelling-houses. But is it as simple as that? It may be possible to argue that the nature of the relationship between the owners of the property and the young occupants is such that these flats cannot properly be described as dwelling-houses:

- the provision of the accommodation may be institutional in nature;
- staff may have access to the property at all times (such that the young adults do not enjoy the "private" domestic existence to which the HMRC guidance refers, as quoted above);
- the young people may be genuinely referred to by all parties as "clients" or perhaps as "service users" rather than as "tenants";
- the nature of the relationship may clearly be that of carer and cared for, rather than of landlord and tenant;
- occupation of the properties may be restricted to young people under the care of local authorities, rather than to the general public.

In short, is it possible to argue that although the properties are *in construction terms* ordinary flats, they are *in usage terms* more akin to "a hospital, a prison, a nursing home or hotel (run as a trade and offering services)" rather than to a private dwelling-house? The point is, to the authors' knowledge, untested.

Law: CAA 2001, s. 35
Guidance: CA 11520, 20020, 23060

4.14.3 Student accommodation

According to HMRC at CA 11520:

> "A University hall of residence may be one of the most difficult types of premises to decide because there are so many variations in student accommodation. On the one hand, an educational establishment that provides on-site accommodation purely for its own students, where, for example, the kitchen and dining facilities are physically separate from the study-bedrooms and may not always be accessible to the students, is probably an institution, rather than a 'dwelling-house'. But on the other hand, cluster flats or houses in multiple occupation, that provide the facilities necessary for day-to-day private domestic existence (such as bedrooms with en-suite facilities and a shared or communal kitchen/diner and sitting room) are dwelling-houses. Such a flat or house would be a dwelling-house if occupied by a family, a group of friends or key workers, so the fact that it may be occupied by students is, in a sense, immaterial."

Original interpretation

Before December 2008, HMRC accepted that a university hall of residence was not a dwelling-house. Since that time, there have been various adjustments to the HMRC view and a rather more complex picture now emerges.

Interpretation between December 2008 and October 2010

HMRC Brief 66/08 was issued on 29 December 2008 to "clarify" the HMRC view on the application of s. 35 to "university halls of residence and similar facilities". According to the Brief, HMRC "recognise that the provision of student accommodation has evolved since expressing our view in CA11520 and so we will be updating our guidance to reflect this". The wording of this revised guidance was that:

> " 'Communal' areas are not dwelling houses. Areas to which tenants do not have access are also not dwelling houses. However, all other areas are dwelling houses."

HMRC gave the following example at the time:

Old HMRC example

A student accommodation block has three floors, each with ten en-suite 'study bedrooms' that are individually lockable. Each floor also has a kitchen and TV room which are for the use of the ten occupants. The building has air-conditioning equipment located in the attic and a boiler located in the basement – only maintenance personnel have access to these areas.

In this example the kitchen and TV room are communal areas and not dwelling houses. The stairs and corridors which give access to other areas are also communal and are not dwelling houses. Tenants do not have access to the roof and attic and so they are not dwelling houses. However, the individual study bedrooms are dwelling houses.

Interpretation since October 2010

However, representations were made to HMRC that this view was still incorrect, and the matter was also reviewed in the light of the earlier *Uratemp* decision. This then led to a third HMRC interpretation of the rules, with the publication of R&C Brief 45/10 on 22 October 2010. This revised guidance stated that:

> "On further reflection, HMRC have concluded that the definition based on the presence of the facilities required for day-to-day private existence is a better everyday description, bearing in mind that the question remains essentially one of fact, so that unusual or controversial cases may still need to be considered in the light of their individual facts and circumstances.
>
> Returning to the example of student accommodation ..., HMRC have concluded that the better view is that each flat in multiple occupation comprises a dwelling-house, given that the individual study bedrooms alone would not afford the occupants 'the facilities required for day-to-day private domestic existence'. In other words, the communal kitchen and lounge are also part of the dwelling-house. The common parts of the building block (such as the common entrance lobby, stairs or lifts) would not, however, comprise a 'dwelling-house'."

This, then, is the current interpretation.

See case study 4 in **Appendix 2** for an illustration of a claim for communal areas in residential accommodation.

Law: CAA 2001, s. 35
Guidance: CA 11520, 20020, 23060; HMRC Brief 45/10

Historic claims

This raises the issue of what happens if a claim is made now for expenditure incurred before HMRC revised their view.

For expenditure incurred on or after 22 October 2010, it is clear that HMRC will apply the new interpretation.

HMRC stated in HMRC Brief 45/10 that:

> "In relation to capital expenditure incurred before 29 December 2008 claims made in returns for open years and filed before 22 October 2010 relying on R&C Brief 66/08 will also be accepted."

By implication, any claims submitted now will have to be on the basis of the October 2010 interpretation, whenever the expenditure was incurred.

Confusingly, HMRC also stated in HMRC Brief 45/10 that:

> "In relation to capital expenditure incurred on or after 29 December 2008 but before 22 October 2010 HMRC will either accept capital allowances claims in returns made in respect of communal areas on the basis of the view as set out in R&C Brief 66/08 or on the basis of the view as previously set out in CA11520 and CA23060."

This is an odd statement, as it appears to be saying that if expenditure was incurred in that interim period of about 22 months, a claim could be made on the basis of either the original interpretation (student accommodation is not a dwelling-house) or the December 2008 interpretation (it was a dwelling-house but communal areas were outside the restriction). However, it seems highly improbable that HMRC are really stating that they will allow claims to be made indefinitely on the basis of an interpretation they now believe to be incorrect. Furthermore, the HMRC view of how the rules apply does not have the force of law, and it seems very likely that any court or tribunal would apply the law consistently on the basis of the more restrictive interpretation that has applied since October 2010.

Law: CAA 2001, s. 35
Guidance: CA 11520, 20020, 23060; HMRC Brief 45/10

4.14.4   Furnished holiday lettings

As already noted, the dwelling-house restriction does not apply for a (UK or EEA) furnished holiday lettings business (see, generally, **3.4** and **3.6**).

However, the business will only qualify as such where the relevant conditions are met, for example in relation to the number of days for which the property is let.

If those conditions are not met, the business will be an ordinary property business, and the dwelling-house restriction will potentially apply (but see **3.2** for a discussion of "serviced accommodation"). The HMRC view is that "a person's second or holiday home or accommodation used for holiday letting is a dwelling house".

The question may then arise of how far the restriction curtails the right to claim plant and machinery allowances. The restriction only applies for expenditure "incurred in providing plant or machinery for use in a dwelling-house". The use of the terminology "in a dwelling-house" would appear to curtail the effect of the restriction. The restriction would certainly not appear to apply to a swimming pool that is shared between various holiday cottages, for example. It is also very possible that the wording prevents any restriction for a private swimming pool in the grounds of a single holiday cottage.

These matters are considered in greater depth in *Furnished Holiday Lettings: A Tax Guide*, written by John Endacott and available from Claritax Books.

4.14.5   Replacement of domestic items

A new form of tax relief was introduced in 2016 to allow landlords of residential dwelling-houses to deduct costs incurred on replacing furnishings, appliances and kitchenware that are used by the tenants of the property. The relief has been generally referred to as "replacement furniture relief". The relief is not given by way of capital allowances but brief coverage is included here for the convenience of readers.

The relief replaced, for expenditure incurred from 1 or 6 April 2016, the former "wear and tear" allowance. (For accounting periods spanning 1 April 2016, a split is made into two notional periods, with apportionment on a time basis unless that produces an unjust or unreasonable result.)

The new relief is available for individuals, companies and other entities (such as trusts or collective investment schemes). The item in question must be provided solely for the use of the lessee of the property. The stated intention behind the relief is "to give relief for the cost of replacing furnishings to a wider range of property businesses as well as a more consistent and fairer way of calculating taxable profits".

The new relief is given for the capital cost of *replacement* items, so does not apply for the first expenditure on a particular type of asset. The relief is calculated as the cost of a like-for-like (or nearest modern equivalent) replacement asset. If the replacement item is an improvement on the old one, the deduction is limited to the amount of the expenditure that would have been incurred on one that was substantially the same. Any costs incurred in disposing of the old asset – and any incidental costs of purchasing the new one – may be added to the claim, but any proceeds from its disposal must be deducted. The rules are modified where the old item is part exchanged for the new one.

The relief is available for the cost of replacing a "domestic item". This is defined to mean "an item for domestic use (such as furniture, furnishings, household appliances and kitchenware)". The relief does not apply for **Fixtures**.

The relief is not given where capital allowances are available for the expenditure. This is of particular significance for furnished holiday let properties: capital allowances may be claimed for such properties, so the replacement furniture relief is not available. Nor is the newer relief available where the landlord derives rent-a-room receipts from the property and those receipts are brought into account in calculating the rent-a-room profits (per ITTOIA 2005, s. 793 or 797).

Law: ITTOIA 2005, s. 311A; CTA 2009, s. 250A

4.15 Employments and offices

4.15.1 Introduction

In principle, it is open to an employee or office holder to claim capital allowances for certain expenditure incurred for work purposes. Such allowances are given as a deduction from earnings (and any balancing charge is taxed as additional earnings).

In reality, however, various important restrictions apply to capital allowances claims by holders of an office or employment.

The *Employment Income Manual* contains extensive guidance on the HMRC attitude to capital allowances claims by employees, including the following points.

It is not necessary to capitalise very small items of office equipment ("such as cheap pocket calculators or staplers"). Where any deduction is available for such items, such deduction should be given under ITEPA 2003, s. 336 (deductions for expenses), rather than by way of capital allowances. HMRC have also stated, in a helpsheet, that employees would normally claim under s. 336 (rather than by way of capital allowances) for "small tools, such as electric drills, or protective clothing such as safety boots or helmets".

Books may be treated the same way if they are likely to be of only temporary use or value, but relief should be claimed by way of capital allowances "if, exceptionally, an employee has to purchase a substantial work of reference likely to have a long useful life".

HMRC do not generally accept that an employee can claim plant and machinery allowances for a briefcase (EIM 36720). Some fairly extensive guidance is given on computers used by employees for work purposes and paid for by the employee (EIM 36730) but the guidance is quite old and in reality the position is untested.

Guidance: EIM 36510, 36710*ff*; HMRC helpsheet 252: *Capital Allowances and Balancing Charges*

4.15.2   Vehicles and bicycles

No plant or machinery allowances are given for a car, van, motorcycle or bicycle owned by the employee; the cost of such a vehicle or cycle is not qualifying expenditure (see also **9.1.3**). The employee may instead obtain tax relief through the system of mileage allowances and relief.

4.15.3   Necessarily

Any other expenditure incurred by the holder of an office or employment will be qualifying expenditure only if it is "necessarily provided" for use in the performance of the duties of the office or employment.

The definition of "necessarily provided" is notoriously tight and was tested in the *Williams* case, where a television newsreader was denied plant and machinery allowances for clothing she wore when presenting. The tribunal held that the clothing in question presented "no special feature either in construction, purpose or position". Principles from the earlier *Hillyer v Leeke* case were applied. Broadly, the requirement to use the item in question must be imposed by the nature of the employee's duties, and not by the personal circumstances of the employee.

HMRC guidance in relation to this "necessarily" condition includes the following:

> "If the expense is substantial, it would be reasonable to expect the contract of employment to include a specific reference to the

requirement to incur it. If there is nothing explicit in the contract, find out whether the employee has approached the employer to provide the item, or to reimburse its cost, and, if so, with what response. If the employer is not prepared to bear the cost and advances the view that the expense is not considered necessary this will clearly weaken the taxpayer's claim, though without being entirely conclusive."

If allowances are due, an adjustment will be required (on a "just and reasonable basis") if the item in question is used partly for private purposes. The "wholly and exclusively" principle that applies to general employee expenses does not apply for capital allowances.

The *Telfer* case is worth referring to where the question of "necessarily provided" needs to be considered in a capital allowances context. The taxpayer lost the case on the basis that the caravans being considered did not, in the circumstances, function as plant. Nevertheless, the tribunal did not accept HMRC's argument in relation to the necessity test:

"We accept that the test imposed by section 36(1)(b) CAA goes beyond a legal requirement by the employer that the asset concerned is provided by the employee and requires an examination of whether or not the duties of the employment objectively require the provision of the asset. In this case, the duties of Mr Telfer's employment did objectively require him to live on site 'in his own outfit'. The duties required Mr Telfer to be on site at all times, and to be ready to move to another site at the Caravan Club's discretion, and on any realistic basis this means that those duties required him to live in his caravan on site. The caravans were used (as shelter and living accommodation) by Mr Telfer in the performance of the duties of his employment(s)."

Law: CAA 2001, s. 36(1), 205*ff.*

Cases: *Hillyer v Leeke* (1976) 51 TC 90; *Williams v HMRC* [2010] UKFTT 86 (TC); *Telfer v HMRC* [2016] UKFTT 614 (TC)

Guidance: EIM 36560

4.15.4 Entertaining

No plant and machinery allowances can be given for employees who use plant or machinery for the purposes of business entertaining. See, generally, **5.8.4**.

4.15.5   *Intermediaries*

The intermediaries ("IR35") rules may apply where a worker would be regarded as an employee if his or her services were provided directly to the client, rather than through an intermediary. Changes to the rules were made from April 2017, shifting the responsibility in some cases to public authority employers rather than to the intermediary.

The tax legislation seeks to prevent a double charge to tax when the intermediary makes a payment to the worker from income which has already been subject to PAYE.

The legislation uses the term "end-of-line remuneration" where a person receives a payment or benefit from the paying intermediary. The amount of that end-of-line remuneration may be reduced (but not so as to create a tax loss) by various amounts, including:

> "the amount of any capital allowances in respect of expenditure incurred by the paying intermediary that could have been deducted from employment income under section 262 of CAA 2001 if the payee had been employed by the 40 public authority and had incurred the expenditure."

Law: ITEPA 2003, s. 61W

4.16   Contributions

Special rules apply where a person makes a contribution to the cost of an item qualifying for capital allowances. Those rules are addressed at **Chapter 31** below.

4.17   Timing of expenditure

4.17.1   *Normal rules*

The normal rules as to the timing of expenditure, as discussed at **1.5** above, apply for plant and machinery as they do for other allowances. In particular, see:

- **1.5.3** for the general rule;
- **1.5.4** for cases where payment is due after four months; and
- **1.5.5** for milestone contracts.

Certain additional rules apply, however, specifically for plant and machinery allowances, as below.

4.17.2 Pre-trading expenditure

A person may incur expenditure for the purposes of the trade, or other qualifying activity, before that trade or other activity has started. In such a case, the expenditure is treated as incurred on the first day on which the activity is in fact carried on. See case study 1 in **Appendix 2** for an illustration of this.

The relevant legislation (s. 12) reads (emphasis added):

> "For the purposes of this Part, expenditure incurred for the purposes of a qualifying activity by a person *about to* carry on the activity is to be treated as if it had been incurred by him on the first day on which he carries on the activity."

HMRC interpret this (at CA 23020) as follows (again, with emphasis added):

> "Treat expenditure incurred *before* a qualifying activity begins as incurred on the first day that the person who incurred the expenditure carries on the qualifying activity."

It is certainly arguable that "about to" means something closer than many years later, but the HMRC guidance glosses over this point and the authors are not aware that HMRC have ever argued it in practice.

This rule is disapplied for the purposes of determining entitlement to annual investment allowances (s. 38A(4): see **5.3**) or first-year allowances (s. 50: see **5.4**).

Law: CAA 2001, s. 12
Guidance: CA 23083

5. Allowances and charges

5.1 Introduction

5.1.1 Overview

The main content of this chapter is an illustration of the various different types of allowance for plant and machinery, but it also addresses some more difficult scenarios and shows how effect may be given to allowances and balancing charges. First-year tax credits are dealt with at **5.11**.

5.1.2 Choosing the correct type of allowance

The writing-down allowance (WDA) may be seen as the default allowance for plant and machinery. However, the rate of tax relief may in certain circumstances be accelerated by claiming a first-year allowance (FYA) or an annual investment allowance (AIA).

As a general principle, a business will wish to claim allowances as fast as possible. This will involve maximising any claims for FYAs or AIAs, and ensuring that assets attracting a slower rate of WDA will as far as possible be the subject of a claim to accelerated allowances instead. If, for example, a business buys both integral features and general plant and machinery in the same period, it will normally wish to claim AIAs against the integral features.

Example

A particular business is entitled to maximum AIA in the period of £25,000 (perhaps because other connected companies have absorbed the balance of the AIA to which it would have been entitled). For simplicity, say that the business incurs exactly £25,000 of expenditure on integral features and the same level of expenditure on other plant and machinery.

If it claims AIAs on the integral features, its total claim will be £29,500, consisting of AIA of £25,000 and WDAs of £4,500 (calculated as £25,000 at 18%).

If it instead claims AIAs on the other plant and machinery, the AIA figure of £25,000 will remain unchanged. However, the WDAs on the integral features will be calculated at just 6% (for periods beginning from April

2019), giving a figure of £1,500. In this case, the total claim for the year will therefore be just £26,500.

The difference is (in principle, at least) one of timing only, and the future allowances in the second scenario will be higher to compensate for the initial disadvantage.

Exceptionally, a business may wish to claim a lower rate of capital allowance. This could arise, for example, if personal allowances will be lost for a sole trader or if a company wishes to maximise losses in a future year to offset against other profits.

Businesses owning fixtures need to claim allowances before selling the property; failure to do this will deny allowances to any future owner (and will thus potentially depress the value). This is explored in detail at **Chapters 12 to 14** below.

Guidance: CA 23100*ff.*

5.1.3   *Final chargeable period*

Various special rules apply to the final chargeable period, and the legislation contains a formal definition of that term.

For the main pool, or for a special rate pool, the final chargeable period is the chargeable period in which the qualifying activity is permanently discontinued.

For a class pool under s. 107 (overseas leasing), the term denotes the chargeable period at the end of which there can be no more disposal receipts in any subsequent chargeable period.

The definition of the term for the purposes of a single-asset pool is more complicated. The normal rule is that it is the first chargeable period in which any disposal event given in s. 61(1) occurs: see **5.5.2**. However, there is no final chargeable period:

- just because plant or machinery starts to be used partly for other purposes (s. 206(4): see **5.8**);
- at the relevant cut-off for a short-life asset (s. 86(2) and s. 87(2): see **15.3**); or
- for a single ship pool (s. 132(2): see **Chapter 20**).

Law: CAA 2001, s. 65

5.2   Annual investment allowances

5.2.1   *Introduction*

The annual investment allowance (AIA) gives immediate tax relief for certain types of expenditure, up to a defined limit. It is available for most capital expenditure on plant and machinery.

Example 1

Jack runs an independent bookshop. During a particular accounting year he incurs just two items of capital expenditure: a shelving unit costing £10,000 and a new till for £600.

Jack claims AIAs on the combined total of £10,600. His taxable profits for the year are reduced by the full amount of the £10,600. (If he has capital expenditure from earlier years, on which he has not yet had full tax relief, he may be entitled to WDAs on that other expenditure as well. He cannot, however, claim AIAs this year for expenditure incurred in the past.)

AIAs may be claimed by businesses of any size. As, however, there is a cap on the amount of AIA that may be claimed in any year, and as associated businesses generally have to share a single allowance (see **5.2.10** and following paragraphs below) the allowance is of less benefit to the largest businesses and to businesses that are part of larger groups of companies.

The key conditions for claiming AIAs are that the person concerned must incur "AIA qualifying expenditure" (see **5.2.2**) and must own the plant or machinery at some time during the chargeable period for which the claim is made.

An AIA can only be made for the chargeable period in which the expenditure is incurred (one of the many things that went wrong for the ill-advised taxpayer in *Tevfik*). It cannot be used for expenditure incurred in an earlier period, whether or not other allowances have already been claimed on that expenditure.

Example 2

Deborah spends £20,000 in June 2017 on some fixtures in her office. She only becomes aware in November 2021 that the can claim plant and machinery allowances on those fixtures. She draws accounts up to 31 December.

As long as she still owns the fixtures in question, Deborah may make a capital allowances claim for a later year – perhaps for the year to 31

December 2020 or by amending the return for the previous year. However, she will be able to claim WDAs only, as the AIA claim was only possible for the year in which she actually incurred the cost. Unless her accounts are under HMRC enquiry, it is too late now for Deborah to change her claim for the year to 31 December 2017.

Example 3

Donna has a balance brought forward on her capital allowances pool of £6,000. She incurs no new expenditure in the year. She is not entitled to claim AIAs on the £6,000 as the expenditure is not incurred in the later year.

Subject to the overall limits for the year in question (see **5.2.4** below), the person claiming the AIA may claim in respect of all of his qualifying expenditure or in respect of only part of it, as he chooses. If an AIA claim converts a profit to a loss, or augments an existing loss, the full amount of the loss may be relieved in the usual way.

A person might choose to claim a lower amount of AIA to avoid loss of the personal income tax allowance, for example. As a point of practice, the allowance may also be partly disclaimed so as to negate a balancing charge that would otherwise arise.

Example 4

Eddie buys a new van for £14,000 and sells his old one for £6,000. The value of the main pool at the start of the year was just £4,500. Eddie may claim AIAs of £14,000 and take the balancing charge of £1,500. Or he may reduce the AIA claim to £12,500, adding the balance of £1,500 to the main pool to ensure that no balancing charge arises. There is no tax difference.

Law: CAA 2001, s. 51A
Case: *Tevfik v HMRC* [2019] UKFTT 600 (TC)
Guidance: CA 23080*ff.*

5.2.2   AIA qualifying expenditure

AIAs are given only for "AIA qualifying expenditure". This means that the expenditure on the plant or machinery must be incurred by an individual, a partnership whose members are all individuals, or by a company.

It follows that partnerships with a corporate member may not claim AIAs. The *Hoardweel Farm Partnership* case concerned a claim for AIA where a partnership had a corporate partner. The decision was primarily one of fact, as it was argued that the corporate partner had been dormant. However, the business accounts indicated that the company had used a partnership capital account and AIAs were denied.

Another partnership argument was raised in *Drilling Global Consultant*, though it never stood any real chance of success. The case concerned a limited liability partnership and the appellant contended that the LLP, with its corporate member, should be regarded as a company; reference was made to various sections of CTA 2009 dealing with the nature of partnerships. On this basis, it was contended that the LLP was a qualifying person for the purposes of claiming AIAs. It was also suggested that there was no good reason to exclude mixed partnerships from claiming AIAs. And it was argued that, in reality, there was no partnership. None of these arguments prevailed, however: the person claiming the allowance was not a qualifying person and HMRC's stance could not be successfully challenged.

Partnerships with a partnership as a member are also denied AIAs. This, at least, appears to be the correct interpretation of the rules and was the line HMRC take, according to a query considered in *Taxation* magazine of 25 September 2013. It had been argued that the second partnership could be looked through by virtue of ITTOIA 2005, s. 863, which states that, for income tax purposes, "all the activities of the limited liability partnership are treated as carried on in partnership by its members (and not by the limited liability partnership as such)".

AIAs are not available for trusts, or for partnerships with a trust as a member.

Although there are a few "general exclusions" (see **5.2.3** below), the AIA is available for a wide range of expenditure. Specifically, AIAs may be claimed on the cost of integral features and other special rate expenditure, as well as on expenditure on general plant and machinery. AIAs are thus available for all vehicles except cars, for fixtures in property, business machinery, office equipment, etc.

Law: CAA 2001, s. 38A
Cases: *Hoardweel Farm Partnership v HMRC* [2012] UKFTT 402 (TC); *Drilling Global Consultant LLP v HMRC* [2014] UKFTT 888 (TC)
Guidance: CA 23084

5.2.3 General exclusions

Expenditure is not AIA qualifying expenditure if a claim is precluded by any of the following "general exclusions":

- expenditure incurred in the chargeable period in which the qualifying activity is permanently discontinued (see below);
- expenditure on a car (see **9.2** for the definition used for these purposes);
- certain expenditure incurred for the purposes of a ring-fence trade;
- expenditure incurred in connection with a change in the nature or conduct of another person's trade or business, where the obtaining of an AIA is a main benefit;
- where an item of plant or machinery provided for other purposes starts to be used for the qualifying activity;
- use for other purposes of plant or machinery provided for long funding leasing; or
- where an asset has been received as a gift (s. 14).

There is one possible exception to the above, where there is pre-trading expenditure on mineral exploration and access.

In contrast to the rules for FYAs (see **5.4.2**) there is no general exclusion for leased assets. This is a deliberate policy difference and was spelt out in the original *Budget Note* that introduced the AIA in 2008 (BN12, para. 18).

Most of the exclusions are self-explanatory, but the fourth bullet requires more explanation. This is obviously an anti-avoidance measure, designed to prevent a person from multiplying his entitlement to AIAs. HMRC have illustrated the way it might work as follows.

HMRC example

Smithson Plc is a business that has already used up its AIA for its current chargeable period. It wants to buy a lathe for £50,000. It makes a loan of £50,000 to Dan, a higher rate taxpayer, who buys the lathe for his new qualifying activity of operating the lathe, thus obtaining the AIA, with fixed supply and sale contracts with Smithson Plc. The lathe is installed in Smithson Plc's factory and operated by its workforce on a subcontract basis. The tax saving is shared by Smithson Plc and Dan through the contract price.

The anti-avoidance legislation means that Dan is not entitled to the AIA and so the scheme does not work.

Law: CAA 2001, s. 38B
Guidance: CA 23084

Permanently discontinued

The question of whether a trade has been permanently discontinued is one of fact, and there are no special capital allowances rules to determine the matter. Nevertheless, the point was considered in the context of the AIAs in *Keyl v HMRC*. The taxpayer had transferred his business as a going concern to a company, and that represented a permanent discontinuance of the trade he had previously carried on. The tribunal held that the unincorporated trade had ceased on 31 March, and that the new trade in the company had begun on 1 April:

> "In the scintilla of time before midnight on 31 March 2009 Mr Keyl's trade ceased. In the scintilla of time after midnight, CC Ltd commenced its trade."

Given the above finding of fact, it followed that the trade was permanently discontinued in the earlier chargeable period, and no AIAs were available for that period. The decision was subsequently upheld by the Upper Tribunal, which ruled that "a discontinuance of a trade at the end of a chargeable period is a discontinuance of that trade in that period". This is therefore an important consideration for a sole trader or partnership that is intending to incorporate, and care should be taken if significant expenditure is being incurred. See **18.5.4** for a detailed discussion of connected party transactions, including the question of elections under sections 198 and 266.

Case: *Keyl v HMRC* [2014] UKFTT 493 (TC), [2015] UKUT 383

5.2.4   Amount of annual investment allowance

The AIA was only introduced in 2008 but the amount of relief that may be given in any one year has already fluctuated wildly. The maximum AIA for corporation tax purposes has been as follows since that time:

	£
From 1 January 2019	1,000,000
1 January 2016 to 31 December 2018	200,000
1 April 2014 to 31 December 2015	500,000
1 January 2013 to 31 March 2014	250,000
1 April 2012 to 31 Dec 2012	25,000
1 April 2010 to 31 March 2012	100,000
1 April 2008 to 31 March 2010	50,000

The figures relate to *expenditure incurred* in the periods indicated (and not, for example, to the date of claim or to the accounting date). The March/April dates (but not the December/January dates) are adjusted by five days for income tax purposes (e.g. with 6 April in lieu of 1 April).

Transitional rules apply whenever the maximum rate changes: see **5.2.6** and following paragraphs below.

If a chargeable period is greater or less than one year, the relevant figure is increased or reduced *pro rata*. So if a company has a chargeable period of six months ending on 31 December 2019, its maximum AIA claim will be £500,000. For corporation tax purposes, a chargeable period cannot exceed 12 months.

HMRC specifically accept that the calculation may be made either on a daily basis or – where the period in question consists of whole calendar months – on a monthly basis.

Businesses that are associated with one another in some way may have to share a single amount of AIA: see **5.2.9**.

If a person incurs AIA qualifying expenditure in excess of the threshold, AIA is simply claimed on an amount up to the limit. Any excess may be subject to a claim for WDAs in the same period.

Example 1

A company (with no complications re associated or group companies) has a value of £80,000 in its main capital allowances pool at the start of the year. Assume that the rate of available AIA is £200,000 for the period in question.

The company incurs new AIA qualifying expenditure of £400,000 in the year, of which £160,000 is on integral features and £240,000 is on general plant and machinery.

The company can claim AIAs on the whole of the £160,000, and on £40,000 of the £240,000. It can claim WDAs on the balance brought forward of £80,000 and also on the £200,000 of new expenditure not covered by the AIA claim. Assuming an 18% WDA rate, the total claim for the year will therefore be £250,400 (£200,000 AIA plus £50,400 WDA).

A company made a bold but ultimately unsuccessful attempt to work around the AIA limit by claiming tax relief under the provisions for the replacement and alteration of tools (CTA 2009, s. 68 and ITTOIA 2005, s. 68, both now repealed). Turners (Soham) Ltd had incurred some £33 million of expenditure on the replacement of vehicles and vehicle parts for its road haulage trade (nearly 400 "tractor units" (the front ends of articulated lorries), 171 trailers of various sorts, and 46 tankers). Having initially claimed capital allowances, the company made an "error or mistake" claim, seeking a deduction under the predecessor legislation for s. 68. The company was not successful, for a variety of technical reasons that have little practical relevance today.

Law: CAA 2001, s. 51A; FA 2013, s. 7, Sch. 1

Case: *Turners (Soham) Ltd v HMRC* [2019] UKFTT 131 (TC)

Guidance: CA 23080*ff.*; https://tinyurl.com/nwpdb5rw (periods more or less than a year)

Disposals

Technically, and in contrast to the position for FYAs, AIA expenditure is pooled in the normal way and the AIA claim then reduces the available qualifying expenditure within the pool. Any disposal proceeds must be allocated to the appropriate pool, and may not be directly netted off against new expenditure.

Example 2

C Ltd has a balance of £10,000 on its main pool at the start of the year. As there are a number of group companies that are claiming allowances, the AIAs for the year in question are capped at £25,000.

In the year, C Ltd sells a machine for £12,000 and buys a replacement for £40,000. There are no other transactions.

C Ltd can claim AIAs of £25,000. The pool value is calculated as £10,000 brought down, plus new expenditure of £40,000, less AIA claim of £25,000, less sale proceeds of £12,000. This gives a pool balance of £13,000. WDAs are given on this figure.

Where appropriate, separate calculations must be performed for the main and special rate pools.

Law: CAA 2001, s. 58(4A)
Guidance: CA 23086

5.2.5   Pre-trading expenditure

A little care is needed with the treatment of pre-trading expenditure.

The easy starting point is that expenditure can only qualify for AIAs if it is incurred on or after 1 or 6 April 2008.

Another key principle is that AIAs are only given for the chargeable period in which the expenditure is incurred. If a person discovers in 2018 that he could have made a claim for expenditure incurred in June 2011, no AIAs can be claimed. (However, if the assets are still owned, WDAs will be due.)

There is a general principle (s. 12: see **4.17.2**) that pre-trading expenditure is treated as incurred on the first day of trading. However, this rule is ignored *for the purposes of determining whether or not expenditure is qualifying AIA expenditure* (s. 38A(4)).

This rule is unlikely to have any practical effect now but can be illustrated by reference to the time when the AIA rules were introduced. If a person incurred expenditure in February 2008 and started trading on 1 October 2008, the expenses would be treated for capital allowances purposes generally as incurred on 1 October 2008. However, no AIAs would be available as that general principle was ignored for the purposes of determining whether it was AIA expenditure.

Suppose, however, that a new company buys machinery in March 2019, starts trading on 1 July 2019, and buys further machinery during its year to 30 June 2020. The rule in s. 38A(4) has no relevance as the expenditure is qualifying AIA expenditure whether it is incurred in March 2019 or on 1 July 2019. Under the general principle of s. 12, the earlier expenditure is treated as incurred on 1 July 2019. The company already has expenditure that may absorb the whole AIA limit for the year, and (if so) cannot claim additional AIA in respect of the earlier amount. This is the case even though that expenditure was in fact incurred in an earlier period for which a separate AIA limit would have been available if the company had been trading.

Law: CAA 2001, s. 38A(5), 51A(2)
Guidance: CA 23083

5.2.6   Transitional rules when limit changes – overview

Transitional rules apply wherever a chargeable period spans the date on which the AIA limit changes.

The rules can be complex, and were especially difficult in relation to periods that spanned two changes. This possibility arose because of the reduction in the AIA in April 2012 followed by its increase in January 2013: companies with accounts drawn up to 28 February 2013, for example, had to calculate their entitlement to AIAs using three different thresholds (£100,000, £25,000 and £250,000).

The former Chancellor promised a period of stability, with a fixed rate of £200,000 from 1 January 2016, on a "permanent" basis. As such, the complexities were briefly reduced. In reality, however, nothing is permanent in tax, and a temporary (two-year, but later extended to three-year) increase was announced in the 2018 autumn Budget, effective from 1 January 2019.

The rules applying in relation to the increase in the threshold from £200,000 to £1,000,000 in January 2019 are covered at **5.2.7** immediately below. See **5.2.8** for the rules that will apply when the threshold reduces from £1,000,000 to £200,000 from January 2022.

5.2.7   Transitional rules – threshold rises (January 2019)

The transitional rules when the AIA threshold increases can be more complex than they seem, so care is needed.

The rules described in this section apply where the accounting period spans a single change in the AIA threshold, and where that change is an increase in the amount of AIA that may be claimed. This was the case, for example, for the change from January 2019, when the AIA limit was increased (initially for two years) from £200,000 to £1,000,000. Accounts drawn up to 30 April 2019, for instance, will include eight months for which the annual AIA limit was £200,000 and four months for which it was £1,000,000.

The legislation uses the expression "first straddling period" to refer to any chargeable period that begins before 1 January 2019 but ends on or after that date. (The "second straddling period" denotes a period beginning before 1 January 2022 (extended from 2021 as originally planned), when the allowance is reduced once more, and ending on or after that date – see **5.2.8** below).

For the period in which the threshold rises, it is necessary to go through two separate calculations. First, the maximum AIA for the whole accounting period must be calculated, but it is then also necessary to consider whether a cap applies for expenditure incurred during that part of the overall period for which the lower threshold applied, i.e. in the part of the overall chargeable period that falls before 1 January 2019.

Overall limit

Calculating the overall limit for the chargeable period is not difficult. It is achieved by looking at each period individually and by then aggregating the results.

The actual chargeable period, where it spans 1 January 2019, must be split into two notional periods:

- the first such notional period runs from the start of the actual chargeable period to 31 December 2018; and
- the second notional period starts on 1 January 2019 and ends at the end of the actual chargeable period.

The AIA limit is calculated for each notional period, and the amounts for the two periods are aggregated to give an overall maximum allowance.

Example 1

A company draws accounts up for the year to 30 April 2019.

Its actual accounting period is split into two notional periods. The first runs from 1 May 2018 to 31 December 2018, and the second from 1 January 2019 to 30 April 2019.

The maximum AIA for the first notional period is calculated as £133,333 (£200,000 x 8/12). The maximum for the latter period is calculated as £333,333 (£1,000,000 x 4/12). Thus the maximum AIA for the company for the actual chargeable period is, with rounding, £466,667.

If, for example, the company incurred AIA qualifying expenditure of £500,000 in April 2019, it would be able to claim AIAs on the maximum amount of £466,667.

The computation may be made on either a daily basis or – where the period in question consists of whole calendar months – on a monthly basis.

Cap

The above calculation is, however, subject to a further restriction for expenditure in the part of the overall period that falls before the increase in the AIA threshold.

In other words, the legislation caps the amount of AIA that may be given for expenditure incurred in the (notional) period ending 31 December 2018. AIAs for such expenditure may not exceed the figure calculated as the maximum AIA that would have been due for the actual chargeable period (ending on 30 April 2019) if the changes applying from January 2019 had not been made.

The resulting figure is not the same as that calculated for the notional period as above (£133,333). This is because the maximum due for expenditure incurred in the first eight months of the 12 month period to 30 April 2019 would have been £200,000 (the annual limit for the year) and not £133,333.

Example 2

Suppose that the company in the example immediately above had instead incurred the expenditure of £500,000 as follows: £420,000 in August 2018 and £80,000 during April 2019.

The maximum AIA for the whole period is still initially calculated as £466,667. However, the claim for expenditure in August 2018 is capped at £200,000, being the amount that would have been available had the changes not been made. The overall AIA claim for the actual chargeable period is therefore capped at £280,000.

Further complications arise if two or more businesses have to share a single AIA figure: see **5.2.9** below.

Law: CAA 2001, s. 51A; FA 2019, s. 32 and Sch. 13

Guidance: https://tinyurl.com/39tcypdx (AIA temporary increase)

5.2.8   Transitional rules – threshold falls (January 2022)

The rules described in this section will apply for periods spanning 1 January 2022, the date on which the maximum AIA falls back from £1,000,000 to £200,000 (FA 2019, Sch. 13, para. 2, as subsequently extended by *Finance Bill* 2021).

Two separate calculations will need to be made.

The first computes the maximum AIA for the *whole* of the chargeable period spanning the date of the change.

A second calculation further restricts the amount of AIA that can be claimed for expenditure incurred in the period from the date of the reduction (in this case, 1 January 2022) to the end of the transitional chargeable period.

Overall cap on AIA for transitional period

The first step, then, is to compute the maximum AIA that can be given for expenditure incurred in the whole chargeable period. In this respect, the change has retrospective effect, in that the maximum AIA that can be claimed for expenditure in 2021 can be reduced by the change from January 2021.

This calculation is made by a simple apportionment of the maximum figures for each part of the overall period.

Example 1

A company draws accounts up for the year to 31 March 2022.

That period includes nine months for which the maximum was £1,000,000, and three months for which it is £200,000. So we add (£1,000,000 x 9/12) to (£200,000 x 3/12) and this gives us a result of £800,000.

So whatever the timing of the expenditure, the maximum AIA that can be claimed for expenditure incurred during the year to 31 March 2022 can never exceed £800,000, even though the headline rate for the calendar year 2021 is £1,000,000.

The following table shows the maximum AIA for chargeable periods for companies drawing accounts up for the year to the dates shown.

Table 1 – maximum AIA for whole of the transitional chargeable period spanning 1 January 2022

Chargeable period y/e (2022)	Overall maximum AIA
	£
31 January	933,333
28 February	866,667
31 March	800,000
30 April	733,333
31 May	666,667
30 June	600,000
31 July	533,333
31 August	466,667
30 September	400,000
31 October	333,333
30 November	266,667
31 December	200,000

Further cap for expenditure incurred on or after 1 January 2022

A further cap restricts the amount of AIA that can be claimed for qualifying expenditure incurred in the transitional period but on or after 1 January 2022. So in the case of accounts drawn up for the year to 31 March 2022, for example, there is a restriction on the amount of AIA that can be claimed for expenditure incurred in the three-month period from 1 January to 31 March 2022.

For this period, the maximum AIAs that can be given are those that would be available for a notional standalone period covering those three months. That notional three-month period would have its AIA calculated as 3/12 of the new lower figure of £200,000, which gives an amount of just £50,000.

So although AIAs could be given for expenditure of up to £800,000 incurred in the overall accounting period to 31 March 2022, AIAs for expenditure incurred in the first three months of the calendar year 2022 are capped at just £50,000 in total.

The following table shows the maximum AIA for expenditure incurred between 1 January 2022 and the end of the transitional chargeable period, for companies drawing accounts up for the year to the dates shown.

Table 2 – maximum AIA for expenditure incurred from 1 January 2022 to end of transitional period

Chargeable period y/e (2022)	Maximum AIA for period from 1 Jan 2022
	£
31 January	16,667
29 February	33,333
31 March	50,000
30 April	66,667
31 May	83,333
30 June	100,000
31 July	116,667
31 August	133,333
30 September	150,000
31 October	166,667
30 November	183,333
31 December	200,000

Worked examples

The next four examples all assume that accounts are drawn up to 31 March 2022. In each case, it is assumed that we are concerned with a standalone company which is in principle entitled to a full amount of AIAs.

Example 2

A Ltd incurs qualifying expenditure of £760,000 in June 2021, and of £200,000 in January 2022. The company's AIA claim is restricted to the maximum overall amount of £800,000.

Example 3

B Ltd incurs the same expenditure but the other way round. So it spends £200,000 in June 2021 and £760,000 in January 2022.

The overall cap of £800,000 still applies, but this time the further restriction bites as well. There is no problem with the £200,000 of expenditure before the change, but the maximum AIA for the first three months of 2022 is £50,000. So the overall AIA will be capped at £250,000.

B Ltd may wish to see if it can bring forward some of its expenditure into the latter part of 2021 (or possibly postpone some of it until after 31 March, but depending also on its future expenditure plans).

Example 4

C Ltd spends £900,000 in November 2021 and nothing further in the first three months of 2022.

C Ltd can claim AIAs of £800,000. Note that although the whole expenditure is incurred before the date of change, and is less than the threshold applying at the time, the change from 1 January 2022 has the retrospective effect of reducing the maximum amount of the claim.

Example 5

D Ltd incurs no qualifying expenditure on plant or machinery until February 2022, at which point it spends £180,000.

D Ltd can claim AIAs of just £50,000 for the year to 31 March 2022. If it had spent the money two months earlier or two months later, it would have been able to claim AIAs for the whole of the £180,000.

Tax planning required

It will be clear that careful tax planning is needed with regard to the timing of large projects of capital expenditure. The next, albeit reasonably extreme, example illustrates how much can be at stake.

Example 6

E Ltd, which is not a member of a group of companies, draws accounts up to 31 January and is contemplating a major project of capital expenditure on plant and machinery. Its total claim will be in the region of £1,400,000.

If it incurs the expenditure in December 2021, its maximum AIA will be £933,333 (per table 1 above). If it defers the expenditure to February 2022, its maximum will be £200,000 (the standard maximum for 12-month chargeable periods beginning after 1 January 2022). But if the expenditure is all incurred in January 2022, its AIAs will be capped at just £16,667 (see table 2 above).

If it can stagger the expenditure, it may be possible to claim AIAs on most of the cost. Failing that, the company may well wish to consider advancing or deferring the expenditure to avoid the first month of 2022.

In technical terms

The above examples and tables show how the rules are applied in practice. The statutory principles underlying that practical outcome are as follows.

A chargeable period beginning before 1 January 2022 and ending on or after that date is referred to as "the second straddling period".

The legislation requires that second straddling period to be divided into two notional chargeable periods. The first begins on the first day of the actual chargeable period and ends on 31 December 2021. The second starts on 1 January 2022 and ends on the last day of the actual chargeable period. The maximum AIA is calculated for each of these periods (bearing in mind the lower figure that always applies for periods of less than 12 months) and the total is aggregated. This gives the maximum AIA for the whole period.

The maximum AIA for expenditure incurred in the second notional period, beginning on 1 January 2022, is the amount calculated for that second notional period. The result will be a proportion of the new lower figure of £200,000, the proportion calculated according to the length of the notional period starting from 1 January 2022.

The computation may be made on either a daily basis or – where the period in question consists of whole calendar months – on a monthly basis.

Law: CAA 2001, s. 51A(5); FA 2014, Sch. 2, para. 4; FA 2019, s. 32 and Sch. 13(2)
Guidance: CA 23085

5.2.9   Restrictions on claiming AIAs (overview)

Various restrictions may apply to deny AIAs altogether, or to restrict the amount that may be claimed. The thinking behind this is explained by HMRC as follows:

> "One of the main objectives underlying the AIA is the aim of keeping the rules as simple as possible, while safeguarding the AIA from abuse through fragmentation and the artificial creation of multiple allowances. In broad terms, the current rules provide that each business is entitled to one AIA, but in order to guard against fragmentation, 'related' businesses that are controlled by the same person must share one AIA."

These may be summarised as follows:

- companies generally: see **5.2.10**;
- groups of companies: see **5.2.11** and **5.2.12**;
- other companies under common control: see **5.2.13**;
- qualifying activities under common control: see **5.2.14**;
- transfer and long funding leaseback (s. 70DA(2): see **7.3.5**);
- plant or machinery used partly for other purposes (s. 205: see **5.2.15**);
- partial depreciation subsidies (s. 210: see **5.9**); and
- anti-avoidance cases (s. 217, 218A, 229A(2) and 241: see **22.3.2**).

See also **Chapter 23** (s. 236: additional VAT liabilities).

Law: CAA 2001, s. 51A(10), (11), 51K
Guidance: CA 23082

5.2.10   Restrictions on AIAs for companies

A company may obviously carry on more than one qualifying activity. However, it is entitled only to one amount of AIA in respect of all such activities.

Subject to the further restrictions for groups, or for companies under common control, the company may allocate its single AIA to its AIA qualifying expenditure as it wishes.

Law: CAA 2001, s. 51B, 51K

5.2.11   Groups of companies

Broadly speaking, a group of companies must share a single AIA.

More specifically, a single AIA must be shared between a company which, in a given financial year, is a parent undertaking of one or more companies, and those other companies. The companies may allocate the single AIA between them as they wish: it does not have to be shared equally between them.

The term "parent undertaking" is defined by reference to s. 1162 of the *Companies Act* 2006 (see reference below). At its simplest level, a company is a parent undertaking in relation to a subsidiary undertaking if it holds a majority of the voting rights in the latter company. The definition is, however, extended to take account of powers to appoint or remove directors, the right to exercise a dominant influence, and various other factors.

For AIA purposes, a company ("P") is a parent undertaking of another company ("C") in a financial year if P is a parent undertaking of C at the end of C's chargeable period ending in that financial year.

The position is more complex where groups of companies are under common control: see **5.2.12**.

Law: CAA 2001, s. 51C, 51K

Guidance: www.legislation.gov.uk/ukpga/2006/46/section/1162

5.2.12   Groups of companies under common control

The restrictions outlined at **5.2.11** become more complex where two or more groups of companies are controlled by the same person and are also related to one another. All such companies are entitled to share just a single AIA, which they may allocate between them as they wish. The single allowance applies to the AIA qualifying expenditure incurred by the companies in chargeable periods ending in the financial year in question.

For these purposes, a group of companies means a company that is a parent undertaking of one or more other companies, and all those other companies. See **5.2.11** for comment on the term "parent undertaking".

Law: CAA 2001, s. 51D, 51K

Control

For these purposes:

- a company is said to be controlled by a person in a financial year if it is controlled by that person at the end of its chargeable period ending in that financial year; and
- a group of companies is said to be controlled by a person in a financial year if the company that is the parent undertaking is controlled by that person at the end of its chargeable period ending in that financial year.

As regards the meaning of "control" for a body corporate, reference is made to s. 574(2): see **32.9.4**. For a company that is not a body corporate, control broadly means the power of a person to secure that the affairs of the company are conducted in a particular way.

Law: CAA 2001, s. 51F

Related

A company ('C1') is said to be related to another company ('C2') in a financial year if the 'shared premises condition' or the 'similar activities condition' (or both) are met in relation to the companies in that year.

Where C1 is related to C2 in a financial year, C1 is also related to any other company to which C2 is related in that financial year.

A group of companies ('G1') is said to be related to another group of companies ('G2') in a financial year if in that year a company which is a member of G1 is related to a company which is a member of G2.

Where G1 is related to G2 in a financial year, G1 is also related to any other group of companies to which G2 is related in that financial year.

The "shared premises" condition is met in relation to two companies in a financial year if, at the end of the relevant chargeable period of one or both of the companies, the companies carry on qualifying activities from the same premises.

The "similar activities" condition is met in relation to two companies in a financial year if more than half of the turnover of each company for the chargeable period ending in that year is derived from qualifying activities within the same "NACE classification" (listed at CA 23090).

Law: CAA 2001, s. 51G
Guidance: CA 23090

5.2.13   Other companies under common control

There is a restriction of the available AIA where two or more companies are not caught by the "groups of companies" rules (see **5.2.11** and **5.2.12** above) but where they are controlled by the same person, and also related to one another, in the financial year in question.

Such companies are entitled to just one AIA between them in respect of the AIA qualifying expenditure incurred in chargeable periods ending in the financial year in question. The companies may allocate the AIA as they wish.

The definitions of "control" and of "related" are as explained at **5.2.12** above.

Law: CAA 2001, s. 51E, 51K

5.2.14   Qualifying activities under common control

Just as rules seek to avoid the proliferation of AIAs for companies or groups of companies, so too are AIAs restricted for others carrying on two or more related qualifying activities.

The restriction applies where two or more qualifying activities are, in a given tax year:

- carried on by a qualifying person other than a company;
- controlled by the same person; and
- related to one another.

For these purposes, a qualifying activity is carried on by a qualifying person in a given tax year if it is carried on by that person at the end of the chargeable period ending in the tax year.

In these circumstances, a single AIA limit is shared between all the qualifying activities carried on by the qualifying person or persons in respect of the relevant AIA qualifying expenditure. The AIA may be allocated as the person or persons choose.

For these purposes, the concepts of "control" and "related" are defined as below.

Law: CAA 2001, s. 51H, 51K

Control

A qualifying activity is said to be controlled by a person in a tax year if it is controlled by that person at the end of the chargeable period for that activity which ends in that tax year.

A qualifying activity carried on by an individual is controlled by the individual who carries it on.

A qualifying activity carried on by a partnership is controlled by the person (if any) who controls the partnership, as defined at s. 574(3) (see **32.9.4**).

Where partners who between them control one partnership also between them control another partnership, the qualifying activities carried on by the partnerships are treated as controlled by the same person.

Law: CAA 2001, s. 51I

Related

A qualifying activity ('A1') is said to be related to another qualifying activity ('A2') in a tax year if the "shared premises condition" and/or the "similar activities condition" is met in relation to the activities in the tax year.

Where A1 is related to A2 in a tax year, A1 is also related to any other qualifying activity to which A2 is related in that tax year.

The shared premises condition is met in relation to two qualifying activities in a tax year if, at the end of the relevant chargeable period for one or both of the activities, the activities are carried on from the same premises.

The similar activities condition is met in relation to two qualifying activities in a given tax year if, at the end of the relevant chargeable period for those activities ending in that tax year, the activities are within the same "NACE classification" (as defined).

For these purposes, the "relevant chargeable period" is defined as the chargeable period for the activity that ends in the tax year in question.

Law: CAA 2001, s. 51J

5.2.15 Plant or machinery used partly for other purposes

A person may use plant or machinery partly for the purposes of a trade (or other qualifying activity) and partly for private purposes (or some other purpose that is not for the qualifying activity). In such cases, any AIA for expenditure on the item "must be reduced to an amount which is just and reasonable having regard to the relevant circumstances".

In particular, regard must be had to the extent of the anticipated other use.

Example 1

Tony is a sole trader who offers a car valeting service. He buys some computer equipment for £1,500 which he uses for keeping his business records and for operating a business website. He also uses the computer for private purposes, and the private use is estimated as one third of the total.

His AIA claim is reduced to £1,000, and no further allowances may be claimed on the equipment.

The AIA claim must still be reduced if the cost is more than the AIA limit.

Example 2

Another sole trader incurs qualifying expenditure of £240,000 at a time when the AIA limit is £200,000. He uses the item 20% for private purposes.

Without the private use, he could have claimed AIAs of £200,000. With the private use, this must be reduced to £160,000. He can also claim restricted WDAs on the balance of £40,000 (£240,000 less the full AIA amount of £200,000).

Law: CAA 2001, s. 205
Guidance: CA 23087

5.2.16 Short and long chargeable periods

A business may have two or more chargeable periods ending in a tax or financial year. If so, each must be considered independently so as to decide whether or not the related activities conditions are met for the purposes of s. 51C, s. 51D, s. 51E or s. 51H.

Where a chargeable period exceeds 12 months (which is not possible for a company), additional AIA may be due, subject to some fairly complex computational provisions.

Law: CAA 2001, s. 51L, 51M, 51N

5.3   Writing-down allowances

5.3.1   Introduction

The basic principle of the writing-down allowance (WDA) is that tax relief for capital expenditure is given over a number of years, very roughly mirroring the accounting concept of depreciation.

WDAs for plant and machinery are calculated year by year on the reducing value rather than on the original cost of an asset. If a single asset costs £10,000 and is written off at 18% per year, for example, it would attract allowances of £1,800 in year one, with the balance of £8,200 carried forward. In the second year, allowances would be calculated as £1,476 (£8,200 at 18%) and so on.

In reality, allowances are rarely given for a single asset in isolation (the main exception being where an item is used partly for private purposes). Instead, the concept of pooling ensures that allowances are calculated collectively on a pool of assets, taking account of any additional purchases in the year, and also of any disposal proceeds.

Example

A new limited company spends £20,000 on an asset in year one and claims WDAs of £3,600, carrying forward the balance of £16,400.

In year two, it spends a further £15,000. The £15,000 is added to the £16,400 and allowances are calculated on the total figure of £31,400. If allowances are once more at 18%, this produces a year two claim of £5,652, with £25,748 carried forward.

There are no purchases or sales in year three, so allowances of £4,635 are claimed, leaving £21,113 to carry forward.

In year four, the asset originally costing £20,000 is sold for £4,000 and a replacement is bought for £23,000. The pool value is now calculated as £40,113 (£21,113, plus new expenditure of £23,000, less disposal proceeds of £4,000). If allowances are still at 18%, the claim for the year will be £7,221, with £32,892 to carry forward.

In practice, the position is made more complicated as AIAs (see **5.2**) will often be available. Also, some expenditure is excluded from the main pool and is instead allocated to (for example) the "special rate" pool (attracting allowances at a lower rate) or to a single-asset pool, where allowances for each item must be calculated separately (see **5.3.2**).

Special rules apply to ships, where a postponement option is given (see, briefly, **Chapter 20**).

Law: CAA 2001, s. 53*ff.*

5.3.2 Pooling

Technically, WDAs and balancing allowances may only be claimed if expenditure is pooled, even though some items are in single-asset pools (a nice statutory oxymoron). This underlying principle has gained greater significance since April 2012 in relation to fixtures in property (see **Chapter 12**).

If a person carries on more than one qualifying activity (e.g. a trade and a property business) the pools for the different activities must be kept separate.

Qualifying expenditure on plant or machinery is allocated to the main pool unless it has to be allocated to a class pool or to a single-asset pool.

Class pools

These are used for:

- special rate expenditure (s. 104C: see **Chapter 17**); and
- overseas leasing expenditure (s. 107: see **Chapter 19**).

Where appropriate, separate class pools are required for the two different types of expenditure: special rate expenditure and overseas leasing expenditure are not merged into a single class pool.

Single-asset pools

These are necessary for various types of asset (e.g. short-life assets, and any assets that are used partly for private purposes by a sole trader or a partner). See **5.3.7** for more detail.

Most businesses will have a main pool and, increasingly, a special rate expenditure pool (e.g. for integral features, for certain expenditure on cars and for long-life assets). Sole traders will typically also have one or more single-asset pools for vehicles (or other assets) used partly for private purposes.

Law: CAA 2001, s. 53, 54
Guidance: CA 23210

5.3.3   *Entitlement to writing-down allowances*

Similar principles govern the entitlement to WDAs for each of the pools. The legislation requires a comparison of two figures for the pool and period in question: the available qualifying expenditure ("AQE") and the total of any disposal receipts that must be brought into account ("TDR"). See **Chapter 4** for a detailed definition of "qualifying expenditure" and see **5.5** for commentary on disposal receipts.

If TDR exceeds AQE, the person will be liable to a balancing charge (see **5.7**).

If AQE exceeds TDR, a writing-down allowance will normally be due. The main exception is for the final chargeable period, where a balancing allowance will instead be due: see **5.6**. There are also particular rules for special rate cars in certain circumstances (s. 104F: see **9.4.4**) and for overseas leasing, where allowances are in some cases prohibited (s. 110(1): see **Chapter 19**).

Law: CAA 2001, s. 55

5.3.4   *Rate of writing-down allowances – main pool*

The rate of WDA for the main pool is 18%.

The maximum allowance is proportionately reduced if the chargeable period is less than a year, or if the qualifying activity is carried on for only part of the chargeable period. This latter scenario could arise, for example, with a company that starts to carry on a second trade, for which allowances will need to be computed separately.

If the chargeable period is more than a year, the maximum allowance is increased (but this cannot apply for a company, as its chargeable period can never exceed 12 months).

A person claiming WDAs may require the allowance to be reduced to a specified amount, thus carrying forward a higher figure to the following period.

A higher rate of relief applies for ring-fence trades. Different rules apply for special rate expenditure (see **5.3.5** below) and for overseas leasing (s. 109: see **Chapter 19**). See also **5.3.6** re small pools.

Law: CAA 2001, s. 56

Guidance: https://tinyurl.com/nwpdb5rw (periods more or less than a year)

5.3.5   *Rate of writing-down allowances – special rate pool*

The rate of WDA for the special rate pool is 6%, having reduced from 8% for periods beginning on or after 1 or 6 April 2019 (for corporation tax and income tax respectively). See below for transitional rules that apply for periods spanning those dates.

As for the main pool, the maximum allowance is proportionately reduced if the chargeable period is less than a year, or if the qualifying activity is carried on for only part of the chargeable period. If the chargeable period is more than a year, the maximum allowance is increased (but this cannot apply for a company, as its chargeable period can never exceed 12 months).

A person claiming WDAs may require the allowance to be reduced to a specified amount, thus carrying forward a higher figure to the following period. This may be appropriate, for example, in the case of a sole trader who only needs a smaller level of capital allowances to take his income down to the level of the personal allowance.

See also **5.3.6** re small pools.

Transitional rules – April 2019

The reduction in the special rate from 8% to 6% is straightforward for chargeable periods beginning on or after the "relevant day" – 1 April 2019 for corporation tax purposes and 6 April 2019 for income tax. For periods spanning those dates, a hybrid rate applies.

The hybrid rate has to be calculated if the chargeable period begins before the relevant day, but ends on or after that day. The effect is to give so many days' worth at the older 8% rate, and so many at the lower 6% rate.

The statutory formula for the hybrid rate for the special rate pool is:

$$(8 \times BRD/CP) + (6 \times ARD/CP)$$

where:

> **BRD** is the number of days in the chargeable period *before* the relevant day;
>
> **ARD** is the number of days in the chargeable period *on or after* the relevant day; and
>
> **CP** is the number of days in the chargeable period.

Where the resulting figure would have more than two decimal places, it is rounded up to the nearest second decimal place.

This is illustrated in the following examples:

Example 1 – limited company

C Ltd draws accounts up to 30 June. For the year to 30 June 2019, its hybrid rate of WDA for the special rate pool is calculated as follows:

$$(8 \times 274/365) + (6 \times 91/365)$$

Rounded up to the second decimal place, this gives a WDA rate of 7.51% for the year in question.

The same principles are applied for income tax, but with slightly different figures as the relevant day falls instead on 6 April 2019.

Example 2 – unincorporated business

Dave, a sole trader, also draws accounts up to 30 June. For the year to 30 June 2019, the hybrid rate of WDA for his special rate pool will be calculated as follows:

$$(8 \times 279/365) + (6 \times 86/365)$$

Rounded up to the second decimal place, this gives a WDA rate of 7.53% for the year in question.

Law: CAA 2001, s. 104D

5.3.6   Small pools

As allowances are given year by year on the reducing balance, an ongoing business may have to prepare annual capital allowance computations for tiny amounts of expenditure. The administration costs of preparing such a computation could easily outweigh the benefits of making any claim.

For this reason, the concept of the "small pool" was introduced to allow the remaining balance on a pool to be written off in one go. This concept is available for both the main pool and the special rate pool.

The small pool rules operate where, in the year, the value of the pool does not exceed £1,000. That value is calculated as available qualifying expenditure ("AQE") less the total of any disposal receipts that must be brought into account (TDR). In other words, the amount brought forward must be added to any additional expenditure in the year. Any disposal proceeds must then be deducted. If the result does not exceed £1,000 then the whole amount may be written off in one go.

Example – unincorporated business

Eva runs a small business. At the start of Year 2, she has a brought forward figure of £3,000 in the main pool and of £1,020 in the special rate pool. She incurs no new expenditure in the year.

After claiming allowances at the appropriate rates for the two pools, so say £540 and £62 respectively, she carries forward £2,460 in the main pool and £958 in the special rate pool.

If she again incurs no new expenditure in Year 3, she can claim allowances of £443 in the main pool but of the full amount of £958 in the special rate pool.

A person may still claim a smaller amount if that is preferable. So, in this example, Eva could reduce the claim on either or both pools if she so wished.

A further example is given at CA 23225.

If a period of account is not of exactly 12 months, the small pools allowance is adjusted accordingly. HMRC give the example of a 17 month period, for which the allowance would be £1,417. (However, periods in excess of 18 months will be split into two or more periods, each of up to 12 months: see **1.6.2**.)

Law: CAA 2001, s. 56A
Guidance: https://tinyurl.com/nwpdb5rw (periods more or less than a year)

5.3.7 Single-asset pools

Single-asset pools, as would be expected, contain just one asset each. Such pools are required for the following:

- short-life assets (s. 86: see **Chapter 15**);
- ships (s. 127: see **Chapter 20**);
- plant or machinery provided or used partly for purposes other than those of a qualifying activity (s. 206: see **5.8**);
- payments of partial depreciation subsidy (s. 211: see **5.9**); and
- contribution allowances (s. 538: see **Chapter 31**).

The most common use of single-asset pools is where an asset is used partly for the purposes of the qualifying activity and partly for other purposes (see also **5.8**). Typically, this will apply for sole traders (or business partners) who make private use of a car or other asset. However, the rule also operates where an asset is used – perhaps by a large company trading in different tax jurisdictions – partly for the purposes of a UK trade and partly for other purposes.

The mechanism of the single-asset pool enables a restriction to be imposed on the amount of any writing-down allowances, to reflect private or other disqualifying use. The restriction must reflect "the extent to which it appears that the plant or machinery was used in the chargeable period in question for purposes other than those of the person's qualifying activity".

If an asset was first used only for business purposes, but starts to be used partly for other purposes, that will constitute a disposal (see **5.5.2**). The disposal value is then used to create a new single-asset pool for the asset in question, for the same chargeable period.

The amount carried forward is to be calculated as if full allowances had been given.

Example – unincorporated business

Julie runs a bakery business as a sole trader. She has a van on which WDAs are claimed annually. Assume that WDAs are available at 18% in all relevant years.

In Year 1, the brought down value of the van is £14,000. Julie has used the van 10% for private purposes. Her WDAs are calculated as £2,268 (£14,000 x 18% x 90%). The amount carried forward is £11,480, calculated as £14,000 less an unrestricted amount of £2,520.

In Year 2, Julie has sold her private car and now uses the van one quarter for private purposes. Her allowances for the year are calculated as £1,550 (£11,480 x 18% x 75%). The amount carried forward is £9,414.

If a person disclaims the allowance, wholly or partially, the unrelieved qualifying expenditure carried forward is not reduced or, as the case may be, is only proportionately reduced.

Law: CAA 2001, s. 53, 54, 65, 206, 207

Final chargeable period

The final chargeable period for a single-asset pool is normally the period in which the disposal occurs. A balancing adjustment will therefore normally be made as soon as the asset is sold.

Example – (cont.)

Continuing with the example of Julie above, assume that the van is sold in Year 3 for £5,000.

Julie will be entitled to a balancing allowance, before private use adjustment, of £4,414. The private use adjustment must be just and reasonable having regard to the relevant circumstances, including in particular the extent of non-business use in the year in question.

The statutory requirement re adjusting for private use is slightly ambiguous. In an extreme example, the owner may have made substantial private use of an asset for many years, but may dispose of it early in the chargeable period without making any private use at all. It is suggested that the private use in the period in question will normally be an acceptable measure, but that an averaging process should be applied if that result is clearly not "just and reasonable". HMRC favour an averaging approach in all cases.

Law: CAA 2001, s. 207
Guidance: CA 27005

Very large assets – reduction in qualifying use

An anti-avoidance rule operates in the case of very substantial assets, where there is a fall in the extent of use of an asset for qualifying activities. The restriction only applies if the market value of the asset exceeds the balance in the single-asset pool (for the chargeable period in which the change of circumstances occurs) by more than £1 million. HMRC give the example of an aircraft used partly for activities outside the scope of UK tax.

Law: CAA 2001, s. 208
Guidance: CA 27300

5.3.8   *Available qualifying expenditure*

Overview

In practice, this concept ("AQE") is normally straightforward. In simple terms, AQE consists of new qualifying expenditure allocated to a given pool for a given period, plus any unrelieved amounts brought forward in that pool from the previous period.

However, there are many complicating factors that do occasionally need to be considered. These can be addressed under the following four headings:

- definition of qualifying expenditure allocated to the pool for the period in question;
- definition of unrelieved qualifying expenditure brought forward;
- other amounts specifically included by statute as available qualifying expenditure; and
- amounts that are specifically excluded from the definition.

This general rule is subject to s. 220 (allocation to chargeable periods of expenditure incurred on plant or machinery for leasing under a finance lease: see (briefly) **Chapter 22**).

Law: CAA 2001, s. 57

Qualifying expenditure

Certain key principles govern the allocation of qualifying expenditure to a particular pool:

- An amount cannot be allocated in a given chargeable period if it has already been taken into account in determining qualifying expenditure for an earlier period.
- It cannot be allocated to a pool for a chargeable period before that in which the expenditure is incurred.
- It may only be allocated to the pool for a particular period if the person owns the plant or machinery at some time in that period.

The way these rules operate for late claims, perhaps many years after the expenditure is incurred, is considered at **1.4.2** above.

Technically, expenditure is still pooled even if an AIA is claimed. If, for example, a person incurs £20,000 of qualifying expenditure on integral features, and claims AIA on the full amount, the £20,000 is still added to the pool. However, the available qualifying expenditure is then reduced by that same amount. This may seem a pointlessly academic exercise, but it has a bearing when disposal proceeds are brought into account. It is also relevant for the rules for fixtures as they have applied since April 2012.

If FYAs are claimed, no amount is allocated to the pool for that chargeable period. In any later period, the amount that may be added to the pool is reduced by the FYAs claimed. Any such net amounts *must* be allocated to the pool (even though the value at that stage may well be zero) if they have not previously been added and if there is a disposal event in relation to the assets in question.

Law: CAA 2001, s. 58

Unrelieved expenditure brought forward

Unrelieved expenditure brought forward is straightforward. It is the available qualifying expenditure for the earlier period, less any disposal proceeds and less any WDAs made for the period in question.

If a person claims full WDAs under the small pools rules (see **5.3.6**) then there will be nothing to carry forward.

There can obviously be no amount to carry forward as unrelieved qualifying expenditure from the final chargeable period.

Special rules apply for those switching to the cash basis for calculating taxable profits (see, generally, **1.9**).

Law: CAA 2001, s. 59

Amounts included by statute in available qualifying expenditure

The following further amounts are included in calculating available qualifying expenditure:

- net costs of demolition (s. 26(3): see **4.5**);
- short-life assets not disposed of before the cut-off date (s. 86(2) and s. 87(2): see **15.3**);
- overseas leasing – standard recovery mechanism (s. 111(3));
- where plant or machinery starts to be used partly for other purposes (s. 206(3): see **5.8**);

- where a partial depreciation subsidy is paid (s. 211(4): see **5.9**); and
- in various other circumstances involving ships (s. 129*ff.*), ring-fence trades (s. 165(3)), oil extraction (s. 161C(2)).

Law: CAA 2001, s. 57(2)

Amounts excluded from available qualifying expenditure

A person's available qualifying expenditure does not include any expenditure that is excluded by the following rules:

- rules against double relief (s. 8(4) and 9(1));
- transfer and long funding leaseback (s. 70DA);
- certain anti-avoidance rules re oil (s. 166(2));
- restrictions where other claims are made in respect of fixtures (s. 185(2), 186(2), 187(2)); and
- restrictions under various general anti-avoidance provisions (s. 218(1), 228(2), 229A, 242(2), 243(2)).

Law: CAA 2001, s. 57(3)

5.4   First-year allowances

5.4.1   Introduction

If a business can claim AIAs for the whole of its expenditure in a given year, it will not normally need to worry about first-year allowances (FYAs), though there may now be an exception to this general principle in relation to the temporary FYAs introduced from April 2021 – see **5.13**.

On the other hand, FYAs may be very valuable for larger businesses, for group companies (that have to share a single AIA), and for businesses with exceptionally high expenditure in a given year.

The following categories of expenditure may qualify for accelerated tax relief by means of FYAs, though these are subject to the general exclusions at **5.4.2** and to the further restrictions considered at **5.4.3**:

- cars with zero CO_2 emissions (s. 45D: see **5.4.6**);
- zero-emission goods vehicles (s. 45DA: see **5.4.7**);
- plant or machinery for a gas refuelling station (s. 45E: see **5.4.8**);
- electric vehicle charging points (s. 45EA: see **5.4.9**);

- plant or machinery for use wholly in a ring-fence trade (s. 45F: see **5.4.10**);

- plant or machinery for use in designated assisted areas (s. 45K: see **5.4.11**);

- expenditure – incurred by companies within the charge to corporation tax – at certain designated freeport sites (s. 45O: see **5.12**); and

- expenditure – incurred by companies within the charge to corporation tax – qualifying (at various rates of FYA) under the rules introduced in FA 2021 under the heading of "super-deductions and other temporary first-year allowances", which are covered separately at **5.13** below.

With the exception of the temporary allowances mentioned in the last bullet above, FYAs can be claimed at 100% in all cases, such that the full cost may be written off for tax purposes for the chargeable period in which the cost is incurred. However, a person may claim a reduced allowance if preferred.

The 100% allowance represents a huge acceleration of tax relief. If the alternative to claiming 100% FYAs is to allocate the expenditure to the special rate pool then (at 6% per year on the reducing balance basis) it would otherwise take 12 years to obtain tax relief for just *half* of the overall expenditure. (In practice, however, AIAs will often be available where FYAs are not.)

The person incurring the expenditure must own the plant or machinery at some time during the chargeable period in which the expenditure is incurred.

FYAs may *only* be claimed for the chargeable period in which the expenditure is incurred. If, for example, a person makes a belated plant and machinery claim some years after incurring the cost, no FYAs (or indeed AIAs) will normally be due as the year will usually be closed for tax purposes under normal self-assessment principles. As long as the asset is still owned in that later period, however, it will still be possible to claim WDAs.

If an asset is bought and sold in the same year, the correct approach is to give full FYAs on the cost and then to set the disposal proceeds against the pool value in the usual way, rather than simply giving FYAs on the net loss in the year. This is made clear by the wording in s. 58(5) and (6). Once more, however, this rule is varied in respect of the temporary FYAs introduced in FA 2021 (see **5.13**).

For the purposes of determining whether FYAs are available, it is necessary to ignore the rule (s. 12) that normally treats pre-trading expenditure as incurred on the first day of the qualifying activity.

Unlike the treatment of AIAs and WDAs, there is no need to restrict FYAs if the accounting period is shorter than 12 months. Conversely, FYAs cannot be increased for longer periods of account.

FYAs must be restricted on a just and reasonable basis to take account of any private use by a business proprietor (s. 205(1)).

Law: CAA 2001, s. 39, 50, 52, 58, 205(1)

Guidance: https://tinyurl.com/nwpdb5rw (periods more or less than a year)

5.4.2   General exclusions

Eight general exclusions prevent expenditure from qualifying for FYAs (and these exclusions apply equally for the temporary FYAs, including the "super-deduction", introduced from April 2021, and also for plant and machinery in freeport tax sites).

No FYAs are available:

- for the chargeable period in which the qualifying activity is permanently discontinued;
- for cars (as defined at s. 268A: see **9.2**) – except that this does not apply to electric or other zero-emission cars qualifying for FYAs by virtue of s. 45D (see **9.6**);
- for expenditure that would be long-life asset expenditure but for the transitional provisions at Sch. 3, para. 20 (see **16.4** and also below);
- for plant or machinery for leasing (see below);
- in certain cases where a change is made with a specific view to obtaining FYAs (again, see below); or
- where any of the following applies:
  - s. 13 (use of asset provided originally for other purposes: see **4.10.1**);
  - s. 13A (use of asset provided originally for long funding leasing: see **4.10.2**); or
  - s. 14 (use of qualifying plant or machinery received as a gift: see **4.10.4**).

The meaning of "expenditure that would be long-life asset expenditure but for the transitional provisions at Sch. 3, para. 20" (in the third bullet point above) is rather obscure and was explored in the *Daarasp* case. The tribunal in that case grappled with the meaning and concluded as follows:

> "On balance and not without some misgivings because of the rather curious result which this achieves, we agree with Mr Thornhill that the better construction of general exclusion 5 is that it only operates to exclude long-life asset expenditure which is otherwise excluded by paragraph 20 of Schedule 3."

Case: *Daarasp LLP v HMRC* [2018] UKFTT 548 (TC)

Ships and railway assets

The former restriction for ships and railway assets no longer applies. For expenditure incurred before April 2020, this allowed businesses incurring expenditure on such assets to consider the use of enhanced capital allowances (ECAs) for energy-saving and water-saving technology. However, the ECA scheme ceased for expenditure incurred from April 2020.

Law: FA 2013, s. 70
Guidance: http://webarchive.nationalarchives.gov.uk/20140109143644 /http://www.hmrc.gov.uk/budget2013/tiin-2011.pdf

Leasing

The leasing restriction applies whether the activity is in the course of a trade or otherwise. For these purposes, the letting of a ship on charter, or of any other asset on hire, is specifically treated as leasing.

The plant or machinery may be provided for leasing under an "excluded lease of background plant or machinery for a building" (see s. 70R).

HMRC accept that "plant provided predominantly with an operative is more than mere hire". Again, HMRC acknowledge that "the supply of plant or machinery with an operator, by a business, is the provision of a service and not mere hire". To meet this condition, the operator should remain with the equipment during its use and should operate it personally in all but exceptional circumstances. HMRC go on to comment as follows:

> "Plant or machinery may be provided with an operator on some occasions and without on others. Where, at the time the

expenditure is incurred, it is intended that the asset will be predominantly provided with an operator, the precise facts and use of the asset will have to be considered, but generally we accept that FYAs are due."

Finally, HMRC "accept that the provision of building access services by the scaffolding industry amounts to a construction operation and is therefore more than mere hire". This would not apply, though, to businesses that simply supply scaffolding poles for use by others.

The above approach by HMRC reflects the decision in the 2002 case of *Baldwins Industrial Services*. However, the more recent *MGF* decision indicated that the HMRC guidance did not go far enough. HMRC argued that the company merely hired out the equipment in question, and that FYAs were therefore not due. A complicating factor was that the associated design service was provided through a separate company. As summarised in the findings of the tribunal, the HMRC argument was that "the appellant merely provided plant hire, and that the design service simply supported the hire and was not integral to it. In any event it was provided by a separate company directly to the customer".

MGF, by contrast, argued that the design was integral to the business. In finding for the company, the tribunal held that the services provided "cannot fairly be described merely as the leasing of plant" as the appellant was "providing an overall service beyond the leasing of assets". The following paragraphs demonstrate the thinking of the tribunal:

"49. It should be noted that HMRC guidance does not have the force of law. The cases referred to in the guidance and by the parties are illustrative of the types of issues that can arise when considering the nature of services provided during the course of construction projects. However we did not find these cases or the 1996 Act helpful in construing the CAA 2001. They deal with different terminology used in a different context to that of the CAA 2001. There is no reference in the CAA 2001 to construction operations. General Exclusion 6 is of general application and not limited to the construction industry. It simply refers to the provision of plant and machinery for leasing.

50. The provisions of the CAA 2001 itself are wide and at first sight appear to cover plant and machinery for leasing whether or not the leasing takes place together with other services. However we accept that where the leasing is provided together with something else the circumstances may be such that what is being provided can no longer be described simply as the leasing of plant.

173

51. We agree with HMRC's guidance to the extent that there is a distinction to be drawn between leasing of assets and the provision of services which include the use of assets. HMRC accept that the exclusion will not apply where assets are provided for use together with the provision of further services, unless those further services are merely subsidiary to the hiring of the asset. The appellant did not take issue with the test stated in those terms, but contended that the services in the present case were more than merely subsidiary. They were a key element of what the customer was purchasing.

52. The application of such a test inevitably involves a question of degree. In particular whether the service provided with the leasing makes the overall package something more than merely leasing assets. The paradigm case in a construction context may be that referred to in the HMRC guidance. The supply of plant or machinery such as a crane with an operator. However, whilst that supply may be at one end of a spectrum there will be other cases, not necessarily involving supplies of operators or labour, that amount to more than the leasing of assets for these purposes.

53. In the light of our findings of fact we are satisfied that the design service was supplied by the appellant."

The question of where the boundary lies between leasing and service provision is not clear cut and the case is a useful reminder that HMRC's guidance is open to challenge in similar cases.

Law: CAA 2001, s. 46

Cases: *Baldwins Industrial Services plc v Barr* [2002] EWHC 2915 (TCC); *MGF (Trench Construction Systems) Ltd v HMRC* [2012] UKFTT 739 (TC)

Guidance: CA 23115

Deliberate attempt to obtain FYAs

No FYAs are available in some circumstances where the expenditure incurred:

"is connected with a change in the nature or conduct of a trade or business carried on by a person other than the person incurring the expenditure".

The restriction applies if the obtaining of the FYA is:

"the main benefit, or one of the main benefits, which could reasonably be expected to arise from the making of the change".

According to HMRC guidance, however, this restriction was:

> "intended to stop a large business that is not entitled to FYA getting round the restriction of FYA to SMEs by parking an asset in a small business".

In other words, it relates primarily to an earlier time when FYAs were more generally available to all but the largest businesses.

Law: CAA 2001, s. 46
Guidance: CA 23110

5.4.3   Specific exclusions and restrictions

Various further restrictions apply to FYA claims, as follows:

- transfer and long funding leaseback: no FYA for lessee (s. 70DA(2): see **Chapter 7**);
- reduction of FYA if asset provided partly for purposes other than those of qualifying activity (s. 205: see **5.4.12**);
- reduction of FYA if it appears that a partial depreciation subsidy is or will be payable (s. 210: see **5.9**);
- cap on FYAs for expenditure on plant and machinery for use in designated assisted areas (s. 212U: see **5.4.11**); and
- anti-avoidance: no FYA in certain cases (s. 217, 229A(2), 241: see **22.3.2**).

Account must also be taken, where appropriate, of s. 236 (FYAs re additional VAT liabilities: see **Chapter 23**).

A person may obviously not claim an AIA and an FYA in respect of the same expenditure. Nor may FYAs be claimed for the same expenditure under two or more headings.

Law: CAA 2001, s. 52, 52A

5.4.4   Energy-saving plant and machinery

Introduction

FYAs (at 100%) were formerly given for expenditure on new (unused) assets that qualify as "energy-saving plant or machinery". This category of expenditure ceased to qualify for FYAs from 1 or 6 April 2020.

Until the end date in 2020, the rules were subject to the general exclusions considered at **5.4.2** above, and to the restrictions where there are payments under the *Energy Act*.

These allowances (together with those for environmentally beneficial plant and machinery, which also ended in April 2020: see **5.4.5** below) were often referred to as "enhanced capital allowances" (or "ECAs").

Full details were included in earlier editions of this book, up to and including the 2019-20 edition.

Law: CAA 2001, s. 45A, 45B

5.4.5   Environmentally beneficial plant and machinery

Introduction

Subject to the general exclusions considered at **5.4.2** above, FYAs (at 100%) were formerly given for expenditure on assets that qualified as "environmentally beneficial" plant and machinery. As with energy-saving technology (above), these accelerated allowances ceased to be available for expenditure incurred from April 2020.

The tax provisions were intended to "promote the use of technologies, or products, designed to remedy or prevent damage to the physical environment or natural resources". In practice, they related mostly to the preservation of water supplies.

These allowances (together with those for energy-efficient plant and machinery) were often referred to as "enhanced capital allowances" (or "ECAs").

Full details were included in earlier editions of this book. (If purchasers of this edition still need the earlier rules, the publishers may (at their discretion) provide, without charge, a PDF of the equivalent sections from the 2019-20 edition.)

Law: CAA 2001, s. 45H; SI 2003/2076 (as amended)
Guidance: CA 23135

5.4.6   Cars with low CO₂ emissions, and electric cars

Most cars are specifically denied FYAs (by virtue of one of the general exclusions: see **5.4.2** above). However, an exception has been made for certain cars with very low CO_2 emissions and for certain electrically propelled cars.

From April 2021, FYAs are only available for cars with zero emissions, which in practice largely restricts the allowances to electric cars only, but which leaves the door open for other zero-emission technologies.

Unused

FYAs are available only for the first buyer of the vehicle, as it must be "unused and not second-hand". HMRC accept that this condition is met "even if it has been driven a limited number of miles for the purposes of testing, delivery, test driven by a potential purchaser, or used as a demonstration car".

The question has been raised about dealers who may pre-register a car, perhaps to meet sales targets: is the car still unused? The matter is not entirely free from doubt if the dealer does technically become an owner rather than merely an agent, but if the dealer is a retailer who has clearly not used the car in any general sense, it is thought that the vehicle will still be treated as unused and not second-hand when sold to the first "real" owner.

Extended definition of "car"

See **9.2** for the definition of "car" as it applies for most capital allowance purposes. However, for the purposes of claiming FYAs, the definition is extended to include a hackney carriage (taxicab).

Expenditure to 31 March 2025

These rules have repeatedly been extended, but with ever stricter thresholds applying if the allowances are to be claimed. The end date has now been set as 5 April (or 31 March) 2025 (SI 2021/120).

Electric cars

A car qualifies as electrically propelled for these purposes if it is propelled solely by electrical power and if that power is derived from:

- a source external to the vehicle; or
- an electrical storage battery which is not connected to any source of power when the vehicle is in motion.

Low-emission cars

A car qualifies as having low emissions if it has a qualifying emissions certificate (as defined) showing an official CO_2 emissions figure not exceeding a given level, as per the following table:

Date expenditure incurred	Threshold
From 1 April 2021	0g/km
1 April 2018-31 March 2021	50g/km
1 April 2015-31 March 2018	75g/km
1 April 2013-31 March 2015	95g/km
Before 1 April 2013	110g/km

HMRC have announced that, from April 2021, there will be four new boxes on form CT600 to allow reporting of zero-emission cars independently of other FYAs within the "Allowances and Charges in Calculation of trading profits and losses" section of the return.

Pooling

Although cars qualifying under this heading can attract FYAs at 100%, the cars should still be pooled as this will have a bearing on future balancing charges.

If there is private use by a business proprietor (*not* by a director or employee), the car will be in a single-asset pool, so that allowances can be restricted to reflect the private use. The rate of WDA will still depend on the car's emission levels.

In all other cases, a low-emission car will be in the main pool. A future sale of the car will not usually trigger a balancing charge as the proceeds will merely be set against the ongoing balance in the main pool. If the owner chooses to claim less than the full FYA, WDAs will be given in the normal way within the main pool.

Law: CAA 2001, s. 45D, 205(1), 268A-268C
Guidance: CA 23153

Exclusions

The general exclusions discussed at **5.4.2** above may prevent FYAs from being given for electric and low-emission cars.

FYAs are not available if the vehicles are acquired for leasing.

Law: CAA 2001, s. 46

5.4.7   Zero-emission goods vehicles

Subject to the exclusions discussed below, FYAs are available for expenditure incurred before 1 or 6 April 2025 (now extended from

2021) (for corporation tax and income tax respectively) on certain zero-emission goods vehicles. The deadline has been repeatedly extended.

The vehicle must be registered and must also be "unused and not second-hand" (regarding which, see **5.4.6** above).

A goods vehicle is usually a van, but is in fact defined to cover any "mechanically propelled road vehicle which is of a design primarily suited for the conveyance of goods or burden of any description".

The vehicle qualifies as having zero emissions if it cannot in any circumstances emit CO_2 by being driven. HMRC have given the following further guidance in relation to the meaning of this term:

> "Vehicles only qualify for the relief if they cannot in any circumstances emit CO2 when driven. This includes vehicles propelled by an electric motor powered by an onboard electric storage battery or hydrogen fuel cell. Where a vehicle is fuelled by hydrogen as a substitute for a carbon based fossil fuel a claim for capital allowances will only be admitted if such a vehicle cannot also be directly powered by a carbon emitting fuel.
>
> Hybrid vehicles may be driven by electric motor, with the battery being charged by an on-board fossil fuel generator, or by switching between electric motor and internal combustion engines. In both cases the vehicles may emit CO2 when driven and are not zero-emission."

Various exclusions apply, explained below.

Law: CAA 2001, s. 45DA (as amended); FA 2015, s. 45(2)

Exclusions

The general exclusions discussed at **5.4.2** above may prevent FYAs from being given for zero-emission goods vehicles. Vans used for leasing will not qualify, for example.

Zero-emission vehicles used for a variety of specified activities are also precluded from qualifying for FYAs. The restrictions apply to businesses engaged in fisheries, aquaculture and (where performed for third parties) certain waste management activities.

Further restrictions have applied where the expenditure is related to state aid or certain other specified grants or subsidies. It is thought that this restriction will no longer apply following the UK's departure from the EU.

Law: CAA 2001, s. 45DA, 45DB

Private use

If there is private use by a business proprietor (*not* by a director or employee), the car will be in a single-asset pool, so that allowances can be restricted to reflect the private use.

Law: CAA 2001, s. 54(3), 205, 206

5.4.8   Gas refuelling stations

Subject to the general exclusions outlined at **5.4.2** above, FYAs are given for expenditure incurred up to 31 March 2025 (extended from 2021) on certain plant or machinery for a gas refuelling station. (The deadline was previously extended from April 2018.)

The plant or machinery must be "unused and not second-hand".

Qualifying expenditure must be on plant or machinery installed at a gas refuelling station for use solely for or in connection with refuelling road vehicles with natural gas, biogas or hydrogen fuel. This is defined to include:

- any storage tank for natural gas, biogas or hydrogen fuel;
- any compressor, pump, control or meter used for or in connection with refuelling vehicles with natural gas, biogas or hydrogen fuel; and
- any equipment for dispensing natural gas, biogas or hydrogen fuel to the fuel tank of a vehicle.

The provisions do not extend the normal definition of plant and machinery, so the premises in which the plant is installed would (in principle) not qualify as plant or machinery in their own right.

There is no statutory requirement for the refuelling station to be open to the public, or to be used for cars. HMRC confirm, for example, that FYAs would be due under this heading for an operator of a fleet of commercial vehicles who installs a gas refuelling station.

For these purposes, "biogas" is defined to mean "gas produced by the anaerobic conversion of organic matter and used for propelling vehicles". It is a non-fossil fuel that can act as a substitute for natural gas.

"Hydrogen fuel" is defined as "a fuel consisting of gaseous or cryogenic liquid hydrogen which is used for propelling vehicles".

Law: CAA 2001, s. 45E (as amended)
Guidance: CA 23155

5.4.9   Electric vehicle charging points

FYAs at 100% are given for expenditure incurred in the "relevant period" on electric vehicle charging points. The relevant period began on 23 November 2016 and is now due to end on 31 March 2023 (corporation tax) or 5 April 2023 (income tax) (the end date having been extended by FA 2019, s. 34).

HMRC guidance confirms that the allowances are available to "businesses of all sizes".

The charging points must be "installed solely for the purpose of charging electric vehicles". For these purposes, an electric vehicle is defined as "a road vehicle that can be propelled by electrical power (whether or not it can also be propelled by another kind of power)". An electric vehicle charging point is defined to mean a facility for charging an electric vehicle. HMRC have confirmed that eligible expenditure includes the costs of:

- the charging point itself;
- alteration of land for the purpose only of installing the qualifying plant or machinery in question; and
- plant or machinery installed for the sole purpose of providing the charging point with the necessary supply of electricity.

The plant or machinery in question must be "unused and not second-hand".

FYAs under this heading are subject to the usual "general exclusions" – see **5.4.2**. However, expenditure not qualifying for the FYAs may still qualify for other plant and machinery allowances. HMRC give the example of where expenditure is incurred "partly for purposes beyond the facility for charging electric vehicles".

To enable HMRC to monitor claims under these rules, additional boxes will from April 2020 need to be completed on CT and income tax self-assessment returns. These will show the amount claimed and the amount of any balancing charges.

Law: CAA 2001, s. 45EA

Guidance: CA 23156; *Capital Allowance – Electric Charge Points: initial equality impact assessment* – see https://tinyurl.com/yxlfppxv

5.4.10 Ring-fence trades

Certain expenditure incurred by a company wholly for the purposes of a ring-fence trade may also qualify for FYAs. Particular rules apply, not covered in this book, with further new rules introduced in FA 2021 in relation to the super-deduction and other temporary FYAs (see **5.13**).

A ring-fence trade is one involved with the extraction of oil or gas in the UK or UK Continent Shelf.

Law: CAA 2001, s. 45F, 45G

Guidance: CA 23157

5.4.11 Plant or machinery for use in designated assisted areas

Certain enterprise zone expenditure qualified for FYAs under this heading if incurred by companies in the eight-year period beginning with the date on which the area in question was designated (but see below). This represents a change (introduced in 2016) from the fixed end dates that formerly applied.

At the time of the Budget in March 2020, the following announcement was made, extending the end date in many cases:

> "Enhanced first year allowances for investment in new plant or machinery within designated assisted areas within Enterprise Zones were introduced in 2012 and were initially available for investment over a 5-year period but this was later extended to 8 years. The period commences from when the area is treated as designated.
>
> By 31 March 2020, 8 years will have elapsed since the introduction of these enhanced first year allowances. The government has announced at Budget March 2020 that these capital allowances will remain available for expenditure incurred in relation to all areas, whenever designated, until at least 31 March 2021."

This change was implemented by SI 2020/260. At the time of writing, in April 2021, the authors are not aware of any further extension, so these allowances appear to have come to an end.

The usual "general exclusions" apply (see **5.4.2**).

The background to the provisions was explained in an information note published by HMRC. The incentives can vary between and even within zones, so the benefits of investment in a particular geographical region should be assessed on a case-by-case basis.

Allowances under these rules are not to be confused with the enterprise zone allowances that were formerly available under the code for industrial buildings allowances (IBAs). These allowances offered immediate tax relief for the whole of the qualifying expenditure where the relevant conditions were met (former CAA 2001, s. 299). The rules were considered in the Upper Tribunal case of *Cobalt v HMRC*.

Law: CAA 2001, s. 45K; SI 2015/2047; SI 2020/260
Case: *Cobalt Data Centre 2 LLP and Cobalt Data Centre 3 LLP v HMRC* [2019] UKUT 342 (TCC)
Guidance: www.hmrc.gov.uk/tiin/tiin690.pdf

Designated areas

The enhanced allowances were not available for all enterprise zones, only for a limited number of designated assisted areas within certain specified zones. HMRC maps at www.gov.uk/government/publications /enterprise-zones show which areas qualify.

Primary use

The expenditure must be incurred on the provision of plant or machinery for use primarily in an area which (at the time the expenditure is incurred) is a "relevant area" (as defined, but broadly a designated assisted area).

Although the test is one of "primary" use, a further exclusion applies if the company intends the plant or machinery to be used partly in a non-designated area and the obtaining of FYAs is a main purpose.

If the use to which the plant and machinery is put changes (within, broadly, a five year period from its first use), expenditure may be treated as never having been first-year qualifying expenditure. This can arise if the plant or machinery starts to be used primarily in an area that is not a designated assisted area, or if it is held for use in such a non-designated area. Any change must be notified to HMRC within three months of a person becoming aware that the return needs to be amended accordingly.

Law: CAA 2001, s. 45K, 45L, 45N; SI 2014/3183; SI 2018/485

Qualifying activities

The expenditure must be incurred by a company that is within the charge to corporation tax for the purposes of a qualifying activity that is either a trade or one of the undertakings (mines, transport, etc.) listed at CTA 2009, s. 39(4).

A further condition is that the expenditure must be incurred for one of the following purposes:

- a business of a kind not previously carried on by the company;
- the expansion of an existing business; or
- the starting up of an activity that "relates to a fundamental change in a product or production process of, or service provided by, a business carried on by the company".

The last condition above is met only if the expenditure on the relevant plant and machinery "exceeds the amount by which the relevant plant or machinery is depreciated in the period of 3 years ending immediately before the beginning of the chargeable period in which the expenditure is incurred". For these purposes, "relevant plant or machinery" is defined to mean plant or machinery being used at the end of the period of the three year period for the purposes of the product, process or service in question.

Law: CAA 2001, s. 45K(6)-(8)

Nature of the plant or machinery

The asset in question must be "unused and not second-hand".

It must not be "replacement expenditure". This is defined to mean new plant or machinery that is intended to perform the same (or a similar) function as other plant or machinery on which the company has previously incurred qualifying expenditure, but which has been superseded by the new plant or machinery. However, relief is not denied to the extent that the new assets are capable of, and intended to perform, a "significant additional function" that enhances the capacity or productivity of the qualifying activity. This is to be determined on a just and reasonable basis.

Law: CAA 2001, s. 45K(9)-(13)

EU restrictions

To comply with EU restrictions ("state aid" etc.), FYAs were not available under this heading if, at the time of the claim, the person incurring the expenditure was (or formed part of) any of the following types of undertaking:

- fisheries and aquaculture sectors, as covered by Council Regulation (EC) No 104/200;
- coal, steel, shipbuilding or synthetic fibres sectors;
- the transport sector or related infrastructure;
- relating to energy generation, distribution or infrastructure;
- relating to the development of broadband networks;
- the management of waste of undertakings (but this does not include the management of waste of the company itself or of certain related businesses); or
- various specified agricultural activities.

Allowances were also denied if the person incurring the expenditure was:

- in difficulty for the purposes of the General Block Exemption Regulation; or
- subject to an outstanding recovery order following a European Commission decision declaring an aid illegal.

Expenditure was also excluded if it was incurred in certain circumstances where the company was not an SME for the purposes of the *General Block Exemption Regulation*.

FYAs were also denied under this heading if certain grants were made by way of state aid or by way of other means specified by Treasury order. Allowances already given could be withdrawn if such grants were subsequently made.

If allowances fell to be denied by virtue of these provisions, the company had to give notice to HMRC within three months of first becoming aware of that fact. The notice had to be in writing (s. 577(1)).

Law: CAA 2001, s. 45M

Cap for those spending more than 125 million euros

No further FYAs were given in respect of a particular designated assisted area if allowances under s. 45K had previously been made in respect of expenditure of 125 million euros in respect of that area on the same investment project. If the current expenditure took the total over that figure, FYAs were restricted accordingly.

Law: CAA 2001, s. 212U

5.4.12   Plant or machinery used partly for other purposes

A person may use plant or machinery partly for the purposes of a trade (or other qualifying activity) and partly for private purposes (or some other purpose that is not for the qualifying activity). In such cases, any FYA for expenditure on the item "must be reduced to an amount which is just and reasonable having regard to the relevant circumstances".

In particular, regard must be had to the extent of the anticipated other use.

Example

Dan is a sole trader taxi driver who buys a new, low-emission car that qualifies for FYAs (see, generally, **5.4.6**). The car costs £20,000. In discussion with his accountant, Dan estimates that his private use of the car will be 10%.

As his profits for the year are not high, he does not need the full amount of the available FYA. In fact, a calculation shows that he needs £10,500 to cover his profits above the level of his personal allowance.

Dan may therefore wish to claim FYAs (before private use adjustment) of £11,667. The 10% restriction then brings the actual claim down to £10,500.

The amount available to carry forward to the next year is £8,333 (not £9,500: see below). Further restrictions will then apply to future WDAs, based on actual private use in later years.

As FYAs are normally given at 100%, there is usually no balance to carry forward. This is not always the case, however, as a person may choose to restrict the allowances to less than the full amount, as just illustrated. (Historically, some FYAs have in any case been given at less than 100%.)

Where allowances are restricted for private or other non-business use, any balance carried forward is calculated as if the full allowance had been given.

Law: CAA 2001, s. 205
Guidance: CA 23087

5.4.13   First-year tax credits

See **5.11** for the treatment of first-year tax credits.

5.5   Disposals

5.5.1   Introduction

A person who has claimed plant and machinery allowances on a particular asset will in certain circumstances have to bring a disposal receipt into account. This will have the effect either of reducing current or future allowances, or of creating a balancing charge.

The term "disposal event" is used to denote any event that requires such a disposal value to be brought into account.

Law: CAA 2001, s. 60

5.5.2   Disposal events

The main disposal events are listed as follows:

- the person ceases to own the plant or machinery;
- the person loses possession of the plant or machinery in circumstances where it is reasonable to assume that the loss is permanent;
- the plant or machinery has been in use for mineral exploration and access and the person abandons it at the site where it was in use for that purpose;
- the plant or machinery ceases to exist as such (as a result of destruction, dismantling or otherwise);
- the plant or machinery begins to be used wholly or partly for purposes other than those of the qualifying activity;
- the plant or machinery begins to be leased under a long funding lease; and
- the qualifying activity is permanently discontinued.

The above is taken directly from s. 61. However, s. 66 (see **5.5.6**) also lists numerous other provisions that may require a disposal value to be brought into account.

The taxation of the UK property income and gains of non-resident companies changes from April 2020, broadly bringing them within the scope of corporation tax rather than income tax. *Finance Act* 2019 amended ITTOIA 2005, s. 362 so that the latter section does not have effect when an existing UK property business is brought within the charge to corporation tax rather than income tax. This ensures that the changing tax regime will not trigger a disposal event under s. 61 of CAA 2001, a welcome transitional provision.

Law: CAA 2001, s. 61(1), 66; FA 2019, Sch. 5, para. 8

5.5.3　Disposal values – general rules

In practice, the disposal value of an item of plant or machinery is normally simply the amount received by way of disposal proceeds (net of any selling costs). Nevertheless, the legislation contains an array of different circumstances in which a different disposal value needs to be brought into account.

The starting point (at s. 61) is a table of disposal values, as follows:

	1. Disposal event	2. Disposal value
1.	Sale of the plant or machinery, except in a case where item 2 applies.	The net proceeds of the sale, together with– a. any insurance money received in respect of the plant or machinery as a result of an event affecting the price obtainable on the sale, and b. any other compensation of any description so received, so far as it consists of capital sums.

	1. Disposal event (cont.)	2. Disposal value
2.	Sale of the plant or machinery where– a. the sale is at less than market value, b. there is no charge to tax under ITEPA 2003, and c. the condition in subsection (4) [see note below] is met by the buyer.	The market value of the plant or machinery at the time of the sale.
3.	Demolition or destruction of the plant or machinery.	The net amount received for the remains of the plant or machinery, together with– a. any insurance money received in respect of the demolition or destruction, and b. any other compensation of any description so received, so far as it consists of capital sums.
4.	Permanent loss of the plant or machinery otherwise than as a result of its demolition or destruction.	Any insurance money received in respect of the loss and, so far as it consists of capital sums, any other compensation of any description so received.
5.	Abandonment of the plant or machinery which has been in use for mineral exploration and access at the site where it was in use for that purpose.	Any insurance money received in respect of the abandonment and, so far as it consists of capital sums, any other compensation of any description so received.
5A.	Commencement of the term of a long funding finance lease of the plant or machinery.	The greater of– a. the market value of the plant or machinery at the commencement of the term of the lease, and b. the qualifying lease payments [defined at s. 61(5A)].

	1. Disposal event (cont.)	2. Disposal value
5B.	Commencement of the term of a long funding operating lease of the plant or machinery.	An amount equal to the market value of the plant or machinery at the commencement of the term of the lease.
6.	Permanent discontinuance of the qualifying activity followed by the occurrence of an event within any of items 1 to 5B.	The disposal value for the item in question.
6A.	Disposal event to which s. 62A applies.	The relevant transition value (see s. 62A).
7.	Any event not falling within any of items 1 to 6A.	The market value of the plant or machinery at the time of the event.

The condition referred to in item 2(c) is met by the buyer if:

- the buyer's expenditure on the acquisition of the plant or machinery cannot be qualifying expenditure for the purposes of either the plant and machinery rules or the rules for research and development allowances, or
- the buyer is a dual resident investing company connected with the seller.

This is subject to the general limit on the amount of the disposal value and to various other provisions regarding disposal values: see the remaining parts of **5.5** below.

The term "market value" is defined to mean, in relation to any asset, the price the asset would fetch in the open market.

Law: CAA 2001, s. 61(2), 577(1)

5.5.4   *General limit on disposal values*

By bringing in a disposal value, a person is restricting the allowances claimed for a particular item. So if an asset is bought for £100 and sold for £30 some years later, the person will obtain tax relief on the net amount of £70.

The plant and machinery rules do not, however, impose a tax charge on a disposal profit (though such a profit may be charged to tax in other ways, for example as a capital gain). For this reason, the disposal value to be brought into account is capped at the amount of qualifying expenditure that the person has previously included in the capital allowances computation.

So if the asset bought for £100 is later sold for £120, the amount to bring in as a disposal value is capped at £100. The effect is that the person will – over the years – obtain no net allowances on the asset in question.

If none of the qualifying expenditure has been included in a capital allowances computation, by the seller or by a connected person, no disposal value is brought into account.

These simple principles are subject to two exceptions.

First, a person may acquire an asset from a connected person. In such a case, the disposal value is capped at the qualifying expenditure incurred by whichever party to the transaction (or to any of a series of transactions) incurred the greatest expenditure.

Example – unincorporated business

Adam buys a machine for £20,000 and sells it for £100 to Eve, who is a connected party. She later sells it for £25,000. Her disposal value is capped at £20,000 rather than at £100. (For a further example, see HMRC's *Capital Allowances Manual* at CA 23260.)

Special rules also apply by virtue of s. 239 (see **Chapter 23**) where there is an additional VAT rebate.

Law: CAA 2001, s. 62, 64

5.5.5   *Disposal values – other issues*

Apportionments

When the figure to be used for the disposal value is the figure of net proceeds of sale, the apportionment rules of s. 562 should not be overlooked. In particular, where two or more items are sold together, the net proceeds of sale of any given item must be calculated as "so much of the net proceeds of sale of all the property as, on a just and reasonable apportionment, is attributable to that item". The point is considered more fully at **12.8**.

Law: CAA 2001, s. 562

Disposal giving rise to employment tax charge

If a disposal of plant and machinery is by way of gift, and gives rise to a tax charge under ITEPA 2003, the disposal value for capital allowances purposes is nil. This ensures that an employer obtains full tax relief on the value of an asset transferred to an employee, just as the employer would obtain relief (in a different way) for a normal salary payment to an employee.

An employer cannot also claim a trading deduction for the cost in these circumstances. HMRC make the point that the capital allowances provision only applies to a gift, and that "a gift cannot have been made wholly and exclusively for the purposes of the trade". That reasoning does not strike the author as very sound, but the end result is undoubtedly correct – an employer may bring in a nil disposal value, or may claim a business deduction if the circumstances justify it, but may not claim double tax relief.

It is possible that the recipient will pay no tax on the gift – if, for example, it is transferred as part of a redundancy package and is exempt under the relevant provisions (see ITEPA 2003, s. 403). The disposal value is still nil for capital allowances purposes in such circumstances.

Law: CAA 2001, s. 63(1)
Guidance: CA 23250

Disposals to charities, etc.

There is a nil disposal value where a person carrying on a "relevant qualifying activity" makes a gift of plant or machinery (used in the course of that activity) to certain charitable or other institutions.

The following activities are qualifying for these purposes:

- a trade, profession or vocation;
- an ordinary UK property business;
- a UK furnished holiday lettings business;
- an ordinary overseas property business; or
- an EEA furnished holiday lettings business.

The gift may be made:

- to a charitable trust within the meaning of ITA 2007, Pt. 10;
- to a charitable company within the meaning of CTA 2010, Pt. 11;

- to a registered club within the meaning of CTA 2010, Pt. 13, Ch. 9 (community amateur sports clubs);
- to a body listed at CTA 2010, s. 468 (various heritage bodies and museums); or
- for the purposes of a designated educational establishment within the meaning of ITTOIA 2005, s. 110 or CTA 2009, s. 106 (gifts to educational establishments).

This is subject to anti-avoidance provisions within ITTOIA 2005 and CTA 2009 (where the donor or a connected person receives a benefit attributable to the gift) and ITA 2007 and CTA 2010 (tainted charity donations, etc.).

Law: CAA 2001, s. 63; ITTOIA 2005, s. 109; ITA 2007, s. 809ZM; CTA 2009, s. 108; CTA 2010, s. 939F

Gifts to others

There is some doubt about the correct tax treatment where a business gives away an item of plant or machinery, perhaps to save decommissioning and other disposal costs.

The disposal rules clearly apply in these circumstances: it is not necessary to identify a sale as such, as s. 61 specifies that a disposal value must be brought into account where a person "ceases to own" the asset in question.

A reader has argued that item 4 of the table at s. 61 would apply in these circumstances, on the grounds that the gift is the "permanent loss of the plant or machinery otherwise than as a result of its demolition or destruction". If that is the case, then the disposal value to be brought into account will be "any insurance money received in respect of the loss and, so far as it consists of capital sums, any other compensation of any description so received". That would result in a nil disposal value for the previous owner.

The alternative argument is that a gift cannot be described as a "loss". If this is correct, then we would be within item 7 of the table, and the market value would need to be brought into account.

The author fears that the second reading of the legislation is likely to be preferred by HMRC, not least to prevent an unintended tax-saving opportunity. It should be remembered, by way of background, that the recipient will be able to claim allowances based on the market value of the item (s. 14 – see **4.10.4**). The treatment of the recipient has no direct bearing on the treatment of the previous owner, though if the legislation is balanced as it should be we may expect that the former owner will similarly be required to bring market value in for the disposal.

Further anti-avoidance considerations will apply if the parties are connected.

Law: CAA 2001, s. 61

Other cases where the disposal value is nil

The disposal value of plant or machinery is also taken to be nil where the expenditure has been treated as incurred on plant or machinery by virtue of s. 27(2) (thermal insulation, personal safety, etc.).

Law: CAA 2001, s. 63(5)

Non-resident companies migrating into the charge to corporation tax

A particular issue arises where a non-resident company migrates into the charge to corporation tax. While non-resident, such a company will be liable to income tax and can claim capital allowances accordingly. If the company becomes UK resident, it will instead become liable to corporation tax. Although there has been no disposal of any assets, the question may arise of whether this constitutes a disposal and re-acquisition for capital allowances purposes.

The point was the subject of correspondence between HMRC and the CIOT in 2014 and 2015, and there was a difference of opinion on the correct application of the tax rules in these circumstances.

Legislation has been introduced to take effect from April 2020, to provide clarity on this point – see **5.5.2** above.

Law: CAA 2001, s. 61; ITTOIA 2005, s. 362

Foreign permanent establishment

A UK resident company may election for certain "exemption adjustments" to be made under CTA 2009, s. 18A (profits or losses of foreign permanent establishments).

In such cases, the disposal value is in some circumstances to be taken as the "transition value" – thus ensuring that there is no balancing allowance or balancing charge.

Law: CAA 2001, s. 62A

Leased assets: arrangements reducing disposal value

An anti-avoidance rule operates where certain arrangements are entered into with the effect of reducing the disposal value of an asset in so far as it is attributable to rentals payable under the lease.

The disposal value for capital allowance purposes at the time the lessor disposes of the leased assets, or otherwise ceases to be within the charge to tax in respect of that activity, is computed as if the arrangements had not been entered into.

Law: CAA 2001, s. 64A

5.5.6   *Further rules relating to disposal values*

The following provisions require different disposal values to be brought into account in particular circumstances:

Provision	Detail	Coverage
68	hire-purchase etc.: disposal value on cessation of notional ownership	Chapter 6
70E	long funding leases: disposal events and disposal values	Chapter 7
72, 73	grant of new software right: disposal value	8.4
88, 89	short-life assets: disposal at under-value or to connected person	15.7, 15.8
104E	special rate expenditure: avoidance cases	17.5.1
108, 111, 114	overseas leasing: disposal values in various cases	19.2
132, 143	ships: ship used for overseas leasing etc.; attribution of amount where balancing charge deferred	Chapter 20
171	oil production sharing contracts: disposal values on cessation of ownership	Chapter 21
196, 197	fixtures: disposal values on cessation of notional ownership and in avoidance cases	10.6
208	effect of significant reduction in use of plant or machinery for purposes of qualifying activity	5.8
208A	cars: disposal value in avoidance cases	9.4.4

Provision	Detail	Coverage
211	effect of payment of partial depreciation subsidy	5.9
218ZB	disposal of plant or machinery in avoidance cases	Chapter 22
228K-228M	disposal of plant or machinery subject to lease where income retained	Chapter 22
229	hire-purchase: disposal values in finance leasing and anti-avoidance cases	Chapter 22
238, 239	additional VAT rebates	Chapter 23

5.6 Balancing allowances

A balancing allowance will arise for the final chargeable period (see **5.1.3**) if, for any given pool, AQE exceeds TDR.

See **5.3.8** and **5.5** for a full discussion of these terms, but broadly the allowance will be available where the value brought down at the start of the final chargeable period, plus any additions in that period, exceed any disposal proceeds.

In the final chargeable period, no AIA or FYA or WDA may be claimed, so the balancing allowance is the mechanism whereby all unused relief is made available.

Example 1 – balancing allowance

Joanna is retiring from her business. She has drawn accounts up to 30 June each year but now has a final set of accounts for the six months to 31 December.

At the start of the final chargeable period, she has a value brought down in the main pool of £2,400. She buys a paper shredder in the year for £150 and she sells some office equipment for £300.

She cannot claim any first-year or WDAs. Nor is she entitled to an AIA. However, she obtains a balancing allowance of the full amount of £2,250 (AQE of £2,550 less TDR of £300).

There is no automatic balancing adjustment simply because a business no longer owns any assets in the pool.

Example 2 – no balancing allowance

Greg operates a simple business that requires one large machine. He has had the machine for some years and its written down value is £20,000. He decides to sell it, obtaining proceeds of £3,000, and he then hires a new machine, paying monthly rentals.

In this scenario, Greg will not be entitled to any balancing allowance. Rather, he can simply claim WDAs on £17,000, carrying the remaining balance forward and claiming on the reducing balance year by year thereafter.

Again, there is no balancing adjustment merely because an asset is acquired and disposed of in the same chargeable period.

Example 3 – no balancing allowance

Kirk is a sole trader electrician with several employees. He has a general pool at the start of the year with a value of £18,000. In the year he buys a second hand van for £12,000 for use by one of his employees. He does not drive the van himself at any time. The van is stolen later in the year and Kirk receives insurance proceeds of £10,000.

Kirk can claim AIAs on the cost of £12,000. The insurance proceeds are set against the value brought down of £18,000, leaving a figure of £8,000. Kirk can claim WDAs of £1,440, carrying forward the balance of £6,560.

The same principles apply to the other pools, the position for each being calculated separately. It is quite possible that there may be a balancing allowance on one pool and a balancing charge on another. See also the rules relating to small pools (at **5.3.6**).

For a single-asset pool, a balancing adjustment normally arises when the asset is sold (but see **5.1.3** for exceptions). This is illustrated at **5.3.7**.

Different rules apply to special rate cars where the discontinued activity is continued by a relevant company (s. 104F: see **9.4.4**). There are also restrictions on allowances for overseas leasing in certain circumstances (s. 110(1): see **Chapter 19**).

Adjustments to the allowances due will be needed where there is private use of the asset (by a business proprietor or family member, but not by a director or employee). See **5.4.12** for a full discussion.

Law: CAA 2001, s. 55(2), (4)

5.7 Balancing charges

A balancing charge is the method whereby allowances that have been given are partially or wholly clawed back. Such a charge arises fairly rarely for an ongoing business, as disposal proceeds will normally simply reduce the balance in the continuing pool of expenditure.

Example 1 – no balancing charge arises

Tempest Ltd, with no entitlement to AIAs, has a balance of £1,200 brought forward in its main pool. In the year in question, it incurs further expenditure of £3,000 and sells some old items for £1,500 (being less than their original cost).

No balancing charge arises. The new expenditure is added to the amount brought forward, and the disposal proceeds are deducted. WDAs are given on the net figure of £2,700.

A balancing charge will arise, however, if the proceeds (capped at original cost) exceed the total of expenditure brought forward and new expenditure in the year. In technical terms, there is a balancing charge where TDR exceeds AQE: see **5.3.8** and **5.5.3** for a detailed explanation of these terms.

Example 2 – balancing charge does arise

Othello Ltd, also with a balance of £1,200 brought forward in its main pool, incurs no further expenditure but sells some old items for £1,500 (being less than their original cost).

This time, the £1,500 is offset against the balance brought forward and a balancing charge is imposed of £300.

In practice, most businesses will be entitled to AIAs. The same overall net result will usually be achieved whether the full AIA is claimed or whether it is restricted to cover a balancing charge.

Example 3 – balancing charge may arise

Hamlet Ltd has a value brought down of £2,000. It incurs new capital expenditure in the year of £10,000 and sells an old machine for £2,400.

If it claims full AIAs on the new expenditure, it will receive AIAs of £10,000 and will suffer a balancing charge of £400. Its net allowances for the year will be £9,600.

It may instead restrict its AIA claim to £9,600. The balance of £400 is therefore added to the value brought forward, exactly matching the disposal proceeds. There is no balancing charge and the net allowances are still £9,600.

Once more, adjustments should be made as appropriate where there is private use of the asset (by a business proprietor or family member, but not by a director or employee). See **5.4.12** for a full discussion.

Law: CAA 2001, s. 55(3)

5.8   Assets used partly for other purposes

5.8.1   Introduction

Allowances (and balancing charges) may be reduced if there is private use of an asset on which allowances are claimed.

The restriction applies where there is use of an asset for purposes other than those of the qualifying activity. In practice, that usually means private use so (for brevity) reference is made in this **5.8** to private use. It could also include, however, such circumstances as use of a substantial asset (e.g. an aeroplane) partly for the purposes of an overseas trade that is not a qualifying activity.

The adjustment is needed for private use by a business proprietor, including a partner unless he or she is taxed as an employee. No adjustment is required where the private use is by a director or employee: such private use is taxed through the employment tax rules and does not affect the employer's capital allowance computation. See, however, **5.8.3** below.

Example – private use

Romulus and Remus are each in business. Romulus is a sole trader but Remus has incorporated his business.

In the year, they both buy computer equipment for £1,500. In each case, the equipment is used one third for private purposes.

Romulus must restrict his allowances (AIA or WDA or – in other circumstances – FYA or a balancing allowance) so that he claims on just £1,000 of the £1,500. Remus' company, however, can claim tax relief on the full amount of £1,500.

Depending on the nature of the asset, the director or employee making the private use may be liable to tax on a benefit in kind (and the employer may face a Class 1A National Insurance liability) on the provision of that benefit.

Law: CAA 2001, s. 205

5.8.2 Mechanics

The legislation recognises that a different approach is required for different types of allowance. For a WDA or balancing allowance, the restriction can reflect the actual extent of private use. In the case of an AIA or an FYA, by contrast, it will be necessary to base a restriction on *predicted* private use.

The restriction of AIAs is considered at **5.2.15**. And see **5.4.12** for the restriction for FYAs.

Allocation to single-asset pool

Assets with private use (or otherwise used only partly for the purposes of the qualifying activity) are allocated to a single-asset pool. Once more, this does not apply to an asset used for the private purposes of a director or employee, though this is subject to the point made at **5.8.3** below.

WDAs, and balancing allowances and charges, are then calculated according to the extent of actual use of the asset for non-qualifying purposes. See **5.3.7**.

Law: CAA 2001, s. 206
Guidance: CA 27005

5.8.3 But is it plant?

The restrictions for private use described above are statutory mechanisms for giving a "fair" amount of capital allowances where plant or machinery is used partly for other purposes.

There is also, though, a potential catch for certain types of asset that are used privately, even where that private use is by a director or employee. This is because of the more fundamental question of whether such an asset will qualify for capital allowances in the first place.

If the asset is *machinery*, there is no problem. If, for example, the company buys a helicopter and it is used for the director's private purposes, allowances will still be due (and the director will probably have a large personal tax charge on the benefit in kind).

The definition of *plant*, however, depends on the context in which the asset is used. If an item is used only for private purposes, it may be that it does not constitute plant at all. HMRC illustrate this with the following example:

> "Assets such as paintings and furniture provided for the director's home are unlikely to be plant. They will not be apparatus with which the company's trade is carried on."

This view was given approval in the case of *Mason v Tyson*.

As regards cars that are far more expensive than would be required for the purposes of the trade alone, see **9.7**.

Case: *Mason v Tyson (HMIT)* (1980) 53 TC 333
Guidance: CA 27100

5.8.4   *Use for business entertainment*

No plant and machinery allowances are given for an asset to the extent that it is used for providing business entertainment. The asset is treated as in use for purposes other than those of the qualifying activity. This also covers cases where the item in question is used for such purposes by an employee of the person carrying on the activity.

The term "entertainment" includes, for these purposes, any kind of hospitality, but the exclusion does not extend to anything provided for employees of the person carrying out the qualifying activity (unless its provision for them is incidental to the provision of entertainment for others). In this context, directors and anyone engaged in the management of a company are treated as employees.

The exclusion of allowances does not apply if a person is using the asset simply to provide something that he provides in the ordinary course of the qualifying activity, whether for payment or by way of advertising to the general public. This relaxation applies as along as it is a function of the person's qualifying activity to provide it.

Law: CAA 2001, s. 269

5.9   Partial depreciation subsidy

Allowances are restricted if the person claiming is entitled to receive a "partial depreciation subsidy". This is a sum that meets all of the following criteria:

- It is payable directly or indirectly to a person who has incurred qualifying expenditure for the purposes of a qualifying activity.

- It is paid in respect of (or it takes account of) part of the depreciation of the plant or machinery resulting from its use for the purposes of that activity.

- It is neither treated as taxable income of that person nor taken into account in calculating the profits of any qualifying activity he carries on.

HMRC give the example of an employee who uses an asset owned personally for work purposes, and who receives a payment from his or her employer to cover some or all of the depreciation. Given the third condition listed above, this pre-supposes that there is no tax charge on the employee as a result of the payment.

Allowances are restricted if it appears that such a subsidy is payable, or will be payable, to him in the period during which the asset will be used for the purposes of the qualifying activity.

Both AIAs and FYAs are reduced to an amount that is "just and reasonable having regard to the relevant circumstances". In the case of FYAs, the balance carried forward is nevertheless reduced by the full amount before the adjustment.

WDAs, and balancing allowances and charges, are also reduced on the same basis, and the expenditure is allocated to a single-asset pool to achieve this. If the expenditure has already been allocated to a different pool, a disposal value must be brought into account and the same figure is then used as the qualifying expenditure for the single-asset pool. This applies only to the first occasion on which such a subsidy is received.

Any reduction in the amount of WDA is again ignored when calculating the balance carried forward. But if the WDA is partly or fully disclaimed in any year, the reduction does not apply or only applies proportionately.

Law: CAA 2001, s. 209-212
Guidance: CA 27500

5.10   Giving effect to allowances and charges

5.10.1   Introduction

As a general principle, allowances are given by treating them as an expense of the qualifying activity. Balancing charges are treated as a taxable receipt of that activity.

This general principle is applied and sometimes modified depending on the nature of the activity, as below.

Law: CAA 2001, s. 247-262A

5.10.2   Trades

Allowances for those carrying on a trade are given effect in calculating the profits of the trade, treating an allowance as a trading expense and any balancing charge as a trading receipt.

This is subject to restrictions where there is "avoidance involving allowance buying". These restrictions apply only to companies that enter into arrangements for an "unallowable purpose" – broadly speaking, to obtain a tax advantage for the company itself or for someone else.

Where assets are provided for leasing in the course of a trade, and the loss derives from the resulting plant and machinery allowances, income tax loss reliefs are restricted in certain circumstances. To avoid the restriction, a person must (broadly) carry on the trade for a continuous period of at least six months, and must devote substantially the whole of his time to carrying the trade on.

Law: ITA 2007, s. 75; CAA 2001, s. 247, 212A-212S
Case: *Johnson v HMRC* [2012] UKFTT 399 (TC)

5.10.3   Ordinary UK property businesses

Allowances for those carrying on an ordinary UK property business (see **3.3**) are given effect in calculating the profits of the business, treating an allowance as an expense of that business and a balancing charge as a business receipt.

Law: CAA 2001, s. 248

5.10.4   UK furnished holiday lettings businesses

Allowances for those carrying on a UK furnished holiday lettings business (see **3.4**) are given effect in calculating the profits of the business, treating an allowance as an expense of that business and a balancing charge as a business receipt.

For profits calculated in this way, the provisions of CTA 2010, s. 65 apply (UK furnished holiday lettings business treated as a trade for purposes of loss reliefs, etc.).

Law: CAA 2001, s. 249

5.10.5   Ordinary overseas property businesses

Allowances for those carrying on an ordinary overseas property business (see **3.5**) are again given effect in calculating the profits of the business, treating an allowance as an expense of that business and a balancing charge as a business receipt.

Law: CAA 2001, s. 250

5.10.6   EEA furnished holiday lettings businesses

Allowances for those carrying on an EEA furnished holiday lettings business (see **3.6**) are given effect in calculating the profits of the business, treating an allowance as an expense of that business and a balancing charge as a business receipt.

For profits calculated in this way, the provisions of CTA 2010, s. 67A apply (letting of EEA furnished holiday lettings accommodation treated as a trade for purposes of loss reliefs, etc.).

Law: CAA 2001, s. 250A

5.10.7   Professions and vocations

Allowances for those carrying on a profession or vocation are given effect in calculating the profits of that activity, treating an allowance as a trading expense and any balancing charge as a trading receipt.

Law: CAA 2001, s. 251

5.10.8   Mines, transport undertakings, etc.

The qualifying activity may involve one of the concerns listed at ITTOIA 2005, s. 12(4) or at CTA 2009, s. 39(4) (mines, transport undertakings, etc.).

In this case, allowances are once more given effect in calculating the profits of that concern, treating an allowance as an expense and any balancing charge as a receipt.

Law: CAA 2001, s. 252

5.10.9   Companies with investment business

The rules are somewhat more complicated for those whose qualifying activity consists of managing the investments of a company with investment business.

As a broad principle, allowances for any given chargeable period are deducted from any income of the business for the period. Balancing charges are treated as income of the business.

It is possible, however, that there will be more allowances than can be used in this way. If so, the excess allowances are treated as management expenses referable to the accounting period in which the company is entitled to the allowances.

There can be no duplication of allowances. So if allowances are due under some other provision, they may not also be given under CAA 2001, s. 253 (or under s. 270HE as the case may be).

These rules are still subject to the provisions in CTA 2010, s. 682(3) and s. 699(3) (restrictions on the deduction of management expenses: notional accounting periods).

Law: CAA 2001, s. 253; CTA 2009, s. 1233
Guidance: CA 29320

5.10.10 Long-term business

The expression "long-term business" was substituted for "life assurance business" from, broadly, 1 January 2013. Various particular rules apply, much amended by FA 2012, but these are not covered in this book.

Law: CAA 2001, s. 254-257, 261
Guidance: *Life Assurance Manual*

5.10.11 Friendly societies

See SI 2008/1942 for various modifications made to CAA 2001 in certain circumstances where a friendly society carries on business other than life or endowment business.

Law: CAA 2001, s. 257A
Guidance: *Life Assurance Manual*

5.10.12 Special leasing

The meaning of "special leasing" is explained at **3.8** above. Different rules govern the way effect is given to allowances for income tax and corporation tax purposes.

Income tax

Allowances are normally given by deducting them from any income a person receives from special leasing of plant and machinery in the current tax year.

However, a restriction applies if the lessee does not use the asset in question, for the whole of part of the tax year, for the purposes of a qualifying activity he is carrying on. In this case, the allowance (or a proportionate part of it) may only be given effect by deducting it against the person's current year income from the particular asset in question.

The allowance is given effect at Step 2 of the calculation in ITA 2007, s. 23. Excess allowances may be carried forward and set against future income of the same description.

A balancing charge is treated as income liable to income tax.

Law: CAA 2001, s. 258

Corporation tax

Broadly similar principles apply for corporation tax purposes. Once more, allowances are given and charges made in calculating the income from special leasing. However, this is again subject to more restrictive rules if the plant or machinery was not used by the lessee for the purposes of a qualifying activity throughout the tax year; the allowances may then only be offset against the company's current year income from that particular special leasing.

As long as the plant or machinery was used by the lessee for the purposes of a qualifying activity, any excess allowances may be offset against the other profits of the company, for the same accounting period. They may also then be carried back and set against the profits of any previous accounting period ending within the "carry-back period". This is the period of the same length as the current account period, ending at the start of the current accounting period. However, if the preceding period began before the start of the carry back period, the total deductions for these allowances and for losses must not exceed a proportionate part of the profits of the earlier part of the period.

Example

A company draws up accounts to 31 March each year, but after its accounts to 31 March 2021 it draws accounts up to 31 December 2021 and then to 31 December each year thereafter.

Excess management charges arising in the year to 31 December 2022 may be offset against profits in the nine months to 31 December 2021. They may also be set against one quarter of the profits arising in the year to 31 March 2021.

A claim to offset against profits of the same or of an earlier period must be made within two years from the end of the accounting period in which the company is entitled to the allowances in question.

Where a company carried on a business in partnership with other persons, and the business includes the leasing of plant or machinery, restrictions may apply to prevent the offset against other profits of the same or previous years.

Different rules apply for special leasing where the company is carrying on "long-term business" (see, briefly, **5.10.10** above).

Law: CAA 2001, s. 259-261A

5.10.13 Employments and offices

For employees and office holders, allowances are given as a deduction from the taxable earnings from the employment or office in question. Balancing charges are treated as earnings of the employment.

Allowances are not given for cars owned by employees even if used for work purposes: see **9.1.3**.

Law: CAA 2001, s. 262

5.11   First-year tax credits

5.11.1   Introduction

First-year tax credits were formerly available for companies (only) that were loss-making and that had incurred expenditure on "energy-saving" or "environmentally beneficial" plant and machinery (see **5.4.4** and **5.4.5** respectively). Full details were included in earlier editions of this book. (If purchasers of this edition still need the earlier rules, the publishers may (at their discretion) provide, without charge, a PDF of the equivalent sections from the 2019-20 edition.)

Cessation of scheme of tax credits

FYAs for expenditure on energy-saving and environmentally beneficial technology ceased from April 2020. The associated scheme for tax credits therefore also came to an end for all expenditure incurred by companies after 31 March 2020.

Law: FA 2019, s. 33

5.11.2   Clawback of credits

Overview

Tax credits are clawed back (and the losses are for other purposes restored) if there is a disposal of "tax-relieved" plant or machinery within the clawback period, as defined.

For these purposes, an asset is said to be tax-relieved if any expenditure on it was relevant first-year expenditure in respect of which an FYA was made for the chargeable period for which the first-year tax credit was paid.

The clawback period starts when expenditure is incurred on the tax-relieved asset, and ends four years after the end of the chargeable period for which the tax credit was paid.

A payment may also become excessive if the company amends its return or if an enquiry into the return concludes that an excessive claim had been made.

Law: CAA 2001, Sch. A1, para. 24, 25

Disposal

An extended definition of "disposal" applies for these purposes. The term includes any event listed at s. 61(1) (see **5.5.2**). However, the company is also treated as making a disposal if there is a change in the ownership of the item in relation to which a "continuity of business provision" applies. This expression is defined to mean any enactment "under which anything done to or by the company which ceases to be the owner of the item is treated, for the purpose of making allowances and charges under this Act, as having been done to or by the person who becomes the owner of the item".

Normal rules apply to determine disposal values (see **5.5.3**), except that market value is (for these purposes only) substituted if:

- the company disposes of the item to a connected person for less than its market value; or

- there is a change in the ownership of the item in relation to which a continuity of business provision applies.

Law: CAA 2001, Sch. A1, para. 25

Mechanics

The clawback provisions apply where, after a disposal, the amount (or the aggregate of the amounts) of the original expenditure on the retained tax-relieved plant and machinery is less than the amount of loss surrendered in the chargeable period for which the first-year tax credit was paid. The appropriate part of the loss surrendered in that period is then treated as if it were not a surrenderable loss. This appropriate part is known as the "restored loss".

The relevant percentage of the restored loss is then used to calculate the amount of the first-year tax credit to be clawed back. The relevant percentage means the applicable percentage (e.g. 12.67%) for the chargeable period for which the tax credit is paid. For earlier chargeable periods (broadly, those ending before 1 April 2018, but subject to the transitional provisions), the relevant percentage was 19%.

The rules err in favour of the company in some circumstances, as illustrated in this example (the principles of which have been discussed by the author with HMRC, who have confirmed that the result shown below is correct):

Example

A company has a profit of £80,000 before deducting first-year allowances of £300,000, giving it a surrenderable loss of £220,000. It claims a repayment of £41,800 (£220,000 at 19%).

The company subsequently sells an asset that was part of the £300,000 but that cost £35,000. The cost of the tax-relieved plant that is retained is £265,000, which still exceeds the surrendered loss of £220,000. As such, the clawback provisions are not triggered.

The amount of the restored loss is calculated using the formula (LS – OERPM) – (OE – DV) – ARL, where:

> **LS** is the amount of loss surrendered in the chargeable period for which the first-year tax credit was paid;
>
> **OERPM** is the amount (or the aggregate of the amounts) of the original expenditure on the retained tax-relieved plant and machinery after the item is disposed of;

OE is the aggregate of the amount of the original expenditure on the item disposed of, and the amounts of the original expenditure on any items of tax-relieved plant and machinery that the company has previously disposed of;

DV is the aggregate of the disposal value of the item disposed of, and the disposal values of any items of tax-relieved plant and machinery that the company has previously disposed of; and

ARL is the amount of the restored loss (or the aggregate of the amounts of the restored loss) on any previous application of these rules.

If the result of the formula is negative, the amount of the restored loss is nil.

HMRC have illustrated the above with the following example at CA 23191:

HMRC example

On 1 October 2010 a company spends £200,000 on various items of energy saving P&M and claims FYA on the full amount. It makes a loss after deduction of the FYA of £50,000 which it surrenders for a first-year tax credit of £9,500. In the year to 31 December 2012 the company sells all this plant and machinery for £170,000. The restored loss is £20,000 and the tax credit clawed back £3,800. The company keeps the tax credit that relates to the loss on disposal (i.e. £30,000 @ 19% = £5,700). Following the claw back the company will have losses of £20,000 available to carry forward at 31 December 2010.

Where the clawback provisions apply, the tax credit paid to the company is "treated as if it ought never to have been paid". If the company becomes aware on a given date that a return has on that basis become incorrect, it must notify HMRC within three months of that date. Assessments may then be made or adjusted as necessary. Interest is charged from the date the payment being recovered was made.

Law: CAA 2001, Sch. A1, para. 24, 26, 27
Guidance: CA 23189, 23191

5.12   Freeport tax sites – first-year allowances

5.12.1   *Introduction and overview*

The general background to freeport tax sites – including an overview of the tax benefits, and details of the requirement for such sites to be designated by regulations – is given at **1.14** above.

This section focuses solely on the 100% FYAs available for expenditure on certain plant or machinery for use in freeport tax sites. In some of the official government guidance notes, the term "enhanced capital allowance" is used to refer to this scheme, but it is technically just another type of FYA.

In practice, companies will wish to consider how best to balance claims under this heading with claims for the super-deduction as outlined at **5.13** below. It may be that the 130% super-deduction will be claimed for main rate expenditure, and the 100% FYA will be available for special rate expenditure incurred in freeports.

5.12.2   *Conditions*

Key conditions for claiming FYAs for freeport tax sites are:

- The plant or machinery must be for use primarily in an area that is designated as a freeport tax site at the time the expenditure is incurred. See **5.12.3** for a discussion of the implications of this, and for associated anti-avoidance rules.

- The plant and machinery must be unused and not second-hand.

- The expenditure must be incurred for the purposes of a trade or of certain concerns listed at ITTOIA 2005, s. 12(4) or CTA 2009, s. 39(4) (mines, transport undertakings, etc.).

- The expenditure must be incurred on or before 30 September 2026.

- The company incurring the expenditure must be within the charge to corporation tax. (Note that this condition does *not* apply for freeport SBAs – see **24.14**).

- The expenditure must not be caught by any of the general exclusions of s. 46 (see **5.4.2** above, but also the note below about leased assets).

Various important restrictions are imposed by these conditions.

211

Most notably, these FYAs are available only for companies (not for individuals, partnerships or trusts, for example).

They are also given only for trades and certain specified concerns. As such, the FYAs are not available for professions or vocations, for employees, or for property businesses of any type (including FHL properties).

The general exclusions prevent FYAs for most cars, and for leased assets (but see also **5.13.1** below re the super-deduction).

These conditions may, within certain parameters, be varied or even repealed by regulation, without the need for new primary legislation. For example, conditions may be imposed relating to accounts or other records.

Law: CAA 2001, s. 45O, 45P

5.12.3   Use within a freeport site

The first condition listed in the section above is that the plant or machinery must be for use primarily in an area that is designated as a freeport tax site at the time the expenditure is incurred. This has important implications.

Most obviously, it follows that expenditure will not qualify if it is incurred before the specific site has been designated.

It may be that the company will intend the plant or machinery to be used partly in an area that is not a freeport tax site. This is not in itself a problem, in that the test is whether plant or machinery is *primarily* for use in the designated area. As such, unrestricted FYAs may in principle be claimed if this test is met. However, a company may be party to a transaction (or scheme or arrangement) precisely with a view to obtaining FYAs under these rules (or greater FYAs than would otherwise be available) for the "non-freeport part" of the expenditure. Where this is the case, FYAs will be denied for that non-freeport part on a just and reasonable basis.

Another potential complication is that the actual or intended use of the plant or machinery may change, and this can lead to a clawback of the FYAs. More specifically, the expenditure will be treated as never having been qualifying expenditure under these rules if, at any "relevant time":

- "the primary use to which the plant or machinery is put is other than in an area which, at the time the expenditure was incurred, was a freeport tax site"; or

- "the plant or machinery is held for use otherwise than primarily in an area which was a freeport tax site at that time".

The clawback can be for up to five years. In more detail, the relevant time is a time within the "relevant period" in which the plant or machinery is owned by the company incurring the expenditure, or by a party connected with that company. So the clawback does not apply if the company has disposed of the asset in question to an unconnected third party.

The relevant period is a period of five years beginning with the day on which the plant or machinery is first:

- brought into use for the purposes of a qualifying activity carried on by the company; or
- (if earlier) held for such use.

Where the clawback applies, HMRC may make or amend any such assessments as may be needed to implement the denial of FYAs.

If a person who has made a return becomes aware that this clawback applies, the person must give notice to HMRC within three months of becoming so aware.

Law: CAA 2001, s. 45Q, 45R

5.13   Super-deductions and other temporary first-year allowances

5.13.1   Introduction and overview

The concept of the "super-deduction" – first mentioned in the 2021 March Budget – provides for temporary FYAs, whereby the capital allowances available can exceed the cost of the asset in question. So, for example, a company incurring costs of £10,000 in a given period may obtain tax relief in that period on £13,000.

The legislation is given in FA 2021, and references throughout this 5.13 are to the clause numbering as published in the *Finance Bill* 2021, covering clauses 9 to 14.

Terminology

The terms "super-deduction" and "super-deduction expenditure" refer only to the FYAs that are given at 130% for main rate expenditure.

The parallel provisions for special rate expenditure, giving FYAs at 50%, instead use the concepts of "SR allowance" and "SR allowance expenditure" (see **5.13.4**).

These are all explained more fully below, but as the rules differ in some significant ways it is important to maintain these differentiating terms.

Law: FB 2021, cl. 9(2), (3)

Timing of expenditure

The new FYAs are given for expenditure incurred from 1 April 2021 to 31 March 2023 inclusive. The normal capital allowances rules about timing of expenditure do initially apply, including s. 5 (when capital expenditure is incurred – see **1.5** above) and s. 50 (supplementary rule about timing of expenditure for FYAs, which disapplies the pre-trading expenditure rule in s. 12 – see **5.4.1** above).

However, no allowances are due under the scheme if the expenditure is incurred "as a result of a contract" entered into before 3 March 2021. In technical terms, s. 5 is then disapplied and the expenditure is treated as incurred when the contract is entered into, irrespective of any unconditional obligation that there may be.

Law: FB 2021, cl. 9(2), (6)

Conditions

Key conditions of the scheme are as follows:

- The rules apply to expenditure on plant and machinery, that must be acquired "unused and not second-hand".
- The expenditure must be incurred from 1 April 2021 to 31 March 2023 (see below).
- The scheme is only available for companies within the charge to corporation tax (so not for sole traders or others paying income tax).
- The eight general exclusions at s. 46(2) (see below) apply to deny allowances under this temporary regime, as they do to deny other FYAs.
- There is a very broad anti-avoidance provision, preventing the claiming of these FYAs in various contrived circumstances, or if there is any attempt to exploit shortcomings in the legislation (see **5.13.5**).

Law: FB 2021, cl. 9(2)

General exclusions

The general exclusions referred to in the penultimate bullet above are given at s. 46 and are covered in depth at **5.4.2**. These deny FYAs for various types of asset and in various circumstances. For example, FYAs are not available for most cars, or for plant or machinery received as a gift.

General exclusion 6 denies FYAs for plant and machinery for leasing (in contrast to the treatment of AIAs, which are *not* denied for leased assets – contrast s. 38B (AIAs) and s. 46 (FYAs)). Specifically, the FYA exclusion applies to expenditure on "the provision of plant or machinery for leasing (whether in the course of a trade or otherwise)". A Treasury answer on 16 March 2021 confirmed that this would also apply to "investment in plant and machinery intended to be subsequently leased", adding a reference to safeguards in the legislation to prevent abuse (see **5.13.5** below).

In principle, this provision prevents the claiming of FYAs (including the super-deduction and the SR allowance) for fixtures in a property that is to be rented out. So the new FYAs are not available for landlords running a property business. (As regards the question of serviced accommodation, see **3.2** above.)

However, the position on this in relation to the new temporary allowances is not fully clear at the time of writing (April 2021), so readers should check for the latest guidance. It has been widely reported that HMRC may in practice allow the FYAs for:

- communal plant provided by landlords of properties that are leased to more than one tenant; and
- capital contributions by landlords to tenant fit-out costs.

Law: CAA 2001, s. 46; FB 2021, cl. 9(2)(d)

Other key features

Relief of 130% is available for main rate expenditure, and of 50% for special rate expenditure (see **Chapter 17** for a more general discussion of special rate expenditure), with different rules applying for each.

There are various complexities, including transitional rules for periods spanning 1 April 2023, special disposal rules for assets for which a super-deduction has been claimed, and in certain other circumstances.

A variant of the scheme, applying to ring-fence trades (involved with the extraction of oil or gas in the UK or UK Continent Shelf) is not covered in this book.

Law: FB 2021, cl. 9(1)

5.13.2 Super-deduction for main rate expenditure

Chargeable periods ending before 1 April 2021

The 130% deduction is potentially available, in the form of an FYA that is called a super-deduction, for a company that meets the key conditions at **5.13.1** above, and that incurs expenditure on plant and machinery that is not special rate expenditure.

No transitional rules apply in April 2021; it is merely necessary to ensure that the expenditure is incurred from 1 April 2021 and that it is not under a contract entered into before 3 March 2021.

Example 1

A Ltd runs a care home and spends £10,000 in July 2021 on installing upgraded baths and basins. It can claim capital allowances of £13,000, potentially saving corporation tax of £2,470. (The 24.7% tax saving is 1.3 multiplied by the corporation tax rate of 19%.)

Expenditure qualifying in this way is referred to in the legislation as "super-deduction expenditure" and the first-year allowance in question is called a "super-deduction".

Law: FB 2021, cl. 9(2)

Chargeable periods spanning 1 April 2023

The position is more complex at the end of the two-year temporary period for which these FYAs are given. For a chargeable period (the "relevant period") ending on or after 1 April 2023, a lower percentage applies (the "relevant percentage") rather than 130%.

The relevant percentage is determined as follows:

- divide the number of days in the relevant period before 1 April 2023 by the total number of days in that period;
- multiply that figure by 30; and
- add 100 to the result.

Example 2

B Ltd draws accounts up for the year to 31 December 2023.

> 90 days out of 365 fall before 1 April 2023.
>
> 90/365 = 0.2466.
>
> 30 x 0.2466 = 7.4 (the *Explanatory Notes* show this rounding).

Add 100 to give the relevant percentage of 107.4%.

Note that this is the percentage applying for expenditure incurred in the period from 1 January to 31 March 2023. No FYAs are given for expenditure incurred from 1 April 2023 onwards.

The following rates will therefore apply for companies with 12-month accounting periods (assuming rounding up to one decimal place).

Chargeable period y/e	Relevant percentage
31 March 2023	130%
30 April 2023	127.6%
31 May 2023	125%
30 June 2023	122.6%
31 July 2023	120%
31 August 2023	117.5%
30 September 2023	115%
31 October 2023	112.5%
30 November 2023	110%
31 December 2023	107.4%
31 January 2024	104.9%
29 February 2024	102.6%
31 March 2024	0%

So the reality is that the figure can drop below 130% from as early as 2 April 2022.

The same principles are applied for shorter accounting periods, for which it will be necessary to work through the calculations.

See **5.13.6** below for an example illustrating the rather complex interaction of these provisions with the AIA transitional rules that will apply as the AIA threshold reduces from £1 million to £200,000.

Law: FB 2021, cl. 11(1), (2), (5)

Additional VAT liabilities

The concept of capital allowances for an additional VAT liability is explained in full in **Chapter 23**. Very broadly, additional VAT paid by the owner of an asset may constitute qualifying expenditure for capital allowances purposes.

In principle, the 130% super-deduction is available for such additional VAT liabilities, according to the normal principles explained in **Chapter 23**. However, a lower figure applies for such liabilities if the chargeable period ends on or after 1 April 2023.

In such cases, the percentage to be used depends on whether the person becomes entitled to the super-deduction in respect of the additional VAT liability before 1 April 2023:

- If so, the "relevant percentage" is to be used, rather than the standard figure of 130%. The relevant percentage is the same as that explained above.
- If the person does not become entitled before 1 April 2023, the figure of 100% is used.

Law: FB 2021, cl. 11(3)-(5)

5.13.3 Disposals of assets where super-deduction made

The normal disposal value rules are modified in the event of any disposal event (normally a sale, but see **5.5.2** for a general discussion, and **10.6** in the context of disposals of fixtures) occurring on or after 1 April 2021, where a super-deduction has been given for the expenditure in question. NB the rules in this paragraph apply only for the purposes of the 130% super-deduction; they have no relevance for the 50% allowance for special rate expenditure

The first key difference is that there is a balancing charge for the period in which the disposal event occurs. In other words, the disposal proceeds are not set against the reducing pool value (the usual treatment for disposal proceeds, which typically, though not invariably, prevents an immediate balancing charge for an ongoing business).

The second key difference is that the amount that has to be brought into account by way of a disposal value may be higher than would normally be the case.

It may be that where expenditure is incurred, only some of it is subject to a super-deduction claim. In this case, the modified disposal rules apply only to that part. The *Explanatory Notes* to the *Finance Bill* 2021 illustrate this as follows:

> "The amount of the disposal value subject to the balancing charge is reduced if a company claims a super-deduction for only part of its qualifying expenditure on the plant or machinery and pools other expenditure incurred on the asset or claims another first-year allowance in respect of it. This might happen, for example, if a company incurs expenditure in stages on plant or machinery that is constructed over a period of time and part of the expenditure is incurred after 1 April 2023."

Calculation of balancing charge

The way the modified rules apply varies according to the timing of the disposal. This appears to be an anti-avoidance measure to prevent a company buying an asset, claiming a super-deduction, and then very quickly selling the asset.

If the disposal occurs in a chargeable period that ends before 1 April 2023, the amount of the disposal value is multiplied by 1.3 ("the relevant factor").

Example 1

C Ltd draws accounts up to 31 December each year.

In June 2021, it spends £200,000 on a large machine, and claims a super-deduction. It therefore claims allowances of £260,000 in the year to 31 December 2021.

An industry development effectively renders the machine obsolete just a few months after the purchase. The company therefore sells it in September 2022, receiving just £30,000.

Although the company has a value of £100,000 in its main pool, as a result of other historic expenditure, it cannot offset the disposal proceeds against that pool value.

Instead, it must incur a balancing charge for the year to 31 December 2022. That balancing charge is calculated as £30,000 x 1.3 = £39,000.

If the disposal occurs in a chargeable period that begins before 1 April 2023 but ends on or after that date, a different relevant factor (rather than 1.3 as in the example above) is used.

The relevant factor is in such cases determined as follows:

- divide the number of days in the chargeable period before 1 April 2023 by the total number of days in that period;
- multiply that figure by 0.3; and
- add 1 to the result.

Example 2

D Ltd draws accounts up to 31 December each year.

In the same way as C Ltd in **Example 1** above, D Ltd spends £200,000 on a large machine, and claims a super-deduction. It therefore claims allowances of £260,000 in the year to 31 December 2021.

D Ltd sells the machine in September 2023, receiving £30,000. Once more, it cannot set the disposal proceeds against any remaining pool values, but must incur a balancing charge for the year to 31 December 2023.

There are 90 days in the chargeable period that fall before 1 April 2023, and there are 365 days in the whole period.

The calculation of the relevant factor is therefore as follows:

$$(90/365 \times 0.3) + 1$$

The relevant factor is therefore 1.074.

The balancing charge will therefore be £32,220.

If the disposal event is in a chargeable period beginning on or after 1 April 2023, there is no enhancement of the disposal proceeds. In a straightforward case where the super-deduction has been claimed for the whole cost of certain plant or machinery, the balancing charge will simply equal the disposal proceeds. In other cases, only the relevant proportion of the disposal proceeds will give rise to an automatic balancing charge, with the remainder of the proceeds being set against the value of the main pool.

Example 3

E Ltd draws accounts up to 31 March each year. The company buys an asset for £500,000 in February 2022, and claims a super-deduction of

£650,000. The asset retains its value and the company sells it again in May 2023, receiving back the £500,000 it paid.

The company incurs a balancing charge of £500,000, but permanently retains the tax relief on the "super" element of £150,000.

What would the position be, though, if the disposal proceeds *exceeded* the original cost?

There is a general principle for plant and machinery allowances that the disposal value to be brought into account is limited to the qualifying expenditure incurred on the asset in question (s. 62 – see **5.5.4**). All FYAs are calculated as "a percentage of the first-year qualifying expenditure" (s. 52(3)) – see **5.4**). It follows that where the super-deduction is given, what changes is the percentage of the qualifying expenditure that gives rise to an FYA. The underlying figure of qualifying expenditure remains unchanged. The disposal proceeds are therefore still capped at the costs actually incurred rather than at any higher figure.

Example 4

Adapting **Example 3** above, suppose that E Ltd sold the asset in May 2023 for £800,000 rather than just £500,000?

The disposal proceeds (and the balancing charge) would still be capped at £500,000.

Law: CAA 2001, s. 52, 62; FB 2021, cl. 12

5.13.4   SR allowance for special rate expenditure

Introduction

As already noted above, the terms "super-deduction" and "super-deduction expenditure" refer only to the FYAs that are given at 130% for main rate expenditure. The parallel provisions for special rate expenditure, giving FYAs at 50%, instead use the concepts of "SR allowance" and "SR allowance expenditure".

The general principles described at **5.13.1** apply equally for the purposes of the SR allowance, and reference should be made to that part of this commentary to ensure that a person is entitled to claim in the first place. For example, SR allowances are only available for companies within the charge to corporation tax, and the allowances are not available for leased assets (including fixtures in rental properties, but with a possible exception for multi-let properties – see **5.13.1** above), for second-hand assets, or for expenditure incurred before 1 April 2021.

The super-deduction rules described at **5.13.2** and **5.13.3** above do *not* apply to the SR allowance, so the SR rules are more straightforward. For example, there is no concept of a reduced SR allowance for chargeable periods spanning 1 April 2023.

Law: FB 2021, cl. 9(3)

Calculation of allowances

Expenditure that otherwise meets all the conditions for the super-deduction, but that is special rate expenditure, qualifies under this heading for 50% FYAs.

Example 1

M Ltd draws accounts up to 31 December each year. In January 2022, it incurs qualifying expenditure of £800,000. Analysis shows that this needs to be apportioned as £350,000 to main rate expenditure and £450,000 to special rate expenditure.

M Ltd can claim as follows:

- super-deduction of £350,000 x 130% = £455,000; *plus*

- SR allowance of £450,000 x 50% = £225,000.

So M Ltd can claim total FYAs of £680,000, and has a further £225,000 of qualifying expenditure still to be relieved.

See **5.13.6** below for the mechanics of giving that further relief.

Balancing charges on disposal

Where an asset is sold, and the 50% SR allowance has previously been claimed on the cost, any disposal proceeds will give rise to a balancing charge.

In straightforward cases, the balancing charge will simply be half of the disposal proceeds. The other half of the proceeds will be deducted from the balance of the special rate pool.

Example 2

In April 2022, N Ltd incurs qualifying special rate expenditure of £200,000. It claims an SR allowance of £100,000 and the balance of the expenditure is taken to the special rate pool.

Some years later, N Ltd disposes of the asset in question, receiving proceeds of £40,000.

Half of this amount will trigger an immediate balancing charge, i.e. of £20,000. This charge will arise for the chargeable period in which the disposal event occurs.

The other half of the proceeds is taken to the special rate pool, reducing the balance in that pool by £20,000. This will *not* normally produce a balancing charge, but will instead reduce the value on which future WDAs can be claimed.

The normal rules for disposal events and disposal values apply (see **5.5** above), so in some cases a disposal value will need to be brought into account using market value or some other figure.

It may be that only part of the expenditure was subject to an SR claim. In this case, an appropriate apportionment will be needed, and the SR balancing charge will be limited to the part of the expenditure on which an SR allowance was made.

5.13.5   Anti-avoidance

Unsurprisingly, the temporary FYAs (both the super-deduction and the equivalent SR allowances) are subject to some strict anti-avoidance measures. The legislation states that tax advantages caught by these measures are to be counteracted by the making of such adjustments as are just and reasonable.

The concept of a "tax advantage" is already in the capital allowances rules (at s. 577(4)), and is discussed at **22.3.3** below.

The anti-avoidance rules for the temporary FYAs talk of a "relevant" tax advantage. An advantage is said to be relevant if it is "connected with a super-deduction or an SR allowance". That is broad, but will normally refer to the obtaining of an FYA or the avoidance of a balancing charge.

The concept of "arrangements" is widely defined to include "any agreement, understanding, scheme, transaction or series of transactions (whether or not legally enforceable)". The arrangements must have been entered into on or after 3 March 2021.

The relevant tax advantage is caught by these rules if it is obtained "as a result of relevant arrangements". Arrangements are said to be relevant where two conditions are met:

- First, the purpose, or one of the main purposes, of the arrangements must be to obtain a relevant tax advantage.
- Second, it must be reasonable, in all the circumstances:

- o "to conclude that the arrangements are, or include steps that are, contrived, abnormal or lacking a genuine commercial purpose; or
- o to regard the arrangements as circumventing the intended limits of relief under CAA 2001 or otherwise exploiting shortcomings in that Act."

The concept of the "intended limits of relief" is very broad (and has already been used in other parts of the tax legislation, for example in relation to losses). The wording obviously seeks to ensure that any attempt to circumvent the intended purpose and limitations of the relief will fail.

Adjustments may be made by way of an assessment or modification of an assessment, or otherwise by amending or disallowing a claim for a FYA or any other tax claim.

5.13.6   Interaction with AIAs and WDAs

The way the temporary FYAs interact with the rules for AIAs and WDAs can be complex.

AIAs and WDAs only

The temporary FYA rules (i.e. both the super-deduction for main rate expenditure and the SR allowance for special rate expenditure) are restricted to companies within the charge to corporation tax. For sole traders, partnerships of individuals, trusts and others within the charge to income tax, the temporary FYAs are not available. The only option for these entities is to claim AIAs or WDAs.

For companies that are engaged solely in running a property business (i.e. where the income is rental income), the same is true. This is because FYAs are denied for leased assets (with one possible exception – see **5.13.1** above) whereas AIAs and WDAs are available for such assets.

The temporary FYAs are available only for assets that are unused, so they are not available, for example, for a company buying an existing commercial property. Once more, the company can instead claim AIAs and WDAs.

FYAs (and also AIAs) are denied for nearly all cars.

In other cases, however, a company may need to decide whether to claim the new FYAs or to opt for AIAs or even just WDAs.

Mixing with other allowances

Where AIAs are claimed, WDAs may also be claimed on the remainder of the expenditure in the same year. So if the AIA limit is £200,000, and there is expenditure of £250,000, it is possible to claim AIAs for the £200,000 and also to claim WDAs in the same period for the £50,000.

For FYAs, the position is different. This will not be an issue in practice for the super-deduction, but will be relevant in the context of the 50% SR allowance. So if there is qualifying SR expenditure of £100,000, allowances at 50% can be claimed, so £50,000, but WDAs can only be claimed on the other £50,000 from the following year.

The technical justification of this can be found in the contrasting wording of s. 58(4A) and s. 58(5). The latter subsection, in particular, makes the position clear.

For completeness, s. 52A ensures that AIAs and FYAs (or different types of FYA) may not be claimed on the same expenditure.

The problem of disposals

For main rate expenditure, the preferred option in most cases will be to claim the super-deduction at 130% (or at the lower rates, but still more than 100%, that apply as the super-deduction is phased out).

In the event of an early disposal, however, this may not be so straightforward. There would appear to be at least three considerations here:

- First, the disposal proceeds may be enhanced where the super-deduction (but not the SR allowance) has been claimed. This is not a problem in itself, as the enhanced proceeds can never exceed the amount on which the super-deduction has been claimed. So a company may spend £1,000 and claim a super-deduction of £1,300. However, the worst-case scenario is that the balancing charge will be £1,300, and it may well be less than that.

- Second, however, is the fact of the balancing charge itself. A company that has claimed these enhanced FYAs will always incur a balancing charge when receiving disposal proceeds at a later date. By contrast, a company claiming AIAs will offset any disposal proceeds against its appropriate pool(s) (main rate and/or special rate) and will usually avoid a balancing charge because of the interaction with other expenditure incurred over the years.

- There is the further complication of the expected increase in the rate of corporation tax from 1 April 2023. It is possible that an allowance may be relieved at just 19% but that the corresponding balancing charge will be taxed at 25% (or even at 26.5% for companies with profits between £50,000 and £250,000).

Example 1

Z Ltd incurs qualifying super-deduction expenditure of £100,000 in December 2021. It claims allowances of £130,000 and saves corporation tax of £24,700 (£130,000 at 19%).

It sells the same asset in May 2024, i.e. during its accounting period ended 30 September 2024, receiving proceeds of £70,000.

It incurs a balancing charge of £70,000 and this increases its taxable profits for the period from £100,000 to £170,000. As such, the balancing charge of £70,000 is liable to corporation tax at the marginal rate of 26.5%, and the tax cost is £18,550.

Overall, the company has still received net tax relief (of £6,150), but with other figures the company could in fact lose out overall.

Case study – interaction of allowances

This case study aims to illustrate some of the complexities that businesses and their advisers will wish to consider.

Example 2 – case study

Y Ltd draws accounts up each year to 30 June. It has no associated companies and its taxable annual profits are in the region of £3 million.

The company is paying for the construction of a substantial new office, under a contract entered into in August 2021. It anticipates that the total cost will be £10 million, of which £3.8 million is expected to qualify for plant and machinery allowances. (The balance, but excluding the land cost, will be the subject of a claim for structures and buildings allowances. This element is not covered in this case study, but see **Chapter 24** for full details.)

To plan its borrowings and cash flow, Y Ltd wants to estimate the capital allowances that will be available to it. It advises that the anticipated timing of the qualifying expenditure of £3.8 million is as follows:

| | Main rate | Special rate |
	£	£
2021 – Q4	-	200,000
2022 – Q1	200,000	300,000
2022 – Q2	400,000	900,000
2022 – Q3	400,000	500,000
2022 – Q4	800,000	100,000
Total	1,800,000	2,000,000

Annual investment allowances

If it relies on AIAs and WDAs only, the company would be able to claim as follows:

| Year ended | Main rate | Special rate |
	£	£
30 June 2022	-	300,000
30 June 2023	-	200,000

The maximum AIA that can be claimed for the whole period spanning 1 January 2022 is £600,000 (see Table 1 at **5.2.8**). However, the maximum that can be claimed for expenditure from 1 January to 30 June 2022 is just £100,000 (see Table 2 at that same reference).

So all of the £200,000 in the last quarter of 2021 can be claimed, plus £100,000 of the remaining expenditure in the year. It makes sense to claim AIAs for special rate expenditure first, so that the remainder attracts a higher rate of WDAs.

For the following year, the AIA claim will be for just £200,000, as that is the AIA cap that is expected to apply from that time.

Super-deduction

The company will probably wish to claim the SD for the main rate expenditure (subject to the caveats under "the problem of disposals" above).

For the year ended 30 June 2022, it has qualifying SD expenditure of £600,000 (i.e. the main rate expenditure incurred in quarters 1 and 2 of

2022). It can therefore claim FYAs on this of £780,000 (i.e. £600,000 x 1.3).

For the following period, it has qualifying SD expenditure of £1.2 million (i.e. the main rate expenditure incurred in quarters 3 and 4 of 2022). By now, the SD allowances are already being phased out, so the SD percentage will now be 122.6% (see **5.13.2**). So FYAs on this expenditure will be £1,471,200.

SR allowance

The SR allowance is available at 50% for the special rate expenditure for which no AIAs have been claimed.

So for the year ended 30 June 2022, SR allowances can be claimed on the special rate expenditure incurred (£1.4 million), less the amount of £300,000 on which AIAs have been claimed. So the SR allowance is £1.1 million at 50%, so £550,000. The company is *not* entitled to claim WDAs on the remainder of the expenditure until the following year, though it can obviously claim for any other expenditure already in its special rate pool.

For the following period, the SR allowance will be 50% of £400,000 (qualifying expenditure of £600,000, less AIAs claimed of £200,000). So the SR allowance will be £200,000. WDAs at 6% can now be claimed on the special rate expenditure brought forward from the previous year, which will include the other half of the expenditure on which the SR allowance was claimed in that earlier year.

6. Hire purchase and assets provided by lessees

6.1 Introduction and overview

6.1.1 Background

One of the conditions for claiming plant and machinery allowances is that the person who incurs the expenditure must, as a result, own the asset in question. This can cause problems in certain circumstances, including for fixtures (see **Chapter 10**) and for hire purchase contracts.

The nature of a hire or lease purchase arrangement is that a person (the lessee) has use of an asset but that the provider (lessor) retains ownership until a final instalment has been paid. The capital allowances rules ensure that the lessee rather than the lessor is entitled to allowances, as long as the lessee has the right to acquire the asset at the end of the contract.

HMRC use the terms "hire purchase" and "lease purchase" synonymously.

Guidance: CA 23310

6.1.2 The basic rule

Subject to an anti-avoidance exception considered at **6.1.3**, plant and machinery is treated as owned by the person carrying on a qualifying activity (or corresponding overseas activity) where all of the following conditions are met:

- the person (i.e. the lessee) incurs capital expenditure on the provision of plant or machinery for the purposes of the activity;
- the expenditure is incurred under a contract;
- the contract provides that the person shall or may become the owner of the plant or machinery on the performance of the contract.

In these circumstances, the plant or machinery is treated as incurred by that person and not by any other person. The actual owner (lessor) is therefore not able to claim allowances.

These rules thus allow the person using the asset to meet the fundamental requirement of owning the plant or machinery as a result of incurring expenditure on it. An effect of this is that abortive expenditure (which does not normally qualify, as the ownership condition is not met – see **4.1.2**) may qualify in the case of an HP contract, for example if a deposit is paid for a machine that is never in fact supplied. However, the HMRC view is that a disposal value must be brought into account as soon as the taxpayer ceases to be entitled to the benefit of the contract.

Law: CAA 2001, s. 11(4)(b), 67
Guidance: CA 23350

6.1.3 HP contracts accounted for as finance leases

A special provision applies if the contract is one which, in accordance with generally accepted accounting practice (GAAP), falls (or would fall) to be treated as a lease.

For periods of account beginning on or after 1 January 2019, the scope of the provision is extended so that it also covers lessees who adopt International Financial Reporting Standard 16 ("IFRS 16"), referred to as an IFRS 16 lessee. In this case, the provision applies, where the person is a lessee under a right-of-use lease, if the contract "would fall to be treated in that person's accounts as a finance lease were that person required under generally accepted accounting practice to determine whether the lease falls to be so treated".

The special hire purchase rules outlined above will in such a case apply only if the contract falls (or would fall) to be treated by the lessee in accordance with GAAP as a finance lease.

This provision is not intended to catch ordinary transactions, as explained in the *Explanatory Notes* to Finance Bill 2006:

> "Such circumstances will only occur where the contract has been artificially structured to gain a tax advantage that was not envisaged when section 67 was originally enacted and the lessee will be entitled to relief for all his expenditure."

In this case, the asset is treated as not owned by either party to the transaction. HMRC have explained the effect as follows:

> "The person buying the asset under the lease purchase contract (the lessee) is not treated as the owner of the asset during the duration of the contract unless that person would treat the contract as a finance lease in accordance with generally accepted accounting practice.

For example, a contract that contains an option for the lessee to buy the asset for market price at the end would not be treated as a finance lease by the lessee. This means that the lessee is not treated as the owner of the asset until they actually buy the asset and so it cannot get PMA until it pays the option price.

If the contract would not be treated as a finance lease by the lessee, the lessee is not treated as the owner and cannot claim PMA but the legislation that stops anyone else being treated as the owner still applies. So if the seller has claimed PMA the seller has to bring a disposal value to account."

Law: CAA 2001, s. 67(2A)-(2C); FA 2019, Sch. 14
Guidance: CA 23310

6.2   Timing of expenditure

As soon as the plant or machinery is brought into use for the purposes of the qualifying activity, the person is treated for capital allowances purposes as incurring all the capital expenditure that is to be incurred by him under the contract thereafter. HMRC have given the following example to illustrate this:

HMRC example

Bob enters into a contract on 24 May 2017 to buy a computer from Robbie. He pays £5,000 on 24 May 2017 when he enters into the contract and then there are five payments of £1,000 at yearly intervals. He brings the computer into use on 4 July 2017. Bob is treated as owning the computer from 24 May 2017 onwards, the date of the contract, and Robbie is treated as ceasing to own it. Bob can claim PMA on the initial payment of £5,000 then. He can claim PMA on the five payments on £1,000 each of which he has still to make when he brings the computer into use on 4 July 2017.

Law: CAA 2001, s. 67(3)
Guidance: CA 23310

6.3   Deemed disposals

It is possible that a person will be treated as owning plant or machinery under the hire purchase rules but will cease to be entitled to the benefit of the contract without actually ever owning the asset in question. In these circumstances, the person is treated as making a disposal of the plant or machinery at the time he ceases to be entitled to the benefit of the contract.

The disposal value will consist of any "relevant capital sums", defined to mean any capital sums that the person:

> "receives or is entitled to receive by way of consideration, compensation, damages or insurance money in respect of (a) his rights under the contract, or (b) the plant or machinery".

If the asset has already been brought into use for the purposes of the qualifying activity before the deemed disposal, the disposal value must also include any capital expenditure treated (under s. 67(3)) as having been incurred when the plant or machinery was brought into use (but which has not in fact been incurred).

Anti-avoidance provisions operate in certain circumstances if the person carrying on the qualifying activity assigns the benefit of the contract to someone else (see **22.4**).

Law: CAA 2001, s. 67(4), 68, 229
Guidance: CA 23310

6.4 Hire purchase and fixtures

The hire purchase rules do not apply to fixtures (as defined for capital allowances purposes: see **10.2**). Nor do they prevent the operation of the special fixtures rules from applying to a hire purchase contract.

If a person is treated under the hire purchase rules as owning plant or machinery, and the item in question subsequently becomes a fixture but the person is not treated as owning the asset under the fixtures rules, the person must bring a disposal value into account at that time.

Law: CAA 2001, s. 69
Guidance: CA 23320

6.5 Plant or machinery provided by lessee

A lessee is treated as owning plant or machinery (if he does not in fact do so) if all of the following conditions are met:

- under the terms of a lease, he is required to provide plant or machinery;
- he incurs capital expenditure on the provision of that plant or machinery for the purposes of a qualifying activity that he carries on; and
- the plant or machinery is not a fixture.

The meaning of "incurs capital expenditure on the provision of plant or machinery" in this context was touched on in the *Inmarsat* case (which was reported in 2019 but was still concerned with the predecessor CAA 1990 legislation and which is of limited ongoing relevance). The tribunal decided that expenditure on satellite launch costs could not be equated with expenditure incurred "on the provision of" the satellites themselves.

For these purposes, a lease is defined to include any tenancy and also an agreement for a lease if the term to be covered by the lease has already begun. It does not include a mortgage.

The lessee is treated as being the owner of the plant or machinery, as a result of incurring the capital expenditure, for as long as it continues to be used for the purposes of the qualifying activity.

The ending of the lease does not trigger a disposal for the lessee, but the *lessor* is required to bring a disposal value into account if:

- the plant or machinery continues to be used for the purposes of the lessee's qualifying activity until the lease ends;

- the lessor holds the lease in the course of a qualifying activity; and

- on or after the ending of the lease, a disposal event occurs in respect of the plant or machinery at a time when the lessor owns the plant or machinery as a result of the requirement under the terms of the lease.

In these circumstances, the lessor must bring a disposal value into account in the "appropriate pool" for the chargeable period in which the disposal event occurs.

The "appropriate pool" means the pool that would be applicable in relation to the lessor's qualifying activity if:

- the expenditure incurred by the lessee had been qualifying expenditure incurred by the lessor; and

- that qualifying expenditure was to be allocated to a pool for the chargeable period in which the disposal event occurs.

Law: CAA 2001, s. 70
Case: *Inmarsat Global Ltd v HMRC* [2019] UKFTT 558 (TC)

7. Long funding leases

7.1 Introduction, overview and proposals for change

7.1.1 Introduction

This chapter contains an overview of the complex rules relating to long funding leases (LFLs), originally introduced in FA 2006. Unlike other sections of this book, this one does not purport to give full coverage of the LFL regime, so the pages that follow should be treated as an introduction to the topic rather than as a definitive guide. HMRC's *Business Leasing Manual* contains extensive guidance on long funding leases. See also the *Capital Allowances Manual* beginning at CA 23800.

In a discussion document issued by HMRC on 9 August 2016, the following explanation was provided of the rationale behind the LFL regime:

> "Prior to the introduction of the long funding leasing regime in 2006 the taxation of leasing of plant or machinery had followed the legal form of the arrangement with capital allowances available to the lessor as owner of the plant or machinery.
>
> For some leases the Long Funding Lease regime changed this. The Long Funding Lease regime allocates capital allowances to lessees under longer term leases where the arrangement results in the lessee having substantially all the benefits and obligations associated with ownership. These leases were identified with the help of accounting concepts and classifications derived from accounting rules. The effect was to bring tax and accounting treatment together in most respects for long funding finance leases. The same accounting rules are used elsewhere for lease taxation, particularly in anti-avoidance provisions."

The LFL rules apply for both income tax and corporation tax purposes. The broad effect is to give plant and machinery allowances to the lessee (as economic owner) rather than to the lessor (the legal owner).

The underlying principle is that a long funding lease is in essence a scheme that allows a lessee to borrow money with which to buy the assets in question. According to HMRC, therefore, the legislation:

"corrects a long-standing distortion in the tax system which meant that those who acquired assets under certain kinds of leases were treated differently from those who financed their acquisitions with debt".

In technical terms, expenditure incurred by a lessor is not qualifying expenditure for the purposes of claiming plant and machinery allowances if it is incurred on the provision of plant or machinery for leasing under a long funding lease. Allowances are instead given to the lessee, but subject to various criteria being met (including a requirement for the lessee to claim the allowances in a return).

Special rules apply for income tax and corporation tax purposes for calculating profits for the parties involved with long funding lease transactions. Those rules are beyond the scope of this book but see, respectively, ITTOIA 2005, Pt. 2, Ch. 10A and CTA 2010, Pt. 9, Ch. 2.

When the LFL rules were introduced, long and complex commencement and transitional provisions applied. These are not considered here.

Law: CAA 2001, s. 34A; FA 2006, Sch. 8, para. 15-27

Guidance: CA 23805; HMRC discussion document of 9 August 2016: "Lease Accounting Changes: Tax Response"

7.1.2   Changes from 2019

The discussion document referred to above indicated that the LFL rules might be subject either to modification or to a complete overhaul. In the event, modest changes have been introduced in connection with the new standard for lease accounting (IFRS 16) which has effect for periods of account beginning from the start of 2019.

The following paragraphs, taken from the *Explanatory Notes* to the *Finance (No. 3) Bill* 2017-2019 (in relation to clause 35 and Schedule 13) provide an overview of the thinking behind the changes:

"Entities applying FRS 101 or IFRSs will be required to adopt IFRS 16 for periods of account beginning on or after 1 January 2019 which will change the accounting treatment for leases. The change will mainly affect the treatment for the lessee.

Currently, lessees and lessors are required to make a distinction between finance and operating leases. Where the lessee has substantially all the risks and rewards incidental to the ownership of an asset, it recognises a finance lease asset and liability on its balance sheet. Where the lessee does not have substantially all the

235

risks and rewards incidental to the ownership of the asset, it recognises lease payments as an expense over the lease term, and is considered to have an operating lease. This treatment will continue under FRS 102, the main Financial Reporting Standard applicable in the UK and Republic of Ireland.

The new accounting standard (IFRS 16) will remove the distinction between finance leases and operating leases for a lessee (but not a lessor). Going forward, under IFRS 16, a lessee will recognise all leases on its balance sheet other than certain exempted leases which are short term or of low value.

This measure introduces legislative changes to ensure that certain rules which relied upon the distinction between finance and operating leases will continue to operate as intended, providing certainty and stability for businesses, and ensuring that taxation of lessees is broadly consistent regardless of which accounting framework is adopted.

...

The long funding lease rules in Part 2 of CAA 2001 provide that where a plant or machinery lease is, in substance, a funding lease for the lessee (because the effect of the lease is substantially equivalent to the lessee having borrowed funds to acquire the asset) the lessee is entitled to claim capital allowances on the asset even though they are not the legal owner. The legislative changes ensure that those rules will continue to apply as intended for an IFRS 16 lessee.

A lessee of plant and machinery using IFRS 16 will have a long funding finance lease if the lease is not short and it meets either the lease payments test or the useful economic life test. There is no need to distinguish between long funding operating leases and long funding finance leases for a lessee using IFRS 16 because all leases will be accounted for in the same way. The legislative changes will ensure that a lessee using IFRS 16 with a long funding finance lease will be able to adjust the deduction claimed in certain circumstances where the rentals increase or decrease. The legislative changes make several simplifications to the tests to identify a long funding lease which are not connected to the accounting standard changes."

7.2   Meaning of "long funding lease"

7.2.1   Overview

The LFL rules only apply if a lease can be classified as a long funding lease. This test may be broken down into two parts:

- it must be a "funding lease" (see **7.2.2** and **7.2.3**); and
- it must meet certain other criteria (see **7.2.4**).

Subject to certain exceptions, a lease is not treated as a long funding lease for the lessee unless he makes a tax return to that effect.

It is possible that, at the commencement of the term of a plant or machinery lease, the plant or machinery is not being used for the purposes of a qualifying activity carried on by the person concerned, but that it subsequently begins to be used for the purposes of such an activity carried on by that person. In that case, the plant or machinery lease is a long funding lease if (apart from s. 70H: requirement for tax return) the plant or machinery lease would have been a long funding lease at its inception had the plant or machinery been used at that time for the purposes of a qualifying activity carried on by the person in question.

In some circumstances, the lessor will already be entitled, at the start of the lease term, to claim capital allowances. In these circumstances, the lease is not treated as a long funding lease. It is therefore essential for a lessee, who hopes to claim plant and machinery allowances, to find out whether or not the lessor has a prior right to claim.

Law: CAA 2001, s. 70G, 70H, 70Q

7.2.2   Meaning of "funding lease"

Subject to certain exceptions (see **7.2.3**), a funding lease is defined to mean a plant or machinery lease that meets at least one of the following conditions at its inception:

1. **The finance lease test**: broadly, where the lease would fall to be treated as a finance lease or as a loan under generally accepted accounting practice.

2. **The lease payments test**: the present value of the minimum lease payments (as defined at s. 70YE) is equal to at least 80% of the market value of the leased plant or machinery, less any grants receivable towards the purchase.

3. *The useful economic life test*: the term of the lease is more than 65% of the remaining useful economic life of the leased plant or machinery.

If none of these conditions is met, the lease is not a funding lease and the LFL rules do not apply. An exception applies for a lease of cushion gas.

Law: CAA 2001, s. 70J, 70N, 70O, 70P
Guidance: BLM 20210

7.2.3   Leases that are not "funding leases"

Certain types of plant or machinery lease are specifically held not to be funding leases. The LFL rules therefore cannot apply to these, as follows.

Hire purchase

If s. 67 applies (hire purchase, etc. – see **Chapter 6**), and if the lease is the contract in question, it is not treated as a funding lease and the LFL rules are not applicable.

Succession of leases

A plant or machinery lease is not a funding lease if:

- before the start of the lease term, the lessor has leased the plant or machinery under one or more other plant or machinery leases;
- in the aggregate, the terms of those other leases exceed 65% of the remaining useful economic life of the plant or machinery at the start of the term of the earliest of them; and
- none of those earlier leases was a funding lease.

For these purposes, all persons who were lessors of the plant or machinery before 1 April 2006 are treated as if they were the same person as the first lessor of the plant or machinery on or after that date.

Transitional rule

A plant or machinery lease is not a funding lease if:

- before 1 April 2006, the plant or machinery had, for a period or periods totalling at least 10 years, been the subject of one or more leases; and

- the lessor under the plant or machinery lease was also lessor of the plant or machinery on the last day before 1 April 2006 on which the plant or machinery was the subject of a lease.

Law: CAA 2001, s. 70J

7.2.4   *Exclusions*

Even if a lease is a funding lease, it will fall outside the definition of "long funding lease" if it is:

- a short lease (see **7.2.5**);
- an excluded lease of background plant or machinery for a building (see **7.2.6**);
- excluded by s. 70U (plant or machinery leased with land: low percentage value) (see **7.2.7**).

Law: CAA 2001, s. 70G(1)

7.2.5   *Short leases*

The definition of "short lease" was amended (and simplified) for leases entered into from 1 January 2019. A lease of up to (and including) seven years is a short lease and is therefore unaffected by the LFL rules. Formerly, the condition was five years, but with special provisions for leases of between five and seven years.

Anti-avoidance rules apply where there are arrangements in place for leasing the same asset under different leases. More complex rules also apply to arrangements involving a sale and finance leaseback or a lease and finance leaseback.

Law: CAA 2001, s. 70I

7.2.6   *Background plant and machinery*

A lease is not treated as a long funding lease if it is "an excluded lease of background plant or machinery for a building".

The point here is that fixtures are often leased with a building (a "mixed lease") and the fixtures could fall foul of the LFL rules in leases exceeding five years. This would have the effect of denying plant and machinery allowances to the lessor. To get round this, the legislation designates certain assets as "background plant or machinery" and states that the lease in question will not be treated as a long funding lease.

The exemption from the LFL rules does not apply if the amounts payable under the lease are variable by reference to the plant and machinery allowances available to the lessor, or if the mixed lease is specifically designed to get round the LFL rules.

The Treasury issued an order (SI 2007/303, the *Capital Allowances (Leases of Background Plant or Machinery for a Building) Order*) which specifies the treatment of various types of expenditure.

The overall effect of the rules is that fixtures installed by a landlord will normally fall within one of the categories of expenditure that qualify as background plant and machinery. Typically, the tenant will pay for the cost of trade-specific fixtures.

If a landlord does meet the cost, or part of the cost, of items that are not allowed (such as storage or manufacturing facilities) the LFL rules will need to be watched to ensure that they do not prevent a claim for capital allowances.

Law: CAA 2001, s. 70R, 70T

Assets deemed to be background plant or machinery

The following categories of fixture are specifically deemed to be background plant or machinery:

- lighting installations including all fixed light fittings and emergency lighting systems;
- telephone, audio-visual and data installations incidental to the occupation of the building;
- computer networking facilities incidental to the occupation of the building;
- sanitary appliances and other bathroom fittings including hand driers, counters, partitions, mirrors, shower and locker facilities;
- kitchen and catering facilities for producing and storing food and drink for the occupants of the building;
- fixed seating;
- signs;
- public address systems; and
- intruder alarm systems and other security equipment including surveillance equipment.

This "positive" list takes priority over the exclusions specified immediately below.

Law: SI 2007/303, reg. 3

Assets deemed not to be background plant or machinery

Plant or machinery used for any of the following purposes will not constitute background plant or machinery unless it is in the first list above:

- storing, moving or displaying goods to be sold in the course of a trade, whether wholesale or retail;
- manufacturing goods or materials;
- subjecting goods or materials to a process;
- storing goods or materials:
  - which are to be used in the manufacture of other goods or materials,
  - which are to be subjected, in the course of a trade, to a process,
  - which, having been manufactured or produced or subjected in the course of a trade to a process, have not yet been delivered to any purchaser, or
  - on their arrival in the UK from a place outside the UK.

Law: SI 2007/303, reg. 4

Further assets deemed to be background plant or machinery

The following categories of plant or machinery are again specified to be background plant or machinery, but in this case subject to the exclusions immediately above:

- heating and air conditioning installations;
- ceilings which are part of an air conditioning system;
- hot water installations;
- electrical installations that provide power to a building, such as high and low voltage switchgear, all sub-mains distribution systems and standby generators;
- mechanisms, including automatic control systems, for opening and closing doors, windows and vents;
- escalators and passenger lifts;

- window cleaning installations;
- fittings such as fitted cupboards, blinds, curtains and associated mechanical equipment;
- demountable partitions;
- protective installations such as lightning protection, sprinkler and other equipment for containing or fighting fires, fire alarm systems and fire escapes; and
- building management systems.

Law: SI 2007/303, reg. 2

7.2.7 Plant or machinery leased with land – low percentage value

Subject to further anti-avoidance measures, certain *de minimis* exemptions apply. Broadly, these operate where the market value of non-background plant and machinery is less than (or equal to):

- 10% of the aggregate market value of all the background plant or machinery leased with the land; and also
- 5% of the market value of the land, including both buildings and fixtures.

For these purposes, market value is determined "on the assumption of a sale by an absolute owner of the land free from all leases and other encumbrances".

Law: CAA 2001, s. 70U
Guidance: BLM 21600

7.3 Effects of LFL rules

7.3.1 Overview

For leases that are *not* subject to the LFL regime, normal principles apply such that:

- the lessor pays tax on the full amount of rents received but claims capital allowances on the cost of the plant or machinery that is leased; and
- the lessee deducts the full amount of rents paid under the lease in calculating his taxable income.

As indicated above, this changes for leases within the LFL regime. In these cases, a lessor may not claim capital allowances for expenditure on the provision of plant or machinery for leasing. Allowances may instead be given to the lessee, where all the necessary conditions are met. The statutory route for achieving this outcome depends on whether the lease is a finance lease or an operating lease.

An important point to watch is that the question of whether or not a lease is a LFL is determined separately for the lessor and the lessee.

The following paragraphs summarise the key effects of the LFL legislation.

Law: CAA 2001, s. 34A

7.3.2   *Entitlement to allowances – overview*

A lessee may claim plant and machinery allowances if he carries on a qualifying activity and incurs expenditure (whether or not it is capital in nature) on the provision of plant or machinery for the purposes of the activity under a long funding lease.

The person is treated as owning the plant or machinery at any time when he is the lessee under the LFL, whether or not the lease is regarded as a long funding lease from the lessor's point of view.

The lessee is treated as having incurred capital expenditure on the provision of the plant or machinery at the commencement of the term of the LFL.

The amount of the expenditure that is treated as incurred depends on whether the lease is a long funding *operating* lease (see **7.3.3**) or a long funding *finance* lease (see **7.3.4**).

A long funding finance lease has formerly been a LFL that meets the finance lease test formulated at s. 70N(1)(a). This test is met where, broadly, the lease would fall to be treated as a finance lease or as a loan under generally accepted accounting practice. For periods of account beginning from 1 January 2019, the definition also encompasses – in relation to a lessee only – a right-of-use lease (as defined) that is an LFL meeting the lease payments test of s. 70O or the useful economic life test of s. 70P. However, the extended definition does not apply to a lease that was, before a relevant change of classification (as defined) a long funding operating lease.

Any LFL that is not a long funding finance lease is a long funding operating lease.

Law: CAA 2001, s. 70A, 70YI(1)

7.3.3 Allowances for a long funding operating lease

If the LFL is a long funding operating lease (see **7.3.2** immediately above), the amount of capital expenditure treated as incurred is the market value of the plant or machinery at the later of:

- the commencement of the term of the lease; or
- the date on which the plant or machinery is first brought into use for the purpose of the qualifying activity.

The lease itself is ignored in determining market value.

There are no rules providing for additional capital allowances if the lessor incurs further expenditure on the asset (in contrast to the rules applying for the purposes of long funding finance leases, considered below). Relief for any increased rentals will therefore be given as revenue expenditure.

Law: CAA 2001, s. 70B, 70YI
Guidance: BLM 42020

7.3.4 Allowances for a long funding finance lease

The calculation is more complex if the LFL is a long funding finance lease (or one that would fall, under generally accepted accounting practice (GAAP) to be treated as a loan).

In summary, the lessee's capital expenditure is the present value of the minimum lease payments at the later of:

- the commencement of the term of the lease; or
- the date on which the plant or machinery is first brought into use for the purpose of the qualifying activity.

The present value, calculated on the assumption that accounts are prepared in accordance with GAAP, is the amount that would be treated as the present value of the minimum lease payments in the lessee's accounts at the appropriate date.

Law: CAA 2001, s. 70C; FA 2004, s. 50

Additional capital expenditure

Lessees under long funding finance leases (or leases accounted for as loans) are entitled to further allowances if the lessor incurs additional expenditure on the asset. The corresponding increase in the present value of the minimum lease payments qualifies for plant and machinery allowances.

Law: CAA 2001, s. 70D
Guidance: BLM 42020

7.3.5   Transfer and long funding leaseback

Restrictions (including a denial to the lessee of AIAs and FYAs) apply where there is a transfer and long funding leaseback. For anyone needing to consider these complex rules, the case of *Cape Industrial Services* provides useful background to many of the issues arising.

The restriction applies where:

- a person (S) transfers plant or machinery to another person; and

- after the transfer the plant or machinery is available for use by S or a person connected to S under a plant or machinery lease that is a long funding lease.

A further anti-avoidance measure (by way of an amendment to s. 70DA) was introduced by FA 2015, with effect from 26 February 2015. The intention was explained in the *Explanatory Notes* as follows:

"Where the restriction applies the qualifying expenditure of S (the transferor) or CS (a person connected with the transferor to whom the plant or machinery is made available) under a long funding lease is restricted to nil. The restriction applies if S is not required to bring a disposal value into account and S or a linked person acquired the plant and machinery without incurring either capital expenditure or qualifying revenue expenditure. No capital expenditure will have been incurred in cases where, for example, plant or machinery has been transferred to a person as part of a statutory transfer of property or where the whole cost of the asset has been met by another person."

Law: CAA 2001, s. 70DA
Case: *Cape Industrial Services Ltd & Anor v HMRC* [2020] UKFTT 162 (TC)

7.3.6 Disposals

A person who is the lessee of plant or machinery under a LFL, and who is treated under the LFL rules as having incurred qualifying expenditure, will have to bring a disposal value into account if:

- the lease terminates;
- the plant or machinery begins to be used wholly or partly for purposes other than those of the qualifying activity; or
- the qualifying activity is permanently discontinued.

The amount of the disposal value is given by the formula:

$$(QE - QA) + QR$$

where:

QE is the person's qualifying expenditure on the provision of the plant or machinery;

QA is the qualifying amount (as defined, and as amended from 2019); and

R is the sum of any "relevant rebate" and of certain other "relevant lease-related payments" (as defined in each case).

Law: CAA 2001, s. 70E
Guidance: CA 23825

8. Software

8.1 Introduction

Computer software may not naturally fall within the definition of "plant or machinery", especially if it is provided in electronic form. For capital allowances purposes, however, it may be treated as such, subject to certain fairly simple conditions.

Computer software includes both programs and data.

Before capital allowances are considered, however, it is necessary to determine whether the expenditure is in fact capital at all, or whether it may simply be written off as a revenue cost.

8.2 Capital or revenue expenditure

Normal principles are applied to determine whether expenditure on software is capital or revenue in nature. HMRC guidance in the *Business Income Manual* still refers to (and reproduces in full) a *Tax Bulletin* originally published in 1993. Considering how fast computer technology has developed over the past 20 years, there are obviously limitations on how useful such old advice can now be. It still refers, for example, to the provision of software on floppy discs.

The following principles, condensed and adapted from that extensive HMRC guidance, would seem to remain relevant and correct today:

- where software is acquired along with associated hardware it may be appropriate to apportion the expenditure (but this is unnecessary if both are treated as capital in nature and if no short-life asset election is made);
- an expected life of two years or less may be taken as a broad guideline for treating software costs as revenue in nature;
- a lump sum payment for a licence to use software will not necessarily be capital – regard should be had to the terms of the agreement and to the expected life of the software;
- the medium for providing software (e.g. whether it is downloaded or bought with a CD) is immaterial;
- a short-life asset election is allowed (and should be made in most cases);

- regular payments akin to a rental are revenue in nature and the timing of deductions follows correct accounting practice.

HMRC have also commented that:

"Many large businesses incur significant expenditure not only on developing new computer systems but also on piecemeal adaptation or improvement of existing systems. It follows that a good deal of expenditure incurred on computer programming etc will be of a revenue nature."

Guidance: BIM 35800*ff.*

8.3 Software treated as plant

For the purposes of claiming capital allowances, computer software is treated as plant.

Companies, however, will normally claim a tax deduction for software costs through the intangibles regime, rather than by way of capital allowances. A company may, though, elect under CTA 2009, s. 815 to disclaim relief under that regime. In that case, HMRC have confirmed that capital allowances may be claimed, and in a written answer on 17 March 2021, the Financial Secretary to the Treasury wrote that "in this case, the super-deduction will be available" (see, generally, **5.13**).

Where the intention is to claim capital allowances, three deeming provisions are required to ensure that allowances may be given. These provisions operate where a person carrying on a qualifying activity incurs capital expenditure in acquiring, for the purposes of the qualifying activity, a right to use or otherwise deal with computer software. In such cases, plant and machinery allowances are given as if:

- the right and the software to which it relates were plant;
- the plant were provided for the purposes of the qualifying activity; and
- (for as long as the person is entitled to the right) the person owned the plant as a result of incurring the capital expenditure.

Law: CAA 2001, s. 71

8.4   Disposal values

8.4.1   *Value to use*

A person who has incurred qualifying expenditure on computer software (or the right to use it or otherwise deal with it) may grant a right to someone else to use it in some way. If so, the person may be required to bring into account a disposal value if the consideration for the grant consists of a capital sum (or would consist of such a sum if the consideration were in money).

This requirement applies unless there has been a prior disposal event under s. 61(1)(e) or (f), respectively covering use for purposes other than those of the qualifying activity, and permanent discontinuance of the activity. That earlier disposal event must have taken place while the person owned the software (or had a right to use or deal with it), but before the grant of the right.

The figure used as the disposal value will be the market value of the right granted, at the time of the grant, if the grant is for consideration that does not consist entirely of money, or if all of the following conditions are met:

- the consideration given (if any) is less than market value;
- there is no tax charge under ITEPA 2003 (i.e. as employment income); and
- the expenditure incurred by the grantee does not qualify for allowances as either plant and machinery or research and development; or
- the grantee is a dual resident investing company connected with the grantor.

In any other case, the disposal value will be the net consideration in money received for the grant, together with any relevant insurance proceeds and any other compensation that consists of capital sums.

Law: CAA 2001, s. 72

8.4.2   *Increase in disposal value for other purposes*

As a general principle, there is an overall limit on disposal values that must be brought into account for capital allowances purposes (s. 62: see **5.5.4**).

A special rule applies in relation to computer software for the sole purpose of calculating and applying that overall limit, as there may be a

249

series of disposal values. In such a case, the total disposal values that must be brought into account cannot exceed the qualifying expenditure.

HMRC have illustrated this principle as follows:

HMRC example

Bruce buys computer software for £15,000. The cost Is qualifying expenditure. He grants Stephen a licence to use that software for £10,000. When he does that he has to bring a disposal value of £10,000 to account. 6 months later he grants a licence to Clarence for £8,000. The disposal value he has to bring to account then is restricted to £5,000 because £10,000 of the cost of £15,000 was used up when Bruce granted the lease to Stephen.

Law: CAA 2001, s. 73
Guidance: CA 23430

9. Cars (and other vehicles)

9.1 Introduction

9.1.1 Overview

Plant and machinery allowances are generally available for cars and other vehicles used for the purposes of a qualifying activity.

As for other assets, the rules ultimately allow tax relief for the depreciation that the vehicle suffers over the period of ownership. In the case of cars, however, the timing of that relief is severely delayed by the capital allowances rules, with the result that the tax saving normally lags way behind the true rate of commercial depreciation.

The rate at which tax relief is given for cars is dictated mainly by the level of emissions produced by the vehicle when driven. The tax rules are used to motivate employers and others to buy cars with lower emissions, rewarding such behaviour with earlier tax relief.

In appropriate cases, it may be possible to claim full (100%) allowances under the scheme for Research and Development (see **Chapter 26**) as an alternative to claiming under the rules for plant and machinery.

9.1.2 Structure of the legislation

The concept of "main rate car" (discussed at **9.3.2** below) is contained in the chapter of the legislation dealing with special rate expenditure (beginning at s. 104A), while various other key definitions are relegated to the "supplementary provisions" chapter, starting from s. 268A.

Expenditure on cars will normally go into either the main plant and machinery pool (see **5.3.4**) or the special rate pool (see **5.3.5**). In each case, expenditure on the cars will thus be merged with other assets (e.g. computers or air conditioning systems) in one or both of these pools. Where there is private use of a vehicle (e.g. by a sole trader) it is allocated to a single-asset pool (though private use by a director or employee is not treated as private use for capital allowances purposes).

9.1.3 Employees and directors

Employees and directors are not able to claim capital allowances on cars that they own personally, even if used for business purposes. The exclusion extends to other vehicles and to bicycles. Instead of claiming allowances, owners of vehicles and bicycles may instead claim tax relief under the system of authorised mileage relief.

Employers, of course, may claim allowances for cars owned by the business but driven by directors or employees (and no adjustment is made to the capital allowances computation for private use of the vehicle in such circumstances).

Law: CAA 2001, s. 36

9.2 Definition of "car"

9.2.1 General rule

In most cases, it will be obvious if any given vehicle is a car, but there are some borderline circumstances where the matter is not entirely clear cut. For this reason, there is a statutory definition that applies for the purposes of the capital allowances rules. Care should be taken not to rely unthinkingly on the way a vehicle is categorised for other tax purposes; absurd though it is, slightly different definitions apply for company car purposes, for capital allowances, for Vehicle Excise Duty and for VAT. Nevertheless, many of the case law decisions relating to employment taxes are also relevant for capital allowance purposes.

According to the capital allowances definition, a "mechanically propelled road vehicle" will be treated as a car unless it falls within one of the following definitions:

- a motorcycle (see **9.2.2** below);
- a vehicle of a construction primarily suited for the conveyance of goods or burden of any description (see **9.2.3**); or
- a vehicle of a type not commonly used as a private vehicle and unsuitable for such use (see **9.2.4**).

By default, therefore, a mechanically propelled vehicle that is designed to drive on the roads will be treated as a car, even if it would not be so treated under any normal definition. See **9.2.2** (quadbikes) and **9.2.5** (motor homes) for examples of vehicles that are treated as cars for these tax purposes.

Law: CAA 2001, s. 268A
Guidance: CA 23510

9.2.2   Motorcycles

Motorcycles are excluded from the capital allowances definition of "cars". Motorcycles are therefore not affected by the special capital allowances regime applying for cars.

In practice, a key effect of this is that annual investment allowances may be given for motorcycles.

A motorcycle is defined as "a mechanically propelled vehicle, not being an invalid carriage, with less than four wheels and the weight of which unladen does not exceed 410 kilograms".

Quadbikes

As quadbikes have four wheels, they are not motorcycles. It follows that if they are road vehicles they will be treated as cars for capital allowances purposes (unless it can be argued that they are exempt on one of the other statutory grounds).

Law: *Road Traffic Act* 1988, s. 185(1); CAA 2001, s. 268A(1)(a)
Guidance: CA 23510

9.2.3   Conveyance of goods or burden

A vehicle will not be treated as a car for capital allowances purposes if it is "of a construction primarily suited for the conveyance of goods or burden of any description" (referred to in other statutory contexts as a "goods vehicle"[1]).

The first point to note is that the definition is concerned with the *construction* of the vehicle, and not with the way it is used. HMRC guidance in relation to company cars from an employment tax perspective is directly relevant here.

People are not "goods or burden" (*Bourne v Norwich Crematorium*) so a vehicle that is constructed to carry people is not (by virtue of this rule, at least) exempt from being treated as a car.

---

[1] The term "goods vehicle" is not used in this section of the capital allowances legislation, but exactly the same wording *is* used to define a goods vehicle elsewhere in the plant and machinery rules (s. 45DA re first-year allowances for zero-emission vehicles). Identical wording in relation to a "goods vehicle" is also used in the employment tax legislation (ITEPA 2003, s. 115(2)).

HMRC take the view that "the fact that the manufacturer or dealer describes the vehicle as a 'commercial vehicle' is not conclusive". Nevertheless, such a description is likely to be a relevant factor as the manufacturer knows more about the construction than anyone else.

HMRC interpret the word "primarily" in a literal way, arguing that "[if] neither purpose predominates with regard to the construction of the vehicle, the vehicle is not primarily suited for either purpose and this means that it does not escape from being a car".

HMRC also take the view that a vehicle with side windows behind the driver and front passenger doors will normally be treated as a car. Similarly, the HMRC view is that the vehicle will usually be a car if it is fitted (or is capable of being fitted) with additional seating behind the driver's row of seats. See **9.2.9**, however, for the treatment of double cab pick-ups.

In most cases, a commonsense approach will determine the correct status of the car, and it is difficult to fault the following HMRC comments:

> "Most estate cars (or indeed cars with some sort of boot) are suited to the dual purpose of carrying passengers and some cargo or luggage. But it is clear that what they are primarily suited for is the conveyance of passengers.
>
> In contrast, a standard transit van is also capable of carrying a driver plus a passenger (occasionally two) as well as cargo, but it is clear that what it is primarily suited for is the conveyance of goods or burden.
>
> A vehicle will not automatically satisfy this test simply because it has only one row of seats. There are certain sports cars and leisure vehicles that can only seat a driver and one passenger, but that are quite clearly not primarily suited for carrying goods or burden."

The dividing line between cars and vans was explored in some depth in the Upper Tribunal *Coca-Cola* case (and in the earlier hearings in that case). The Upper Tribunal held that the FTT had drawn an incorrect conclusion from the presence of a seat for the driver, but had nevertheless been entitled overall to reach its decision. The earlier tribunal had concluded that "the accommodation of seating for passengers in the front section pointed against the construction of the [vehicles in question] being primarily suitable for the carriage of goods or burden". The FTT had also been entitled to conclude that the vehicles had no overall "primary suitability", with the result that they were not to be treated as goods vehicles.

Law: ITEPA 2003, s. 115(2)

Cases: *Bourne (HMIT) v Norwich Crematorium Ltd* (1964) 44 TC 164; *Payne, Garbett and Coca-Cola European Partners Great Britain Ltd v HMRC* [2017] UKFTT 655 (TC); *HMRC v Payne, Garbett and Coca-Cola European Partners Great Britain Ltd* [2019] UKUT 90 (TCC)

Guidance: EIM 23110, 23120

Modifications to the vehicle

It is necessary to consider the nature of the vehicle's construction at the time the vehicle is acquired, rather than at the point when the vehicle was originally made. This is not identical to the considerations that arise for employment tax purposes, but the HMRC guidance from that context may still be relevant in determining whether the vehicle acquired is a car or something else.

HMRC will wish to establish whether any modifications are "sufficiently permanent and substantial in scale to have altered the original manufactured construction of the vehicle". In this respect, the HMRC view is that:

- changes such as sliding out the rear seats, but leaving the seat mountings and seat belt fixtures in place, or placing temporary coverings over the rear side windows do not change the original construction of the vehicle; but

- changes such as permanent removal of the rear seats and all associated fittings, possibly accompanied by the welding in of a new load base, and the replacement of glass rear side windows by permanently welded-in fibreglass or metal panels, may well change the original construction of the vehicle.

For this reason, the description on the original Vehicle Excise Duty registration document is not conclusive as the vehicle may since have been modified. The point was touched on in the case of *Jones v HMRC*, where a Land Rover Discovery that had been altered was held to be a car rather than a goods vehicle. Unfortunately the reasoning in that case was not as clear and coherent as it might have been, but it appears that the tribunal simply felt that the modifications did not fundamentally alter the structure of the car.

HMRC do not accept that painting a vehicle in a particular way (e.g. to include an advertisement for the employer's products) would change the type of vehicle.

Case: *Jones v HMRC* [2012] UKFTT 265 (TC)
Guidance: EIM 23110, 23115, 23125

9.2.4   Not suitable for use as a private vehicle

A vehicle is not treated as a car for capital allowances purposes if it is:

- of a type not commonly used as a private vehicle; *and*
- unsuitable to be so used.

Both conditions must be met if the vehicle is to avoid being treated as a car for these purposes. So, for example, a particular vehicle may be of a type rarely used for private purposes but actually be perfectly suitable for such use. Such a vehicle meets the first test but fails the second. It follows that it will be treated as a car unless it falls into one of the other categories of exempted vehicles listed at **9.2.2**.

Type not commonly used as a private vehicle

Certain vehicles are clearly of a type not commonly used as a private vehicle. Some emergency vehicles (for example ambulances or fire engines) and large buses are cases where this first condition is clearly met.

HMRC accept, based on case law precedents, that modifying a vehicle may establish a different "type". Specifically, HMRC accept that a new type of vehicle may be created by the addition of fixed, flashing blue lights, of dual controls, or of a rooftop sign or loud speaker.

In the *Auto School of Motoring* case, the judge commented as follows:

> "It seems to me that a car which has dual control equipment installed is in an important respect different from a car which has not got dual control equipment. I do not think that it is sensible to regard such cars as belonging to the same type of vehicle. The fact that by a certain amount of work a car with dual controls could be reconverted to a car of the ordinary conventional type by removing the dual control equipment seems to me ... to be neither here nor there."

If such modifications have taken place, it is still necessary to consider whether the modified vehicle is of a type not commonly used as a private vehicle. In respect of a dual control car, the judge went on to give a clear indication that a dual control car "was a kind of vehicle not commonly used as a private vehicle".

HMRC accept that fire engines, agricultural tractors, buses, back-hoe loaders and diggers are all of a type not commonly used as a private vehicle.

It might be argued that a rare car is, by virtue precisely of its rarity, "of a type not commonly used as a private vehicle". HMRC specifically reject this view:

> "A vehicle that in itself is not of a common model because there are not very many of them, for example a luxurious sports car, is still of a type of vehicle that is commonly used as a private vehicle and suitable for that use. The type in that instance is a sports saloon."

A luxurious sports car would, in any case, be suitable for private use and would therefore fall at that second hurdle (see below).

Law: ITEPA 2003, s. 115(1)(d)
Cases: *Bourne (HMIT) v Auto School of Motoring (Norwich) Ltd* (1964) 42 TC 217; *Gurney (HMIT) v Richards* [1989] BTC 326
Guidance: EIM 23125, 23130

Unsuitable for private use

If it has been shown that the vehicle is of a type not commonly used as a private vehicle, it will also be necessary to demonstrate that it is unsuitable for such private use. According to HMRC:

> "The words unsuitable for use as a private vehicle should be taken to mean unsuitable for use by members of the public generally. So, with regard to any vehicle under consideration, the key question to pose is; what are the features of this vehicle that make it unsuitable to be used privately?
>
> One example of a feature that will make a vehicle unsuitable to be used privately is the fact that it is of a type that ordinary members of the public are legally barred from driving."

For example, HMRC specifically accept that:

> "Where a vehicle that would otherwise be treated as a car ... is an emergency vehicle because it has blue flashing lights and/or

audible warning devices, you can accept that it is of a type not commonly used as a private vehicle and unsuitable to be so used."

In the *Auto School of Motoring* case, the judge commented that:

"I should be very slow to say that a car which had got dual control equipment at the feet of what would normally be a passenger sitting in the nearside seat was a type of car which was suitable to be used as a private vehicle."

In that case, then, both parts of the test were met. Similarly, in *Gurney v Richards*, the judge gave the view that:

"a vehicle which is altered so that, without being reconverted, it cannot be used lawfully on a road by a member of the public ... cannot be said to be of a type commonly used as a private vehicle, nor in my judgment can it be described as suitable for such use."

As a general principle, however, HMRC take the view that "the fact that a car has been modified in some way will not make it either illegal or unsuitable for use as a private vehicle". More specifically, the HMRC guidance goes on to say that "the fact that a car is usually kept loaded with goods or equipment does not mean that it is unsuitable for use as a private vehicle if all that is necessary to make it suitable is to unload the items in question".

The mere painting of a car will not change its type or make it unsuitable for private use.

Generally, HMRC argue that:

"Irrespective of their use in practice, there is nothing that renders most vehicles inherently unsuitable for private use. Indeed the marketing of many whose status might otherwise be uncertain is aimed at illustrating how well fitted they are for private use."

Law: ITEPA 2003, s. 115(1)(d)

Cases: *Bourne (HMIT) v Auto School of Motoring (Norwich) Ltd* (1964) 42 TC 217; *Gurney (HMIT) v Richards* [1989] BTC 326

Guidance: EIM 23135, 23140

9.2.5 Motor homes

The question of whether a "motor home" is a car for tax purposes has been tested in the courts (*Morris v R & C Commrs*). The case was concerned with the question of whether the vehicle was a company car for employment tax purposes, but the principles are equally valid in this capital allowances context.

Mr Morris was a pharmacist and worked for his own company, County Pharmacy Ltd. The company provided the director with a motor home that was used as a mobile office. The vehicle was also used to buy stock and was available to the director for his private use for leisure purposes.

The case considered both the construction of the vehicle and the question of whether it was commonly used as a private vehicle and suitable for such use. The court ruled that such a vehicle was correctly treated as a car for tax purposes.

The motor home was not of a construction primarily suited for the conveyance of things rather than people; it was not, in fact, well suited for carrying goods and the judge commented that that exemption could not possibly apply to a motor home. The fact that it was in fact used to buy and carry stock did not mean that the vehicle was primarily suited for the conveyance of goods or burden.

The court therefore had to consider whether the motor home was of a type commonly used as a private vehicle and suitable to be so used. The "obvious problem" here was that motor homes are sold mainly for the recreational market and are both commonly used as private vehicles and suitable for such use.

The vehicle was patently not a motorcycle (or, in the employment tax context, an invalid carriage), so it fell clearly within the statutory definition of "car" and was to be taxed accordingly.

Law: ITEPA 2003, s. 115
Case: *Morris v R & C Commrs* [2006] BTC 861
Guidance: EIM 23155

9.2.6   Taxis

Most taxis are treated in the same way as any other cars, with the result that annual investment allowances are denied for most taxis.

HMRC guidance is that "Hackney carriages (traditional 'London black cab' type vehicles)" should not be treated as cars for capital allowances purposes (so AIAs are available for such vehicles). No clues are given as to why this should be the case. In statutory terms, however, there are only certain options. Such vehicles are clearly not motorcycles, and it is surely impossible to argue that hackney cabs are primarily suited for carrying goods rather than people. The special treatment must therefore be on the basis that a London cab is "not commonly used as a private vehicle *and* unsuitable for such use" (emphasis added – both halves of the test must be met).

It is a question of fact whether the London cab, or indeed any other vehicle, can be said to have met these tests. Factors that may have influenced the HMRC treatment of London cabs would include the lack of a front seat, the unusual arrangement of the passenger seats, and the very small boot space.

Most taxis will clearly be cars for capital allowances purposes, and only WDAs will be due (at the standard or "special" rate as appropriate, depending on emission levels).

Law: CAA 2001, s. 38B, 268A
Guidance: CA 23510

9.2.7   Invalid carriages

An invalid carriage does not fall within any of the exemptions at **9.2.1** above, and is thus treated as a car for capital allowances purposes (but not for the purposes of calculating a benefit in kind, where an additional exemption applies).

Law: *Road Traffic Act* 1988, s. 185(1); CAA 2001, s. 268A

9.2.8   Off-road and multi-purpose vehicles

HMRC comment on these types of vehicle as follows:

> "Luxury off road vehicles, four wheel drive recreational vehicles and multi-purpose vehicles will usually count as cars."

Such vehicles are not normally designed or constructed primarily for carrying goods or burden, and they are not unsuitable for private use. HMRC do acknowledge, however, that there are certain commercial variants that may not be properly classified as cars. The test is one of construction rather than use.

Guidance: EIM 23145

9.2.9   Double cab pick-ups

According to HMRC, these vehicles normally have the following features:

- a front passenger cab that contains a second row of seats and is capable of seating about four passengers, plus the driver;

- four doors capable of being opened independently, whether the rear doors are hinged at the front or the rear (two door versions are normally accepted as vans); and
- an uncovered pick-up area behind the passenger cab.

These are considered by HMRC to be suitable for private use (though that view might possibly be challenged before a tax tribunal). Such a vehicle would on that basis be classified as a car unless it can be shown that it is designed primarily for carrying goods or burden.

HMRC do acknowledge that some such vehicles, but not all, are vans rather than cars. As such, HMRC comment that:

> "It is not possible on first principles to come up with a single categorisation for all double cab pick-ups. Nor is it possible to give a blanket ruling on any particular makes, as the standard vehicle may have been adapted in the factory, by the dealer, or once acquired. So each case will depend on the facts and the exact specification ... ."

Luxury fittings or accessories, such as leather seats or digital radio, are likely to be unhelpful if seeking to argue that the vehicle is designed primarily for the conveyance of goods or burden.

On the other hand, HMRC do accept that a double cab pick-up with a payload of one tonne or more should not be treated as a car.

Guidance: CA 23510

9.2.10   *Land Rover Defender Station Wagons*

The HMRC view is that these are cars for the purposes of applying the company car tax rules. If so, they would also be treated as cars for capital allowance purposes.

Guidance: EIM 23155

9.2.11   *Dual control cars*

HMRC accept that dual control cars used by driving schools are not cars for capital allowances purposes.

Guidance: CA 23510

9.2.12 Emergency vehicles

Emergency vehicles are not treated as cars for capital allowance purposes.

Guidance: CA 23510

9.2.13 Funeral businesses

The definition of "car" can be particularly pertinent for a funeral business. A hearse and a limousine can each cost in the region of £100,000, and the denial of annual investment allowances for cars is a serious consideration for expenditure of that magnitude.

It seems clear that the hearse is outside the definition of "car". It is not of a type commonly used as a private vehicle and it is unsuitable for such use. So there would appear to be no problem.

The limousine is closer to the line. It seems reasonably clear that it is not of a type commonly used as a private vehicle, but is it unsuitable for such use? It would be hoped that HMRC would take a reasonable line in the context of a funeral business (assuming the proprietors of the business do not in fact use the vehicle for any private purposes), but it might be worth a tribunal hearing if not.

The argument that a funeral limousine is unsuitable for private use would turn mainly on cost and practicality. The fuel consumption is obviously very poor, though that in itself is not a particularly strong argument as the same could be said of many vehicles that are undoubtedly used privately. A weightier argument is perhaps that the vehicle would simply be too long for many day-to-day purposes; parking at Tesco or on the road would be very impractical, and the vehicle would be difficult to manoeuvre on many narrower streets. On the other hand, HMRC might take the line that a very wealthy individual might use a limousine for private purposes and engage a chauffeur, so that parking as such is not an issue.

9.3 Calculation of allowances – overview

9.3.1 Introduction

The rate at which capital allowances are given for cars is now determined principally by the level of emissions.

Expenditure on cars is normally allocated either to the main plant and machinery pool or to the special rate pool, depending on the level of emissions. In broad terms, cars with lower emissions are called "main rate" cars and attract standard allowances, while cars with higher emissions are treated as "special rate expenditure" and thus attract a slower rate of tax relief.

Where there is private use of a car by a business proprietor, the cars are allocated to individual ("single asset") pools, so that the necessary adjustments may be made.

See **9.5** regarding AIAs and **9.6** re first-year allowances.

9.3.2   *Main rate cars*

A "main rate car" is allocated to the main pool of plant and machinery (and therefore attracts allowances at the standard rate). Any other car normally goes to the special rate pool, but subject to a complication where there is a private use.

The following vehicles are currently (from April 2021) classified as main rate cars:

- cars with an official CO_2 figure that does not exceed 50g/km;
- any car first registered before March 2001; and
- cars that are electrically-propelled.

The above figure of 50g/km applies for expenditure incurred on or after 1 April 2021 (corporation tax) or 6 April 2021 (income tax). The great majority of non-electric cars will now attract allowances at just 6% per year. This is obviously a deliberate policy, whereby tax relief lags way behind commercial depreciation, designed to push company fleet policies towards greener cars.

A figure of 110g/km applied for expenditure incurred from April 2018 to 31 March or 5 April 2021. For the five years before that date, the equivalent figure was 130g/km, and it was 160g/km before April 2013.

See **5.4.6** for a discussion of first-year allowances for cars.

Electrically propelled

For these purposes, a car is electrically propelled if it is propelled *solely* by electrical power. That power must be derived from a source external to the vehicle or from an electrical storage battery that is not connected to any power source when the car is moving.

Anti-avoidance

Anti-avoidance legislation is in place to prevent the exploitation of loopholes that would allow a business to re-allocate cars to the main rate pool. These only apply where the qualifying activity has included making cars available to others and where that activity has been permanently discontinued.

Law: CAA 2001, s. 104AA, 268B; SI 2021/120

9.3.3 Cars with higher emissions

Any car that is not a main rate car, as defined above, is normally allocated to the special rate pool and attracts allowances at a slower rate: see **9.4.3** below.

Law: CAA 2001, s. 104A(1)(e)

9.4 Writing-down allowances

9.4.1 Overview

In practice, allowances for cars are nearly always given by means of WDAs. As for other assets, these WDAs will give some initial tax relief in the year in which the car is bought, with ever-reducing levels of relief in subsequent years. This is achieved through the system of "pooling" (see **5.3.2**) whereby expenditure on cars is merged with other expenditure.

Example

A company draws accounts up to 31 December each year. At 1 January, the value of its main capital allowances pool is £80,000. In the year it buys a company car for one of its directors at a cost of £26,000 and some computers for £14,000. It also sells some old office furniture for £2,000. Assume that the emissions figure of the car is 107g/km (the significance of which is explained at **9.3.2** above).

The expenditure will all be merged into one main "pool" for the purposes of calculating capital allowances. (In practice, the company may be able to claim AIAs on the cost of the computers, but assume for present purposes that those have been allocated to another group company.)

The total value in the pool will therefore be calculated as £118,000: the amount brought forward, plus the expenditure in the year, less the disposal proceeds. Assuming that allowances for the year are given at 18%, the value of the WDAs will be £21,240. The remaining value of £96,760 will be carried forward to the following year.

There is no question of restricting allowances for private use of a vehicle by a director or employee (but a restriction would apply to the capital allowances if a car or other asset was used privately by a sole trader or by a partner in a partnership).

As the expenditure is pooled with other assets, the sale of a car will not normally produce any balancing allowance or charge; instead, the proceeds will simply reduce the value in the ongoing pool. The practical effect of this is often to delay the timing of tax relief, as cars generally depreciate at a faster rate than the rate of WDAs (especially those cars with higher emissions) (but see **9.4.2** below where there is private use).

9.4.2   Main rate cars

As noted above, a main rate car is allocated to the main pool for the purposes of calculating WDAs. Currently, therefore, such cars will attract allowances at 18%.

Private use

A main rate car is, however, allocated instead to a separate "single asset" pool if there is any private use. (Private use does not for these purposes include use by a director or employee of a company.)

WDAs are then calculated using the same rate that would otherwise apply (i.e. depending on the level of emissions) and the resulting allowances are then restricted to reflect the level of private use.

Example

Pete is a sole trader who buys a car for £20,000. It has low emissions and is therefore a main rate car. One quarter of the use is for private purposes.

The car must be kept out of the main pool. Assuming a WDA rate of 18%, Pete's allowances for Year 1 will be £2,700 (£20,000 x 18% gives £3,600, from which one quarter is deducted). The amount carried forward to the next year is, however, calculated by subtracting the full £3,600 from the cost, rather than the amount as amended for private use. So the figure carried forward is £16,400.

Using the same principles, allowances for Year 2 will be £2,214, and the amount carried forward will then be £13,448.

Although the private use restriction permanently reduces the allowances that are given, the effect can be partially countered by an advantage in terms of timing of relief. This is because an asset with private use is dealt with in its own single-asset pool and the disposal will therefore trigger a balancing adjustment. For cars, that adjustment will normally be a balancing allowance (as the tax relief given by way of capital allowances tends to lag behind the real depreciation rate of the car).

Law: CAA 2001, s. 65(2), 104A

9.4.3   Other cars

If a car is not a main rate car, because its emissions are too high to qualify as such, it will instead be allocated to the special rate pool (see, generally, **Chapter 17**), where it will attract allowances at just 6% (formerly 8%).

If the car is used privately, however, the vehicle will once more be allocated instead to a single-asset pool, where an appropriate adjustment for private use must be made after calculating the 6% allowance. The same principles apply as illustrated at **9.4.2** above.

Law: CAA 2001, s. 104A(1)(e)
Guidance: CA 23535

9.4.4   Anti-avoidance

The rate of allowances for most cars lags behind the true commercial rate of depreciation. In the case of special rate cars, attracting allowances at just 6% (formerly 8%) per year, this can represent a significant cash flow disadvantage: a car that loses half of its value in two to three years will have to wait until the ninth year of ownership to gain tax relief for half of the cost if relying on writing-down allowances.

Groups of companies

To counteract attempts to circumvent these disadvantages, various anti-avoidance measures are in place. The intention of one such rule was explained in the *Explanatory Notes* to the Finance Bill of 2009 as follows:

> " ... to prevent the artificial generation of balancing allowances by groups of companies who engineer the cessation of a group company's business of providing cars, only for another company in the group to continue a similar activity."

The rule operates only where the qualifying activity carried on by a company has been permanently discontinued and where that activity was (or included) the making available of cars to other persons. Where the conditions are met, restrictions to balancing allowances and WDAs may apply. There is an extended HMRC example at CA 23560 to illustrate this.

Law: CAA 2001, s. 104F

Connected parties

Where allowances are restricted under s. 217 or s. 218 (connected party transactions: see **22.3.2**), the legislation also restricts the artificial creation of balancing allowances for cars that have been allocated to single-asset pools. This is achieved by using market value (or cost, if lower) as the disposal value, and the higher value is then used as the buyer's purchase cost. HMRC have illustrated this as follows with what is now a rather old example, but still in place in 2018 (and note that the rate of WDA would from April 2019 be just 6% rather than 10%):

HMRC example

A buys a car for £100,000 in 2017. It produces high CO_2 emissions and therefore qualifies for WDAs at the special rate only. It is used for non-business purposes 50% of the time. The expenditure is allocated to a single asset pool and WDAs are claimed at the special rate, restricted for the private use element. A sells the car to his son B in 2018 for £5,000, although the market value of the car is £95,000 on that date. A's disposal value is £95,000 rather than £5,000 and if B is able to claim capital allowances, his qualifying expenditure is also £95,000.

Law: CAA 2001, s. 208A
Guidance: CA 23555

9.4.5   Other vehicles

If a vehicle is not treated as a car for capital allowances purposes, allowances will be calculated as they are for other assets. AIAs will be due, subject to the usual conditions, and WDAs will be given at the standard rate in the main pool.

9.4.6   Fixed rate deduction

As an alternative to claiming capital allowances, some unincorporated businesses have the option of claiming mileage allowances. This is obligatory for employees (see **9.1.3**) and is an option for the self-employed and for unincorporated property businesses.

As a general principle, no mileage allowances may be claimed if the car has already been subject to a capital allowances claim. Once mileage allowances are claimed, any residual capital allowances value is written off. The effect of this was expressed as follows in the *Explanatory Notes*:

> "This prevents unrelieved capital expenditure on a particular vehicle, being carried forward for capital allowances purposes for that property business, when mileage rates have been used for that vehicle for that same property business."

Law: CAA 2001, s. 59; ITTOIA 2005, s 94E

9.5   Annual investment allowances

No AIAs are available for cars.

This lends importance to the technical definition of "car" – as discussed in detail at **9.2** above. In particular, it should be borne in mind that motorcycles and black London taxis are accepted as falling outside the definition of "car" and that AIAs are therefore available for these vehicles. AIAs are also given for vans.

Example

A business spends £20,000 to buy a car (which has emissions of 140g/km) and £12,000 to buy a motorcycle. Both are used by employees for both work and private purposes. The business incurs no other capital expenditure in the year.

Full tax relief may be claimed in the year for the motorcycle by way of an AIA of £12,000. The £20,000 will be joined to the special rate pool of expenditure and allowances will be calculated accordingly. No restriction is made for the private use.

Law: CAA 2001, s. 38B, 268A

9.6   First-year allowances

As a general principle, no first-year allowances (FYAs) are available for cars. This is subject to exceptions, however.

FYAs are available for new (unused) cars if the vehicle "is electrically propelled" or "has low CO_2 emissions". The rules are discussed in detail at **5.4.6** above. These FYAs are not available if the car is bought for leasing.

FYAs are also available for zero-emission goods vehicles. The rules are explained at **5.4.7** above.

Law: CAA 2001, s. 45D, 45DA, 46(2), 268A

9.7   Very expensive cars

The HMRC view is that very expensive cars may still be subject to a restriction of capital allowances if "there is a blatant incongruity between the asset provided for the director or employee and the commercial requirements of the business". This is based on the principles brought out in the *Northiam Farms* case.

The author's opinion, however, is that the principles of that case no longer apply. The case was heard before the introduction of the rules for benefits in kind, at a time when companies were subject to income tax. Any restriction would more recently have been under CAA 2001, s. 77, but this could only apply where "the car is used partly for purposes other than those of the qualifying activity".

HMRC now accept that:

> "expenditure incurred by an employer in providing an asset for a director's or employee's private use as part of a remuneration package, thus giving rise to liability under ITEPA, is incurred wholly and exclusively for the purposes of the qualifying activity".

The benefits in kind legislation now, of course, imposes a tax charge on the employee that is already related to the value of the car. There are also rules restricting capital allowances where there is private use of an asset. There seems no more reason to disallow the car costs in such circumstances than to disallow remuneration paid to a director. Any HMRC approach on these lines should be robustly challenged, asking on what statutory authority it is made.

Case: *G H Chambers (Northiam Farms) Ltd v Watmough* (1956) 36 TC 711
Guidance: CA 27100

9.8   Short-life assets

Cars can never be treated as a short-life asset, but there is no reason in principle why a van should not be so treated (unless it is used partly for purposes other than those of the qualifying activity).

It will normally be beneficial to claim short-life asset treatment for a van if it is likely to be sold within approximately eight years for less than its capital allowances written-down value. See, generally, **Chapter 15.**

Law: CAA 2001, s. 84

9.9   Car hire

The treatment of car hire costs is not strictly a capital allowances issue. In broad terms, however, there is a fixed 15% disallowance of car hire costs if the vehicle's emissions exceed a given threshold. That threshold reduces from 110g/km to just 50g/km from April 2021.

The 15% restriction is not applied to maintenance or similar costs, if these are identified separately in the rental agreement.

Law: CAA 2001, s. 104AA; ITTOIA 2005, s. 48*ff*; FA 2013, s. 68; SI 2021/120

10. Fixtures in property – principles and definitions

10.1 Introduction

10.1.1 Overview

The topic of fixtures in property is one of the more difficult areas of capital allowance law, but it also offers some of the most neglected tax planning opportunities. Recent changes to the relevant legislation make this an increasingly dangerous area to ignore.

The point at issue is the claiming of plant and machinery allowances for parts of the cost of a property, whether newly built, extended or acquired from a third party.

A set of accounts will typically divide fixed assets into categories such as goodwill, freehold or leasehold property, and either "plant and equipment" or "fixtures and fittings". This division sets up a distinction between the property on the one hand and the fixtures on the other. For capital allowances purposes, this distinction has to be broken down, as the fixtures rules relate specifically to assets (such as lighting or central heating) that qualify for plant and machinery allowances despite being part of the property: see the definition at **10.2** below.

Important changes were introduced to the rules for claiming allowances for fixtures, especially in the context of property that is being bought and sold. These changes were in FA 2012 and took effect, in principle, from April 2012, but transitional rules meant that the main effects of the changes were not felt until April 2014.

This chapter deals with the underlying statutory principles, including the tax definition of "fixture". **Chapter 11** looks at fixtures claims for new capital expenditure (newly built property, extensions and capitalised renovation costs). Allowances for the property buyer are covered at **Chapter 12** while the seller's perspective is given at **Chapter 13**. Finally, **Chapter 14** contains a number of worked examples showing how the fixtures rules operate in practice across a number of different scenarios.

10.1.2 Cash flow

One objection that is made against a capital allowances claim is that the claim may be no more than a cash flow exercise. This is a complex issue, and the permutations have changed as a result of the rules introduced in

FA 2012. However, there are several reasons of principle why claims for allowances should not be neglected.

First, a cash flow advantage is worth having: almost any business would take the view that a tax saving now, offset by an equivalent tax cost in five years from now, is likely to be beneficial. This is particularly true if the tax saving comes at a time of high expenditure (when a property is bought) and the tax cost comes at a time when the business has received additional funds (as the property has been sold).

Second, the vendor has an important say in the disposal value to be brought into account, so it is impossible to predict that there will be a complete re-capture of allowances given (or, indeed, any re-capture at all). In reality, it is rarely the case that a well advised seller will give up the whole value of allowances.

The third reason is now the most important of all. Any purchaser of a property will be denied allowances for the fixtures unless the vendor has first captured the value of all those fixtures (the so-called "pooling requirement"). A vendor who has not addressed the issue will therefore often be forced to do so at the time of sale: the worst possible moment, when under pressure to complete the sale. Not only will such a vendor have lost out on the advantages of an early claim, but the resulting delays will put him or her at a negotiating disadvantage and can in some cases even jeopardise the whole sale process.

10.2 Definition of "fixture"

10.2.1 The meaning of "fixture"

The term "fixture" is defined to mean "plant or machinery that is so installed or otherwise fixed in or to a building or other description of land as to become, in law, part of that building or other land". The legislation adds, though the addition is in practice superfluous, that the term includes "any boiler or water-filled radiator installed in a building as part of a space or water heating system".

Nearly every property contains substantial numbers of fixtures, covering everything from boilers and radiators, to electrical and water systems, to toilets and basins, and lifts.

HMRC guidance explains that the term "fixture" has the same meaning for the capital allowances fixtures legislation as it does for property law. The guidance then continues as follows:

"Property law distinguishes between chattels and fixtures. A chattel is an asset which is tangible and moveable. A chattel may become a fixture if it is fixed to a building or land. For example, before it is installed in a building as part of a central heating system, a central heating radiator is a chattel. Once installed, it becomes a fixture.

The courts have developed two tests for determining whether an asset is a fixture or a chattel:

- the method and degree of annexation,
- the object and purpose of annexation.

The first test is not conclusive. Some degree of physical affixation is required before a chattel becomes a fixture. If the asset cannot be removed without serious damage to, or destruction of, the building or land, that is strong evidence that it is a fixture. But it is neither a necessary nor a sufficient condition.

The second test is now accorded greater significance by the courts than the first. The courts look at the purpose and intention of the asset and its affixation. If, when viewed objectively, it is intended to be permanent and effect a lasting improvement to the property, the asset is a fixture. If the attachment is temporary and is no more than is necessary for the asset to be used and enjoyed, the asset remains a chattel.

Where a property is leased, property law distinguishes between tenant's fixtures and landlord's fixtures. A tenant's fixture is one installed by the tenant which may be removed by the tenant during or at the end of the lease. For example shop fittings are frequently installed on this basis. This distinction is not relevant for the fixtures legislation. The rules on fixtures apply to both tenant's and landlord's fixtures."

In the *Business Income Manual*, HMRC comment as follows:

"If the object is only temporarily attached to a building, such as a fridge freezer plugged into a wall socket in a kitchen, and the attachment is no more than is necessary for the object to be used and enjoyed, then it is not a fixture and remains a separate asset."

In reality, there is a substantial volume of case law (property law rather than tax law) on the distinction. The 1943 decision in *Bingham* held that an object resting on land merely due to its own weight and to gravity was a chattel rather than a fixture (even if the item was heavy). However, as

HMRC state above, there is a more enduring principle that the *purpose* of the annexation must be considered rather than merely its physical nature. In *Hodgson*, therefore, a distinction was made between blocks of stone piled up (without mortar or cement) to form a dry stone wall (fixtures), and the same stones piled up for convenience in a builder's yard (chattels).

Further references may easily be found. One helpful approach may be to search online for the expression *Quicquid plantatur solo, solo cedit*, Latin for "whatever is affixed to the land [or, literally, soil] belongs to the land".

Law: CAA 2001, s. 173(1)

Cases: *Hulme v Bingham* (1943) KB 152; *Holland v Hodgson* (1872) LR 7 CP 328

Guidance: BIM 46910; CA 26025

10.2.2   Fixture or chattel?

HMRC's SDLT manual gives some examples of items that will normally be treated as fixtures rather than as moveable chattels:

- fitted kitchen units, cupboards and sinks;
- agas and wall mounted ovens;
- fitted bathroom sanitary ware;
- central heating systems;
- intruder alarm systems.

By contrast, the following items will, according to that guidance, "normally be regarded as chattels":

- carpets (fitted or otherwise);
- curtains and blinds;
- free standing furniture;
- kitchen white goods;
- electric and gas fires (provided that they can be removed by disconnection from the power supply without causing damage to the property);
- light shades and fittings (unless recessed).

The treatment of fitted carpets is arguably not clear cut. There is certainly a possible argument that carpet tiles that are glued in place should be treated as fixtures. The point is considered in some depth in the *Botham* case.

SDLT is included as part of the purchase price when buying fixtures, and would be included when making an apportionment using the agreed formula (see **12.8.2**).

Case: *Botham v TSB plc* (1996) 7P&CRD1
Guidance: SDLTM 04010

10.3   Other definitions

10.3.1   *"Interest in land"*

In most cases, a person can only claim allowances for fixtures in property if he has some underlying interest in the land. The interest will normally be either a freehold or a leasehold. More specifically, the term covers all of the following:

- the fee simple estate in the land or an agreement to acquire such an estate;
- in relation to Scotland, the interest of the owner or an agreement to acquire such an interest;
- a lease (see **10.3.2**);
- an easement or servitude or an agreement to acquire an easement or servitude; and
- a licence to occupy land (see **10.3.3**).

An interest in land may be conveyed or assigned by way of security. HMRC have given the following advice in that respect, illustrating the distinction between a legal and a beneficial interest:

> "If an interest in land is conveyed or assigned by way of security and subject to a right of redemption, then so long as the right of redemption exists the interest held by the creditor is treated as held by the person having the right of redemption. ... For example, if a freehold property is mortgaged, the freehold interest is sometimes held in law by the person who grants the mortgage. However, the interest is treated for the purposes of the fixtures legislation as being held by the person who mortgages the property."

HMRC go on to illustrate that as follows:

HMRC example

Xanadu Properties Plc owns Kane House. It needs to raise cash so it takes out a mortgage on Kane House with Barset Bank. Once Kane House is mortgaged Barset Bank might become its legal owner, but Xanadu Properties Plc is still treated as the owner of Kane House for the purposes of the fixtures legislation.

The Land Registry document in the above example might show Xanadu Properties Plc as having the title absolute, but Barset Bank might be named as the proprietor in the "charges register" section of the document.

It has been asserted that HMRC would accept that informal permission to occupy land – falling short of a lease or formal licence to occupy – would be accepted as an interest in land. The authors have not seen written evidence of this and it is obviously preferable to formalise the arrangement if possible. See also **10.3.3** below.

Law: CAA 2001, s. 175
Guidance: CA 26100

10.3.2 *"Lease"*

For the purposes of the fixtures rules, a lease is defined to mean:

- any leasehold estate in (or, in Scotland, lease of) the land, whether in the nature of a head-lease, sub-lease or under-lease; or

- any agreement to acquire such an estate or (in Scotland) lease.

This definition does not apply, however, in the context of leasing plant or machinery.

Law: CAA 2001, s. 174(4)
Guidance: CA 26100

10.3.3 *"Licence to occupy"*

HMRC have given the following guidance on the meaning of a licence to occupy in this context:

"A licence to occupy land is not an interest in land for the fixtures legislation unless it is an exclusive licence. A licence to occupy is a permission to enter and remain on land for such a purpose as enables the licensee to exert control over the land. It is this level of control that suggests that a licence to occupy must be an exclusive licence. The idea of exclusive occupancy is also supported in part by ratings law that says that there can only be one occupier of land. It follows that where a person can enter onto land for a subordinate purpose, such a licence of entry would be something less than a licence to occupy."

The 1996 case of *Decaux v Francis* showed that a right to enter property for maintenance purposes fell short of a licence to occupy land. (Note, however, that the circumstances of that case would now be covered by the rules for equipment lessors – see **10.5.3** below.)

In more general terms, there is no definitive guidance on what constitutes a licence to occupy. Take, for example, the position of a property owned jointly by a married couple and used entirely for the purposes of a trade carried on by a limited company that they control. *HM Customs & Excise Business Brief* 21/1999 suggested that a licence to occupy would normally involve the payment of consideration. On the other hand, it might be argued (quite forcefully) that if the owners actively cooperate to arrange for the company to take over full use of the property, then they are clearly granting an unwritten licence to occupy, even if no payment is made.

Energy efficiency

It is understood that the restrictions regarding energy efficiency can cause practical difficulties in this area. The author has seen a case where a pension fund was acquiring a property and wished to grant a 10-year lease to a limited company that was a connected party, so that the company could refurbish the property and modernise its electrical systems. However, the SSAS would have been committing an offence if (from 1 April 2018) it granted a new tenancy to the company while the property had an energy efficiency standard of F or G (SI 2015/962, reg. 22(a)).

So the company could not be granted a lease until it had incurred the expenditure, and it could not incur the expenditure until it was granted a lease. One proposed solution was to grant the future lessee a licence to occupy while it performed the required work. However, HMRC take the view that the licence must be exclusive if it is to amount to a qualifying interest in land, and an exclusive licence is likely to constitute a tenancy, which would amount to letting, and which would therefore infringe the energy efficiency regulations.

Counsel was asked to advise on the above scenario and proposed a solution as follows. The SSAS was recommended to grant a lease on a conditional basis, which would allow it to register a valid exemption (online, on the national PRS exemptions register). The exemption would last for six months, during which period the company could complete the necessary work.

Case: *J C Decaux v Francis* (1996) Sp C 84

Guidance: CA 26100; https://www.gov.uk/government/publications/the-private-rented-property-minimum-standard-landlord-guidance-documents

10.4   The problem of ownership

One of the key conditions for giving plant and machinery allowances is that of ownership. Section 11(4) of CAA 2001 reads as follows:

> "The general rule is that expenditure is qualifying expenditure if—
>
> (a)   it is capital expenditure on the provision of plant or machinery wholly or partly for the purposes of the qualifying activity carried on by the person incurring the expenditure, and
>
> (b)   the person incurring the expenditure owns the plant or machinery as a result of incurring it."

Most of the time, this condition poses no problems. However, particular issues arise from point (b) above in relation to fixtures in property. Suppose, for example, that a tenant with 20 years remaining on a lease installs air conditioning in the property. Legally, the building belongs to the landlord; as the air conditioning – once installed – forms part of the property, it immediately belongs to the landlord.

Without special rules, the landlord could not obtain allowances on the expenditure as he has not incurred the cost and the tenant could not claim allowances as he does not own the air conditioning system.

The point came to a head in the case of *Costain Property Investments Ltd.* The Courts considered the meaning of the terms "belong" and "belonging" and concluded that they were ordinary English words to be interpreted in an ordinary sense. If a person merely had the right to use an asset for a limited period then it could not be said that the asset belonged to him. Landlords' fixtures could therefore not be said to belong to a leaseholder:

> "he cannot remove them from the building, he cannot dispose of them except as part of the hereditament and subject to the provisions of the lease and for the term of the lease."

Although it felt compelled to reach that decision, the Court could see no reason of principle to justify the outcome:

> "I cannot, however, regard the state of the law as satisfactory. The purpose of the statutory provisions must be to encourage investment in machinery and plant. In this case very large sums were expended on such investment but, under the enactment as it stands, nobody will receive the tax allowance in respect of it. The freeholder will not, because the freeholder did not incur the expenditure and is not carrying on the trade. And the taxpayer will not because the items did not belong to the taxpayer. The Revenue are unable to suggest any policy reason why a person in the position of the taxpayer should be refused relief. It is to be hoped that the ambit of the legislation will be reconsidered."

The legislation was indeed reconsidered and new provisions relating to fixtures were introduced from 1985. Those provisions, as amended since their introduction, can now be found in CAA 2001 at Chapter 14 of Part 2.

See **10.3.1** above for an illustration of the difference between legal and beneficial ownership.

Law: CAA 2001, s. 172*ff.*

Case: *Costain Property Investments Ltd v Stokes* [1984] BTC 92

10.5   Deemed ownership

10.5.1   Introduction

To overcome the problem of ownership identified at **10.4** above, the fixtures rules create a legal pretence of ownership so that plant and machinery allowances may be given for fixtures in certain defined circumstances.

The following are identified in the legislation as potential claimants of capital allowances by virtue of the special fixtures rules:

- persons with an interest in relevant land;
- equipment lessors;
- energy service providers;
- purchasers of land giving consideration for fixtures;
- purchasers of land discharging the obligations of an equipment lessee;

- purchasers of land discharging obligations under energy services agreement;
- incoming lessees (with different rules according to whether or not the lessor is entitled to allowances).

Each of the above is considered in turn in the following paragraphs.

The rules described here are subject to special provisions if the fixtures in question are the subject of a long funding lease (see **Chapter 7**), and in certain other circumstances involving such long funding leases.

HMRC seem to have had a moment of forgetfulness about the existence of these deemed ownership provisions, as alluded to at paragraph 85 of the First-tier Tribunal judgment in *Cheshire Cavity Storage*. As stated in that judgment:

> "The appellant could only speculate on why HMRC held this view, as although the appellants were only tenants of the sites under which the cavities were created, since 1985 the law has been that in some circumstances a tenant can obtain capital allowances for expenditure on leasehold property."

Fortunately, however, HMRC did not pursue the point at the appeal, and the tribunal accepted that the ownership condition was satisfied.

Law: CAA 2001, s. 172, 172A

Case: *Cheshire Cavity Storage 1 Ltd and EDF Energy (Gas Storage Hole House) Ltd v HMRC* [2019] UKFTT 498 (TC)

10.5.2   *Persons with an interest in relevant land*

This is an important category. It treats a person as owning fixtures, for the purposes of claiming plant and machinery allowances, where:

- he incurs capital expenditure on plant or machinery, for the purposes of a qualifying activity he is carrying on;
- the plant or machinery becomes a fixture; and
- the person has an interest in the relevant land at the time the item in question becomes a fixture.

This therefore covers the classic case of a tenant who installs plant or machinery in the property owned by his landlord.

An interest in land will typically be a freehold or leasehold interest, but see **10.3.1** above for a fuller definition.

"Relevant land" is the building or other description of land of which the fixture becomes part. In relation to boilers and water-filled radiators, the relevant land is the building in which that item is installed as part of a space or water heating system.

The legislation recognises that there may be different interests in the same land and, broadly, gives the right to claim allowances to the person with the lowest interest – the tenant rather than the landlord in a simple tenancy arrangement. If landlord and tenant wish to share the cost of installing plant or machinery, the tenant will be able to claim under these rules. The landlord will be able to make a contribution and to claim allowances by virtue of the special rules for such contributions (s. 537: see **31.3.2**).

HMRC confirm that if two people with the same level of interest incur expenditure on the same fixture, they can each claim for the expenditure they incur. For example, two tenants may agree to share the cost of a new lift or a reception area desk.

Law: CAA 2001, s. 173(2), 176
Guidance: CA 26150

10.5.3   Equipment lessors

A person may buy equipment and lease it to a tenant, who installs it as a fixture in leased property. In technical terms, there is an equipment lease where:

- a person incurs capital expenditure on the provision of plant or machinery for leasing;
- an agreement is entered into for the lease of the plant or machinery, directly or indirectly from that person to another person;
- the plant or machinery becomes a fixture; and
- the agreement is not an agreement for the plant or machinery to be leased as part of the relevant land.

Without special rules, no allowances would be due to the lessor, as ownership has legally passed to the freeholder of the property. Nor would any allowances be due to the tenant or to the landlord, as they have not incurred capital expenditure.

The equipment lessor may make a joint election with the tenant to treat the lessor as owning the fixture. The election is not possible if the two parties are connected. Subject to that, the election normally takes effect from the time the lessor incurs the qualifying expenditure. However, it takes effect instead from the time the equipment lessee begins to carry on the qualifying activity, if the equipment lessor incurs the capital expenditure before that time.

Various conditions and exclusions apply. In particular, one of the following sets of conditions must be met:

Qualifying activity

- the equipment lease must be for the purposes of a qualifying activity carried on by the equipment lessee;
- the equipment lessee would have been entitled to fixtures allowances if he had incurred the expenditure directly; and
- the plant or machinery is not for use in a dwelling-house.

Right to sever

- the item in question becomes a fixture by being fixed to land that is neither a building nor part of a building;
- the equipment lessee has an interest in the land when taking possession of the plant or machinery in question;
- under the terms of the equipment lease, the equipment lessor is entitled to sever the plant or machinery, at the end of the period for which it is leased, from the land to which it is then fixed (and will then own it);
- the nature of the asset and the way it is fixed to land are such that its use on one set of premises does not, to any material extent, prevent it from being used (once severed) for the same purposes on a different set of premises;
- the equipment lease would fall to be treated, under generally accepted accounting practice, as an operating lease in the accounts of the equipment lessor; and
- the plant or machinery is not for use in a dwelling-house.

Affordable warmth programme

A third option existed for expenditure incurred by the end of 2007.

Law: CAA 2001, s. 174, 177-180
Guidance: CA 26200

282

10.5.4   Energy service providers

Overview

A provider of "energy services" may be treated as owning fixtures as a result of capital expenditure he has incurred. Without special rules, no allowances would be due to the provider as that person does not have an interest in the land.

According to HMRC guidance:

> "An energy services provider is a business that provides a range of energy management services, including the provision, operation and maintenance of plant or machinery, aimed towards reducing their client's energy bills. They are contracted by other businesses (clients) to manage their energy usage. This can take a variety of forms, from giving advice on how to reduce energy consumption, negotiating lower supply charges with energy providers, to designing, installing, operating and maintaining facilities on the client's premises to achieve energy efficiencies or savings."

This must be under a formal energy services agreement and is subject to a joint election by the provider and his client. Once more, certain restrictions and conditions apply.

Detail

The following conditions must be met if an energy services provider (abbreviated below to "the provider") is to be treated as incurring expenditure on fixtures so as to be able to claim allowances:

- there must be a formal energy services agreement (see below);
- the provider must, under the terms of that agreement, incur capital expenditure on plant or machinery;
- at the time the plant or machinery becomes a fixture, the client must have an interest in the relevant land, but the provider must have no such interest;
- the asset in question must not be provided for leasing;
- it must not be provided for use in a dwelling-house;
- the operation of the plant or machinery must be carried out "wholly or substantially" by the provider or by a person connected with him;

- the provider and the client must not be connected persons;
- the client would (normally, but see below) have been entitled to claim allowances under CAA 2001, s. 176 were it not for the election;
- the two parties must elect for these rules to apply.

The time limit for submitting the election is, for corporation tax purposes, two years from the end of the chargeable period in which the capital expenditure is incurred. For income tax purposes, the deadline is the normal self-assessment deadline for amending a return for the tax year in which the chargeable period ends (i.e. 31 January some 22 months after the end of that tax year).

An election is normally possible only if the client would have been entitled to allowances under s. 176 ("Person with interest in relevant land having fixture for purposes of qualifying activity": see **10.5.2**); the allowances for the provider are then given in lieu of the allowances that would have been due to the client. However, this requirement does not apply if the plant or machinery belongs to a class specified by Treasury order.

Definition of "energy services agreement"

An energy services agreement is defined to mean an agreement between the provider and another person "with a view to saving energy or using energy more efficiently". The agreement must cover all of the following:

- the design of plant or machinery, or one or more systems incorporating plant or machinery;
- obtaining and installing the plant or machinery;
- the operation and maintenance of the plant or machinery, and
- the amount of any payments in respect of the operation of the plant or machinery to be linked (wholly or in part) to energy savings or increases in energy efficiency resulting from the provision or operation of the plant or machinery.

Law: CAA 2001, s. 175A, 180A
Guidance: CA 23150

10.5.5   Purchasers of land with fixtures

This is the category that applies most frequently. It covers an ordinary purchase of a commercial property, where:

- plant or machinery has become a fixture;
- a person thereafter acquires an interest in the relevant land (which must exist before the purchaser acquires it, so the granting of a new lease is not covered under this section, though the assignment of an ongoing leasehold interest from one tenant to another would be);
- the amount paid by the purchaser for the interest is, or includes, a capital sum; and
- that capital sum falls to be treated as expenditure on the provision of a fixture.

Where these conditions are met, there is a disposal of the fixtures by the vendor and an acquisition by the new owner. Subject to various conditions, the new owner can then claim allowances on an amount paid for the fixtures in the property. Determining that amount can be straightforward (where an election is made) or complicated (where a valuation apportionment is needed), and the rules were subject to important changes in FA 2012.

Prior right

The new owner is not, however, entitled to claim allowances to the extent that someone else has a prior right to the allowances. A person will have a prior right if he owns the fixture immediately before the property sale, and makes a claim for capital allowances. HMRC have illustrated the point as follows:

HMRC example

Xanadu Properties Plc owns the freehold of Kane House, an office block, which it leases to its tenant, Budokan Computers. Xanadu Properties Plc installs central heating before it leases Kane House to Budokan computers and claims PMAs on the central heating. Budokan Computers installs air conditioning on which it claims PMAs. After the air conditioning has been installed in Kane House, Budokan assigns its lease to Shangri-la Software for a capital sum.

After the assignment of the lease Shangri-la Software can claim PMAs on the air conditioning but not on the central heating. Xanadu Properties Plc has the freehold interest in the relevant land (Kane House) and a prior right in relation to the central heating. The air conditioning is different. Budokan computers had a leasehold interest in the relevant land for the air conditioning when they installed it and they no longer have it after the assignment of the lease. Shangri-la Software has acquired that interest.

In other words, it is important when acquiring a tenanted property – whether from the landlord or the tenant – to be clear about which parties have a right to claim allowances on which fixtures. This will in turn determine the expenditure on which the buyer can claim allowances. In addition to the split between landlord and tenant, as illustrated in the HMRC example immediately above, it is possible that there will be integral features for which neither party has been able to make a claim.

These rules are subject to transitional provisions if the purchase of the interest in the land was before 24 July 1996 (Sch. 3, para. 34).

Law: CAA 2001, s. 181, 562
Guidance: CA 26250

10.5.6   *Purchaser of land discharging existing obligations*

A person acquiring land may take on the legal liability for an equipment lease; HMRC give the example of a lift that is leased to a trading company. If the new owner pays a capital sum to discharge the obligations under the equipment lease, the fixture is treated as belonging to the person as a consequence of that payment. Plant and machinery allowances can then be claimed accordingly.

Once more, this is subject to the question of whether another person has a prior right.

Equivalent rules apply where the new owner discharges obligations under an energy services agreement.

These rules are subject to transitional provisions if the purchase of the interest in the land was before 24 July 1996 (Sch. 3, para. 35).

Law: CAA 2001, s. 182, 182A
Guidance: CA 23150, 26300

10.5.7   *Incoming lessees – overview*

An incoming tenant (lessee) may incur capital expenditure (a lease premium) on land that contains fixtures. Where the necessary conditions are met, the tenant may be treated as the owner of the fixtures for the purposes of claiming capital allowances. The intention of the legislation is therefore to resolve the question of who is entitled to claim where two (or more) persons have an interest in the land.

Section 183 deals with the position where (broadly) the lessor is entitled to claim allowances. See **10.5.8** below.

Section 184 covers the situation where the lessor is not entitled to claim. See **10.5.9** below.

In practice, the distinction is less clear cut, as explained in the commentary that follows.

Where the transaction does not involve the granting of a new lease, but is rather the sideways assignment of an existing lease, different rules apply – see **10.5.10** below.

Finally, see **10.5.11** below for a complex worked example involving various different transactions.

Law: CAA 2001, s. 183-184
Guidance: CA 26350

10.5.8   Incoming lessees – lessor entitled to allowances

If the lessor is entitled to allowances for the chargeable period in question (or would be so entitled if liable to tax – see below) then the lessor and lessee must make a joint election (under s. 183) if the lessee is to be treated as owner of the fixtures as a result of incurring the capital expenditure.

An election under s. 183 may not be made if the lessor and lessee are connected.

The point here is that the election is made where the landlord has met the conditions for claiming allowances, but where the intention is to pass the value of the allowances to the tenant. The landlord has incurred the expenditure and in normal legal terms owns the fixtures in question (under general principles, discussed at **10.4** above), even once the tenant has paid a lease premium. However, the effect of the election under s. 183 is that the tenant is *treated as* the owner of the fixtures from the time the lease is granted. (Section 190 ensures that the landlord is treated as disposing of the fixtures at the same time (see **10.6.4**).) In this way, the right to claim allowances may be passed from landlord to tenant.

The s. 183 election may be made if:

- the lessor is in fact entitled to an allowance; or
- the lessor is not so entitled, but "would be if he were within the charge to tax".

287

So it can apply, for example, to a charity or pension fund that grants a lease to a tenant.

Experience suggests that these elections are often not considered in practice, especially where the person granting the lease is a non-taxpayer.

These rules are subject to transitional provisions if the lease was granted before 24 July 1996 (Sch. 3, para. 36).

Election practicalities

Where an election is made under s. 183, it will also be appropriate to make an election to determine the transfer value under s. 199 (see **12.7.4**). Indeed, the pooling and fixed value requirements will need to be met in most circumstances as the conditions of s. 187A(1) (discussed in detail in **Chapter 12**) will normally be met. If, however, the landlord is a non-taxpayer (typically a charity or a pension fund), the pooling and fixed value requirements may not apply if the non-taxpayer has owned the property since before April 2012 – see **12.3.5**.

The legislation does not specify the mechanics of making an election under s. 183, other than the two-year time limit. It would be good practice, though, to include the same types of details as are required by statute for an election under sections 198 and 199 (and indeed, as just noted, the s. 183 election will usually be accompanied by an election under s. 199). It is therefore recommended that the election should include the names of the parties, their tax references, details of the land that is the subject of the lease, details of the fixtures, and the date of the transaction.

The following, though having no official status, would appear to be a reasonable model for an election:

> **Election under section 183 of the Capital Allowances Act 2001**
>
> In this election:
>
> **The property** means [details]
>
> **The lessor** means [name, address, taxpayer reference]
>
> **The lessee** means [name, address, taxpayer reference]
>
> **The lease** means the lease granted by the lessor to the lessee on [date]
>
> **The lease date** means the date on which the lease was granted

The fixtures means all the fixtures (as defined at s. 173(1) of the Capital Allowances Act 2001) in the property, as summarised in the Schedule below.

This election is made on [date] between the lessor and the lessee in relation to the fixtures in the property.

We, the lessor and the lessee, hereby jointly elect under section 183 of the Capital Allowances Act 2001 that the lessee is to be treated from the lease date as the owner of the fixtures as a result of incurring capital expenditure on the lease.

Signature of lessor (with date):

Signature of lessee (with date):

[Schedule of fixtures to be added.]

Law: CAA 2001, s. 183, 199
Guidance: CA 26350

10.5.9 Incoming lessees – lessor not entitled to allowances

Section 184 needs to be considered, instead of s. 183 (above), if the lessor is not able to claim allowances. Section 184 would apply, for example, to a builder who is within the charge to tax but who is unable to claim allowances as the property is trading stock rather than a capital investment.

However, s. 184 will not apply if the inability to claim arises simply from the fact that the lessor is not within the charge to tax. So if a charity cannot claim allowances, but would have been able to claim had it been a non-charity (as any other relevant conditions are met) then s. 184 will not apply (but s. 183 will instead need to be considered, as covered at **10.5.8** above).

Where s. 184 applies, the right to claim allowances is (broadly speaking) automatically granted to the incoming lessee. As long as the lessor has not used the fixture for any qualifying activity, the lessee may be treated as owning the fixture without any election (s. 184).

This is, however, subject to the possibility that a third party may have a prior right in relation to the fixture (see **10.5.5** above).

These rules are also subject to transitional provisions if the lease was granted before 24 July 1996 (Sch. 3, para. 37).

Integral features

On the face of it, there can be an odd outcome in relation to integral features.

Suppose, for example, that a landlord grants a new lease to a tenant, charging a lease premium. There are no connected parties or other particular complications. Suppose that the landlord acquired the property before April 2008 and was therefore unable to claim for certain integral features.

Section 183 does not apply to the integral features on the grant of a lease because the lessor was not entitled to claim, per s. 183(1)(b).

If the lessor has not used the fixtures for the purposes of any qualifying activity, then ownership is treated as passing automatically to the lessee under s. 184.

But if the lessor has used the assets in question for the purposes of a qualifying activity – e.g. the property was previously let out – then the condition in s. 184(1)(c) is not met.

The technical summary would seem to be as follows:

- under general property law principles, the fixtures in question continue to belong to the lessor;
- deemed ownership does not pass to the tenant under s. 183, as the condition in s. 183(1)(b) is not met;
- deemed ownership does not pass to the tenant under s. 184, as the condition in s. 184(1)(c) is not met;
- deemed ownership does not pass to the tenant under s. 181, as the condition in s. 181(1)(b) is not met; and
- (for completeness), deemed ownership does not pass to the tenant under s. 176, as the condition in s. 176(1)(d) is not met.

So although the tenant is incurring capital expenditure on integral features that in principle qualify for allowances, he or she is not entitled to claim for the cost of those items. It would appear that the first claim will only be possible when the freehold comes to be sold, and it is possible that the items in question will by then have been stripped out such that no claim can be made.

Law: CAA 2001, s. 183-184
Guidance: CA 26350

10.5.10 Assignment of an existing lease

Different issues will arise where an existing lease is assigned by an outgoing tenant to a new one. In the simplest scenario, this is therefore where the position changes from Landlord with Tenant 1, to Landlord with Tenant 2 (i.e. because Tenant 1 has gone and has assigned its leasehold interest to Tenant 2).

This scenario does not come within either s. 183 or s. 184, because both of those sections only apply where a person "grants a lease" (i.e. a new lease).

Example 1

A Ltd, a property investor who is carrying on a qualifying activity, acquired the freehold interest in a new property in 2006, paying £500,000. A Ltd granted a 99-year lease to B Ltd in 2007 for £480,000, but no election under s. 183 was signed and it is now too late for such an election. A Ltd is therefore still treated as the owner of the fixtures in the property.

B Ltd assigns the lease to C Ltd some years later for £520,000. All the parties are unconnected.

C Ltd has incurred capital expenditure of £520,000 and wishes to claim capital allowances.

A Ltd and C Ltd cannot sign an election under s. 183, as A Ltd is not granting a new lease (and indeed is not even a party to the transaction) so C Ltd needs to find another way of gaining deemed ownership of the fixtures, if a claim is to be allowed.

Turning to s. 181 (purchaser of land giving consideration for fixture), it would seem to be clear that that section cannot apply either. This is because C Ltd has paid the £520,000 to B Ltd. As B Ltd does not own the fixtures, no part of the consideration can be treated as expenditure on the fixtures – whatever B Ltd is selling for the £520,000 cannot include something that B Ltd does not own.

The reason, of course, is that A Ltd has an entitlement to claim allowances for the fixtures in question. Indeed, it is possible that the whole discussion will alert A Ltd to that entitlement, and that a belated claim will now be made. That is acceptable as long as A Ltd is still carrying on a qualifying activity, and as long as the fixtures that are the subject of the claim are still in the property.

In summary, there is no "second chance" for a new tenant to claim allowances if the original lease is assigned by the old tenant, and if that old tenant was unable to claim allowances.

Different issues will arise, of course, if B Ltd incurred further capital expenditure on the property. B Ltd is able to claim for the cost of these fixtures by virtue of s. 176 (see **10.5.2** above). In principle, there will be no problem in transferring entitlement to claim for such further fixtures from B Ltd to C Ltd, subject to meeting the usual conditions (including the pooling and fixed value requirements (i.e. with a s. 198 election)).

Integral features

The issues become more complex when we consider those integral features that did not qualify for relief before April 2008 (typically cold water systems, general lighting, general electrical works). The issues are brought out in the following example.

Example 2

Charles, who is carrying on a property business, acquires a freehold property in 2003. He grants a lease to William in 2007 and no s. 183 election is signed. William incurs no new capital expenditure, and duly assigns the lease to Harry some years later, receiving a capital payment. All parties are unconnected.

As in **Example 1** above, there is a general bar on Harry claiming allowances for the original expenditure on the property. Is there any difference, though, in relation to those integral features (e.g. the cold water system) that did not qualify before April 2008?

In this case, we know that neither Charles nor William could claim allowances, as their capital expenditure on the cold water system was incurred before April 2008 (see, generally, **4.11**). So does that then give a clear run to Harry?

The answer would appear to be No. Although nobody has a prior right to claim, we need to come back to first principles.

In property law, fixtures belong to the landlord. They can only be treated for capital allowances purposes as belonging to the tenant if the CAA 2001 rules create the fiction of ownership. The fact that Charles is unable to claim allowances for the cold water system does not mean that ownership of that system is deemed to pass to anybody else.

Harry is incurring capital expenditure when acquiring the leasehold interest, but he cannot buy something that does not belong to the person to whom he is making the payment. So the sum paid by Harry to William for the lease assignment cannot be treated as expenditure incurred partly on the cold water system.

For the time being, therefore, nobody can claim allowances for the cold water system. If Charles disposes of his freehold interest, the new owner of that interest will in principle be able to claim for the integral features.

The above is the writer's opinion of the matter. It has not, to his knowledge, been confirmed either in case law or by HMRC.

10.5.11 Worked example

The following example, adapted from a real case worked on by the authors, brings together the various strands covered at **10.5.7** to **10.5.10** above.

Example

Builder Ltd, a property developer, built a new property in 2002 and immediately granted a 999-year lease to Pension Fund. Pension Fund in turn granted a 21-year lease to Trader Ltd in 2003, in return for a capital sum and a notional annual rent. No thought was given at this time to an election under s. 183.

Builder Ltd sold the freehold interest to Top Investor Ltd in 2009.

Pension Fund sells its long leasehold interest to Client Ltd in 2021, in return for a capital payment of £500,000.

At this stage, therefore, the chain of ownership is freehold (Top Investor Ltd), long lease (Client Ltd), short sub-lease (Trader Ltd).

All parties are unconnected.

Client Ltd wishes to know if it is entitled to claim allowances.

Taking the transactions in chronological order, the following results would appear to arise.

2002: original build. Builder Ltd is a property developer, and is therefore not incurring capital expenditure. For this reason, it cannot claim allowances.

2002: grant of long lease to Pension Fund. This transaction falls within s. 184. It is not within s. 183 because Builder Ltd cannot claim allowances even though it is within the charge to tax. Ownership therefore passes to Pension Fund. However, Pension Fund is not within the charge to tax, and is therefore unable to claim allowances.

2003: grant of short lease to Trader Ltd. Deemed ownership of the fixtures did not pass to Trader Ltd under s. 183, as no election under that section was signed (and it is now much too late to rectify that, as there is a two-year time limit). Nor does deemed ownership pass under s. 184, as the condition in s. 184(1)(b) is not met: even though Pension Fund cannot claim allowances, this is because it is not within the charge to tax. So Trader Ltd cannot claim allowances and deemed ownership stays with Pension Fund.

2009: sale of freehold interest by Builder Ltd to Top Investor Ltd. There are two possible interpretations here.

a. Under the first interpretation, the transaction falls within s. 181 (see, generally, **10.5.5**). Top Investor has paid a capital sum to acquire the property, which by definition includes the fixtures therein. Nobody has a prior right to claim (per s. 181(3)) as no other person is entitled to claim allowances, as already illustrated above. At this stage, therefore, there is a valid claim by Top Investor.

b. The alternative view, however, is that Builder Ltd cannot sell something that it does not own. As already shown above, the deemed ownership of the fixtures in the property has passed from Builder Ltd to Pension Fund (and the fact that Pension Fund cannot claim does not change that underlying principle). It would therefore seem to follow that no part of the consideration paid by Top Investor Ltd to Builder Ltd "falls to be treated ... as expenditure on the provision of the fixture" (per s. 181(1)(c)).

In the author's opinion, the second interpretation is to be preferred. Assuming that this is correct, it means that Pension Fund still owns the fixtures, even though it cannot claim allowances. This would apply equally to those integral features that did not qualify before April 2008.

2021: assignment of long lease by Pension Fund to Client Ltd. Assuming that interpretation (b) above is correct, Client Ltd is the first person entitled to claim allowances for the fixtures in the property. This being the case, Client Ltd may make a claim based on an apportionment of the cost it pays to acquire the leasehold interest. There is no restriction to historic cost (as the condition in s. 185(1)(d) is not met).

Law: CAA 2001, s. 183-184
Guidance: CA 26350

10.6   Disposal events

10.6.1   Introduction

As we have seen, capital allowances are often given for fixtures by means of a statutory sleight of hand: the legislation creates a pretence of ownership, so that – for example – the tenant of a property can be treated as owning fixtures even though, in property law terms, those fixtures belong to the landlord.

If there is only a deemed ownership of fixtures, it follows that there cannot be an actual disposal. So to continue with the example of the tenant, he claims allowances *as if* he were the owner of the property. For this reason, the disposal rules that apply for most plant and machinery cannot normally apply to fixtures as a person cannot dispose of something he does not really own.

The legislation therefore includes its own special rules relating to the disposal of fixtures. HMRC explain all this in the following terms at CA 26500:

> "Since the person who gets PMAs on a fixture is not the true owner of the fixture but the person that is treated as owning it (**the virtual owner**) actual cessation of ownership is no use as a disposal event for fixtures. The other disposal events work normally. There is legislation in Sections 188-189 that says when you should treat the virtual owner of a fixture as ceasing to own it."

As noted at **5.5.6**, the cessation of (notional) ownership of a fixture is a disposal event for the purposes of calculating plant and machinery allowances (and charges). Particular rules can then be applied according to the nature of the notional ownership.

10.6.2   Person ceases to have qualifying interest

A person who has been treated as the owner of a fixture under any of the following provisions is treated as ceasing to own the fixture at the time he ceases to have the qualifying interest:

- person with interest in land having fixture for purposes of qualifying activity: s. 176 (see **10.5.2**);

- purchaser of land giving consideration for fixture: s. 181 (see **10.5.5**);

- purchaser of land discharging obligations of equipment lessee: s. 182 (see **10.5.6**);

- purchaser of land discharging obligations of client under energy services agreement: s. 182A (see **10.5.4**);

- incoming lessee where lessor entitled to allowances: s. 183 (see **10.5.7**); or

- incoming lessee where lessor not entitled to allowances: s. 184 (again, see **10.5.7**).

Acquisition of ownership by lessor or licensor

If, on the termination of a lease or licence, the outgoing lessee or licensee is treated under these rules as ceasing to be the owner of a fixture, the lessor or licensor is treated as the owner of the fixture from the time of the termination of the lease or licence.

Law: CAA 2001, s. 188, 193

10.6.3 Identifying the qualifying interest

As a general rule, the qualifying interest for these purposes is the interest in the relevant land, or the lease, referred to in the sections in question as identified at **10.6.2** above. However, this is subject to the following exceptions.

If a person's qualifying interest is an agreement to acquire an interest in land, and that interest is subsequently transferred or granted to that person, the interest transferred or granted is treated as the qualifying interest.

If a person's qualifying interest ceases to exist as a result of its being merged into another interest acquired by that person, that other interest is treated as the qualifying interest.

If the qualifying interest is a lease and, on its termination, a new lease of the relevant land (with or without other land) is granted to the lessee, the new lease is treated as the qualifying interest.

If the qualifying interest is a licence and, on its termination, a new licence to occupy the relevant land (with or without other land) is granted to the licensee, the new licence is treated as the qualifying interest.

If the qualifying interest is a lease and, with the consent of the lessor, the lessee remains in possession of the relevant land after the termination of the lease without a new lease being granted to him, the qualifying interest is to be treated as continuing so long as the lessee remains in possession of the relevant land.

Law: CAA 2001, s. 189
Guidance: CA 26500

10.6.4   Lessors and incoming lessees

If s. 183 applies (incoming lessee where lessor entitled to allowances: see **10.5.7**), the lessor is treated as ceasing to own the fixture when the lessee begins to be treated as the owner.

Law: CAA 2001, s. 190

10.6.5   Severance of fixtures

A person who has been treated as the owner of a fixture by virtue of the special fixtures rules is treated as ceasing to be the owner if:

- the fixture is permanently severed from the relevant land (so that it ceases to be a fixture); and
- once it is severed, it is not in fact owned by that person.

Law: CAA 2001, s. 191

10.6.6   Cessation of ownership by equipment lessor

An equipment lessor may have been treated as the owner of a fixture by virtue of the rules in s. 177 (equipment lessors: see **10.5.3**). He may then be treated as ceasing to be the owner at the earliest of the events mentioned below.

Assignment of rights

If the equipment lessor at any time assigns his rights under the equipment lease, he is treated as ceasing to be the owner of the fixture at that time.

In such a case, the assignee is treated thereafter as having incurred expenditure (i.e. the consideration given by him for the assignment) on the provision of the fixture, and thus as being the owner of the fixture. The assignee is then treated for any future application of these rules as being the equipment lessor who owns the fixture under s. 177.

Law: CAA 2001, s. 192, 194

Discharge of financial obligations

If the financial obligations of the equipment lessee under an equipment lease are discharged, the equipment lessor is again treated as ceasing to be the owner of the fixture at that time.

For these purposes, the equipment lessee is, in a case where the financial obligations of the equipment lessee have become vested in another person, the person in whom the obligations are vested when the capital sum is paid.

In this case, the equipment lessee is treated as having incurred expenditure, consisting of the capital sum, on the provision of the fixture, and thus as owning it from the time of payment.

Law: CAA 2001, s. 192, 195

10.6.7 Cessation of ownership by energy services provider

An energy services provider who has been treated as the owner of a fixture (under s. 180A: see **10.5.4**) is treated as ceasing to be the owner of the fixture at the earliest of the following times.

Assignment of rights

If the energy services provider at any time assigns his rights under the energy services agreement, he is treated as ceasing to be the owner of the fixture at that time.

In such a case, the assignee is treated thereafter as having incurred expenditure (i.e. the consideration given by him for the assignment) on the provision of the fixture, and thus as being the owner of the fixture. The assignee is then treated for any future application of these rules as being the equipment lessor who owns the fixture under s. 180A.

Law: CAA 2001, s. 192A, 195A

Discharge of financial obligations

If the financial obligations of the client in respect of the fixture under an energy services agreement are discharged, the energy services provider is again treated as ceasing to be the owner of the fixture at that time.

For these purposes, the client is (if the financial obligations of the client have become vested in another person), a reference to the person in whom the obligations are vested when the capital sum is paid.

In this case, the client is treated as having incurred expenditure, consisting of the capital sum, on the provision of the fixture, and thus as owning it from the time of payment.

Law: CAA 2001, s. 192A, 195B
Guidance: CA 23150

10.7   Disposal values

As with disposals of plant and machinery generally, the disposal value to be brought into account depends on the nature of the event triggering the disposal. However, other than in certain special circumstances (e.g. involving connected parties or avoidance cases), the disposal value is capped at the expenditure incurred on the provision of the asset by the person making the disposal.

For a normal sale of the qualifying interest at or above market value, the sale price for the vendor is specifically linked to the part of the price on which the buyer can claim plant and machinery allowances as expenditure on fixtures.

In certain other cases, market value is substituted. This will be the case if there is a transfer of the qualifying interest other than by way of sale, or if the fixture is severed. It will also apply if the fixture starts to be used wholly or partly for purposes other than those of the qualifying activity (which can cause a problem, for example, if a person owning a furnished holiday let (FHL) property starts to use the property for leasing to a tenant in circumstances that no longer qualify for the special FHL rules).

If the qualifying interest is sold for less than market value, market value is used unless the buyer's expenditure qualifies for plant and machinery allowances (in which case the disposal value is again linked to the amount on which the buyer can claim allowances). This is subject to an exception if the buyer is a dual resident investing company connected with the seller.

A different value is used in certain other cases. For example, the value is nil if the qualifying interest expires and the person does not receive any capital sum (e.g. by way of compensation).

299

A detailed table is given at s. 196, to which reference should be made as appropriate. The HMRC version of the table, given at CA 26700, may be preferred as it is easier to digest than the table itself.

When the figure to be used for the disposal value is the figure of net proceeds of sale, the apportionment rules of s. 562 should not be overlooked. In particular, where two or more items are sold together, the net proceeds of sale of any given item must be calculated as "so much of the net proceeds of sale of all the property as, on a just and reasonable apportionment, is attributable to that item". The point is considered more fully at **12.8**.

Fixtures elections will be required in most cases where there is a sale of the property (see **12.2.3**).

Anti-avoidance

Anti-avoidance provisions at s. 197 provide for a different disposal value if the disposal event is linked to a scheme or arrangement of which a main purpose is the obtaining by the taxpayer of a plant and machinery tax advantage.

It is not thought that this provision is invoked frequently, but it is part of HMRC's armoury. The effect would be that the company making the disposal would have to bring in a higher disposal value than might otherwise be the case. Essentially, allowances already given would be preserved but no balancing allowance (or later WDAs) would be available.

Example

Company A identifies qualifying expenditure of £100,000 in a residential property that is briefly used for FHLs purposes. It claims allowances of perhaps £14,000 (i.e. some at 18% and some at 6%) and has a pool value of £86,000.

Company A sells the property to connected Company B, which intends to use it for letting to tenants. As this is an ordinary property business, and as the property is a dwelling-house, it will not qualify for capital allowances (s. 35). The parties sign an election with a figure of £2 (being £1 each for integral features and other fixtures). Company A therefore hopes to claim allowances of a further £85,998.

HMRC assert that the transaction was undertaken purely to obtain additional capital allowances and it therefore invokes s. 197. The

£14,000 already claimed would be retained, but the additional allowances of £85,998 would be denied.

Law: CAA 2001, s. 35, 197, 562
Guidance: CA 26700

10.8   Capital gains tax

It is sometimes asserted that any claim for capital allowances on the fixtures in the property will result in a higher capital gains tax bill (or corporation tax bill on the capital gain) when the property comes to be sold at some future date. The thinking is that if, say, £50,000 of costs are allocated to fixtures rather than to the property then the base cost of the property is reduced accordingly and a higher gain will eventually ensue.

Despite the apparent logic of this approach, it is simply incorrect; this is because the division between property on the one hand, and fixtures on the other, is a false one.

The evidence for this is in TCGA 1992, s. 41(1), as follows:

> "Section 39 shall not require the exclusion from the sums allowable as a deduction in the computation of the gain of any expenditure as being expenditure in respect of which a capital allowance or renewals allowance is made, but the amount of any losses accruing on the disposal of an asset shall be restricted by reference to capital allowances ... ."

In other words, making a claim for capital allowances does not increase any capital gains tax charge when the property comes to be sold. The only impact a capital allowances claim can have is if the property is later sold at a loss, in which case there is a restriction on the tax relief that might have been given at that time.

The topic is covered in depth at section **1.10** above.

10.9   Claims

A person is said to make a claim in respect of a fixture if he makes an actual claim or if he includes the cost in a tax return (or an amendment to a return) as qualifying expenditure.

Law: CAA 2001, s. 202

Amending a return

A person is obliged to notify HMRC if a return becomes incorrect for any of the following reasons:

- withdrawal of approval for the purposes of s. 180 (affordable warmth programme);
- any of sections 181(2), 182(2), 182A(2) or 184(2) (where another person has a prior right to claim) applies;
- s. 185 applies (restriction on qualifying expenditure where another person has claimed an allowance);
- a fixtures election is made under s. 198 or s. 199; or
- s. 200(4) applies (reduction in amount which can be fixed by an election).

The notice must be given within three months of the person becoming aware that something has become incorrect. All such assessments and adjustments may then be made as are necessary to rectify the matter. The notice must be in writing (s. 577(1)).

Law: CAA 2001, s. 203

10.10 Appeals

A tax tribunal may determine any question, if material to two or more persons, as to whether any plant or machinery has become, in law, part of a building or other land. The rules are subject to the provisions of TMA 1970, Pt. 5 (especially s. 48(2)(b)). Each of the persons concerned is entitled to be a party to the proceedings.

If a tribunal has to determine any issue relating to a fixtures election under s. 198 or s. 199, it must do so separately from any other questions in those proceedings. Each of the persons who has joined in the election is entitled to be a party to the proceedings and the tribunal's determination has effect as if made in an appeal to which each of those persons was a party.

Law: CAA 2001, s. 204

11. Fixtures claims for new buildings

11.1 Tax relief for part of the construction cost

Where a person incurs capital expenditure on constructing, improving or extending a commercial property, a part of that cost will normally qualify as expenditure on fixtures. Plant and machinery allowances can then be claimed for the cost of those fixtures.

If, for example, a business builds a new office block for its own purposes, that office block will contain substantial numbers of fixtures. These will include the entire lighting and electrical costs, the whole of the hot and cold water system, toilets and other sanitaryware, all air conditioning and central heating, any lifts, and much else besides.

Example

A company buys some land for £500,000 and then pays £1 million to build a new care home. Equipping the home with moveable furniture (beds, chairs, tables, etc.) costs a further £140,000. Analysis shows that £425,000 of the build cost and the whole of the additional costs qualify for allowances, the former category qualifying as "fixtures" in the capital allowances sense.

At 20%, the £565,000 has the potential to save the company tax of £113,000.

To quantify a claim in these circumstances, it is necessary to analyse the overall costs of the project. Pinning down the concept of "plant" is notoriously difficult, with a host of statutory provisions, and case law stretching back well over a century (see, generally, **4.3**). Nevertheless, the principles for claiming allowances for fixtures in newly built property are clear: simply identify those parts of the overall construction expenditure that qualify as plant or machinery. A portion of overheads will also qualify: see **11.5** below.

The reference above to "commercial" property is important. This term is essentially to be contrasted with residential property, for which allowances are much more restricted (see, generally, **4.14**).

11.2 Changing tax landscape

Changes to the rules for claiming allowances for fixtures were introduced in FA 2012 and became fully effective from April 2014.

The changes *directly* affect only those who are buying or selling property. In the past, the right to claim allowances was preserved indefinitely and would pass to a new owner if the property was sold without any claim being made by the vendor; the only condition was that the fixtures still formed part of the property at some point during the period for which a claim was eventually made. That principle has changed as a result of the FA 2012 changes, with a formal "pooling requirement" in place since April 2014. As such, even a loss-making business may need to include the fixtures in its capital allowances computations, so as to retain their value for a future owner and thereby prevent a drop in the value of the property.

For this reason, the FA 2012 changes have also had an impact on those who are not immediately involved in buying or selling property, but who are currently paying to build, extend or adapt an existing property, or who perhaps incurred expenditure on a property many years previously but did not fully address the capital allowances issues at the time.

Advantages of earlier claims

Owners will almost certainly be required, before the property is sold, to identify the fixtures and to bring the value of those fixtures into the business tax computations. Although the owners can still choose to leave that exercise until the point of sale, there are numerous potential benefits of identifying the fixtures sooner. In particular:

1. Memories fade and records get lost. By conducting the exercise at the time the capital expenditure is incurred, accuracy is ensured and professionals involved with the work can be asked for their input if necessary. As it is simpler at this stage, the exercise may also cost less in terms of professional fees.

2. Cash flow. The value of a claim for fixtures in property can typically offer significant tax savings. If a business can use the allowances in any way, to reduce current tax liabilities or to reclaim tax that would otherwise be payable, it is obviously preferable to do that.

3. Retention of benefit of allowances. When a property is sold, the two parties will need to agree a transfer value for the fixtures. This is entirely a matter for negotiation, but a common starting point is to suggest that the vendor should retain the value for which relief has already been given, and transfer the remaining value to the purchaser. So if fixtures

costing £100,000 are identified several years before the sale of the property, and if the vendor has enjoyed tax relief on £60,000 of that value, it is quite possible that the parties will agree to transfer the fixtures to the new owner at the written-down value of £40,000. If the purchaser is driving the claim, by contrast, he or she may expect to have a much greater slice of the cake.

4.   Preventing the loss of allowances. Capital allowances are only available for capital expenditure, so the potential to claim will be lost if the property is refurbished and if (or to the extent that) the replacement items are written off as revenue expenditure.

5.   One thing less to worry about at the time of sale. Selling a private residence can be complex enough, but selling a business is often much more so. If capital allowances are left to the time of sale, they will certainly present one more headache at that time. Furthermore, a vendor who is keen to complete a sale, and who is already worrying about any number of warranties and indemnities, may well be tempted to give up more than would otherwise be the case in terms of capital allowances.

From the accountant's point of view, there is the additional factor that if he or she does not address these issues for the client, there is a high chance that the client will be approached by other specialists, who may or may not provide the best advice to the client. So instead of providing high value advice for the client, genuinely offering legitimate tax savings, there is the risk that the accountant will be on the back foot because of a failure to flag up the opportunities.

If the business is making losses, and cannot use the capital allowances, that will obviously change the perspective. Even here, the vendor is likely to be asked to bring the value of the fixtures into his computations before sale but the owner may decide that he will leave it until the point of sale, rather than incurring costs to harness a form of tax relief that he cannot use.

11.3   Formulating the claim

The methodology for calculating the claim will in practice depend on the size of the project – if expenditure on a new commercial property runs into millions of pounds, a more sophisticated approach will be needed than for a small extension to an existing building. Nevertheless, the principles to be applied will be the same.

Many but not all accountants will be able to formulate a claim for fixtures in a newly built property, but they will need to know what information to obtain from the builders or surveyors. It will also be essential to have a thorough knowledge of what constitutes qualifying expenditure. The claim should almost certainly be built up on a spreadsheet and it will be essential to split the costs into at least three headings: general plant and machinery, integral features and non-qualifying expenditure. Professional fees and preliminary costs will need to be apportioned, but some degree of thought as to the correct nature of apportionment will be needed, as discussed at **11.4** and **11.5** below.

For all but the smallest projects, it will be necessary to have a very detailed breakdown of the costs. It is not good enough just to have broad headings – and to "take a view" on whether the expenses in question will qualify or not – as this approach will not stand up to HMRC scrutiny.

The analysis of the expenditure should almost certainly not be viewed as a simple tax compliance exercise that is completed within the accountant's agreed fee structure. It is a valuable tax planning exercise that is worth doing properly, and the starting point may be to ensure that the client has some understanding of the potential tax savings, and therefore values the exercise that is needed to obtain those savings.

For most sizeable projects, the surveyor will have prepared a Bill of Quantities. This will include a detailed breakdown of the pricing of the project, prepared before work is begun.

The Bill of Quantities will provide the key starting point to allow for an analysis of the costs of the project. It will be clear at a glance that some items do not qualify for allowances at all; typically, this will include substructures, steelwork, external walls and so on. Other items will immediately be seen to qualify, whether as integral features or as general plant; little time should be needed, for example, to deal with the cost of baths and WCs in a care home (as these will clearly qualify, though some analysis may be needed even here to identify any water-saving technology for which first-year allowances may be available until April 2020). Still further items may need to be broken down, either because the wording is not precise enough for tax purposes (e.g. "refurbishment work to existing bedrooms") or because the necessary division between integral features and general plant imposes a requirement for more detail (e.g. for certain mechanical installations).

As the Bill of Quantities has been prepared in advance of the work carried out, it will have certain limitations. A key point is that it will contain provisional sums, and these will need to be resolved. Similarly, there will inevitably be "variations" along the way as the work is put into practice and as complications arise. The client (or for larger projects his professional advisers on the building side) should be able to provide a reconciliation from the Bill of Quantities to the final figure of expenditure that is actually incurred. The capital allowances spreadsheet must obviously reflect those changes.

The Bill of Quantities will relate only to the main contractor, and to other subcontractors paid by him. Typically, there will be a range of other suppliers of one sort or another. In practical terms, it may be preferable to have one overall spreadsheet with a front summary page, and with separate pages for the analysis of the main contractor costs and for each of the other suppliers.

Some professional costs will need to be allocated to particular categories of expenditure; for example, the costs of a mechanical engineer may relate entirely to mechanical and electrical work. Other costs will need to be apportioned across the entire project, and others still may be disallowed in full. The various issues are addressed in more depth at **11.4** below.

No Bill of Quantities

In some cases, the paperwork will not be adequate to prepare a claim for allowances. This may be the case if the work was undertaken many years previously, for example.

In these circumstances, other approaches are available, and a claim should in principle still be possible. At the simplest, it may be that old files contain at least some analysis of the capital expenditure, giving sufficient detail to formulate an acceptable claim. In more complex cases, a professional valuer – with an understanding of capital allowances law so that he knows what he is looking out for – will be able to survey the property and create a proper computation of the costs incurred, using building cost indexation as necessary. The pros and cons of involving external surveyors are touched on at **12.8.3** below.

11.4   Professional fees

A proportion of professional fees will be treated as expenditure on plant or machinery.

HMRC guidance in relation to these costs used to be as follows, before the guidance was updated in July 2012:

> "It is not appropriate simply to apportion the fee by reference to the building costs of the plant and machinery and of other assets as that will commonly overstate the extent to which the services relate to the provision of the plant and machinery."

However, this guidance has been updated to reflect more recent case law developments, including in particular the *Wetherspoon* cases, which addressed the correct treatment of £4.8 million of professional costs. The parties in that case agreed that the structural engineer's fees should be allocated proportionally but disagreed about the treatment of the fees charged by the planning supervisor. In the end, the tribunal adopted a fairly simple apportionment approach, as discussed more fully at **11.5** below.

HMRC guidance now includes the following:

> "Where preliminaries and professional fees are paid in connection with a building project that includes the provision of plant or machinery, only the part, if any, which relates to services that can properly be regarded as on the provision of plant or machinery can be qualifying expenditure for PMA [plant and machinery allowances].
>
> Establishing the part which relates to such services needs to be determined on a case by case basis. There is no one correct answer for all cases. For some cases it may be necessary to carry out a detailed analysis of the individual costs to determine whether, or the extent to which each should properly be apportioned to particular plant or machinery expenditure. In other cases, it may only be possible to apportion the costs between items which do, or do not, qualify for PMA. (This is sometimes called "the pro rata approach").
>
> ...
>
> For most small construction projects ... the use of the pro rata approach will generally be acceptable (unless it is clear that an apportionment approach would be demonstrably inappropriate without opening any enquiry). So, for such smaller claims, enquiries should not be opened simply because a business has made a pro rate apportionment of professional fees and preliminaries. Indeed, even if other aspects of any wider capital allowance claim are subject to an enquiry, a challenge to a pro rata

approach to professional fees and preliminaries should not be made solely because the business has used a pro rata methodology.

It may be that the amount of the professional fees or, perhaps more particularly, preliminaries, looks unusually high ... . However, the advice of the Valuation Office (see CA12300) **must** be sought in any such case where the initial fact finding seems to suggest that particular costs are unusually high because the costs may have been incorrectly classified as either relevant professional fees or preliminaries.

In larger construction projects ... there will often be other capital allowances aspects that need to be enquired into and it may be that one aspect of a wider review of the capital allowance claim will be the treatment of professional fees and preliminaries. If a business has decided to pro rata such costs then the advice of the Valuation Office **must** be sought before challenging the treatment adopted by the business.

If, unusually, in relation to any larger construction project, it is considered that the only cause of concern is that the costs have been apportioned on a pro rata basis, the advice of the Valuation Office **must** be sought before opening any enquiry."

Broadly speaking, the correct approach is that if a more accurate approach can be obtained from a reasonable amount of work then that should be done, but a pro-rata apportionment is likely to be accepted where the work involved for a more accurate assessment would be disproportionate.

Fees of a mechanical or electrical engineer may well qualify in full, but will need apportionment between general plant and integral features. On the other hand, some legal fees may be too remote from the provision of plant or machinery and may not qualify at all. Fees for a structural engineer, a quantity surveyor or an architect are all examples of professional costs where some apportionment will usually be required between qualifying and non-qualifying elements.

Cases: *J D Wetherspoon plc v HMRC* (2007) Sp C 657; *J D Wetherspoon plc v HMRC* [2009] UKFTT 374 (TC); *J D Wetherspoon plc v HMRC* [2012] UKUT 42 (TCC)
Guidance: CA 20070

11.5   Overheads and preliminary costs

These categories of expenditure are likely to arise in almost any project, and it is important to identify the part of the costs that may be claimed as qualifying expenditure on plant and machinery.

Broadly speaking, the term "overheads" will include support activities where the cost is not known at the outset, whereas the "preliminaries" category will cover lump sum payments, insurance and similar items that may be reasonably predicted at the outset. In practice, the distinction is not clear cut, however, and in *Wetherspoon* the term "overheads expenditure" was used to cover "the preliminaries costs and professional fees incurred".

Overheads

Overhead costs should be apportioned in a reasonable way between the different categories of expenditure: those qualifying as standard plant or machinery, those qualifying as special rate expenditure (e.g. integral features) and those not qualifying at all.

In *Wetherspoon*, for example, the parties agreed that a cost of some £54,000 relating to site supervision and management "was a project overhead which should be apportioned equally to each and every item of main project expenditure".

Cases: *J D Wetherspoon plc v HMRC* (2007) Sp C 657; *J D Wetherspoon plc v HMRC* [2009] UKFTT 374 (TC); *J D Wetherspoon plc v HMRC* [2012] UKUT 42 (TCC)

Preliminary costs

According to HMRC, preliminaries:

> "are indirect costs incurred over the duration of a project on items such as site management, insurance, general purpose labour, temporary accommodation and security".

In *Wetherspoon*, the following comment was made:

> "Preliminaries generally refers to the building contractor's necessary costs which are not usually tangibly reflected in the finished works as opposed to costs directly related to the quantity of items of work, i.e. materials, tradesmen and site labour, tools and small plant. Costs concerned with the works as a whole are preliminaries being commonly referred to as the contractor's site-related overheads."

The same case defined preliminaries to mean "global costs covering several different items which are not readily attributable to specific items". On the other hand, it also made the point that :

> "the expression 'preliminaries' is not a precise expression. Items which might be treated as preliminaries in one contract or tender might not be so treated in another. While some costs, such as portable toilets, are not capable of meaningful attribution to measured work, other costs may be capable of meaningful attribution, albeit with varying degrees of difficulty. All, however, will be integral parts of the construction costs of the measured work to the extent that they can be properly apportioned to such work. A cost properly attributable to one item of work cannot properly be apportioned among the whole."

It will be appropriate to apportion these unallocated costs across the various elements of the building project. A pro-rata apportionment should normally be used unless there are particular reasons for allocating more or less of the overall figure to particular headings.

HMRC guidance is that "only the part, if any, which relates to services that can properly be regarded as on the provision of plant or machinery can be qualifying expenditure". However, recent case law suggests that that may be unduly harsh an interpretation.

In some instances, it will be clear that particular costs relate to parts of the overall expenditure that do not qualify (e.g. to a steel frame for a building) or that do qualify (e.g. to the hot and cold water system). In such cases, the preliminary costs should – as far as is reasonably possible – be allocated on an accurate basis between non qualifying items, items qualifying as integral features (or other special rate expenditure), items qualifying as general plant or machinery, and possibly to some items qualifying for first-year allowances.

In *Wetherspoon* again, it was held that an apportionment on the above lines was appropriate, and that businesses should not be expected to spend a disproportionate amount of time on the exercise:

> "In a case such as the present where the capital expenditure to which the preliminaries relate involves a multiplicity of items many of them relatively small we consider that a pro-rata apportionment is in principle reasonable and is justified as being in accordance with generally accepted accounting practice. ...
>
> We do not consider that it can have been the intention of Parliament that if a taxpayer is to be entitled to include

preliminaries in capital expenditure claimed it should be necessary to enter into a detailed assessment in order to allocate the preliminaries."

In the Upper Tribunal, this approach was "unhesitatingly" approved, such that the HMRC appeal on the question of preliminaries "entirely fails".

The HMRC guidance at CA 20070, as still worded in 2021, may be flawed in suggesting that professional and preliminary costs may be allowed only "if they relate directly to the acquisition, transport and installation of the plant or machinery".

Timing of tax relief

Preliminary costs and professional fees may be incurred before the main expenditure. In this case, the question can arise of when tax relief can be claimed.

As a general principle, such costs should be linked to the actual expenditure on the underlying assets, by directly attributing the costs to the work in question. If that main expenditure has not yet been incurred, it would seem to be the case that no relief can yet be claimed for the associated preliminary and professional costs. In statutory terms, the fundamental condition for claiming plant and machinery allowances – that the person must own the asset – is not yet met, as no asset has yet been acquired or created. The accounting approach would be to treat the costs as prepaid expenses, carried forward accordingly on the balance sheet.

If the project proves to be abortive, no relief will in principle be due. This is because no tangible asset will come into existence. See also the case of *ECC Quarries* discussed in the *Business Income Manual* at BIM 35325.

Cases: *ECC Quarries Ltd v Watkis* (1975) 51 TC 153; *J D Wetherspoon plc v HMRC* (2007) Sp C 657; *J D Wetherspoon plc v HMRC* [2009] UKFTT 374 (TC); *J D Wetherspoon plc v HMRC* [2012] UKUT 42 (TCC)
Guidance: BIM 35325; CA 20070

11.6   Sampling

In the very largest cases, HMRC will in principle allow "sampling" as the basis of a claim for capital allowances on fixtures. In the past, HMRC stated that this may be permitted where "there would be a considerable and demonstrable burden involved for the business in analysing the expenditure for the whole population" [i.e. of properties].

The aim will therefore be to identify the proportion of overall expenditure that qualifies, whether as general fixtures or as integral features, in those properties, and then to apply the same percentage to other properties.

Guidance beginning at CA 20075 states that the following principles should apply:

- the option for using a sampling basis may be available "where a taxpayer incurs significant expenditure in a chargeable period on a number of properties that contain fixtures that qualify for PMA";
- the approach is for use with fixtures only (not chattels);
- the example given is of a company that "acquires a number of similar sized retail units and fits them out in their 'corporate style' to create a standard type of shop".

Earlier HMRC guidance (in *R&C Brief* 24/12 of August 2012) also suggested the following, though these are not reproduced in the HMRC manual:

- the number of *sample* properties must be at least 15, and HMRC will often insist on a higher number;
- HMRC will require evidence that the sample chosen is random;
- HMRC will also require a certain "confidence level", with a higher requirement if the claim exceeds £25 million.

It may well be that the omission is deliberate as one of the authors received the following further information from HMRC's specialist capital allowances team in June 2013:

> "The principles published in R&C Brief 24/12 are the (broadly) correct ones and are the ones we now tell operational colleagues to follow in relation to any sampling claim.
>
> However the consultation responses raised an important question in relation to smaller businesses. We decided to hold off updating the sampling guidance until we were able to give an element of greater certainty in relation to smaller businesses."

Sampling can cause problems when the property comes to be sold. Suppose, for example, that a fast food restaurant with outlets all over the country sells one of its shops to an independent retailer. If no actual capital allowances analysis has taken place of the shop in question then this certainly raises issues, when it comes to completing an election under s. 198, about how to demonstrate which fixtures have been the subject of a claim. Here, even more than in other cases, it will be important for the buyer to have a full discussion with the vendor so as to reach agreement on the detailed content of the fixtures election. This is particularly true since the introduction of the pooling and fixed value requirements (see **12.2**).

11.7 Extensions and refurbishments

Where a building is not newly constructed, but has work done to it, the first question will be to determine whether or not the expenditure is capital in nature. The distinction is considered at **1.5.2**. Any extension will be capital, whereas a refurbishment may be wholly or partly revenue expenditure.

For any capital expenditure on an existing building, the same principles apply as they do for newly constructed property. Once more, it will be necessary to divide up the total cost between elements that qualify as fixtures and those that do not.

Care is needed if integral features are being replaced on a significant scale, as such expenditure may be automatically treated as capital for these purposes (s. 33A: see **4.11.6**).

11.8 Repairs and renewals

When property comes to be sold, the parties must remember that a fixtures election can only cover items on which the vendor has incurred capital expenditure: s. 198 applies only if "the disposal value of a fixture is required to be brought into account" for capital allowances purposes, which will only be the case if capital expenditure has been incurred on the fixture in question.

Example

An office radiator is damaged and replaced, with the cost of the replacement written off as revenue expenditure. When the property comes to be sold, the radiator should – in principle – be excluded from the fixtures election as it is not an item on which the vendor has claimed or could claim capital allowances.

For the purchaser, the cost of the radiator is capital expenditure. It is open to the buyer to claim allowances for the cost of the radiator over and above any figure in the s. 198 election. (The pooling and fixed value requirements do not apply as the conditions in s. 187A(1)(b) and (d) are not met, as the vendor did not incur capital expenditure and was therefore not entitled to claim allowances.)

Note that it does not make any difference whether or not the vendor had claimed allowances on the old, damaged radiator. If so, that value has given the vendor a permanent tax reduction. If not, the opportunity to claim allowances for the original cost is lost from the end of the chargeable period in which the old radiator is scrapped.

12. Fixtures claims – allowances for the buyer

12.1 Introduction

Few areas of tax are as poorly understood – and as often neglected – as those that relate to fixtures in commercial property that is being bought or sold. Changes introduced from April 2012 and April 2014 have created a growing awareness of this as a technical area that needs to be addressed, and attention should be paid as much to capital allowances (for both parties) as to the computation of the vendor's capital gain.

This chapter explains the legalities and the practical issues that arise from the buyer's point of view. The seller's perspective is covered in **Chapter 13**.

Every commercial property contains plant or machinery that is affixed to the building, i.e. "fixtures". Lighting systems and toilets are examples of fixtures that can be found in nearly every such building.

When the property changes hands, ownership of the fixtures forming part of the property will by definition be transferred. The transaction therefore constitutes (a) the sale of fixtures by the vendor and (b) the acquisition of the same fixtures by the purchaser. As in other circumstances where plant or machinery is bought and sold, this raises capital allowance considerations for both parties.

In principle, but subject to some exceptions, the capital allowances disposal value for the vendor will have to be the same as the acquisition value for the buyer. In practice, it is quite possible that the parties will not, for commercial reasons, need to allocate a value to the fixtures forming part of the property: if a building is sold for £800,000, there is no reason in principle why that £800,000 should be broken down into its constituent elements (bricks, roof, electrical systems, and so on). It follows that some mechanism is needed to agree the transfer value of those items – the fixtures – that are relevant for capital allowances purposes.

Statutory context

In statutory terms, the key change in 2012 was the introduction of sections 187A and 187B into CAA 2001. These sections come under the heading "Restrictions on Amount of Qualifying Expenditure" which is part of Chapter 14 (Fixtures) of Part 2 (Plant and Machinery Allowances). Section 187A is given the heading "Effect of changes in ownership of a fixture" and s. 187B is entitled "Section 187A: supplementary provision".

Land contamination

The special relief for the costs of decontaminating land – land remediation relief – is not part of the capital allowances legislation and is therefore beyond the scope of this book. Nevertheless, the relief should – in appropriate cases – be considered alongside capital allowances when buying land. Brief coverage is therefore included at the end of this chapter (at section **12.12**).

12.2   Conditions for the buyer to claim allowances

12.2.1   Overview

The purchaser of a property will by definition have incurred capital expenditure (assuming, of course, that he is not trading in property, in which case these rules will not apply) and will, as a result, own the property. The fundamental conditions for claiming plant and machinery allowances – capital expenditure resulting in ownership – are therefore met (per s. 11: see **4.1.2**).

For most property acquisitions since April 2014, however, two further conditions must be met if the buyer is to obtain any allowances: the pooling requirement and the fixed value requirement. These two requirements apply in most but not all circumstances, as explained at **12.4** and **12.5** below.

If these two requirements are imposed by the legislation in the circumstances of the deal but are not met, the purchaser – and all future owners of the property – will be denied allowances for the fixtures in question.

If the required conditions are not met, the past owner must still bring in a disposal value in the usual way (normally triggering a balancing charge) – even though the new owner will be denied the chance to claim plant and machinery allowances for the fixtures in question. The vendor's perspective is considered in detail in **Chapter 13** below, but this aspect of the legislation means that both parties to a property transaction will have a strong incentive to reach an agreement on the capital allowances aspects of the deal.

317

A third requirement – the disposal value statement requirement – is imposed in much rarer circumstances, as explained at **12.6** below.

Law: CAA 2001, s. 187A(3)

12.2.2 Pooling requirement (in brief)

First, the *vendor* must have added the qualifying expenditure to his tax computations – to the extent that he is permitted to do so. This is known as the pooling requirement, and is considered in greater depth at **12.4** below.

Example

A Ltd bought a property in 2009 and is now selling it to B Ltd. B Ltd can only claim allowances for fixtures in the property if A Ltd has added them to its own computations first. So A Ltd must add to its own computations the maximum possible value for fixtures in the property if B Ltd is to be able to claim.

However, this only applies if A Ltd is entitled to claim, and each fixture must in principle be considered separately. If A Ltd had bought the property before April 2008, however, it will probably not be entitled to claim allowances for certain integral features, such as the cold water system and general lighting. These fixtures, then, would not be covered by the pooling requirement.

12.2.3 Fixed value requirement (in brief)

The second condition that must be met, if the purchaser is to make any claim for capital allowances, is that the two parties to the transaction must formally determine a transfer value for all the fixtures in the property (including any integral features) that have been included in the vendor's capital allowances computations. This is called the fixed value requirement, and is considered in depth at **12.5** below.

In nearly all cases, this means that an election must be signed under s. 198 to agree the value at which the fixtures will be transferred. The figure in the election will provide the capital allowances disposal value for the vendor and the acquisition value for the purchaser.

Example

One of the assets in the property being sold by A Ltd to B Ltd in the example above is an air conditioning system that A Ltd installed at a cost of £20,000. The two parties must allocate a value to that system by signing a fixtures election. The value allocated to the system does not have to be market value but may be anywhere between zero and £20,000: this is entirely a matter of negotiation between the parties.

Once a valid election has been submitted, the figure is binding on both parties and on HMRC. It is also irrevocable.

Given that a fixtures election is (normally) the only way to secure the purchaser's entitlement to allowances, it is vital that the election should be correctly completed, and submitted within the required timeframe. The technicalities of an election are covered at **12.7** below.

12.2.4 Additional claim for the purchaser

As mentioned above, there may be fixtures on which the vendor has been unable to claim allowances. Almost certainly, these will be such assets as are now categorised as integral features (see, generally, **4.11**) and that did not qualify if purchased before April 2008.

As the vendor is not entitled to claim for these items, the pooling requirement and the fixed value requirement do not apply to them. Nevertheless, the purchaser is in principle entitled to claim for these assets as well.

The value of these additional items will need to be calculated using an apportionment principle. This is explained in depth at **12.8** below, but it is worth noting here that the value to be attributed to such items is often much higher than their apparent market value.

12.2.5 Costs incurred by the purchaser

The purchaser may incur professional or other costs in relation to the property acquisition. Although no allowances are allowed for the legal costs of acquisition, for example, it is possible that the purchaser of a property will need to engage – for example – the costs of a structural or mechanical engineer. The treatment of these costs will depend on all the facts, but if they have to be capitalised it is possible that they will qualify for allowances, in part or in whole.

12.2.6 The cost of delay

The tax effect of the various requirements is to prevent allowances for the current (new) owner where the conditions are not met. Failure by the *past* owner to handle allowances correctly will therefore mean that the *current* owner can lose out. (The new rules have no direct bearing on the tax position for the past owner, but a vendor can easily incur a balancing charge if he fails to handle the disposal correctly. See **13.1**.)

Example

The owner of a care home is now selling it, having acquired it six years ago. Although some fixtures have been the subject of a claim for plant and machinery allowances, no claim has been made for other expenditure.

The property is sold for £1 million and it is computed that the potential capital allowances value of the fixtures is £350,000. However, allowances have been claimed only on one fifth of the total. The fixtures that have been subject to a claim are listed out and an election is signed in the amount of £40,000.

The former owner submits his tax computations using that agreed figure of £40,000. Three years later, the new owner realises that a claim could have been made for the remaining fixtures in the property, but it is now too late for the former owner to amend his tax computations. The value is permanently lost.

This clearly has very important implications for professional advisers working with the purchaser. For this reason, it is essential to address the matters as part of the sale and purchase process.

The need for the past owner to make a claim did not apply until (broadly) April 2014: see **12.3.8** below.

Law: CAA 2001, s. 187A, 187B

12.2.7   Summary of buyer's position

The main claim to be made by the purchaser of a property will therefore be determined by the fixtures election. If the vendor owned the property before April 2008, the purchaser will also need to consider a claim based on an apportionment approach for certain additional fixtures. It is also possible that certain professional or other acquisition costs will qualify for allowances. Finally, and entirely outside the scope of the pooling and fixed value requirements, relief may be due also for moveable items of plant and machinery (chattels).

In their essence, then, the rules are not difficult. In practice, of course, there can be many complicating factors. The critical issue for the buyer, though, is to gain legal certainty that the vendor has captured the value of the fixtures in his capital allowances computations. Equally essential is the requirement to submit, in time, a valid fixtures election.

Difficulties may arise if the seller (or his adviser) has a poor understanding of capital allowances. There may be unjustified fears that the making of a capital allowances claim will increase a capital gains tax liability, or there may be a perception that any claim will be almost worthless because the fixtures are now old. Both of these are in principle wrong.

It may also be that the seller is simply unwilling to incur the costs of making a proper capital allowances claim, where any benefit will just pass to the new owner. If the amounts at stake are substantial, the buyer may wish to consider paying for the preparation of a claim (or may, of course, simply refuse to proceed with the purchase unless the allowances are sorted out). It may also be necessary to reassure the seller that the inclusion of a properly computed capital allowances claim will not cause problems of any sort with HMRC.

Finally, the new rules recognise that the past owner is not necessarily the person selling the property. This is because the "past owner" as defined for these purposes must have been entitled to claim allowances. If the actual seller is not entitled to claim allowances, probably because he is not carrying on a qualifying activity or because he has owned the property as trading stock, it will be necessary to look back to earlier periods of ownership. However, this will only be the case where the earlier party owned the property on or after 1 or 6 April 2012 (the "commencement date" – see **12.3.8**).

Law: CAA 2001, s. 11, 187A, 187B

12.3   When the pooling and fixed value requirements apply

12.3.1   Introduction

In the great majority of cases, a person buying a property will need to ensure that the changes introduced in FA 2012 – primarily the pooling and fixed value requirements, as outlined at **12.2** above – are met. However, there are exceptions and the details are quite complex.

The FA 2012 rules only apply where four specified conditions are met. If the requirements are not met, but allowances would have been due for the new owner under the rules applying before April 2012, allowances continue to be due in the same way. In other words, the changes applying from April 2012 merely impose new conditions that have to be met in certain circumstances; if those circumstances do not arise, the new restrictions do not operate. So if one or more of these conditions is not met, the person acquiring the property can ignore the pooling and fixed value requirements (as well as the disposal value statement requirement: see **12.6** below) when determining if a claim can be made.

Each of the four conditions is considered in turn below.

Law: CAA 2001, s. 187A(1)

12.3.2   New expenditure

The starting point is that a person must be treated as owning a fixture as a result of incurring capital expenditure on its provision. The expenditure must have been incurred for the purposes of a qualifying activity (e.g. a trade) carried on by the person incurring the expenditure.

Typically, the rules will apply where a person buys a commercial property (e.g. a shop, an office or a care home). All commercial property contains a certain level of fixtures (such as lighting or central heating).

The person owning the fixture as a result of incurring the expenditure is referred to in the legislation as "the current owner" and the expenditure in question is called "new expenditure".

Law: CAA 2001, s. 187A(1)(a)

12.3.3   Historic expenditure

The next condition for the new rules to apply concerns previous owners. The fixture in question must have been treated as owned at a "relevant earlier time" (see **12.3.6**) by a person as a result of that person incurring other capital expenditure on its provision.

Once more, the expenditure must have been incurred for the purposes of a qualifying activity carried on by that earlier person. Furthermore, that person must have been entitled to claim plant and machinery allowances on the fixture in question (whether or not he in fact did so).

The earlier capital expenditure is referred to as "historic expenditure". The term "past owner" is given to the person incurring that historic expenditure. If there was more than one amount of historic expenditure then the past owner is the person by whom the expenditure was most recently incurred. The past owner is typically but not always the vendor.

The past owner is a person who has in the past been entitled to claim allowances for historic expenditure on a fixture. This would therefore exclude a non-taxpayer (e.g. a charity or pension fund), as explained more fully below in relation to the fourth condition.

The past owner must be treated as having owned the plant or machinery in question as a result of incurring historic expenditure for the purposes of a qualifying activity carried on by him. The resulting ownership must be at a relevant earlier time.

A key point is that the past owner must, by definition, have incurred capital expenditure. If the current owner buys a newly built property, the expenditure incurred by the builder will have been revenue rather than capital expenditure. The builder is not a past owner for these purposes, as he did not incur capital expenditure on the property. Or the current owner of a property may pay to have it fitted out with new fixtures; once more, the new rules will not apply as there has been no earlier capital expenditure on the provision of the fixtures.

The typical scenario where the rules *will* apply is where a person buys a used commercial property.

Law: CAA 2001, s. 187A(1)(b), (2)

12.3.4   Contribution allowances

This will arise less frequently in practice, but the rules do not apply where the fixture was treated as owned as a result of historic expenditure (i.e. per the second condition above) only by virtue of s. 538 (the special rules for contribution allowances: see **31.3**). So the pooling and fixed value requirements are not imposed in those circumstances.

Law: CAA 2001, s. 187A(1)(c)

12.3.5   Past owner able to claim allowances

The rules will not apply if no past owner (as defined) was entitled to claim allowances for the fixtures in question. Here, as throughout the fixtures rules, it is important to remember that the capital allowances legislation works – in theory – on an asset-by-asset basis. So if a person has been entitled to claim for Asset 1 but not for Asset 2 then the FA 2012 provisions apply to the former but not to the latter.

This rule may prevent the imposition of the FA 2012 restrictions in two typical circumstances.

First, the principle will be relevant in relation to certain integral features acquired before April 2008. As a result of changes introduced in 2008, a broader range of assets started to qualify for plant and machinery allowances. Certain items now classified as integral features did not normally qualify for relief if they were owned before that date.

Example 1

Charlie bought an office building in 2002 and is now selling it. He meets all the conditions in respect of most of the fixtures in the property, so the pooling and fixed value requirements must be met if the purchaser is to claim allowances. However, Charlie is not entitled to claim allowances for the cost of the general lighting, for example.

It follows that the pooling and fixed value requirements do not apply to the lighting costs. The new owner (Dave), however, is entitled to claim for the costs, and the quantum of the claim must be established by applying apportionment principles. Charlie has no interest in this part of the claim, but he will need to cooperate with Dave regarding all the remaining fixtures in the property.

Another circumstance in which this condition will not be met is when the vendor has owned the property since before April 2012 (the date from which, broadly speaking, the FA 2012 rules apply) and is a non-taxpayer.

Example 2

A pension fund has owned the freehold of a block of offices since 2010 and is now selling them. The pension fund is treated here as the only past owner, as it has owned them since before the FA 2012 rules were introduced. As a non-taxpayer, the pension fund has not been entitled to claim allowances. As such, the conditions of s. 187A(1) are not met and the pooling and fixed value requirements are not imposed on the buyer.

It follows that the buyer will make a claim on an apportionment basis, though its claim will be restricted (by virtue of s. 185 – see **12.7.5**) if a previous owner has in fact made a claim for plant or machinery allowances.

It may be the case that both of these principles are involved in a single transaction.

Example 3

Edward bought a new office building in 2002 and sold it to Fiona in 2015. Fiona, who has confirmed that the property has been trading stock in her accounts, is now selling it to George.

As s. 187A(1)(d) refers to a person who was entitled to claim an allowance, the legislation cannot apply in this scenario to the lighting costs. Edward was not able to claim for the costs of general lighting as he owned the property before April 2008. Fiona could not claim as she did not incur capital expenditure (see s. 187A(1)(d)). So the pooling and fixed value requirements do not apply in these circumstances to the lighting costs. George can claim allowances for those costs on an apportionment basis, in addition to whatever other amounts may be claimable.

A particular issue is known to have arisen in practice where a business owner claimed industrial buildings allowances, which would therefore prevent the same owner from claiming plant and machinery allowances for the same assets – see **1.7.1** above. If a person chose to claim IBAs for certain expenditure (which, as IBAs ceased altogether in 2011, must have been before the new legislation at s. 187A was enacted in 2012) can it still be said that the person "was entitled to claim [a plant and machinery allowance] in respect of the historic expenditure"?

On the one hand it may be argued that as the person had in fact claimed IBAs he was not entitled to claim plant and machinery allowances. This interpretation would mean that the conditions of s. 187A are not met and that the pooling and fixed value requirements are therefore not imposed. On the other, it may be argued that the person chose to claim IBAs but could have chosen to claim PMAs, and that he is therefore indeed caught by the wording.

A reader of this book raised the point with HMRC, who are understood to have responded that "the s. 187A provisions do not apply if the past owner was not entitled to claim plant and machinery allowances due to having already claimed allowances under Part 3". In the author's view, this is the correct interpretation of an ambiguous point, for three reasons.

First, an alternative interpretation would produce an impossible result in practice, as it would impose the pooling and fixed value requirements in circumstances in which these are not capable of being met (as the past owner does not have the option of claiming PMAs). This is unjust and there is no reason of principle why such an outcome should be imposed.

Second, it is worth noting that there could never be, and could never have been, any attempt to exploit the ambiguity so as to gain an unintended tax advantage. This is because, as noted above, the chance to claim IBAs came to an end before the new legislation was enacted.

Lastly, the stricter interpretation would seem to remove any grounds for retaining s. 186, which imposes a partial restriction on allowances that may be claimed by the new owner where the previous owner had claimed IBAs. As s. 186 remains on the statute book, its purpose can only be to address circumstances in which the past owner claimed IBAs but the new owner is to claim PMAs. But such circumstances could not exist if the stricter interpretation is made of this provision.

Law: CAA 2001, s. 187A(1)(d)

12.3.6   Relevant earlier time

The pooling and fixed value requirements are only imposed if the plant or machinery was owned, by a person entitled to claim allowances, at a "relevant earlier time".

The relevant earlier time is normally the time ending before the sale that is being considered. More technically, it is the time ending immediately before the date on which the current owner is first treated as owning the plant or machinery as a result of incurring the new expenditure. This is subject to two exceptions.

First, the commencement and transitional rules need to be considered. See **12.3.8** below for fuller details but essentially this means that periods of ownership before 1 or 6 April 2012 are for these purposes ignored. The second example at **12.3.5** immediately above shows why the pooling and fixed value requirements would not be imposed, for example, if the current vendor is a non-taxpayer who has owned the property since before April 2012.

The second, much rarer, exception relates to fixtures that have been detached from the property, which HMRC explained well in the *Explanatory Notes* to the relevant Finance Bill.

> "New subsection (5) ensures that the legislation does not apply where there has been a sale of an asset that is no longer a fixture at the time of sale, unless that sale is to a connected person. For example: company A owns a building, containing an antique copper water heater, which it strips out and sells to an architectural salvage dealer. Company B, not connected with company A, buys the copper water heater from the dealer and installs it in a property it owns. Company B is not required to establish the disposal value brought into account by Company A and is not precluded from claiming allowances based on what it paid for the asset."

Although rare in practice, it is possible for the current owner and the past owner to be the same person.

Law: CAA 2001, s. 187A, 187B

12.3.7 Non-resident landlords

A particular issue may arise in practice for non-resident landlords who own commercial property in the UK.

The details of the scheme are beyond the scope of this book, but HMRC provide extensive guidance. The scheme applies to the UK rental income of persons whose "usual place of abode" is outside the UK. Letting agents, and in some cases tenants, have an obligation to deduct tax from the rental income and to pay it over to HMRC, though HMRC may authorise them not to deduct tax in certain cases.

Where the obligation is in place, a letting agent must deduct tax at the basic rate of income tax from quarterly rental income less certain deductible expenses.

Example

A letting agent collects rent of £4,000 in the period in question and calculates that there are deductible expenses of £500. The basic rate of tax is 20%. The agent must deduct tax of £700 (20% of the net £3,500) and account for it to HMRC.

Expenses that may be deducted are those that are paid in the quarter that the agent "can reasonably be satisfied are deductible under the Tax Acts in computing the profits or gains of that business". The clear HMRC view is that that excludes a claim for capital allowances.

However, the special scheme does not impose a new tax charge in itself but – rather like PAYE – is merely a mechanism for collecting tax. It is open to the landlord to submit a tax return and to claim relief for all expenses that are due and, in particular, for capital allowances. According to the HMRC guidance, "letting agents cannot deduct capital expenses whereas landlords may be entitled to capital allowances".

There is an obvious risk that non-resident landlords will be unfamiliar with the capital allowances rules, especially the more complex ones relating to property fixtures. If they perceive that they are already receiving relief for most expenses, they may be disinclined to worry about the potential value of capital allowances. When they come to sell, however, they are in the same position as anyone else as far as the pooling requirement and fixed value requirement are concerned: they are entitled to claim and must do so if the new owner is not to lose out on valuable relief.

Law: ITA 2007, s. 971; SI 1995/2902

Guidance: www.gov.uk/government/uploads/system/uploads/attach ment_data/file/420961/notes-letting-agents-tenants.pdf

12.3.8 Commencement and transitional rules

The general principle is that the new legislation has had effect in relation to new expenditure incurred since 1 or 6 April 2012 ("the commencement date") for corporation tax and income tax respectively. This, however, is subject to two important provisos.

First, the rules do not apply if the past owner's period of ownership fell entirely before the commencement date. The statutory mechanism is to say that such a period is to be regarded as not occurring at a relevant earlier time (see **12.3.6** immediately above). As HMRC have confirmed, "neither the pooling requirement nor requirements to fix formally the value of fixtures apply in relation to such a period of ownership".

The second limitation on the scope of the new rules concerned the two year transitional period from 1 April 2012 to 31 March 2014 (but 6 April 2012 to 5 April 2014 for income tax purposes). During that period, the pooling requirement was not imposed. In other words, the requirement for the old owner to have made a claim did not apply for sales in the period to 31 March or 5 April 2014.

There was no similar relaxation of the fixed value requirement as the legislation merely says the following:

> "Section 187A(3)(a) of CAA 2001 (imposition of the pooling requirement) does not apply if the period for which the plant or machinery is treated as having been owned by the past owner as a result of incurring the historic expenditure ends no later than the end of the period of 2 years beginning with the commencement date."

So if the vendor had not claimed, and the sale took place before April 2014, this was not a problem for the purchaser, who could still claim for fixtures in the property. But if the vendor had claimed allowances for a particular fixture, the requirement to sign a fixtures election (or, exceptionally, to go to a tax tribunal) was imposed for sale and purchase transactions from April 2012.

Law: FA 2012, s. 187A(5), (10), Sch. 10, para. 11, 13

12.4 The pooling requirement

Now that the FA 2012 rules are fully operational, the pooling requirement must be satisfied in all cases, if the current owner is to obtain allowances. If this condition is not met, the new owner (and all future owners) will be denied all plant and machinery allowances for the fixtures in question.

In accordance with s. 187A(4):

> "The pooling requirement is that–
>
> (a) the historic expenditure has been allocated to a pool in a chargeable period beginning on or before the day on which the past owner ceases to be treated as the owner of the fixture, or
>
> (b) a first-year allowance has been claimed in respect of that expenditure (or any part of it)."

The distinction here is a technicality with regard to the way the plant and machinery pooling system works where there is an FYA claim – what matters is whether the fixtures in question have been included in a past owner's capital allowances computation (typically, but not always, in the computation of the person now selling the property).

As emphasised above, the concern is with the treatment of the *historic* expenditure, so the issue arises in respect of the past owner's tax computations. The pooling requirement is met if the past owner has claimed an FYA or has added the expenditure in question as qualifying expenditure to a plant and machinery pool (typically the main pool or the special rate pool). There is no requirement that allowances should actually have been claimed on the asset in question: they can be added to the pool but writing-down (and other) allowances can be disclaimed if necessary.

It may be that there are assets on which the vendor is not able to claim allowances – normally integral features such as general electrical wiring, general lighting and cold water systems, where the costs were incurred before April 2008, and did not at that time qualify as plant or machinery. To the extent that the vendor is not allowed to claim allowances, the pooling requirement is not imposed.

Example

Oldco Ltd draws accounts up to 31 December and sells a property on 1 November 2021. Oldco incurred capital expenditure on fixtures back in

2003 but has not bothered to claim plant and machinery allowances as the company has trading losses and is therefore not paying corporation tax. No calculation has been made of the qualifying expenditure incurred in 2003.

The company is free to make such a claim for any year in which the assets in question are still owned.

The pooling requirement will be met only if the expenditure is added, as far as permitted, to Oldco's capital allowances pool. The last chance to do this is in the computations for the year to 31 December 2021, being the last chargeable period that starts "on or before the day on which the past owner ceases to be treated as the owner of the fixture". If Oldco does not do this, the new owner will be denied allowances on all the fixtures in question. In this case, the new owner's only claim will be in respect of integral features on which the vendor was not entitled to claim allowances.

The fixtures legislation has always been worded on the basis that each individual fixture is considered in isolation. In practice, this would be wholly impractical as a building may contain many thousands of identifiable fixtures, but the principle will be enforced if it makes a difference. Where, for example, there is a reference to claiming an FYA in respect of the expenditure "or any part of it" that cannot be taken to mean that a claim made on one fixture somehow covers any other fixtures.

The pooling requirement does not mean that the value of the allowances has to be shared between the old and the new owners. At one extreme, it will be possible for an old owner to claim allowances and to retain their full value by putting a zero value into the fixtures election. By contrast, the old owner can add the full value to his capital allowances pool but then disclaim allowances; this still meets the pooling requirement but by putting the maximum figure into the fixtures election, the entire value can be transferred to the new owner. In most cases, a middle way is agreed between the purchaser and the seller, so that each party enjoys tax relief on part of the value of the fixtures.

See Case study 6 in **Appendix 2** for an illustration of this.

Law: CAA 2001, s. 187A(4)

12.5   The fixed value requirement

12.5.1   Introduction

In practice, the fixed value requirement normally means simply that the two parties to a property transaction must sign an election – under section 198 of CAA 2001 – to determine the value at which fixtures in the property are to be transferred from vendor to purchaser. That value, which will be part of the overall price paid for the property and not a separate figure alongside that price, will be used as the vendor's disposal value for the fixtures and as the purchaser's acquisition cost for capital allowances purposes.

The fixtures election is the way the requirement is met in the overwhelming majority of cases. It is not, however, the only possible way.

12.5.2   When the requirement must be met

The fixed value requirement has to be met in most but not all cases. The point depends on the technical statutory mechanism by which the past owner is obliged to bring into account a disposal value for the fixture in question. The requirement applies where that obligation is imposed by items 1, 5 or 9 of the Table at s. 196.

Section 196 is the section of the plant and machinery legislation determining the disposal value for fixtures. The table is complex with many internal cross references and readers should check the detailed legislation in appropriate cases. The HMRC summary, from the *Explanatory Notes* issued with the Finance Bill legislation in March 2012, reads as follows:

> "The relevant disposal events are items 1, 5 or 9 in that Table. Item 1 covers the case of a market value sale; item 5 covers the case of an incoming lessee paying a capital sum for the lease, which sum falls to be treated in whole or part as expenditure on the provision of the fixture; and item 9 covers the case of a past owner, who permanently discontinues his business, followed by a sale of the qualifying interest in the property, including its fixtures.
>
> This last case should be distinguished from the example given in relation to new subsection 10 below, where there is a significant gap between the past owner ceasing his business and later deciding to sell the property, so that the capital allowances disposal event occurs on the earlier occasion."

In practice, item 1 will apply to most sales and item 5 will apply in most cases where the tenant makes a capital sum under a lease (i.e. a lease premium).

A few definitions are given to interpret the fixed value requirement. These differ according to whether the case falls within items 1 or 9 of the s. 196 Table on the one hand, or within item 5 of that Table on the other.

Cases falling within items 1 or 9:

- *Affected parties* are the past owner and the purchaser from the past owner.
- *Apportionable sum* means the sale price.
- *Election* is an election under CAA 2001, s. 198.
- *Relevant two year period* is the period of two years beginning with the date when the purchaser from the past owner acquires the qualifying interest.

Cases falling within item 5:

- *Affected parties* are the past owner and the lessee.
- *Apportionable sum* means the capital sum given by the lessee for the lease.
- *Election* is an election under CAA 2001, s. 199.
- *Relevant two year period* is the period of two years beginning with the date when the lessee is granted the lease.

The way these terms are applied in practice is explained at **12.5.3** and **12.5.4** below.

Law: CAA 2001, s. 187A(5), (9)

12.5.3 *Details of the requirement*

In accordance with s. 187A(6):

"The fixed value requirement is that either–

(a) a relevant apportionment of the apportionable sum has been made, or

(b) the current owner has obtained the statements mentioned in subsection (8), or copies of them, (directly or indirectly) from the persons who made them and the case is one where the purchaser from the past owner or, as the case may be, lessee was not

> entitled to claim an allowance under this Part in respect of capital expenditure incurred on the fixture."

The first of these two options will apply in most cases – the requirement to make a "relevant apportionment", and this will be considered first. See **12.5.5** for an explanation of the relatively rare circumstances in which (b) above will apply.

12.5.4   Relevant apportionment

In most cases, the first of these options will apply and there will need to have been "a relevant apportionment of the apportionable sum". This concept is subject to a further statutory definition (at s. 187A(7)), as follows:

> "... a relevant apportionment of the apportionable sum is made if—
>
> (a)   the tribunal determines the part of the apportionable sum that constitutes the disposal value, on an application made by one of the affected parties before the end of the relevant 2 year period, or
>
> (b)   an election is made, in respect of the apportionable sum, by the affected parties jointly—
>
> (i)   before the end of the relevant 2 year period, or
>
> (ii)   if an application is made as mentioned in paragraph (a) and not determined or withdrawn by the end of that period, before that application is determined or withdrawn."

Although worded in this way, the practical reality is that (b) rather than (a) will apply in the overwhelming majority of cases. In other words, the normal route is that the two parties will simply agree to sign an election to determine the transfer value of the fixtures.

If the parties cannot agree the amount to include in a fixtures election, it will be necessary to take the matter to a tax tribunal (i.e. option (a) above). This is likely to arise rarely in practice, partly because of the costs involved but also because it means that the sale and purchase agreement will be unable to give closure on the matter. Nevertheless,

HMRC did make the following point in their response (para. 3.31) to the consultation document:

> "The Government wishes to place on record that the proposal to make section 198/199 CAA elections the norm, should not be seen as detracting, in any way, from the right of either the seller or the purchaser to insist upon a just and reasonable apportionment of the sale value of a property to its fixtures."

The circumstances in which a person might go to tribunal are likely to be where the issue of capital allowances has not been resolved before the property sale. (If the matter is still open before the sale goes through, the resolution of capital allowances is likely to form part of the negotiation process.)

Example

A Ltd recently sold a restaurant to B Ltd. A Ltd had claimed allowances for fixtures in the property costing £140,000 but (owing to a misunderstanding between the solicitors and the accountants) the question of capital allowances was not resolved before the sale completed.

B Ltd approaches the vendor shortly after completion and asks for a fixtures election to be signed with a figure of £80,000, thus allowing B Ltd to claim allowances on that figure. The written down values in A Ltd's capital allowances pools are just £25,000, so this will create a balancing charge of £55,000 for A Ltd. The director of A Ltd is under no legal obligation to sign an election, and refuses to do so.

B Ltd might in these circumstances ask a tribunal to determine the disposal value for these purposes. The resulting figure may well be higher than the £80,000 that has been proposed (for the reasons explained at **12.8** below).

In reality, A Ltd is not taking good advice in refusing to sign the election. Even if B Ltd does not go to a tribunal (which will mean, in the absence of an election, that B Ltd cannot claim allowances for any of the fixtures), A Ltd will still have to bring in a disposal value. That disposal value is likely to be higher than £80,000 and could be as high as £140,000. (This is explained more fully at **Chapter 13** below).

Two lessons can be drawn from this example. First, it can be seen why it is essential to agree the issues before the sale and purchase transaction is completed. Second, it is almost invariably in the interests of both parties to sign a fixtures election, even though the figures to go into the election will be a matter for negotiation. Going to the tribunal is likely to be expensive in terms of professional advice, and will create an uncertain outcome for both parties.

Leaving aside the possibility of going to a tribunal, and of certain other rare complications considered later in this chapter, the practical effect of the new rules may be easily summarised: the new owner can make a plant and machinery claim for fixtures if:

- the vendor has brought the cost of those fixtures into a capital allowances computation relating to a period before the sale (even if no allowances have in fact been claimed); and
- the two parties have signed and submitted a valid fixtures election.

The purchaser may also be able to claim if the vendor was not entitled to do so, typically in relation to integral features owned before April 2008.

Law: CAA 2001, s. 187A(6), (7)

12.5.5   Statements

If there is no relevant apportionment, another possible approach exists where there is a non-taxpayer who has been unable to claim allowances.

A non-taxpayer (such as a charity or a pension fund) is still entitled to sign an election under s. 198 when acquiring fixtures, and should always do so. However, if it has been overlooked then the legislation allows this to be rectified when the non-taxpayer subsequently sells the property. This may be achieved by obtaining statements both from the last owner who was able to claim allowances and from the intervening owner who was not. (These statements are not to be confused, however, with the "disposal value statement requirement" that is explained at **12.6** below).

This was explained by HMRC in the *Explanatory Notes* to the Finance Bill as follows (at paras. 13 to 15):

> "Persons who are not entitled to claim an allowance (such as charities that are not chargeable to tax) buying property from 'past owners' are entitled to make a section 198 or 199 of CAA election, or to apply to the tribunal for a determination of the fixtures value, if they wish to do so. They may wish to do so, in order to enable a future business purchaser to claim in respect of those fixtures, thereby potentially enhancing or protecting the value of their property investment. If they duly elect or apply to the tribunal, they will then be able to provide the election notice

or tribunal determination to a new owner, on a later sale, thereby establishing the new owner's entitlement to allowances on those fixtures.

However, it is possible that non-taxpayers, such as charities, may have scant knowledge or awareness of the capital allowances legislation and may therefore inadvertently omit to follow either of the election or tribunal procedures for making a fixtures' apportionment. Of course, it may be that the non-taxpayer had informally agreed with the seller that the seller could return a nil disposal value for the fixtures, precisely because the non-taxpayer was uninterested in the capital allowances. Indeed, it could even be that the non-taxpayer obtained the property for a somewhat lower price in consequence of allowing this. In such a situation, the expenditure on the fixtures would have been written off in full in the hands of the seller and it would be in accordance with the underlying policy for those fixtures to have a nil value in the hands the current owner, purchasing the property from the non-taxpayer. However, in a case where it can be formally demonstrated by the past owner that he returned a specific disposal value for those fixtures, and that it is too late for the non-business purchaser to fix an apportionment with him, a narrowly defined exception from the normal rule appears to be justified.

New subsection (8) therefore provides that, in these circumstances, if the current owner obtains a written statement made by the 'purchaser from the past owner' (in our example, say, a charity) that new subsection (6) (a) has not been met and is no longer capable of being met, and also a written statement made by the past owner of the actual amount of the disposal value that the past owner, in fact, brought into account, then the "fixed value requirement" would be regarded as met in that way. The expression 'purchaser from the past owner' in subsection (6)(b) means, in effect, an intermediate owner or lessee who was not entitled to claim an allowance, and who acquired an interest in the fixtures from a "past owner", who was so entitled to claim."

In other guidance, HMRC use the terminology of preserving allowances where there has been an "intervening owner" who has been unable to claim allowances for the fixtures. The following example illustrates the point:

HMRC example

Adam sells a building to a charity in 2015 then the charity sells the building to Ben in 2018. Here the charity is the intervening owner between Adam and Ben.

The charity can't claim PMA for capital expenditure they incurred on the fixtures. But Adam and the charity can make an election agreeing the apportionment (or apply to the tribunal to decide the value).

When the charity sells the building these documents can be passed to the new owner, Ben. This will satisfy the fixed value requirement and pass on the entitlement to PMA to Ben.

But the intervening owner, the charity, doesn't consider making a joint election with Adam.

To avoid losing allowances in these circumstances, Ben can satisfy the fixed value requirement if he gets both a written statement:

- from the charity (intervening owner) stating that an election was not made and can no longer be made
- made by Adam showing the disposal value that he brought in

The wording of this HMRC example is grammatically and logically flawed, but the intended meaning is reasonably clear. The key point is that two separate statements are required. The last owner who was entitled to claim allowances must provide a statement of the disposal value that he was required to bring in, and the intervening owner must provide a statement that no election was signed when it acquired the property and that it can no longer sign such an election.

This approach should be seen very much as repairing an imperfect earlier handling of the issues. It is much cleaner for all parties if an election is properly signed on the occasion of the purchase by the charity from the previous owner. Nevertheless, there may be circumstances in which the provisions could be useful.

Example 2

Buyer Ltd is buying a property from a pension fund in April 2019. The pension company bought it from a connected party, Oldco Ltd, in February 2017. Oldco Ltd draws accounts up to 30 September each year.

Oldco Ltd and the pension fund could and should have signed a fixtures election under s. 198, for any fixtures for which Oldco had claimed, but are now out of time to do so.

Suppose that Oldco Ltd had claimed for some fixtures but had overlooked the possibility of claiming for others.

With regard to the fixtures for which it had claimed, it is *required* to bring a disposal value into account, even though no election was signed (s. 187B(6)). Assuming that it does indeed do this, Buyer Ltd will be able to claim per the wording at s. 187A(8)(b), using the "disposal value that the past owner has in fact brought into account".

For the overlooked fixtures, it is still open to Oldco Ltd to amend its accounts for the year to 30 September 2017, as the fixtures were still owned at some point in that year. So if the additional claim is for, say, £100,000, it can add this qualifying expenditure to its capital allowances computations for that year. Once more, no fixtures election is possible as it is out of time (more than two years since the disposal to the pension fund) but Oldco must bring a full disposal value into account, which (using normal valuation principles) is likely to be £100,000. This will in turn allow Buyer Ltd to claim for the £100,000.

There is no tax cost to Oldco for this whole exercise, assuming that it was intending to bring correct disposal values into account in the first place. However, there is some work involved and Buyer Ltd will therefore wish to get Oldco's legal commitment to doing what is necessary, before completing the purchase.

Law: CAA 2001, s. 187A(6)(b)

Guidance: www.gov.uk/guidance/plant-and-machinery-allowances-on-fixtures-when-theres-a-change-of-ownership

12.5.6   Burden of proof

The legislation specifies that it is for the current owner (i.e. the buyer) to show whether or not the fixed value requirement applies and (if it does) that it is satisfied. Failing this, no allowances can be claimed by the new owner.

The fixed value requirement only applies if the past owner is required to bring in a disposal value, which in turn can only apply if that past owner has brought a cost figure into his capital allowances computations (whether or not any allowances were in fact claimed).

The new owner can be asked to produce to HMRC a tribunal decision, an election or a statement to prove that the necessary condition is satisfied.

Before April 2012, arguments could arise as to whether any claim had previously been made by the vendor. There could be strong circumstantial evidence that no such claim had been made but the matter was often not free from doubt.

HMRC took the line that it was for the claimant to prove that there had been no earlier claims. The *West Somerset Railway* case had held that the onus was on the taxpayer to show that no person had previously been entitled to claim, even though this was acknowledged to be "an almost impossible task". This stance was, once more, supported in the *Tapsell* case, where the tribunal held that "the burden of proof must lie with the Appellants to show that there had been no previous claim made by the vendors to capital allowances". The taxpayers in that case failed to discharge the burden of proof.

The fact that a claim had been made by a previous owner did not, of course, mean that all future claims were barred. However, if a previous owner had claimed allowances then the question arose of whether any disposal value had been brought in by that owner. The arguments could then be complex – if the previous owner should have brought in a disposal value, but did not, where did that leave the claim for the new owner? This issue has created real difficulties in practice.

See also case studies 6 and 8 in **Appendix 2** for an illustration of some of the practical issues arising.

Law: CAA 2001, s. 187B(1)

Cases: *West Somerset Railway plc v Chivers* [1995] STC 1; *Tapsell & Anor (t/a The Granleys) v HMRC* [2011] UKFTT 376 (TC)

12.6   The disposal value statement requirement

12.6.1   When the requirement must be met

According to HMRC guidance, the "disposal value statement requirement" is likely to apply only very infrequently.

The *Explanatory Notes* to the Finance Bill (at para. 17) explain this as follows:

> "This provision is designed to cater for a very small subset of disposal events that may have occurred, other than by virtue of an immediate sale of, or grant of a lease of, the fixtures by a person

carrying on a qualifying activity. The requirement would apply if, for example, a past owner had previously permanently ceased his business activity, finalising his cessation accounts and tax return, in which he would have been required to bring the market value of the fixtures, at that time, into account, in accordance with item 7 of the Table in section 61 of CAA. If, some years later, he then decided to sell his former business premises with its fixtures to a purchaser, "the disposal value statement requirement" would apply."

The point here is that the past owner may be required to bring a disposal value into account even though the property has not been sold: for example, if the qualifying activity simply comes to an end but without a disposal of the property. If he then does sell the property some years later, it will not be possible to enter into an election with the buyer to fix the value of the fixtures (as the requirements of s. 198(1) will not be met and it may in any case be too late). Instead, the new owner can ask the past owner for a written statement giving details of the disposal value that that past owner was required to bring into account. However, the past owner should not delay making the statement: even though it may not be needed until some years after the disposal is brought into account, there is a two year time limit for the past owner to make the written statement.

Example

Sam has leased out some offices for many years but the last property becomes vacant in May 2019. He does not actively look for new tenants and so he draws up his final property leasing accounts to 31 May 2019. He is considering whether to give the property to his two adult children, but in the end decides to sell it, and the sale goes through in September 2021.

As the property business ceased in 2019, Sam has to bring a disposal value into account for the fixtures in the 2019accounts, using market value. No further disposal value is brought into account in 2021, and no fixtures election is then possible.

As long as Sam made a disposal value statement within two years from the May 2019 date on which the business ceased, the new owner can obtain a copy of the statement and will then be able to claim allowances for the fixtures in the property using those figures.

In technical terms, the disposal value statement requirement applies if the past owner has to (or has had to) bring a disposal value into account in accordance with certain specified provisions. Those provisions are items 2 or 3 of the Table at s. 196, and item 7 of the Table at s. 61.

Item 2 at s. 196 applies where the fixture ceases to be owned because of a sale at less than market value. The purchaser must be unable to claim plant or machinery or research or development allowances on the fixture (or must be a dual resident investing company connected with the former owner).

Item 3 at s. 196 applies in certain circumstances where the qualifying interest continues in existence or would so continue but for its becoming merged with another interest.

Item 7 at s. 61 applies where market value is used as the disposal value in certain rare but specified circumstances.

Law: CAA 2001, s. 187A(10)

12.6.2   Details of the requirement

For the requirement to be met, the past owner must make a written statement no later than two years after the date on which he ceased to own the plant or machinery. The statement must show the disposal value of the fixtures that the past owner is (or has been) required to bring into account.

The requirement is only treated as met, however, if a further condition is met. This further condition is that the current owner has obtained the past owner's statement, or a copy of it. The statement or copy may be obtained either directly or indirectly.

HMRC illustrate this rather odd-seeming provision as follows (at para. 18 of the *Explanatory Notes* to the Finance Bill):

> "If, for example, the immediate purchaser is not a business, but a later purchaser is a business, the later purchaser may obtain the required statement either directly from the past owner, or indirectly from the intermediate owner, who sold the property to the current owner. As with the "fixed value requirement", an intermediate purchaser, who is not a business should ensure that he obtains this written statement from the past owner, if he wants to make sure that he is able to pass on an entitlement to claim on those fixtures to a future owner. However, the later owner is free to try to obtain the statement, or a copy of it, directly from the past owner, if the past owner is still contactable and willing to oblige."

Law: CAA 2001, s. 187A(11)

12.7 Fixtures elections

12.7.1 Introduction

Apportionments that involve valuations and negotiations inevitably come with a price tag in terms of professional time. In many cases, the complications and expense may be avoided with a fixtures election. If a valid election is submitted, it takes precedence over any other apportionment.

The fixtures election was introduced for chargeable periods ending on or after 19 March 1997 (the date of Royal Assent to FA 1997). Between 1997 and April 2012, such elections were often not used in practice: sometimes this was deliberate policy, as one party (usually the purchaser) sought to gain an advantage through using an apportioned value; but all too often it was because the parties failed to realise the possible advantages until it was too late, or simply relied (imprudently) on the wording in the sale and purchase agreement.

Under the rules applying since April 2012, the election has come into its own and should now be seen as the standard way of dealing with transfer values for fixtures. Indeed, it is no longer open to the parties to make any other apportionment in most circumstances.

The key points regarding an election are as follows:

- It should be signed (but see below) jointly by seller and purchaser and must normally (but once more see below) be submitted within two years of the date of sale (or of the grant of the lease).
- It must specify the amount fixed as the sale price for a particular fixture (but see below where, as is almost certainly the case in practice, there are multiple fixtures).
- The amount fixed by the election does not have to correlate to market value but may not exceed the cost that the seller has brought into account for the fixture for capital allowances purposes.
- Nor may the amount fixed by election for the fixtures exceed the overall sale price of the property.
- The election is binding on both parties and on HMRC.

There is nothing in the relevant legislation that explicitly states that the election must in fact be signed. In a major discussion, where it suited HMRC to argue that an unsigned election was valid, HMRC have stated in

2016 that "there is nothing stated in the legislation that the certificates need to be signed by both parties" and that "the signing of the elections is not necessary to make them valid". It is not known how this point was ultimately resolved with HMRC, but the author's view is that a signature by both parties is indeed a requirement for a valid election. There is a statutory provision stating that "the seller and the purchaser may jointly, by an election, fix the amount ..." which clearly implies that the parties must both sign the election.

The election is irrevocable. However, if the figure included in the election proves – because of circumstances arising after the making of the election – to be higher than the statutory maximum, the election is treated for capital allowances purposes as having been made in the maximum allowable amount. As the election attributes part of the sale value to fixtures, the remaining amount (if any) of the sale price must be adjusted accordingly, so that it correctly reflects the expenditure attributable to the property that does not constitute fixtures.

Election not possible in some circumstances

An election under s. 198 is only possible where the disposal value of the fixture has to be brought into account in accordance with items 1 or 9 of the table at section 196. Normally, this means that it may be made when there is a sale of a property at not less than market value. No election is possible if the vendor is a non-taxpayer (such as a pension fund) or if the vendor has held the property on trading account rather than as a capital asset (i.e. the vendor is a property developer or is simply involved with buying and selling properties as trading stock). A *purchaser* who is a non-taxpayer should still sign an election.

An election is also possible (with one exception for dual resident investing companies) if the sale is at less than market value if it is to a person who can claim allowances under the plant and machinery rules or under the rules for research and development allowances. And again an election is possible if the permanent discontinuance of the qualifying activity is followed by a sale of the qualifying interest in the property.

An election is not possible in relation to other, less common, types of disposal. No election may be made, for example, if the fixture starts to be used wholly or partly for private purposes, or if the permanent discontinuance of the qualifying activity is followed by the demolition or destruction of the fixture.

An election may be made under s. 199 where a lessee pays a capital sum on acquisition: see **12.7.4**.

Law: CAA 2001, s. 198-201

Dividends in specie

Sometimes, ownership of a property may be passed from subsidiary to parent company by way of a dividend *in specie*. This would not constitute a sale, and so the disposal will be under item 3 rather than item 1 of the table at s. 196. It follows that an election under s. 198 will not be possible.

The pooling requirement under s. 187A will still be imposed on the subsidiary, but the fixed value requirement will not be imposed as the conditions in s. 187A(5) are not met. Instead, the transfer has to take place at market value, with allowances transferred to the parent company.

In these circumstances, the disposal value requirement applies (per s. 187A(10)). This means that there is a requirement, which must be met within two years of the transfer date, for the subsidiary to make a written statement of the disposal value it has been required to bring in and to provide a copy to the parent company by the same deadline. If that condition is not met, the subsidiary would still have to bring in a market value disposal (s. 187B(6)) but the acquiring parent company would not be able to claim any allowances (s. 187A(3)).

Law: CAA 2001, s. 187A, 187B(6), 196, 198

Furnished holiday lettings

A particular issue may arise in relation to furnished holiday let (FHL) properties.

As discussed at **4.10.3**, special rules apply where a property is switched between an FHL business and an ordinary property business (s. 13B). In these circumstances, the person will be treated as making a disposal from the first business but then as incurring notional expenditure on new plant or machinery for the purposes of the other activity.

The figure to use for the notional expenditure is the lower of market value at the date the property is transferred and the amount of the actual expenditure. This can cause problems because of the interaction with the s. 35 restriction for dwelling-houses.

Example 1

Caroline runs an FHL business and also an ordinary property business with longer term lets, with four properties in each. All the properties are residential in nature.

As a result of particular local factors, one of the FHL properties has not generated as much income as she hoped, and she therefore decides to transfer its use to her other business and to let the property out to a longer term tenant.

Caroline has claimed allowances for fixtures in the property, as the s. 35 restriction does not apply to FHL properties. When she transfers the property to the other business, she must bring a disposal value into account at market value (restricted to cost). No s. 198 election is possible as the disposal is not under either item 1 or item 9 of the table at s. 196 (and it therefore fails to meet the fundamental condition for an election as stated at s. 198(1)).

Although the fixtures are now in use for the purposes of a new qualifying activity (an ordinary property business), the s. 35 restriction will this time prevent Caroline from claiming allowances for fixtures in the property.

This rule does work both ways, however, and Caroline will be able to start claiming allowances for fixtures if a property that has formerly been used for an ordinary property business starts to be used for an FHL business.

A possible solution for Caroline in the above example might be to sell the property to a related business. However, this might produce an unacceptable SDLT liability. Caroline would also need to consider the anti-avoidance provisions of s. 197 (see **10.7**).

Timing of election

An election must normally be "made" within two years of the date of sale (or of the grant of the lease). This time limit does not refer to the election being signed but to its being submitted to HMRC ("An election must be made by notice to an officer of Revenue and Customs no later than 2 years after the date ..."). The notice must be in writing (s. 577(1)).

This is varied if the fixed value requirement applies (or may apply) and if an application is made to the tax tribunal to determine the "apportionable sum" for the sale price. If the application is not determined by the normal time limit date, the election may be submitted at any time before the tribunal determines the application or the application is withdrawn. If the two-year time limit has passed, it is therefore essential that the election should be submitted *before* any application to the tribunal is withdrawn.

Example 2

Vendor Ltd and Buyer Ltd are unable to agree an amount to include in their fixtures election. Vendor's view is that the fixtures in the property are almost worthless, whereas Buyer is computing the value on a replacement basis and believes that a far higher valuation is justified. The sale takes place on 1 June 2019 and the case is expected to be heard by the tax tribunal in August 2021. In July 2021, the parties decide to withdraw the case as they have reached agreement. The election will only be effective if it is submitted before the case is formally withdrawn.

No election will be needed, of course, if the amount is in fact determined by the tribunal.

Law: CAA 2001, s. 201(1), (1A)

Amending a return

A person is obliged to notify HMRC if a return becomes incorrect as a result of making a fixtures election under s. 198 or s. 199.

The notice must be given (in writing – s. 577(1)) within three months of the person becoming aware that something has become incorrect. All such assessments and adjustments may then be made as are necessary to rectify the matter.

Law: CAA 2001, s. 203

12.7.2 Multiple fixtures in one election

A typical property will contain hundreds, or probably thousands, of different fixtures.

Strictly speaking, an election is made on a fixture by fixture basis (s. 198 referring to the part of the sale price that is incurred "on the provision of *the fixture*") but this would be wholly impractical in reality.

As such, HMRC will allow "a degree of amalgamation of assets where this will not distort the tax computation". This raises a number of important points of practice to ensure that the validity of the election is not open to challenge (which, since April 2012, could potentially be hugely expensive for the buyer, and which could also cause the vendor to be hit by an unexpected balancing charge).

More than one property

HMRC never allow a single election to cover the fixtures in more than one property.

Identification

An essential starting point is to ensure that the election properly and clearly identifies all the assets covered. All too often, an election purports to cover "all the fixtures and fittings" or "all the plant or machinery" in a particular property. This is inappropriate as an election can only cover *fixtures* in the capital allowances sense.

A care home (for example) will have beds, tables and other items that are plant and machinery but not fixtures. Indeed, the authors have seen all too many cases where an appendix lists out all the items that the election purports to cover, but including a host of moveable items of furniture that are clearly not fixtures.

Given that one of the requirements for a valid election is that the notice of election must provide "information sufficient to identify the plant or machinery" it may well be argued that such an approach renders the election invalid. If one global figure is given for all such items, there will also necessarily be a failure to show the amount allocated to the fixtures proper.

In the past, it was often in HMRC's interests for the election to work, but in the future it is the purchaser (and often also the vendor) who will lose out if an election is invalid and it is not difficult to envisage an HMRC challenge over this sort of issue.

In theory, an election could be worded to cover "all the fixtures in the property" but this can cause various problems, and best practice would certainly involve the use of one or more schedules in which the fixtures are identified. Indeed, some have argued that such wording would lead to an invalid election on the basis that the statutory requirement to identify the plant or machinery in question has not been met – a view that (to the knowledge of the authors) has not been tested in the courts. In any case, care would be needed to ensure that a prior claim had been made for all the fixtures in the property, as the inclusion of an item for which no claim had previously been made would again risk invalidating the election.

Another possible complication here would be the treatment of revenue expenditure.

> **Example**
>
> Vendor Hotel Ltd has claimed all possible capital allowances following a major refurbishment five years before the sale. Just recently, however, a wash basin in a bedroom was cracked and replaced and the cost was written off as revenue expenditure. The cost of the basin has therefore not been subject to a claim for capital allowances and it follows from the wording of s. 198(1) that it cannot be included in the fixtures election. For this reason, there is a further problem with the wording "all the fixtures in the property".

Another potential error in this area would be to include fixtures that do not even exist; this can arise if standardised lists are used that may, for example, include a lift or an air conditioning system, even though such assets are not present in the property in question.

Integral features

An election covering multiple assets will need to have separate figures for integral features and other assets. HMRC guidance explains this as follows (and NB the 8% rate referred to reduces to 6% from April 2019):

> "Following the introduction of the new classification of 'integral features' in respect of relevant expenditure incurred on or after 1 April 2008 (CT) or 6 April 2008 (IT), it will be necessary to distinguish between–
>
> (i) fixtures that are "integral features" and so qualify for WDAs at the 8% rate in the special rate pool, and
>
> (ii) fixtures that qualify for WDAs at the 18% rate in the main P&M pool; ...
>
> To do otherwise would clearly have the potential to distort the tax computation, which would be unacceptable. So, following the FA08 changes, it is now less likely that you will be able to accept an election covering all the fixtures in a particular property without requiring some apportionment of value between the two groups identified above."

Once more, it may be argued that failure to make this distinction between integral features and other fixtures included in the election may render the election invalid.

In practice, a further step is required to ensure that clarity is gained for all parties (and to eliminate the risk that the election could be declared invalid on these grounds). This is because some assets (e.g. central heating systems) will be main rate expenditure for the vendor (i.e. if they were bought before April 2008) but will be special rate expenditure for the buyer. Good practice therefore dictates that the distinction between integral features and other fixtures should be taken a step further. This can be achieved by including in the election separate schedules, and separate figures, for three categories of expenditure (rather than simply distinguishing between special rate and main rate expenditure, which can be ambiguous).

There is no specific guideline about the way the election should work when the nature of an asset is different for seller and buyer. It is always good, though, to remember the first principles, which are that an election is in theory made on an asset by asset basis, but that that theory can be ignored as long as the tax computations are not distorted. As such, it is good practice to divide the election by showing separate figures and separate schedules for each of the following categories:

- assets that have always been general fixtures (e.g. toilets);
- assets that were general fixtures for the seller but that are now special rate (e.g. lifts); and
- assets (bought by the seller since April 2008) that are special rate expenditure for both seller and buyer.

(If the seller could not claim for particular assets, because they were bought before April 2008 and did not then qualify, they will not be included in the election as the seller has not been able to claim and the condition in s. 198(1) is therefore not met. The buyer will nevertheless claim for these, in addition to any amounts included in the election.)

Law: CAA 2001, s. 198
Guidance: CA 26850

12.7.3   Requirements for a valid election

The election under s. 198 or 199 must include the following and will be invalid if any of these items is missing:

- the amount fixed by the election;
- the name of each of the persons making the election;
- information sufficient to identify the fixture(s) covered by the election;

349

- information sufficient to identify the relevant land;
- particulars of the interest acquired by the purchaser (or, as the case may be, particulars of the lease granted);
- the unique taxpayer reference (UTR) of each of the parties, or a statement that one or both does not have a UTR.

A person who has made an election must include a copy when subsequently making a tax return "for a period which is the first period for which he is making a tax return in which the election has an effect for tax purposes in his case". This is a separate and additional requirement to the two-year time limit within which the election must be "made" (i.e. submitted to HMRC), though in practice (in all normal circumstances) the election will only have to be sent in once by each party to the transaction.

For those working in partnership, references to a tax return are to returns made under TMA 1970, s. 12AA. In other words, the election must accompany the partnership return.

The normal rules relating to claims and elections (TMA 1970, s. 42 and Sch. 1A for income tax; FA 1998, Sch. 18, para. 54-60 for corporation tax) are disapplied for these purposes.

Law: CAA 2001, s. 201
Guidance: CA 26850

Invalid elections

Breaching any of the above conditions will invalidate the election. As discussed above, this can cause major problems for both vendor and purchaser.

Amount fixed by the election

The fixtures election was introduced by FA 1997. *Explanatory Notes* were published at the time, and these made it clear that an election should have an actual figure:

> "The amount apportioned to the fixture must be quantified, and therefore cannot be given as a formula or algorithm."

Vendor must have disposal value

An election is only possible if the vendor is required to bring in a capital allowances disposal value. If, for example, the vendor is a builder who has constructed the property, the disposal by the builder will be of trading stock, so no election will be possible.

This rule also means that a person who has not claimed allowances on a particular fixture will have no disposal value, so no fixtures election may be made in respect of that item. In the past, this meant that the right to claim allowances on the fixture in question normally passed to the buyer, but since April 2014 this has been reversed: a buyer can claim *only* if the seller has first included the item in a capital allowance computation (unless the vendor was not permitted to claim allowances).

Law: CAA 2001, s. 198-201

Nominees and legal owners

The beneficial ownership of a property is not always the same as the legal ownership. The distinction can be complex and is beyond the scope of this book but (broadly) the legal owner will be shown in official documents (e.g. at Land Registry) whereas beneficial ownership has been defined as "an interest in the economic benefit of property". Beneficial ownership can give a right to live in a property, for example, and may also bestow a financial share in the property. See also the HMRC illustration of this principle at **10.3.1** above.

A reader of this volume told the authors of a property that was being sold by two nominee companies on behalf of an (unnamed) beneficial owner. The two nominee companies were dormant, and were thus not able to claim allowances (i.e. as they were not carrying on a qualifying activity). Capital allowances had been claimed, however, by the beneficial owner.

The draft legal agreement required the two nominee companies to sign the election, and provided their UTRs. The reader rightly assumed that whilst the nominee companies no doubt had authority to sign the election on behalf of the beneficial owner, the election had to show the beneficial owner's UTR. The reader checked the matter out with HMRC's capital allowances technical division. HMRC confirmed that "it is the beneficial owner that needs to appear on the s198 election".

Receivers

In a technical submission in March 2014, the Chartered Institute of Taxation raised with HMRC a particular issue about the signing of fixtures elections.

The point concerned a *Law of Property Act* (LPA) receiver who is acting at the request of a lender, but who is legally the agent of the defaulting borrower. The CIOT pointed out that without the permission of the defaulter (which would rarely be given), the receiver would not be able to sign an election or to apply to the tribunal for a value to be assigned to fixtures.

HMRC duly responded to this concern in June 2014, acknowledging that "a receiver has no direct power to ensure that a vendor pools the qualifying expenditure in a chargeable period beginning on or before the day of sale". HMRC argued that the position remains broadly as it was before the enactment of FA 2012, on the basis that HMRC have always required purchasers to provide details of how past owners have treated their disposals for capital allowances purposes.

Rather than agreeing to amend the legislation, HMRC committed to "keeping watch on the effects it has in practice". When pressed by the CIOT, HMRC's technical adviser commented as follows:

> "Changes to the law are, of course, a matter for the Government and Parliament, but if you have any evidence of the scale of the issue (volume and value of property sales by receivers, proportion of cases in which vendors cannot be contacted etc) then we would be pleased to take account of this as part of the normal policy review process."

Readers may also like to refer to an article on this topic in the September 2014 issue of *Tax Adviser*.

12.7.4   Capital sums given by lessees on grant of lease

The most common scenario for which a fixtures election is made is when a property is sold from one user to another. However, an election may also be made where a lessee pays a capital sum on the grant of a lease. In such a case, the election must be signed by the lessor and the lessee.

In technical terms, the election may be made in these circumstances where the disposal value of a fixture has to be brought into account in accordance with item 5 of the table in s. 196 ("Cessation of ownership of the fixture under section 190 because the lessee has become the owner under section 183": see, generally, **10.5.7**).

The same principles apply here as for a sale and purchase, but in this case the election fixes the part of the overall capital sum that is treated as incurred by the lessee on the provision of the fixture. The figure used in the election must not exceed the actual capital sum paid. Nor may it exceed the amount of the capital expenditure which was treated as incurred by the lessor on the provision of the fixture (or of the plant or machinery which became the fixture).

The rules are once more subject to cases where there is a prior claim for different types of allowance (see **12.7.5** immediately below), certain avoidance cases affecting disposal values (s. 197: see **10.7**), and the other general rules about elections discussed in this chapter (s. 200 and 201).

Law: CAA 2001, s. 199

12.7.5   Restrictions where allowances already claimed

Various restrictions apply where a previous owner has already claimed allowances on a particular fixture, whether under the plant or machinery rules or otherwise. The nature of the restriction depends on the allowances previously claimed. For previous plant and machinery claims, the point is covered immediately below. See **12.10** for commentary in respect of claims for other allowances.

Law: CAA 2001, s. 9

Previous claim for plant and machinery allowances

The most common scenario is where a property with fixtures is sold by the old owner, who has claimed plant and machinery allowances, to the new owner. The old owner will have to bring a disposal value into account.

In this case, the new owner's qualifying expenditure may not exceed the disposal value that has to be brought into account by the vendor (though the cost of any building alterations allowable under s. 25 may be added: see, generally, **4.4**). The disposal value will nowadays be agreed by signing a fixtures election, but the principle remains relevant in respect of previous owners.

Example 1

A Ltd sells a hotel for £2.5 million to B Ltd. A Ltd has claimed plant and machinery allowances on fixtures costing £400,000.

To meet the fixed value requirement, the two companies must sign a fixtures election. The amount in the election is capped at £400,000.

Example 2

C Ltd sells a hotel for £2.5 million to D Ltd. C Ltd has not claimed plant and machinery allowances for fixtures in the property, but it goes back to review the computations from 2005, when it bought the property.

No election was signed at that earlier time, but an apportionment exercise is carried out which reaches a value of £300,000 for the fixtures in the property. C Ltd is able to contact the previous owner – Z Ltd – who advises that the cost of those fixtures was £250,000.

Z Ltd's disposal value for those fixtures is capped at that cost figure of £250,000. It follows that C Ltd's qualifying expenditure for those items is similarly capped at £250,000. As such, the figure for the fixtures election to be signed by C Ltd and D Ltd will similarly be capped at £250,000 for those original fixtures. If C Ltd added new fixtures during the period of ownership, the total figure for the election may exceed £250,000.

The cap is set by reference to the amount the previous owner was *required* to bring into account, even if that was not in fact done. This is clear from the wording of the legislation at s. 562(3), and was confirmed in the *Glais House* case reported in early 2019. As the tribunal noted in that case:

> "This does of course leave HMRC in a difficult position in that they would undoubtedly wish to see symmetry between the figure for the disposal value which was actually brought into account in the capital allowance computations of [the vendor] and the figure for the acquisition costs in the capital allowance computations of [the appellant / buyer]."

The HMRC view is that the onus to work out the disposal value of the former owner lies with the new owner who wishes to claim allowances, failing which allowances may well be denied. This issue has been partly resolved by virtue of the changes that have applied from April 2012 and 2014.

In some cases, the past owner will not be the person from whom the buyer acquires the property, as that person may have acquired the fixture as revenue expenditure (or may be a non-taxpayer such as a pension fund). HMRC have illustrated this as follows:

> "Cassandra Plc constructs an office block for its own use and claims PMA on the fixtures in the building. Three years later it sells the office block to Spencer Moore Ltd, a firm of property dealers.

When Cassandra Plc sells the office block it has to bring a disposal value to account because it has treated its expenditure on the fixtures as qualifying expenditure. Spencer Moore Ltd's expenditure on the office block is revenue expenditure and so it cannot claim PMA on the fixtures. Spencer Moore Ltd then sells the office block to Terence Ltd who intend to use it has their headquarters. If Terence Ltd claims PMA on the fixtures in the office block its qualifying expenditure is limited to Cassandra Plc's disposal value."

In practice, this arises most frequently with non-taxpayers. If Trader A sold to Pension in 2003, and Pension is selling to Trader B today, the rule will ensure that Trader B's acquisition cost is capped at the disposal value that was brought in *or that should have been brought in*, by Trader A. In the absence of an election at the time of sale by Trader A, a proper apportioned value should have been brought in.

The current and past owner may even be the same person. This will arise if the property is sold and leased back and an election is signed under s. 183 (see **10.5.7**) in respect of the leaseback.

The restriction is not imposed in certain circumstances where the item in question was previously sold otherwise than as a fixture (as long as the buyer and seller were not then connected).

Law: CAA 2001, s. 185, 198(3), 562(3)
Case: *Glais House Care Ltd v HMRC* [2019] UKFTT 59 (TC)
Guidance: CA 26400

More than one previous owner

It is quite possible, of course, that the property will have had more than one previous owner. In principle, it is then necessary to cap the qualifying expenditure at the lowest historic disposal value.

Example 3

A had a property built in 1991 and claimed full plant and machinery allowances, amounting to £100,000, for all the fixtures in the property. A sold the property to B in 1998 and an election under s. 198 was signed with a figure of just £1 to cover all the fixtures.

Assume that B sold to C in 2000, and C in turn sold the property in 2004 to D, the present vendor. E Ltd is planning to acquire the property from D in January 2022. All parties have been traders or property landlords.

What, though, is the treatment of the original fixtures, assuming that they still form part of the property at the start of 2022?

A's disposal value for the fixtures was £1, and this in turn caps B's acquisition cost at the same figure (per s. 198(2)). B's future disposal value is similarly restricted to £1 (per s. 62(1)). Following the same logic forwards, E Ltd's qualifying expenditure on the original fixtures is capped at £1.

It is likely that additional fixtures will have been added along the way, and those will need to be considered separately. E Ltd will also be able to claim for integral features on which no claim has previously been possible.

Two other points are important to note.

First, it must be borne in mind that the fixtures election was only introduced by FA 1997, and elections have only been possible in relation to disposals on or after 19 March 1997. Before that date, the only possibility was a just and reasonable apportionment.

Second, the significance of the July 1996 date can easily be misunderstood, but was explained well in the *Explanatory Notes* when the legislation was amended in FA 1997:

> "[The former legislation], which applied where an interest in land which includes a fixture was acquired from a person who has claimed allowances on the fixture, restricted the amount on which allowances could be claimed by the purchaser to the disposal value of the vendor. New Section 56B extends this rule to apply generally where allowances have been claimed in respect of that asset by a previous owner ... and restricts the amount on which allowances can be claimed by the new owner to the disposal value of the last owner to claim allowances."

The position is more complicated if there has been an owner who has not been able to claim allowances (e.g. a pension fund or a charity). In these circumstances, it is still necessary to restrict the value to the lowest disposal value of anyone who has owned the property (s. 185). However, no account needs to be taken of anyone who ceased to own the property before 24 July 1996.

Example 4

J sold a property to a pension fund in February 2006. The pension fund sells it to X in October 2021.

Although the pension fund does not have to bring in a disposal value (as it has not been able to claim any allowances), J's disposal value will still restrict the qualifying expenditure incurred by X. As such, X will be able to claim allowances on three elements:

- fixtures on which J claimed allowances, restricted to J's disposal value;
- integral features on which J was not able to claim allowances;
- any other fixtures on which no claim has been made (as long as they are still in the property in October 2021, but whether or not they were already in the property at the time of J's sale to the pension fund).

If J's disposal to the pension fund had been 10 years earlier, in February 1996, there would be no restriction by reference to J's disposal value. This better outcome arises only where there has been no owner since 24 July 1996 who could have claimed allowances.

The FA 2012 rules do not operate to restrict the allowances available here as (broadly) nobody owing the property since April 2012 has been able to claim allowances.

Law: CAA 2001, s. 185; Sch. 3, para. 38

Uncertainty

The reality is often that the history of previous claims is unknown, or at best incomplete. A vendor may be under pressure to establish the maximum claim so that a fixtures election can be put in place and the new owner can benefit from the allowances. But the vendor may be uncertain about the nature of any claims made by a previous owner.

The background is that any claim by a current owner is restricted by reference to the disposal value of a previous owner. In principle, no claim is possible unless that disposal value can be established. Simple disregard of that starting point could leave the claimant exposed to a clawback of any allowances, and possibly to financial penalties as well. Cautious vendors may therefore wish to take the line that no claim should be submitted.

Arguably, however, this is handing more to HMRC than is necessary. Assume that it can be shown that no fixtures elections have been signed. It then follows that an earlier vendor who made a claim would have been required to bring a disposal value into account. That disposal value would in turn be capped at the historic cost of the fixtures in question, so a valuation exercise may be required to establish those figures (assuming that cost details are not available).

Example 5

A built an office in 1995 for £500,000 and sold it to B in 2000 for £1.2m. B is now selling it to C, for a figure of £1.5m. C wants B to maximise his claim and to transfer the value over to C by election. B knows that no election was signed back in 2000.

If A made no claim for capital allowances on the fixtures, B could make an unrestricted claim now, based on an apportionment approach as at the 2000 acquisition date, without regard to historic cost. However, as it is possible that A made a claim, it should be assumed that he did so, in which case the claim would be based on the (probably lower) historic cost figure. If A claimed for a particular fixture, he should have brought a disposal value into account on transfer of the property to B. That figure would almost certainly be higher, initially, than the historic cost, but the disposal value would be capped at cost. If the original cost can be calculated (using a valuation approach), B should be able to claim accordingly (i.e. on the lower of the historic cost or the transfer value in 2000).

If an exercise is properly carried out on the above lines, and if the approach is fully disclosed to HMRC, it is thought that the resulting claim will be justifiable, even if subject to possible negotiation with HMRC. Sometimes, however, no claim will be possible, at least in relation to certain fixtures. See case study 5 in **Appendix 2** for an illustration of this.

Law: CAA 2001, s. 62, 185, 562

12.7.6 Election practicalities for vendor and purchaser

The key element of the fixed value requirement, in most cases, is that "an election is made, in respect of the apportionable sum, by the affected parties jointly". In this respect, the motivation of the two parties is now more complex than it was before April 2012.

Previously, it was normally in the interests of the vendor to ensure that an election was signed. Failing this, a "just and reasonable apportionment" would be required and this would often result in a higher sale value for the fixtures, producing a balancing charge for the vendor and potentially valuable allowances for the purchaser. The position for the purchaser was more balanced – an election gave certainty but would often reduce the value of the allowances to a lower level than might otherwise have been available.

If the vendor did not make any capital allowances claim for particular fixtures, and if it could be shown that no previous owner had made a claim, this almost always worked to the advantage of the purchaser. The purchaser could make a claim based on apportioned cost (s. 562) and there would be no restriction to historic cost because no earlier claim had been made (s. 185).

Under the rules as they have applied since April 2014, this thinking is turned on its head and the ambiguity for the purchaser as to whether or not an election should be signed disappears at a stroke. If there is no election, or if no claim has been made by the vendor, no allowances will be due to the purchaser for any fixtures on which the vendor could have claimed relief. Any buyer will therefore need a legally binding agreement that the vendor will add the maximum permitted value to his capital allowances computations by way of allowable costs of fixtures, and will then sign and submit an election. The amount to be included in the election will need to be agreed as part of the contractual negotiations.

The respective interests of both parties will need to be considered here. As a starting point, substantial work may be involved in formulating a claim and the vendor may have no interest in making such a claim (i.e. if the full value is to be passed on to the buyer). It may be that the purchaser will pay for the work involved, but the vendor's tax computations will then need to include information supplied by professionals engaged by the purchaser – numerous potential issues arise in relation to professional indemnity and so on. To give just one example, it may be that the vendor's accountants (whether justifiably or not) do not accept that the claim made by the purchaser's advisers is valid.

It is not all one-sided, however. If the vendor *has* made a claim for particular fixtures, it is essential from his own point of view to submit a valid fixtures election. Failure to do this will mean that his disposal value must be calculated on a just and reasonable basis, which could result in a large balancing charge (see **Chapter 13**). In reality, the parties are likely to cooperate as they both wish the sale and purchase of the property to go ahead (which is a key reason why a legal agreement should be reached in relation to the allowances before the sale is completed).

Notifying HMRC

If a person has submitted a tax return, and the return becomes incorrect as a result of the making of a fixtures election, the person must give notice (in writing – s. 577(1)) to that effect to HMRC. The time limit for doing this is three months from the day on which the person becomes aware that the return is now incorrect (s. 203: see **10.1.7**).

12.7.7 What figures should go into the election?

It is almost always the case that both parties to a transaction will wish to sign an election under s. 198 (or, as the case may be, s. 199), so to that extent there is a common interest in ensuring that a valid election is prepared and then submitted within the required timeframe.

By contrast, the amount to go into a fixtures election will be a matter for negotiation. The only statutory rule relating to this matter is that the vendor's disposal value is capped at his capital allowances cost in relation to any given fixture. So if a new radiator was installed at a cost of £100 then the disposal value of that radiator cannot exceed £100. Where, as is usually the case, the single election covers many different fixtures, this principle should still be borne in mind.

Beyond that, the figure to go into the election will be purely a matter for negotiation between the parties (though the figure in the election cannot exceed the sale price of the property). Once a valid election is signed, it is binding on both parties and on HMRC, and is irrevocable. There are some guiding principles that may help to determine the appropriate value to include in the fixtures election.

Vendor's tax written down value

A common starting point will be to consider the vendor's tax position. If an asset was bought some years ago for £100,000 and allowances have been given over the years, it may be that the tax written down value will now be, say, £30,000. (In practice, most assets are pooled, so this is a notional figure, but it is usually possible to gain some idea of what that figure might be.)

If the vendor sells the property, it may be that he will therefore agree to include a figure of £30,000 in the election in relation to the fixture in question. The practical effect is that the vendor will retain the tax benefits that he has already enjoyed (£70,000), and the purchaser will claim tax relief on the remaining £30,000.

The more aggressive vendor

If the vendor is in a strong negotiating position, he may wish to take a more robust stance and insist on keeping most or even all of the tax relief. There is nothing in principle to prevent him from seeking a £1 value for the fixtures election (or, more typically, £1 each for the integral features and for the remaining fixtures).

In this way, the vendor will enjoy the full tax benefit of the allowances that are available for fixtures in the property. If the vendor has owned the property since before April 2008, there will be integral features on which he has been unable to claim (and which will therefore be excluded from the election). He will effectively be saying to the purchaser: "You can have the benefit of those integral features on which I have been unable to claim, but I am keeping the capital allowances for all the other fixtures."

If a commercial vendor is selling to a non-taxpayer, such as a charity or local authority or pension fund, the buyer will have no immediate interest in the capital allowances, though those allowances will potentially increase the value of the property if it comes to be sold again in the future. As the allowances are of more immediate value to the vendor than to the buyer, it is more likely that the parties will agree a very low figure for the fixtures election, thus passing most of the benefit to the vendor.

Conversely, it may be that the seller has claimed substantial capital allowances in the past but has a high level of trading losses that will be wasted once the business is sold. In these circumstances, it will make sense for the seller to accept a high election figure, and consequently a possibly substantial balancing charge. If properly advised, and if the seller's overall negotiating position is strong, the seller may be able to ask for a higher sale value to reflect the valuable allowances that will thereby be passed to the new owner.

The stronger buyer

In many cases, of course, the vendor's overwhelming objective will be to sell the property, and capital allowances may be offered up as part of the deal. In this case, the buyer may be able to insist on a high value in the capital allowances election.

The vendor in these circumstances will have to decide whether the loss of allowances is a price worth paying to ensure that the deal goes ahead.

If the vendor has trading losses that will absorb any balancing charge then this may not be a problem in practice. Indeed, in these circumstances the vendor may willingly offer a high value in the election and (as suggested above) may perhaps seek to negotiate a somewhat higher sale price to reflect the fact that the buyer is gaining valuable tax relief.

Another factor that may have a bearing on the position is where the buyer is having to drive the whole capital allowances exercise. If the vendor has not claimed allowances for fixtures in the property, the buyer may well insist on an exercise to capture their value so that the pooling requirement (see **12.4**) is met. In some cases, the buyer will even be paying for the technical work needed to achieve that, and in these circumstances the buyer may insist on having the benefit of most or possibly all of the allowances. On the other hand, the vendor should also be aware that he holds some of the cards: to the extent that he has made a claim, he will certainly wish to sign a fixtures election, but if there are assets on which no claim has been made he is in a stronger position.

Example

Helen has just sold a small office that she has owned for many years. The buyer, Jack, demonstrates that Helen could have claimed allowances for fixtures in the property. Jack says that he will carry out a capital allowances exercise and he wants Helen to add the claim to her final tax computations, and then sign a fixtures election with figures equal to the whole of the claim, thus transferring the entire value to Jack.

Helen has missed out on some tax relief but there is no benefit to her in adding the figures to her computations and then transferring the whole benefit to Jack. Indeed, there is likely to be some cost to Helen in terms of accountancy fees, and there is always the possibility of HMRC enquiries into the details of the claim.

As the deal has already gone through (and there is therefore no commercial pressure on her to cooperate) Helen has the option of doing nothing at all, and in some cases that will be the right decision. On the other hand, she may have a tax liability and if she can retain the benefit of some of the allowances then she may agree to the whole exercise. Perhaps the deal will be that she keeps one third of the benefit, for example (by choosing a figure for the election that will achieve that end).

If Helen has losses, or if for some other reason she has no tax liability, she may be willing to cooperate on the basis that Jack underwrites her entire accountancy costs relating to the matter.

What will the tribunal do?

One other factor may influence the value to go into a fixtures election. The purchaser of a property has no power to force the vendor to meet the pooling requirement (beyond a refusal to go ahead with the purchase, of course – which is one reason why the purchaser should always insist on sorting out capital allowances before the deal goes ahead). Once the vendor has pooled the capital expenditure, on the other hand, the balance of power shifts rather more in the buyer's favour. The vendor, having made a claim, will have to bring in a disposal value and there are three ways in which that value will be determined: an apportionment, an election or a tribunal determination.

If the fixed value requirement is not met – no election and no tribunal ruling – the vendor will have to bring in a full apportioned value. This is explained in full at **13.1** below, but is potentially a very expensive option for both parties, effectively handing back all tax relief permanently to the Treasury. So this will never be the chosen outcome and is only likely to arise where things have gone wrong.

The fixed value requirement is normally met by way of an election but if the parties cannot agree the figures for the election, there is always the possibility of a tribunal ruling on the matter. The figure to be allocated by a tribunal will normally be computed using apportionment principles, and is likely to pass a high percentage of the value of the fixtures to the purchaser. This is explained more fully at **12.8.2** below.

The attitude of the two parties is likely to be influenced by the desire to complete the transaction, and the capital allowances tail will rightly not wag that commercial dog. With that important proviso, however, it will be seen that a vendor who has included the value of the fixtures in his computations is unlikely to be in a position to insist on a very low fixtures value in the election.

12.7.8   Jointly owned property

The legislation does not appear to give a clear cut answer on the use of elections for jointly owned property. So if a property is jointly owned, and is then sold to a third party, should there be two separate elections or just the one?

It is thought likely that HMRC would in practice accept a single election covering all three parties, as long as the respective disposal values are clear. The more correct view, though, would appear to be that each of the vendor parties should sign a separate election showing their respective shares of the assets in question.

In technical terms, s. 571 deals with "parts" of plant and machinery, and s. 270 deals with "shares" of plant and machinery. In this case, each of the vendors owns a share of the assets, and the legislation effectively says that the shares should be isolated to their respective owners, and that the capital allowances rules should then be applied as if the share were a separate asset.

12.7.9   Sample election under s. 198

The following is an example of an election that might be used in the case where a freehold property is sold by a limited company to an unconnected partnership.

The election includes three different categories of asset, which have been given names for identification (main rate fixtures, special rate fixtures, changed status fixtures). These are not statutory terms, but the legislation does in theory require a separate election for each fixture (which would be impossible in practice) and the view of the authors is that this is an appropriate way of achieving the clarity for both parties that the legislation demands.

> We hereby elect under section 198 of the *Capital Allowances Act 2001* to fix the amount that is to be treated for the purposes of Part 2 of that Act as the part of the sale price that is on the provision of the specified fixtures.
>
> In this election:
>
> - "main rate fixtures" means fixtures that are correctly allocated to the main pool by both parties;
> - "special rate fixtures" means fixtures that are correctly allocated to the special rate pool by both parties;
> - "changed status fixtures" means fixtures that were main rate expenditure for the seller but that are special rate expenditure for the buyer.
>
> **The property:** the whole of the premises at 1 High Street, Anytown, Newshire, AT1 1AA.
>
> **Title number:** ANY12345.
>
> **Interest acquired:** freehold.
>
> **Price paid:** £1.2 million
>
> **Date of transaction:** 1 February 2019.
>
> **Seller:** Yellow Ltd, whose registered office is 12 High Street, Anytown, Newshire, AT1 1AB. Unique Tax Reference: 11111 22222.

Buyer: The Green Partnership, 10 The Grange, Othertown, Oldshire, OT3 4ZZ. Unique Tax Reference: 33333 44444.

Main rate fixtures covered by this election: as listed in the attached Schedule 1.

Special rate fixtures covered by this election: as listed in the attached Schedule 2.

Changed status fixtures covered by this election: as listed in the attached Schedule 3.

Amount fixed for main rate fixtures: £25,000.

Amount fixed for special rate fixtures: £50,000.

Amount fixed for changed status fixtures: £5,000.

Signature of seller (with date) ....

Signature of buyer (with date) ....

The schedules will be an important part of the election, and must only include fixtures (in their capital allowances sense – see **10.2**) so there should be no mention of any moveable chattels such as chairs or tables).

Schedule 1 must list only items that have qualified as main rate expenditure for the vendor and that will continue to qualify as such for the new owner (e.g. WCs, basins, manufacturing equipment).

Schedule 2 must list only items that are properly treated as special rate expenditure by both parties (e.g. a lift or an air conditioning system which, in either case, has been installed by the vendor since April 2008).

Schedule 3 must list only items that were main rate expenditure for the vendor but that must be categorised as special rate expenditure by the purchaser. This will cover items that already qualified as plant and machinery when they were acquired by the vendor before April 2008 but that must now be treated as integral features for the purchaser (e.g. an air conditioning system bought or installed by the vendor before April 2008).

Each list should then be broken down either in detail or at least into broad categories. For example, Schedule 3 may (depending on the facts of the case) be divided between lifts, heating systems and air conditioning equipment. Whilst a figure would ideally be allocated to each category, HMRC will in practice normally accept a generic figure for each schedule, as long as there are no special factors that would cause this to distort the tax computations for either party.

12.8   Apportionments

12.8.1   Principles

The whole concept of the "apportionment" remains valid after the changes applying from both April 2012 and April 2014, albeit subject to some important differences in the ways the apportionment is now used in practice.

Strictly speaking, the fixtures election is no more than an "election to apportion [the] sale price" (according to the heading of the relevant statutory provision). Indeed, the fixtures election was introduced (in the words of the *Explanatory Notes* that accompanied the legislation that became FA 1997) because the standard apportionment procedure "has been criticised as costly and inappropriate where figures have been agreed between the parties". The FA 1997 legislation "remove[d] this burden by allowing the purchaser and vendor jointly to elect to determine the amount apportioned to the fixtures".

So apportionment remains as the underlying principle and an election is simply one way to determine the apportioned amount. Under the rules as amended by FA 2012, however, the election has now become not just one option but very much the normal way of determining the apportioned value. Nevertheless, there are many circumstances in which an election is not possible, and in these cases an apportionment is still required.

The statutory foundation for apportionments is found at s. 562, the first three subsections of which are fundamental and are therefore reproduced below:

> "**562(1)** Any reference in this Act to the sale of property includes the sale of that property together with any other property.
>
> **562(2)** For the purposes of subsection (1), all property sold as a result of one bargain is to be treated as sold together even though–
>
> > (a)   separate prices are, or purport to be, agreed for separate items of that property, or
> >
> > (b)   there are, or purport to be, separate sales of separate items of that property.
>
> **562(3)** If an item of property is sold together with other property, then, for the purposes of this Act–

(a)   the net proceeds of the sale of that item are to be treated as being so much of the net proceeds of sale of all the property as, on a just and reasonable apportionment, is attributable to that item, and

(b)   the expenditure incurred on the provision or purchase of that item is to be treated as being so much of the consideration given for all the property as, on a just and reasonable apportionment, is attributable to that item."

The effect of this is that there is a statutory requirement to find a "just and reasonable apportionment" when a property containing fixtures is sold. This applies even if the single transaction is supposedly split into several separate parts or if separate prices are agreed for particular assets.

What this means is that the law overrides, for capital allowances purposes, whatever is contained in a sale and purchase agreement regarding the split of an overall proceeds figure between different assets. So if the agreement says that the proceeds should be £200,000 to goodwill, £2 million to the property and £5,000 to "fixtures and fittings", the capital allowances law states that these figures should be ignored unless they represent a "just and reasonable apportionment" (or unless an election is signed).

In practice, all sorts of problems arise, including in particular the following:

- some advisers are still unaware that the law has this effect, though the FA 2012 changes have certainly forced capital allowances more clearly onto the agenda;

- HMRC have, in practice, often failed to apply their own rules and interpretations (though they added some further guidance in 2017 – see below);

- the term "fixtures and fittings" is often used at best unclearly and at worst incorrectly: for capital allowances purposes, the term "fixture" has a very specific meaning (see **10.2**) that excludes any moveable items of furniture. Nevertheless, it is common to see legal documentation that confuses the looser accounting meaning of "fixtures and fittings" with the narrower capital allowances term;

- the question of what constitutes a "just and reasonable apportionment" is far from intuitive for most accountants and

367

tax advisers, who naturally think in terms of the current market value that would be achieved if the fixtures in question were to be sold separately. In reality, valuation specialists have for years had an agreement in place with HMRC that requires a completely different approach.

HMRC guidance

HMRC added a new page to the *Capital Allowances Manual* in early 2017, which includes the following guidance to tax officers in relation to apportionments:

> "If you find out that an apportionment has been made you should check with the buyer/seller's district to make sure that the buyer/seller has used the same apportionment in their capital allowance computations as your taxpayer. You should not accept your taxpayer's computations if different figures have been used."

As far as fixtures are concerned, the matter will normally now be settled by an election. However, the same principles apply to other plant and machinery, including moveable chattels. (Rather confusingly, HMRC give an example in which they refer to fixtures, but they are obviously not using the term in its capital allowances sense.)

Guidance: CA 12100

12.8.2 Reaching the apportioned value

The correct valuations to use for a capital allowances apportionment have been thrashed out between surveyors and HMRC and are published in the *Valuation Office Agency – Capital Gains & Other Taxes Manual*. Reference should be made to that manual (web address at the end of this section) and in particular to Part 3, entitled "Approach to Apportionments".

The approach does not have any statutory basis but it is well established. The principles also gained approval in the 2015 *Bowerswood House* case heard at the First-tier Tribunal, discussed below. HMRC's guidance also refers to the much earlier case of *Salts v Battersby* to support the assertion that "the underlying aim of any method of apportionment should be to apportion the purchase price in proportion to the values of the constituent parts that go to make up the property".

According to the HMRC guidelines, the apportioned value of plant and machinery is to be calculated using the formula:

Purchase Price x A/(A + B + C)

where:

A is the replacement cost of qualifying items of plant and machinery;

B is the replacement cost of the whole building, excluding qualifying items of plant and machinery; and

C is the bare site value.

In practice, this formula may be simplified (as HMRC guidance confirms) to the following:

Purchase Price x A/(B + C)

where:

A is the replacement cost of qualifying items of plant and machinery;

B is the replacement cost of the whole building, *including* qualifying items of plant and machinery; and

C is the bare site value.

The formula is then illustrated by HMRC with the following example (apostrophes corrected):

HMRC example

This example is to illustrate the effect of the formula for arriving at the plant and machinery value on the acquisition of a building that is say 20 years old. The total replacement cost of the building is £6 million, the replacement cost of the qualifying items of plant and machinery is £1.5 million and the bare site value is £2 million. The purchase price, as the building is now 20 years old, is however only £5 million.

Apportioned value of the Plant and Machinery:

£5 Million x (£1.5m ÷ (£6m + £2m)) = £937,500

As can be seen, the apportioned value of the plant and machinery is £937,500 compared with its replacement cost of £1.5 million, reflecting the fact that its value will be less due to its age. That value, however, is probably considerably higher than the original cost of the plant and machinery 20 years ago.

Even though we are dealing with an ageing building, the replacement costs used in the formula are not written down because the obsolescence factor is reflected in the purchase price. The effect of the formula is therefore to reduce the value of the plant and machinery in the same proportion that the purchase price bears to the total of the replacement cost of the whole building and the bare site value. The effect of the formula is also to write down the values of all the elements of the property, including the land. Although land does not of course depreciate in value with age the bare site in this case is encumbered by an ageing building. The full bare site value is not actually realisable because it would not be economic to demolish the building until its value was exhausted.

The key point from the above HMRC guidance and example (and the point that often causes surprise) is that the value apportioned to the plant and machinery is often much higher than both its original historic cost and the (possibly negligible) amount it would attract if sold separately from the property. Where a claim has been made by the vendor, the valuation will through statutory restrictions be capped at the vendor's historic cost, but that is a second stage that needs to be viewed separately. For all sorts of practical reasons, it is necessary to understand in isolation how the apportioned valuation is to be calculated. Unless the figures are immaterial, a professional valuation – from surveyors with experience and expertise in valuing fixtures as well as land and property – will be required if a valuation is to be reached that gives the taxpayer the best result whilst still being fully defendable to HMRC.

Since the introduction of the FA 2012 rules, and especially since the transitional rules came to an end in April 2014, it has been necessary to reach an agreed transfer value for fixtures in virtually every case. Although the value may in practice be agreed by making a joint election, the negotiations about the figure to include in the election may take account of the principles regarding apportioned values, as outlined in the paragraphs above. Similarly, a tax tribunal would be expected to apply those principles if required to settle a valuation disagreement between two parties, unless it takes the radical step of setting the (non-statutory) principles aside in favour of a new approach.

Tribunal approval for the apportionment

As mentioned above, the *principle* of the apportionment is statutory, but the *formula* is not. It was therefore helpful to see that the long-agreed basis for making apportionments received clear approval in the First-tier Tribunal cases of *Bowerswood House*.

In that case, which concerned a conservatory-type enclosure for a swimming pool, the taxpayer argued that the apportionment formula was unnecessary "where the value of assets can be separately identified for capital allowances purposes". Essentially, it was argued that a replacement value should be found for the plant, an agreed value should be used for the land, and the value of the building would then be the balancing figure.

The tribunal rejected this, commenting:

> "We consider that approach is flawed. It does not identify the value of all assets purchased on the same basis. It identifies the replacement cost of the assets qualifying for capital allowances and simply leaves all other assets to be valued by reference to a balancing figure. In our view that does not amount to a just and reasonable apportionment."

Instead, the tribunal accepted the non-statutory but very well established formula that has been used by HMRC and taxpayers for many years. The formula does indeed use replacement value as its starting point but, crucially, does so "for all the assets being purchased including the building". The tribunal noted that that approach "has been used over many years in this context" and that it did give a just and reasonable apportionment in this case.

Cases: *Salts v Battersby* [1916] 2 KB 155; *Bowerswood House Retirement Home Ltd v HMRC* [2015] UKFTT 94 (TC)

Guidance: www.voa.gov.uk/corporate/Publications/Manuals/Capital GainsTaxManual/sect3/toc.html

12.8.3   *Using a professional valuer*

Many accountants and tax practitioners will have come across niche capital allowances firms, and may have an ambivalent relationship towards such firms. There is frankly a huge range in the level of knowledge and expertise of these firms. Some have a proper in-depth understanding of the tax angles, as well as the necessary specialist valuation skills. There is no regulation in this area, though, and some self-styled experts actually have a frighteningly poor understanding of the complex tax rules, so it is crucial for a business to find the right advisers.

The approach to a capital allowances claim depends on the nature of the project. For a newly built property, there may be tender documents with full post-build reconciliations, in which case the actual costs incurred can be analysed in depth (with a proper allocation of professional fees and overhead costs).

Even for a new building, though, it may be that – for a variety of reasons – no adequate breakdown is available of the costs incurred. In this case, the surveyor's valuation experience is needed to calculate the appropriate figures. This will involve a site visit, allowing the surveyor to identify and record the different elements for which valuations are required. A calculation of cost can then be made, typically using one of the Spon's Guides to value the fixtures in the context of the overall project. Where necessary, current figures can be indexed back (not with RPI but with specialist building price indices) to ensure that the end result will stand up to HMRC scrutiny if challenged.

Different issues arise where a used property is bought. Although the transfer value will now need to be settled by election, it may well be the case that an apportionment is required in respect of the historic acquisition of the property by the current vendor. Such an apportionment requires a valuation of three elements: the fixtures in the property, the rest of the property and the land on which it stands. These figures must be established as at the date of purchase, which may be many years before the exercise is being carried out. Typically, the surveyor will be working with little or no historic information regarding the property, so a thorough survey will be needed.

The property will need to be measured (as costs per square metre will form part of the calculation) and particular attention will be paid to mechanical and electrical installations, as these will form a core part of the eventual claim. Reconstruction costs will be computed, taking account of the location of the property and the date on which it was built.

Although no capital allowances are available for the cost of land, the apportionment formula needs to include a land valuation, and again this must be as at the time the property was acquired. Different methods are available for valuing land, but the comparative method is typically used, whereby similar land transactions are identified and any variable factors are adjusted as necessary. Again, it is necessary to ensure that the claim can stand up to scrutiny, so in appropriate cases the resulting valuation may need to be supported by means of residual calculations and/or by reference to the Valuation Office's Property Market Report.

Accountants and tax advisers engaging a valuation professional will obviously wish to take appropriate steps to protect their clients' interests. In many cases, a constructive and long term relationship between accountant and professional valuer may be possible. Some valuers will be prepared to make a payment to the referring accountant, if only to cover any costs the accountant incurs in acting as initial go-between and in providing accounting information.

12.9   Charities, pension funds and other non-taxpayers

12.9.1   Introduction

It might be thought that bodies that do not pay income tax or corporation tax on their profits – such as pension funds, charities or local authorities – will not have to worry about the capital allowances rules for fixtures. This is not necessarily the case.

12.9.2   Non-taxpayer as buyer

A charity (for example) that is buying a commercial property, and that cannot use capital allowances, may nevertheless wish to protect the value of those allowances for a future owner. Similar considerations apply to pension funds. For simplicity, however, the point is illustrated below in relation to a charity.

All other things being equal, the property will have a higher market value when the charity sells it if allowances are available. So how can the charity protect that value?

Suppose that the charity in question is buying a corner shop from a retailer. The advice to give to the charity will depend on achieving a balance between the commercial and tax considerations.

The fact that the buyer is a charity does not remove either the pooling requirement or the fixed value requirement. Even though the charity cannot use any allowances, consideration should be given to protecting them for the future. This may mean going through the same commercial hoops for the charity as for a commercial business in relation to capital allowances. So the charity should consider signing an election in order to protect the value of the allowances (and therefore the full commercial value of the property) on a future sale.

The charity may, understandably, be reluctant to incur the costs of a capital allowances exercise now, when the benefits may only arise in the future (if at all). If the charity in this scenario is planning to strip the property out and start again then there is probably no point in doing the work. However, the balance of cost and reward may be different if the charity does not intend to alter the property in any significant way and expects to sell it on in the fairly near future.

Example

A charity, to meet its goals, needs a high street presence in a particular town for a period of three or four years. After reviewing the options, it prefers to buy a property and re-sell it, rather than paying rent. The property costs £450,000 and it is estimated that the historic cost of the fixtures is in the region of £125,000.

The vendor of the property in question is an independent retailer that bought the shop when it was newly built in June 2012. The vendor has been making substantial trading losses and has not given any thought to capital allowances.

The fact that the buyer is a charity does not prevent the FA 2012 rules from applying in this scenario. The pooling requirement must be met if any future owner is to be able to claim allowances for the fixtures in the property. The vendor will not be interested in claiming allowances but the charity could insist that this exercise is carried out as a condition of buying the property. Possibly, the charity will be willing to pay for the exercise.

Suppose, therefore, that a capital allowances analysis is undertaken, and that £125,000 of qualifying expenditure is added to the capital allowances pools (split between general fixtures and integral features). An election is signed to transfer the fixtures to the charity at their full cost of £125,000. (In the past, no fixtures election would have been possible at the time the charity buys the property, if it does not have a Unique Taxpayer Reference, but that is no longer a requirement – s. 201(3)(f).) Before any election is signed, however, it will first be necessary for the past owner – who is selling to the charity – to meet the pooling requirement.

At this point, there is no tax benefit to either party, as nobody can actually use the allowances. However, the charity has now captured the value of the allowances and can pass that value to a future owner.

In 2022, the charity sells the property to another retailer and it fetches £480,000. No election can be signed at this time, as the disposal by the charity does not meet the condition in s. 198(1): it has made no claim, so it does not have to bring a disposal value into account. An apportionment must therefore be made (s. 562), but with a restriction to historic cost (s. 185).

The rules in s. 187A still apply, and the "past owner" is the original retailer rather than the charity (per the definitions in that section). If the pooling requirement and fixed value requirement had not been met at the time of the sale to the charity, the new owner in 2022 would have been denied all allowances, but subject to the special rules for intervening owners, explained at **12.5.5** above.

If the original vendor had been a profitable retailer – say a major supermarket chain that was selling off an unwanted corner shop – there would probably be a different balance of priorities.

Assume that the original vendor is Tesco, for example, and that maximum allowances have been claimed by the supermarket. The pooling requirement has been met and the charity might once more wish to protect the future value of the fixtures by signing an election. In this case, however, Tesco will have an interest in keeping the figure in the election as low as possible, thus retaining any allowances already enjoyed and securing the full value of any remaining allowances for the future. In this case, the relative bargaining powers will be different and the charity's best overall commercial decision may be to accept a very low figure for the election. When the charity comes to sell the property later, it will be on the basis that minimal allowances will be due for the new owner.

12.9.3   Non-taxpayer as vendor

This topic is covered at **13.4** below.

12.10   Restrictions for earlier claims

12.10.1 Introduction

Restrictions apply where a previous owner has included expenditure in a capital allowances computation and is required to bring in a disposal value.

12.10.2 Fixtures on which plant and machinery allowances have been claimed

If a previous owner has included the cost of a fixture in a plant and machinery claim, the new owner's allowances are restricted accordingly. This is considered in depth at **12.7.5**.

The restriction does not apply if the old owner claimed by way of contribution allowances (see, generally, **31.3**).

Law: CAA 2001, s. 185

12.10.3 Fixtures on which industrial buildings allowances have been made

If there is no change of owner, and a person has already claimed IBAs, it is not possible for that same person to start claiming plant and machinery allowances on the same expenditure, even though the phasing out of IBAs meant that some of the costs effectively went unrelieved.

The position is different, however, if a previous owner claimed industrial buildings allowances (IBAs) on a building that included fixtures. The new owner will not be able to claim IBAs, as the rules for these have now been repealed, but may still be able to claim plant and machinery allowances for fixtures in the property.

As always, it is important to bear in mind that – strictly speaking – each fixture is considered in isolation. So if there is a complicated scenario, it may be necessary to isolate those assets on which IBAs have been claimed from those on which they have not.

Where a particular fixture has in the past been the subject of an IBA claim, the legislation restricts the new owner's claim to a proportionate part of the residue of qualifying expenditure immediately after the sale. The residue is calculated in accordance with the IBA rules immediately before they were repealed.

If the total consideration for the transfer exceeds "R" (see below), the maximum allowable amount is capped using the formula:

$$(F/T) \times R$$

where:

F is the part of the consideration for the transfer by the past owner that is attributable to the fixture;

T is the total consideration for that transfer; and

R is the residue of qualifying expenditure that would have been attributable to the relevant interest immediately after that transfer, calculated on the assumption that the transfer was a sale of the relevant interest, immediately before the repeal of the IBA rules.

To apply this, it is necessary to remember what happened when IBAs were phased out. First, balancing adjustments were abolished. Then IBAs as such were phased out and finally themselves abolished.

The concept of the "residue of qualifying expenditure" (RQE) could be quite complicated, but in simple terms it covered the qualifying costs less any IBAs actually given. In some circumstances, notional expenditure also had to be written off. When there was a balancing charge, this was (broadly speaking) added back, so that the RQE *after* the sale was often higher than the RQE *before* the sale. Once there were no more balancing charges, this did not apply so the RQE remained low.

Example

A building cost £1m. IBAs were claimed totalling £400k before IBAs were abolished. The RQE is £600k.

The property is bought some years later for £1.4m.

Without the restriction, the allowable cost of a given fixture would have been £10,000.

With the restriction, the allowable cost is restricted to £4,286 ((10,000/1,400,000) x 600,000).

(That is the way the legislation presents it. Arguably, the more logical presentation would be to show it as 10,000 x (600,000/1,400,000). It makes no difference to the result.)

For the avoidance of doubt, there can be no interaction between sections 186 (as illustrated above) and 198 (fixtures election).

If an asset has been subject to an IBA claim, s. 186 will apply. As the former owner claimed IBAs, he cannot also have claimed PMAs. As he did not claim PMAs, the condition in s. 198(1) is not met. So any asset on which the vendor claimed IBAs should always be excluded from the fixtures election.

If an asset has not been subject to an IBA claim, s. 186 will not apply.

Law: CAA 2001, s. 9, 186

Separate parts of the property

The restriction only applies to capital expenditure for which a claim has previously been made. It is possible that IBAs could not be claimed for part of a property, e.g. for an office where the cost of the office was more than 25% of the overall build cost. In this case, no IBAs would have been claimed on the office part and it would now be possible to claim for fixtures in that part (assuming they are still in the property at the time of the claim). To meet the pooling requirement, that claim would have to be made by the vendor before the property is sold.

Integral features and previous IBA claims

A particular issue arises in relation to integral features, where the wording of the legislation appears to produce an unexpected result. This can be illustrated as follows.

If a seller ("S") sells a property to a buyer ("B"), B may obviously wish to claim for the cost of integral features. If S has owned the property since before April 2008, and the fixtures in question were in place before that date, B will in principle have an unrestricted claim on items that did not qualify before the integral feature rules were introduced. This will normally be the case, for example, with general electrical work, lighting systems and cold water systems.

Suppose, though, that the building was an industrial building and that S claimed IBAs for, say, 5 full years and then the reducing elements as the allowances were phased out. Assume, for the moment, that IBAs were claimed on the whole construction cost. (The alternative, of course, would have been that the seller claimed plant and machinery allowances on some fixtures and IBAs on the remaining construction costs.)

As a general principle, B can still claim allowances for fixtures in the property, adjusted for the IBA rules about residues of qualifying expenditure as described above. In statutory terms, s. 9 initially blocks the fixtures claim if there has been a previous IBA claim, but s. 9(2) unblocks it where s. 186(2) applies. This would apply, for example, to a lift that was installed at the time of construction, but the cost of which was simply included in the overall IBA claim.

But suppose the item in question is an integral feature, of a type that would not have qualified as plant and machinery before April 2008. It appears in this case that s. 186(2) does not now apply. This is because s. 186 applies only if the past owner has claimed an IBA "in respect of expenditure which was or included expenditure on the provision of plant or machinery". In the case of an electrical system, for example, this would not in the past have constituted "expenditure on the provision of plant or machinery". As such, s. 186 does not apply. It then follows that s. 9(2) also does not apply.

The rather odd effect is that a person seems to be precluded from claiming allowances now for items that did not previously qualify as plant and machinery, but only if an IBA claim was made. It is not clear whether HMRC would take the point in practice – one reader has suggested to the author that HMRC did not do so in one particular case – but it is worth being aware of the possible restriction that could apply in these circumstances.

Law: CAA 2001, s. 9, 186

12.10.4 Fixtures on which business premises renovation allowances have been made

Allowances are restricted if a past owner has claimed business premises renovation allowances (BPRAs: see **30.1**) and the new owner wishes to claim plant and machinery allowances for fixtures.

The rules apply where:

- a past owner has at any time claimed BPRAs in respect of qualifying expenditure;
- there has been a BPRA balancing event (per s. 360N(1): see **21.3.6**) as a result of which an asset ceased to be owned by the past owner;
- the asset was or included plant or machinery; and
- the current owner makes a claim for plant and machinery allowances in respect of expenditure incurred on the provision of the plant or machinery at a time when it is a fixture.

Any excess over the maximum allowable amount if left out of account in determining the current owner's qualifying expenditure. That maximum amount is given by the formula:

$$(F/T) \times R$$

where:

F is so much of the proceeds from the balancing event as are attributable to the fixture;

T is the total amount of the proceeds from the balancing event; and

R is the qualifying expenditure incurred by the past owner on the asset in question, less any BPRAs given (net of any BPRA balancing charges) in respect of that asset.

The current owner may be the person who acquires the asset from the BPRA claimant, or it may be any person who is later treated as the owner of the plant or machinery in question.

Law: CAA 2001, s. 186A

12.10.5 Fixtures on which research and development allowances have been made

Allowances are restricted if a past owner has claimed research and development allowances (RDAs) and the new owner wishes to claim plant and machinery allowances for fixtures.

The rules apply where:

- a past owner has at any time claimed RDAs in respect of qualifying R&D expenditure;
- the past owner has ceased to own some or all of the relevant assets;
- the asset was or included plant or machinery; and
- the current owner makes a claim for plant and machinery allowances in respect of expenditure incurred on the provision of the plant or machinery at a time when it is a fixture.

Any excess over the maximum allowable amount is left out of account in determining the current owner's qualifying expenditure. That maximum amount is given by the formula:

$$(F/T) \times A$$

where:

F is the part of the consideration for the disposal of the R&D asset by the past owner that is attributable to the fixture;

T is the total consideration for that disposal; and

A is the smaller of the disposal value of the R&D asset when the past owner ceased to own it, and so much of the R&D expenditure as related to the provision of the asset in question.

The current owner may be the person who acquires the asset from the R&D claimant, or it may be any person who is later treated as the owner of the plant or machinery in question.

Law: CAA 2001, s. 187

12.11   CPSEs

12.11.1 Introduction

Accountants or others advising in relation to property transactions will often be asked by the legal teams to respond to queries on the commercial property standard enquiries (CPSE) form. This form is sent by the solicitor acting for the buyer as a way of gathering essential information from the vendor.

CPSEs in general cover much more than capital allowances, but section 32 of the form (as updated in February 2014) deals with capital allowances for plant and machinery. An understanding of the principles explained in this chapter will allow an intelligent response to the matters raised.

It is essential that accountants and lawyers dealing with capital allowances should be clear about who is taking ultimate responsibility for handling them correctly. In many cases, the solicitors will expressly not accept responsibility for these or for certain other tax matters. In such cases, the advice must come from elsewhere to avoid the costly errors that can potentially be made.

12.11.2 Problem areas

The CPSEs certainly act as an aid to eliciting the correct information, but should not be viewed as a checklist of all the questions it is necessary to ask the vendor at the time of sale. More often than not, it will be necessary to ask additional questions at the outset, or follow-up questions once the replies to the CPSEs have been received.

Certain problems may arise from the wording of the CPSE forms. To give one example, question 32.2 asks if the vendor has claimed allowances or allocated any expenditure on fixtures to a capital allowances pool. So a vendor who has claimed for any fixtures at all will answer "Yes".

The next question (32.3) opens with the words "If you have not pooled any expenditure ...". It would appear that the intended meaning is "If there is any expenditure that you have not pooled". However, another perfectly normal interpretation of the question is to read it as saying "If you have not pooled any expenditure at all". As the vendor has already answered "Yes" to 32.2, on the basis of having made a partial claim, he may legitimately answer "Not applicable". However, this can cause confusion and may lead to a significantly reduced claim for the buyer (and possibly a contractual claim against the vendor).

Example

Your client is buying a care home, and the normal CPSE queries are raised.

The vendor states that the property has been held on capital account and that he has indeed claimed allowances or allocated expenditure to a capital allowances pool. He therefore says "Not applicable" to the question that begins with the words "If you have not pooled any expenditure". All of the remaining queries in the main part of the form (up to and including 32.8) are similarly marked as "Not applicable".

In response to the supplementary enquiry 32.9, the vendor replies as follows: "When we bought the home, we agreed a figure of £25,000 for fixtures and fittings. We also claimed £10,000 for a new lift when we built the extension in 2010, and £6,000 for new furniture at the same time."

Section (f) at 32.9 is marked as "Not applicable" and section 32.10 is completed with contact details for the vendor's accountant.

So what should you advise your client, who is buying the property?

It might be thought that a fixtures election should be signed with a figure of perhaps £15,000 (being a share of the £25,000 plus £10,000) and that a transfer value of perhaps £2,000 should be agreed for the furniture that was bought in 2010. So on this basis the purchaser would be entitled to claim £17,000.

In reality, this approach fails to address many of the relevant issues, and a claim of £17,000 for the buyer may only be a fraction of what he could potentially claim. At the very least, we need to establish the following:

1. What did the £25,000 represent? Did it cover only fixtures, or also chattels? Was an election signed? What did the legal agreement actually say? It may be that a much higher figure can be pooled by the vendor at this late stage, and that that value can then be transferred by election to the buyer.

2. When was the property bought? This will allow us to consider a claim for integral features: if it was before April 2008, there will be items on which the purchaser can claim, over and above whatever is in the fixtures election.

3. Has there been other capital expenditure since the vendor acquired the property? Such expenditure must be pooled by the vendor if the purchaser is to be able to claim.

4. We need to know more about the extension. Nothing has been said about the extension costs themselves, which will certainly include both integral features and other fixtures. Once more, these must be pooled by the vendor before any value is transferred by election to the purchaser.

In summary, there are far too many permutations at present and some detailed further enquiries must be made before proper capital allowances advice can be given to the buyer.

It will normally be necessary to analyse all the expenditure in the accounts that has been allocated as "Additions to Property" so that a proper appraisal may be made of all of the expenditure.

12.11.3 Revenue or capital account

There is a point to watch in respect of the very first of the CPSE questions, which asks whether the vendor holds the property on capital or revenue account.

A developer or property trader may reply "revenue" and this may give the buyer a freer hand to claim allowances. (Even here, there are various possible outcomes, depending on when the property was built and when the current vendor acquired it.)

If the vendor has owned it as trading stock, however, it will not be possible for the vendor to meet either the pooling requirement or the fixed value requirement. (And the vendor cannot sign a fixtures election as the condition of s. 198(1) is not met.)

However, there is always a risk that HMRC will argue with the vendor that the property was in fact a capital asset: that will not often happen, but it is a possibility. That would mean that the pooling and fixed value requirements *would* have to be met, and time limits would have to be watched.

12.11.4 Agreeing to elect

There is little benefit to the buyer in agreeing to have a s. 198 election in place unless the figures – or at least the principles that will determine those figures – are agreed before the transaction takes place. It is *not* necessary to sign the election in the typically frenetic days leading up to completion of the deal, but the contract needs to commit both parties to submitting a valid election and should also clearly specify the basis on which the figures will be agreed.

In principle, if the buyer is willing to pay for a further capital allowances exercise, then he or she needs a commitment from the seller that the latter will pool the additional qualifying expenditure and will also pass it on in full to the buyer by way of an election. It may be appropriate for the buyer to commit to defending the claim in the event of any HMRC enquiry into the figures.

12.11.5 Structures and buildings allowances

The relevance of CPSEs is not limited to plant and machinery allowances. In particular, they will be of growing importance in relation to structures and buildings allowances, for the reasons given at **24.2.2** below.

12.12   Land remediation relief

This special relief for the costs of remedying contamination or dereliction of land is not part of the capital allowances legislation and is therefore beyond the scope of this book. Nevertheless, the relief should – in appropriate cases – be considered alongside capital allowances when buying or regenerating land.

Very briefly, relief is given of up to 150% of the costs incurred, which may be revenue or capital in nature. The relief is available for developers as well as traders and property investors, but is only given to companies (and not, for example, to individuals or to partnerships, though corporate members of partnerships may claim relief in respect of their share of the partnership's remediation expenditure). Loss-making companies can claim a tax credit, i.e. a cash repayment from HMRC.

The relief is typically given for the costs of removing asbestos from buildings, or knotweed or arsenic from land; petrol, diesel and cyanide are other contaminants that commonly feature in claims for relief. Relief is not available if the contamination was caused by the claimant company in the first place, so it is normally given only if the land was in a derelict or contaminated state when it was acquired (though an exception is made for knotweed, which can often be caused by fly-tipping and which may therefore have been outside the control of the vendor).

Incidental and professional costs may form a legitimate part of a claim for this relief. It is worth bearing in mind that qualifying costs may not be immediately visible, for example if they are classified as earthworks, excavation costs, or something similar.

Law: CTA 2009, Pt. 14
Guidance: CIRD 60000

12.13   Checklist for buyer of existing property

This section is intended to serve as a capital allowances *aide-memoire* for anyone buying an existing property.

12.13.1   Determine nature of property

Capital allowances are generally available for commercial (i.e. non-residential) properties, including hotels, care homes, offices, factories and many other property types. Allowances are also available for properties meeting the furnished holiday letting criteria.

No allowances are generally due for landlords of residential property, though allowances *are* available for the communal parts of residential blocks.

Certain property types (e.g. student accommodation and so-called houses of multiple occupation) need to be considered on their own merits, depending on the design and use of the property.

12.13.2   Find out about the vendor (and previous owners)

The buyer's entitlement to claim allowances depends very much on the vendor's tax status and claims history.

If (and to the extent that) the vendor is entitled to claim plant and machinery allowances, the pooling requirement will apply. The buyer will only be able to claim allowances for fixtures if the value of these has first passed through the vendor's capital allowances computations.

It may be that the vendor was entitled to claim for some fixtures but not others. This could arise, for example, if the vendor bought the property before April 2008 and was therefore unable to claim for some items now classified as integral features (typically, general lighting, other general electrical costs, and cold water systems). The pooling requirement will not apply to fixtures for which nobody before the current buyer has been able to claim allowances.

If the vendor has not been able to claim allowances (e.g. because it is a charity or a pension fund), it will be necessary to find details of any other owners of the property going back to at least April 2012, and possibly much earlier.

12.13.3 Quantify the claim

For any fixtures for which the vendor has made a legitimate claim, the amount of allowances available to the buyer will be determined by making a valid fixtures election under s. 198. (The only alternatives are to go to tribunal, with all the costs and uncertainty that that entails, or to give up the right to claim allowances.) The buyer's professional adviser should negotiate carefully the figures to go into the election, and must ensure that the fixtures election is valid and is made within statutory time limits.

In many cases, the vendor will have claimed for some fixtures but not all. In technical terms, the pooling requirement will have been met for some fixtures but not others. It is vital, from the buyer's point of view, that the vendor should pool any fixtures on which the vendor is entitled to claim allowances, and these should then be added to the fixtures election. The buyer's professional advisers should not take at face value a statement from the vendors that all fixtures have been pooled, but should explore the correctness of that claim.

It may be that there are fixtures (e.g. certain items bought by the vendor before April 2008) on which the vendor is not able to claim allowances. These fixtures will not be subject to the pooling or fixed value requirements (and will thus be excluded from the fixtures election) but should be the subject of a separate claim by the buyer. This will require a just and reasonable apportionment, which should certainly be carried out by an experience valuer. No negotiation is needed with the vendor on these assets, though the vendor may be able to provide useful background details.

Beware of the various restrictions that may apply – see below.

12.13.4 Restrictions

The right to claim plant and machinery allowances for a given fixture may be restricted or denied for a variety of reasons, and care should be taken to establish entitlement in all cases. This non-exhaustive list covers some of the most common restrictions:

- The pooling requirement may apply even if the current vendor is not entitled to claim – e.g. if a corner shop was bought by a charity in May 2014 and is now being sold, it will be necessary to look back at the 2014 transaction (s. 187A(1)).

- If the current transaction, or an earlier transaction in relation to the same property, is/was between connected parties, or had a tax avoidance motive, various restrictions can apply (s. 213 to 218ZA and later sections).

- Where any previous owner (not just the current vendor) has claimed plant and machinery allowances for a given fixture, the legislation normally imposes a cap (equal to that earlier sale figure) on any future claim for the same fixture (s. 62 and s. 185). A due diligence process may be needed, to check whether that may in fact be the case.

- Equivalent restrictions apply where a past owner claimed any of various other types of capital allowance (IBAs, BPRAs, RDAs) (s. 186 to 187).

- Where a lease has been granted, some complex rules need to be considered to determine whether the landlord or tenant is entitled to claim (s. 183 and s. 184).

12.13.5   Protecting the buyer

There are certain key steps that the professional adviser should take to protect the interests of the buyer of a commercial property in relation to capital allowances. According to the circumstances, and the amounts involved, these steps may appropriately be taken by the solicitor acting for the buyer, by the buyer's accountant, or (see **12.13.6** below), by a specialist capital allowances firm.

- Check the entitlement to claim allowances, taking account of all relevant factors, including past ownership and all earlier claims to plant and machinery or other allowances.

- Where details of earlier claims are not known, ensure that proper procedures are followed to determine the extent of any valid claim now.

- Check whether the vendor has met the pooling requirement in respect of all eligible fixtures. The starting point for this may be to raise commercial property standard enquiries, and to review very critically the answers received.

- Take appropriate steps to ensure that the vendor pools, before the sale, all other fixtures that have not previously been included in the vendor's capital allowances computations but that the vendor is entitled to pool.

- Negotiate a transfer value for all the fixtures.
- Encapsulate that transfer value in a fixtures election, ensuring that the election is valid and timely.
- Undertake a proper valuation exercise to determine the just and reasonable apportionment figure for any fixtures that cannot be covered by a fixtures election.

12.13.6 *Capital allowances specialists*

Accountants and legal advisers will need to decide whether it is necessary or desirable to engage the services of a capital allowances specialist. Where valuations are needed, any estimate made by an accountant without valuation expertise is likely to be way off the mark.

All specialist firms will be able to carry out valuations, but only some are competent to advise on the underlying CAA 2001 technicalities, providing written evidence to support (and if necessary defend) any claim made. Those instructing specialist firms will need to be acutely aware of that distinction, so that they know to what extent they may depend on the advice received.

Some capital allowances specialists are competent to carry the entire burden of the capital allowances aspects: reviewing paperwork, negotiating with the vendor, fully checking entitlement to claim, making proper elections, and providing figures for the accountant to include in an income tax or corporation tax return. Other specialists are not competent to do this.

13.   Fixtures claims – the seller's perspective

13.1   Why the vendor needs to sign a fixtures election

The FA 2012 rules, which introduced the pooling and fixed value requirements, are entirely concerned with the tax claims that may be made by the new ("current") owner. If the requirements are not met, the new expenditure incurred by the person acquiring the property "is to be treated as nil".

The legislation goes on to specify, however, that the question of whether any claim can be made by the purchaser does not affect "the disposal value (if any) which falls to be brought into account by the past owner (as a result of having made a claim in respect of the historic expenditure)".

On a quick reading, it may therefore be thought that the FA 2012 changes, introducing the pooling and fixed value requirements, are of no interest to the vendor. In practice, however, there will be an indirect effect on the vendor, and the cost of overlooking this aspect can be very high.

Fixtures elections (under s. 198) are now the norm rather than the exception. They provide certainty of tax treatment for the vendor in relation to any fixtures that are covered by the election.

Failure to sign an election may have disastrous consequences for the vendor, as well as denying all allowances to the new owner.

Example

Bill incurred qualifying expenditure of £200,000 many years previously and claimed allowances in full. The written down value of his capital allowances pool is just £5,000 and he is now selling to Mike. Mike has asked to sign a fixtures election with a figure of £60,000. Bill refuses as he will suffer a balancing charge of £55,000.

If no election is signed, and if the tribunal is not asked to set a transfer value for the fixtures, Mike will not be entitled to any allowances, as the fixed value requirement has not been met. However, Bill's disposal value will then be calculated using apportionment principles. It is quite possible that his disposal value will be much higher than £60,000 and he could end up with a balancing charge of up to £195,000.

For this reason, it is usually in the interests of *both* parties to sign an election, though the actual figures to put into the election may be much more difficult to agree.

At one level, there is nothing new here. It has been the case for many years that a vendor who has not signed an election has been required to bring in a proper disposal value. However, the HMRC perspective is likely to change significantly as a result of the FA 2012 changes. In the past, any failure by the vendor to bring in a disposal value was typically matched by a lower claim by the purchaser; HMRC were not exactly accepting of this approach, but it was what often happened in practice. Now, however, the outcome is very different: if the fixed value requirement is not met, the purchaser cannot claim allowances, but HMRC can still go after the vendor to bring in a proper disposal value. In other words, HMRC can now have their cake and eat it, as illustrated in the example above.

Law: CAA 2001, s. 187B(6)

13.2 The figure to go into the election

A vendor who has claimed allowances for fixtures in the property will almost certainly wish to sign an election to determine the disposal value, as illustrated at **13.1** immediately above.

The question of the amount to put in the election is another matter, however. There are lots of permutations here, and the issues are addressed in detail at **12.7.7** above.

13.3 The pooling requirement

Since April 2014, the buyer has only been able to claim allowances if the past owner has first made a claim for FYAs or has included the cost of the fixtures in a capital allowances pool.

In this respect, the buyer will be completely in the hands of the seller – if the latter makes no claim for certain fixtures, even though he could do so, the opportunity for the buyer or for any future party to claim allowances for those fixtures will be lost forever.

At one level, this means that the seller is in a stronger negotiating position: the default starting position is that the buyer cannot claim any allowances unless the seller makes a claim first.

If the buyer is being well advised, the vendor will be asked to pool any remaining capital expenditure as a condition of the transaction going ahead. If this is not done, there will still be a short period of opportunity following the sale, but the vendor will then hold all the cards. This is examined at **12.7.7** and see especially the example at that section.

Risk of penalties for vendor

A practical issue may arise if the vendor (or his professional adviser) does not really understand the fixtures rules and is reluctant to pool expenditure in his tax computations because of a risk of penalties.

The penalty rules at FA 2007, Sch. 24, Pt. 1 include the concept of an "error in taxpayer's document attributable to another person". A penalty can be payable by a person (referred to in the legislation as "T") if T provides another person ("P") with certain documentation which leads P to understate his tax liability. In these circumstances, both T and P are potentially liable to a penalty.

The bar for such a penalty is set high, however, as T is only liable to a penalty is he *deliberately* supplies false information or *deliberately* withholds relevant information. This is very different from the day-to-day test of taxpayer negligence.

Example

Thomas, who has never claimed capital allowances for fixtures, is selling a property to Peter. As part of the commercial discussions, it is agreed that Peter's advisers will conduct a capital allowances exercise and will identify qualifying expenditure on fixtures. Thomas will then include the identified figure in his final tax computations and will sign an election under s. 198, transferring the whole value to Peter.

Suppose that Peter's advisers include, in the qualifying expenditure, certain items (e.g. the cost of fixed partition walls) on which allowances are not in fact due. Thomas will not personally benefit from that fact, as the full value is being passed to Peter. However, could Thomas still be liable for a penalty?

On the basis of the wording at Sch. 24, para. 1A, Thomas will only be liable if he deliberately provides a false document. In the view of the authors, it would be very difficult for HMRC to sustain an argument that there was a deliberate act on the part of Thomas in these circumstances.

In summary, there would not appear to be a risk to the vendor of a property who simply agrees, in good faith, to amend his final capital allowances computations to take account of information provided by the buyer's professional advisers.

This general principle would obviously not apply if there were to be blatant fraudulent collusion on the part of the seller and buyer – deliberately overstating the value of the fixtures, and perhaps agreeing to share the resulting tax savings (in which case both parties would already be liable to penalties in any case).

13.4   Charities and other non-taxpayers

If a charity or pension fund that is now selling the property has owned it since before April 2012, the FA 2012 changes can be ignored.

Section 187A, which imposes the pooling and fixed value requirements, only applies if the "past owner" was entitled to claim plant and machinery allowances in respect of the expenditure (s. 187A(1)(d) and s. 187A(2)).

In simple terms, if the vendor was a pension fund, and was therefore unable to claim allowances, this condition is not met, and so the various requirements in s. 187A are not imposed. In considering whether there is any other "past owner", any period of ownership falling before April 2012 is ignored for the purposes of determining whether s. 187A applies.

If the charity bought the property after April 2012 and is now selling, the purchaser will need to consider the application of the FA 2012 rules by reference to the person from whom the charity acquired the property. The charity will ideally have signed a fixtures election when buying the property (see **12.9.2** above).

14.   Fixtures claims – worked examples

14.1   Buying a new property from a developer

The FA 2012 rules, now at sections 187A and 187B of CAA 2001, do not apply in these circumstances, as there is no past owner who was entitled to claim plant and machinery allowances. As such, there is no pooling requirement and no fixed value requirement.

The new owner will need to analyse the costs and to claim for those items that constitute fixtures for capital allowances purposes, allocating as necessary to the main pool or to the special rate pool.

14.2   Buying from an owner who had the property built in 2009 and who has claimed all possible allowances

This is a relatively straightforward scenario, as the property was built after April 2008 (when the integral features rules were introduced) and the owner has made all possible claims.

The pooling requirement has here been met already, so the only focus needs to be on the fixed value requirement. Almost certainly, this means that that two parties will sign a fixtures election.

Care must be taken to ensure that the election separates main rate expenditure from special rate expenditure (mostly integral features). The parties must also ensure that the election is valid, and is submitted in time, as it will be very expensive if HMRC can demonstrate that no valid election is in place.

14.3   Buying from an owner who had the property built in 2005 and who has claimed all possible allowances

This differs from the last scenario above in relation to integral features. As the current vendor has owned the property since before April 2008, it is unlikely that he or she will have been able to claim for certain key items, including cold water systems and general electrical (including lighting) costs. These items did not normally qualify as plant or machinery before April 2008.

For all *other* fixtures, the treatment is the same as outlined at **14.2** immediately above.

For those items for which the vendor was not permitted to claim allowances, the s. 187A and 187B provisions do not apply. In technical terms, this is because the condition at s. 187A(1)(d) is not met in relation to these items: the vendor was not entitled to claim in respect of the expenditure in question. As such, the purchaser can claim on an apportionment basis – with no restriction to historic cost – for these additional items.

The purchaser's claim will therefore contain both elements – figures from the fixtures election, plus an additional claim for those integral features that did not qualify for allowances before April 2008.

14.4 Buying from an owner who bought the property new in 2009 but who has claimed no allowances

Assuming that the vendor is entitled to claim allowances, the purchaser and all future owners will be denied allowances unless the vendor meets the pooling requirement. This does not mean that the vendor has to retain any part of the value of the allowances, but it does mean that the fixtures must pass through the vendor's capital allowances computations.

Once the sale and purchase contract has been signed, there is no incentive for the vendor to co-operate with the new owner: an amount of work will be needed to formulate the claim, and the tax computations will have to reflect both the purchase cost and the agreed disposal value for the fixtures. This is the main reason why it is essential for the purchaser to ensure that capital allowances issues are addressed before formally agreeing to the purchase.

If the vendor has the construction cost details, it will usually be possible to apportion these by creating a spreadsheet analysis. If the details are no longer available, a valuation exercise can be carried out to determine that portion of the purchase cost of the property that qualifies as incurred on fixtures, split as necessary between integral features and main rate expenditure. In each case, the claim must be adjusted to take out of the equation any fixtures that were scrapped before the start of the accounting period in question.

The two parties must ensure that a valid fixtures election is put in place to determine the transfer values of the fixtures.

14.5 Buying from an owner who bought the property new in 2005 but who has claimed no allowances

For those items for which the vendor was not permitted to claim allowances, the s. 187A and 187B provisions do not apply. In technical terms, this is because the condition at s. 187A(1)(d) is not met as the vendor was not entitled to claim in respect of the expenditure in question. As such, the purchaser can claim on an apportionment basis – with no restriction to historic cost – for these additional items.

All the other fixtures are subject to the pooling requirement, and the principles outlined at **14.4** above will apply.

14.6   Buying from an owner who bought the property second hand but who has claimed few or no allowances

This is a common scenario in practice, and is where it starts to get more complicated.

Example

Venus is currently selling an office building to Pluto. The following facts are established:

- Mars had the property built in 1998.
- Mars sold it to Venus in 2004.
- The paperwork from 2004 does not make reference to capital allowances.
- We do not know whether or not Mars made a claim, and Mars can no longer be contacted.
- Venus confirms that no fixtures election was signed in relation to the 2004 purchase.
- Venus has not claimed for any property fixtures, with the exception of £12,000 for a new boiler in 2010.

The technical problem here is the fact that we do not know whether or not Mars claimed any allowances. However, this is not fatal to the claim now. There are two possibilities in relation to any given fixture: Mars did not claim, or Mars did claim.

No claim by Mars

If Mars did not claim, then Venus has an unrestricted right to claim for any fixtures in the property. As the construction costs are not available, this should be done using an apportionment principle, establishing the value of the fixtures at the time Venus acquired the property in 2004. This should only include fixtures that are still in the property in the year for which Venus will now claim.

It is essential for Venus to go through this process if Pluto is to be able to claim allowances for the fixtures in question (the pooling requirement).

Suppose, however, that the sale documents have already been signed and Venus refuses to engage with the exercise at all, or to claim any new allowances.

There is nothing that Pluto can now do to force Venus to make a retrospective claim for fixtures acquired when the property was bought from Mars, or added since. The tax tribunal has no jurisdiction in this matter.

Pluto can, however, go to tribunal to establish a transfer value for the boiler that was installed in 2010. In practice, it is in the interests of both parties to agree a transfer value and it should be possible to deal with the matter simply with a fixtures election.

As Venus acquired the property before April 2008, Pluto can also claim for those integral features (cold water systems, general lighting, other general electrical wiring) that did not then qualify for allowances. Pluto does not need any cooperation from Venus to claim for these items. A valuation exercise will be needed to establish the appropriate figures.

Mars claimed allowances

But what is the position if Mars did claim, or may have claimed?

Essentially, the outcome is the same. We know that there was no fixtures election, so Mars had a statutory obligation to bring in a disposal figure based on an apportioned value. That same value then provides the acquisition cost for Venus.

Of course we do not know whether or not Mars in fact brought such a disposal value into account, but this is not our problem – the same principle still applies for establishing the capital allowances cost for Venus.

On this basis, the pooling requirement once more applies (and, again, there is nothing that Pluto can do to force Venus to pool the expenditure in question, other than refusing to go ahead with the purchase).

14.7   More than one owner before the present vendor

The example immediately above showed that a claim should be possible even where there is uncertainty about claims made by a previous owner. However, there is more difficulty where there have been several previous owners.

Example

Andy paid for a pub to be built in 1992. He sold it to Bert in 1999. Bert sold it on to Charlie in 2006 and Charlie is now selling it to Doug. Andy has since died and Bert now lives in the Bahamas, with no interest at all in any tax matters.

Charlie checks his paperwork and confirms that no fixtures election was signed when he bought the pub in 2006. The sale and purchase agreement from the time shows a figure of £5,000 allocated to "fixtures, fittings, plant and machinery".

Charlie has trading losses and is not really interested in capital allowances, but he is keen to sell the property and therefore wants to help Doug if he can. Doug wishes to make the best possible capital allowances claim.

In practice, Charlie and Doug can agree a reasonable figure for the chattels in the pub – tables, chairs, stools, etc.

The fixtures, though, present a problem. Once he has bought the property, the onus will be on Doug to prove that a valid claim can be made. The complication here is that a fixtures election may have been signed when Andy sold the pub to Bert in 1999, and it is possible that the figure in the election will have been just £1. That would then cap Bert's acquisition cost of the fixtures at the same £1, and this would in turn mean that neither Charlie nor Doug can claim more than £1 for those fixtures.

The sale by Andy to Bert was a long time ago, however, and fixtures in a pub suffer a good deal of wear and tear. So it is possible that many of the fixtures that were then in place have since been replaced. If that is the case, a claim should be possible for those replacement fixtures, as in the previous example above.

As Charlie owned the property before April 2008, Doug will also have an unrestricted chance to claim for any integral features on which Charlie was unable to claim. That is likely to include general electrical wiring and non-specialist lighting, as well as most or all of the cold water supply.

In relation to this last example, it should be remembered, however, that the fixtures election was only introduced by FA 1997, and has only been available for chargeable periods ending on or after 19 March 1997 (see **12.7.1**). So if the first sale had been in January 1997, rather than in 1999, the problem would not arise as no election could then have been signed.

14.8 Buying from an owner who has claimed some allowances for fixtures

In practice, it is often the case that the vendor has claimed for certain more obvious fixtures, but has overlooked others. Typically, a claim will have been made for toilets and lifts, but overlooked for fitted cupboards and for the hot and cold water systems.

The principle to remember here is that each fixture is – in theory – dealt with on an asset by asset basis. Although this would be impossible to implement in practice, the technicality must be respected where, as here, it makes a difference.

The purchaser should therefore establish a clear list of those fixtures for which claims have or have not been made. If there are fixtures for which the vendor could have claimed, but has not, the pooling requirement will apply to those fixtures. The fixed value requirement will then apply to all fixtures on which the vendor has made a claim.

15. Short-life assets

15.1 Introduction

15.1.1 Overview

Nobody is obliged to use the short-life asset rules. Nevertheless, the right to make an election is a useful one that can accelerate tax relief in certain circumstances.

An election may be made for any asset where such treatment is not ruled out (see **15.6** for a discussion of the exclusions). There is no test as to whether the asset will in fact have a working life of a certain period.

An election for such treatment must be made by the person incurring the expenditure (see **15.4**).

Where an election is made, a nominated asset is removed from the main "pool" of plant and machinery. Capital allowances are then calculated instead on the asset in isolation, within a "single-asset pool". (The concept is a contradiction in terms, but such is the statutory wording.) Any tax advantage comes at the time the asset is sold or scrapped, at which point there may be an acceleration of the allowances that would otherwise have been given.

Law: CAA 2001, s. 83

15.1.2 Relevance

The benefit of the short-life asset election varies according to other capital allowances changes. The election is mainly of value in cases where expenditure in the year has exceeded the level of available AIAs. With that value now settling down at £200,000 (and indeed subject to an increase to £1,000,000 in 2019 to 2021), short-life asset elections will tend to be relevant only for larger businesses, for companies that are part of a large group (where the AIA has to be shared between group members) and in circumstances where there is an exceptional level of expenditure in the year (e.g. if a commercial property is bought).

Short-life asset elections are of greater relative value where the main rate of WDAs is reduced. For example, the reduction from 20% to 18% created a longer delay in giving tax relief for assets that are not subject to an SLA election.

An SLA election only has any beneficial effect if the asset is disposed of within a given period of approximately eight years, in each case counting from the end of the chargeable period. The details of this are discussed at **15.3** below, but the change means that many more assets have been able to benefit from the election.

Law: CAA 2001, s. 83
Guidance: CA 23620

15.2   Effect of election

The effect of making an election is one of timing only. It has no bearing on the overall quantum of plant and machinery allowances that may be claimed. An election will usually mean that the business obtains tax relief for the actual depreciation of the asset over the period of ownership.

Example – effect of election

Amir buys some machinery in Year 1 for £20,000 and sells it in Year 3 for £7,000. He has already used up his AIA for Year 1 on other purchases. He has a range of other assets in his main capital allowances pool. Assume a WDA rate of 18% throughout.

If Amir simply adds the new machine to his main plant and machinery pool, he will obtain allowances of £3,600 in Year 1, £2,952 in Year 2 and £2,421 in Year 3. By the time the asset is sold, therefore, he will have had tax relief on just £8,973, even though his actual depreciation suffered over the period of ownership is £13,000. He will eventually receive allowances on the rest of the £13,000 but this will be by way of ever reducing amounts over future years.

By making an election for SLA treatment, Amir will receive the same allowances in Year 1 and Year 2, but will receive a balancing allowance in Year 3 instead of the WDA of £2,421. This balancing allowance will be calculated by starting with the original cost of £20,000 and deducting the allowances already received in Years 1 and 2 (£6,552). From this net amount of £13,448, the disposal proceeds of £7,000 are deducted and he can claim a balancing allowance in Year 3 of £6,448.

Possible downsides of election

An SLA election may occasionally be disadvantageous. This will be the case if the asset in question is sold, within approximately eight years, for more than its tax written-down value. As the election is irrevocable, it is not possible to go back and undo it.

In the example concerning Amir above, the written down value at the start of Year 3 was £13,448. If Amir had sold the machine for £17,000 instead of £7,000, he would have suffered a balancing charge of £3,552.

Once more, the issue is one of timing only, but the effect in such a case is to accelerate the recovery by HMRC of allowances that have already been given.

For some businesses, the additional record-keeping may be perceived as a further disadvantage. If a short-life asset election is made, it will be necessary to isolate the asset in the business records so that any disposal proceeds may be properly taken into account. Indeed, it will be necessary to know even if the asset is scrapped so that a balancing adjustment may be made at that time. If the business already keeps a fixed asset register, which in many circumstances is good practice anyway, this should not be an issue in practice.

15.3   Eight-year cut-off – short-life asset pool

15.3.1   Overview

The short-life asset election will only have an effect if the asset in question is sold or scrapped within a specified period. This period is counted from the end of the chargeable period in which the asset was acquired. The period is broadly of eight years (but was four years for expenditure incurred before April 2011).

In simplified terms, the item in question is transferred back into the main pool (or, for certain cars, the special rate pool: see **15.3.4**) if there is no disposal of the asset within that eight year period. The tax effect is (normally) then the same as if no election had been made.

In technical terms, it is necessary to allocate expenditure that is to be treated as a short-life asset to a single-asset pool, known as the short-life asset pool. The taxpayer must then determine whether the final chargeable period for the short-life asset pool has occurred before the eighth anniversary of the end of the relevant chargeable period. The concept of the "final chargeable period" is considered in detail at **5.1.3** but it is broadly, for the purposes of a short-life asset pool, the period in which a disposal is brought into account.

The "relevant chargeable period" is the chargeable period in which the qualifying expenditure was incurred on the provision of the short-life asset. If the expenditure was incurred in different chargeable periods, it is necessary to use the first such period in which any of the qualifying expenditure on the item was incurred.

The test is whether a disposal value has been brought into account in a chargeable period *ending by* the eighth anniversary of the end of the period of account. A little care is needed if there is a change in the date to which accounts are drawn up.

The meaning of "chargeable period" differs for income tax and corporation tax purposes, so these are considered in detail below.

Law: CAA 2001, s. 86

15.3.2 Income tax

For income tax purposes, a chargeable period means a period of account.

Where capital allowances are being offset against the profits of a trade (or profession or vocation), the period of account is simply the period for which trading accounts are drawn up. In any other case, it is the tax year ending on 5 April.

Example

Morse, a sole trader, draws accounts up to 31 December each year. He bought a piece of equipment for his business in May 2011 and made a short-life asset election in his tax computations for the year to 31 December 2011.

Morse changed his accounting date by drawing up a 16-month period of accounts to 30 April 2014, retaining the 30 April date thereafter.

The asset is scrapped in June 2019 and it is necessary to determine whether or not he can claim a balancing allowance. For this purpose, he must work out whether or not the final chargeable period for the short-life asset pool has ended on or before the eighth anniversary of the end of the relevant chargeable period.

The relevant chargeable period was the year ended 31 December 2011, being the period of account in which the expense was incurred. The eighth anniversary is therefore 31 December 2019. Although the asset was scrapped before that date (and indeed within eight years of the date on which the asset was bought) the chargeable period in which that occurs is the year ended 30 April 2020. As such, the chargeable period has not ended before the eighth anniversary (31 December 2019) so no balancing allowance is available.

The short-life asset pool comes to an end and the written-down value is transferred into the main pool at the start of the period to 30 April 2021.

See **1.6.2** if it is necessary to address the question of overlapping periods of account, of gaps between such periods, or of periods exceeding 18 months.

Law: CAA 2001, s. 6, 86

15.3.3   Corporation tax

The position is simpler for corporation tax purposes, but the same underlying principles apply.

The test is whether a disposal value must be brought into account in any accounting period that ends by the eighth anniversary of the end of the accounting period in which the original expenditure was incurred.

If there is no change of accounting date, this is simple.

Example 1

Lewis Ltd draws accounts up to 31 December each year. It bought a machine in October 2013 and made a short-life asset election.

A balancing adjustment will be made if there is a disposal of the asset by 31 December 2021. If there is no such disposal, the machine will be transferred into the main pool as at 1 January 2022.

Again, it is a little more complicated if there has been a change of accounting date.

Example 2

Hathaway Ltd drew accounts up to 31 December each year but had a short period of account to 30 September 2017. It bought a machine in October 2014 and made a short-life asset election.

A balancing adjustment will only be made if there is a disposal of the asset in a chargeable period ending by 31 December 2022. As such, a balancing adjustment will be made only if there is a disposal by 30 September 2022, being the last day of the last accounting period ending by the eighth anniversary.

If enough was at stake in relation to a disposal in the last three months of 2022, it would be open to the company to draw up a short period of accounts to 31 December 2022.

Law: CAA 2001, s. 86

15.3.4 Cars

Cars cannot normally be the subject of a short-life asset election (see **15.6.2**). Exceptionally, an election may be made for certain cars used by disabled drivers.

If a car that is treated as a short-life asset is still retained at the end of the eight-year period, it will be transferred to the special rate pool, rather than the main pool, if it is not a main rate car (as defined: see **9.3.2**).

Law: CAA 2001, s. 86(5)

15.4 Procedure for election

15.4.1 Procedure

A short-life asset election, which is irrevocable, must be made to an officer of HMRC and must specify:

- the plant or machinery that is the subject of the election;
- the amount of expenditure incurred; and
- the date on which the expenditure was incurred.

The tax officer is then required to make any assessment or adjustments needed to give effect to the election.

Law: CAA 2001, s. 85, 577(1)
Guidance: CA 23640

15.4.2 Time limit

The election must be made in writing within a specified time limit.

For corporation tax purposes, the limit is two years from the end of the chargeable period in which the expenditure was incurred.

For income tax purposes, the normal self-assessment deadlines apply. As such, the election must be made by the normal time limit for *amending* a tax return for the tax year in which the relevant chargeable period ends. For an income tax trade, for example, the time limit is 31 January some 22 months after the end of the tax year in which the period of account ends.

Example

Hobson, a GP practising on his own, draws accounts up to 30 November each year. He buys some equipment for the surgery in April 2017.

The period of accounts ends in November 2017, falling in 2017-18. The time limit for the election is 31 January 2020.

If qualifying expenditure is incurred in different chargeable periods, the time limit is by reference to the first chargeable period in which any of the expenditure was incurred.

Example 2 – HMRC example

Jackson buys a computer in his accounting period ended 31 July 2010. If he wants to make a SLA election he must do it by 31 January 2013.

If Jackson incurs the expenditure on the computer in two instalments, half in his accounting period ended 31 July 2010 and half in his accounting period ended 31 July 2011 the time limit for making a SLA election is still 31 January 2013.

Law: CAA 2001, s. 85
Guidance: CA 23640

15.4.3   Many assets in one election

A short-life asset election is, strictly, made on an asset-by-asset basis, each item of plant or machinery going into its separate single-asset pool. However, HMRC are prepared to break that rule in practice in certain specific circumstances, as per the following extract from CA 23640:

> "If separate identification of the SLAs acquired in a chargeable period is impossible or impracticable, then you should accept an election which gives information about the assets by reference to batches of acquisitions, with their costs aggregated and shown in one amount provided that you are satisfied that–
>
> - the assets are not specifically excluded, and
> - the election gives enough information for it to be clear what is and what is not covered by it.

> Strictly, each SLA should go into its own separate pool and so that [sic] the allowances on it are calculated separately. This may not be practicable where assets are held in large numbers. In cases like that capital allowance computations which give the correct statutory result, and do not abuse the short life asset provisions,

should be accepted even if there is not a separate computation for each asset."

The HMRC guidance then includes the following example:

HMRC example

Alice runs a restaurant and, every year, buys glasses to use in the business. She agrees with her Inspector that the glasses have an actual life of three years and that nothing is received for the remains.

She has used her AIA annual amount on other expenditure. She spends £1,200 on wine glasses in the year ended 30 June 2010 and makes a SLA election. She can make a single capital allowance calculation for that expenditure of £1,200 and claim a balancing allowance in the year ended 30 June 2013 based on a disposal value of nil. None of the glasses bought in the year ended 30 June 2010 should still exist by then because they have an actual life of 3 years and Alice will not have received anything for the remains.

If Alice spends £1,500 on glasses in the year ended 30 June 2011 and makes another SLA election, that expenditure is put into a separate pool.

If in the year ended 30 June 2013 Alice sells the broken glass for recycling for £50 and the £50 is not treated as a trading receipt, then it should be treated as disposal proceeds.

If the disposal proceeds cannot be tied to any particular acquisition, then they should be treated as disposal proceeds of the earliest period for which a short life asset pool is in existence.

If the broken glass cannot be related to any particular acquisition of glasses, the £50 should be treated as disposal proceeds of the pool for the expenditure of £1,200 incurred in the year ended 30 June 2010.

Law: CAA 2001, s. 86(1)
Guidance: CA 23640

15.5 Assets provided for leasing

Although various restrictions apply to prevent leased plant and machinery from being classified as a short-life asset, there is an exception for certain assets that will be used for a qualifying purpose within a designated period (s. 122 to 125: overseas leasing: see **Chapter 19**).

In such a case, it is possible that the asset will cease to be used other than for a qualifying purpose before the four or eight year cut-off period. If so the balance in the short-life asset pool is transferred at that point to the main pool. Although the short-life asset pool therefore comes to an end, there is no final chargeable period and no balancing adjustment.

Law: CAA 2001, s. 87
Guidance: CA 23650

15.6   Cases where election not allowed

15.6.1   Introduction

There are various circumstances in which an election for short-life asset treatment is ruled out. These are considered in turn under the headings that follow.

Law: CAA 2001, s. 84
Guidance: CA 23620

15.6.2   Cars

Short-life asset elections are not permitted for cars (as defined at s. 268A: see **9.2**).

The only exception is for hire cars for disabled persons, i.e. cars that are provided wholly or mainly for hire to, or for the carriage of, disabled persons in the ordinary course of a trade. A disabled person is one who is in receipt of any of the following:

- a disability living allowance (payable under the *Social Security Contributions and Benefits Act* 1992, or equivalent Northern Ireland legislation) because of entitlement to the mobility component;
- certain personal independence payments made under the *Welfare Reform Act* 2012 (or corresponding Northern Ireland provisions);
- an armed forces independence payment under a scheme established under s. 1 of the *Armed Forces (Pensions and Compensation) Act* 2004; or
- a mobility supplement (as defined).

Law: CAA 2001, s. 84, 268D
Guidance: CA 23510, 23620

407

15.6.3   Special rate expenditure

No short-life asset election may be made for special rate expenditure (as defined: see **17.2**). Once more, the only exception is for hire cars for disabled persons (as defined at s. 268D: see **15.6.2** above).

Law: CAA 2001, s. 84
Guidance: CA 23620

15.6.4   Leasing

No SLA election is permitted where plant or machinery is used for leasing. However, this restriction does not apply to:

- a hire car provided for a disabled person (as defined at s. 268D: see **15.6.2**); or
- plant or machinery to be used within a designated period for a qualifying purpose (overseas leasing per s. 122 to 125: see **Chapter 19**). A qualifying period is broadly 10 years from the date on which the person first uses the plant or machinery, but the more complex definition is given at s. 106.

SLA treatment is also ruled out for plant or machinery that is the subject of special leasing (per s. 19: see **3.7**).

Again, no SLA election is possible where allowances are only allowed at 10% by virtue of s. 109 (certain plant and machinery for overseas leasing: see **Chapter 19**). Nor may an SLA election be made if plant or machinery is leased to two or more persons jointly in circumstances such that s. 116 applies (overseas leasing (mitigation)).

Law: CAA 2001, s. 84
Guidance: CA 23620

15.6.5   Other restrictions

An SLA election is also not permitted:

- where expenditure is incurred partly for the purposes of a qualifying activity and partly for other purposes (s. 205: see **5.2.15**);
- for deemed expenditure that qualifies by virtue of s. 13 (asset provided originally for other purposes: see **4.10.1**);
- for assets qualifying by virtue of s. 13A (asset provided originally for long funding leasing: see **4.10.2**);

- where plant and machinery allowances are claimed (by virtue of s. 14: see **4.10.4**) for items received by way of a gift;
- where expenditure has to be allocated to a single-asset pool under s. 211 (partial depreciation subsidy: see **5.9**);
- for a ship.

Law: CAA 2001, s. 84
Guidance: CA 23620

15.7   Sales at less than market value

An anti-avoidance rule applies if:

- there is a disposal of an asset at less than market value;
- no election has been made in relation to the disposal under s. 89(6) (certain disposals to connected persons: see **15.8** below); and
- there is no charge to tax under ITEPA 2003 (i.e. for a director or employee).

In this case, the disposal value to be brought into account is the market value of the asset. This prevents the creation of an artificial balancing allowance.

This rule is disapplied in the case of certain transfers to a national authority made under s. 1(2) of the *Railways Act* 2005.

Law: CAA 2001, s. 88; *Railways Act* 2005, Sch. 10, para. 2(4)
Guidance: CA 23660

15.8   Disposal to connected person

Special rules apply if a person disposes of a short-life asset to a connected person before the end of the eight-year cut-off.

The asset is treated automatically as a short-life asset in the hands of the connected person acquiring the plant and machinery. The eight-year cut-off is calculated as it would have been for the transferor.

The parties may elect to transfer the asset across at its written-down value, such that no balancing adjustment is made.

Where an election is made, certain restrictions for first-year and other allowances (s. 217 and 218: see **22.3.2**) and for assets that are sold and leased back (s. 225: see **22.5**) are disapplied.

The time limit for an election is two years from the end of the chargeable period in which the disposal occurs.

If no election is made, market value will apply to the disposal, as explained at **15.7** above.

Law: CAA 2001, s. 89
Guidance: CA 23660

16. Long-life assets

16.1 Introduction

The long-life asset rules operate to slow down the rate at which plant and machinery allowances are given for certain assets that are expected to have a long useful life. Two key issues arise to allow effect to be given to that intention: identification of the assets affected, and the mechanical aspects of slowing down the allowances for those assets.

Originally, the mechanics of giving slower tax relief formed part of the long-life asset provisions themselves. Since April 2008, however, long-life assets are treated as just one form of "special rate" expenditure; allowances are therefore now given according to the rules applying to such expenditure (see **Chapter 17**). As such, the main function of the long-life asset rules is now simply to identify the assets that must be allocated to the special rate pool.

Law: CAA 2001, s. 101, 102

16.2 Definition of long-life asset

16.2.1 General rule

Expenditure is treated as "long-life asset expenditure" if:

- it is incurred on the provision of a long-life asset for the purposes of a qualifying activity; and
- it is not excluded from such treatment by specific provision.

Plant or machinery is classified as a long-life asset if it has a certain "useful economic life". This is defined to mean a period that begins when the plant or machinery is first brought into use by any person for any purpose, and ends when it is no longer used or likely to be used *by anyone for any purpose* as a fixed asset of a business. This therefore differs from the FRS15 definition that looks at expected use in the particular business.

The plant or machinery will be a long-life asset if:

- it is new, and can reasonably be expected to have a useful economic life of at least 25 years; or

- it is second hand, but could reasonably have been expected when new to have a useful economic life of at least 25 years.

Exclusions

The following types of asset may be excluded, but subject to the conditions outlined at **16.2.2** to **16.2.4** below.

- certain fixtures;
- (formerly) ships and railway assets;
- cars.

There is also an important provision regarding the level of expenditure, which in practice saves many businesses from the effects of the long-life asset rules (see **16.3**).

Useful economic life

The useful economic life begins when the asset is first brought into use by any person. For these purposes, HMRC have stated that the construction of the asset or the fact of its being held as trading stock will not be counted as "use". According to HMRC:

> "The long-life asset test looks at the expected life estimated by reference to the facts when capital allowances are first claimed or when the asset was first brought into use if earlier. This will depend on the way in which the asset is likely to be used in that business and, if it is likely to be sold in working order, by any subsequent owner. It may be dependent on physical deterioration through use or effluxion of time, reduced by economic or technological obsolescence, or directly governed by extraction or consumption as in the case of equipment in a mine."

Whole or part

According to HMRC, the 25-year test must be applied to the whole of the plant or machinery, and not to its component parts:

> "The rule in CAA 2001, s. 571 that any reference to plant or machinery includes a reference to a part of any plant or machinery cannot be used to exclude parts that are likely to be replaced within 25 years. This is because the legislation defines the asset to be a long-life asset if it has a useful economic life of at least 25 years. Where the asset as a whole falls to be treated as long-life

under this rule, there is nothing in the legislation that then allows part of the asset to be excluded from the long-life asset rules.

...

You should use the concept of the entity or entirety as developed by the Courts in cases about whether expenditure on a replacement part is allowable as expenditure on a repair in deciding what is the whole of the item of plant or machinery. You should not accept that the 25 year test can be applied to part of an item of plant or machinery if the cost of replacement of that part without improvement would be allowable ... as a repair to the plant or machinery as a whole."

Elsewhere, HMRC give the example of a lift with an expected life of 30 years. This will be treated as a long-life asset even if parts of the lift are likely to be replaced in less than 25 years.

This can work both ways, however, and HMRC give the example of a claim for an underground cable system with ducting, and comment:

"Where the ducting is installed as a direct incident of the installation of the cabling, the costs of the ducting and the associated excavation are, for capital allowance purposes, part of the costs incurred on the provision of the cabling regardless of the treatment in the accounts. In these circumstances, if the cabling is not itself a long-life asset, the long-life asset rules are not separately applicable to the ducting."

Improvements

Again, HMRC have given guidance on how improvements to assets would be treated for the purposes of the long-life asset rules:

"If there is expenditure on an improvement to an asset, you should apply the long-life test to the part of the plant or machinery that represents the improvement. This is because the improvement is treated as a separate asset for the plant and machinery legislation. The useful economic life of the improvement is the period from when the improvement is brought into use until the part representing the improvement is likely to cease to be used. For example, suppose that a printing press has an expected working life of 30 years when it is new. After 25 years there is a major refurbishment that extends the expected working life of the press to 20 years from the refurbishment. The capital expenditure on the refurbishment has a useful economic life of 20 years and is not caught by the long-life asset rules."

Law: CAA 2001, s. 90, 91
Guidance: CA 23720

16.2.2 Fixtures

Fixtures are not automatically preserved from the long-life asset rules. However, expenditure is not treated as long-life asset expenditure if the plant or machinery is a fixture for use in a building that is used:

- wholly or mainly as a dwelling-house, hotel, office, retail shop or showroom; or
- for purposes ancillary to any such use.

HMRC accept that the "wholly or mainly" condition is met "if at least 75% of the building measured on a reasonable basis, for instance by cost or floor area, is used for purposes within the list of excluded buildings".

For these purposes, the term "fixture" is defined as for the fixtures legislation generally (see **10.2**).

The term "retail shop" is defined to include "any premises of a similar character where a retail trade or business, including repair work, is carried on". This picks up the definition that was used in the former provisions for industrial buildings allowances. The *Kilmarnock* case brought out a distinction between a retail business on the one hand and a retail shop on the other. HMRC also make the following points:

"The meaning of shop was also considered in various rating cases. Those cases established that premises to which the public has access for the purposes of having wants supplied or particular services rendered are shops. This means that a building does not have to be premises where goods are sold over the counter to be a shop. For example, buildings occupied by laundrettes, banks, undertakers, jobbing builders and shoe repairers are shops.

Trade customers are not the public and so a building which serves only trade customers is not a retail shop. A wholesaler's premises are not a retail shop if all the customers are trade customers. If, however, the public are allowed to shop at a wholesaler's premises it will be a retail shop even if most of the customers are trade customers."

Where fixtures are provided for other premises, they will be subject to the long-life asset rules in the same way as any other assets. However, it is then necessary to look at the expected life of the asset, and not of the building as a whole. HMRC give the example of a lift in a factory: if the lift has an expected life of 20 years it will not be treated as a long-life asset even though the building may last for 50 years.

Law: CAA 2001, s. 93

Case: *Kilmarnock Equitable Co-operative Society, Ltd v CIR* (1966) 42 TC 675

Guidance: CA 23720, 32221, 32311

16.2.3   Ships and railway assets

Certain expenditure incurred on ships and "railway assets" was not treated as long-life asset expenditure. However, this exclusion only applied for expenditure before the end of 2010.

Law: CAA 2001, s. 94, 95

Guidance: CA 23730

16.2.4   Cars and motorcycles

Expenditure on a car or motorcycle is never treated as long-life asset expenditure. The same definitions are used here as for other plant and machinery purposes: see **9.2**.

Law: CAA 2001, s. 96

16.2.5   Aircraft

HMRC and the British Air Transport Association have reached an agreement on the application of the long-life asset rules to certain jet aircraft. HMRC have also provided guidelines on the treatment of aircraft that do not fall within the terms of that agreement.

For aircraft purchased from 1 July 2014, HMRC will "no longer assume a useful economic life of 25 years or more, but consider whether a new jet aircraft is a long life asset or not based on the facts of the particular aircraft and its use or intended use". HMRC have also commented that:

> "Useful economic life of a jet aircraft will depend on the pattern of use by the owner. The owner's own assessment of the likely useful life should be taken into account when considering whether a jet aircraft has a useful economic life of at least 25 years or not."

HMRC will normally follow the accounting treatment of the useful economic life of the fuselage. If this does not lead to a clear conclusion, HMRC may take account of the following factors:

- available industry data on the useful economic life of similar aircraft;

- the operating model and utilisation of aircraft by the person incurring expenditure;

- regulatory requirements likely to impact upon useful economic life (e.g. in relation to age, noise, emissions);

- the options available to customers in disposing of their aircraft assets (e.g. evidence of a viable second-hand market).

HMRC take the view that:

"an aircraft purchased in its ready-for-service configuration is a single entirety and so the expenditure should not be split between long life and normal life asset treatment".

Similarly, HMRC treat "engines, interiors, landing gear and all other components fitted to the aircraft" as part of the aircraft and not as separate "entireties in their own right".

(This guidance was originally provided to one of the authors by HMRC in February 2017. See now the guidance in the *Capital Allowances Manual*.)

Guidance: CA 23781-23783

16.2.6   *Greenhouses*

There was formerly an agreement between HMRC and the NFU concerning the long-life asset treatment of greenhouses. The agreement only ran until the end of 2005 and the HMRC view is that (for expenditure incurred from the start of 2006), each case must be dealt with on its particular facts. The explanation given is that:

"HMRC's expectation when entering into the agreement was that as a result of technological advances glasshouses constructed in the future might have longer useful economic lives."

Guidance: CA 23785

16.2.7   Printing equipment

Guidance is given by HMRC on the application of the long-life asset rules to printing equipment. The guidance covers pre-press equipment, printing presses and finishing equipment.

For modern equipment that is bought new, each case will be considered on its merits but HMRC instruct their staff that "unless there are exceptional circumstances you should accept that modern printing equipment purchased new and unused is unlikely to have an expected useful economic life of 25 years or longer". As such, the equipment will not normally have to be classified as a long-life asset.

For the purchase of second-hand printing equipment, the HMRC guidance reads as follows:

> "Where second-hand printing equipment is acquired the treatment will depend on whether or not the seller claimed capital allowances on it. If it is acquired from a person who has claimed capital allowances on the asset the buyer will obtain the same treatment as the seller. If the seller treated the asset as a long-life asset the buyer will obtain relief at the rate for the special rate pool. If the seller received writing down allowances in the main pool the buyer will also receive them at that rate.
>
> If the asset is acquired from a dealer in second-hand equipment, or another person who has not claimed capital allowances on the particular asset, then the general approach outlined above will be applied. A key additional factor to those outlined above will be the age of the equipment on acquisition."

Guidance: CA 23790

16.3   Monetary limit

16.3.1   Introduction

The legislation includes a "monetary limit". The idea is to provide a *de minimis* exemption from the effects of the long-life asset restrictions.

As a simple example, a sole trader who incurs £40,000 of expenditure in a given year will not have to worry about the long-life asset rules as the expenditure is below the threshold. This means that the expenditure will not be treated by the long-life asset rules as special rate expenditure and, unless there are other reasons to allocate it to the special rate pool, it will qualify for WDAs at the standard rate rather than the reduced rate.

In technical terms, expenditure is not long-life asset expenditure if:

- it is expenditure to which the monetary limits apply (see **16.3.2**); and
- it is incurred in a chargeable period for which the relevant monetary limit is not exceeded (see **16.3.3**).

Care is needed with second-hand assets, which may be classified as long-life asset expenditure even though the limit is not exceeded: see **16.4.1**.

Law: CAA 2001, s. 97
Guidance: CA 23740

16.3.2   Expenditure to which limit applies

Different rules apply according to the person who incurs the qualifying expenditure.

Individuals

For an individual, the limits apply for a given chargeable period if:

- the expenditure is incurred by him for the purposes of a qualifying activity carried on by him; and
- the whole of his time is, in that chargeable period, substantially devoted to the carrying on of that qualifying activity.

This is subject to the exclusions outlined below.

According to the *Explanatory Notes* issued when the long-life asset rules were introduced, the purposes of the "whole of his time" rule was "to ensure that the effect of the *de minimis* limit is not multiplied through application to separate trades carried on by the same persons and to different partnerships with common members".

Partnerships

For a partnership, the limits apply for a given chargeable period if:

- all members of the partnership are individuals (so a partnership with corporate members will not qualify);
- the expenditure was incurred by the partnership for the purposes of a qualifying activity carried on by it; and
- throughout that chargeable period, at least half of the partners devote the whole or a substantial part of their time to the carrying on of that qualifying activity.

HMRC have commented that "where there are changes in the numbers or involvement of partners during the chargeable period, this [last] condition is applied by looking at the parts of the period before, between and after the changes separately".

Again, this is subject to the exclusions outlined below.

Companies

The limits apply to expenditure incurred by companies, subject only to the exclusions below. However, the limit is reduced if there are associated companies: see **16.3.3** below.

Trusts

There is no monetary limit exemption for trusts.

Exclusions

The monetary limits do not apply for any of the above categories if the expenditure is:

- incurred on the provision of a share in plant or machinery;
- treated as incurred on the provision of plant or machinery as a result of s. 538 (contribution allowances for plant and machinery: see **31.3**);
- incurred on the provision of plant or machinery for leasing (whether or not the leasing is in the course of a trade).

Law: CAA 2001, s. 98
Guidance: CA 23740

16.3.3   Amount of limit

As a starting point, the monetary limit is £100,000, but this is subject to the following.

If the chargeable period is shorter or (for an individual or partnership) longer than 12 months, the limit is proportionately reduced or increased.

The monetary limit has to be shared if, in a given chargeable period, a company has one or more associated companies. (This is a technical change, introduced in 2021. Formerly the test was whether one or more companies are "related 51% group companies").

The rules in CTA 2010, Pt. 3A (see sections 18E to 18J) are applied for these purposes to determine whether companies are associated.

Example

A company draws accounts up for the nine months to 31 December and it has two associated companies in that period.

The monetary limit will be £100,000 x 9/12 x 1/3 = £25,000.

Law: CAA 2001, s. 99; CTA 2010, s. 279F
Guidance: CA 23740

16.3.4   Exceeding the limit

The monetary limit is exceeded in any given chargeable period if the total specified expenditure exceeds the limit as above. Expenditure is only specified for this purpose if it is long-life asset expenditure (or would be, but for the monetary limit rules) and is expenditure to which the monetary limits apply (see **16.3.2** above).

So, for example, any expenditure on assets to be used for leasing will not be counted for the purposes of determining whether the monetary limit has been exceeded. HMRC illustrate this with the following example:

> "Janis draws up her accounts to 31 December each year. Her spending in 2010 on long-life assets is £90,000 on a machine to be let and £80,000 on a machine for use in her manufacturing business. The long-life asset rules apply to the £90,000 but not to the £80,000 as that is below the *de minimis* limit."

In other words, the £90,000 is caught (assuming that it has an expected useful life of at least 25 years) because leased assets cannot benefit from the monetary limit exemption. However, the same £90,000 is then ignored in calculating the monetary limit, because it is not expenditure to which the monetary limits apply. It follows that the £80,000 is considered without reference to the leased machine and is therefore below the limit and exempt on that basis.

If the £90,000 machine had not been used for leasing, the whole of the £170,000 (not just the excess over £100,000) would be subject to the long-life asset rules.

Expenditure falling in different chargeable periods

Under the terms of a contract for the provision of plant or machinery, the expenditure may be treated as incurred in different chargeable periods.

For these purposes only, all of such expenditure is treated as falling into the first chargeable period in which any of it is in fact incurred.

HMRC illustrate this with the following example.

HMRC example

Jim draws up his accounts to 31 December each year. In 2010 and 2011 expenditure on long-life assets is £150,000 under one contract, payable in 2 instalments – £80,000 on 11 December 2010, £70,000 on 11 July 2011 and £90,000 under a second contract payable on 1 December 2011. For the purposes of the monetary limit the whole £150,000 is treated as incurred in 2010 and the limit for that chargeable period has been exceeded. The expenditure of £90,000 is treated as incurred in 2011 and is below the limit. Expenditure of £80,000 in 2010 and £70,000 in 2011 is therefore subject to the long-life asset rules.

Law: CAA 2001, s. 100
Guidance: CA 23740

16.4   Anti-avoidance

16.4.1   Later claims

Once an asset has been classed as a long-life asset, that treatment will continue for a future owner as well, unless it is a fixture used for one of the excluded types of trade (hotels, etc. – see **16.2.2**). This is illustrated by HMRC with the following example:

> "Jackson buys a new printer with an expected life of 30 years for £40,000 and a binder from Lowell for £50,000. The binder was treated as a long – life asset when Lowell owned it. Jackson's total expenditure is £90,000, which is less than the monetary limit.
>
> The printer is not treated as a long-life asset because Jackson's total expenditure is less than the monetary limit, but the binder is treated as a long-life asset as it was treated as one in Lowell's hands.
>
> If the printer had cost Jackson £60,000, it would also have been treated as a long-life asset as Jackson's total expenditure of £110,000 would then have exceeded the monetary limit."

Imported assets

HMRC policy is to apply the long-life asset rules to a second-hand asset brought into the UK from abroad if it was reasonable to expect that the asset would have a useful economic life of at least 25 years when it was new. It is irrelevant that the remaining life when it is imported is less than 25 years.

Law: CAA 2001, s. 103
Guidance: CA 23750

16.4.2   Disposal values

Anti-avoidance rules apply to prevent taxpayers from getting round the effects of the special rate legislation (s. 104E: see **17.5.1**).

17. Special rate expenditure

17.1 Introduction and overview

The special rate expenditure rules apply to slow down the rate at which tax relief is given for certain classes of asset.

To achieve this effect, certain types of expenditure are designated as "special rate" and are normally allocated to a "special rate pool". This pool attracts plant and machinery allowances at a slower rate than other assets; from April 2019, the rate is reduced from 8% to 6% (compared with a standard rate of 18%), with hybrid rates for periods spanning that date.

If an asset falls into one of the categories of special rate expenditure, but is used partly for private or certain other purposes, it is allocated to a single-asset pool but allowances are still given at the slower rate.

Various anti-avoidance measures apply to ensure that the rules cannot easily be sidestepped.

Law: CAA 2001, s. 104A-104G
Guidance: CA 23220

17.2 Definition of "special rate expenditure"

The concept of special rate expenditure has existed since April 2008, since when the categories affected have gradually been expanded. Changes are always made in relation to expenditure incurred from 1 April of a given year for corporation tax purposes and from 6 April for income tax purposes.

The following assets are currently classed as special rate expenditure:

- thermal insulation within s. 28 (see **4.7**);
- integral features within s. 33A (see **4.11**);
- long-life assets within CAA 2001, Pt. 2, Ch. 10 (see **16.2**);
- higher-emission cars, i.e. cars that are not "main rate" cars (per s. 104AA: see **9.3.2**) (from April 2009);
- cushion gas (per s. 70J(7): see also **17.5.3**) (corporation tax only);
- solar panels.

It is possible that part of the capital expenditure on particular assets will be special rate expenditure and part will not. In that case, the two parts are treated as expenditure on separate items of plant and machinery, using a just and reasonable apportionment to allocate the expenditure between the two notional assets.

Law: CAA 2001, s. 104A, 104B

17.3 Pooling

The concept of pooling generally is explained at **5.3.2** above.

Special rate expenditure that is pooled is allocated to a "class pool" known as the special rate pool. The term "class pool" indicates that the expenditure is outside the main plant and machinery pool, but that allowances do not have to be calculated on an asset-by-asset basis.

All special rate expenditure will be allocated to the special rate pool if it is incurred wholly and exclusively for the purposes of a qualifying activity, and if there is no requirement to allocate it to a single rate pool. (See **5.3.7** for details of expenditure that must be allocated to a single rate pool, but the main categories are short-life assets and any assets that are used partly for private purposes.)

Law: CAA 2001, s. 104C

17.4 Allowances

17.4.1 *Writing-down allowances*

The rate of WDA for the special rate pool reduced in April 2019 from 8% to 6%. With one exception (see below), the 6% rate applies to all special rate expenditure, even if it is in a single-asset pool because of private use.

As for the main pool, the maximum allowance is proportionately reduced if the chargeable period is less than a year, or if the qualifying activity is carried on for only part of the chargeable period. If the chargeable period is more than a year, the maximum allowance is increased *pro rata*.

The special rate pool is subject to the "small pools" rule whereby expenditure may be written off in one go once it falls below a given threshold: see **5.3.6**.

A person may require the allowance to be reduced to a specified amount, thus carrying forward a higher figure to the following period.

See **5.3.5** for details of the transitional rules applying at April 2019.

There is one exception to the 6% figure for special rate expenditure. If the expenditure is incurred wholly for the purposes of a ring-fence trade (oil industry), the rate is 10%.

Law: CAA 2001, s. 104D

Assets with private use

Paradoxically, an unincorporated business may possibly enjoy a better rate of tax relief for an asset that is used partly for private purposes. Take, for example, a private jet that is bought by a wealthy sole trader and that is used for genuine business purposes. Assume for present purposes that it is classified as a long-life asset and that WDAs are due only at 6%. And assume that the jet is sold at a significant loss after three years.

If there is no private use, the jet will be in the special rate pool, possibly joining higher-emission cars, integral features and various other types of expenditure. When the jet is sold the proceeds will be deducted from the pool but allowances will continue at just 6% indefinitely.

If there is private use, the rate is still 6% and must now be adjusted for the element of private use. When the jet is sold there will be a balancing adjustment and, if the sale is at a loss, there may be a significant balancing allowance.

This may obviously work the other way if the full cost is recovered at the time of sale.

Law: CAA 2001, s. 54, 55, 65, 104D(2), 206

17.4.2   Annual investment allowances

AIAs are available for special rate expenditure, subject to normal principles (see, generally, **5.2**).

17.5   Other provisions

17.5.1   Disposal value – anti-avoidance rules

A notional value is used as the disposal value if there is a disposal event in relation to special rate expenditure and if the event is part of, or occurs as a result of, a scheme or arrangement of which a main purpose is the obtaining of a tax advantage in relation to plant and machinery allowances.

Law: CAA 2001, s. 104E

17.5.2   Special rate cars – anti-avoidance rules

Anti-avoidance rules apply in certain cases where a company has incurred expenditure on special rate cars and the company's qualifying activity is permanently discontinued. The rules are considered at **9.4.4** above.

Law: CAA 2001, s. 104F

17.5.3   Cushion gas

When the concept of cushion gas was introduced from 1 April 2010, rules were introduced to deal with disposals of gas that had been acquired partly before and partly since that date.

As a general principle, disposals are taken on a Last In First Out basis. If this means that a disposal relates both to new and to old expenditure, it is treated as constituting two separate disposal events.

Law: CAA 2001, s. 104G

18. Partnerships and successions

18.1 Introduction and statutory overview

Partnerships and business successions raise particular issues in relation to capital allowances.

For most types of capital allowance, a general set of principles (starting at s. 557) is used to determine entitlement to allowances. However, those principles are specifically disapplied in the case of plant or machinery allowances.

For plant and machinery allowances (the subject of this chapter) the rules relating to partnerships and successions are contained in Chapter 20 of Part 2 of CAA 2001, beginning at s. 263.

Law: CAA 2001, s. 557

18.2 General principles – partnerships

The general rule is that partnership changes are ignored for the purposes of claiming plant and machinery allowances, as long as at least one person carrying on the activity before the change continues to do so thereafter. The ongoing partnership continues to claim allowances as if anything done by former partners had been done by the present partners.

18.3 Calculation of allowances for partnership

Particular rules apply in respect of all types of allowances and charges for plant and machinery where:

- a qualifying activity has been set up and is at any time carried on in partnership;
- there has been a change in the persons engaged in carrying on the qualifying activity; and
- if the qualifying activity is a trade or property business, a further condition is met, as below.

For income tax purposes, the further condition is met if a person carrying on the trade or property business immediately before the change continues to carry it on after the change. For corporation tax purposes, a company carrying on the trade or property business in partnership immediately before the change must continue to carry it on in partnership after the change

For these purposes, the term "qualifying activity" does not include an office or employment.

Any annual investment allowance, first-year allowance or writing-down allowance is made to the present partners. The allowance is calculated as if the present partners had at all times been carrying on the qualifying activity and as if everything done to or by their predecessors had been done to or by them.

Similarly, any balancing allowance or balancing charge is made to or on the partners carrying on the qualifying activity at the time of the event that triggers the balancing adjustment. Once more, the calculation is made as if everything done to or by their predecessors had been done to or by the partners at the time of the event.

Law: CAA 2001, s. 263

18.4 Partnership using property owned by partner

Assets owned by partners individually, but used for the purposes of a qualifying activity carried on by the partnership, are treated as partnership property for the purposes of calculating allowances, deductions and charges.

This scenario may be seen, for example, in the case of a professional partnership where the partners own their cars personally but use them for the purposes of the partnership business. The partners are not permitted to submit individual capital allowances computations but must instead claim plant and machinery allowances as part of the partnership return.

There is no disposal event if:

- plant or machinery is used for the purposes of a qualifying activity carried on in partnership;
- a sale or gift of the plant or machinery is made by one or more of the partners to another partner or to other partners; and
- the plant or machinery continues to be used after the sale or gift for the purposes of the qualifying activity.

These rules do not apply if the asset in question is let by the partner to the partnership, or if the partner receives a payment that is deductible in calculating the taxable profits of the partnership activity.

This can raise some quite difficult technical issues in relation to business premises owned by partners who leave the partnership.

Example

Doctors A, B and C are in partnership and respectively own 40%, 35% and 25% shares in the surgery from which the practice activities are carried out. Fixtures have been claimed for the property, which is not shown on the balance sheet. No rent is paid outside the accounts, so allowances are given to the partnership rather than to the partners individually, but the partners take account of their respective shares in the property as part of their profit sharing arrangements.

Partner C is retiring but wishes to retain his 25% share of the property. If a new partner, D, is taken on then C will consider selling his share to D. In the meantime, C will be paid a rent from the date of his retirement.

Before the change, the property has been used for one qualifying activity (the medical practice) but after the change it is used by C for a different qualifying activity (an ordinary property business carried on by C). As allowances for different activities have to be calculated separately (per s. 11(3)), it follows that a mechanism is needed to determine the disposal value and acquisition value of the 25% share for the two activities respectively. It seems clear that these arrangements do not constitute a sale of the 25% share of the property, as C cannot sell to himself. Assuming that this is the correct interpretation, we are not within items 1 or 9 of the table at s. 196, so it follows that no fixtures election can be signed (in accordance with the wording of s. 198(1)). Rather, the fixtures in the 25% share are to be treated as passing at market value, in accordance with item 12 of the table at s. 196.

C's retirement does not have any bearing on the capital allowances treatment of the remaining 75% of the property.

Law: CAA 2001, s. 264
Guidance: CA 29020

18.5   Successions

18.5.1   Introduction

The term "succession" is used to describe the situation where one person takes over (i.e. succeeds to) a qualifying activity that was previously carried on by someone else. (An employment is not treated as a qualifying activity for these purposes.)

It is a question of fact to determine whether a person has succeeded to the business or has merely taken over some assets. The concept of the business succession goes back in tax law to the first half of the nineteenth century, when business life was in some ways simpler than today. A full discussion of the meaning of succession is beyond the scope of this book, but (broadly speaking) the legislation envisages a transfer of a business or identifiable part of a business. The fact that the new business may not be "isolated, separated, kept apart, and distinct from all other businesses of the successor" does not prevent it from being a succession (*National Provincial* case).

The legislation uses the term "relevant property" to cover any assets that:

- were owned by the predecessor immediately before the succession and were in use (or provided and available for use) for the purposes of the now discontinued qualifying activity; and

- are in use (or provided and available for use) for the purposes of the new qualifying activity immediately after the succession but without being sold.

This last wording ("without being sold") is important, as explained below.

Law: CAA 2001, s. 265

Case: *Bell v The National Provincial Bank of England, Ltd* (1903) 5 TC 1

18.5.2   General rule

The general rule for successions is that any relevant property given by the old owner to the new is treated as sold at market value by the predecessor to the successor at the time of the succession.

The person acquiring the plant and machinery can claim WDAs accordingly, but is not entitled to either FYAs or AIAs.

HMRC example

Clark runs a record shop. He transfers the business including the cash register to Harris free of charge. Clark is treated as selling the cash register to Harris at its market value when Harris took over the business. Harris is treated as buying the cash register at its market value. He can claim WDAs but not FYA on the cash register.

A more likely scenario is perhaps the incorporation of a business where, in some circumstances, assets may be gifted to the newly formed company. See, however, **18.5.6** for a more detailed example involving an incorporation.

This general rule is subject to some important exceptions, as explained below.

Law: CAA 2001, s. 265
Guidance: CA 29030

18.5.3   Exceptions

The general rule (see **18.5.2** above) is subject to a number of important exceptions.

Connected persons may instead elect to transfer assets at tax written-down value: see **18.5.4**.

Connected parties not so electing are subject to various anti-avoidance provisions, explained generally at **Chapter 22**.

The general rule will not apply where the assets in question are sold rather than being given. See **18.5.5**.

Different rules apply where individuals succeed to a business under the terms of a deceased person's will, or under intestacy rules: see **18.5.8**.

In the case of a trade or property business the rules apply only where the following condition is also met:

- (for income tax purposes), no person carrying on the trade or business immediately before the succession continues to carry it on after the succession; or

- (for corporation tax purposes), no company carrying on the trade or business in partnership immediately before the succession continues to carry it on in partnership after the succession.

The point here is that where at least one person continues to carry on the trade or business then there is no cessation for tax purposes, so capital allowances continue to be computed for the ongoing business without regard to the change in personnel.

18.5.4 Connected persons: election to transfer at written down value

Where there is a succession to a business, connected persons (see below) may be able to elect to override the general rule described at **18.5.2** immediately above. Specifically, the predecessor and the successor may jointly elect for different treatment if they are connected with each other and if each is within the charge to tax on the profits of a qualifying activity.

The joint election must be made within two years from the date of the succession.

If there is no succession to the business, no election is possible and normal principles are applied. This applies even between connected parties, though in this case subject to general anti-avoidance considerations (see, generally, **Chapter 22**).

Effect of election

Where an election is signed, relevant plant or machinery is treated as sold by the predecessor to the successor at the time of succession at a price which gives rise to no balancing adjustment (i.e. at the capital allowances written down value). The election may be made whether or not the plant or machinery has actually been sold or transferred.

The term "relevant plant or machinery" covers any plant or machinery that:

- was owned by the predecessor immediately before the succession and that was then in use (or provided and available for use) for the purposes of the qualifying activity; and

- is owned by the successor immediately after the succession and is then in use (or is provided and available for use) for the purposes of the qualifying activity.

Subject to the restriction explained below, allowances and charges for plant and machinery are calculated for the successor as if everything done to or by the predecessor had been done by the successor. Assessments may be made and adjusted as appropriate to give effect to this principle.

Again subject to the restriction explained below, the following provisions do not apply if an election is made:

- s. 104E (special rate expenditure: avoidance cases – see **17.5.1**);
- s. 108 (overseas leasing: disposal values – see **19.2**);
- s. 265 (general rule re successions – see **18.5.2** above).

Law: CAA 2001, s. 267
Guidance: CA 29040

Order of disposals

There is no requirement that all of the assets have to be transferred to the successor, and a planning point may arise if some other assets are to be sold off.

Example

Oldco is transferring its business to its connected company Newco.

Oldco's capital allowances written down value is £800,000. This is split into assets that are to be transferred (£650,000) and assets that are to be sold off at auction (£150,000). The latter category is expected to reach a price at auction of £200,000.

If both disposals take place in the same accounting period, it is not clear from the legislation whether or not this gives rise to a balancing charge of £50,000. If the auction proceeds are put through first, this appears to ensure that there is no balancing charge. But if the connected transfer takes place first, a balancing charge appears to arise. (In other circumstances, of course, this might instead be a balancing allowance.) Section 55(1)(b) simply requires a total of the disposal receipts for the period in question, and does not require that the disposals are dealt with in chronological order.

To ensure that the balancing charge does not arise, there would appear to be two options. One is to split the transactions across two separate accounting periods – auction in the first and transfer in the second. Alternatively, the assets could all be transferred first to the successor company, and used briefly for its qualifying activity, before the unwanted assets are sold off at auction.

Restrictions on effect of election

For corporation tax purposes only, a restriction applies in the case of a "business of leasing plant or machinery" if the parties make an election under s. 266.

433

In such a case, both s. 266(7) (in connection with special rate expenditure) and s. 267 (effect of election under s. 266) are disapplied in relation to any plant or machinery which (in determining whether the business is a business of leasing plant or machinery on the relevant day) falls within CTA 2010, s. 410(6) (if the business is carried on in partnership) or within CTA 2010, s. 387(7) (in any other case).

Law: CAA 2001, s. 267A

Connected persons

The predecessor and successor are connected with each other if any of the following applies:

- they would be treated as connected persons under s. 575 (see **32.9.5**);
- one of them is a partnership and the other has the right to a share in the assets or income of that partnership;
- one of them is a body corporate and the other has control over that body;
- both of them are partnerships and another person has the right to a share in the assets or income of both of them;
- both of them are bodies corporate, or one of them is a partnership and the other is a body corporate, and (in either case) another person has control over both of them.

No election is possible if the successor is a dual resident investing company, or if s. 561 applies (transfer of UK trade to a company in another member State).

Law: CAA 2001, s. 266

Interaction with fixtures election

As a result of the changes to the fixtures rules applying since April 2012, an election under s. 266 should routinely be accompanied by a fixtures election under s. 198.

In the past, a person electing under s. 266 would never have contemplated a fixtures election. Under s. 187A, however, the "fixed value requirement" is imposed where the former owner has made a claim for allowances for fixtures. As such, the new owner will (in simplified terms) be able to claim allowances only if there is an election under s. 198 (or an apportionment that is agreed by the tax tribunal).

Section 187A applies if the past owner has to bring in a disposal value in accordance with items 1, 5 or 9 of the table at s. 196. The effect of a s. 266 election is that there is no balancing allowance or charge, but the way this result is achieved is that plant and machinery is treated as sold at tax written down value (s. 267). This seems to take it squarely within item 1 of the table ("a sale of the qualifying interest").

In short, it seems that parties making an election under s. 266 will also (rather oddly) need to make a fixtures election, which must presumably be in the same amount as regards any particular fixture, under s. 198. But that does not quite get us out of the woods, as the election under s. 198 relates only to fixtures, whereas that under s. 266 specifically relates to *any* plant or machinery. This is messy as separate pools are not maintained for fixtures.

A fixtures election is, strictly speaking, made on an asset-by-asset basis. In practice, that rule is never imposed but there must be sufficient information to prevent any tax distortion. The election should clearly identify all the fixtures that it covers and care should be taken to include only fixtures as defined for capital allowances purposes (specifically excluding any moveable chattels).

No apportionment as such is required for the purposes of the s. 266 election. In practice, however, it will be clear that the amounts in the fixtures election will be a subset of the amounts in the s. 266 election, with the balance relating to plant and machinery other than fixtures.

This is going to arise whenever a s. 266 situation includes a transfer of a property. One suspects that the interaction was simply overlooked when the new fixtures rules were introduced.

The author raised this point for confirmation with the HMRC capital allowances specialists who replied as follows:

> "In our view there has to be two elections and the s. 267 election is the key election as this makes the transfer a sale whether or not it would otherwise have been one and that then places the taxpayer in s. 196 event 1 and the requirement to make a s. 198 election.
>
> [One point] which supports our view that two elections are required is that in many circumstances the amount fixed by the s. 267 election will also relate to other plant and machinery that is not within the scope of Chapter 14 so it is not possible to say that in each and every case the amount fixed by the s. 267 election is the amount fixed by the s. 198 election. We think that in such

circumstances the s. 198 election should always be less than the s. 267 election but this is not considered to be a high risk area and we would expect most practitioners to have apportioned based on the opening statement of affairs or something similar. We intend to mention the interaction at CA 29040 in the draft guidance which we expect to release for comment shortly."

That guidance was duly introduced and confirms that "the amount in the section 198 election cannot exceed that amount in the section 266 election".

There may now be circumstances in which a s. 266 election would previously have been made, but in which no such election would now be needed. However, it should be borne in mind that the election applies to any plant or machinery (including chattels) whereas the s. 198 election applies only in relation to fixtures.

Law: CAA 2001, s. 198, 266, 267
Guidance: CA 29040

18.5.5 Assets sold not given

Where an election is made for connected party successions (see **18.5.4**), it does not matter whether the assets are sold or given.

In other cases, the special rules for successions apply only where the assets are given rather than sold.

Where assets are sold, normal principles will therefore apply. For plant or machinery other than fixtures, the disposal value will normally be determined by item 1 of the table at s. 61(2) (see **5.5.3** above).

For fixtures, the more complex provisions of Chapter 14 of Part 2 of CAA 2001 will have to be considered, discussed in depth in **Chapters 12 to 14**. The transfer value for fixtures will normally be determined by making an election under s. 198.

18.5.6 Incorporation – by way of example

The various permutations considered in the preceding sections may be illustrated by considering a business incorporation.

Example

John is a sole trader whose business has grown and who has decided to incorporate. He owns a machine that cost £60,000 and that is now worth

£40,000. John was not able to claim AIAs because of other expenditure and the tax written down value of the machine is £25,000.

John may:

- sell the machine to the company for a notional figure of £1, potentially gaining a balancing allowance (as item one in the table at s. 61 will apply to give a disposal value of just £1);
- transfer the machine at its tax written down value of £25,000, and sign an election (per **18.5.4** above), thus avoiding any balancing adjustment; or
- give the asset to the company but sign no election, in which case he will have to bring in the market value of £40,000, potentially producing a substantial balancing charge.

Law: CAA 2001, s. 265
Guidance: CA 29030

18.5.7   Successions – extended example

This extended example brings together some of the principles explored in the preceding parts of this section **18.5**.

Example

A partnership incurs capital expenditure on a property and decides a few years later to incorporate the business. It is accepted, as a fact, that the company is succeeding to the business formerly carried on by the partnership.

It has made a claim for fixtures in the property of £300,000 and has also claimed £40,000 for moveable items (chairs, tables, etc.) which are plant but which do not constitute fixtures for capital allowances purposes. As far as possible, the goal is to retain the value of the allowances in the partnership.

The disposal of a property will by definition involve the disposal of the fixtures as part of the property. The capital allowances treatment for the fixtures is clear: an election must be signed (s. 198) by the two parties, and this will determine the capital allowances transfer value of the fixtures (but *not* of the moveable plant and machinery).

There is no requirement for the figure in the election to be "reasonable". By having a very low figure in the election – typically £1 each for integral features and for the other fixtures – the value of the capital allowances is retained by the partnership.

In this case, there are therefore various options.

Option 1 – plant or machinery is given

If the plant and machinery is *given* to the company, and no s. 266 election is made, the position is as follows.

All of the plant and machinery (fixtures and chattels) is treated as sold at market value (s. 265(1)(b)).

As we have a deemed sale, we are within item 1 of the table at s. 196. This in turn means that an election under s. 198 is possible (in accordance with the wording at s. 198(1)).

An election therefore can (and indeed must) still be signed in respect of the fixtures, to determine the tax value at which these are transferred across. As explained above, this can be done for a total figure of perhaps £2.

The non-fixtures are then treated as sold at market value (s. 265(2)(b)). The apportionment rules (s. 562) apply when calculating the market value, but the market value of chattels will generally be low.

Option 2 – plant or machinery is sold

If the plant and machinery is *sold* to the company, and no s. 266 election is made, the position is as follows.

The plant and machinery is in this case *not* "relevant property" for the purposes of s. 265 (see s. 265(3)(b) – "without being sold").

As we have an actual sale, we are within item 1 of the table at s. 196. Once more, this means that an election under s. 198 is possible.

Here too, therefore, an election must be signed in respect of the fixtures, to determine the tax value at which these are transferred across. Once more, this can be done for a total figure of perhaps £2.

In this case, the sale proceeds of the chattels must be brought into account (item 1 of the table at s. 61). So in theory these items could be sold for £1. However, the apportionment rules (s. 562) will in this case clearly apply. Although the market value of chattels will generally be low, they are not likely to have a market value of just £1.

Option 3 – election under s. 266

The final option is to sign an election under s. 266. The election may be made whether or not the plant or machinery has actually been sold.

This would mean that both the fixtures and the chattels would be transferred across at tax written-down value. So the partnership would not suffer any balancing charge, but nor would it receive any balancing allowances.

An election under s. 198 is still required in these circumstances, as explained at **18.5.4** above. Once more, however, we must remember that the election under s. 198 relates only to fixtures. By contrast, that under s. 266 specifically relates to *any* plant or machinery.

It is thought that the s. 198 election will necessarily override the s. 266 election, and that it is therefore possible to have £2 (say) for the fixtures, with the chattels being transferred at written-down value. However, neither the legislation nor the HMRC guidance really addresses the interaction between the two elections, and there is therefore perhaps a small risk of signing an election under s. 266 where (as in this example, and as is typically the case) the main value lies in the fixtures. (In other words, the outcome of a s. 198 election on its own is clear cut, but the s. 266 election just possibly clouds the issue.)

It would be possible, of course, to calculate the tax written-down values, and to ensure that the s. 266 election reflects those values in full, and that the s. 198 election reflects those values in relation to the fixtures only. The benefit of this would be to provide certainty. In short, the partners will get the benefit of the allowances as already enjoyed, and will gain certainty, but not maximum tax relief (as some of the relief will be given to the company at a lower tax rate than that potentially enjoyed by the partners).

The better option, however, would appear to be to forgo the s. 266 election, and (ideally) to sell the chattels from the partnership to the company. This could be done for just £1, but the apportionment rules of s. 562 will be in point, and an apportioned value should be applied to the chattels. It is thought that this will be more than £1 but, in any case (per s. 62), it cannot exceed the historic cost of the items in question (£40,000 in this example), and is likely to be much less than those figures. A specialist capital allowances valuer would be qualified to give a view on the appropriate value, and a full disclosure should be made of this valuation, to protect against any future discovery assessment.

If, for example, it is agreed that the market value of the chattels is £10,000, this would give total capital allowances disposal proceeds of £10,002 (i.e. to include £2 for the fixtures). This protects the capital allowances position of the fixtures (where most of the value lies), gets quite close to an ideal outcome and should not be provocative to HMRC.

18.5.8 Successions by beneficiaries

A person may elect for particular rules to apply if:

- he succeeds to a qualifying activity (other than an office or employment) as a beneficiary under the will or on the intestacy of a deceased person who carried on the activity, and
- all of the persons carrying on the activity before the succession permanently cease to carry it on.

If an election is made, "relevant plant and machinery" is treated as if it had been sold to the beneficiary at the time of the succession. The transfer value is the lower of the market value of the assets at the time and the unrelieved qualifying expenditure that would have been taken into account in calculating the amount of any balancing allowance if the disposal value of the plant or machinery had been nil. This calculation is made for the chargeable period in which the qualifying activity of the deceased person was permanently discontinued. In other words, the sale price is the lower of market value and the expenditure left in the pool at the time of death, after deducting any disposal values (to persons other than the beneficiary) for the chargeable period in which the death occurs.

Subsequent disposals

If the beneficiary later sells an asset in respect of which an election is made, the disposal proceeds are restricted to the amount of qualifying expenditure incurred by the deceased, rather than to the transfer value at the time the beneficiary took ownership of the item. HMRC have illustrated this as follows:

> "Jim runs a coffee shop. When he dies Ray inherits the business and makes an election under s. 268. One of the assets that Ray takes over is a car that had cost Jim £30,000. The value at which Ray takes it over is £20,000. If Ray sells the car for £25,000, that is

the disposal value. It is not restricted to £20,000, the value at which Ray took over the car."

Law: CAA 2001, s. 268
Guidance: CA 29050

19. Overseas leasing

19.1 Phasing out

The term "overseas leasing" (formerly, "foreign leasing") refers to the leasing of plant or machinery to a person who is not resident in the UK and who does not use the asset exclusively for earning profits that are chargeable to tax in the UK.

The above definition is, however, subject to phasing-out provisions. Broadly, the special rules do not apply for leases that have been finalised since 1 April 2006.

Overseas leases finalised since that date are now subject instead to the provisions relating to long funding leases (see **Chapter 7**).

The rules relating to overseas leasing are not covered in depth in this book.

Law: CAA 2001, s. 105
Guidance: CA 24000*ff.*

19.2 Overview of effect

The background to the overseas leasing rules is explained as follows by HMRC:

> "When plant or machinery that qualifies for capital allowances is leased, other than on a short-term basis, the lessor usually shares the benefit of the capital allowances he, she or it expects to receive with the lessee by taking the capital allowances into account when the rent is fixed. In this context the benefit of capital allowances broadly means the extent to which such allowances are given at a rate greater than the commercial depreciation of the plant or machinery.
>
> The overseas leasing legislation reduces to 10% the annual rate of capital allowances on plant or machinery that is leased to a person resident overseas. The annual rate of WDA on plant or machinery used for overseas leasing is reduced to ensure that leases of plant or machinery to lessees with little or no connection to the UK are not tax subsidised. Sometimes there are no allowances at all when plant or machinery is used for overseas leasing.

The overseas leasing legislation applies to expenditure incurred on the provision of plant or machinery that at any time in the designated period is used for overseas leasing that is not protected leasing. Where the overseas leasing legislation applies WDAs are given at an annual rate of 10%. If the lease has certain properties there are no WDAs at all."

The reductions in the rate of allowances for special rate expenditure, from 10% to 8% with effect from April 2012 and from 8% to just 6% from April 2019, do not apply for the purposes of the overseas leasing rules.

Law: CAA 2001, s. 105, 109, 126; FA 2011, s. 10
Guidance: CA 24010

20. Ships

20.1 Overview

Plant and machinery allowances are available for ships, with preferential treatment allowed in specified circumstances.

The specialist rules are not covered in depth in this book, but the following HMRC summary gives a useful overview:

> "Ships are treated more generously than other assets by the capital allowance system. A shipowner can claim a WDA (or an FYA if available) and then postpone it [see CA 25200]. This means that the allowance need not be taken in the chargeable period for which it is claimed but can be taken in a later chargeable period provided that the qualifying activity is still being carried on. Shipowners can also defer balancing charges arising in respect of ships by setting them off against expenditure on new shipping [see CA 25300].

> There is no definition of ship in the *Capital Allowances Act* 2001 and so you should give ship its ordinary meaning. Treat any vessel registered by the Maritime Coastguard Agency as a ship as a ship for capital allowance purposes. The *Merchant Shipping Act* 1995 defines a ship as including every description of vessel used in navigation. Accept that anything which is covered by the *Merchant Shipping Act* 1995 definition of ship is a ship for capital allowance purposes. This means that you should treat any vessel which is capable of being manoeuvred under direct or indirect power as a ship.

> Oil-rigs and platforms, accommodation barges, light and weather ships etc. are not generally regarded as ships. They do not normally move about and are not used in navigation. Semi-submersible oil-rigs and similar vessels in the oil and gas industry may be ships, depending on the use made of them. This use-based approach was followed by the Court of Appeal in *Clark v Perks* (2001) [which held that a semi-submersible drilling rig could be considered as a ship]. As a result, you should not automatically accept that all such vessels qualify as ships."

Note that the deferral option referred to in HMRC's first paragraph quoted above does not apply in relation to a super-deduction or an SR allowance (temporary FYAs introduced in FA 2021) (FB 2021, cl. 9(9)). See, generally, **5.13** above.

The question of what constitutes a ship has been considered several times in the employment tax context relating to seafarers (see below). Care is needed in that, for those other purposes, there is a statutory provision whereby a ship does not include an offshore installation. Nevertheless, the reasoning of the various cases may be helpful for capital allowances purposes.

The First-tier Tribunal in *Szymusik* rejected an HMRC argument that a deep sea diver worked "from" rather than "on" a ship.

The mechanics of giving preferential allowances for ships involve the use, by default, of a "single ship pool".

Law: CAA 2001, s. 127-158; ITEPA 2003, s. 385

Cases: *Clark (HMIT) v Perks; Macleod (HMIT) v Perks; Guild (HMIT) v Newrick & Anor* [2001] BTC 336; *Palmer v HMRC* [2007] BTC 126; *Torr v HMRC* (2008) Sp C 679; *Spowage & Ors v HMRC* [2009] UKFTT 142 (TC); *Szymusik v HMRC* [2020] UKFTT 154 (TC)

Guidance: CA 25000*ff.*

20.2   Smaller vessels

The rules are not restricted, as a whole, to larger vessels, so they could be of interest, for example, to a fisherman with a relatively small boat.

It may be worthwhile for the owner of the vessel to use the special rules and to allocate the expenditure to a single ship pool, a type of single-asset pool (see, generally, **5.3.7**). If there is also a disposal of another ship in the same year, however, such treatment may not be beneficial. The point is illustrated by HMRC at CA 25150.

20.3   Main object

The legislation contains a rather curiously worded provision which states that a ship is not treated as being used for a qualifying purpose if a main purpose of the transaction "was to obtain a writing-down allowance determined without regard to section 109 (writing-down allowances at 10%) in respect of expenditure incurred by any person on the provision of the ship or aircraft".

The interpretation of this part of the legislation was considered in the *Lloyds TSB* decision, which went in favour of HMRC in the Court of Appeal. There was a similar outcome in *Lloyds Bank Leasing*.

Cases: *Lloyds TSB Equipment Leasing (No 1) Ltd v HMRC* [2014] STC 2770; *Lloyds Bank Leasing (no. 1) Ltd v HMRC* [2015] UKFTT 401 (TC)

21. Mining and oil industries

21.1 Overview

The rules relating to plant and machinery allowances are applied in a particular way for those involved with mineral extraction trades. This chapter contains a brief overview of those rules.

For these purposes, the terms "mineral extraction trade" and "mineral exploration and access" have the same meanings as they do in the context of mineral extraction allowances: see **Chapter 25.**

For the purposes of giving plant and machinery allowances, expenditure incurred by a person is treated (subject to the proviso below) as incurred for the purposes of the trade if it is:

- on the provision of plant or machinery for mineral exploration and access; and
- in connection with a mineral extraction trade that he carries on.

Since April 2014, this principle has not applied if, when the expenditure is incurred:

- the person is carrying on the trade but the trade is not at that time a mineral extraction trade, or
- the person has not begun to carry on the trade and, when the person begins to carry on the trade, the trade is not a mineral extraction trade.

For these purposes, the concept of commencement of trade is considered without applying the special rules of s. 577(2).

Law: CAA 2001, s. 159, 160
Guidance: *Oil Taxation Manuals*

21.2 Pre-trading expenditure

Pre-trading expenditure is broadly treated as incurred on the first day of trading. More specifically, it covers capital expenditure incurred:

- before the day on which a person begins to carry on a trade that is a mineral extraction trade, but

- only if there is no prior time when the person carried on that trade and the trade was not a mineral extraction trade.

However, plant and machinery allowances are not given if the assets in question are sold, demolished, destroyed or abandoned before the first day of trading. In these circumstances, mineral extraction allowances are given instead: see **25.2.2**.

Law: CAA 2001, s. 161

21.3 Offshore oil infrastructures

Writing-down allowances are available for certain decommissioning expenditure incurred by a person carrying on a trade of oil extraction. Various conditions and definitions apply.

Law: CAA 2001, s. 161A-161D

21.4 Ring-fence trades

Ring-fence trades (which are oil-related activities) are treated as a separate qualifying activity for the purposes of giving plant and machinery allowances.

Various special provisions apply, relating in particular to "general decommissioning expenditure" (as defined).

In *Marathon Oil*, it was held that certain substantial payments made to a subsidiary company were not incurred on decommissioning plant or machinery and, therefore, did not give rise to allowances under this heading.

Law: CAA 2001, s. 162-165
Case: *Marathon Oil UK LLC v HMRC* [2017] UKFTT 822 (TC)

21.5 Other provisions

Other particular rules relate to:

- anti-avoidance in the context of transfers of interests in oil fields; and
- oil production sharing contracts.

Law: CAA 2001, s. 166-171

22. Anti-avoidance

22.1 Introduction

Anti-avoidance measures are covered only briefly in this book. They would add considerably to the length of the overall text but they are by their nature of limited application to most practitioners. Furthermore, the very existence of the complex rules has the paradoxical effect that they rarely apply in practice: as the rules exist, people do not take the measures that the rules are designed to address.

This chapter must be seen as an introductory overview to the anti-avoidance provisions rather than a full explanation of how they operate.

22.2 Allowance buying

Restrictions apply where there is "avoidance involving allowance buying". These restrictions apply only to companies that enter into arrangements for an "unallowable purpose" – broadly speaking, to obtain a tax advantage for the company itself or for someone else.

See, very briefly, **5.10.2**.

Law: CAA 2001, s. 212A-212S
Guidance: CA 28300

22.3 Relevant transactions

22.3.1 Overview

Restrictions apply to certain "relevant transactions" (including the simple sale of an asset) falling into any of three categories:

- those between connected persons (s. 214);
- those carried out for the sole or main benefit of getting plant and machinery allowances (s. 215); or
- certain sale and leaseback transactions (s. 216).

In each case, the buyer's qualifying expenditure is restricted to the amount of the seller's disposal value, and the buyer is not entitled to FYAs or AIAs. The more detailed rules are considered below, but still only as an overview.

Assessments may be made or adjusted as necessary to give effect to the various restrictions.

Law: CAA 2001, s. 213, 231

22.3.2   Connected persons

If two connected persons enter into a relevant transaction, no FYAs or AIAs are given to the person acquiring the asset (referred to here as "the buyer" though the rules still apply if the asset has been given).

If the seller has had to bring into account a disposal value as a result of the transaction, the buyer's expenditure is then restricted to that amount. In any other case, the buyer's qualifying expenditure is restricted to the lowest of the following figures:

- the market value of the asset in question;
- (if the seller incurred capital expenditure on acquiring the plant or machinery) the amount of such expenditure;
- (if a person connected with the seller incurred capital expenditure on acquiring the plant or machinery) the amount of such expenditure.

The HMRC view is that these restrictions apply to gifts between connected persons, a point discussed in detail at **4.10.4** above.

However, these rules do not apply to sale and finance leasebacks (which are, instead, subject to the rules of s. 225).

The scope of the rules was extended from 26 February 2015 to catch situations where the seller or transferor (or a person connected with them) has previously acquired the plant and machinery without incurring capital expenditure or an arm's length amount of revenue expenditure. In these circumstances, the expenditure qualifying for allowances is nil.

The rules are also subject to the provisions of s. 218ZA(3) (see below). The rules are relaxed for manufacturers and suppliers making sales in the ordinary course of business, as long as there is no tax avoidance motive.

The meaning of "connected" is determined (subject to one extra element for local authorities) in connection with s. 575 (see **32.9.5**).

Example

Company A buys a property for £1m and sells it at a later date to Company B for £2m. Company B wishes to claim for plant in the property.

If the parties are at arm's length, A's disposal value for any fixtures is capped at cost, say £200k. B's acquisition cost is therefore capped at this figure. If A has failed to claim for certain fixtures and does not now do so, the value of those fixtures is lost permanently to B, because of the pooling requirement introduced by FA 2012 (see **11.2.7**).

However, B can also claim on any integral features on which A was unable to claim because of the different rules applying before April 2008. Such a claim will be calculated on an apportioned basis, without restriction to A's historic cost.

If the parties are connected, B will not be able to claim allowances for the integral features (see **4.11.7**). There may be assets other than fixtures on which A could have claimed but did not. In that case, B is entitled to make a claim (as the FA 2012 restrictions apply only to fixtures). As the parties are connected, however, s. 218 operates to restrict the purchase price for B. If the current market value exceeds A's cost, the claim will be restricted to that cost.

Law: CAA 2001, s. 214, 217, 218, 230, 232

22.3.3   *Transactions to obtain tax advantages*

Allowances are restricted if a transaction has a main purpose of obtaining more favourable capital allowances treatment than would otherwise be the case. FYAs and AIAs are denied. WDAs are also restricted or denied altogether.

A person is said to obtain a tax advantage if he obtains an allowance or greater allowance, or if he avoids or secures the reduction of a charge (s. 577(4)).

AIAs are also denied if arrangements have a main purpose of obtaining such an allowance that would not otherwise be due.

For transactions taking place on or after 25 November 2015, tax advantages received are cancelled in certain defined circumstances. According to the *Explanatory Notes* to the 2016 *Finance Bill*, the provision addresses a number of avoidance schemes where "the common theme is that the amount to be taken into account under the scheme as disposal value for capital allowances purposes is significantly less than the actual value of the plant or machinery being disposed of". The changes are designed to "prevent companies from artificially lowering the disposal value of plant and machinery for capital allowances purposes, and make any payment received for agreeing to take responsibility for tax deductible lease related payments subject to tax as income".

The interpretation of s. 215 was explored in the *Daarasp* case, where it was agreed that the test is an objective one. The tribunal in that complex case explored the concept of "other party" but the wording of the section has since changed so the case is unlikely to be of much relevance in interpreting the section in future.

Law: CAA 2001, s. 215, 217, 218ZA, 218ZB, 218A
Case: *Daarasp LLP v HMRC* [2018] UKFTT 548 (TC)

22.3.4   Sale and leaseback

Allowances are restricted for sale and leaseback transactions.

No first-year allowances or annual investment allowances are given if, after the sale, the plant or machinery is (very broadly) still used for the purpose of a qualifying activity carried on by the seller or by a connected person.

The buyer's qualifying expenditure is restricted to the amount of the seller's disposal value.

Writing-down allowances are also restricted in some circumstances, broadly where there is a deliberate tax advantage.

Once more, the rules are relaxed for manufacturers and suppliers making sales in the ordinary course of business, as long as there is no tax avoidance motive.

Law: CAA 2001, s. 216, 217, 218, 218ZA, 230

22.4   Hire purchase

22.4.1   Assignment

A person who buys an asset under a hire purchase agreement may assign the benefit of the contract before it is brought into use. If the anti-avoidance measures apply (such that the allowances for the assignee would have to be restricted) s. 68(3) does not apply. This is the provision that normally provides the disposal value where a person ceases to be entitled to the benefit of a contract before plant or machinery is brought into use. Instead, an alternative calculation applies, as explained at **22.4.3** below.

Law: CAA 2001, s. 229(2)

22.4.2   Timing of expenditure

When a person acquires an asset on hire purchase, the hirer can normally claim allowances on the full amount of the expenditure once the asset is brought into use – see, generally, **Chapter 6**.

Where the asset is leased out under a finance lease, however, these provisions are disapplied. In such a case, capital allowances will instead be given as the expenditure is incurred.

Law: CAA 2001, s. 229(3)

22.4.3   Disposal value

When the above provisions apply, but a person is treated as ceasing to own plant or machinery by virtue of s. 67(4) (see **6.3**), the disposal value will be the total of any relevant capital sums and any capital expenditure that the person would have incurred if he had wholly performed the contract. However, the person is deemed (for the sole purpose of bringing a disposal value into account) to have incurred that capital expenditure in the chargeable period in which he is treated as ceasing to own the plant or machinery.

For these purposes, "relevant capital sums" are capital sums that the person receives or is entitled to receive by way of consideration, compensation, damages or insurance money in respect of his rights under the contract, or of the plant or machinery.

The purpose of this legislation was summarised as follows when CAA 2001 was enacted:

> "In anti-avoidance cases, the assignee's qualifying expenditure may (depending on the circumstances) be limited to the disposal value brought into account by the assignor.
>
> Section 229 is designed to protect the assignee in an anti-avoidance context from an unduly depressed disposal value, by including the expenditure that will be incurred under the contract if it is wholly performed in the disposal value."

Law: CAA 2001, s. 229(3)-(7)

Guidance: CAA 2001, *Explanatory Notes, Annex 1, Change 27*

22.5   Other anti-avoidance measures

Other anti-avoidance measures in relation to plant and machinery, but not covered in this book, include the following:

- finance leases and certain operating leases (s. 219-220);
- sale and finance leasebacks (s. 221 and 225);
- sale and leaseback: election for special treatment (s. 227-228);
- finance leaseback: parties' income and profits (s. 228A-228C, 228G-228J);
- disposal of plant or machinery subject to lease where income retained (s. 228K-228M);
- restriction of qualifying expenditure in case of certain leased assets (s. 228MA-228MC);
- restriction on hirer's allowances where transfer followed by hire purchase, etc. (s. 229A);
- arrangements whereby non-taxable consideration is received when taking over tax deductible lease obligations in respect of plant and machinery (CTA 2010, s. 894A).

22.6   Further references

Other anti-avoidance rules to which reference is made in this book include the following:

- timing of expenditure: see **1.5.6**;
- integral features – connected parties: see **4.11.7**;
- annual investment allowances – prevention of multiplication of allowances: see **5.2.2**;
- single-asset pools – reduction in qualifying use of very large assets: see **5.3.7**;
- disposals to charities – benefits attributable to gifts: see **5.5.5**;
- allowance buying – companies with an unallowable purpose: see **5.10.2**;
- tax credits with a disqualifying purpose: see **5.11.9**;
- hire purchase – artificially structured contracts: see **6.1.3**;
- short leases – same asset leased under different leases: see **7.2.5**;
- cars re-allocated to main rate pool: see **9.3.2**;

- cars: various other measures to counter acceleration of allowances: see **9.4.4**;
- short-life assets – sales at less than market value: see **15.7**;
- long-life assets – various measures: see **16.4**;
- special rate expenditure – disposal values: see **17.5.1**; and
- special rate cars – permanent discontinuance of company's qualifying activity: see **17.5.2**.

23. Additional VAT liabilities and rebates

23.1 Introduction

23.1.1 Capital allowances implications

There may be capital allowances implications when a person incurs an "additional VAT liability" or receives an "additional VAT rebate". This chapter deals with the implications in relation to plant and machinery allowances.

The background is explained by HMRC as follows:

> "The VAT payable on an asset is usually determined by the first use of that asset. This is particularly an issue for businesses which make both taxable and exempt supplies for VAT purposes.
>
> The VAT Capital Goods Scheme (which applies to large capital items of capital expenditure) adjusts the VAT due if the use of an asset changes during the period of ownership. If the mix of use changes, for VAT purposes, from taxable to exempt a further amount (called an additional VAT liability) is payable by the taxpayer. This reflects the fact that too much VAT was originally claimed by the taxpayer (based on the initial use). Conversely, if the mix of use changes, for VAT purposes, from exempt to taxable a higher proportion of the input tax originally incurred by the taxpayer (called an additional VAT rebate) is payable by Customs to the taxpayer.
>
> The VAT Capital Goods scheme applies to computers and computer equipment worth £50,000 or more (and applies over the first 5 years of the asset's life) and to land and buildings worth £250,000 or more (over a 10-year period)."

The guidance explains that, broadly, additional VAT paid by the owner of an asset is qualifying expenditure for capital allowances purposes and that the receipt of a VAT rebate is a disposal event if a person receives an additional VAT rebate while owning the asset at some time in the chargeable period in which the rebate is made.

See **5.13.2** for guidance on the temporary super-deduction in the context of additional VAT liabilities.

Guidance: CA 29230

456

23.1.2 Terminology

An additional VAT liability and an additional VAT rebate are amounts that a person becomes, respectively, liable to pay or entitled to deduct, by way of adjustment under the VAT capital items legislation in respect of input tax.

The time when a person incurs an additional VAT liability, or when an additional VAT rebate is made to a person, is the last day of the period:

- that is one of the periods making up the "VAT period of adjustment" applicable to the asset in question under the VAT capital items legislation; and

- in which the increase or decrease in use giving rise to the liability or rebate occurs.

The term "VAT period of adjustment" is defined to mean a period specified under the VAT capital items legislation by reference to which adjustments are made in respect of input tax.

Law: CAA 2001, s. 234, 547, 548

23.2 Additional qualifying expenditure

A person is treated as incurring additional qualifying expenditure if he:

- has incurred actual ("original") qualifying expenditure; and

- incurs an additional VAT liability in respect of the original expenditure at a time when the plant or machinery is provided for the purposes of the qualifying activity.

The additional liability is treated as qualifying expenditure incurred on the same plant or machinery as the original expenditure, and which may be taken into account in determining the person's available qualifying expenditure for the chargeable period in which the additional VAT liability accrues.

First-year allowances

If a person incurs additional qualifying expenditure on an asset that attracted first-year allowances (FYAs), and the asset is still used for the purposes of a qualifying activity, the additional expenditure also qualifies for FYAs. The rate of allowance is the same as applied originally, even if the earlier regime has since been withdrawn (e.g. the 40% rate for certain expenditure incurred by SMEs, that is no longer available generally). The FYA is given, however, for the chargeable period in which the VAT liability accrues.

This does not apply (so no FYAs are due) if the asset is used for overseas leasing that is not protected leasing. Nor are allowances due in certain cases involving anti-avoidance provisions.

Law: CAA 2001, s. 236, 237, 241

Annual investment allowances

If a person incurs additional qualifying expenditure on an asset that attracted AIAs, and the asset is still used for the purposes of a qualifying activity, the additional expenditure is also treated as AIA qualifying expenditure, for the chargeable period in which the liability accrues. Normal principles and limits apply.

This does not apply (so no AIAs are due) if the asset is used for overseas leasing that is not protected leasing. Nor are allowances due in certain cases involving anti-avoidance provisions.

Law: CAA 2001, s. 236, 237, 241

Writing-down allowances

If no AIAs or FYAs are due, but the asset is still in use for the purposes of the qualifying activity when the person incurs an additional VAT liability, the liability is added to the appropriate pool of expenditure for the year in which it arises.

Law: CAA 2001, s. 235

23.3 Additional VAT rebate generating disposal value

23.3.1 General rule

An additional liability may arise if a person who has incurred qualifying expenditure receives an additional VAT rebate in respect of that original expenditure. The rule only applies if the person owns the plant or machinery on which the original expenditure was incurred at any time in the chargeable period in which the rebate is made.

If there would otherwise be no disposal value to be brought into account in respect of the asset for the chargeable period in which the rebate accrues, the disposal value is the amount of the rebate.

If, by contrast, there would already be a disposal value for that period, the amount of the rebate must be brought into account as an addition to that disposal value.

Law: CAA 2001, s. 238

23.3.2   *Limit on disposal value*

A cap is placed on the amount of the disposal value where certain conditions are met. The cap, equal to the amount of the original expenditure reduced by any additional VAT rebates already taken into account, applies if:

- a person is required to bring a disposal value into account in respect of any plant or machinery; and
- any additional VAT rebate has been made to him in respect of the original expenditure.

If the VAT rebate is the only reason for a disposal value to be brought into account, the value is limited to the amount of the original expenditure reduced by the amount of any disposal values brought into account in respect of the plant or machinery as a result of any earlier event.

If a person required to bring the disposal value into account has acquired the plant or machinery as a result of one or more transactions between connected persons, and an additional VAT rebate has been made to any party to the transaction(s), the amount of the disposal value is limited to the greatest "relevant expenditure" of any of the parties. The relevant expenditure of a party is that party's qualifying expenditure on the provision of the plant or machinery, less any additional VAT rebate made to that party.

Law: CAA 2001, s. 239

23.4   **Short-life assets**

A person is entitled to a further balancing allowance if he:

- was entitled to a balancing allowance for the final chargeable period for a short-life asset pool for a qualifying activity;
- incurs, after the end of that period, an additional VAT liability in respect of the original expenditure on the short-life asset; and

- has not brought the liability into account in determining the amount of the balancing allowance.

The amount of the additional allowance is equal to the additional VAT liability for the chargeable period of the qualifying activity in which that liability accrues.

Law: CAA 2001, s. 240

23.5 Anti-avoidance

Various anti-avoidance measures apply in relation to additional VAT liabilities and rebates. These include:

- restrictions on FYAs and AIAs (mentioned at **23.2** above);
- a substitution for the anti-avoidance measures normally applying under s. 218;
- cases where lessors do not bear the non-compliance risk; and
- elections under s. 227 (sale and leaseback or sale and finance leaseback).

Assessments (and adjustments of assessments) may be made as necessary to give effect to the anti-avoidance measures.

Law: CAA 2001, s. 241-246

OTHER ALLOWANCES

24. Structures and buildings allowances

24.1 Introduction and overview

24.1.1 Background and purpose

Structures and buildings allowances (SBAs) are given for the construction costs of non-residential properties and structures.

The economic purpose of SBAs was explained in the *Explanatory Notes* to the relevant *Finance Bill*, as follows:

> "... to address a gap in the current capital allowances system, where no relief has been available for most structures and buildings. It is intended explicitly to stimulate investment in commercial activity – specifically on new commercial structures and buildings, the necessary works to bring them into existence and the improvement of existing structures and buildings, including converting existing premises to qualifying use."

A technical note issued by HMRC on 29 October 2018 (*Capital allowances for structures and buildings* – referred to throughout this chapter as "the 2018 technical note") also comments on the desire to improve the UK's international competitiveness. The note states that the SBA "represents a long-term commitment" to that goal, suggesting that SBAs should be around for many years to come.

The expected annual cost to the Exchequer (and therefore presumably the expected annual saving for taxpayers) is shown as rising to £585 million by the tax year 2023-24 (HMRC policy paper of 18 June 2019). However, the rate of allowance has been increased since then (from 2% to 3%), and an enhanced SBA is also now available for certain freeport sites, so the potential tax savings are now higher.

The introduction of the SBA reversed the general trend of abolishing numerous types of property-related capital allowances, including industrial buildings allowances, agricultural buildings allowances, flat conversion allowances and business premises renovation allowances, all of which had been removed in the decade before SBAs were introduced.

Broadly speaking, the allowance is available for expenditure incurred on or after 29 October 2018 (the Budget date on which the introduction of the SBA was announced). Allowances are available for UK taxpayers for buildings and structures in the UK or overseas.

Avoidance provisions seek to ensure that this start date cannot be manipulated.

The allowance is now given at a flat rate of 3% per annum. The rate was increased (from 2%) from 1 April 2020 (corporation tax) or 6 April 2020 (income tax). Where a chargeable period spans the date of change, allowances may be claimed at the rate of 2% per year for days before the change and 3% thereafter.

2% was the rate of allowances originally given for industrial buildings, but that the IBA rate was subsequently doubled to 4%. The very low rate means that SBAs are not particularly attractive for many taxpayers, though the increase to 3% obviously helps to some extent.

For the purposes of this allowance, the term "building" is specifically defined to include any "structure" (FA 2019, s. 30(13)).

24.1.2   SBAs at a glance

The key features of the SBA regime are as follows:

- Allowances are given at a flat rate of 3% (formerly 2%) per year, but at a higher rate for freeport tax sites.
- Allowances are available for commercial buildings and structures, but not for residential property. No allowances are given for land costs.
- The first use of the building, after the qualifying expenditure has been incurred, must be non-residential.
- There are no first-year allowances, annual investment allowances or balancing adjustments. Strictly speaking, there are no writing-down allowances either – just "allowances".
- The right to claim allowances until they are exhausted passes to the new owner when a building is sold. The new owner is required to obtain appropriate documentation to underpin the right to claim.
- The person claiming the allowances must have the relevant interest in the building. Special rules apply for certain leases of 35 years or more.
- Allowances are given for new construction costs incurred from 29 October 2018, as long as no contract for the construction

works was entered into before that date. Allowances are not available for a purchase after that date where the construction expenditure was incurred before that date.

- Allowances are also given for capital renovation and conversion costs.

- Allowances can only be given once the building or structure has been brought into qualifying use. Thereafter, allowances may continue to be given during periods of disuse. However, no further allowances are given once the building is entirely demolished.

- Allowances cease if the building is brought into residential use.

- Allowances are not available under the SBA regime for property fixtures (including both integral features and other fixtures). The cost of fixtures must therefore be isolated and claimed separately under the regime for plant and machinery allowances.

- Various anti-avoidance measures apply, notably in relation to the start date of 29 October 2018, to costs in excess of market value, and to other avoidance arrangements.

24.1.3   Legislation

The relevant legislation is at Part 2A of CAA 2001 ("Structures and buildings allowances"), beginning at s. 270AA.

Part 2A is broken down as follows:

- Introduction (Chapter 1 – s. 270AA to 270AB).

- Qualifying expenditure (Chapter 2 – s. 270BA to 270BN).

- Freeport qualifying expenditure (Chapter 2A – s. 270BNA to 270BNC).

- Qualifying use and qualifying activities (Chapter 3 – s. 270CA to 270CG).

- The relevant interest in the building or structure (Chapter 4 – s. 270DA to 270DE).

- Calculating the allowance: supplementary provision (Chapter 5 – s. 270EA to 270EC).

- Highway undertakings (Chapter 6 – s. 270FA to 270FC).

- Additional VAT liabilities and rebates (Chapter 7 – s. 270GA to 270GC).

- Adjustment for pre-April 2020 allowance (Chapter 7A – s. 270GD).
- Giving effect to allowances (Chapter 8 – s. 270HA to 270HI).
- Supplementary provisions (Chapter 9 – s. 270IA to 270IH).

The legislation was introduced by FA 2019 and by SI 2019/1987. The regulations also make amendments to other sections of CAA 2001:

- s. 1 (capital allowances);
- s. 2 (giving effect to allowances);
- s. 3 (claims);
- s. 6E (NI rate activity cases);
- s. 7 (prevention of double allowances);
- s. 262AB and following sections (co-ownership schemes);
- s. 536 and 537 (and new 538A) (contributions);
- s. 544 (management assets);
- s. 546 (additional VAT liabilities and rebates); and
- s. 573 (transfers treated as sales).

Similarly, the regulations make amendments to other legislation, as follows:

- TCGA 1992, s. 24 and new s. 24A (disposal on destruction of asset); new s. 37B (consideration on disposals); s. 39 and new s. 39A (exclusion of certain expenditure); s. 41 (restriction of losses); s. 52 (supplemental); s. 103D (CoACS);
- ITTOIA 2005, s. 96A and 96B (capital receipts – cash basis);
- ITA 2007, s. 123 (losses with capital allowances connection);
- CTA 2009, s. 1147 (contaminated land); s. 1233 (excess capital allowances);
- FA 2009, Sch. 61 (alternative finance investment bonds);
- CTA 2010, s. 682 (management expenses); s. 699 (group management expenses);
- FA 2012, s. 78(3) (management assets); and
- SI 2012/3008 (friendly societies).

Law: FA 2019, s. 30; SI 2019/1087

24.1.4   Tax returns

HMRC guidance confirms the following practical points in connection with the claiming of these allowances:

> "This allowance will be claimed as a deduction as part of a customer's main tax return (Income Tax Self Assessment (ITSA) and Corporation Tax (CT)). Therefore, we would expect the customer to be able to claim the allowance when completing their return online.
>
> The allowance will be claimed as part of the customer's current annual process and, therefore, should not create any additional users.
>
> We want customers to be able to claim the allowance both digitally and, where applicable, in paper format – therefore, HMRC is introducing additional boxes on all relevant tax returns to capture the allowance.
>
> This will allow HMRC operators to be able to identify when this allowance has been claimed to analyse its impact and identify any non-compliance."

Guidance: HMRC Impact Assessment (4 November 2019) – *Capital Allowances – Structures and Buildings Allowance: initial equality impact assessment*

24.2   Conditions for claiming allowances

24.2.1   General principles

Three core conditions must be met for these allowances to be available:

- the construction of a building or structure must begin on or after 29 October 2018 (but see **24.3.1** where the actual construction was after that date but where the contract was entered into before that date);
- qualifying expenditure must be incurred on or after that date on its construction or acquisition (see **24.5**);
- the first use of the building or structure, after the qualifying expenditure is incurred, must be non-residential use (see **24.4.2**).

For the purposes of the last bullet above, if a building or structure has fallen into disuse, but was in non-residential use before the period of disuse began, it is treated as continuing to be in non-residential use (see **24.4.1**).

In relation to any given qualifying activity (see **24.4.3**), a person is entitled to an allowance for a given chargeable period if:

- the person has the relevant interest (see **24.6**) in the building or structure, in relation to the qualifying expenditure, in respect of any day in the chargeable period;
- the building or structure is in non-residential use; and
- that day falls:
  - on or after the building or structure is first brought into qualifying use by the person (or, if later, after the day on which the qualifying expenditure is incurred); and
  - within the specified period (see below) from the day on which it was first brought into non-residential use (or, if later, from the day on which the qualifying expenditure was incurred).

A person ceases to be entitled to an allowance if the building or structure is demolished (see **24.4.4** below). See **24.4.2** below where the building or structure is brought into residential use.

For the last bullet above, the period referred to is normally 33.33 years, i.e. based on the current 3% per annum, and has the effect that allowances are lost for periods when nobody can claim allowances. This principle remains correct, though the actual figure depends on when allowances are first claimed. The rule, whatever the precise figure in any given case, would appear to cover the position where construction costs are incurred by the Crown or by another person not in the charge to UK tax, or where income from the qualifying activity is not within the charge to UK tax.

For freeport expenditure, the specified period is 10 years – see **24.14**.

Law: CAA 2001, s. 270AA; FA 2019, s. 30(1)

Guidance: HMRC Technical Note (29 October 2018) – *Capital allowances for structures and buildings*

24.2.2 *Evidence of qualifying expenditure – the allowance statement requirement*

A person who is in principle entitled to an allowance under the rules described immediately above is nevertheless treated as having no qualifying expenditure unless the "allowance statement requirement" is met. This will have important implications in relation to commercial property standard enquiries (CPSEs – see, generally, **12.11**, where these are explained in detail in relation to plant and machinery allowances) where a property is acquired from a third party.

The allowance statement requirement is imposed on the person making the claim, referred to in the legislation as the "current owner".

If the current owner was the person who incurred the qualifying expenditure, then he is the one who must make the allowance statement.

If the building or structure was acquired from a previous owner, who used the building or structure (other than for residential use), then the current owner must obtain an allowance statement (or a copy thereof) from a previous owner (but not necessarily from the owner from whom the property was acquired). This is the case even if the previous owner was unable to claim SBAs because, for example, it was a government body or a non-UK resident person with no UK income.

The allowance statement has no prescribed format but must be in writing and must identify the building or structure to which it relates. It must then include the following details:

- the date of the earliest contract for the construction of the building or structure;
- the amount of the qualifying expenditure incurred on its construction or purchase; and
- the date on which the building or structure was first brought into non-residential use.

In the first of the above bullets, the original intention was that the contract for constructing the building had to be in writing, if the allowance statement requirement was to be met, but this has been amended. The *Explanatory Notes* issued at the time of the March 2020 Budget confirm that the change "enables persons with an oral contract to be able to comply with the allowance statement requirement, without which a claim cannot be made".

The earlier proposed requirement, that the statement should also include such information as HMRC may require, has been removed. However, HMRC state that taxpayers should keep information about the earliest construction costs, such as "formal contracts, emails or board meeting notes". It is not necessary to record the amount of SBA claimed, as any amounts not claimed are simply lost.

HMRC have stated that for extensions or renovations completed after the structure is first used, "you can record separate construction costs on the allowance statement or create a new allowance statement". This is also confirmed in an example at CA 91400, concerning a food-testing consultant (Jane), who buys a property and spends additional money fitting it out:

> "Jane's additional fit out costs may qualify for the SBA, to the extent that the costs do not relate to the provision of plant, as a new SBA claim for a new 50 year period starting from the day the laboratory comes into use. Jane must create a new allowance statement or add to the existing one to show clearly the amount of her new qualifying expenditure, the date it was incurred and the date the new assets came into use."

The HMRC example is still worded this way in April 2021, but the 50 years would now be 33.33 years.

HMRC have confirmed that the statement does *not* need to be included routinely with the return, but "should be retained as part of business records that may be required to be produced during a check by HMRC into any claim". HMRC also make the point that the allowance statement does not replace the need for the business to retain other records, such as invoices to show the amount of construction expenditure incurred.

In March 2021, the government announced that it would legislate to ensure that statements "include the date qualifying expenditure is treated as incurred when the allowance period commences from this date". This is to ensure that subsequent owners know that they can use this date rather than the date on which the asset was brought into use.

Where the qualifying expenditure includes freeport qualifying expenditure (see **24.14**), a statement is not treated as being a valid allowance statement unless it states the amount of such freeport qualifying expenditure.

Law: CAA 2001, s. 270IA; FA 2020, Sch. 5, para. 7
Guidance: CA 91400, 94650, 94700; https://www.gov.uk/guidance/claiming-capital-allowances-for-structures-and-buildings

24.3 Timing of expenditure

24.3.1 *Commencement*

The rules here apply equally to buildings or structures, but this has for convenience been shortened here to "buildings".

Allowances are available only for expenditure incurred from 29 October 2018. This creates obvious temptations to re-draft any agreements that were put in place shortly before that date, and the legislation seeks to prevent taxpayers from bending the rules in this way. It does this first by imposing specific deadlines, but then also with a series of anti-avoidance measures.

First, a condition for obtaining SBAs is that the construction of the building must begin on or after 29 October 2018 (s. 270AA(1)(a)).

For these purposes, the construction is treated as beginning before 29 October 2018 (so that allowances are denied) "if any contract for works to be carried out in the course of the construction of that particular building or structure (whether or not the contract also relates to the construction of other buildings or structures) is entered into before that date" (s. 270AB).

The HMRC view is that a contract may consist simply of "an email exchange confirming works will take place".

In practice, the contract date will usually precede the construction date, though there may be cases where the contract is in fact entered into only after the construction works have begun. In other cases, such as where work is done "in house" by employed workers, there may be no contract at all.

The qualifying expenditure must also be incurred on or after that date (s. 270AA(1)(b)).

Anti-avoidance rules (see **24.11**) seek to ensure that these rules cannot be manipulated so as to enable allowances to be claimed.

Law: CAA 2001, s. 270AB; FA 2019, s. 30(1)(a), 30(9)
Guidance: CA 90200; HMRC Technical Note (29 October 2018) – *Capital allowances for structures and buildings*

24.3.2   *Pre-trading expenditure*

If a person incurs expenditure, for the purposes of a trade or other qualifying activity, before the date on which that activity begins, the expenditure is treated as incurred on that commencement date.

A proposed restriction, whereby pre-trading expenditure could only qualify if incurred in the seven years prior to commencement, has been removed from CAA 2001. At the time of writing, s. 30(5) of FA 2019 still refers to a seven-year limit, but this would appear to be an oversight, as para. 3.35 of the June 2019 "Summary of Responses" document states that the government "has removed the seven-year restriction". HMRC guidance at CA 91600 makes no reference to a seven-year restriction.

This provision does not, however, allow for expenditure incurred before 29 October 2018 to qualify. (So the seven-year question will not be a practical consideration until at least late 2025.)

Law: CAA 2001, s. 270BN; FA 2019, s. 30(5)

Guidance: CA 91600; HMRC Technical Note (29 October 2018) – *Capital allowances for structures and buildings*

24.4 Qualifying use

24.4.1 Core tests

The FA 2019 legislation states that regulations must specify what is qualifying use. It also specifies that qualifying use must be restricted to use for "prescribed business purposes".

A number of main tests are imposed:

- expenditure must have been incurred on or after 29 October 2018;
- the building or structure must be in qualifying use;
- expenditure must be qualifying expenditure; and
- allowances must be denied for expenditure on the acquisition of land or rights in or over land.

In summary, qualifying use is non-residential use for the purposes of a qualifying activity carried on by the person with the relevant interest, where that use is not insignificant.

See **24.7.2** below where a property is put to multiple uses.

Law: CAA 2001, s. 270CE; FA 2019, s. 30

Guidance: HMRC Technical Note (29 October 2018) – *Capital allowances for structures and buildings*

Insignificant use

A building or structure that is only used for the purposes of a particular activity to an insignificant extent is not treated as used for those purposes. This must be determined on a just and reasonable basis.

According to HMRC:

> "Nominal use of a building will not enable it to qualify for the SBA. Whether or not a building is used to a significant extent should be determined on a reasonable basis taking into consideration the relevant facts and circumstances. For example, a building in non-residential use by a seasonal business such as a theme park, which is not open all year, is unlikely to be in insignificant use only because of the limited number of months that it is open each year."

HMRC have also commented as follows:

> "In the context of a building, insignificant use will most likely refer to the number of days of use for the qualifying activity out of the total available. However, it may be appropriate to consider the specific use in the context of the overall pattern of use of the building to decide whether or not that use was insignificant."

Although there is no specific guidance on quantifying "insignificant", HMRC examples at CA 92200 suggest that two days out of 11 months (or indeed out of seven months) would be insignificant, but two days out of just part of a month might not.

Guidance: CA 92100, 92200

Periods of disuse

It is important to understand how the above tests of "qualifying use" interact with the conditions for claiming allowances explained at **24.2** above.

A quick reading of the core tests above would suggest that allowances will be denied for periods in which the property is not in any use (as it is not then in non-residential use). However, this is not how it actually works: the legislation confirms that relief will continue to be available for such periods, with no prohibition on the allowances available (a different treatment to that which had originally been proposed).

So once entitlement to claim has been established, and as long as the building or structure is neither demolished nor turned to residential use, allowances will continue to be available.

The way this works in statutory terms is that the building or structure must be in actual (non-residential) use to trigger the initial ability to claim allowances – the core test as above. But allowances continue thereafter – by virtue of the wording in s. 270AA(2)(b)(i) and

s. 270AA(3) – without the need for continuing actual use. The default position is therefore that allowances continue to be available (for each person with a relevant interest) once they have started to be given, unless there is non-residential use or demolition, until the 33 and a third (formerly 50) years have expired.

Law: CAA 2001, s. 270AA, 270CE

Guidance: CA 92100, 92900; HMRC Introductory note to draft secondary legislation (13 March 2019)

24.4.2 *Residential use*

A condition for claiming allowances is that the property must be in non-residential use (defined, perhaps unnecessarily, to mean that it must be in use that is not residential use).

Allowances are not available where a property is in residential use. If a person is already entitled to claim allowances, the entitlement ends when the building or structure is brought into residential use.

Furthermore, it is a condition that the *first use* of the building, after the qualifying expenditure is incurred, must be non-residential. If this condition fails, no allowances are due under the SBA code. For this reason, it is essential to understand when qualifying expenditure is said to be incurred, as discussed in depth at **24.5.2** below.

The legislation in this area is somewhat different from that envisaged in the earlier consultation, which proposed to give a full definition of "dwelling-house". Instead, what we now have is a longer list of purposes that constitute residential use.

A building or structure is said to be in residential use if it is used as, or for purposes ancillary to use as, any of the following:

- a dwelling-house (see below);
- residential accommodation for school pupils;
- student accommodation (see below);
- residential accommodation for members of the armed forces;
- a home or other institution providing residential accommodation (whether for children or adults), except where certain personal care is provided (see below);
- a prison or similar establishment.

Similarly, a property will be treated as being in residential use if it falls within the definition in the *Housing Act* 2004, Sch. 14, para. 4 (buildings in England or Wales occupied by students and managed or controlled by educational establishment etc.), or corresponding provisions having effect in Scotland or Northern Ireland.

A building or structure situated on land that is (or is intended to be) occupied or enjoyed with a building or structure that is in residential use as a garden or grounds is treated as being in residential use. (In the words of the June 2019 HMRC document, this clarifies that "assets used for purposes ancillary to residential use include those assets situated on land within the curtilage of a residential structure or building".)

HMRC guidance also states the following:

> "A building is treated as being in residential use if it is ancillary to a residential building, or situated on land intended to be occupied or enjoyed with a building in residential use. For example, swimming pools located in the grounds of a dwelling and facilities, gyms, cinemas and car parks provided as facilities for dwelling houses such as a block of flats would be ancillary and therefore excluded from SBA."

No allowances are given for *any part* of a building or structure that is used as a dwelling-house, even if it is used for other purposes as well. The technical note (at para. 27) made it clear that the denial of allowances for "shared areas which cover both use as a dwelling and commercial use" was a conscious departure from the approach that applies for plant and machinery allowances.

The technical note also specified that allowances are not available for work spaces within domestic properties, such as home offices. This appears to be confirmed in the legislation at s. 270CF(4) (though it seems to the writer that the statutory wording is somewhat ambiguous, and not as watertight as it ought to be).

The June 2019 "Summary of Responses" document from HMRC (i.e. following a consultation process) provided further insights, with the following comments:

> "It is acknowledged that the definition of 'residential' is wide; for example, serviced apartments may well contain non-residential facilities including a concierge, gyms or swimming pools.

However, we consider that they nevertheless remain residential accommodation and will not qualify as a result."

Law: CAA 2001, s. 270AA(3), 270CF; FA 2019, s. 30

Guidance: CA 92500; https://www.tax.org.uk/policy-technical/ submissions/capital-allowances-structures-and-buildings-ciot-comments; https://assets.publishing.service.gov.uk/government/uploads/ system/uploads/attachment_data/file/809373/Capital_allowances_for_ structures_and_buildings_consultation_summary_of_responses.pdf

Student accommodation

As with plant and machinery allowances (see **4.14.3**), defining "student accommodation" can be difficult.

For the purposes of claiming SBAs, a building is said to be in use as student accommodation if both of the following conditions are met:

- the accommodation is purpose-built, or is converted, for occupation by students; and
- it is available for occupation by students on at least 165 days of each calendar year.

The concept of being occupied by students is defined to encompass occupation "exclusively or mainly by persons who occupy it for the purpose of undertaking a course of education (otherwise than as school pupils)".

HMRC guidance adds that "where student accommodation is managed by or on behalf of an educational establishment, it will be in residential use for the purposes of the SBA".

Law: CAA 2001, s. 270CF
Guidance: CA 92700

Dwelling-house

As noted above, the statutory restrictions refer to "residential use" and one subset of residential use is use as a dwelling-house. As there is no statutory definition of "dwelling-house" it is necessary to consider the ordinary meaning of the term, and many of the principles applying for plant and machinery allowances will apply here as well.

According to HMRC:

> "A dwelling-house is a building, or a part of a building; its distinctive characteristic is its ability to afford to those who use it the facilities required for day-to-day private domestic existence."

This can include a second/holiday home, but does not include a hospital, nursing home or hotel that is run as a trade with services offered.

In relation to flats, the HMRC guidance is as follows:

> "A block of flats is not a dwelling-house although the individual flats within the block will be, and the common areas are likely to be ancillary to the dwelling-houses within the block."

HMRC also draw an important distinction between serviced apartments and hotels:

> "A hotel is primarily a provision of accommodation on a temporary basis as part of a trade providing other services, whereas serviced apartments may be used longer term by occupants such that each apartment forms a dwelling-house as with any other form of short-let residential accommodation, and will therefore not qualify for the SBA."

Law: CAA 2001, s. 270CF
Guidance: CA 92600

Accommodation with personal care

As noted above, most homes providing residential accommodation will constitute "residential use", but there are exceptions where the accommodation is provided with personal care for persons in need of such care by reason of old age, disability, past or present dependence on alcohol or drugs or past or present mental disorder.

HMRC have given the following guidelines in relation to care provided for older people:

> "This does not include general accommodation for persons of old age. Only care home accommodation which provides personal care where the persons occupying are in need of such services qualifies for the SBA.
>
> 'Personal care' does not include remote monitoring, for example in caretaker-managed independent living, or the provision of meals. It involves administering of personal hygiene, feeding, medication or therapy, such as physiotherapy.

General accommodation for persons of old age, and which is delivered through self-contained individual apartments (as opposed to individual rooms within a communal building) is considered to be in residential use."

With a growing range of options for housing older people, there are likely to be grey areas around the boundary between residential and non-residential accommodation.

Law: CAA 2001, s. 270CF
Guidance: CA 92800

24.4.3   Qualifying activities

The legislation lists the following types of qualifying activity:

- a trade (and the 2018 technical note specified that this would include a ring-fence trade in the oil and gas sector);

- an ordinary UK property business (defined as for the purposes of claiming plant and machinery allowances – see **3.2** above);

- an ordinary overseas property business (once more, defined as for the purposes of claiming plant and machinery allowances – see **3.4** above);

- a profession or vocation;

- the carrying on of a concern listed in ITTOIA 2005, s. 12(4) or CTA 2009, s. 39(4) (mines, quarries and other concerns);

- managing the investments of a company with investment business (and although the statutory mechanism is different, this is again defined as for plant and machinery allowances – see **3.6** above).

Note that furnished holiday lettings (whether in the UK or abroad) are *not* a qualifying activity (and see **3.2** above for a broader discussion of the question of serviced accommodation). Residential property letting is also excluded as the building is in residential use.

Law: CAA 2001, s. 270CA, 270CB, 270CD
Guidance: CA90450

Profits to be chargeable to tax

In all cases, the activity is a qualifying activity to the extent only that any profits or gains from the activity are chargeable to tax (or would be so chargeable, if there were any such profits or gains).

Permanent establishment

A special rule has applied since 19 July 2011 in relation to any business carried on through one or more permanent establishments outside the UK by a company in relation to which an election under CTA 2009, s. 18A has effect (exemption for profits or losses of foreign permanent establishments).

Such a business is treated for SBA purposes as a separate activity and is to be regarded as "an activity all the profits and gains from which are not, or (if there were any) would not be, chargeable to tax".

Law: CAA 2001, s. 270CA, 270CC

Use for a property business

There is statutory guidance as to what constitutes use for a property business. The condition is that the person with the relevant interest in the building or structure must be entitled (whether under the terms of a lease or otherwise) to rents or other receipts "of such amounts as may reasonably have been expected to have been payable if the transaction had been between persons dealing with each other at arm's length in the open market". This may, in HMRC's words, include "allowing for any customary and reasonable periods of reduced or nil rents as would be expected in transactions between persons acting at arm's length".

The concepts of "rent" and "other receipts" are defined here as for the purposes of ITTOIA 2005, s. 266. (See HMRC's *Property Income Manual* for detailed guidance on these definitions.)

HMRC guidance confirms that entitlement to rents and other receipts "may arise under the terms of a lease or otherwise".

Law: CAA 2001, s. 270CG
Guidance: CA 92300

24.4.4   Demolition

No further claims may be made for qualifying expenditure once the property is demolished.

This is a change from what was originally envisaged (per the 2018 technical note) where a "shadow SBA" had been contemplated. The reason for the change of approach was explained as follows (in the "introductory note" to the draft legislation published on 13 March 2019):

"Demolition would usually be considered a disposal event for capital gains purposes. As informed by discussion with stakeholders, any unrelieved expenditure would therefore be claimed as a deduction in arriving the capital gains computation. This would avoid businesses having to continue with 'shadow' SBA claims, after the structure or building has been demolished or where interest in land may have expired, whilst at the same time ensuring investors remain able to claim relief for all qualifying construction costs."

Further HMRC guidance re demolition now includes the following:

"Where the entirety of a building is demolished, it will cease to qualify for SBA. The remainder of any unclaimed SBA on the costs of the building will be lost. SBA claimed will be added to consideration (even where the consideration is nil) in the Capital Gains computation.

Demolition only applies to the demolition of an entire building. Where parts of a building, such as a single wall, are demolished, any capital costs of demolition or restoration works are covered under the capital renovation and conversion provisions."

Law: CAA 2001, s. 270AA(4)
Guidance: CA 91500

24.5   Qualifying expenditure

24.5.1   *General principle*

The legislation distinguishes between two types of qualifying expenditure:

- capital expenditure incurred on construction (see **24.5.2**); and
- capital expenditure incurred on a purchase (see **24.5.3**).

Certain other amounts (renovation costs, conversion costs, incidental repairs, and site preparation costs) are treated as construction costs for these purposes (see **24.5.5**).

Expenditure is not qualifying expenditure, however, if it is excluded expenditure under any of the following provisions:

- s. 270BG (acquisition or alteration of land) (see **24.5.6**);
- s. 270BH (market value rule) (see **24.5.7**); or
- s. 270BI (provision of plant or machinery) (see **24.5.8**).

See also **24.5.9** for comment on other excluded costs.

If the first use of a building is residential use, the qualifying expenditure is nil.

The 2018 technical note provided some further clarity on the scope of qualifying expenditure, as follows:

> "the construction of new structures and buildings that are intended for commercial use, the necessary works to bring them into existence and the improvement of existing structures and buildings, including the cost of converting existing premises for use in a qualifying activity."

The note also makes it clear that overseas structures and buildings may qualify, as long as the business entity is within the charge to UK income tax or corporation tax. Provisionally (but the point was raised for public feedback), "the structure or building will qualify for SBA where it is in use by the person claiming the relief for a qualifying activity and to the extent the profits of the activity are chargeable to tax in the UK".

It also states that "structures and buildings include offices, retail and wholesale premises, walls, bridges, tunnels, factories and warehouses". The term "structure" is of course much wider than the term "building" (in that most buildings are structures, but many structures – e.g. roads, bridges, tunnels – are not buildings). Although the statutory provisions are different, and care is needed accordingly, readers may find it helpful to refer to section **4.2.3** above, which discusses the concept of "structure" in the context of plant and machinery claims.

Law: CAA 2001, s. 270BA

24.5.2   *Construction costs*

Capital expenditure is treated as qualifying capital expenditure where:

- it is incurred on the construction of a building or structure; and
- either:
  - the relevant interest in the building or structure has not been sold, or
  - it has been sold only after the building or structure has been brought into non-residential use.

See **24.6** for the meaning of "relevant interest".

HMRC list the following as expenditure that is treated as incurred on the construction of a building:

- professional fees relating to the design and construction of a building (provided that the building is actually constructed);
- costs incurred in preparing the site for construction (including demolition of any existing structure or building);
- construction costs of the building;
- capital renovation and conversion costs;
- capital fitting out works;
- capital repairs, incidental to capital renovation or conversion, for which the cost is not available as a deduction in computing the profits of the qualifying activity.

Guidance: CA 93110

Expenditure incurred at different times

Where subsequent qualifying expenditure is incurred on the property, allowances will be claimed separately for that later expenditure, for a new period of 33.33 years beginning from that time. The concept of pooling is therefore not applied. An example illustrating this is available at CA 90350.

The legislation allows for three different possibilities in relation to the timing of expenditure. Expenditure incurred on different days after the property has been brought into non-residential use may be treated as incurred on any of the following:

- the latest day on which qualifying capital expenditure is in fact incurred;
- the first day of the chargeable period following the period in which the above date falls; or
- the first day of the chargeable period following the period in which qualifying capital expenditure is in fact incurred.

This is a simplification measure to avoid having to keep track of large numbers of separate costs, each with a different start date, but at the cost of accepting a delay in making the claim. As HMRC acknowledge, a business may wish "to decide whether the delay in claiming the SBA is a suitable trade-off for a simpler computation". The point is illustrated with an extended example at CA 93450.

The requirement was originally going to be that the expenditure was incurred after the property was brought into "qualifying use" but this has been changed to refer instead to "non-residential use". The reason for the change was explained in the *Explanatory Notes* issued with the draft legislation at the time of the March 2020 Budget: "Before this amendment the easement was only available where the building was in qualifying use and therefore was not available to civil society organisations or other bodies not chargeable to tax."

Law: CAA 2001, s. 270BB; FA 2020, Sch. 5, para. 5

Buildings

There is no statutory definition of this term, but HMRC guidance includes the following:

> "The dictionary definition of a building is a substantial structure for giving shelter and so you should treat any item constructed with walls and a roof as a building provided that it is of reasonably substantial size. An item that is too small or insubstantial to be a building, such as a tool shed, may be a structure.

> Works within the curtilage of a building do not necessarily qualify simply because they are within the curtilage of a qualifying building, and need to be examined in their own right against the conditions for relief."

Guidance: CA 90250

Structures

In this case, HMRC guidance includes the following:

> "There is no definition of structure in the SBA legislation, so the word takes its everyday meaning.

> You should treat something as a structure if it has been erected or constructed and is distinct from the earth surrounding it.

> Areas that have undergone construction works such as underpinning structural works are structures.

> Land that retains its character as land is not a structure, even if it has been cultivated or modified in some way. For example, grass or earthed surfaces such as tennis courts, rough areas, greens and fairways in golf courses, grass football pitches, and grass bowling greens are not usually structures."

HMRC then provide the following examples of structures (though the list is obviously non-exhaustive):

- roads
- a constructed hard surface, such as a concrete or asphalt car park tunnels
- walls
- bridges
- aqueducts
- dams
- hard tennis courts
- fences
- permanent terracing and seating areas at sports grounds
- artificially constructed parts of golf courses, such as bunkers
- embankments.

Guidance: CA 90300

Burden of proof

The legislation puts the onus firmly on the taxpayer to prove that the qualifying construction expenditure has been incurred.

So the qualifying expenditure consists only of "the sum of those items of expenditure the actual amount of which can be shown". There is therefore no room for saying that such an amount is likely to have been incurred on the balance of probabilities – if no actual amounts can be shown, then the qualifying expenditure is nil.

For this reason, it will not be acceptable to use estimated amounts of overall qualifying expenditure. However, an estimate is not the same as an apportionment: for example, the SBA rules specifically require the fixtures elements to be taken out (see **24.5.8** below). It follows that a precise figure of actual overall expenditure must be the starting point, excluding any estimated elements, and that a proper apportionment methodology must be used to ensure that the respective claims under the SBA rules and the plant and machinery rules are correct.

HMRC guidance includes the following apportionment examples (which predate the increase from 2% to 3%):

Example 1 – HMRC example

Easybuilding Limited incurs £1.8 million capital expenditure constructing a mixed-use development, comprising retail outlets on the ground floor with student accommodation above, for use in its property business. For the purposes of SBA, the retail space qualifies, but the student accommodation does not.

One-sixth of the development cost relates to the retail space and so, assuming in this instance that it is just and reasonable to apportion the overall expenditure in this way, the qualifying expenditure is £300,000 (one-sixth of £1.8 million). Therefore, the annual SBA is 2% × £300,000 = £6,000.

Example 2 – HMRC example

Fastbuild Limited incurs £2 million capital expenditure constructing a mixed-use development, comprising offices and residential accommodation, for its property business. For the purposes of SBA, the office space qualifies, but the residential accommodation does not.

The development's total Gross Internal Area is 10,000 square metres, of which 6,000 relates to offices and, in this case, the facts indicate a reasonable apportionment should be made on an area basis. Therefore, on a just and reasonable basis, the qualifying expenditure is £1.2 million ((6,000 ÷ 10,000) × £2 million). The annual SBA is 2% × £1.2 million = £24,000.

Where a property is being put to different uses, a just and reasonable apportionment will be required, following standard capital allowances principles. This could apply, for example, if:

- the same building is used for two or more qualifying activities (where allowances will need to be calculated for each);
- part of the building is used for a qualifying activity and part for a different activity that does not qualify;
- part of the building is used for mixed purposes.

However, no allowance is available for use within a dwelling-house, so an office at home does not qualify.

See CA 91900 for an extended example illustrating these possibilities.

Law: CAA 2001, s. 270BM
Guidance: CA 91800, 91900

24.5.3 Sale by someone other than a developer

The legislation here (and again at **24.5.4** below) refers to a *sale by* a person other than a developer rather than, as might be expected, a *purchase from* such a person. Tempting though it is to turn this around, it is safer to stay with the statutory wording.

The rules are different depending on whether or not the building or structure has been used (for any purpose).

Unused buildings or structures

Where a building or structure (shortened to just "building" in this section) is sold by someone other than a developer, but before the building is first used, the qualifying capital expenditure incurred by the purchaser is the lesser of the amount paid and the actual construction costs.

Specifically, this rule applies where:

- capital expenditure has been incurred on the construction of the building;
- the relevant interest in the building is sold before the building is first used;
- a capital sum is paid by the purchaser for the relevant interest; and
- the rules described at **24.5.4** below (sale by a developer) do not apply.

Where these conditions are met, the purchaser is treated as incurring qualifying expenditure when the capital sum is paid. If the buyer pays a deposit, with the balance on completion, the entire amount is treated as being incurred on the date of completion.

If this section applies more than once, because there are several sales before the building is first used, the "lesser of" rule is applied only in relation to the last such sale.

In these circumstances, an apportionment will be required to exclude the cost of the land. Similarly, the capital sum that may qualify for SBAs will include SDLT attributable to the building but not to the land. In principle, the same restriction applies to legal and surveyor costs.

Guidance: CA 93500, 93550

Used buildings or structures

It is important to note that the sale of a used building or structure (other than by a developer – see **24.5.4** below) does not give rise to new qualifying expenditure for the buyer.

The buyer of such a used property can (in principle) still claim allowances, as the fundamental condition is met: the buyer now has the relevant interest. The buyer therefore continues to claim by taking over the residue of qualifying expenditure previously incurred by the seller or by a previous owner.

HMRC example (using old rate of 2%)

Tom's period of account runs from 1 January to 31 December. Tom constructs a building costing £1 million which is brought into qualifying use on 1 April. For the chargeable period during which the building is brought into use, Tom can claim £1 million × 2% × (9 ÷ 12) = £15,000. For subsequent years, Tom will be able to claim £1 million × 2% = £20,000 per year.

If Tom sells the building to Veronica, Veronica can claim the SBA on the original construction costs, at the same rate of 2% per year, which is £20,000 per year for the remainder of the 50 year period. The purchase price Veronica pays does not change the amount of the SBA available.

Note, however, that this has an important implication for residential property. A condition for claiming allowances is that the first use of the building, after the qualifying expenditure is incurred, must be for non-residential use. So even if the buyer is intending to use the property for commercial purposes, no allowances will be available for the earlier construction costs, as this condition was not met when that earlier qualifying expenditure was incurred.

Law: CAA 2001, s. 270AA(1)(c), 270BC
Guidance: CA 91300

24.5.4   Sale by a developer

Different rules are needed when the sale is by a developer who is constructing and selling buildings in the course of a development trade. This is because such a developer will have incurred revenue rather than capital expenditure.

The statutory rules make a distinction here between the sale of an unused or used building or structure (once more shortened to just "building" in this section for ease of reference).

In each case, the following definitions apply.

A "developer" is defined as "a person who carries on a trade which consists in whole or part in the construction of buildings or structures with a view to their sale". HMRC have stated that "the fact that a person subcontracts the actual construction work, and/or elements of the sale/transfer process does not prevent them from being a developer."

An interest in a building or structure is said to be sold by the developer in the course of the development trade "if the developer sells it in the course of the trade or (as the case may be) that part of the trade that consists in the construction of buildings or structures with a view to their sale".

Law: CAA 2001, s. 270BF
Guidance: CA 93600

Unused buildings or structures

The rules immediately below apply where a developer incurs expenditure on the construction of a building and then sells the relevant interest in the course of his development trade before the building is first used.

In most cases, the sale of the relevant interest by the developer will be the only sale of that interest before the building is first used. Where this is the case, and where the purchaser pays a capital sum to acquire the relevant interest, that capital sum will be the qualifying capital expenditure. The construction cost is not relevant.

Example 1

A builder buys land for £300,000 and constructs a warehouse at a cost of £500,000. He sells the brand new property for £1.2 million to a trading entity that will use it for storage of its trading stock.

The qualifying SBA expenditure will be an apportioned part of the £1.2 million (i.e. to exclude the land element).

It is possible, however, that the sale by the developer will not be the only sale before first use of the building. In this case, if the purchaser pays a capital sum for the relevant interest on the last sale, the qualifying capital expenditure will be the lesser of:

- the amount so paid; and
- the amount paid for the relevant interest on its sale by the developer.

Example 2

Suppose that the trading entity, from the first example above, makes a decision to relocate its storage facility after it has committed to buy the warehouse. It therefore decides to sell the property, without at any stage occupying it for its own trade, and it is able to find a willing buyer at an agreed price of £1.25 million.

The first company is not able to claim SBAs as the property has not been brought into use. The new owner, however, will be able to claim on £1.2 million (being the lesser of £1.2m and £1.25m), once more adjusted to exclude the land element.

In either case, the qualifying expenditure is treated as incurred by the purchaser when the capital sum is paid.

Law: CAA 2001, s. 270BD
Guidance: CA 93650

Used buildings or structures

In some instances, the developer will incur expenditure on a building or structure that is used before the relevant interest is sold by the builder during the course of his development trade.

In these circumstances, the rules are applied as if the expenditure on the construction had been qualifying capital expenditure. This then determines the tax position for the person to whom the relevant interest is first sold and for any person who subsequently acquires the relevant interest.

Example 3

A builder constructs a small office block with the intention of selling it at a profit. The land cost was £200,000 and the construction costs amounted to £350,000.

The market is slow and the builder is unable to sell the property. It therefore leases it out on a short lease with a three-month notice period. Two years later, a buyer is found and the property is sold for £600,000.

Although the buyer is in reality the first to incur capital expenditure, the rules are applied as if the £350,000 costs incurred by the builder had been capital rather than revenue expenditure. SBAs for the new owner will therefore be based on this figure.

Law: CAA 2001, s. 270BE

Apportionments

Where a property is bought from a developer, the technical guidance states that "an apportionment of the purchase cost from the developer will be required to separate the amount of the cost that is attributable to the land". The legislation itself refers to "assets representing expenditure for which an allowance can be made" under the SBA rules and to "assets representing other expenditure".

The statutory requirement, where any apportionment has to be made between expenditure for which an allowance can be made and other expenditure, is that the apportionment is to be made on a just and reasonable basis.

Law: CAA 2001, s. 270BL, 562; FA 2020, Sch. 5, para. 6

24.5.5   Renovations, conversions and incidental repairs

Certain renovation, conversion and repair costs are treated as if the expenditure in question "were capital expenditure on the construction of that part of the building or structure for the first time".

Specifically, this treatment applies to expenditure that a person incurs:

- on the renovation or conversion of a part of a building or structure; or
- on repairs to a part of a building or structure that are incidental to the renovation or conversion of that part.

For these purposes, the renovation (etc.) is treated as if it were construction of that part for the first time, for the purposes of applying the timing test (re beginning on or after 29 October 2018) (s. 270AA(1)(a) and s. 270AB – see **24.2** and **24.3** above).

So if a property is built in 2010 and renovated in 2020, no allowances can be claimed for the original costs, but allowances are in principle available for the renovation costs.

Similarly, capital expenditure may be incurred on residential accommodation in 2020, which will not qualify, but the property may then be converted to business use some time later. The original construction costs cannot qualify for SBAs, but the conversion costs can.

If both the original expenditure and the renovation/conversion costs qualify, the two elements must be separately recorded for the purposes of claiming allowances.

Expenditure on such costs is treated as capital expenditure if it is not tax deductible, as a revenue cost, in calculating the profits of the qualifying activity for tax purposes.

According to HMRC, "if a property requires renovation, the renovations are brought into use when the renovated parts of the building begin to be used".

These rules are modified for freeport expenditure – see **24.14** below.

Law: CAA 2001, s. 270BJ
Guidance: CA 91200, 93200

24.5.6   *Excluded expenditure – acquisition or alteration of land*

Allowances are specifically *not* available for:

- expenditure on the acquisition of land, or rights in or over land;
- or for the costs of altering land (but see below re site preparation costs).

For these purposes (other than in relation to land remediation), the word "land" does not include buildings or structures.

Expenditure on any of the following is specifically categorised as excluded expenditure, on which allowances are denied:

- expenditure on or in connection with seeking planning permission, including fees and related costs;
- fees, SDLT (and equivalent Scottish and Welsh taxes) and other incidental costs attributable to the acquisition, insofar as these relate to land rather than to the building or structure.

The 2018 technical note, at para. 20, included "the costs of public inquiries" as one of the disallowable incidental costs.

The term "planning permission" is defined according to the relevant planning enactment, as in turn defined at s. 436(2) in relation to mineral extraction allowances.

Law: CAA 2001, s. 270BG
Guidance: CA 94010, 94100

Altering land

This concept is defined to include:

- land reclamation;
- land remediation (see below); and
- landscaping (other than so as to create a structure).

Law: CAA 2001, s. 270BG(4)

Land remediation

The term "land remediation" is defined:

- in relation to land in a contaminated state, by reference to CTA 2009, s. 1146 (contaminated land remediation);
- in relation to land in a derelict state, by reference to CTA 2009, s. 1146A (derelict land remediation),

in each case including relevant preparatory activity as defined in those respective sections.

References to land being in a contaminated or derelict state for the purposes of the above bullet points have the same meaning as in Part 14 of CTA 2009.

Law: CAA 2001, s. 270BG(5)

Site preparation costs

Capital expenditure on preparing land as a site for the construction of a building or structure may be treated as if it were expenditure on the actual construction, and may thereby qualify for allowances.

However, these costs will not be allowed if the site preparation falls within the meaning of altering land, as described above. (In other words, the rules denying allowances for the alteration of land take precedence over those allowing allowances for site preparation costs.)

If allowances are in principle available for land preparation costs, the land preparation is treated as construction for the purposes of applying the timing test (re beginning on or after 29 October 2018) (s. 270AA(1)(a) and s. 270AB – see **24.2** and **24.3** above).

Law: CAA 2001, s. 270BK
Guidance: CA 93250

24.5.7   Excluded expenditure – market value rule

There is a broad principle that qualifying expenditure is restricted to market value.

Expenditure is excluded expenditure, on which allowances are denied, if and to the extent that it exceeds:

- in a case where the qualifying capital expenditure under s. 270BC or s. 270BD is the capital sum paid for the relevant interest (i.e. for unused buildings and structures), the market value of the interest; and

- in any other case, the "market value amount" (see below) of the works, services and other matters to which it relates.

The market value of the interest is defined by reference to s. 577(1), i.e. as the price that it would fetch in the open market.

The "market value amount" is defined to mean the amount of expenditure that it would have been normal and reasonable to incur on the works, services or other matters:

- in the market conditions prevailing when the expenditure was incurred; and

- on the assumption that the transaction (as a result of which the expenditure was incurred) was between persons dealing with each other at arm's length in the open market.

Law: CAA 2001, s. 270BH
Guidance: CA 94200

24.5.8   Excluded expenditure – plant and machinery

Claims can be made under the plant and machinery regime for fixtures in commercial properties, including integral features. Such fixtures obviously continue to qualify for plant and machinery allowances.

There is a general principle (at CAA 2001, s. 7) that prevents any double claiming of relief. It follows that expenditure on which plant and machinery allowances are claimed will have to be excluded from the SBA claim, a point reinforced at s. 270BI (and confirmed at para. 23 of the technical note).

In fact, though, the division between plant on the one hand and the rest of the building or structure on the other is mandatory rather than optional. The wording of the relevant provision is (with emphasis added) that expenditure that constitutes capital expenditure on the provision of plant or machinery for the purposes of Part 2 **is** excluded expenditure. So a taxpayer does not have the option of simply claiming SBAs on everything. Indeed, HMRC guidance confirms that the SBA rule "excludes capital expenditure on the provision of plant or machinery from being qualifying expenditure for SBA, whether plant and machinery allowances have been claimed or not".

Similarly, if the costs are deductible under other provisions, such as those for land remediation relief, SBAs will not be given for the expenditure (para. 24).

Dividing qualifying expenditure between fixtures (the costs to be claimed under the plant and machinery regime) and non-fixtures (to be claimed under the SBA rules) will be a key element of tax planning. The former will give much faster tax relief, protection against higher taxation of capital gains (see **24.10**), and greater flexibility as between seller and buyer on disposal of the property.

Example

A Ltd constructs some offices for £2 million, excluding land costs. It calculates that one quarter of the cost relates to fixtures, and accordingly claims plant and machinery allowances of £500,000, all available as annual investment allowances. The company also claims SBAs on the balance of £1.5 million, at 3% per year.

After seven years, it sells the offices to an unconnected pension fund for £3 million, again excluding the land element.

Once more, it is calculated that one quarter of the cost is properly allocated to fixtures. However, the pension fund is willing to sign a fixtures election (see **12.7**) for just £1. A Ltd is therefore able to retain the full benefit (minus £1) of the plant and machinery allowances for the fixtures.

A Ltd has claimed SBAs of £315,000 (£45,000 per year for seven years), and it retains these in full when the property is sold (as there are no SBA balancing adjustments). However, its capital gain would be £1 million, but this is increased by the £315,000 of SBAs that it has enjoyed. The fact that plant and machinery allowances have been claimed (and, in this case, retained) for the fixtures has no bearing on the computation of the gain.

The tax relief for the fixtures is immediate and permanent, whereas the relief under the SBA regime is given much more slowly and is then effectively reversed (not by way of a balancing charge but through higher taxation of the capital gain) when the property comes to be sold.

It is possible, of course, that the vendor's capital gain will simply be rolled over into a new purchase, in which case this may not be a problem in practice, or may at least be an issue that is deferred.

Law: CAA 2001, s. 270BI
Guidance: CA 90250, 94300

24.5.9   Excluded expenditure – other costs

In addition to the exclusions already covered above, HMRC list the following as non-allowable SBA costs:

- any structure located in the grounds of a residence;
- any costs on which other types of allowance have been claimed;
- financing / loan costs;
- capitalised interest;
- the costs of public enquiries;
- legal expenses;
- marketing, promotion, agency or arrangement costs associated with the legal transfer of a relevant interest;
- costs associated with the acquisition of franchise rights or intellectual property;
- costs for which a grant or contribution is received.

Guidance: CA 93110; https://www.gov.uk/guidance/claiming-capital-allowances-for-structures-and-buildings

24.6   Relevant interest

24.6.1   General principle

SBAs are, broadly speaking, claimed by the person who has the relevant interest in the building.

The general principle is that the relevant interest, in relation to any qualifying expenditure, is the interest in the building or structure to which the person who incurred the expenditure on its construction was entitled when the expenditure was incurred. This is subject to modification for highway undertakings (see **24.8.2**) and where a lease is terminated.

Two different people may each have a different type of relevant interest in the same building. So if A Ltd constructs a building at a cost of £1 million, it will have the relevant interest in relation to that expenditure. If the company then grants a lease to B Ltd, and B Ltd incurs capital expenditure of £50,000 to alter the building in some way, B Ltd has the relevant interest in relation to the £50,000. Subject to the complications outlined at **24.6.3** below, each company can in principle claim SBAs for its respective qualifying expenditure.

One person may have more than one interest, with one such interest reversionary on the other(s). In such a case, the reversionary interest is the relevant interest. In HMRC's words, "the reversionary interest is the interest which reverts back to the person incurring the expenditure". Elsewhere, it has been described as "any interest the enjoyment of which is postponed".

As HMRC explain:

> "Since construction expenditure may be incurred at different times and by different people there may be several relevant interests in a building. This could result in more than one claim for a building, with different persons claiming qualifying expenditure on the building attributable to their own relevant interests."

Where the relevant interest in a building or structure is sold, the seller (rather than the purchaser) is the one treated as having the relevant interest on the day of transfer.

As a point of practice, good record-keeping will be essential. A property may be built one year, extended some time later, renovated, partly demolished, extended some more, and so on. Over a period of several decades, keeping track of the different interests may be quite complex, whether this is done by adding to the original statement of expenditure or creating a series of separate documents.

Law: CAA 2001, s. 270DA
Guidance: CA 90510

24.6.2   *Interest acquired on completion of construction*

A modified rule applies where a person incurs expenditure on the construction of a building or structure and is entitled to an interest in it on or as a result of the completion of the construction. In this case, the person is treated as having had that interest when the expenditure was incurred.

Law: CAA 2001, s. 270DB

24.6.3   Creation of a subordinate interest (e.g. a lease)

As a general principle, the granting of a lease, or the creation in another way of a subordinate interest, does not extinguish the existing relevant interest. So a freeholder who has the relevant interest, and who grants a 10-year lease to a tenant, will not thereby lose the relevant interest. The freeholder will continue to claim SBAs as before (though the tenant will claim for qualifying expenditure it then incurs – see **24.6.1** above).

Where a very long lease is granted, however, this becomes more akin to a sale (and where a building is sold, the right to claim allowances is in principle passed to the new owner). The guidance notes initially give two extreme examples to illustrate the underlying principle here:

- A 999-year lease may be granted for a large premium followed by a peppercorn rent: the practical effect of this is very similar to a sale, and the legislation seeks to ensure that the lessee, rather than the lessor, will be entitled to claim the allowance.

- By contrast, a lease granted at full market rent, with no lease premium paid at the outset, would not be equivalent to a sale and the lessor would still be entitled to claim SBAs.

So where "the granting of a lease is substantially no different from a purchase of the interest in land" (as worded in the technical note of 29 October 2018), the legislation treats this in some circumstances as the sale by the grantor to the tenant, so that the right to claim allowances passes to the tenant. Where the lease comes to an end, however, the entitlement to any remaining SBAs will revert to the lessor/landlord.

The legislation sets the cut-off point at 35 years, with modified rules applying for leases of 35 years or more. More specifically, the rules are modified where:

- qualifying capital expenditure has been incurred on the construction or acquisition of a building or structure;

- a lease is granted out of the interest which is the relevant interest in relation to the qualifying expenditure; and

- the "effective duration of the lease" (see below) is equal to, or exceeds, 35 years.

In these circumstances, the rules require a comparison of the market value of the retained interest in the building or structure and the amount of the capital sum given as consideration for the lease (see below).

If the market value of the retained interest is less than one third of the capital sum paid, then two consequences follow:

- the lessee is treated as acquiring the relevant interest in the building or structure on the grant of the lease; and
- when the lease expires, or is surrendered, the lessor is treated as re-acquiring the relevant interest from the lessee.

Law: CAA 2001, s. 270DC, 270DD
Guidance: CA 90800

Capital sum

Where a lease premium is paid, a part of the amount paid may fall to be treated as a revenue rather than a capital sum received, for the purposes of calculating the lessor's profits (see ITTOIA 2005, s. 277 and CTA 2009, s. 217 for income tax and corporation tax purposes respectively).

As the guidance explains:

> "The tax rules treat part of the premium received on the grant of a lease as income and the amount that is treated as being disposal proceeds is reduced accordingly. This means that for shorter leases a very large proportion of a premium is treated as income. The capital gains rules then treat the grant of a lease as a part disposal and a proportionate part of the cost of the asset is deducted from the proceeds to calculate the chargeable gain."

(See also **1.5.2** for comment on the tax treatment for the payer.)

In such cases, any amount treated as revenue rather than capital under those provisions is excluded for these SBA purposes from the capital sum when making the comparison with the market value retained.

Computation of element taxable as income

The existing rules for premiums for short leases (up to 50 years) are given at ITTOIA 2005, s. 287 (for income tax) and at CTA 2009, s. 227 (for corporation tax). The amount of the premium taxable *as income* is given by the formula:

$$P \times (50 - Y)/50$$

where:

P is the amount of premium paid; and

Y is the number of complete periods of 12 months, excluding the first, in the duration of the lease.

See the *Property Income Manual* at PIM 1205 or the *Capital Gains Manual* at CG 70900 for an illustration of how the calculation is made.

Law: CAA 2001, s. 270DD(3)

Effective duration

The effective duration of a lease is, for these purposes, to be determined in accordance with the rules at ITTOIA 2005, s. 303 or CTA 2009, s. 243 (property income – calculation of profits of property business – lease premiums).

Law: CAA 2001, s. 270DD(4)

Definitions and general principles

See **24.13** for various general principles and definitions that apply in relation to leases for all SBA purposes.

Example 1

Ariana owns the freehold of a property and grants a 30-year lease to Taylor, charging a premium and an annual rent.

The lease is for less than 35 years, so no calculations are needed. Ariana continues to claim allowances and Taylor has no right to do so.

Example 2

Scarlett owns the freehold of a commercial property and grants an 80-year lease to Amber, charging a premium of £300,000 and an annual rent of £50,000. The value of the retained interest is calculated as £75,000.

This time, a calculation must be made as the lease exceeds 35 years.

The market value of the retained interest (£75,000) is less than one third of the capital sum paid (£300,000). Amber is therefore treated as acquiring the relevant interest at the time the lease is granted. She therefore takes over from Scarlett the right to claim allowances from that date.

Example 3 – HMRC example

The market value of a retail outlet is £1,000,000. A 50 year lease is granted to a lessee for a capital sum of £750,000. The lessor's retained interest in the property is £250,000. This is exactly one third of the capital sum, so the relevant interest does not pass to the lessee.

If the 50 year lease had been granted for a capital sum of £750,001, leaving the lessor's retained interest at £249,999, the value of the retained interest is less than a third so the relevant interest would pass to the lessee.

When considering the market value condition described above, the capital sum given to acquire the relevant interest is treated as excluding the amount that is brought into account as a receipt in calculating the lessor's profits for the purposes of ITTOIA 2005, s. 277 or CTA 2009, s. 217.

Guidance: CA 90600

24.6.4   Merger of leasehold interest

It is possible that the relevant interest is a leasehold interest that is extinguished because the person entitled to the interest acquires the interest that is reversionary on it.

Where this happens, the interest into which the leasehold interest merges becomes the relevant interest.

Example 1 – HMRC example

Andy, the freeholder, constructs a commercial building and grants Betty a 40-year lease, which meets the conditions for Betty to be treated as acquiring the relevant interest. Betty subsequently incurs fit-out expenditure which is qualifying expenditure for SBA. At that point, Betty is able to claim SBA separately on the construction expenditure and also on the fit-out expenditure.

Before the end of the lease, Betty buys the freehold interest from Andy. At that point the leasehold interest is extinguished, but because the leasehold interest is merged with the freehold interest, Betty may continue to claim SBA on both the construction and fit-out expenditure, despite the lease ending.

The natural ending of a lease does not, however, constitute the merger of a leasehold interest.

Example 2

Freeholder Ltd grants a 20-year lease to Tenant Ltd. Freeholder Ltd continues to claim any allowances in relation to expenditure it has incurred.

Tenant Ltd incurs new expenditure on fitting out the property. It has the relevant interest in the fit-out expenditure, and can claim SBAs until the end of the lease term. At that point, entitlement to claim SBAs on the fit-out expenditure ceases (and there is no balancing adjustment).

This is subject to the rules in s. 270IG, which in certain circumstances treat the lease as continuing.

Example 3

[This extended example is adapted from several different examples at CA 90800.]

Rebecca constructs an office building and incurs £1,000,000 of qualifying expenditure. She grants a 40-year lease to Asjad, meeting the conditions that transfer the right to claim to Asjad.

When Asjad brings the building into qualifying use, he is entitled to claim SBA on £1,000,000 for the duration of the lease.

Asjad now incurs £500,000 of capital expenditure on fitting out the office building to his required specifications. As Asjad has the relevant interest, in the £500,000 expenditure, he can claim SBA on this expenditure for the duration of the lease. The record of expenditure and calculation of SBA for this additional capital expenditure must be kept separately from that of the original construction costs of the building.

After 40 years, when the lease expires, the relevant interest for the £1,000,000,reverts to Rebecca. Rebecca is now entitled to claim any remaining SBA on the original qualifying expenditure of £1,000,000. The entitlement to SBA on the £500,000 of capital improvements is lost because the relevant leasehold interest expires with the lease, so neither Asjad nor Rebecca can continue to claim SBA on any remaining amount.

Rebecca then grants a five-year lease to Charlotte. This lease is not for 35 years or more, so Rebecca retains the relevant interest and can continue to claim the SBA, on £1,000,000, for this period.

Law: CAA 2001, s. 270DE
Guidance: CA 90700, 90800, 90900

24.7   Calculation and claims

24.7.1   General principles

The "basic rule" (rather hidden away at s. 270AA(5)) is that the allowance for a given chargeable period is 3% of the qualifying expenditure (but 10% for freeport tax site expenditure – see **24.14**). So allowances are calculated as a flat rate 3% of the qualifying costs, giving relief on a straight-line basis over 33.33 years.

For periods before 1/6 April 2020, the rate was just 2%, but the higher 3% rate applies whether expenditure was incurred before or after the date of increase. Chargeable periods spanning the April 2020 date will have allowances calculated on an apportioned basis, with some days at the old rate and some at the new.

Example 1

Freda, a sole trader, draws accounts up to 30 June and is entitled to claim SBAs from 1 February 2020 on a property with qualifying expenditure of £100,000.

For the period to 30 June 2020, she can claim SBAs as follows:

100,000 x 2% x 65/366 = £355, plus

100,000 x 3% x 86/366 = £705.

So her total claim for the period is £1,060. Thereafter she will claim at the rate of £3,000 per year.

The following HMRC example illustrates the increase from 2% to 3% for a limited company.

Example 2 – HMRC example

You built a factory costing £900,000. All the contracts for works were entered into on 7 January 2019.

The factory was completed on 21 November 2019 and you started to use it in your engineering business from 1 December 2019. You prepare accounts for each year ending on 31 December.

In your chargeable period to 31 December 2020, you can claim 2% a year for 96 days from 1 January 2020 to 5 April 2020, and 3% a year for 270 days from 6 April 2020 to 31 December 2020.

96/366 × £900,000 × 2% = £4,722; plus

270/366 × £900,000 × 3% = £19,919.

Total claim £24,641 for the year ended 31 December 2020.

Keep a note of all the days you claimed the 2% rate for in this period or an earlier period. If you do not sell or dispose of the structure within 33 and one third years from the start of the allowance period, you may claim for any shortfall in allowances at the end of that time.

Qualifying expenditure is to be calculated separately for each structure or building.

The allowance is proportionately increased or reduced if the chargeable period is longer or shorter than 12 months.

Similarly, a reduction will be made on a proportionate basis if the conditions of s. 270AA(2)(a) or (b) are met for only part of the year. See, for more detail, **24.2.1** above, but broadly this restriction will apply if the person only has the relevant interest for part of the chargeable period, or if part of the period falls outside the period (formerly of 50 years, now of 33.33 years) beginning with the first day of non-residential use. Where a property is sold or acquired part way through a chargeable period, only a proportion of the allowance will therefore be available for that period.

Allowances cease to be given from the date on which a building or structure is demolished (s. 270EA(3)(b)).

The use of a property may change from commercial to residential, in which case allowances will no longer be available for the non-commercial periods of use. Again, an apportionment must be made if the change of use occurs part way through a given chargeable period.

Example 3 – HMRC example

Sadia builds a premises to use as a retail space for her independent clothes shop. As market conditions deteriorate, Sadia decides to convert the building into a residential flat. The day on which the premises starts to be used for a residential purpose is the day on which the entitlement to SBA ceases. The SBA calculation for that chargeable period must be apportioned to the date the residential activity commences.

There is, of course, no question of claiming annual investment allowances, first-year allowances or balancing allowances for SBA expenditure, as these are all plant and machinery concepts that have no place in the SBA rules. The 3% (formerly 2%) allowance is referred to at

FA 2019, s. 30(2) as a writing-down allowance, though the wording within CAA 2001 itself does not use the term. The allowance differs in nature from the plant and machinery writing-down allowance, not least because it is calculated as a straight-line figure rather than on a reducing balance basis.

If relief is not claimed for a given period, that relief is then lost; it cannot be deferred until a later period. It may occasionally be appropriate not to claim the relief because of the interaction with the calculation of a capital gain (see **24.10**).

Although the legislation refers to apportioning by reference to days, HMRC have confirmed that "a reasonable adjustment by reference to months in the period may be acceptable, provided it is used consistently throughout the period of ownership".

Law: CAA 2001, s. 270AA(3), (4), 270EA; FA 2019, s. 30; FA 2020, s. 29
Guidance: CA 91100, 91400; https://tinyurl.com/yxjh2f8r (HMRC guidance re SBAs)

No balancing adjustments

A property sale will not give rise to any balancing adjustment for the vendor. Instead, the purchaser steps into the vendor's shoes, as it were, and may start to claim allowances in respect of the residue of the qualifying expenditure. The purchaser's claim will therefore be based on the earlier construction cost, and not on the price paid to the vendor. (As the 2018 technical note puts it, "the amount eligible for relief will not be increased where a structure or building is purchased and where it has appreciated in value as this does not represent the cost of construction.")

Allowances for the period in which the sale takes place will be apportioned between the two parties.

Section 30(8)(b) of FA 2019 does include a suggestion that balancing adjustments could arise in certain circumstances. The relevant *Explanatory Note* includes a reference to "how allowances are apportioned or otherwise adjusted". It is thought that this refers to an anti-avoidance measure, as discussed at **24.11** below.

Guidance: https://www.tax.org.uk/policy-technical/submissions/capital-allowances-structures-and-buildings-ciot-comments

24.7.2   Multiple uses

Allowances may be restricted where a building or structure is put to multiple uses. The legislation lists three such circumstances:

- where the building or structure is used for the purposes of two or more qualifying activities – this would seem to cover the situation where there is simultaneous use of the whole building or structure for two qualifying activities;
- where part of the building or structure is in use for a qualifying activity and part for another activity – i.e. separate parts are used for the different activities; or
- part of the building or structure (excluding any area within a dwelling-house) is used both for the purposes of a qualifying activity and for the purposes of another activity – i.e. (at least) part of the property is in simultaneous use for different activities.

Where there is more than one qualifying activity, allowances for each such activity must be separately calculated by apportioning on a just and reasonable basis. In each case, the allowance will be 3% of the appropriate proportion of the qualifying expenditure. In calculating the appropriate proportion, regard must be had to all the activities for which the building or structure is used, and especially to the extent to which it is used for each activity in the chargeable period in question.

Law: CAA 2001, s. 270EB

24.7.3   Interaction with R&D allowances – current rules

In some circumstances, research and development allowances (RDAs) will be claimed in relation to part or all of a property.

The SBA legislation addresses the interaction between the two types of allowance, preventing double relief where RDAs are or have been available. It was discovered that the original legislation was flawed, so the original s. 270EC was replaced for sales taking place on or after 11 March (Budget day) 2020. See **24.7.4** below for the rules that applied to sales before 11 March 2020.

First restriction

A general rule applies to any sale of the relevant interest in a building or structure.

This general rule restricts the amount of SBAs that can be claimed, and the restriction is calculated by deducting the amount of any "Part 6 allowance" that is available to the person buying the relevant interest in the building or structure in question. A "Part 6 allowance" means any research and development allowance in relation to expenditure on constructing or acquiring the building or structure in question.

So if a person buys a property for £1m but can claim £300,000 of RDAs for part of the property, then the maximum figure on which SBAs could otherwise have been claimed is reduced by £300,000.

This restriction cannot reduce the available allowances to below nil.

Law: CAA 2001, s. 270EC(1)-(3), (6)-(8); FA 2020, s. 30, Sch. 5, para. 2

Second restriction

The legislation also imposes another restriction where the following conditions are both met.

- Either the sale in question, or an earlier sale, is by a person entitled to claim RDAs.
- The amount paid for the relevant interest, on any of those sales, has been less than the "ordinary Part 2A amount".

The ordinary Part 2A amount is the total amount of SBAs available in relation to the building or structure in question (i.e. the amount qualifying for SBAs less the amount arising before the time of the sale in question).

In other words, the second restriction applies "when the purchaser pays an amount less than the total remaining structures and buildings allowances available at the time of sale" (from the *Explanatory Notes* to *Finance Bill* 2020).

In these circumstances, the allowances available to the person buying the building or structure are capped at the "permitted maximum". This maximum figure is calculated as follows:

- Start with the lowest sum paid for the relevant interest at the time of any earlier sale by a person entitled to claim SBAs.
- Deduct the total amount of SBAs arising by reference to the building or structure in question since that earlier sale.

Again, it may be helpful to quote from the *Explanatory Notes*, which express the result as follows:

> "The total structures and buildings allowances available collectively to all purchasers following a sale within subparagraph (3) is [sic] restricted to the lowest amount paid on such a sale."

(Subparagraph (3) appears to mean s. 270EC(3), which refers to an earlier sale of the relevant interest by a person entitled to claim SBAs.)

For the purposes of these calculations, it is obviously necessary to take into account allowances actually arising, but account must also be taken of any allowances that would have arisen if the building or structure had been in continuous qualifying use since it was first brought into non-residential use.

Law: CAA 2001, s. 270EC(4), (5), (7); FA 2020, s. 30, Sch. 5, para. 2

24.7.4   Interaction with R&D allowances – sales before 11 March 2020

For sales that took place before 11 March 2020, the interaction of RDAs and SBAs needed to be considered where:

- a building or structure, in respect of which qualifying SBA expenditure has been incurred, was in use for a non-residential purpose; and
- the relevant interest in the building or structure was sold.

The former legislation applied two sets of provisions, as below.

Law: CAA 2001, s. 270EC(1), as formerly enacted

Purchaser entitled to claim RDAs

If the purchaser could claim RDAs, any claim the purchaser makes under the SBA provisions had to be restricted, as would be expected.

The maximum allowances to which the purchaser was entitled were calculated by deducting from the qualifying expenditure the total of:

- the amount of SBAs to which an entitlement arose before the sale of the building or structure (or would have arisen if the building or structure had been in continuous qualifying use since it was first brought into non-residential use); and

- the amount of RDAs to which the purchaser was entitled in respect of qualifying expenditure incurred on the acquisition of the building or structure.

Section 7 (no double allowances – see **1.7.1**) was ignored for the purposes of determining the figure in the first bullet point above.

Law: CAA 2001, s. 270EC(2), (3), as formerly enacted

Seller entitled to claim RDAs

If the seller was entitled to claim RDAs, but the purchaser was not, the total amount on which the purchaser could claim SBAs was again restricted.

The restriction was calculated by deducting from the qualifying SBA expenditure the amount of the SBA to which an entitlement arose by reference to the building or structure before its sale (or would have arisen if the building had been in continuous qualifying use since it was first brought into non-residential use). Section 7 (no double allowances – see **1.7.1**) was ignored for the purposes of determining this figure.

The allowance available to the purchaser was in any case restricted to the capital sum paid by him for the relevant interest.

Law: CAA 2001, s. 270EC(4), (5), as formerly enacted
Guidance: CA 91700

24.7.5   Adjustment for pre-April 2020 allowance

A technical adjustment was introduced in FB 2020, making a transitional provision for anyone entitled to an allowances on 31 March or 5 April 2020 (for corporation tax or income tax purposes respectively). The effect is to rectify any shortfall in allowances by granting a small additional allowance (a fraction of 1% of the qualifying expenditure) in the last chargeable period in which such an allowance is available (i.e. at the end of the 33 and a third years).

This technical amendment will therefore have no practical effect until the second half of the 21st century!

Law: CAA 2001, s. 270GD

24.7.6   Giving effect to allowances

Introduction

The 2018 technical note stated, surprisingly, that allowances would be given as a "deduction from profits" (rather than in calculating the profits), whether the claim is for income tax or corporation tax purposes. Fortunately, this appears to have been an error and has been corrected in the legislation.

The specific methods of giving relief are detailed in the legislation as below.

Trades, professions and vocations

Where the qualifying activity is a trade, profession or vocation, allowances are given in calculating the profits or gains of the activity in question, treating the allowances as an expense of the trade, profession or vocation in question.

Law: CAA 2001, s. 270HA, 270HC

Ordinary property businesses

Where the qualifying activity is an ordinary UK, or ordinary overseas, property business, allowances are given in calculating the profits of that business, treating the allowances as an expense of the property business in question. (No SBAs are allowed for an FHL business.)

Law: CAA 2001, s. 270HB

Mines, transport undertakings, etc.

The qualifying activity may involve one of the concerns listed at ITTOIA 2005, s. 12(4) or at CTA 2009, s. 39(4) (mines, transport undertakings, etc.).

In this case, allowances are once more given effect in calculating the profits of that concern, treating an allowance as an expense of the concern.

Law: CAA 2001, s. 270HD

Companies with investment business

As is the case for plant and machinery allowances (see **5.10.9**), the rules are somewhat more complicated for those whose qualifying activity consists of managing the investments of a company with investment business.

As far as possible, allowances for any given chargeable period are deducted from any income of the business for the period. CTA 2009, s. 1233 (addition of allowances to company's expenses of management) applies only so far as it cannot be given effect in this way. Subject to this paragraph, the Corporation Tax Acts are applied as if the allowances were required to be given effect in calculating the profits of the person's trade for the purposes of CTA 2009, Pt. 3.

There can be no duplication of allowances. So if allowances are due under some other provision, they may not also be given under CAA 2001, s. 270HE.

Expenditure relieved under these provisions is not to be taken into account otherwise than for the purposes of SBAs or as provided by CTA 2009, s. 1233.

These rules are still subject to the provisions in CTA 2010, s. 682(3) and s. 699(3) (restrictions on the deduction of management expenses: notional accounting periods).

Law: CAA 2001, s. 270HE

24.8   Highway undertakings

24.8.1   Application of SBA rules

Structures and buildings allowances may be available for a person who is carrying on a highway undertaking, but who cannot claim the costs of road construction as revenue expenditure.

A highway undertaking is defined, for the purposes of the SBA legislation, to mean so much of any undertaking relating to the design, building, financing and operation of roads as is carried on for the purposes of, or in connection with, the exploitation of highway concessions.

In relation to a road, a highway concession is:

- a right to receive sums from a public body because the road is or will be used by the general public; or

- the right to charge tolls, if the road is a toll road.

A public body is defined to mean the Crown or any government or public or local authority (whether or not in the UK).

The carrying on of a highway undertaking is treated as the carrying on of an undertaking by way of a trade, so references in the SBA rules to a trade include a highway undertaking. Furthermore, a person carrying on a highway undertaking is treated as occupying any road in relation to which it is carried on.

Law: CAA 2001, s. 270FA
Guidance: CA 94510

24.8.2   The relevant interest

For SBA purposes, a highway concession is not treated as an interest in a road.

However, where a person who incurred the expenditure on the construction of the road:

- was not entitled to an interest in the road when that person incurred the expenditure; but

- was at that time entitled to a highway concession in respect of the road,

then the highway concession is treated as the relevant interest in relation to that expenditure.

Law: CAA 2001, s. 270FB

24.8.3   Cases where highway concession treated as extended

A highway concession in respect of a road is treated as extended if:

- the person entitled to the concession takes up a renewed concession (see below) in respect of the whole or a part of the road; or

- that person (or a person connected with that person) takes up a new concession in respect of the whole or a part of the road (or of a road that includes the whole or a part of the road).

However, the concession is to be treated as extended only:

- to the extent that the concession which has in fact ended, and the renewed or new concession, relate to the same road; and
- for the period of the renewed or new concession.

For these purposes, a person is treated as taking up a renewed or a new concession if:

- the person is granted a renewed or new concession; or
- the arrangements for the concession otherwise continue (whether or not the arrangements are legally enforceable).

It does not matter whether the renewed or new concession is on the same terms as the previous concession or on modified terms.

Law: CAA 2001, s. 270FC
Guidance: CA 94525

24.9 Additional VAT liabilities and rebates

24.9.1 Introduction

The background to this concept is explained in some depth (in relation to plant and machinery allowances) at **Chapter 23** above, and reference should be made to that commentary as necessary.

The concepts of:

- additional VAT liability;
- additional VAT rebate; and
- the chargeable period in which (and the time when) an additional VAT liability or an additional VAT rebate accrues,

are all applied for the purposes of SBAs exactly as they are for PMAs – see **23.1.2**.

HMRC guidance at CA 94555 also gives explanations of the underlying VAT concepts. That guidance also includes the following summary of the principles:

"For the purposes of the SBA additional VAT liabilities or rebates only apply to the person with the relevant interest who first makes qualifying use of the building. The qualifying expenditure of any subsequent holders of the relevant interest are not affected because their relief for the SBA is based on the qualifying expenditure incurred by the person who first makes use of the building. It follows that if the first person to use the building does not use it for the purposes of a qualifying activity, then no VAT adjustments are due in respect of any subsequent claim to SBA for that building."

Law: CAA 2001, s. 270GA
Guidance: CA 94555

24.9.2 Additional VAT liabilities

There is a statutory basis for calculating SBAs where:

- a person is entitled to an SBA by reference to qualifying expenditure he has incurred; and
- the person incurs an additional VAT liability in respect of the qualifying expenditure.

The legislation specifies how the SBA is to be calculated for the chargeable period in which the additional VAT liability accrues and for any subsequent chargeable period. In essence, the amount of qualifying expenditure is treated as increased, at the beginning of the chargeable period in which the additional VAT liability accrues, by the amount of the liability.

If, immediately before the end of the "allowance period" (as defined), the person who is entitled to the SBA by reference to qualifying expenditure is the person who incurred that expenditure, that person is entitled to an additional amount of allowance for the chargeable period in which the allowance period ends.

HMRC example (pre-dating increase to 3%)

Terry constructs a workshop for £250,000 plus £50,000 VAT which he reclaims in full. He brings it into use immediately and claims SBA. The annual SBA is £250,000 × 2% = £5,000. During year six he changes the use of the workshop and incurs an additional VAT liability of £2,500 in respect of the original qualifying expenditure incurred on construction of the workshop. His SBA then becomes (£250,000 + £2,500) × 2% = £5,050. In year 50 he can claim an additional £250 allowance for that year being the difference between the £2,500 additional VAT liability and the allowance already received in respect of this £2,250 (£2,500 × 2% × 45).The additional amount is the difference between the amount of the additional VAT liability and the total amount of the allowance to which the person has been entitled during the allowance period in respect of the additional VAT liability.

However, if an additional VAT rebate is made to the person in respect of the qualifying expenditure, this is still subject to the limit on the total allowance given by s. 270GC(4) – see below.

Law: CAA 2001, s. 270GB
Guidance: CA 94570

24.9.3 Additional VAT rebates

There is also a statutory basis for restricting SBAs where:

- a person is entitled to an SBA by reference to qualifying expenditure he has incurred; and
- an additional VAT rebate in respect of the qualifying expenditure is made to that person.

This time, the legislation specifies how the SBA is to be calculated for the chargeable period in which the additional VAT rebate accrues and for any subsequent chargeable period. In essence, the amount of qualifying expenditure is treated as reduced, at the beginning of the chargeable period in which the additional VAT rebate accrues, by the amount of the rebate.

The total SBAs available by reference to the qualifying expenditure incurred by the person is limited to:

- the amount of qualifying expenditure (including the amount of any additional VAT liability treated as qualifying expenditure under s. 270GB, per **24.9.2** above); less
- the amount of any additional VAT rebate.

HMRC example (pre-dating increase to 3%)

Bob constructs a workshop for £250,000 plus £50,000 VAT. He brings it into use immediately and claims SBA. He is restricted to recovery of 50% of the VAT he is charged so the SBA qualifying expenditure is £250,000 + £25,000 = £275,000. The annual SBA is £275,000 × 2% = £5,500. In year six he changes the use of the workshop and accrues an additional VAT rebate of £2,500. His SBA qualifying expenditure then becomes £275,000 – £2,500 = £272,500 and the SBA given for this and future chargeable periods is £272,500 × 2% = £5,450. After 49 years the total SBA given will be (£5,500 × 5) + (£5,450 × 44) = £267,300 and the maximum SBA claimable in year 50 will be £272,500 – £267,300 = £5,200.

Law: CAA 2001, s. 270GC
Guidance: CA 94580

24.10   Capital gains

24.10.1 General principle

For the purposes of calculating any capital gain, whether liable to CGT or to corporation tax, the allowable cost of the asset will be reduced by the amount of relief the vendor has claimed.

This is an important distinction from the way the rules operate where plant and machinery allowances are claimed, where TCGA 1992, s. 41 specifically ensures that a capital gain is not increased by virtue of the fact that allowances have been claimed (though a capital loss may be restricted).

This interaction with the rules for chargeable gains does need careful consideration. Claiming the SBA will clearly offer a cash flow advantage and if the property or structure is held for many years then that advantage may be considerable. In the end, though, much of the benefit may be undone when the property comes to be sold, in terms of a higher CGT or corporation tax bill (see the example at **24.5.8** above).

The vendor of a property does ultimately have some control over the tax treatment of fixtures that are sold, and will typically insist on a fixtures election with such figures as ensure that tax relief that has already been enjoyed is not clawed back at the point of sale. This element of control is missing from the SBA rules, and the best the vendor can hope for is that it will be possible to roll the capital gain over under TCGA 1992, s. 152, thus at least postponing (in some cases indefinitely) the capital gain. However, rollover relief is of limited application, and many commercial property owners will not be able to claim.

This distinction between the two capital allowances regimes underscores the need to ensure that qualifying expenditure on fixtures (including integral features – see, generally, **Chapters 10 to 14** above) is subject to a claim under the plant and machinery code rather than simply claiming everything under the SBA rules, which – as explained at **24.5.8** above – is in any case not permitted as an alternative approach.

Law: TCGA 1992, s. 37B, 39(3B), 41(4A)

24.10.2 *Other CGT considerations*

The SBA rules interact with the provisions for computing capital gains in other ways as well. In particular:

- Negligible value claims (TCGA 1992, s. 24) are modified in relation to certain leasehold interests where a person is entitled to claim SBAs (but with an option to elect to disapply the special rules).

- Contribution allowances (see, generally, **31.3** below) are in certain circumstances modified so as to create a deemed loss for the contributor (see TCGA 1992, s. 24A).

- As noted at **24.10.1** above, the capital gain is in principle increased where there has been an SBA claim. Where the gain is deferred (e.g. where the no gain / no loss provisions apply), the legislation ensures that the higher capital gain is nevertheless retained for a future disposal (TCGA 1992, s. 37B(3)).

- Where a long lease is sold, and the parties are connected, expenditure qualifying for SBAs is not included in the base cost (TCGA 1992, s. 39A).

- The CoACS rules (see **24.12** below) are modified to ensure that the restriction in s. 37B (see **24.10.1** above) is applied where an investor in a CoACS (or in an offshore transparent fund) disposes of units in the fund (see also **24.12** below).

24.11 Anti-avoidance

Some fairly standard anti-avoidance rules are included to counter transactions involving "avoidance arrangements", as widely defined.

The legislation requires the making of "such adjustments as are just and reasonable" and makes it clear that such adjustments may affect "persons other than the person in relation to whom the tax advantage is counteracted". So, for example, an inflated claim by one owner could have an impact on a later owner. This is something that needs to be watched in connection with CPSEs (see **12.11**) when a property is being bought, seeking reassurances that there are no skeletons in the cupboard and/or gaining an indemnity from the vendor.

One example given by HMRC is of a contract that was entered into before 29 October 2018, but then rescinded so that a new contract could qualify for SBAs.

It would appear that one of the just and reasonable adjustments that could be made in these circumstances would be the imposition of a balancing charge, even though that concept does not normally exist for SBA purposes.

See also **24.3.2** regarding anti-avoidance measures that seek to ensure that allowances are not given for a project that was already underway before the SBA rules were brought into effect. And see **24.5.7** regarding values that are not true market values.

Law: CAA 2001, s. 270IB; FA 2019, s. 30(8)(b)
Guidance: CA 94810

24.12 CoACS

24.12.1 Introduction

The concept of the co-ownership authorised contractual scheme (CoACS) is explained at **1.12.5** above. The following paragraphs give a brief overview of how the SBA rules are applied to such schemes.

For SBA purposes, each participant in such a scheme is treated as carrying on the qualifying activity, but only to the extent that the profits or gains arising to the participant from the activity are chargeable to tax (or would be, if there were any).

Law: CAA 2001, s. 270IC

24.12.2 Election

In specified circumstances, the operator of the CoACS may make an election, which will have effect for the first and all future accounting periods. The election is irrevocable (but see s. 262AEA regarding withdrawal of an election under s. 262AB).

Various assumptions are then applied in calculating the amount of the allowances that are due. The operator of the CoACS must then allocate to each participant in the scheme a proportion of the allowances calculated on those assumptions, allocating on a just and reasonable basis.

Law: CAA 2001, s. 270ID, 270IE

24.12.3 Definitions

Definitions applying for the purposes of sections 262AA to 262AF (see, generally, **1.12.5**) are similarly applied for SBA purposes.

Law: CAA 2001, s. 270IF

24.13 Leases

24.13.1 Definitions

For SBA purposes, a lease is defined to include any tenancy and also an agreement for a lease if the term to be covered by the lease has already begun. It does not include a mortgage.

In the case of land outside the UK, a lease includes an interest corresponding to a lease.

In the application of the SBA rules to Scotland:

- a leasehold interest (or leasehold estate) is defined to mean the interest of a tenant in property subject to a lease; and
- a reference to an interest that is reversionary on a leasehold interest or on a lease is read as a reference to the interest of the landlord in the property subject to the leasehold interest or lease.

Law: CAA 2001, s. 270IH

24.13.2 Principles

The following principles apply in relation to the treatment of leases for SBA purposes.

The starting point is that both lessor and lessee may claim for their respective qualifying expenditure, as long as each is carrying on a qualifying activity. Typically the landlord will have a property investment business and the tenant may be carrying on a trade or profession from the property.

The same principles apply to the sale (assignment) of a leasehold interest, as they do to the sale of a freehold interest.

A lease is treated as continuing if it is renewed, extended or replaced.

If a lease is terminated and, with the consent of the lessor, the lessee of a building remains in possession of the building after the termination but without a new lease being granted to the lessee, the lease is treated as continuing so long as the lessee remains in possession.

If, on the termination of a lease, a new lease is granted to the lessee as a result of the exercise of an option available to the lessee under the terms of the first lease, the second lease is treated as a continuation of the first.

If on the termination of a lease, the lessor pays a sum to the lessee in respect of a building comprised in the lease, the lease is treated as if it had come to an end by surrender in consideration of the payment.

It may be that, on the termination of a lease, another lease is granted to a different lessee, and – in connection with the transaction – that second lessee pays a sum to the person who was the lessee under the first lease. In this case, the two leases are treated as if they were the same lease, assigned by the first lessee to the second lessee in consideration of the payment.

Law: CAA 2001, s. 270IG

24.14 Freeport tax sites

24.14.1 Introduction and overview

The general background to freeport tax sites – including an overview of the tax benefits, and details of the requirement for such sites to be designated by regulations – is given at **1.14** above.

This section focuses solely on the enhanced SBAs that are available for certain freeport qualifying expenditure. Where the conditions are met, allowances are given at 10% per year rather than at 3%.

24.14.2 Conditions

To attract enhanced SBAs, qualifying expenditure incurred on the construction or acquisition of a building or structure must be "freeport qualifying expenditure". This requires all of the following conditions to be met:

- The construction of the building (or structure) must begin at a time when the area in which the building is situated is a freeport tax site (Condition A – see **24.14.3**).

- The building must first be brought into qualifying use by the person entitled to the SBA at a time when the area in which it is situated is a freeport tax site, and in any case on or before 30 September 2026 (Condition B – see **24.14.4**).

- The qualifying expenditure must also be incurred within that time and before that date (Condition C).

- The person incurring the qualifying expenditure must be within the charge to either income tax or corporation tax at the time the expenditure is incurred (Condition D). (Note that this differs from the freeport first-year allowances for plant and machinery expenditure, which are available only for companies within the charge to corporation tax – see **5.12**.)

- An allowance statement must state that the person wants the expenditure to be freeport qualifying expenditure (Condition E). The statement must be:

    - made for the purposes of s. 270IA (the allowance statement requirement – see **24.2.2**) by the person who incurred the qualifying expenditure; and

    - relied on for the purposes of the first valid SBA claim for that expenditure.

These rules are "subject to regulations". In other words, they may be varied without the need for further primary legislation.

Law: CAA 2001, s. 270BNA

24.14.3 *Timing of construction*

As noted above, the construction must begin at a time when the area in which the building is situated is a freeport tax site.

For this purpose only, the construction is treated as beginning when the first contract for works to be carried out in the course of the construction of the building or structure is entered into (whether or not the contract also relates to the construction of other buildings or structures).

Law: CAA 2001, s. 270BNA(7)

24.14.4 *Apportionment*

A building or structure may be situated only partly within a freeport tax site. An adjustment to the SBAs available at the 10% rate is required if this is the case at the later of:

- the day on which the building or structure is first brought into non-residential use; and

- the day on which the qualifying expenditure is incurred.

In these circumstances, an apportionment must be made on a just and reasonable basis, so that only an appropriate amount will be treated as freeport qualifying expenditure.

A just and reasonable apportionment will also be required, in the future, if the building is first brought into qualifying use by the person entitled to the SBA partly by 30 September 2026 and partly after that date.

Law: CAA 2001, s. 270BNB

25. Mineral extraction allowances

25.1 Introduction

25.1.1 Overview

Mineral extraction allowances (MEAs) are given for certain capital expenditure that is incurred in connection with mineral extraction. Those claiming include companies working in the oil industry, but also businesses involved with the extraction of minerals such as gravel and sand.

Certain first-year allowances are available on a restricted basis, but the standard rate of annual writing-down allowance is 10% for expenditure on acquiring a mineral asset and 25% for other qualifying expenditure, in each case on a reducing balance basis.

There is (strictly speaking) no concept of "pooling" of assets, so allowances are claimed separately for each qualifying asset. In practice, HMRC accept a grouping of assets provided that individual sources are dealt with separately and expenditure qualifying at different rates is segregated. However, this may cause problems when calculating balancing adjustments.

In more technical terms, allowances are given if a person carrying on a "mineral extraction trade" incurs "qualifying expenditure".

Changes from April 2014

Finance Act 2014 introduced some important changes to the regime for mineral extraction allowances "to confirm the treatment of MEAs where the mineral extraction activity enters or ceases to be within the charge to UK tax". The text of this chapter has been updated accordingly, and should therefore be read as applying only for claims made from 1 or 6 April 2014 (for corporation tax or income tax respectively).

The effect of these changes was summarised in the *Explanatory Notes* to the Finance Bill as follows:

- to confirm that for the purposes of MEAs a mineral extraction trade consists of an activity that is within the charge to UK tax;
- to confirm that the activity of an exempt FPE is treated as a separate mineral extraction trade for the purposes of MEAs;

- to align the treatment of MEAs with the existing principles for plant and machinery allowances; and,
- to confirm that notional allowances will be given automatically in calculating the profits or losses of the exempt FPE as if the exempt FPE were within the charge to UK tax.

Key definitions

The term "mineral extraction trade" is defined to mean a trade that consists of, or includes, the working of a source of mineral deposits, but to the extent only that the profits or gains from that trade are, or (if there were any) would be, chargeable to tax.

"Mineral deposits" are defined to include "any natural deposits capable of being lifted or extracted from the earth", but the deposits must be of a wasting nature.

Geothermal energy is treated for these purposes as a natural deposit.

A "source of mineral deposits" is defined to include "a mine, an oil well and a source of geothermal energy".

Law: CAA 2001, s. 394
Guidance: CA 50410

25.1.2   Mineral exploration and access

This concept is defined to mean:

- searching for or discovering and testing the mineral deposits of a source; or
- winning access to such deposits.

Expenditure on seeking planning permission necessary to enable:

- mineral exploration and access to be undertaken at any place; or
- any mineral deposits to be worked,

is treated as expenditure on mineral exploration and access. Until the passing of FA 2014, this was only the case if planning permission was not granted. That condition has been relaxed and the costs of seeking planning permission are therefore now routinely treated as expenditure on mineral exploration and access rather than as part of the cost of acquiring a mineral asset.

For these purposes, the concept of "seeking planning permission" is defined to include the pursuance of an appeal against a refusal to grant permission.

HMRC explain that expenditure on successful planning permission falls within s. 397: see **25.1.3** below.

According to HMRC:

> "The terms of the planning permission or licence to exploit a mineral deposit will normally require the mine operator to undertake a range of work to make the land fit for future use once the mining operations have ceased. This 'restoration expenditure' is part of the costs of acquiring the rights to the mineral deposits and is qualifying expenditure within s. 395(1)(b)".

Law: CAA 2001, s. 396
Guidance: CA 50220, 50300

25.1.3   *Mineral asset*

This term is defined to mean any mineral deposits or land comprising mineral deposits, or any interest in or right over such deposits or land.

This, however, is subject to an important proviso, explained by HMRC in these terms:

> "The effect of s. 407 is to strip out any expenditure that represents the value of the land disregarding the presence of the minerals. Therefore only the proportion of expenditure attributable to the mineral content of the land is qualifying expenditure."

Expenditure on the acquisition of (or of rights over) mineral deposits (or the site of a source of such deposits) is treated as expenditure on acquiring a mineral asset and not as expenditure on mineral exploration and access. This, however, is subject to the particular provisions concerning second-hand assets. It is also subject to different treatment of planning permission costs (whether or not successful): see **25.1.2** above.

Law: CAA 2001, s. 397, 398
Guidance: CA 50330

25.1.4   *Excluded expenditure*

Expenditure on the following is specifically excluded from being qualifying expenditure:

- the provision of plant or machinery except as provided by s. 402 (pre-trading expenditure on plant or machinery: see **25.2.2**).

- works constructed wholly or mainly for subjecting the raw product of a source to any process, unless the process is designed for preparing the raw product for use as such.

- expenditure on buildings or structures provided for occupation by, or for the welfare of, workers, except as provided by s. 415.

- expenditure on a building if the whole of the building was constructed for use as an office.

If part of a building or structure has been constructed for use as an office, expenditure on the office part is not qualifying expenditure unless it is 10% or less of the capital expenditure incurred on the whole building.

Expenditure incurred by a person for the purposes of a mineral extraction trade is not qualifying expenditure:

- if, when the expenditure is incurred, the person is carrying on the trade but the trade is not at that time a mineral extraction trade; or

- if the person has not begun to carry on the trade when the expenditure is incurred and, when the person begins to carry on the trade, the trade is not a mineral extraction trade.

For these purposes, the concept of commencement of trade is considered without applying the special rules of s. 577(2).

Law: CAA 2001, s. 399
Guidance: CA 50320

25.2   Qualifying expenditure

25.2.1   Overview

The legislation lists four categories of qualifying expenditure:

- expenditure on mineral exploration and access (see **25.2.2**);
- expenditure on acquiring a mineral asset (see **25.2.3**);
- expenditure on certain second-hand assets (see **25.2.4**);

- expenditure on certain works that are likely to become valueless (see **25.2.6**) or on specified restoration costs (see **25.2.8**);

However, this is subject to the rules regarding excluded expenditure (see **25.1.4**). In the case of second-hand assets, certain restrictions apply to limit the amount of qualifying expenditure.

HMRC list the following types of qualifying expenditure:

- the acquisition of mineral deposits and rights;
- exploration and development expenditure;
- restoration costs;
- certain pre-trading expenditure;
- planning permission.

Law: CAA 2001, s. 395
Guidance: CA 50210

25.2.2 Mineral exploration and access

Capital expenditure on mineral exploration and access is qualifying expenditure if it is incurred for the purposes of a mineral extraction trade.

Such expenditure incurred by a person in connection with a mineral extraction trade which that person carries on (then or subsequently) is treated as incurred for the purposes of that trade.

Pre-trading expenditure: general principles

Pre-trading expenditure only qualifies if it meets the conditions specified in s. 401 ("pre-trading exploration expenditure") or s. 402 ("pre-trading expenditure on plant or machinery").

Any pre-trading expenditure qualifying under those provisions is treated as incurred on the first day of trading. For these purposes, pre-trading expenditure means capital expenditure incurred before the day on which the person begins to carry on the mineral extraction trade.

Pre-trading exploration expenditure

These rules apply if a person incurs pre-trading expenditure on mineral exploration and access at a source, and the expenditure is not on plant or machinery.

The amount of the expenditure that is qualifying depends on whether mineral exploration and access is continuing at the source on the first day of trading. If so, the amount of qualifying expenditure is the figure by which it exceeds any "relevant receipts" (see below). If it is not, expenditure only qualifies to the extent that it exceeds any relevant receipts and is incurred in the period of six years ending on the first day of trading.

For these purposes, relevant receipts are capital sums received before the first day of trading by the person who incurred the pre-trading expenditure, so far as reasonably attributable to that expenditure.

Pre-trading expenditure on plant or machinery

These rules apply if a person incurs pre-trading expenditure on the provision of mineral exploration and access at a source and, before the first day of trading, the plant or machinery is sold, demolished, destroyed or abandoned.

Once more, the amount of the expenditure that is qualifying depends on whether mineral exploration and access is continuing at the source on the first day of trading. If so, the amount of qualifying expenditure on the plant or machinery is the figure by which it exceeds any "relevant receipts" (defined differently in this case: see below). If it is not, expenditure on the plant or machinery only qualifies to the extent that it exceeds any relevant receipts and is incurred in the period of six years ending on the first day of trading.

In this case, the amount of the relevant receipts depends on the fate of the plant or machinery. If it has been sold, then the figure is the net proceeds of the sale. If it has been demolished or destroyed, the figure to use is the net amount received for the remains of the plant or machinery, together with any associated insurance money received and any further capital sums received by way of compensation. If the plant or machinery has been abandoned, it is again necessary to take into account insurance proceeds and other capital sums received as compensation.

A balancing allowance may be due in these circumstances: see **25.3.5**.

Expenditure on plant or machinery does not qualify for mineral extraction allowances in any other circumstances.

Law: CAA 2001, s. 399(1), 400, 401, 402

25.2.3 Acquiring a mineral asset

Capital expenditure on acquiring a mineral asset is qualifying expenditure if it is incurred for the purposes of a mineral extraction trade.

This is, however, subject to two restrictions:

- a restriction is imposed in relation to the undeveloped market value of land; and
- a reduction is imposed where premium relief has previously been allowed.

Undeveloped market value

A mineral asset may be an interest in land. However, allowances are not available to the extent that the buyer's expenditure on acquiring the interest is equal to the undeveloped market value.

The concept of the undeveloped market value is defined to mean the amount that (at the time of acquisition) the interest might reasonably be expected to fetch in an open market sale on the assumption that:

- there is no source of mineral deposits on or in the land, and
- it will only ever be lawful to carry out "existing permitted development".

For these purposes, development is existing permitted development if, at the time of the acquisition, it has been (or had begun to be) lawfully carried out, or it could be lawfully carried out under planning permission granted by a general development order. This is subject to the following:

- the rules are adapted for land outside the UK;
- references to the time of acquisition are interpreted without reference to the rules relating to pre-trading expenditure;
- the provisions regarding undeveloped market value do not apply to the buyer's expenditure if an election has been made under s. 569 (election to treat sale as being for alternative amount: see **32.7.3**).

Premium relief

A person may qualify for allowances in respect of land for which income tax or corporation tax relief has previously been given for part of a chargeable premium, (i.e. under ITTOIA 2005 or CTA 2009). In such a case, the allowances due are reduced to reflect the former deduction.

The legislation uses the formula D x (E/T) where:

> **D** is the total amount of deductions made under ITTOIA 2005, s. 60-67 or CTA 2009, s. 62-67;
>
> **E** is the amount of capital expenditure that would have qualified for mineral extraction allowances if the buyer had been entitled to allowances in the earlier chargeable periods; and
>
> **T** is the total capital expenditure incurred on acquiring the interest in the land.

Cessation of use

Allowances may be available if the buildings or structures cease permanently to be used for any purpose at a later date. Allowances are given at that later time, after deducting any allowances already given to the claimant for them under any part of the capital allowances regime except for the assured tenancy rules.

The legislation uses the formula V – (A – B) where:

> **V** is the value of the buildings or structures at the date of the acquisition (disregarding any value properly attributable to the land on which they stand);
>
> **A** is the amount of any other capital allowances made to the buyer (excluding assured tenancy allowances); and
>
> **B** is the amount of any balancing charges made on the buyer, in respect of those buildings or structures or assets in them, under the provisions governing those other allowances.

References to the time of acquisition are interpreted without reference to the rules relating to pre-trading expenditure.

Law: CAA 2001, s. 403, 404, 405, 406

25.2.4   Second-hand assets

Special rules apply where a person carrying on a trade of mineral extraction acquires an asset, and part of the value is attributable to expenditure on exploration and access incurred prior to his acquisition.

The statutory provisions allow for part of the expenditure to be relieved at 25% with the balance at 10%. The HMRC summary of the complex statutory wording is as follows:

> "The expenditure which is treated as attracting the 25% rate is the smaller of:
>
> - the amount of the buyer's expenditure corresponding to the part of the value of the asset attributable to the previous trader's expenditure on mineral exploration and access, and
> - the previous trader's expenditure on mineral exploration and access attributable to the asset acquired by the buyer.
>
> The balance of the purchaser's qualifying expenditure qualifies at the 10% writing down allowance rate."

Equivalent rules apply if assets are acquired from non-traders, to impose a restriction on the amount treated as expenditure on mineral exploration and access attracting the higher 25% rate of writing-down allowances. In HMRC's words:

> "The limit is the amount of the expenditure incurred by the seller on mineral exploration and access in so far as the asset acquired represents that expenditure.
>
> The balance of the acquisition cost qualifies at the 10% writing down allowance rate."

Law: CAA 2001, s. 407, 408, 409
Guidance: CA 50640, 50650

25.2.5 *Restriction re historic costs*

Oil licences

Special provisions apply where a buyer carrying on a mineral extraction trade incurs capital expenditure on acquiring an interest in an oil licence (or on acquiring a mineral asset that is a UK oil licence) for the purposes of that trade.

Law: CAA 2001, s. 410

Restriction to residue of qualifying expenditure

If the previous trader was entitled to an allowance (or liable to a balancing charge) then it is necessary to cap the buyer's qualifying expenditure by reference to that previous trader's residue of expenditure (qualifying expenditure, minus net allowances made to the previous buyer after adjusting for balancing charges). The "previous trader" for these purposes is the last person to have incurred expenditure on acquiring (or bringing into existence) the asset in connection with a mineral extraction trade he was carrying on.

Law: CAA 2001, s. 411

Transfers within group

A mineral asset may be transferred between companies under common control. In this case, the transferee's qualifying expenditure is capped at the level of expenditure incurred by the transferor. This is subject to any election under s. 569: see **32.7.3**. The rules do not apply if s. 410 (above) applies re oil licences.

If the asset transferred is a right or an interest (e.g. a lease created out of the freehold) then a just and reasonable apportionment must normally be made.

If the "undeveloped market value" provisions apply, and the transferee company is carrying on a trade of mineral extraction, the reference to the time of acquisition of the interest is read as meaning the time at which the transferor (or first transferor) acquired it. In defined circumstances, the latest transferee is deemed to have incurred qualifying expenditure on the value of buildings or structures.

For these purposes, a company is a group company in relation to another if one controls the other or if both are under common control.

Law: CAA 2001, s. 412, 413

25.2.6   Works likely to become valueless

Capital expenditure incurred for the purposes of a mineral extraction trade is deemed to be qualifying expenditure if:

- it is incurred on constructing works in connection with the working of a source of mineral deposits; and

- *either* the works are likely to be of little or no value to the last person working the source when the source ceases to be worked;
- *or* the source is worked under a foreign concession and the works are likely to become valueless when the concession ends.

The concept of expenditure on "constructing works" does not include expenditure on acquiring the site of the works or any right in or over the site. According to HMRC, "works" can include railway lines, roads and jetties at the site of mineral extraction. HMRC have also given the following commentary:

> "The costs of gaining access to a deep mine via a shaft are capital, until the target mineral is reached, and fall within mineral exploration and access. Once the target mineral is reached the costs of extracting it are generally revenue.
>
> For an open cast mine, before the deposit can be worked, the operator must win access to the minerals by removing any soil overburden and making the 'first cut' through any layers of rock to reach the target minerals. These costs are part of the capital costs of exploration and access. Subsequent cuts are regarded as revenue and part of working the mineral. Land acquired simply to provide road access to the mineral bearing deposit does not qualify."

A foreign concession is defined to mean any right or privilege granted by the government of, or any municipality or other authority in, a territory outside the UK.

Law: CAA 2001, s. 414
Guidance: CA 50230

25.2.7 *Benefit for overseas employees*

Relief is available for certain infrastructure works and employee welfare facilities. More specifically, expenditure is qualifying expenditure if all of the following conditions are met:

- the expenditure is incurred by a person carrying on a mineral extraction trade outside the UK, for the purposes of that trade;
- it is a contribution consisting of a capital sum to the cost of specified buildings or works (see below);

- the buildings or works are likely to be of little or no value, when the source is no longer worked, to the last person working the source;

- the person does not acquire any asset as a result of the expenditure;

- the person is not entitled to any other tax allowance for the expenditure.

The following types of buildings and works qualify for these purposes:

- buildings to be occupied by people employed at or in connection with the working of a source outside the UK;

- works for the supply of water, gas or electricity wholly or mainly to buildings occupied or to be occupied by such employees;

- works used to provide other services or facilities wholly or mainly for the welfare of such employees or of their dependants.

Law: CAA 2001, s. 415
Guidance: CA 50290

25.2.8   Restoration after cessation of trade

Expenditure on restoration of a site is treated as qualifying expenditure where certain conditions are met. The amount of the qualifying expenditure is the "net cost of restoration" after deducting specified receipts. Such expenditure is treated as incurred on the final day of trading, and is therefore relieved in full as a balancing allowance.

For these purposes, restoration includes landscaping. It also includes works required as a condition of granting planning permission for development consisting of the winning and working of minerals. In relation to land outside the UK, this is applied on the basis of equivalent conditions.

The conditions for the expenditure to qualify are as follows:

- a person has ceased to carry on a mineral extraction trade;

- that person incurs expenditure on the restoration of the site of a source used for the mineral extraction trade (or last used in connection with working such a source);

- the expenditure is incurred within three years from the last day of trading;

533

- the expenditure has not been claimed as a tax deduction in calculating the taxable profits of any trade carried on by that person;
- the expenditure would have qualified for tax relief in calculating trading profits, or by way of mineral extraction allowances, if it had been incurred before the cessation of the trade.

If expenditure qualifies under this provision the whole of the restoration cost (not just the net cost) is disallowed in calculating the person's income for all tax purposes. Conversely, none of the amounts subtracted to produce the net cost is taxable as income.

The net cost of restoration is defined to mean expenditure incurred on restoration costs, less any amounts that are received within three years from the last day of trading and that are attributable to the restoration of the site. This might include, for example, amounts received for spoil or for other assets that are removed from the site, or amounts received for tipping rights.

If an operator permanently ceases to work a particular mineral deposit, but the trade continues, a balancing allowance will normally be due: see **25.3.5**.

Law: CAA 2001, s. 416
Guidance: CA 50280

25.3 Allowances and charges

25.3.1 First-year allowances

FYAs are available only for expenditure incurred wholly for the purposes of a ring-fence trade. Various rules and conditions apply.

Law: CAA 2001, s. 416A-416E

25.3.2 Other allowances and charges

Other than for FYAs, the amount of any allowance or charge is calculated by comparing unrelieved qualifying expenditure ("UQE" – see **25.3.3**) with the total of any disposal receipts that have to be brought into account for that period ("TDR" – see **25.3.4**).

If TDR exceeds UQE, the person is liable to a balancing charge of the excess for that period. However, this is capped at a figure calculated as all allowances for earlier chargeable periods in respect of the expenditure less the total of any balancing charges for those periods in respect of the expenditure.

If UQE exceeds TDR, the person is entitled to a writing-down allowance or, as the case may be (see **25.3.5**) to a balancing allowance.

Companies that migrate to the UK cannot claim allowances for mineral extraction expenditure incurred while the company was outside the scope of corporation tax.

Calculation of writing-down allowances

WDAs are normally given at either 10 or 25% of the amount by which UQE exceeds TDR. The lower percentage applies for qualifying expenditure on the acquisition of a mineral asset and the higher figure for all other qualifying expenditure. (For the avoidance of doubt, these figures are not affected by the changes that reduced the rate of WDAs for plant and machinery.)

The amount of WDA is increased or reduced proportionately if the chargeable period is longer or shorter than one year. It is also proportionately reduced if the mineral extraction trade has been carried on for only a part of the chargeable period.

The amount of the balancing allowance to which a person is entitled is the excess of UQE over TDR.

A person may claim a lower amount of WDA or a lower balancing allowance for any period.

Law: CAA 2001, s. 417, 418
Guidance: OT 26300

25.3.3   Unrelieved qualifying expenditure

A person's unrelieved qualifying expenditure is, for the year in which it is incurred, the whole amount of the qualifying expenditure.

For any later period, it is necessary to deduct any allowances made in respect of the expenditure for earlier chargeable periods, and also the total of any disposal receipts for those earlier periods.

The above is subject to special rules that apply where first-year allowances have been available.

Special rules also apply to a person entering the cash basis. That person's unrelieved qualifying expenditure for the chargeable period ending with the basis period in the tax year that he enters the cash basis will only be the non-cash basis deductible portion of his qualifying expenditure incurred before this chargeable period.

Law: CAA 2001, s. 419, 419A
Guidance: OT 21250

25.3.4   Disposal values and receipts

A disposal receipt is defined to mean a disposal value that a person is required to bring into account in accordance with any of the following provisions:

- CAA 2001, s. 421-425 (considered under the headings below);
- ITA 2007, s. 614BS;
- CTA 2010, s. 918; or
- any other enactment.

The ITA and CTA provisions are concerned with a potential clawback of a major lump sum.

Law: CAA 2001, s. 420

Disposal of (or cessation of use of) an asset

A person must bring into account a disposal value if he has incurred qualifying expenditure on providing assets and if any of those assets is subsequently disposed of, or if it ceases permanently to be used by him for the purposes of a mineral extraction trade (for whatever reason).

The disposal value must be brought in for the chargeable period in which the disposal or cessation occurs.

Law: CAA 2001, s. 421

Use for non-allowable purposes

A person must bring into account a disposal value if he has acquired a mineral asset and if the asset subsequently starts to be used in a way that constitutes development (except as below). It does not matter if the use is by the same or a different person.

No disposal value is brought into account if the development is for the purposes of a mineral extraction trade carried on by the person, or if it is "existing permitted development". Development is within that category if it has been (or had begun to be) lawfully carried out, or if it could be lawfully carried out under planning permission granted by a general development order. The rules are applied with suitable modifications if the land is outside the UK.

Law: CAA 2001, s. 422

Guidance: CA 50430

Disposal values

For the purposes of sections 421 and 422 above, the following disposal values apply.

The disposal value cannot, however, exceed the expenditure on the given asset, but the excess may give rise to a chargeable gain. Any computation of a gain will reflect the undeveloped market value that is excluded from the computation of mineral extraction allowances.

	Event	**Disposal value**
1.	Sale of the asset, except in a case where item 2 applies.	The net proceeds of the sale, together with– (a) any insurance money received in respect of the asset as a result of an event affecting the price obtainable on the sale, and (b) any other compensation of any description so received, so far as it consists of capital sums.
	Sale of the asset where– (a) the sale is at less than market value, (b) there is no charge to tax under ITEPA 2003, and (c) the condition in subsection (4) [see note below] is met by the buyer.	The market value of the asset at the time of the sale.

		Event	Disposal value
3.		Demolition or destruction of the asset.	The net amount received for the remains of the asset, together with– (a) any insurance money received in respect of the demolition or destruction, and (b) any other compensation of any description so received, so far as it consists of capital sums.
4.		Permanent loss of the asset otherwise than as a result of its demolition or destruction.	Any insurance money received in respect of the loss and, so far as it consists of capital sums, any other compensation of any description so received.
5.		Permanent discontinuance of the trade followed by the occurrence of an event within any of items 1 to 4.	The disposal value for the item in question.
6.		Any event not falling within any of items 1 to 5.	The market value of the asset at the time of the event.

The condition referred to in item 2 is met by the buyer if his expenditure on the acquisition of the asset cannot be qualifying expenditure for the purposes of claiming plant and machinery or research and development allowances, or the buyer is a dual resident investing company connected with the seller.

Law: CAA 2001, s. 423
Guidance: CA 50440

Interest in land

If the asset in question is land, the disposal value is restricted by excluding the "undeveloped market value of the interest". This term is defined to mean that the amount that the interest might (at the time of the disposal) reasonably be expected to fetch on a sale in the open market. In applying this test it is assumed that:

- there is no source of mineral deposits on or in the land; and

- it will only ever be lawful to carry out "existing permitted development".

Development is within the latter category if, at the time of the disposal, it has been (or had begun to be) lawfully carried out, or if it could be lawfully carried out under planning permission granted by a general development order. The rules are applied with suitable modifications if the land is outside the UK.

Law: CAA 2001, s. 424

Receipt of a capital sum

A person must bring into account a disposal value if he has incurred qualifying expenditure and if he receives a capital sum which (in whole or in part) can reasonably be attributed to that expenditure, and which is not already brought into account under sections 421 or 422 (see above).

The disposal value to bring into account is so much of the capital sum as is reasonably attributable to the qualifying expenditure.

Law: CAA 2001, s. 425

25.3.5   Entitlement to balancing allowance

As noted at **25.3.2** above, a person may be entitled to a writing-down allowance (WDA) or to a balancing allowance, and rules are needed to determine which type of allowance is given when. Those rules are as follows.

Pre-trading expenditure

A person's entitlement for the chargeable period in which trading begins is to a balancing allowance (rather than a WDA) if the expenditure is qualifying pre-trading expenditure under s. 401 or 402 (see **25.2.2**). Such expenditure is therefore relieved in full on the commencement of trade, rather than being written down over a period of time.

Law: CAA 2001, s. 426
Guidance: CA 50240

Giving up exploration, etc.

A person's entitlement for a chargeable period is to a balancing allowance (rather than a WDA) if the qualifying expenditure is incurred on mineral exploration and access and if:

- he gives up the exploration, search or inquiry to which the expenditure related in that chargeable period; and
- he does not subsequently carry on a mineral extraction trade consisting of or including the working of mineral deposits to which the expenditure related.

Law: CAA 2001, s. 427

Ceasing to work mineral deposits

A person's entitlement for a chargeable period is to a balancing allowance (rather than a WDA) if:

- he permanently ceases to work particular mineral deposits in that chargeable period; and
- the qualifying expenditure is incurred on mineral exploration and access relating solely to those deposits, or on acquiring a mineral asset consisting of (or of part of) those deposits.

If the person is entitled to two or more mineral assets that at any time were comprised in (or otherwise derived from) a single mineral asset, the rule applies only when he permanently ceases to work the deposits comprised in all those mineral assets taken together. For these purposes, if a mineral asset relates to, but does not actually consist of, mineral deposits, the deposits to which the asset relates are treated as comprised in the asset.

Law: CAA 2001, s. 428

Buildings for employees abroad

A person's entitlement for a chargeable period is to a balancing allowance (rather than a WDA) if:

- the expenditure is qualifying expenditure under s. 415 (contributions to buildings or works for benefit of employees abroad: see **25.2.7**), and
- the buildings or works permanently cease, in that period, to be used for the purposes of (or in connection with) the mineral extraction trade.

Law: CAA 2001, s. 429

Disposal of asset, etc.

A person's entitlement for a chargeable period is to a balancing allowance (rather than a WDA) if:

- the qualifying expenditure was incurred on the provision of certain assets; and
- in that period, one or more of those assets is disposed of (or otherwise permanently ceases to be used) by him for the purposes of the mineral extraction trade.

A person's entitlement for a chargeable period is also to a balancing allowance if one of the following events occurs in that period in relation to assets that represent the qualifying expenditure:

- the person loses possession of the assets in circumstances where it is reasonable to assume that the loss is permanent;
- the assets cease to exist as such (as a result of destruction, dismantling or otherwise);
- the assets begin to be used wholly or partly for purposes other than those of the mineral extraction trade.

HMRC have given the following practical advice in relation to disposals and part disposals:

"Where part of an asset is disposed of a claim to a balancing allowance is acceptable in principle under [CAA 2001, s. 575]. This treats the retained part of the asset and the part of the asset disposed of as separate assets.

In the case of a part disposal the taxpayer may find it easier to deduct the disposal receipt from the balance of qualifying expenditure without taking the benefit of the balancing allowance. This is acceptable if the disposal is not to a mineral trader. If it is not then it is necessary to compute the seller's allowances for the part disposed of and the part retained as if each were a separate asset. This is so that the buyer's secondhand cost restriction [under CAA 2001, s. 410] can be computed.

If expenditure has been grouped together for convenience, there is no objection to the practice of deducting the disposal receipt from the balance of qualifying expenditure.

However, a separate computation in respect of individual assets will be required where there are disposals to a mineral extraction trader and it is necessary to apply the secondhand cost restriction rules in [CAA 2001, s. 410]."

Law: CAA 2001, s. 430

Guidance: CA 50470

Cessation of trade

A person's entitlement for a chargeable period is to a balancing allowance (rather than a WDA) if the mineral extraction trade is permanently discontinued in that chargeable period.

However, this is subject to a possible election under CTA 2009, s. 18A (foreign permanent establishment exemption). This allows a trade carried on through one or more permanent establishments outside the UK to be treated as a separate trade. In such cases, special rules apply with regard to disposal values and there is a system of notional allowances.

Law: CAA 2001, s. 431, 431A, 431B, 431C

25.3.6 *Giving effect to allowances and charges*

Allowances are given effect in calculating the profits of a person's mineral extraction trade by treating them as a trading expense. Balancing charges are treated as trading receipts.

Law: CAA 2001, s. 432

25.4 Other issues

25.4.1 *Demolition costs*

The net cost to a person of demolishing an asset that represents qualifying expenditure is added to that qualifying expenditure in determining the amount of any balancing allowance or balancing charge for the chargeable period in which the demolition occurs.

The net cost is the amount (if any) by which the demolition costs exceed any money received for the remains of the asset in question.

The net cost is then not treated as expenditure incurred on a replacement asset.

Law: CAA 2001, s. 433

25.4.2   *Time when expenditure incurred*

For the purposes of calculating mineral extraction allowances, expenditure incurred for the purposes of a mineral extraction trade by a person who is about to carry it on is treated as incurred on the first day of actual trading. However, this does not apply to pre-trading expenditure on mineral exploration and access as this is already covered by the pre-trading expenditure rules of s. 400(4): see **25.2.2**.

This general rule is disapplied in connection with the rules relating to the exclusion of undeveloped market value of land (s. 404(6)) and those relating to cessation of use of buildings or structures (s. 405(4)). See, generally, **25.2.3**.

Law: CAA 2001, s. 434

25.4.3   *Shares in assets*

The MEA rules apply in relation to a share in an asset as they do (per s. 571: see **32.9.1**) to a part of an asset. For these purposes, a share in an asset is treated as used for the purposes of a trade only so far as the asset itself is used for such purposes.

Law: CAA 2001, s. 435

25.4.4   *Meaning of "development"*

The terms "development", "development order", "general development order" and "planning permission" have the meaning given by the respective Planning Acts in relation to England and Wales, Scotland, and Northern Ireland.

Law: CAA 2001, s. 436

25.4.5   *Cash basis*

Special rules may apply where a person carrying on a mineral extraction trade leaves the cash basis in a given chargeable period. The rules apply if the person incurs expenditure when calculating profits on a cash basis that was deductible in calculating the profits of this trade if the expenditure would have been qualifying expenditure if the person was not using the cash basis at the time the expenditure was paid.

Broadly speaking, any amount by which the "unrelieved portion" of expenditure exceeds the "relieved portion" of expenditure is treated as qualifying expenditure incurred in the chargeable period.

The relieved portion is the higher of two figures:

- the amount of that expenditure for which a deduction was allowed in calculating the profits of the trade; or
- the amount of that expenditure for which a deduction would have been so allowed if the expenditure had been incurred wholly and exclusively for the purposes of the trade.

The unrelieved portion is then the remaining amount of the expenditure.

Law: CAA 2001, s. 431D

26. Research and development allowances

26.1 Introduction and overview

Research and development ("R&D") allowances are available if a person incurs qualifying expenditure on R&D. These allowances were formerly known as scientific research allowances.

The allowances are available only for traders. Allowances are not given to a person carrying on a profession or vocation.

Where available, allowances are given in full at the outset. If an asset is sold, demolished or destroyed a balancing charge may arise, though a change of use does not trigger such a charge.

See **26.2** below for the meaning of R&D.

See **26.3** for the definition of qualifying expenditure.

Tax relief is also due for expenditure on R&D that is not capital expenditure. The mechanics of that other relief are beyond the scope of this book.

Law: CAA 2001, s. 437
Guidance: CA 60100*ff.*

26.2 Definition of research and development

26.2.1 Statutory definition

For capital allowances purposes, the concept of research and development (R&D) is defined to cover:

- activities that fall to be treated as R&D in accordance with generally accepted accounting practice; but also
- oil and gas exploration and appraisal.

In relation to the general definition of R&D, reference should be made to the HMRC guidelines in the *Corporate Intangibles Research & Development Manual*, especially paragraph CIRD 81300. Although those guidelines are not specifically addressing capital allowances issues, the *Capital Allowances Manual* at CA 60200 specifically cross refers to them. The *CIRD Manual* in turn picks up the guidelines of the Department for Business Innovation & Skills ("BIS") (regarding which, see the "tinyurl" link below.

545

HMRC guidance is that the second bullet above covers activities carried out for the purpose of searching for petroleum or of ascertaining:

- the extent or characteristics of any petroleum bearing area; or
- the level of reserves of such an area, so that it can be determined whether the petroleum is suitable for commercial exploitation.

The above is, however, subject to the provisions of any regulations made under ITA 2007, s. 1006, so that:

- activities that, as a result of regulations made under s. 1006, are R&D for the purposes of that section are also R&D for capital allowance purposes; and
- activities that, as a result of any such regulations, are not R&D for the purposes of that section are also not R&D for capital allowance purposes.

Law: CAA 2001, s. 437; ITA 2007, s. 1006
Guidance: CA 60200; CIRD 80000*ff.*; https://tinyurl.com/ychgwbe5

26.2.2   Expenditure on R&D

Expenditure on R&D includes all expenditure incurred for:

- carrying out research and development, or
- providing facilities for carrying out research and development.

But such expenditure does *not* include expenditure incurred in the acquisition of rights in (or arising out of) R&D.

HMRC example (from CA 60300)

The Masters of Invention want to used [sic] a patented invention in their research and so they buy the patent rights. The cost of acquiring the patent rights does not qualify for RDA because it is expenditure incurred in acquiring rights arising out of research and development.

In the case of *The Partners of the Vaccine Research Ltd Partnership*, it was held that huge amounts of money purportedly constituting expenditure on R&D did not in fact constitute such expenditure. Nevertheless, a small proportion of the total was held to be qualifying expenditure. According to HMRC:

> "The taxpayers sought to inflate allowance entitlement, so as to get more than would otherwise be available, by entering into

circular finance schemes. It was found that the part of the expenditure that produced no economic activity but rather went into a loop as part of a tax avoidance scheme was not expenditure 'on' the [research and development]."

HMRC guidance states that "expenditure on R&D includes expenditure on providing facilities or assets used by employees carrying on R&D". Examples given include the cost of an expensive car, which could attract 100% allowances under the R&D rules, rather than the much more restricted plant and machinery allowances given for most cars.

HMRC accept that a trader's trade may consist of research and development, and nothing else (e.g. if a group of companies has one company to carry out all of the R&D on behalf of the group). In that case, HMRC accept that "all the assets of that company's trade are used for, or provide facilities for, research and development and so expenditure on them qualifies for RDA unless it is specifically excluded".

Case: *The Partners of the Vaccine Research Ltd Partnership & Anor v HMRC* [2014] UKUT 389 (TCC)
Guidance: CA 20060, 60300, 60400

Dwellings

In principle, expenditure on the provision of a dwelling is also excluded. However, special rules apply if a building is used mainly for R&D but a part of it is used as a dwelling. In such a case, the whole building will be treated as used for R&D as long as no more than a quarter of the capital expenditure incurred on constructing or acquiring the building was referable to the dwelling.

HMRC example (from CA 60300)

The Masters of Invention buy a building for £1 million excluding the cost of the land. It mainly consists of rooms in which research is conducted but there is a flat at the top of the building that the head of research occupies. If the cost of the flat is £100,000 then the whole of the expenditure of £1 million qualifies for RDA because £100,000 is less than one-quarter of £1 million. If, however, the cost of the flat is £300,000 only £700,000 of the expenditure of £1 million qualifies for RDA.

Any apportionment must be made in a just and reasonable manner, ignoring any additional VAT liability or rebate.

Law: CAA 2001, s. 438
Guidance: CA 60300

26.3   Qualifying expenditure

26.3.1   Definition

Qualifying expenditure for capital allowances purposes must be capital expenditure and it must be related to a trade. It may be undertaken either directly by the person carrying on the trade, or on his behalf.

If he is carrying on a trade when the expenditure is incurred, it must relate to that trade. If not, the person must set up a trade after incurring the expenditure, and the trade must be connected to the R&D. The trade, in either case, is referred to as the "relevant trade".

In *Salt v Golding*, it was held that the taxpayer had not incurred capital expenditure on scientific research related to a trade of publishing. Rather, the research related to his profession of author (for which no R&D allowances are available).

HMRC guidance is that there must be a strong link between the trader and the research:

> "You should only treat expenditure as incurred on behalf of a trader if there is a clear, close and direct link between the trader and the research undertaken. The relationship between the person claiming the allowances and the person undertaking the research need not be contractual, but if it is not it must be one of agency, or something similar to agency. The fact that research undertaken by someone else is for a trader's benefit, or is in his interest, is not enough to make the expenditure qualify for RDAs."

HMRC refer to the case of *Gaspet Ltd* in support of this view. In that case, it was held that research undertaken "on behalf of" a person had to involve an agency relationship or something akin thereto (though the relationship did not necessarily have to be on a contractual basis).

The same expenditure must not be taken into account as qualifying expenditure in relation to more than one trade.

Where capital expenditure only meets these conditions in part, it is to be apportioned in a just and reasonable manner.

The concept of R&D being related to a trade specifically includes:

- R&D that may lead to or facilitate an extension of that trade; and
- R&D of a medical nature that has a special relation to the welfare of workers employed in that trade.

In relation to this last point regarding medical research, HMRC comment as follows:

"Medical research which qualifies for RDA does not include research undertaken for the benefit of the community as a whole. However, medical research undertaken for the benefit of the community as a whole may qualify for RDA as research and development which may lead to or facilitate an extension of the trade. For example, medical research undertaken by a drug company for the purpose of its trade may qualify because it is related to its trade of manufacturing drugs."

It is worth making a brief reference here to the 2015 decision in *Hockin*. The case concerned a tax avoidance scheme in which capital allowances were claimed for expenditure on scientific research. As summarised by the tribunal, the scheme sought "to generate up-front reliefs by artificial steps that might enable capital allowances to be claimed for vastly more than the realistic amount that was actually to be spent on undertaking such research". For the great majority of claimants, the details of the case are unlikely to be of any practical interest, but suffice it to say here that the tribunal ruled in favour of HMRC. Furthermore, the view of the First-tier Tribunal was upheld by the Upper Tribunal.

See case study 5 in **Appendix 2** for an example of a claim for R&D allowances. And see **1.5.3** above for discussion of the question of when expenditure is incurred for capital allowances purposes.

See **24.7.3** and **24.7.4** for the interaction of RDAs and the relatively new structures and buildings allowance.

Law: CAA 2001, s. 439

Cases: *Gaspet Ltd v Ellis* (1987) 60 TC 91, [1987] BTC 218; *Salt v Golding* (1996) Sp C 81; *Hockin v HMRC* [2015] UKFTT 325 (TC); *The Brain Disorders Research Limited Partnership and Neil Hockin v HMRC* [2017] UKUT 176 (TCC)

Guidance: CA 60400

26.3.2   Exclusion of land

Qualifying expenditure does not include the cost of acquiring land, or rights in or over land.

This exclusion does not, however, prevent expenditure from qualifying so far as it relates to:

- a building or structure already constructed on the land;
- rights in or over such a building or structure; or
- plant or machinery forming part of such a building or structure (i.e. normally fixtures).

For these purposes, expenditure is to be apportioned in a just and reasonable manner. So if a building is bought it will be necessary to apportion the cost between the part relating to the land and the part relating to the building itself.

Law: CAA 2001, s. 440
Guidance: CA 60400

26.4 Allowances and charges

26.4.1 Allowances

The R&D regime simply has "allowances" on the one hand and balancing charges on the other. The allowances are not referred to as initial, first-year, annual or writing-down allowances.

Allowances are given at 100% of the qualifying expenditure, less any disposal values that have to be brought into account for the period in question.

In the case of pre-trading expenditure, the allowances are given for the first chargeable period in which the trade is carried on. In all other cases, allowances are given only for the chargeable period in which the expenditure is incurred. It follows that a person who fails to make a claim at the appropriate time will not be able to do so later, once the chargeable period in question is out of time for amending a return on normal self-assessment principles.

A person may claim to reduce the claimed allowance to a specified amount. The only benefit of doing this is to reduce a future balancing charge – there is no scope for claiming the allowances in a future year if they have been partly or fully disclaimed at the outset, or indeed if the claim has simply been overlooked. (The only option in such a case may be to see if part of the expenditure qualifies for other allowances – probably as plant or machinery – for which a later claim will be possible if the assets are still owned.)

Any allowances due are treated as expenses of the relevant trade, (and any balancing charges are treated as trading receipts – see below).

From April 2014, the definition of "deductible amount" for the "transfer of deductions" rules in CTA 2010 excludes a trade expense that is treated as such by virtue of s. 450a of CAA 2001, i.e. to the extent that it arises from research and development allowances under that section.

Law: CAA 2001, s. 441, 450; CTA 2010, s. 730B
Guidance: CA 60500, 60800

26.4.2   *Charges*

A balancing charge is imposed if a person is required to bring a disposal value into account for a chargeable period later than that in which the qualifying expenditure was incurred. (If it is in the same period, the disposal value will instead simply reduce the amount of the allowance.)

The balancing charge cannot exceed the allowance made in respect of the qualifying expenditure. Subject to that, the charge will be the amount by which the disposal value exceeds any unclaimed allowance.

Example 1

A company incurs qualifying expenditure of £30,000 in year one, and claims full allowances.

In year three, it has disposal proceeds for the same asset of £40,000. The balancing charge is of £30,000.

Example 2

A company incurs qualifying expenditure of £30,000 in year one, but has some losses brought forward and only claims allowances of £10,000.

In year three, it has disposal proceeds for the same asset of £24,000. There is a balancing charge of £4,000: the unclaimed allowance is £20,000 and the charge is on the excess over that figure.

The above is subject to a complication where there has been an additional VAT disposal value, as explained at **26.5** below.

Any balancing charge that is imposed is treated as a receipt of the relevant trade.

Law: CAA 2001, s. 442, 449, 450

26.4.3   *Disposal events and values*

A disposal value must normally be brought into account if a person ceases to own an asset on which qualifying expenditure has been incurred, or if the asset in question is demolished or destroyed while he still owns it. No disposal value is required, however, if the event gives rise to a balancing charge for the purposes of claiming plant and machinery allowances.

If:

- the asset is sold at not less than market value, the disposal value is the net proceeds of sale;
- the asset is demolished or destroyed, the disposal value is the net amount received for the remains of the asset, plus any related insurance or capital sums of compensation.
- neither of the above applies, the disposal value is the market value of the asset at the time of the event.

Any sale is treated as made at the time of completion or, if earlier, at the time when possession is given.

The fact that a person ceases to use an asset for research and development does not give rise to a disposal event. It is only later, when the asset is sold or destroyed, that a disposal event will arise. (This point is confirmed at CA 60600.)

This is subject to special rules regarding demolition costs (see **26.4.4** below). Different rules apply in relation to the disposal of oil licences.

A person may also be required to bring a disposal value into account under s. 448 (additional VAT rebates: see **26.5** below).

Law: CAA 2001, s. 443, 451

Chargeable period for which value to be brought into account

In practice, the disposal value is normally brought into account for the chargeable period in which the event occurs. There are, however, two special rules to deal with particular circumstances.

If the disposal event occurs *before* the chargeable period for which the allowance in respect of the expenditure is made, the disposal value is to be brought into account for that chargeable period. (This point was addressed in the *Explanatory Notes* for CAA 2001, as Change 51 in Annex 1.)

If the event occurs after the chargeable period in which the relevant trade is permanently discontinued, the disposal value must be brought into account for that period.

Law: CAA 2001, s. 444
Guidance: CA 60600

26.4.4   Demolition costs

A person may incur demolition costs in connection with an asset representing qualifying expenditure. In such a case, the disposal value is reduced by the demolition costs.

If the demolition costs exceed the disposal value, the person is treated as incurring qualifying expenditure equal to the excess. However, this does not apply if, before its demolition, the asset had begun to be used for purposes other than R&D related to the relevant trade.

Expenditure qualifying in this way is treated as incurred at the time of the demolition or, if that is on or after the date on which the relevant trade is permanently discontinued, immediately before the discontinuance. Such expenditure is not treated, for any capital allowance purposes, as expenditure on property that replaces the demolished asset.

Law: CAA 2001, s. 445

26.5   VAT liabilities and rebates

26.5.1   Introduction and terminology

Particular rules apply in respect of an "additional VAT liability" or an "additional VAT rebate".

An additional VAT liability is defined to mean "an amount which a person becomes liable to pay by way of adjustment under the VAT capital items legislation in respect of input tax".

An additional VAT rebate means "an amount which a person becomes entitled to deduct by way of adjustment under the VAT capital items legislation in respect of input tax".

The additional liability is treated as incurred, or the rebate as made, in the last day of the period:

- which is one of the periods making up the VAT period of adjustment applicable to the asset in question under the VAT capital items legislation; and

- in which the increase or decrease in use giving rise to the liability or rebate occurs.

For these purposes, a VAT period of adjustment is defined to mean "a period specified under the VAT capital items legislation by reference to which adjustments are made in respect of input tax".

The chargeable period in which, and time when, the additional liability or rebate accrues are set out in s. 549.

Law: CAA 2001, s. 446, 547, 548, 549
Guidance: CA 60750

26.5.2   VAT liability treated as additional expenditure

If a person has incurred qualifying expenditure, and subsequently incurs an additional VAT liability in respect of that original expenditure, the liability is treated as capital expenditure incurred on the same R&D as the original expenditure.

This rule does not apply, however, if by the time the VAT liability is incurred, the asset has been demolished or destroyed, or the person who incurred the original expenditure has ceased to own it.

Where such an allowance arises, the normal rule about when the allowance is given (per s. 441: see **26.4.1**) is disapplied. Instead, the allowance is available for the chargeable period in which the liability accrues. But if the liability accrues before the chargeable period in which the relevant trade is set up and commenced, the allowance is given for that chargeable period.

Law: CAA 2001, s. 447

26.5.3   Additional VAT rebate

If a person has incurred qualifying expenditure, and subsequently receives an additional VAT rebate in respect of that expenditure, the person must bring the rebate into account as a disposal value (or as an addition to the disposal value that would in any case apply) in respect of the qualifying expenditure.

The rebate is brought into account for the "appropriate chargeable period". Normally, this is the period in which the rebate accrues.

However, if (exceptionally) the rebate accrues before the chargeable period in which the relevant trade is set up and commenced, then the rebate is brought into account for that chargeable period.

Where a VAT rebate is brought into account under these rules, any future balancing charge will be restricted accordingly: see **26.5.4** below.

This rule does not apply, however, if by the time the VAT rebate is made, the asset has been demolished or destroyed, or the person who incurred the expenditure has ceased to own the asset in question.

Nor does the rule apply if the rebate has to be brought into account as a disposal value for the purposes of calculating plant and machinery allowances.

Law: CAA 2001, s. 448

26.5.4   Additional VAT rebate – effect on future balancing charge

If a VAT rebate is made on the basis described at **26.5.3** above, this has the effect of reducing the amount of the "unclaimed allowance".

It is not very easy to make immediate sense of the way this part of the legislation is worded, but the principles were explained clearly in the *Explanatory Notes* issued when CAA 2001 was originally enacted, as follows:

> "The treatment of VAT rebates as disposal values under section 448 means that ... the receipt of the VAT rebate may not lead to a balancing charge because there are unclaimed allowances under section 442(4).
>
> To the extent that an unclaimed allowance shields a disposal value in one chargeable period this section reduces, for later chargeable periods, that unclaimed allowance by the amount shielded so that relief is not obtained more than once."

Law: CAA 2001, s. 449

26.6   Sales treated as being for alternative amount

Anti-avoidance provisions, at s. 567*ff*, apply in certain circumstances where either the "control" test or the "tax advantage" test is met. Broadly, a sale of R&D assets is taken at market value, but subject to a possible election in certain circumstances. See **32.7.2** for details.

27. Know-how allowances

27.1 Introduction and overview

Know-how allowances are given for income tax purposes where a person incurs "qualifying expenditure" (see **27.3**) on the acquisition of "know-how" (see **27.2**).

As with plant and machinery expenditure, a system of pooling is used. Allowances are then given on a reducing balance basis at an annual rate of 25%. (The changes to the rate of writing-down allowances for plant and machinery did not have any impact on the rate of allowances given for patents.)

The allowances are available only to a person carrying on a trade.

For capital allowance purposes, know-how is treated as property and any reference to the purchase or sale of property therefore includes the acquisition or disposal of know-how.

Those paying corporation tax will claim relief for new expenditure on know-how under the regime applying for intangible assets (see CTA 2009, Pt. 8) rather than by way of capital allowances. This has applied for expenditure incurred since 1 April 2002.

Law: CAA 2001, s. 452*ff*; CTA 2009, Pt. 8
Guidance: CA 70000*ff*.

27.2 Definition of know-how

27.2.1 Statutory wording

For capital allowance purposes, the term "know-how" is defined to mean:

> "any industrial information or techniques likely to assist in–
>
> (a)   manufacturing or processing goods or materials,
>
> (b)   working a source of mineral deposits (including searching for, discovering or testing mineral deposits or obtaining access to them), or
>
> (c)   carrying out any agricultural, forestry or fishing operations".

The term "mineral deposits" is then defined to include "any natural deposits capable of being lifted or extracted from the earth" and the legislation then specifies that "for this purpose geothermal energy is to be treated as a natural deposit". HMRC have confirmed that "searching for, discovering or testing mineral deposits or obtaining access to them are working a source of mineral deposits".

The concept of a "source of mineral deposits" is defined to include "a mine, an oil well and a source of geothermal energy".

Law: CAA 2001, s. 452

27.2.2   HMRC guidance

Industrial

In relation to the concept of "industrial", HMRC have written as follows:

> "The expression 'industrial information or techniques' is coloured by the words that follow – 'likely to assist in the manufacture or processing of goods and materials'. This means that only information relevant to industrial or technical processes is within the definition of know-how."

Guidance: CA 70010

Commercial know-how and franchise agreements

HMRC do not accept that these can constitute know-how for these purposes, as explained in the following terms:

> "Things like market research, customer lists and sales techniques are commercial know-how. They do not assist directly in manufacturing or processing operations. Rather, they are concerned with selling goods or materials once they have been manufactured. They are not industrial information or techniques likely to assist in the manufacture of goods or materials or in the working of a mine or in agricultural operations. This means that commercial; know-how is not within the definition of know-how in CAA and so it does not qualify for capital allowances.

> You may get a claim from a person who pays for a franchise agreement that capital allowances are due because all or part of the payment is for know-how. All or part of the payment may be for know-how but it is not likely to be the type of know-how that qualifies for capital allowances. A franchise agreement is essentially a licence to operate a business. Any know-how that is

transferred by a franchise agreement is more likely to be commercial know-how than industrial information and techniques. If so it will not qualify for capital allowances."

Guidance: CA 70030

27.3 Qualifying expenditure

27.3.1 Definition

The term "qualifying expenditure" – in the context of know-how allowances – is always defined in relation to a trade. Subject to the excluded expenditure rules (see **27.3.2**), capital expenditure (see **27.3.3**) on the acquisition of know-how will be qualifying expenditure if the person:

- is carrying on a trade at the time of the acquisition and the know-how is acquired for use in that trade;
- acquires the know-how and subsequently sets up and commences a trade in which it is used;
- acquires the know-how together with the trade or part of a trade in which it was used and the parties to the acquisition make an election under ITTOIA 2005, s. 194 or under CTA 2009, s. 178 (consideration for know-how on disposal of trade to be treated as payment for goodwill unless parties otherwise elect); or
- the person acquires the know-how together with the trade or part of a trade in which it was used and the trade in question was, before the acquisition, carried on wholly outside the UK.

The same expenditure may not be counted for more than one trade.

Qualifying expenditure incurred before the start of the trade in question is treated as incurred when the trade is set up and commenced.

In relation to holding companies, HMRC have commented as follows:

"A holding company may acquire know-how for use in trades carried on by its subsidiary companies. If this happens the holding company may qualify for capital allowances as the know-how is also used in its trade of providing management services to its subsidiaries."

This is obviously subject to meeting the standard definition of "know-how" (see **27.2** above).

Law: CAA 2001, s. 454
Guidance: CA 70040

27.3.2   Excluded expenditure

Already allowable

Expenditure does not qualify for know-how allowances to the extent that the acquisition cost is already tax deductible in some other way.

Connected parties

Expenditure does not qualify if:

- the buyer is a body of persons over whom the seller has control;
- the seller is a body of persons over whom the buyer has control; or
- the buyer and the seller are both bodies of persons and another person has control over both of them.

For the above purposes, a body of persons includes a partnership. HMRC refer to these as "control transactions".

Payment for goodwill

Expenditure is not qualifying expenditure if it is treated as a payment for goodwill under ITTOIA 2005, s. 194(3) or under CTA 2009, s. 178(3) (consideration for know-how on disposal of trade to be treated as payment for goodwill unless parties otherwise elect).

HMRC guidance on the election is given at CA 72300. HMRC accept that "where an election to avoid goodwill treatment is made the payment made by the person acquiring the know-how will normally qualify for writing-down allowances".

Law: CAA 2001, s. 455
Guidance: CA 71000, 72300

27.3.3   Capital or revenue expenditure

The HMRC view is that trade *receipts* for know-how will normally be revenue in nature. Exceptions quoted by HMRC relate to a disposal of know-how as one element of a comprehensive arrangement, and receipts that are wholly or partly attributable to some sort of restrictive covenant.

Similarly, the HMRC view is that "payments made to acquire know-how wholly and exclusively for the purposes of a trade are normally revenue payments and are allowable deductions in computing trading profits" (which means that no capital allowances will be due).

In other cases, however, payments may be capital in nature. It will be necessary to apply normal principles to determine the correct treatment. A know-how payment that includes a "keep-out covenant" (offering protection against future competition from the vendor) may be capital expenditure, applying the principles of *Associated Portland Cement Manufacturers*. A know-how receipt may also be capital if it is "disposed of as one element of a comprehensive arrangement under which a trader effectively gives up an established business in a particular territory" (per HMRC, applying *Evans Medical*).

A payment for know-how that is made in the form of shares may still be correctly treated as a revenue receipt (*Thomsons (Carron) Ltd*).

Guidance: CA 72000, 72200, 73000

Cases: *Associated Portland Cement Manufacturers Ltd v CIR* (1945) 27 TC 103; *Evans Medical Supplies Ltd v Moriarty* (1958) 37 TC 540; *Thomsons (Carron) Ltd v CIR* (1976) 51 TC 506

27.4　Allowances and charges

27.4.1　Overview

Know-how allowances are given by way of writing-down allowances (WDAs) or (occasionally) balancing allowances. Relief may be clawed back through balancing charges.

No initial or first-year allowances are available. Nor is there any equivalent to the annual investment allowance that is given for plant and machinery. The concepts of special rate expenditure and of short-life assets do not apply for the purposes of patent allowances.

A system of pooling applies, so allowances are not calculated separately on each item of qualifying expenditure. The pool grows as new qualifying expenditure is incurred, and reduces as allowances are given or as disposal proceeds are received. A separate pool is needed for each trade in respect of which a person has qualifying trade expenditure.

WDAs are normally given at 25% of the reducing balance of the pool, adjusted for additions and disposals. The figure of 25% is not affected by changes to the rates of plant and machinery allowance.

Law: CAA 2001, s. 456*ff*
Guidance: CA 71100

27.4.2   Calculation

Allowances are calculated by comparing "available qualifying expenditure" ("AQE") with "the total of any disposal values" ("TDV") for each pool for the period in question.

If AQE exceeds TDV, relief is given by way of writing-down allowances (WDAs), except in the final chargeable period, where no WDA is given but where a balancing allowance may instead be available.

The amount of the WDA is normally 25% of the excess of AQE over TDV, but the figure is proportionately increased or decreased if the chargeable period is longer or shorter than one year. It is also reduced proportionately if the trade has been carried on for only a part of the chargeable period. A person claiming a WDA may require the allowance to be reduced to a specified amount (e.g. to avoid the wasting of personal allowances or if it is expected that tax will be paid at a higher rate in a later year).

If a balancing allowance is due (i.e. for the final chargeable period: see below) the allowance is of the whole excess of AQE over TDV.

If, in any given chargeable period, TDV exceeds AQE, a balancing charge is imposed equal to the excess.

Example

Jo is a sole trader who has been in business for several years. He incurs qualifying expenditure of £10,000 in the year to 31 December and claims WDAs of £2,500. The balance of £7,500 is carried forward.

In the following year, he has incurred trading losses and so he decides to claim no allowances.

In Year 3, the trade comes to an end and he receives £1,500 for the know-how. He obtains a balancing allowance of £6,000 at that time.

Law: CAA 2001, s. 456-458

27.4.3   Available qualifying expenditure

This consists of qualifying expenditure allocated to the pool in the chargeable period, plus any unrelieved qualifying expenditure brought forward in the pool from the previous period.

Two rules govern the allocation of qualifying expenditure to a pool:

- qualifying expenditure is not allocated to a pool for a given chargeable period if the amount has already been taken into account in determining the person's available qualifying expenditure for an earlier chargeable period; and

- expenditure may not be allocated to a pool for a chargeable period before that in which the expenditure is incurred.

A person has unrelieved qualifying expenditure to carry forward if, in the period in question, AQE exceeds TDV. The amount to carry forward is the excess, less any writing-down allowance claimed for the period. No amount may be carried forward from the final chargeable period.

This is subject to special rules at s. 461A-462A where a person carrying on a trade enters the cash basis (see, generally, **1.9** above). In these circumstances, no cash basis deductible amount may be carried forward as unrelieved qualifying expenditure from the chargeable period ending with the basis period for the previous tax year. The calculation of any cash basis deductible amount is made on a just and reasonable basis.

Law: CAA 2001, s. 459-461, 461A-462A

27.4.4   Disposal values

A person must bring a disposal value into account for a chargeable period in which he sells know-how on which he has incurred qualifying expenditure. The value to bring into account is the net proceeds of sale, to the extent that they are capital in nature.

No disposal value is brought into account if the consideration received for the sale is treated as a payment for goodwill under ITTOIA 2005, s. 194(2) or CTA 2009, s. 178(2) (consideration for know-how on disposal of trade treated as payment for goodwill, unless parties otherwise elect).

In relation to "keep out covenants" HMRC have written as follows:

> "Sometimes a person who disposes of know-how gives an undertaking which protects the buyer of the know-how against competition from the seller or from other licensees (a keep out

covenant). The undertaking may be absolute or qualified and may or may not be legally valid. Treat any consideration received for the undertaking as consideration received for the disposal of know-how."

Again, this is subject to special rules at s. 461A-462A where a person carrying on a trade has entered the cash basis.

Law: CAA 2001, s. 462, 461A-462A
Guidance: CA 72600

27.4.5   Giving effect to allowances and charges

Allowances are treated as trading expenses, with any balancing charges treated as trading receipts.

Law: CAA 2001, s. 463

27.5   Other issues

27.5.1   Partnership changes

The rules in s. 558 (effect of partnership changes) apply for the purposes of know-how allowances as they do for many other capital allowances.

Law: CAA 2001, s. 557, 558

27.5.2   Successions

The rules in s. 559 (effect of successions) apply for the purposes of know-how allowances as they do for many other capital allowances.

Law: CAA 2001, s. 557, 559

27.5.3   Non-residents

ESC B8 may be relevant for the purposes of double taxation relief involving know-how payments. The concession reads as follows:

"B8 DOUBLE TAXATION RELIEF: INCOME CONSISTING OF ROYALTIES AND "KNOW-HOW" PAYMENTS

Payments made by a person resident in an overseas country to a person carrying on a trade in the United Kingdom as consideration for the use of, or for the privilege of using, in the overseas country any copyright, patent, design, secret process or formula, trademark or other like property may in law be payments the source of which is in the United Kingdom, but are nevertheless treated for the purpose of credit (whether under double taxation agreements or by way of unilateral relief) as income arising outside the United Kingdom except to the extent that they represent consideration for services (other than merely incidental services) rendered in this country by the recipient to the payer."

See also some more extensive guidance in the *International Manual*.

Guidance: INTM 161130

27.5.4   *Divers*

HMRC have issued specific guidance in relation to know-how claims by divers. Details are available in the *Capital Allowances Manual*.

Law: ITTOIA 2005, s. 15
Guidance: CA 74000

28.   Patent allowances

28.1   Introduction and overview

Patent allowances are given for income tax purposes where a person incurs "qualifying expenditure" (see **28.2**) on the purchase of "patent rights" (see **28.3**).

As with plant and machinery expenditure, a system of pooling is used. Allowances are then given on a reducing balance basis at an annual rate of 25%. (The changes in recent years to the rate of writing-down allowances for plant and machinery do not have any impact on the rate of allowances given for patents.)

The allowances are available only to a person carrying on a trade or to someone for whom any income arising from the rights would be liable to income tax.

Those paying corporation tax will claim relief for new expenditure on patent rights under the regime applying for intangible assets (see CTA 2009, Pt. 8) rather than by way of capital allowances. This has applied for expenditure incurred since 1 April 2002.

Tax relief for the cost of establishing a patent (and for certain other related expenditure) is given separately, under ITTOIA 2005, s. 89. This relief applies only to those carrying on a trade (not including a profession or vocation).

Law: CAA 2001, s. 464*ff.*; ITTOIA 2005, s. 89; CTA 2009, Pt. 8
Guidance: CA 75000*ff.*

28.2   Qualifying expenditure

28.2.1   Overview

The term "qualifying expenditure" is defined to mean either "qualifying trade expenditure" or "qualifying non-trade expenditure".

Law: CAA 2001, s. 467

28.2.2   Qualifying trade expenditure

This is defined to mean "capital expenditure incurred by a person on the purchase of patent rights for the purposes of a trade within the charge to tax carried on by the person".

Pre-trading expenditure is treated as incurred on the first day of trading, but this does not apply if the person has, by that date, sold all of the patent rights in question.

For the avoidance of doubt, the legislation makes it clear that the same expenditure may not be counted as qualifying trade expenditure in relation to more than one trade.

As regards the concept of "available qualifying expenditure" see **28.4.3** below.

Law: CAA 2001, s. 468

28.2.3　Qualifying non-trade expenditure

This term covers capital expenditure incurred by a person on the purchase of patent rights if:

- any income receivable by the person in respect of the rights would be liable to tax; but
- the expenditure is not qualifying trade expenditure.

As regards finance leases with a return in capital form (claw back of major lump sum), see ITA 2007, s. 614BRff.

Law: CAA 2001, s. 469; ITA 2007, s. 614BR

28.3　Patents and patent rights

28.3.1　Main definition

The term "patent rights" is defined to mean "the right to do or authorise the doing of anything which would, but for that right, be an infringement of a patent".

There is no tax definition of "patent" but HMRC guidance is as follows:

> "A **patent** consists of rights conferred by letters patent to the exclusive use and benefits of a particular invention. It will last for a specified period. The period for which a patent lasts is often referred to as the term of the patent.
>
> A patent is a form of protection for an inventor. A person who wants to use an invention which has been patented must acquire rights to use the patent or be granted a licence to use it. This lets the inventor control the way in which the invention is used. Once

a patent has been granted the inventor can get income by granting rights or a licence to use it."

Law: CAA 2001, s. 464
Guidance: CA 75010

28.3.2   Future patent rights

Expenditure on buying patent rights specifically includes expenditure incurred on obtaining a "right to acquire future patent rights".

If a person incurs expenditure on obtaining a right to acquire future patent rights, and subsequently acquires those rights, the expenditure is treated as having been expenditure on the purchase of those rights.

For these purposes, a "right to acquire future patent rights" is defined to mean "a right to acquire in the future patent rights relating to an invention in respect of which the patent has not yet been granted".

A sale of patent rights includes a sale of future patent rights as defined for these purposes.

Law: CAA 2001, s. 465

28.3.3   Licences

A person who acquires a licence in respect of a patent is treated as buying patent rights.

The grant of a licence in respect of a patent is treated as a sale of part of the patent rights, except that the grant of an "exclusive licence" is treated as the sale of the whole of the rights. For these purposes, an exclusive licence is defined to mean "a licence to exercise those rights to the exclusion of the grantor and all other persons for the period remaining until the rights come to an end".

Certain sums paid in respect of use by the Crown under s. 55 to 59 of the *Patents Act* 1977, or by overseas governments under corresponding legislation, are treated as use under licence. Sums paid in respect of the use are then treated accordingly for these purposes.

Law: CAA 2001, s. 466, 482
Guidance: CA 75030

28.4 Allowances and charges

28.4.1 Overview

Patent allowances are given by way of writing-down allowances (WDAs) or (occasionally) balancing allowances. Relief may be clawed back through balancing charges.

No initial or first-year allowances are available. Nor is there any equivalent to the annual investment allowance that is given for plant and machinery. The concepts of special rate expenditure and of short-life assets do not apply for the purposes of patent allowances.

A system of pooling applies, with a separate pool for each trade in respect of which a person has qualifying trade expenditure, and a different pool for all of a person's qualifying non-trade expenditure.

WDAs are normally given at 25% of the reducing balance of the pool, adjusted for additions and disposals. The figure of 25% is not affected by changes to the rates of plant and machinery allowance.

Law: CAA 2001, s. 470*ff.*

28.4.2 Calculation

Allowances are calculated by comparing "available qualifying expenditure" ("AQE") with "the total of any disposal receipts" ("TDR") for the period in question.

If AQE exceeds TDR, relief is given by way of writing-down allowances (WDAs), except in the final chargeable period, where no WDA is given but where a balancing allowance may instead be available.

The amount of the WDA is normally 25% of the excess of AQE over TDR, but the figure is proportionately increased or decreased if the chargeable period is longer or shorter than one year. It is also reduced proportionately if the trade has been carried on for only a part of the chargeable period. A person claiming a WDA may require the allowance to be reduced to a specified amount (e.g. to avoid the wasting of personal allowances or if it is expected that tax will be paid at a higher rate in a later year).

If a balancing allowance is due (i.e. for the final chargeable period: see below) the allowance is of the whole excess of AQE over TDR.

If, in any given chargeable period, TDR exceeds AQE, a balancing charge is imposed equal to the excess.

Law: CAA 2001, s. 471, 472

28.4.3   Available qualifying expenditure

This consists of qualifying expenditure allocated to the pool in the year, plus any unrelieved qualifying expenditure brought forward in the pool from the previous chargeable period.

Three rules govern the allocation of qualifying expenditure to a pool:

- qualifying expenditure is not allocated to a pool for a given chargeable period if the amount has already been taken into account in determining the person's available qualifying expenditure for an earlier chargeable period;
- expenditure may not be allocated to a pool for a chargeable period before that in which the expenditure is incurred; and
- expenditure on patent rights may not be allocated to a pool for a chargeable period if, in any earlier period, those rights have been wholly disposed of or have come to an end without any of them having been revived.

A person has unrelieved qualifying expenditure to carry forward if, in the period in question, AQE exceeds TDR. The amount to carry forward is the excess, less any writing-down allowance claimed for the period. No amount may be carried forward from the final chargeable period.

This is subject to special rules at s. 475A and 477A where a person carrying on a trade enters the cash basis (see, generally, **1.9** above). In these circumstances, no cash basis deductible amount may be carried forward as unrelieved qualifying expenditure from the chargeable period ending with the basis period for the previous tax year. The calculation of any cash basis deductible amount is made on a just and reasonable basis.

Law: CAA 2001, s. 473-475A

28.4.4   Disposal value

Normally, a disposal receipt means a disposal value that a person has to bring into account by reason of selling the whole or a part of any patent rights on which he has incurred qualifying expenditure.

The disposal value is then the amount of any capital sums (per CAA 2001, s. 4: see **1.5**) received as proceeds of the sale. The proceeds for these purposes are capped at the capital expenditure incurred by the person on purchasing the rights (such that the worst case scenario is that there is a full claw back of the allowances previously given).

This is subject to different rules where there have been connected party transactions; in these cases, the cap is the amount incurred by whichever of the connected parties incurred the greatest amount of expenditure. HMRC illustrate this as follows:

HMRC example

David, Stephen and Graham are connected. David buys patent rights for £11,000. He sells them to Stephen for £10,000 who then sells them to Graham for £9,000. If Graham sells the rights for £12,000 the limit on his disposal value is £11,000, the amount David paid for the rights. It is not £9,000, the amount Graham paid to Stephen for the rights.

Amounts may also have to be brought into account as disposal receipts for these purposes by virtue of ITA 2007, s. 614BS or CTA 2010, s. 918 (finance leases: claw back of major lump sum).

Again, special rules apply where a person has entered the cash basis.

Law: CAA 2001, s. 476, 477, 477A
Guidance: CA 75120

28.4.5 *Final chargeable period*

For a pool to which qualifying trade expenditure has been allocated, the final chargeable period is the one in which the trade is permanently discontinued.

In relation to non-trade expenditure, it is the chargeable period in which the last of the patent rights on which the person has incurred qualifying non-trade expenditure is wholly disposed of or comes to an end without any of those rights being revived.

Law: CAA 2001, s. 471

28.4.6   Giving effect to allowances and charges

Traders (income tax)

For traders liable to income tax, any patent allowances are treated as trading expenditure, and any balancing charge is treated as a trading receipt.

Law: CAA 2001, s. 478

Others (income tax)

For non-traders liable to income tax, any allowances are deducted from (or set off against) the person's income from patents for the year in question.

Relief is given at Step 2 of the calculation in ITA 2007, s. 23 ("the calculation of income tax liability"). Any excess allowances are carried forward and set against the person's income from patents for the next year in which such income is available for offset, with any further excess being carried forward indefinitely.

Any balancing charge is treated as income assessable to tax.

Law: CAA 2001, s. 479; ITA 2007, s. 23, 24(1)(b)

Corporation tax

As noted at **28.1** above, corporation tax relief for qualifying expenditure incurred since April 2002 will not be given by way of capital allowances. Any allowances or charges still given in connection with old expenditure are treated for traders as trading expenses or receipts. For non-trade expenditure, allowances are deducted from the company's income from patents for the accounting period in question, with any excess carried forward. Balancing charges are taxed as income from patents.

Law: CAA 2001, s. 480

Income from patents

This term is define to include:

- royalties or other sums paid in respect of the use of a patent;
- balancing charges to which the person is liable in respect of patents; and

- amounts on which tax is payable under ITTOIA 2005, s. 587, 593 or 594 or CTA 2009, s. 912 or 918 (taxation of receipts from sale of patent rights).

Law: CAA 2001, s. 483

28.5 Connected persons and tax-structured transactions

The amount of expenditure qualifying for patent allowances will be restricted in certain circumstances. The restriction will apply where there is a sale of patent rights between connected persons, or where it appears that the sole or main benefit for the parties was the obtaining of patent allowances. In such cases, the amount of qualifying expenditure is capped as follows:

- where a disposal value is brought into account by the seller for capital allowances purposes, the cap is that disposal value;
- where the seller is taxed on a sum under either ITTOIA 2005, s. 587 or CTA 2009, s. 912 ("charge to tax on income from sales of patent rights"), the cap is the amount of that sum;
- in any other case, the cap is on the smallest of the following amounts:
- the market value of the rights;
- if the seller incurred capital expenditure on acquiring the rights, the amount of that expenditure;
- if a person connected with the seller incurred capital expenditure on acquiring the rights, the amount of that expenditure.

Law: CAA 2001, s. 481

28.6 Successions

Where a business succession is not treated as the cessation of a trade, allowances are calculated as if the persons carrying on the trade before and after the trade were the same persons.

Law: CAA 2001, s. 557-559

29. Dredging allowances

29.1 Introduction and overview

Dredging allowances are available "if a person carries on a qualifying trade and qualifying expenditure has been incurred on dredging".

See **29.2** for the meaning of "qualifying trade" and **29.3** for the definition of "qualifying expenditure".

There are no first-year allowances, initial allowances or annual investment allowances. Relief is given by way of writing-down allowances or (occasionally) balancing allowances. There are no balancing charges. See **29.4**.

Various other issues arise: see **29.5**.

Law: CAA 2001, s. 484
Guidance: CA 80000

29.2 Qualifying trade

A trade may qualify in one of two ways.

First, it will do so if it "consists of the maintenance or improvement of the navigation of a harbour, estuary or waterway".

Second, it will do so if it is of a kind listed in tables A or B at s. 274. This is part of the now repealed legislation for industrial buildings allowances. The two tables list out qualifying trades and undertakings, broadly including the following:

- manufacturing, processing or storage trades;
- agricultural contracting;
- working foreign plantations;
- fishing;
- mineral extraction;
- undertakings of electricity, water, hydraulic power, sewerage;
- transport or highway undertakings;
- tunnel or bridge undertakings;
- undertakings of inland navigation or of docks.

HMRC accept that a marina is normally a dock undertaking for these purposes.

This initially broad definition is, however, considerably restricted in practice as dredging is then defined to exclude "anything done otherwise than in the interests of navigation".

Subject to the above exclusion, dredging includes the widening of an inland waterway or the "removal of anything forming part of, or projecting from the bed of, the sea or any inland water". The means used for removal are immaterial and it does not matter if the thing to be removed is wholly or partly above water at the time of removal.

HMRC add the following:

> "Dredging is the deepening or widening of a channel for the passage of ships, whether in tidal waters or in an inland waterway. Dredging does not include normal maintenance work on an existing channel."

Dredging carried on by a harbour authority, in order to keep channels clear for navigation, has in any case been held to be revenue expenditure (*Dover Harbour Board*).

If part of a trade satisfies the conditions, the part meeting the conditions is for these purposes treated as a separate trade. An apportionment must then be made of the expenditure.

Law: CAA 2001, s. 484(2)-(4)
Case: *Whelan v Dover Harbour Board* (1934) 18 TC 555
Guidance: CA 80200*ff*, 80400

29.3 Qualifying expenditure

29.3.1 Normal rules

Expenditure on dredging will be qualifying expenditure if it is capital expenditure incurred for the purposes of a qualifying trade. It must be incurred by the person carrying on the trade.

If the trade qualifies under the formal IBA rules (rather than consisting of the maintenance or improvement of the navigation of a harbour, estuary or waterway), a further rule is imposed. In this case, the dredging must be for the benefit of vessels coming to, leaving or using a dock or other premises occupied by the person for the purposes of the qualifying trade.

The following HMRC example (from CA 80500) illustrates qualifying expenditure:

> "Pratt manufactures furniture and sells it wholesale. Manufacturing furniture is a qualifying trade for IBA and so Pratt has a qualifying trade for dredging. He occupies a dock that he uses for importing the materials he uses and sending out the furniture he produces. If he incurs capital expenditure on deepening the dock he can claim dredging allowances."

Where expenditure is incurred only partly for the purposes of a qualifying trade, the capital expenditure must be apportioned on a just and reasonable basis.

The following HMRC example (from CA 80500) illustrates how an apportionment may be needed:

> "Brown owns and operates ships. He uses some of them to transport goods, which is a qualifying trade for IBA, and others to run pleasure cruises, which is not. He occupies a dock that he uses for his trade of operating ships. If he incurs capital expenditure on dredging the dock the expenditure is apportioned between the part of his trade that consists of transporting goods and is a qualifying trade and the part, which consists of running pleasure, cruises and is not. Dredging allowances are given on the part that is allocated to the part trade of transporting goods."

Law: CAA 2001, s. 485
Guidance: CA 80200*ff.*

29.3.2   Pre-trading expenditure

If a person incurs capital expenditure with a view to carrying on a trade or a part of a trade, the expenditure is treated as incurred on the first day of trading. Dredging allowances are given accordingly.

A slightly different rule may apply if a person incurs capital expenditure in connection with a dock or other premises, with a view to occupying the dock or other premises for the purposes of a qualifying trade. If that trade qualifies under the former IBA rules, allowances are given as if the expenditure were incurred on the date the person first occupies the dock or premises for the purposes of the qualifying trade.

Law: CAA 2001, s. 486

29.4 Calculation of allowances

29.4.1 Introduction

Tax relief for qualifying expenditure on dredging is given by way of writing-down or balancing allowances. No other allowances are available and no balancing charges are imposed.

Any allowances due are treated as trading expenses.

Law: CAA 2001, s. 489

29.4.2 Writing-down allowances

To calculate allowances, it is first necessary to identify the "writing-down period". In relation to any qualifying expenditure, that term is defined to mean the period of 25 years beginning with the first day of the chargeable period in which the qualifying expenditure was incurred.

WDAs are available if three conditions are met:

- a person has incurred qualifying expenditure on dredging;
- at any time during the chargeable period in question, the person is carrying on the qualifying trade for which the expenditure was incurred; and
- that time falls within the writing-down period.

The amount of the WDA is normally 4% of the qualifying expenditure, but this figure is proportionately increased or reduced if the chargeable period is longer or shorter than one year.

A person may also ask the allowance to be reduced to a specified amount. If this is done, however, some of the expenditure will never be relieved unless a balancing allowance is later due.

The total amount of any WDAs relating to particular qualifying expenditure, whether claimed by one person or by several, can never exceed the amount of that expenditure.

No WDA is available for the chargeable period in which the person receives a balancing allowance for that expenditure.

Law: CAA 2001, s. 487

29.4.3   *Balancing allowances*

A person may be entitled to a balancing allowance if the qualifying trade is permanently discontinued or is sold.

The allowance will be available where qualifying expenditure on dredging has been incurred, and where the amount of the expenditure exceeds the total amount of allowances previously given in relation to it (whether to the same person or to others).

The balancing allowance, equal to that excess, is made to the last person to carry on the trade before its discontinuance or sale.

The term "permanent discontinuance" does not include a deemed discontinuance under CAA 2001, s. 577(2A) or ITTOIA 2005, s. 18 (effect of company ceasing to trade etc.).

Anti-avoidance measures deny balancing allowances where the buyer has control over the seller, or vice versa, or where both are under common control. Nor is any balancing allowance given if the seller and buyer are connected persons. Finally, no balancing allowance is available if the sole or main benefit of a transaction is the obtaining of certain defined tax advantages.

Law: CAA 2001, s. 488
Guidance: CA 81600

29.5   **Contributions and subsidies**

The normal rules relating to contributions and subsidies do not apply to dredging allowances.

However, a person ("D") who has incurred expenditure is regarded as not having incurred it for the purposes of a trade carried on by him to the extent that it is met by a public body, or by capital sums contributed by another person for purposes other than those of D's trade.

Law: CAA 2001, s. 532(3), 533

30. Former allowances

30.1 Business premises renovation allowances

Business premises renovation allowances (BPRAs) offered tax relief for the costs of renovating or converting certain unused business properties. The scheme broadly expired from April 2017, but qualifying expenditure incurred before 1 April 2017 (for corporation tax) or 6 April 2017 (for income tax) remained eligible.

Allowances were given only to the person who incurred the expenditure. Someone who subsequently bought the property was not able to claim.

Allowances could be clawed back if there was a balancing event in the period of five years from the date on which the premises were brought back into use or were first suitable for letting. The clawback period was seven years for expenditure incurred before April 2014.

Reference should be made to earlier editions of this book for details of the rules as they used to apply. Some readers may also wish to consider the recent *London Luton Hotel* case.

Law: CAA 2001, s. 360A-360Z4
Case: *London Luton Hotel BPRA Property Fund v HMRC* [2019] UKFTT 212 (TC)
Guidance: CA 45000*ff.*

30.2 Assured tenancy allowances

Allowances under this part of the capital allowances legislation were only given for expenditure incurred before 1 April 1992 – now more than 25 years ago.

Allowances were given by reference to construction costs and had to relate to a "qualifying dwelling-house".

The HMRC manual continues to include coverage of the scheme, and reference should be made to the relevant pages in the unlikely event that anybody is advising on the scheme for the first time.

Law: CAA 2001, s. 490-531
Guidance: CA 85200*ff.*

30.3   Flat conversion allowances

The flat conversion allowance scheme was abolished from April 2013, not only for new expenditure but also for earlier expenditure that would otherwise have continued to attract writing-down allowances.

The rules relating to balancing adjustments were not repealed by FA 2012. Broadly speaking, balancing adjustments may be made for up to seven years.

Reference should be made to earlier editions of this book for details of the rules as they used to apply.

Law: FA 2012, Sch. 39, para. 36
Guidance: CA 43000*ff.*

30.4   Other allowances

Guidance on other former allowances may still be found in HMRC's *Capital Allowances Manual.* See, for example, the commentary beginning at CA 30000 regarding industrial buildings allowances and at CA 40000 regarding agricultural buildings allowances. Both of these were withdrawn from April 2008, but with a run-off period to April 2011.

Law: CAA 2001

OTHER PROVISIONS

31. Contributions

31.1 Introduction

If someone contributes to the costs of an asset for a second person, two potential issues arise:

- does the recipient have to reduce his capital allowances claim accordingly?
- can the contributor claim capital allowances for the expenditure incurred?

Different rules apply for different types of allowance, but some broad principles are established.

The position of the recipient is considered at **31.2** below, with the position of the contributor being discussed at **31.3**.

Law: CAA 2001, Pt. 11

31.2 The position of the recipient

31.2.1 General rule

A general rule is given for all types of capital allowances except dredging allowances (regarding which see **29.5**).

This rule, which is subject to exceptions considered below, states that a person ("R" in the legislation, for "recipient") is treated as not having incurred expenditure to the extent that it is met by a public body or by a person other than R. The same rule applies whether the expenditure is met directly or indirectly, and whether the grant is capital or revenue in nature.

For these purposes, the term "public body" covers the Crown and any government or public or local authority, whether in the UK or abroad.

In applying this restriction, HMRC policy is to:

> "treat a non-returnable grant of money given by way of gift, that is, not in return for anything, as a contribution if there is a clear connection between the receipt of the grant and the incurring of the expenditure. The grant should be specifically related to the capital expenditure on the provision of capital assets."

If a person repays part or all of a grant, they are not then entitled to claim capital allowances on their net expenditure. Relief was previously allowed in certain circumstances by virtue of ESC B49, but HMRC instructions now state that "since ESC/B49 has been withdrawn you should refuse to give capital allowances in all cases on a grant repaid because there is nothing in the legislation to allow them".

A repayable loan, however, is not a contribution.

Law: CAA 2001, s. 532
Guidance: CA 14100, 14300

31.2.2   *Northern Ireland regional development grants*

Despite the general rule above, a person is treated as incurring expenditure even to the extent that it is met by a grant made under Northern Ireland legislation if it is declared by Treasury order to correspond to a grant under Pt. II of the *Industrial Development Act* 1982. The relevant Treasury order expired on 31 March 2003, however, and any grants made under later agreements are not exempted by virtue of this provision.

This exception did not, in any case, apply to certain oil-related grants.

Law: CAA 2001, s. 534
Guidance: CA 14200

31.2.3   *Insurance or compensation money*

A person's qualifying expenditure is not reduced by the amount of any insurance or compensation money if the money is received in respect of an asset that has been destroyed, demolished or put out of use.

Insurance receipts may, however, be brought into account separately as disposal receipts. See, for example, **5.5.3** in relation to plant and machinery allowances.

This is illustrated by the following simple HMRC example.

HMRC example

Gary runs a ferry service. One of his boats is destroyed by fire. He uses the insurance moneys to buy a replacement. The insurance moneys are not a contribution to the cost of the replacement. This means that the full cost of the replacement is qualifying expenditure for PMAs. The insurance moneys may be brought to account as a disposal receipt.

Law: CAA 2001, s. 535
Guidance: CA 14200

31.2.4   No tax relief for payer

If the person making the payment cannot claim any form of tax relief, the recipient may be able to ignore the contribution and claim unrestricted capital allowances. This relaxation of the general rule (which does not, however, apply for the purposes of structures and buildings allowances) applies as long as the contributor:

- is not a public body;
- is unable to claim relief under the rules for contributions (considered at **31.3** below); and
- cannot deduct the contribution in calculating the profits of a trade or "relevant activity" that he carries on.

A "relevant activity" includes a profession or vocation. For plant and machinery allowances only, it also includes:

- an ordinary UK property business;
- a UK furnished holiday lettings business;
- an ordinary overseas property business;
- an EEA furnished holiday lettings business;
- a concern listed in ITTOIA 2005, s. 12(4) or CTA 2009, s. 39(4) (mines, transport undertakings etc.); and
- the management of an investment company.

HMRC example

George and Andrew are friends. George is a scriptwriter and Andrew is a shopkeeper. George makes a contribution towards Andrew's expenditure on a new computer. You cannot deduct George's contribution from Andrew's expenditure. George cannot claim capital allowances on the contribution or deduct it in calculating his profits as a scriptwriter.

Law: CAA 2001, s. 536
Guidance: CA 14200

31.2.5   Reverse premiums

A landlord may contribute to a tenant's fitting-out costs. If so, and if the contribution reduces the tenant's qualifying expenditure for capital allowances purposes (in whole or in part), the payment will not (to that extent) be charged as a reverse premium.

This produces a number of different permutations of possible tax outcomes, and the best result in any case may depend on the respective tax positions of both landlord and tenant. In principle, an agreement may be worded so that any contribution is treated as *pro rata* for all elements, or so that it is a contribution only to the shell of the building, or that it is only towards expenditure qualifying for capital allowances. Each will have a different outcome in terms of the tax position of both contributor and recipient.

See also the *Income Tax (Construction Industry Scheme) Regulations* 2005 re the interaction between these reverse premium rules and the definition of "contract payment" for the purposes of the construction industry scheme.

Law: ITTOIA 2005, s. 100(1); CTA 2009, s. 97; SI 2005/2045, reg. 20
Guidance: BIM 41090

31.2.6   NHS meeting particular costs

Doctors and other medical practitioners may receive contributions from the NHS towards either revenue or capital costs.

In principle, normal rules apply, as described above, when the contribution is towards capital costs. As the NHS is a public body, the recipient is not entitled to claim allowances to the extent that the expense has been met by an NHS grant. The HMRC view has been clear that for the balance of the expenditure, however, there is no bar on claiming allowances:

> "Where the practice receives a grant for capital expenditure (for example, computer equipment), only the net cost of the capital asset should be reported in the practice accounts. Similarly, you should calculate any capital allowances due using the net capital cost."

However, it is understood that in 2020 a policy was developing whereby GPs applying for an NHS grant have been required to state that they will not claim capital allowances even on the balance of the expenditure that is *not* covered by the grant. The authors have not seen official confirmation of this, but it is certainly something that recipients will wish to bear in mind when planning cash flow, etc.

Guidance: https://tinyurl.com/6p2h256a (HMRC document HS231: Doctors' expenses (2017), as updated 6 April 2021)

31.3   Allowances for the contributor

31.3.1   Introduction

A person who makes a contribution to someone else's capital expenditure may be entitled to claim capital allowances for some or all of the expenditure.

Different rules apply for plant and machinery, for mineral extraction and for dredging. No other contribution allowances are available.

31.3.2   Plant and machinery allowances

A person may claim plant and machinery allowances where the following conditions are met:

- the person ("C", for "contributor") contributes a capital sum to expenditure on the provision of an asset;
- if it were not for the rules of s. 532(1) (see **31.2.1** above), the expenditure would have been regarded as wholly incurred by another person ("R");
- without those rules, R (if not a public body) would have been entitled to allowances under the plant or machinery provisions (or possibly under the mineral extraction provisions), or R could have allocated the costs to a plant and machinery pool;
- R and C are not connected persons;
- C's contribution is made for the purposes of a trade or "relevant activity" (see **31.2.4**) carried on, or to be carried on, by C.

For these purposes, a public body means the Crown or any public or local authority in the UK.

Where the conditions are met, C can claim plant and machinery allowances as if he had incurred the expenditure on an asset for his own business and as if he owned the asset as a result. This applies for as long as R owns it (or is treated as owning it under normal plant and machinery principles). The expenditure in question must be allocated to a single-asset pool.

HMRC example

Johnny runs a restaurant. June has a market garden where she grows herbs that Johnny uses in the restaurant. June buys new equipment for the market garden and Johnny makes a contribution towards her costs. Johnny's contribution is deducted from June's expenditure qualifying for PMA ... and Johnny can claim PMA on the contribution.

But if Johnny and June are married Johnny cannot claim capital allowances on his contribution because they are connected persons. However June can then claim capital allowances on all of her expenditure – the contribution is within the exception for contributions by someone other than a public body who cannot get relief for it.

If the contribution is made to a public body, perhaps as part of a planning application, care will be needed to ensure that as much tax relief is obtained as possible.

Example

Larkin has applied for planning permission to build a number of office units at an out-of-town location, which are to be let out to small businesses. Permission is granted on the basis that Larkin contributes £20,000 towards the cost of local improvements. Before making the payment, Larkin should try to agree with the planning authority that the payment will be towards plant and machinery – perhaps street furniture, traffic lights or CCTV. As long as it is formally agreed – before the payment is made – that it will specifically constitute a contribution towards the cost of identified plant or machinery (and as long as all the normal conditions are met) then allowances will be due.

If there is a subsequent transfer of C's trade or relevant activity, writing-down allowances for chargeable periods ending after the date of the transfer are made to the transferee instead of to C. (If only part of the trade is transferred, an apportionment is made.)

In practice, contributions are often made by landlords towards costs incurred by tenants.

Example

Hughes is freeholder of a boutique hotel which is leased to Coleridge. Coleridge wishes to add a second lift to the property, at a total cost of £40,000, and Hughes agrees to contribute £15,000 towards the project.

Without the special rules for contribution allowances, Coleridge could claim for the £25,000 but neither party could claim for the £15,000:

Coleridge could not do so because he has not incurred the cost, and Hughes could not do so because of the pecking order rules at s. 176, assigning deemed ownership only to the person with the lower (leasehold) interest.

The contribution allowance rules ensure that each party can obtain relief for his share of the total cost.

Law: CAA 2001, s. 537, 538

HMRC clarification

HMRC have clarified that "where a business makes a contribution to capital expenditure by another business on plant or machinery, capital allowances for the amount covered by the contribution are available to the contributor and not the recipient".

Law: CAA 2001, s. 537, 538; FA 2013, s. 73

Guidance: CA 14400; HMRC TIIN: Capital allowances: contributions towards capital expenditure on plant or machinery

Fixtures elections and fixed value requirement

The question may arise of whether or not a fixtures election may be signed (and therefore whether or not the pooling and fixed value requirements – see **12.5** – are imposed) where contribution allowances have been claimed. The author has seen two opposing views on the matter.

The legislation specifies at s. 538(5) and (6) the rules that apply if there is a transfer of the whole or part of the trade for the purposes of which the contribution was made. According to those subsections, "writing-down allowances for chargeable periods ending after the date of the transfer are to be made to the transferee instead of to the transferor". On this basis, it has been argued that any balance of unclaimed allowances is passed to the new owner at tax written-down value. This is therefore deemed to override any possible election.

The opposing view is that section 538 is merely a deeming provision, whereby the contributor is in certain circumstances treated as owning the plant – and as meeting the other required criteria – so that a claim may be made. On this basis, it has been argued that the deemed owner of the property is within the normal provisions regarding disposals, and that the owner may therefore sign a fixtures election on disposal and indeed would be bound by the fixed value requirement. Under this interpretation, which appears to the writer to be the more correct one, the writing-down allowances made to the transferee would presumably be based on whatever figure was included in the election.

Section 187A (1)(c) makes it clear that the fixed value and pooling requirements are not imposed if the plant or machinery is only deemed to have been owned by the previous owner as a result of the rules for contribution allowances. That does not in itself prevent the parties from signing an election, however.

Furthermore, it is necessary to distinguish between a sale of the property and a sale of the trade for which the contribution was made.

Example

Clive is building a new office and Derek, for the purposes of his own trade, contributes part of the cost and claims allowances accordingly by virtue of s. 538.

If Clive sells the office building, he cannot pass on the value of the allowances to the extent that these are available to Derek, as Clive is deemed not to have incurred the expenditure in question (per s. 532).

But if Derek sells his trade, the new owner of the business may continue to claim allowances, stepping into Derek's shoes for that purpose (s. 538(5), (6)).

31.3.3 Structures and buildings allowances

A person may claim structures and buildings allowances (SBAs) where certain conditions are met. The rules were found to be flawed and were therefore "clarified" for contributions made on or after 11 March (Budget day) 2020. For ease of reference, the rules are given separately below for contributions before and on/after that date.

Contributions made on or after 11 March 2020

For contributions made from 11 March 2020, a person can claim SBAs where the following conditions are met:

- the person ("C", for "contributor") contributes a capital sum to expenditure on the provision of an asset;
- if it were not for the rules of s. 532(1) (see **31.2.1** above), the expenditure would have been regarded as wholly incurred by another person ("R");
- without those rules, R (if not a public body) would have been entitled to allowances under the mineral extraction provisions

or under the SBA provisions (or possibly under the plant and machinery provisions), or R could have allocated the costs to a plant and machinery pool;

- R and C are not connected persons;
- C's contribution is to expenditure that is qualifying expenditure for the purposes of claiming SBAs; and
- C's contribution is made for the purposes of an SBA qualifying activity carried on, or to be carried on:
  - by C or by a tenant of land in which C has an interest (if R is a public body), or
  - by a tenant of land in which C has an interest (if R is not a public body).

For these purposes, a public body is defined to mean the Crown or any public or local authority, whether or not in the UK.

Where the conditions are met, C is treated for the purposes of claiming SBAs as if:

- the contribution were expenditure incurred by C on the construction or acquisition of the building or structure;
- the building or structure were brought into qualifying use, for the purposes of the allowance in relation to the contribution, on
  - the day on which R first brought the building or structure into qualifying use, or
  - (if R is a public body) the earlier of that day and the day on which R first brought the building or structure into non-residential use.

In other words, the contributor may claim allowances when the public body brings the asset into qualifying use, or non-residential use if earlier.

The rules are modified if – at any time in the period beginning with the day on which C made the contribution, and ending with the day on which R first brought the building or structure into non-residential use – C did not have a relevant interest in the building or structure. In these circumstances:

- C is treated for the purposes of claiming SBAs as having had a relevant interest in the building or structure when that period begins; and

- C is not treated as ceasing to have that interest on any subsequent sale of R's relevant interest in the building or structure.

The usual SBA rules regarding the relevant interest (see, in particular, **24.6**) apply *mutatis mutandis* here too.

In determining the day on which R first brings a building or structure into non-residential use, any insignificant use of the building or structure is ignored.

Law: CAA 2001, s. 537, 538A; FA 2020, Sch. 5, para. 3, 9

Contributions made before 11 March 2020

Before the changes were made, a person could claim SBAs where the following conditions were met:

- the person ("C", for "contributor") contributed a capital sum to expenditure on the provision of an asset;
- if it were not for the rules of s. 532(1) (see **31.2.1** above), the expenditure would have been regarded as wholly incurred by another person ("R");
- without those rules, R (if not a public body) would have been entitled to allowances under the mineral extraction provisions or under the SBA provisions (or possibly under the plant and machinery provisions), or R could have allocated the costs to a plant and machinery pool;
- R and C were not connected persons;
- C's contribution was to expenditure that was qualifying expenditure for the purposes of claiming SBAs; and
- C's contribution was made for the purposes of an SBA qualifying activity carried on, or to be carried on:
  - by C or by a tenant of land in which C had an interest (if R is a public body), or
  - by a tenant of land in which C had an interest (if R was not a public body).

For these purposes, a public body was defined to mean the Crown or any public or local authority, whether or not in the UK.

Where the conditions were met, C was treated for the purposes of claiming SBAs as if:

- the contribution were expenditure incurred by C on the construction or acquisition of the building or structure;

- the building or structure were brought into qualifying use by C on the day on which R brought it into qualifying use; and

- for the purposes of section 270AA(2)(b) (see **24.2.1**), the day on which the qualifying expenditure was incurred were the day on which C made the contribution.

As for SBAs generally, the allowance ceased if the building or structure was brought into residential use.

The usual SBA rules regarding the relevant interest (see, in particular, **24.6**) applied *mutatis mutandis* here too. If C did not in fact have a relevant interest on the day on which R brought the building or structure into qualifying use, C was treated as having had the relevant interest on that day. C was not treated as ceasing to have a relevant interest in the building or structure on the subsequent sale of R's relevant interest.

Law: CAA 2001, s. 537, 538A (as formerly worded)

31.3.4   *Mineral extraction allowances*

A person may claim mineral extraction allowances where the following conditions are met:

- the person ("C", for "contributor") contributes a capital sum to expenditure on the provision of an asset;

- if it were not for the rules of s. 532(1) (see **31.2.1** above), the expenditure would have been regarded as wholly incurred by another person ("R");

- without those rules, R (if not a public body) would have been entitled to allowances under the mineral extraction provisions (or possibly under the plant and machinery provisions), or R could have allocated the costs to a plant and machinery pool;

- R and C are not connected persons;

- C's contribution is made for the purposes of a trade carried on, or to be carried on, by C.

For these purposes, a public body means the Crown or any public or local authority in the UK.

Where the conditions are met, C is treated for the purposes of claiming mineral extraction allowances as if:

- the contribution were expenditure incurred by C on the provision, for the purposes of C's trade, of an asset similar to that provided by means of C's contribution; and
- the asset were at all material times in use for the purposes of C's trade.

If there is a subsequent transfer of C's trade or relevant activity, writing-down allowances for chargeable periods ending after the date of the transfer are made to the transferee instead of to C. (If only part of the trade is transferred, an apportionment is made.)

Law: CAA 2001, s. 537, 541, 542

31.3.5   *Dredging allowances*

A person who contributes a capital sum to expenditure incurred by another person on dredging is regarded for the purposes of claiming dredging allowances as incurring capital expenditure on that dredging.

Law: CAA 2001, s. 543

32. Final provisions

32.1 Introduction

The final "Part" of the *Capital Allowances Act* 2001 is entitled "Supplementary Provisions" and contains a variety of Chapters addressing particular issues. Where possible, these have been incorporated into the main text above, but the rest are dealt with in the paragraphs below.

32.2 Partnerships, successions and transfers

32.2.1 Introduction

The rules relating to partnerships and successions for plant and machinery purposes are addressed at **Chapter 18** above. The rules below do not therefore apply for those purposes (though they are in many respects very similar). They are also not relevant for research and development allowances.

Different rules apply to the transfer of an insurance company business, not covered here.

Law: CAA 2001, s. 557

32.2.2 Effect of partnership changes

The provisions described below apply (but not for plant and machinery or certain other purposes, as explained at **32.2.1** above) where the following conditions are met:

- a relevant activity has been set up and is carried on in partnership;
- there has been a change in the persons engaged in carrying on that activity; and
- (for income tax purposes) a person carrying on the relevant activity immediately before the change continues to carry it on after the change, or
- (for corporation tax purposes), a company carrying on the relevant activity in partnership immediately before the change continues to carry it on in partnership thereafter.

Any allowance or charge is made to or on the present partners, i.e. the persons or person for the time being carrying on the relevant activity. The amount of any allowance or charge is to be calculated as if the present partners had always carried on the relevant activity and as if everything done to or by their predecessors had been done to or by the present partners.

For these purposes, a "relevant activity" means any trade, property business, profession or vocation.

Law: CAA 2001, s. 558

32.2.3 Effect of successions

The provisions described below apply (but not for plant and machinery or certain other purposes, as explained at **32.2.1** above) where the following conditions are met:

- a person succeeds to a "relevant activity" that was until then carried on by another person; and

- (for income tax purposes) no person carrying on the relevant activity immediately before the succession continues to carry it on thereafter, or

- (for corporation tax purposes), no company carrying on the relevant activity in partnership immediately before the succession continues to carry it on in partnership thereafter.

Where these conditions are met, the "property in question" (see below) is treated as if it had been sold to the successor at market value when the succession takes place. The successor is not entitled to claim initial allowances.

The "property in question" means any property that was in use for the purposes of the discontinued relevant activity immediately before the succession and (without being sold) is in use for the purposes of the new relevant activity immediately after the succession.

For these purposes, a "relevant activity" means any trade, property business, profession or vocation.

Law: CAA 2001, s. 559

32.2.4   Transfers of trade without a change of ownership

Particular rules apply to certain transfers or divisions of a UK business between qualifying companies resident in different member states (s. 561). Different rules apply to transfers of assets by reason of a cross-border merger (s. 561A).

Where neither of the above applies, the provisions of CAA 2001 are overridden by those of CTA 2010, Pt. 22, Ch. 1 (transfer of trade without a change of ownership). Broadly speaking, a transfer of the whole of a trade is then ignored for capital allowances purposes, with no balancing adjustments made. The successor steps into the shoes of the predecessor.

Law: CAA 2001, s. 560A; CTA 2010, s. 948
Guidance: CA 15420, 15560

32.3   Apportionments

Apportionments are most often encountered in connection with fixtures in property and the practical effects are illustrated in detail at **11.3**. Nevertheless, the following principles are applied for the purposes of all types of capital allowance.

Any reference to the sale of property includes the sale of that property together with any other property. All property sold "as a result of one bargain" is treated as sold together, even if there are apparently separate sales of separate items, or if separate prices are agreed for different elements.

Where one item of property is sold with another, the net proceeds of each item "are to be treated as being so much of the net proceeds of sale of all the property as, on a just and reasonable apportionment, is attributable to that item". Similarly, the expenditure on any given item is determined by using a just and reasonable apportionment of all the expenditure.

For example, a property may be sold that contains fixtures and it may be that the parties allocate different figures to the property on the one hand and to the fixtures on the other. In the absence of any formal election to the contrary, the allocation given by the parties is ignored unless it represents a just and reasonable apportionment.

HMRC instructions to tax officers includes the following:

> "You should ignore any apportionment figures shown in the sale documents if those figures seem unreasonable. You must remember that if the total sales figure has been negotiated at arm's length you cannot change that total sales figure. If you think that the apportionment given by the taxpayer undervalues the assets that have qualified for capital allowances you can only challenge that apportionment if you can also show that something else has been overvalued."

The same principles are applied (with the necessary modifications) to other proceeds such as insurance money or compensation. Again, there is no reason why the principles should not apply to loose plant and machinery (chattels). So if the sale agreement allocates £490,000 to property and £10,000 to "moveable plant and machinery" the allocation may be challenged if the figures are unreasonable. (The formula for apportioning fixtures, discussed in detail at **11.3.2**, would obviously not apply for determining a value to be attributed to the moveable items.)

For the purposes of mineral extraction allowances, these rules are applied as if expenditure on the provision or purchase of an item of property included expenditure on the acquisition of a mineral asset (per s. 397: see **25.1.3**), or of land outside the UK.

Law: CAA 2001, s. 562
Guidance: CA 12100*ff.*

32.4　Procedures for determining disputes, etc.

In the following cases, an application to the tax tribunal is subject to the provisions of TMA 1970, Pt. 5, and each person for whom the issue may be material is entitled to be a party to the proceedings:

- apportionments, other than in respect of plant or machinery allowances;
- determination of market value for:
- the purposes of any issues re plant or machinery allowances;
- disposal value for mineral extraction allowances (per s. 423: see **25.3.4**);
- effect of successions (s. 559: see **32.2.3**);

- sales treated as being for alternative amount (s. 568 or 569: see **32.7.3**); or

- transfers treated as sales (s. 573: see **32.9.3**).

If s. 561 applies (transfer of a UK trade to a company in another member State), then these rules also apply for the purposes of the tax of both company A and company B (per that s. 561), and in relation to the determination of any question of apportionment of expenditure under s. 561(3).

Law: CAA 2001, s. 563, 564

32.5 Tax agreements for income tax purposes

If a person is entitled to a capital allowance for income tax purposes, and enters into a tax agreement with HMRC about the tax year in which the allowance will be given effect, the allowance is treated as having been given effect even though there is no formal assessment for the tax year in question.

The HMRC view is that this is unlikely in practice but "could happen with, for example, a PAYE taxpayer".

Law: CAA 2001, s. 565
Guidance: CA 11150

32.6 Companies not resident in the UK

A company that is not resident in the UK may be within the charge to corporation tax and income tax, in respect of different sources of income.

Allowances related to any source of income are to be given effect only against income chargeable to the same tax as is chargeable on income from that source.

Law: CAA 2001, s. 566

32.7 Sales treated as being for alternative amount

32.7.1 Scope

The provisions described in these paragraphs (**32.7**) apply for the purposes of the following types of allowance only (some of which have since been withdrawn):

- business premises renovation allowances;
- flat conversion allowances;

- mineral extraction allowances;
- research and development allowances; and
- assured tenancy allowances.

The provisions do not apply if s. 561 applies (transfer of a UK trade to a company in another member State).

32.7.2 Terminology

Three key terms need to be defined for these purposes.

Body of persons

This term is defined to include a partnership.

Control test

This test is said to be met if any of the following applies:

- the buyer is a body of persons over whom the seller has control;
- the seller is a body of persons over whom the buyer has control;
- both the seller and the buyer are bodies of persons and another person has control over both of them; or
- the seller and the buyer are connected persons.

Tax advantage test

This test is met if it appears that the sole or main benefit which might be expected to accrue from the sale (or from transactions of which the sale is one) is the obtaining of a tax advantage by all or any of the parties under any capital allowances provision, other than one relating to plant and machinery.

Law: CAA 2001, s. 567

32.7.3 Effect and election

Unless an election is made under s. 569 (below), any sale of property that is not at market value is treated as being at market value if either the control test or the tax advantage test is met.

The parties to a sale may elect for the sale to be treated as being for the alternative amount if the control test is met or if s. 573 applies (transfers treated as sales), but no election is possible if the tax advantage test is met. This election was not available for the purposes of business premises renovation allowances or flat conversion allowances (both now withdrawn).

The alternative amount is the lower of market value and another figure, determined as follows:

- in the case of assured tenancy allowances, the residue of the qualifying expenditure immediately before the sale;
- in the case of mineral extraction allowances, the unrelieved qualifying expenditure immediately before the sale;
- in the case of research and development allowances, the qualifying expenditure represented by the asset sold (unless a research and development allowance is given for the expenditure represented by the asset sold, in which case the figure is nil).

A balancing charge is made on the buyer if, after the date of the sale, an event occurs as a result of which a balancing charge would have been made on the seller if he had continued to own the property, and had done all such things, and been allowed all such allowances, as were done by or allowed to the buyer.

Any election under these rules must be made within two years of the date of the sale.

Further restrictions on elections

No election under these provisions may be made if the buyer is a dual resident investing company.

No election is possible if the circumstances of the sale (or of the parties to it) mean that a relevant allowance or charge will not be capable of being made. An allowance or charge is "relevant" if it is made under any of the five types of allowance listed at **32.7.1** above.

Law: CAA 2001, s. 569, 570

32.8   Avoidance affecting proceeds of balancing event

Balancing allowances, for the purposes of the following allowances (mostly now withdrawn) are/were denied in certain circumstances where there is a scheme or arrangement the main purpose, or one of the main purposes, of which is the obtaining of a tax advantage by the taxpayer:

- business premises renovation allowances;
- flat conversion allowances;
- mineral extraction allowances; and
- assured tenancy allowances.

Law: CAA 2001, s. 570A

32.9 Interpretative provisions

32.9.1 *Parts of assets*

Unless the context requires otherwise, references to an asset of any kind include a part of an asset. This principle applies to all assets, including buildings, structures, works or plant and machinery.

Law: CAA 2001, s. 571

32.9.2 *Sales of property*

References to the sale of property include the exchange of property, and the surrender for valuable consideration of a leasehold interest (or, in Scotland, the interest of the tenant in property subject to a lease). As a result:

- references to the net proceeds of sale and to the price include the consideration for the exchange or surrender; and
- references to capital sums included in the net proceeds of sale or paid on a sale include so much of the consideration for the exchange or surrender as would have been a capital sum if it had been a money payment.

Time of sale

Other than for the purposes of research and development allowances, any reference to the time of a sale is taken to be a reference to the earlier of:

- the time of completion; or
- the time when possession is given.

Law: CAA 2001, s. 572

32.9.3   Certain transfers treated as sales

The transfer of a relevant interest, if not a sale, is treated as a sale for the purposes of claiming structures and buildings allowances.

Formerly, it was also so treated for the purposes of the following types of allowance, all now withdrawn:

- business premises renovation allowances;
- flat conversion allowances; and
- assured tenancy allowances.

Unless there is an election under s. 569 (see **32.7.3**), the sale is treated as being at market value.

These rules do not apply if s. 561 applies (transfer of a UK trade to a company resident in another member State).

Law: CAA 2001, s. 573

32.9.4   Control

In relation to a body corporate ("company A"), "control" means the power of a person ("P") to secure that the affairs of company A are conducted in accordance with P's wishes:

- by means of the holding of shares or the possession of voting power in relation to that or any other body corporate; or
- as a result of any powers conferred by the articles of association or other document regulating that or any other body corporate.

HMRC have clarified that "when a company is in liquidation it is the liquidator, not the company or its members, who has control of the assets of the company".

In relation to a partnership, "control" means the right to a share of more than half of the assets, or of more than one half of the income, of the partnership.

This applies throughout the capital allowances legislation, *other than* for the purposes of defining "connected persons" below (though it also applies in that case where specifically indicated).

Law: CAA 2001, s. 574
Guidance: CA 11650

32.9.5 Connected persons

The question of whether one person is connected with another is determined according to the following rules.

For these purposes only:

- A company includes any body corporate or unincorporated association, but does not include a partnership. A unit trust scheme is treated as if it were a company.
- The term "control" is interpreted (except where indicated) in accordance with CTA 2010, s. 450 and 451 (and *not* in accordance with **32.9.4** above).
- A relative is a brother, sister, ancestor or lineal descendant.
- The term "settlement" is defined per ITTOIA 2005, s. 620. "Principal settlement" and "sub-fund settlement" are defined per TCGA 1992, Sch. 4ZA, para. 1.
- The term "trustee" in the case of a settlement in relation to which there would otherwise be no trustees, means any person:
  - in whom the property comprised in the settlement is for the time being vested, or
  - in whom the management of that property is for the time being vested.

Law: CAA 2001, s. 575A

Individuals

An individual ("A") is connected with another individual ("B") if:

- A is B's spouse or civil partner;
- A is a relative of B;
- A is the spouse or civil partner of a relative of B;
- A is a relative of B's spouse or civil partner; or
- A is the spouse or civil partner of a relative of B's spouse or civil partner.

Law: CAA 2001, s. 575(2)

Trustees

A person, in the capacity as trustee of a settlement, is connected with:

- any individual who is a settlor in relation to the settlement;
- any person connected with such an individual;
- any close company whose participators include the trustees of the settlement;
- any non-UK resident company which, if it were UK resident, would be a close company whose participators include the trustees of the settlement;
- any body corporate controlled by a company as specified within the two bullets immediately above (and the provisions of s. 574, as described at **32.9.4** above *do* apply for this purpose);
- if the settlement is the principal settlement in relation to one or more sub-fund settlements, a person in the capacity as trustee of such a sub-fund settlement; and
- if the settlement is a sub-fund settlement in relation to a principal settlement, a person in the capacity as trustee of any other sub-fund settlements in relation to the principal settlement.

Law: CAA 2001, s. 575(3)

Partners

A person who is a partner in a partnership is connected with:

- any partner in the partnership;
- the spouse or civil partner of any individual who is a partner in the partnership; and
- a relative of any individual who is a partner in the partnership.

But this rule does not apply in relation to acquisitions or disposals of assets of the partnership pursuant to genuine commercial arrangements.

Law: CAA 2001, s. 575(4)

Example

Back in 1989, Andrea sold a commercial property in equal shares to her son Alan and to Brian, who was Alan's business partner. In 1994, Alan sold his half share to Brian and the partnership business ceased at that time. In 1999, Brian sold the property to Brian Ltd, a company of which he was the controlling shareholder.

No capital allowances have ever been claimed, but Brian Ltd is selling the property to an unconnected party in 2016 and the question is raised of a possible claim for fixtures in the property.

To meet the pooling requirement, Brian Ltd must add the value of the fixtures to its tax computations for the year of sale (or for an earlier year if still open). As Brian and Brian Ltd are connected parties, s. 218(3) requires the cost to be restricted to the expenditure incurred by Brian personally. But will his expenditure in turn have to be capped by reference to the expenditure incurred by Andrea and Alan?

Section 575(4) says that Brian will be connected both with Alan (s. 575(4)(a)) and with Andrea (s. 575(4)(c)). However, this will not be the case if the property was a partnership asset and if the sales by Andrea to Brian and by Alan to Brian were "pursuant to genuine commercial arrangements". So if the arrangements were on an arm's length basis, there is no reason to restrict the claim to the original cost incurred by Andrea. If that condition is not met, the costs will be restricted.

Companies

A company is connected with another company if:

- the same person has control of both companies;
- a person ("A") has control of one company and persons connected with A have control of the other company;
- A has control of one company and A together with persons connected with A have control of the other company; or
- a group of two or more persons has control of both companies and the groups either consist of the same persons or could be so regarded if (in one or more cases) a member of either group were replaced by a person with whom the member is connected.

A company is connected with another person ("A") if:

- A has control of the company; or
- A together with persons connected with A have control of the company.

In relation to a company, any two or more persons acting together to secure or exercise control of the company are connected with one another, and with any person acting on the directions of any of them to secure or exercise control of the company.

Law: CAA 2001, s. 575(5)-(7)

APPENDICES

Appendix 1 – Northern Ireland

The *Corporation Tax (Northern Ireland) Act* 2015 is expected to be implemented from a future date, as discussed at **1.13** above. This appendix reproduces the *Explanatory Notes* that were published at the time of the draft legislation, insofar as they relate to capital allowances.

Section 2 and Schedule 1: Capital Allowances

107. Section 2 introduces Schedule 1, which contains amendments of CAA 2001.

Part 1 of Schedule 1

108. Part 1 amends CAA 2001 as set out in the rest of Schedule 1.

Part 2 of Schedule 1

109. Part 2 amends Part 1 of CAA 2001. Although it uses different terms, new section 6A inserted into Part 1 of CAA 2001 imports the definitions of Northern Ireland companies in Part 8B of CTA 2010 into CAA 2001. A "NIRE company" is a company where the large company condition applies and a "Northern Ireland SME company" is one where the SME condition applies.

110. There are also definitions in new section 6B(3) and (4) which refer to Northern Ireland firms (section 357WA) whose profits are determined under Chapter 6 or 7 of Part 8B of CTA 2010 respectively.

111. New section 6C also introduces the term "NI rate activity" for the purposes of CAA 2001. An activity, the profits or losses of which are Northern Ireland profits or losses under Part 8B of CTA 2010, is an "NI rate activity".

112. Under new section 6D the NI rate activity is treated for the purposes of CAA 2001 as a separate trade, distinct from all other activities carried out by a NIRE company or a Northern Ireland SME company. The provision also provides that the NI rate activity carried on by a Northern Ireland firm is to be treated as a separate trade for the purposes of determining the profits of the firm under section 1259 of CTA 2009.

113. New section 6E sets out how allowances are given and charges imposed under the parts of CAA 2001 which deal with: plant and

machinery allowances; business premises renovation allowances; mineral extraction allowances; research and development allowances; and dredging allowances. These rules also cover how allowances and charges are given effect in a company's tax computation. In the case of an allowance or charge related to an NI rate activity, allowances or charges are treated as a deduction from, or addition to, the NI profits or losses of the period as appropriate. In the case of an allowance or charge related to a main rate activity, allowances or charges are treated as deductions from, or additions to, mainstream profits or losses of the period as appropriate. [Note: this is now extended to include structures and buildings allowances.]

Part 3 of Schedule 1

114. Part 3 provides for amendments to plant and machinery allowances under Part 2 of CAA 2001 to take account of the fact that an NI rate activity is subject to a different rate of corporation tax.

115. Paragraph 3 amends section 12 of CAA 2001 to ensure that, if a company incurs expenditure for the purposes of trade for an activity that will, on the company becoming a NIRE company, be an NI rate activity treated as a separate trade, any such expenditure will be treated as incurred on the first day the company is a NIRE company.

116. Similarly, paragraph 3 amends section 12 of CAA 2001 to provide that expenditure incurred by a partnership for the purposes of an activity that will, on the partnership becoming a Northern Ireland Chapter 7 firm, be an NI rate activity treated as a separate trade, will be treated as incurred on the first day the partnership is a Northern Ireland Chapter 7 firm.

117. Paragraph 4 inserts new subsections (2ZA) and (2ZB) into section 15 of CAA 2001. These rules ensure that activities carried out by a company or firm which are treated as separate trades are also treated for the purposes of Part 2 of CAA 2001 as separate qualifying activities.

118. Paragraph 5 inserts new section 51JA which provides for a restriction to Annual Investment Allowance (AIA) available under Chapter 5 of Part 2 of CAA 2001 where the AIA qualifying expenditure is incurred in respect of an NI rate activity in a financial year for which the Northern Ireland rate is lower than the main rate.

119. Paragraph 6 contains amendments of section 61 of CAA 2001 which deals with disposal events and disposal values. Their effect is that where an asset that is used for the purpose of a main rate activity is sold at less than market value to a company that is within the NI CT regime, the sale will in certain circumstances be treated as being at market value.

120. Paragraph 7 sets out new sections 66B, 66C, 66D and 66E. New section 66B ensures that a capital allowances disposal event will not arise where, in an accounting period which starts on or after the commencement day (again, as defined by section 5 of the Act), a company becomes a Northern Ireland SME company and as a result of section 15(2ZA) (as inserted by paragraph 4) any assets are treated as ceasing to be used for the purpose of a main rate activity and beginning to be used for the purposes of an NI rate activity.

121. There are also rules in new section 66B that govern how any unrelieved qualifying expenditure brought forward to the first period where a company has both a main rate activity and an NI rate activity is treated. This includes a just and reasonable apportionment of the unrelieved qualifying expenditure between a main rate activity pool and an NI rate activity pool.

122. New section 66C contains provision about the application to partnerships of the provisions of new section 66B.

123. New section 66D covers the situation where a company that was a Northern Ireland SME company starts to carry on a qualifying activity that is not an NI rate activity. A capital allowances disposal event will not arise in the case of any assets which are consequently treated as ceasing to be used for the purposes of an NI rate activity. Any unrelieved qualifying expenditure previously used for the purposes of an NI rate activity that is to be carried forward is treated as relating to the qualifying activity the company is carrying on.

124. New section 66E contains provision about the application to partnerships of the provisions of new section 66D.

125. Paragraph 8 inserts new Chapter 16ZA into CAA 2001.

126. New section 212ZA deals with qualifying expenditure on plant or machinery which is used partly for NI rate activity and partly for main rate activity. For the purposes of any annual investment allowance or first year allowance the expenditure is to be

apportioned on a just and reasonable basis between the NI rate activity and main rate activity.

127. New section 212ZB requires that where qualifying expenditure is incurred partially for NI rate activity and partially for main rate activity (if it is to be allocated to a pool) it must be allocated to a single asset pool. Where a company is required to bring in a disposal value because an asset previously used for either NI rate activity or main rate activity begins to be used for both activities, an amount equivalent to the disposal value is allocated to a single asset pool for that chargeable period.

128. New section 212ZC deals with allowances and charges on expenditure in a single asset pool by applying a just and reasonable apportionment between the NI rate activity and the main rate activity.

129. New section 212ZD introduces rules dealing with the disposal value to be applied in the case of a significant change of circumstances affecting the use of plant or machinery in a single asset pool under section 212ZC.

130. New section 212ZE provides for the application of the new Chapter 16ZA to partnerships.

131. New section 212ZF defines the phrase "main rate activity" for the purposes of Chapter 16ZA.

132. Paragraph 9 of Schedule 1 amends section 247 of CAA 2001. The inserted subsection (1A) deals with the way in which plant and machinery allowances are given effect in the case of companies within the NI CT regime which have an NI rate activity. Allowances in respect of the NI rate activity are relieved as deductions against Northern Ireland profits of the relevant accounting period.

133. Paragraph 10 of Schedule 1 relates to first-year tax credits payable under Schedule A1 to CAA 2001. It amends Schedule A1 so as to give the Treasury power by order to prescribe a different percentage where the surrenderable loss in question relates to an NI rate activity. [See, however, FA 2018, s. 29(5).]

Part 4 of Schedule 1

134. In Part 4 of Schedule 1, paragraph 11 introduces amendments to section 360Z CAA 2001 to make it clear that where a company or partnership, because of its NI rate activity, is treated as carrying on two separate trades, any business premises renovation allowances, or corresponding charges, relate to the trade the

qualifying building is used in. A just and reasonable apportionment applies where the building is used by both trades.

135. The amendment made by paragraph 12 relates to mineral extraction allowances. It amends section 394 to provide that where a company, because of its NI rate activity, is treated as carrying on two separate trades, both trades will be treated as mineral extraction trades if the separate trades together would be so treated. Any allowance or charge applies separately to each trade.

136. Paragraph 13 amends section 432 so as to provide that mineral extraction allowances are given effect, in the case of a Northern Ireland SME company or a NIRE company, in accordance with section 6E (as inserted by paragraph 2 of Schedule 1 to the Act).

137. Paragraph 14 inserts new section 439A which governs how research and development allowances will be treated where a company or partnership incurs expenditure for the purpose of a trade on an activity that will, upon the company becoming a NIRE company, be an NI rate activity treated as a separate trade. Any such expenditure will be treated as incurred on the first day the company is a NIRE company.

138. Paragraph 15 amends section 450 so as to provide that research and development allowances are given effect, in the case of a Northern Ireland SME company or a NIRE company, in accordance with section 6E (as inserted by paragraph 2).

139. Paragraph 16 amends section 484 so as to provide for the purposes of dredging allowances that, where a company, because of its NI rate activity, is treated as carrying on two separate trades, both trades will be treated as qualifying trades if the separate trades together would be so treated.

140. Paragraph 17 amends section 489 so as to provide that dredging allowances are given effect, in the case of a Northern Ireland SME company or a NIRE company, in accordance with section 6E (as inserted by paragraph 2).

Parts 5 and 6 of Schedule 1

141. Part 5 provides for consequential amendments of CAA 2001.

142. Part 6 sets out rules to cover the transition to the Northern Ireland corporation tax regime for the purposes of CAA 2001.

143. Paragraph 19 defines the "transition period" for a company as the first accounting period in which the Northern Ireland rate applies

to the corporation tax profits and losses of a company or partnership.

144. Paragraph 20 applies to a company or partnership if in the transition period a company is a NIRE company or Northern Ireland SME company or the partnership is a NI Chapter 6 or Chapter 7 firm (as defined by new section 6B, inserted by paragraph 2 of Schedule 1 to the Act). It applies if, as a result of section 6D of CAA 2001 (inserted by paragraph 2), an NI rate activity begins to be treated for the purposes of Part 2 of CAA 2001 (plant and machinery) as a separate qualifying activity. Paragraph 20 provides that any unrelieved qualifying expenditure on plant and machinery to be carried forward into the transition period is to be apportioned on a just and reasonable basis into separate pools for purposes of the NI rate activity and main rate activity. The paragraph provides that this does not create a disposal event.

145. Paragraph 21 also applies to a company or partnership if in the transition period a company is a NIRE company or Northern Ireland SME company or the partnership is a NI Chapter 6 or Chapter 7 firm. It applies if, as a result of section 6D of CAA 2001, an NI rate activity begins to be treated for the purposes of Part 7 of CAA 2001 (know-how allowances) as a separate qualifying activity. Paragraph 21 provides that any unrelieved qualifying expenditure on know-how to be carried forward into the transition period is to be apportioned on a just and reasonable basis into separate pools for purposes of the NI rate activity and main rate activity.

Appendix 2 – Case studies re fixtures

The following case studies are all closely based on real scenarios dealt with by the authors (i.e. for Six Forward Capital Allowances) in recent years. Collectively they demonstrate the practical application of the capital allowances rules to commercial property transactions.

Study 1 – pre-trading expenditure, AIAs, tax planning

This case concerned a producer in the food and drinks sector. The company acquired some derelict buildings and redeveloped them in three phases. The building, as renovated, included a production facility, offices, staff facilities, a restaurant, toilets. There is also now a warehouse, configured for the storage of the product in question.

The business started trading in 2015 but had incurred expenditure in the region of £8.5 million in the seven previous years. The first question to determine was whether there was an existing qualifying activity or whether the expenditure was correctly claimed by virtue of s. 12 (pre-trading expenditure: see **4.17.2**).

Detailed information was only available for around £1.5 million of the expenditure and the accountant had provisionally made a claim for annual investment allowances of £250,000 but for nothing else.

As advisers, we were asked to conduct a full review of the principles of entitlement, and the opportunities arising, using the full array of our services (apportionments, valuations, Land Registry checks, etc.).

The work took eight months, and involved two surveys, five meetings and 35 pieces of correspondence. The end result was a report, fully rooted in correct statutory principles, identifying qualifying expenditure of £2.97 million, producing a tax saving at the rates then in force of £594,000. The saving in the first year was in the region of £120,000.

Law: CAA 2001, s. 11, 12, 15, 21, 23, 33A, 176

Study 2 – definition of plant, scope of s. 22 restrictions

A company spent around £1.7 million on a new marina. The accountant was of the view that no allowances could be claimed because of the restrictions in s. 22 re fixed structures, including a specific reference at item 5 to marinas. We were asked for a second opinion.

Our site visit made it apparent that the marina complex included various different elements, including a perimeter road, fixed berths and several articulated pontoons.

Our analysis of the expenditure revealed that around £900,000 of the expenditure was for structural elements, £500,000 for the pontoons, and £300,000 for identifiable elements of plant and machinery.

The key question was whether the pontoons could qualify, or whether they were properly treated simply as part of the marina, and were therefore denied relief by s. 22.

HMRC guidance is quite clear that floating pontoons are to be treated as plant, even if attached to a pile or other fixed structure. The articulated pontoons in this case were floating pontoons attached to piles in the marina. The HMRC guidance therefore provided clear justification for the claim.

In total, the allowances claimed amounted to around £800,000, leading to a tax saving of more than £150,000. There were possible arguments that we could have had with regard to the pilings, but the client was delighted with a solid claim for nearly half of the expenditure, so we mutually agreed not to pursue a larger but more controversial claim.

Law: CAA 2001, s. 22
Guidance: CA 21215

Study 3 – leaseholders, residential accommodation

A freeholder developed and held five blocks of mixed use property, including a hotel, apartments and offices constructed over three to 19 storeys, along with a basement area providing car parking facilities and access to two plant rooms.

The total construction cost under consideration for a claim, after the sale of some apartments for social housing, was £48m, of which some £14m qualified for capital allowances. A claim for the hotel element was made by the freeholder (there was a trade) but not for the apartments (where there was no qualifying activity).

The freeholder then granted a new lease to a new lessor who in turn granted a new sub-lease to a new lessee for £60m. There was a qualifying activity consisting of the letting of the apartments only. As neither the freeholder nor the lessor had a qualifying activity, and as neither had ever claimed allowances, no disposal value or fixtures election was required (and there was no pooling requirement). Thus, the lessee was entitled to claim, resulting in £4.6m of allowances against the communal areas (7.7%), giving a worthwhile tax saving.

Law: CAA 2001, s. 11, 15, 35, 176, 181, 183, 184, 187A, 198, 199, 201
Guidance: R&C Brief 66/08, 45/10

Study 4 – uncertain property history, R&D allowances

An extensive research and testing laboratory was purchased for £1.6m, complete with workshops and external testing facilities. The installation of certain test machinery required extensive alterations to the building. Upper floor offices provided administration and analytical support and offices on one floor were sub-let.

The vendor, who had purchased pre-2008, was in administration, and cooperation for pooling was attempted but not achieved. The contract was also silent on capital allowances and, given the history, it was not possible to rule out a previous claim. As such, entitlement for most of the fixtures could not be established and a claim for just £80,000 of integral features was made.

However, even though the owner missed out on the ordinary fixtures claim, the client was entitled to claim R&D allowances by virtue of the work across the facility. RDAs of £944,000 were identified and the resulting tax saving was in excess of £200,000.

Law: CAA 2001, s. 11, 15, 33A, 181, 187, 437-440

Study 5 – advising buyer, vendor not understanding rules

Our client was purchasing a care home for £1.1m from an existing operator in "special measures". The vendor had bought the property before 2008 for £1.5m and wanted to elect for £1 for plant and machinery on disposal.

The purchaser was expecting at least a tax written-down value. Following frank discussions and negotiations with the vendor's advisers it transpired that no claim had been made previously and that the vendor's business was to cease. Once the vendor had established that there would be no balancing charge following disposal he agreed to pool the expenditure and to pass allowances on in full via the fixtures election. This resulted in a claim for the purchaser of £275,000 for the main pool and £88,000 for the special rate pool – giving immediate and future tax savings of £69,000.

Law: CAA 2001, s. 11, 15, 187A, 187B

Study 6 – advising buyer, powerful vendor

Our client was purchasing property from an insurance company which had held it since before 2008 and which was asking for elections of £1 each for main pool fixtures and for integral features. The qualifying expenditure totalled more than £1.1 million and the tax saving at stake was in excess of £200,000.

The vendor's advisers told us that the "heads of terms" had agreed the two £1 elections. As the figures were significant we recommended that the purchaser should insist on a different sharing of the tax relief and advised of three options: accept the elections, refuse to sign or split the relief. Meanwhile, we carried out our due diligence work and it transpired that the heads did not in fact mention capital allowances at all.

Our client was keen for the deal to go ahead but asked for allowances to be passed at the tax written-down value. The vendor agreed and the deal went through without further issue.

Law: CAA 2001, s. 11, 15, 187A, 187B

Study 7 – property acquisition by individual

Our client, an individual paying tax at 40%, bought two properties in 2017 from vendors who had owned the buildings since 2002. The previous owners had held the properties from 1999. We were able to establish that no previous claims had been made for fixtures in the properties.

We were not involved in heads of terms but were instructed early enough to draft contract clauses for the pooling and passing of allowances via a fixtures election, satisfying the requirements of s. 187A.

Total expenditure was around £3m, and we identified qualifying expenditure in the region of £675,000. This resulted in total tax savings of £270,000, including a first-year tax saving (using AIAs and WDAs) well in excess of £100,000.

Law: CAA 2001, s. 11, 15, 181, 187A, 198, 201

Study 8 – advising seller, confusion over terminology

A successful sole trader, potentially paying tax at 45%, was selling his business, including the commercial property. Before we were involved, the overall sale proceeds of £880k had already been agreed, provisionally allocated as £500k to land and buildings, £250k to goodwill and £130k to fixtures and fittings.

The vendor had previously identified qualifying expenditure of some £150k on fixtures in the property. These (together with any other plant in the pools) had been written down to a balance of around £80k.

The vendor had (before our involvement) been advised that he would be hit with a balancing charge of £50k. This was not an ideal outcome for the client, as he could benefit from other tax reliefs and pay as little as 10% on any gains on the goodwill and property, whereas he would be paying 45% income tax on the balancing charge. We were advised, however, that this was a price he was willing to pay for the deal to go through.

Unfortunately, the client's advisers had assumed that £130k would be the total disposal value to be shown in the capital allowances computations. When it came to discussing a fixtures election (under s. 198), however, the buyer's advisers were looking for some figure allocated to fixtures, over and above the £130k allocated to "fixtures and fittings".

In other words, this was a classic example of difficulty when using the word "fixtures". The capital allowances definition of the term is clear, and it includes only those items so affixed to the property as to become, in law, part of the property (s. 173). By contrast, the term "fixtures and fittings" is generally used to refer to *moveable* items of plant or machinery. So there is no overlap between the two (though they all constitute plant and machinery).

One option was for the vendor to sign a fixtures election with just £1 allocated to fixtures. NB it is essential that such an election should be signed, to prevent a large balancing charge for the vendor (see s. 187B(6)).

However, the £130k allocated to moveable items only was (on the facts) probably excessive, and was therefore quite likely to be challenged by HMRC; there is no need for a figure in a s. 198 election to be "reasonable", but any figures not covered by an election are open to challenge by HMRC if they do not constitute a "just and reasonable apportionment" (s. 562). It would therefore be safer and probably more correct to allocate a smaller figure to those items, say £40k. In that case, our client would be willing to sign an election with £90k allocated to fixtures, retaining an overall capital allowances disposal proceeds figure of £130k.

It would follow, however, that the reduction from £130k to £40k allocated to fixtures and fittings would have to be matched by an increase in the amount allocated to either goodwill or to land and buildings. Our client would have some increased tax liability as a result, but hopefully only at 10%, and the buyer might have some additional SDLT to pay, but this result would be much better for our client than having a higher figure than £130k allocated to plant and machinery overall.

Appendix 3 – HMRC toolkit

HMRC publish a *Capital Allowances for Plant and Machinery Toolkit*. At the time of writing, the latest version was produced in April 2020 and is said to related to "2020-21 Self Assessment and Company Tax Returns". It may be found in full at https://tinyurl.com/mu63ua7h (shortened link).

The toolkit does not come close to addressing the complexities of the plant and machinery rules (never mind the various other capital allowances regimes), but it does contain a checklist of 28 questions with (in each case) a comment on the risk, the action that may be taken to mitigate that risk, and a more detailed explanation of the underlying issues and of relevant HMRC guidance.

The following summary reproduces the 28 questions and the "Risk" explanation – all in HMRC's words. Some references have also been added (in square brackets) to commentary in this book. The main change since the previous version of the toolkit is at item 22.

ACQUISITIONS

1.   If there have been any assets acquired during the period do they qualify for capital allowances?

There are general conditions that must be satisfied for expenditure to be qualifying expenditure for capital allowances. The expenditure must be capital expenditure on the provision of plant and machinery wholly or partly for the purposes of the qualifying activity that the person incurring the expenditure carries on and the person must own the plant and machinery as a result of incurring the expenditure. [See **4.1.2.**]

2.   Is the amount identified as qualifying expenditure incurred accurate?

The capital allowances computation should accurately reflect the amount of any expenditure incurred in the chargeable period. If adequate records are not maintained the capital allowances computation may not be accurate.

3. Has the qualifying expenditure been adjusted for any VAT reclaimed?

The purchase price of an asset usually includes VAT. Where VAT paid on the acquisition of an asset is allowable as input tax for VAT purposes capital allowances should only be claimed on the cost of the asset net of the VAT input tax reclaimed. In all other cases the VAT paid should be included in the cost of the capital expenditure for capital allowances purposes. If reclaimed VAT is not correctly identified the amount of qualifying expenditure will not be accurate. [See **1.5.2**.]

4. Have all payments been made within four months?

The date on which capital expenditure is incurred may depend on the date that payment is made. If this is overlooked it may result in the expenditure being treated in the wrong period for capital allowances purposes. [See **1.5.4** and **4.17**.]

5. Have any qualifying energy-saving plant and machinery assets been acquired during the period?

The Enhanced Capital Allowance (ECA) energy scheme provides for 100 per cent first-year allowances (FYA) for expenditure incurred on acquiring new energy-saving plant and machinery. It is only available on qualifying technologies or products specified on the Energy Technology List website. If the proper checks are not carried out to ensure that the particular asset acquired qualifies then ECA may be incorrectly claimed. [See **5.4.4** and **5.4.5**. These enhanced allowances are no longer available.]

6. Where any assets have been purchased on hire purchase have they been brought into use?

Where an asset is acquired by instalments under a hire purchase type contract the full amount of the purchase price may not immediately qualify for capital allowances. The date on which the expenditure is treated as being incurred will depend on whether the asset has been brought into use. [See **6.2**.]

DISPOSALS

7. If any assets have been disposed of during the period has the disposal value been included in the capital allowances computation?

Where an asset for which capital allowances, including Annual Investment Allowance (AIA), have been claimed is disposed of, a disposal value should be accounted for even if the balance of expenditure in the pool is nil. If any disposals are overlooked the capital allowances computation will not be accurate. [See **5.5**.]

8. Have the correct disposal values been accounted for?

Where an asset is disposed of the full disposal value should be accounted for in the capital allowances computation. The disposal value will depend on the nature of the disposal event. [See **5.5.3**.]

9. Has the value of any assets disposed of in part exchange for a new asset been accounted for appropriately?

If an asset is disposed of in part exchange for another asset the part exchange value needs to be reflected in the capital allowances computation for the computation to be accurate.

10. Has the correct disposal value for assets purchased on hire purchase been accounted for?

The disposal value for assets purchased under hire purchase agreements will depend on whether or not the contract has been assigned.

Where an asset which is being acquired under a hire purchase contract is disposed of by assigning the contract, the amount to be accounted for will depend on whether the asset has been brought into use for the purposes of the qualifying activity.

NON-BUSINESS USE ADJUSTMENTS

11. Have all business assets used for non-business purposes been identified?

Non-business use of assets often applies to unincorporated businesses, the most common example being private use of motor vehicles. [See **9.4**.]

However, it may also apply to companies. Broadly speaking, company expenditure on assets provided for directors' and/or employees' use as part of their remuneration package is accepted as incurred wholly and exclusively for the purposes of the qualifying activity and consequently for capital allowances purposes. But, there are occasions when there may be non-business use of assets in a company. For example, a company may have an asset which it uses partly for a qualifying activity and partly for an activity not within the charge to UK tax. In these circumstances the capital allowances computation should be adjusted accordingly.

The amount of allowances claimed for assets that are only used partly for the purposes of the qualifying activity should be reduced. If any non-business use is overlooked the capital allowances claim will not be accurate. [See **5.2.15**, **5.4.12** and **5.8**.]

12. Have the allowances for any asset used partly for non-business purposes been reduced?

If the allowances claimed are not reduced in line with the amount of the non-business use the capital allowances computation will not be accurate. [See **5.4.12** and **5.8**.]

13. Is the reduction in the writing-down allowances claimed for an asset with non-business use accurate?

If the extent of non-business use is estimated, the reduction to the allowances claimed may not be accurate. If records are kept they may not be sufficiently robust to ensure an accurate record of non-business use. Apart from vehicles provided to employees as part of their remuneration package, if a business vehicle is a car then the capital allowances claimed are usually restricted to reflect non-business use. [See **9.4.1**.]

14. If a non-business use adjustment was made in an earlier period has the reduction been reviewed to ensure that it is still just and reasonable?

It is common for any non-business use to be discussed only when an asset is first acquired. Any adjustment is then carried forward to later periods. However, personal or business circumstances may change and could affect the correct level of any non-business use, for example moving home or business premises, change of business vehicles etc. [See **5.8.2**.]

15.   Has the balancing adjustment (allowance or charge) of any asset which has been used partly for non-business purposes and has been disposed of been adjusted appropriately?

Where an asset which has been used partly for non-business use is disposed of the amount the balancing adjustment (allowance or change) needs to be restricted by the average non business use over the life of the asset. [See **5.7** and **5.8**.]

16.   Have appropriate adjustments been made for any business vehicles used for journeys between home and work?

Travel between home and work is generally considered to be private/non-business use. If this non-business use is not identified the allowances claimed will not be accurate.

CARS

17.   Have all business vehicles which are cars for capital allowances purposes been identified?

If vehicles are not properly identified as cars, the capital allowances computation may not be accurate. [See **9.2**.]

18.   Have all cars been excluded from the Annual Investment Allowance qualifying expenditure?

Cars are excluded from being eligible for Annual Investment Allowance. If vehicles are not properly identified as cars and excluded, then the capital allowances computation will not be accurate.

19.   Have the correct capital allowances rules for cars been applied?

The capital allowances treatment of qualifying expenditure on cars depends on the date the car was purchased, the carbon dioxide (CO_2) emissions and (for first year allowances) whether the car is new.

Expenditure on a new and unused car from April 2021 which is electric or has CO_2 emissions of 0g/km or less may be eligible for a 100% first year allowance. Expenditure on other cars will only be eligible for writing down allowances, either at the special rate (6%), or the main rate (18%).

Expenditure on a new and unused car between April 2018 and April 2021 which is electric or has CO2 emissions of 50g/km or less may be eligible for a 100% first year allowance. Expenditure on other cars will only be eligible for writing down allowances, either at the special rate (8%), (6% with effect from April 2019) or the main rate (18%). [See **9.3**.]

20. Has a mileage allowance been paid to anyone for use of a vehicle on which capital allowances have been claimed?

Where a mileage allowance has been paid, capital allowances may not be applicable. For example where the vehicle is not owned by the company or business and/or an allowance is paid other than solely for reimbursement of fuel costs.

21. Have any sale proceeds for cars on which first-year allowances have previously been claimed been dealt with correctly?

If a car, on which 100 per cent first-year allowances (FYA) have been claimed, is the only asset for which capital allowances have been claimed the written down value carried forward after FYA is nil.

In these circumstances, if the car is disposed of the proceeds from the disposal should not be overlooked from the capital allowances computation.

GENERAL

22. Has depreciation, impairment, revaluation movements and any profit or loss on sale been added back to the accounts profit in the tax computation?

Depreciation is generally not an allowable expense for tax purposes.

There is a risk that the depreciation, impairment and revaluation movements may not be added back to profit in the tax computation appropriately. Depreciation, impairment and revaluation movements should be added back in the computation even where capital allowances have not been claimed.

23. Are all assets on which expenditure has been incurred still owned by the business at the time of their introduction into the pool for capital allowances purposes?

Whilst capital expenditure is generally incurred when the obligation to pay becomes unconditional see CA11800, there is no legislative restriction on when assets on which qualifying expenditure has been incurred must be brought into the capital allowance pool.

However, expenditure can only be allocated to a pool in a chargeable period if the person owns the plant or machinery at some time in that period.

Where expenditure qualifying for capital allowances is identified following a review and brought into the pool in a period after acquisition there is a risk that the asset(s) has already have been disposed of. [See **1.4.2**.]

24. If the chargeable period is longer or shorter than 12 months have the allowances claimed been increased or reduced appropriately?

Capital allowances are made for a chargeable period. Where the chargeable period is longer or shorter than 12 months the allowances claimed should be apportioned appropriately. [See **5.3.4**, **5.3.5** and **5.4.1**.]

25. Has Annual Investment Allowance only been claimed where there is a qualifying person?

Annual Investment Allowance (AIA) can be claimed for expenditure on general business equipment including long life assets and integral features (but not cars) up to the annual amount. AIA is only available where the expenditure is incurred by a qualifying person.

If AIA is claimed when expenditure is not incurred by a qualifying person the capital allowances computation will be inaccurate. [See **5.2.2**.]

26. Is the Annual Investment Allowance claimed appropriate to the qualifying expenditure incurred in the chargeable period?

Annual Investment Allowance (AIA) can only be claimed in the chargeable period in which the qualifying expenditure is incurred. Where the qualifying expenditure incurred is more than the maximum allowance, the business can only claim this maximum amount. Where the qualifying expenditure incurred is less than the maximum allowance the business can claim AIA up to the amount of qualifying expenditure incurred. [See **5.2.4**.]

27. Have any assets been disposed of, or acquired from, connected parties (this includes transactions made as part of a business incorporation)?

Where an asset is disposed of to, or acquired from, a connected party the allowances available are sometimes restricted. If allowances are not restricted in particular circumstances the computation will not be accurate. [See **22.3.2**.]

28. Has a property together with fixtures that are plant and machinery been acquired or disposed of?

From 1 April 2012 for Company Tax Returns and 6 April 2012 for Income Tax Self Assessment tax returns new rules apply for claiming plant and machinery allowances on fixtures that are acquired with a building. These rules were extended from 1 April 2014 for Corporation Tax and 6 April 2014 for Income Tax. If the new rules are not followed correctly there may be an incorrect claim to capital allowances.

It is for the new owner to show whether or not the new rules apply. If the new owner is not able to supply evidence that the requirements have been met, they will not be able to claim plant and machinery allowances on expenditure on fixtures acquired from a past owner. [See **12.3**.]

Appendix 4 – Historic rates

1. Introduction

For various reasons, it may be necessary to calculate allowances that would have been due in the past. This may relate not only to plant and machinery claims but also to now-defunct regimes such as the one for industrial buildings allowances (where the historic rates may still be relevant for the purpose of calculating the restriction under CAA 2001, s. 186 (see **12.10.3**) for example).

This appendix therefore brings together various historic rates of allowances.

2. Plant and machinery – annual investment allowances

The following table shows the thresholds since AIAs were introduced in April 2008:

	£
From 1 January 2022*	200,000
1 January 2019 to 31 Dec 2021*	1,000,000
1 January 2016 to 31 Dec 2018	200,000
1 April 2014 to 31 December 2015	500,000
1 January 2013 to 31 March 2014	250,000
1 April 2012 to 31 Dec 2012	25,000
1 April 2010 to 31 March 2012	100,000
1 April 2008 to 31 March 2010	50,000

* The reduction to £200,000 was originally to apply from 1 January 2021 but the higher threshold was extended for a further year.

See **5.2** above for details of the complex transitional arrangements that apply when the threshold is changed.

3. Plant and machinery – first-year allowances (current)

Most FYAs are now given at 100% (though taxpayers have the option to restrict the amount if they wish to do so, for example to preserve personal allowances that would otherwise be wasted). These allowances are subject to various "general exclusions".

Different rules apply for the temporary allowances introduced in 2021 (super-deduction and related FYAs)

Type	Available from
Cars with low CO_2 emissions	17 April 2002
Zero-emission goods vehicles	1/6 April 2010
Plant or machinery for a gas refuelling station	17 April 2002
Electric vehicle charging points	23 November 2016
Plant or machinery for use wholly in a ring-fence trade	17 April 2002
Plant or machinery for use in designated assisted areas	1 April 2012 (but according to designation)
Expenditure by companies (only) in designated freeport sites	March 2021 (but according to designation)
Expenditure by companies (only) qualifying for super-deduction or other temporary FYAs	1 April 2021

4. Plant and machinery – first-year allowances (old)

FYAs were formerly available for the following, but again subject to various "general exclusions". Type	Rate	From	To
N. Ireland expenditure by SMEs	100%	12 May 1998	11 May 2002
Expenditure incurred by SMEs	50%	1 July 1997	30 June 1998
Expenditure incurred by SMEs	40%	1 July 1998	31 March 2008
Expenditure incurred by small enterprises	50%	FYs 2004, 2006, 2007 (but not FY 2005) *	
ICT expenditure incurred by small enterprises	100%	1 April 2000	31 March 2004

FYAs were formerly available for the following, but again subject to various "general exclusions". Type (cont.)	Rate	From	To
Expenditure incurred by any business	40%	1 April 2009	31 March 2010 *
Energy-saving plant or machinery	100%	1 April 2001	31 March 2020 *
Environmentally beneficial plant or machinery	100%	1 April 2003	31 March 2020*

* And equivalent income tax periods.

Long-life assets attracted 12% FYAs for expenditure incurred from 1 July 1997 for one year.

5. Plant and machinery – low-emission cars

A car qualifies as having low emissions if it has a qualifying emissions certificate (as defined) showing an official CO_2 emissions figure not exceeding a given level:

Date expenditure incurred	CO2
From 1 April 2021	0g/km
From 1 April 2018	50g/km
1 April 2015-31 March 2018	75g/km
1 April 2013-31 March 2015	95g/km
Before 1 April 2013	110g/km

See **5.4.6** for further details. Equivalent periods apply for income tax purposes (e.g. 6 April rather than 1 April).

6. Plant and machinery – writing-down allowances

WDAs for plant and machinery have been given as follows:

633

Chargeable periods beginning	Standard rate	Special rate
From 1/6 April 2019	18%	6%
From 1/6 April 2012 to 31 March/ 5 April 2019	18%	8%
From 1/6 April 2008 to 31 March/ 5 April 2012	20%	10%
Before 1/6 April 2008	25%	See note *

* A standard 25% WDA rate applied from 26 October 1970 to April 2008. Long-life assets, however, attracted allowances at 6%.

Different rules applied to cars bought before April 2009.

7. Structures and buildings allowances

WDAs are given on a straight-line basis from 29 October 2018, subject to anti-avoidance commencement provisions.

The rate was 2% per annum from the time the allowances were introduced, rising to 3% from 1 April 2020 (6 April 2020 for income tax), whether expenditure was incurred before or after the date of change.

Higher rates apply for expenditure in designated freeports.

8. Industrial buildings allowances

WDAs were given at 4% from 5 November 1962 (formerly 2%) until IBAs were phased out between 2007 and 2011.

Initial allowances were given at various rates in different periods, as below.

Date expenditure incurred	Rate
From 1 November 1993	nil
1 November 1992-31 October 1993	20%
1 April 1986-31 October 1992	nil
1 April 1985-31 Mach 1986	25%
14 March 1984-31 March 1985	50%
11 March 1981-13 March 1984	75%
13 November 1974-10 March 1981	50%

Table of legislation

Taxes Management Act 1970

Welfare Reform Act 2012

Index of cases

General index

Note: with the exception of plant and machinery allowances, entries below are given mainly under the name of the allowance. For example, qualifying expenditure for research and development allowances is indexed under "Research and development" but not under "Qualifying expenditure".